Well-Crafted:

The History of the
Western North Carolina Furniture Industry

Well-Crafted:

The History of the
Western North Carolina Furniture Industry

RICHARD ELLER

Introduction by G. Leroy Lail

Redhawk Publications

The Catawba Valley Community College Press

2550 US Hwy 70 SE

Hickory, NC 28602

Library of Congress Control Number: 2023932724

ISBN: 978-1-959346-07-4

Layout and Design by Melanie Johnson Zimmermann

Cover photo by Fanjoy-Labrenz (courtesy of G. Leroy Lail)

Robert Canipe, Editor

Aurora King, Editor

Tim Peeler, Editor

Claudia Ward-Eller, Editor

Patty Thompson, Project Manager

To June C. Eller and Richard A. Eller, my mother and father who taught me a lot of things I did not want to learn, like perseverance and the value of a hard day's work in a furniture factory.

To the uncounted number of people who came together to create the western NC furniture industry. From beginning to end, their efforts have made all of us who live there very proud. Their product exemplifies their character, strong and enduring.

Table of Contents

---❖---

---∞∾---

Furniture Entrepreneur and owner of Hickory Furniture Mart, G. Leroy Lail

Introduction

Furniture follows fashion. I noticed that as soon as I got into the business back in 1963, when I returned from the Navy. After service as a naval officer during the intense episode known as the Cuban Missile Crisis, my wife Lynn and I came back to Hickory to see what could be done to grow Hickory Furniture Mart.

I love to build and I love to promote. Over the years, I pursued those two major objectives. After each furniture market, we added on to the space available, increasing the size of the Mart with each semi-annual visit from retailers around the country. I was fortunate to envision a design that was a mall, which I had never seen. This arrangement solved the problem that all levels needed to be seen. The solution was a mall. I developed it due to need. Throughout the 1960s and 70s, Hickory Furniture Mart gained a larger share of showroom space, thanks in part to our efforts to promote. It was so popular in fact, that we opened our doors after each market and let the public see all the beautiful furniture being made in the area, some of it crafted by the hands of those who flocked to the "after market sale." It also became a community gathering space, especially around the holidays.

Then, a change occurred in the mid-1980s. Buyers looked for just one place to see all the new lines and make their choices. Many of the families manufacturing furniture started to sell their businesses and take their businesses public. As they were sold, they tended to concentrate their businesss in High Point, not Hickory. By the time the trend reached its inevitable conclusion, I had begun to plan a new chapter for Hickory Furniture Mart, as a retail outlet. Over the course of a few years, we transitioned the Mart from use as a center for wholesale buyers, that was only visited for a ten-day period every April and October, to a 360-day a year facility. We banked on the idea that Hickory and western North Carolina was famous for the furniture it made.

Consumers would come to see the variety and enjoy the prices they could get from furniture manufactured close to where they were shopping. The success of the concept remains evident as thousands flock through the doors looking for those special pieces that make their house a home. As the concept grew, local manufacturers began to share space with a wider array of companies that wanted to be associated with this furniture-rich region.

From very humble beginnings, when no one could even envision an entire industry springing from wood and fabric, the crafting of furniture has become a source of the area's identity, a dominant employer, and a reason for visitors to come, making Hickory one of the most important travel destinations on the East Coast. Along the way, Hickory Furniture Mart celebrated those early days with its annual Furniture Festival, an event designed to make sure the history of the craft of furniture making was not forgotten.

Furniture holds a unique place in our lives. When you go into almost any room, it is there. Its look defines our tastes. Its utility defines our lifestyle. In many ways furniture is an extension of who we are. Selection of the right pieces is not one to be taken lightly, although I see so many people know what they want as soon as they see it. But whether furniture is bought through the process of long study or snap judgement, we all know that it makes a statement.

The responsibility of making furniture that the public wants to show off in their personal spaces is a duty designers and builders have taken on for as long as this region has had homes that needed chairs, tables, and chests. Their work, with all the imagination and innovation they could muster has been crafted into every piece produced. Over time, generation by generation, the collective output has become an immense source of pride. Such a story needed a comprehensive telling, one that documents the advances and setbacks of a variety of entrepreneurs, willing to bet on their ingenuity to advance life for both their customers and the workers who believed in the concept.

Countless numbers of folks have gone into the "shops", their slang for factories, taking the raw lumber at their feet and turning it into a value added product that was useful, durable, and increasingly, fashionable. The success of manufacturers to be able to understand and deliver products that met the needs of people kept buyers coming back for more, which kept the factories producing, and a viable economy rolling along for those, either by birth or sojourn, who call western North Carolina home. They toiled in anonymity waiting for their moment.

Well-Crafted: The History of the Western North Carolina Funiture Industry reflects the many personalities that went in to establishing a business that is known the world over for the product it makes. It is a fascinating epic of how such a collection of companies came to be, what happened to them as they grew and prospered, along with the ones who are no longer around. Step by step this narrative tells the stories, some of them long forgotten, about what it took to make furniture a viable commodity. It was not easy.

Each failure had its way of leading to eventual success. Though they were competitors, collectively they took on an identity that reinforced each other. They challenged the established world of furniture making in the late 19th century, centered around Grand Rapids, Michigan and reoriented the center of furniture-making down south, right where the best wood grew.

Of course, the industry has had its challenges, just like Hickory during the furniture market days, but what started here has proved resilient. Even with the threat of offshoring, the furniture business has rebounded with a plan to not only survive, but thrive. In that way, my experience with Hickory Furniture Mart serves as something of microcosm of the industry itself. Just when you count us out, we are back with a better idea.

Generations of neighbors have worked, laughed, fought, goofed off, commiserated, and retired together in those factories. Their dedication and grit have defied the odds and built a way of life that we now celebrate and can take pride in. Together with the investors, managers all the other jobs it took to run a successful factory, this book attempts to tell their story and honor their life's work. Today, we are the beneficiaries of that work. Remembering what they did, along with all the sacrifices made along the way, is perhaps the best memorial. Professor Richard Eller started with my family tree and has told such a good job of telling the stories of our industry. Please enjoy.

G. Leroy Lail
Conover, North Carolina
May, 2022

Prologue
The Ghost of Furniture Past

Walk into almost any room. What do they all have in common?

Furniture. There to adorn, there to function, there to reveal.

These appliances of comfort and usefulness create a distinct atmosphere, sending messages to all who enter. It's as if furniture serves as a personal extension of the room, well beyond its utility. How we rest, work, and entertain shapes and is shaped by our selection of furniture, making a revealing statement about who we are.

Not everyone puts overwhelming thought into those preferences. Most make quick judgements based on what we like, then act upon those whims. But out of either studied intent or snap decisions, the style of furniture selected says a lot. For anyone making furniture, it becomes a big responsibility to anticipate what people want and craft from that idea, representing the buyer's likes in a tangible way.

The furniture makers of western North Carolina have been building a product that has been met with our approval for almost three centuries. For the first half of that period, pieces were crafted by hand, in the last half, mass produced. While the beauty and artistry of the first period cannot be denied, the output of the latter period dwarfed the first in terms of quantity. Both have found a place in rooms all over the world. An examination of this regional industry, its origin and history is long overdue. To disregard the collective effort of all that spurred development would be the same as saying the hard work of the people who made it happen didn't matter, when quite the opposite is true.

The western piedmont and foothills of the Tarheel state developed their identity from the output of factories both large and small, churning out crates and cardboard boxes filled with case goods and upholstery. At one point, half the population of western North Carolina made a living by contributing to what went out in those boxes. From the experience, they fashioned their own vernacular. The plant where they worked became known as the "shop," likely short for workshop, a holdover from the pre-industrial era. The word used for the coordinated groupings, known as 'suites' (spoken 'sweets' as the French intended), was pronounced locally as 'suits' (like what people wore), the way it was spelled, more or less. Workers came to accept and use a slang term for themselves and what they brought to the process, their value to the industry. They were the 'hands'.

Within the region, ignoring the imprint of the furniture industry would be almost impossible. At one time, just traveling the roads offered constant reminders. Factory smoke billowed proof that something productive was going on. Factory whistles ushered in each new workday, as well as signaled the end. Afternoon driving offered a constant worry of getting caught up in 'shop traffic.' Stores dotted the highways as outlets for almost factory-direct purchase of coordinated rooms of home furnishings, sometimes just a stone's throw from where it was made. The predominance has faded, but reminders remain, some active, others relics.

Generations of people worked, laughed, fought, goofed off, commiserated, and retired together in those factories. They gave their labor and their lives to the idea that they, guided by company leadership, could put out a product of which they all could be proud, all while drawing a paycheck

The work of machine carved details like these ushered in an affinity for industrial furniture during much of the 20th century. Working class people, that could generally not afford such features, were now able to buy pieces that dressed up their homes. (Hickory Furniture Mart Display - Author's collection)

for their efforts in the bargain. For many years, they were successful in that pursuit. In its heyday, the culture was something of a 'garden of Eden' with local people making local decisions, building furniture that impressed the public to reach for their checkbooks and purchase by the trailer load.

Across the region, then across the nation customers welcomed the output of those factories into their homes because furniture upgraded their living spaces. Machines produced intricate scroll work or carved details that many in the industrial era likened to the handiwork of fine crafters from days gone by, something common people could not afford before mass production came to town. Sales catalogs from early twentieth-century firms revealed ornately honed pieces, which impressed homeowners as fancy and thus worthy to own. Since furniture elevated their surroundings they believed, making the buyer feel more affluent and fancy, even though they were working class. Across the economic spectrum, furniture offered status. Also, those pieces sawed, sanded and veneered with machinery represented a new level of comfort and beauty for a flourishing America. The timing for the arrival of a New South industry to fill a need in consumer culture could not have been better.

When the success of the business caught the attention of a national, then international market, things changed. It grew, but simultaneously contracted. The shops got bigger, and more furniture than ever went to a wider range of addresses as faceless conglomerates began buying up local companies, consolidating what were once competitors into step-families that might change with the next corporate arrangement. Those deals condensed the number of operating firms, defining the industry differently. The destabilized landscape became less certain for workers, offering fewer choices for jobs when layoffs occurred.

Then came competition from workers in other places. The discovery that labor from somewhere else could be trained to make case goods at cheaper hourly rates than where it was already established was the same concept that brought manufacturing to the South in the first place. Along with an overwhelming supply of raw material, the harnessing of a local labor force that could be paid less gave companies the fuel they needed to rise in the late 19th century just as the same motivation saw its decline in the early 21st. With a remarkable resilience, the tradition of making furniture in the hills found ways to survive in good both times and bad. The following pages examine those ups and downs.

Furniture production in North Carolina centered around two cities, High Point in the east and Hickory in the west. Initially, the Uwharrie Mountain chain supplied wood to the east, the Brushy mountains to the west. As a result, each created its own sphere of influence. The two regions cooperated but also competed for control. At stake was superiority best showcased by where retailers came to see and buy the latest styles that they in turn would present the furniture to consumers across the country. For thirty years the two markets battled, each claiming to be the "Furniture Capital of the South." Together, they sought to elevate North Carolina as the epicenter of production. But alas, a kingdom can have only one head that wears the crown.

The coronation took place in High Point around 1985. Western manufacturers lost the pleasure and power of showing their own wares on their home turf at the semi-annual furniture market. Companies in the Hickory orbit were forced to take a backseat, at least symbolically, to the agenda of the east, making what came from the foothills look like a sofa out of style, to be discounted and shuffled off the showroom floor. High Point spoke for the entire NC industry and though they gave credit where credit was due when it was due, Hickory and its satellites found themselves outside the spotlight.

The loss of the furniture market for western North Carolina companies was just the first blow. Soon, communities began to rock the

The fertile mountains, traversed first by foot and then by rail. One reason to go there was for the wood contained in the hills. Early entrepreneurs saw the value of those trees. They sawed them down, then cut them into lumber for the coming furniture industry which defined the area. (Image courtesy of the Caldwell Heritage Museum)

pedestal upon which furniture companies had been placed back when they were the only game in town. Amnesia mixed with a little disdain became fashionable after factories started shutting down and politicians who once looked to manufacturers as a source of pride and funding sought to move on to the next industrial sweetheart. Industry diversification became the goal, which some hoped would help the entire region rid itself from the stigma of being a 'furniture town,' complete with all the connotations of low wages and low skilled workers such a designation conjured.

The sentiment was understandable. Living in a one-industry town brought with it not just fewer opportunities, but sweeping generalizations about life in those towns. The sons and daughters of the factory workforce need look no farther than than their parent's recommendation for job entry. If they did travel beyond western North Carolina, admitting where they were from brought the judgement of a wider world that furniture kids may not have even realized.

The negative attitude of outsiders ran counter to how many within the industry saw themselves. The workforce took pride in their product, labored daily, punched the clock regularly, gave a good days work for the wages they received, at least enough to put food on their family's table for decades. To them, the life was uncomplicated, reputable, and steady, as long as the job required their services.

Entering the 21st century, employees faced a new foe, offshoring. By that point, few companies controlled their own destiny. When a plant shut down there was no one in town to blame. Those decisions had been made far away and for reasons that had nothing to do with the local economy. Actually, those choices almost always adversely affected everyone in the community, whether they worked in the business or not. Detesting an executive who said the company was not closing operations fast enough was like hating a biting dog. Sure, the injured party could kick at it, but the dog neither understood nor cared about their anger.

Since it started, the people of western North Carolina's furniture industry have worked in anonymity. Most companies were too busy making furniture to bother with documenting how they did it. Especially after the demise of the western furniture market, the manufacturers of the foothills lost some of their energy, finding themselves on with fewer reasons to trumpet their existence. The factories were still producing a quality product but unless their history was presented in the wider context of High Point as a Tarheel story, and ignore a footnote, the importance of how it came to be was like last year's style.

The disservice of such a fate to all who remember the once proud industry could not stand. The context of its history needed an awakening, not only for those who experienced shop traffic, but more importantly those who didn't. Its legacy and continued importance as a phenomenon unique to the western foothills required a detailed account that documents the ingenuity and effort it took to make it happen.

Would it ever be possible for the furniture manufacturing industry to return to its supremacy, when it presided over the economic and social fabric of the region from which it came? As time moves farther from those glory days, it seems unlikely and maybe even undesirable. However, charting a course for the future of furniture requires knowing where the industry had been. Figuring out where the industry goes by starting with only a current view of the landscape, whenever one begins that forecast, is incomplete. Snap observers have been saddled with an extreme disadvantage as it leaves much of the nuances unexplored. A step back using the time travel apparatus of history offers a better indicator. Examining where an ever changing collective of companies might go in its days ahead based upon their past experiences provides a better lens through which to frame the industry. A fuller knowledge is no guarantee that anyone can completely predict what lies ahead, but it sure is good preparation.

The research presented here allows us to place ourselves in a world that eventually merges with our own, explaining the origin, progress and consequences of the actions undertaken by generations prior. For good or ill, these predecessors paved the way for the circumstances in which the industry now finds itself. From their perspective, everything was possible, so their advantage was in not knowing the long-range implications of the actions they took. We now have both the advantage of knowing how those plans worked out but also the burden of the results. Understanding the pitfalls that befell a once dominant industry keeps us attuned to hazards as we, the inheritors face the future.

As with any comprehensive history, this volume is full of stories about people. How they accomplished their goals remains instructive. Even their failures are worth examining so that we might draw analogies to our own challenges and avoid flawed solutions. In that way, this journey is an epic tale, written for the incidental purpose of our own self-help. But there is more to this voyage. The very idea that individuals would go to the woods, fell trees and think they could create a massive industrial movement is inspiring/quizzical/intimidating. You pick the word that best describes your evaluation. It took blood, sweat, toil, stamina, ingenuity, patience and tears to succeed, and sometimes even that was not enough. But make no mistake. What we have today and what we hope to have tomorrow comes largely from what they created yesterday.

For many who call western North Carolina home, either by birth or sojourn, *Well Crafted: The History of the Western North Carolina Furniture Industry* reveals a lot about the intelligence and grit of people who walked this corner of the earth, last week and last century. Their accomplishments speak to what can be gained when an idea gets to work and produces. Clearly, the vision enacted by one generation affects the next, which subsequently affects the next, and so on, creating an inheritance for whichever generation you are a part. Each of us has to ask ourselves "what kind of a steward am I. Do we build or drift?" These are the collected stories of both, mostly the former, but some of the latter are in there as well.

"When is the best time to plant a tree? Thirty years ago. When is the second best time? Today." Ironically, this Chinese proverb is the perfect adage for this furniture history. So many people who drove what became the furniture industry left scant information about why and how they did their work and how they interpreted the issues they faced. They just did it. Too busy to reflect, the goal of success, whatever that meant to them, became the driving force. In the aftermath of what they left behind, documenting those motives has become a giant jigsaw puzzle. Putting the pieces together remains like questions in any historical inquiry. Many are asked, while the answers are few.

In lieu of a comprehensive study of the furniture industry from thirty years ago, here is one that, like the planting of the tree, comes as the next best thing. Actually, this work is some thirty years in the making and is the

A sign of the times from the golden era of furniture manufacturing in western North Carolina. The back doors of numerous tractor-trailers hailed Lenoir as the center of furniture production. While the claim was arguable in its time, things are not what they used to be. (Author's collection)

better for it. In graduate school, I wrote about the origins of the furniture industry. Those days came before software could organize information and pinpoint important research. Looking back on that work, the story was regrettably incomplete. It needed a more systemized and comprehensive approach to identify trends that offered contextual answers to some of those questions. Thirty years ago, personalities like D.A. Smith, Helen Kelly, and Hill Baker were hidden, their contributions lost to the times in which they were happening. Now, their stories exemplify diverse aspects of an industry coming together, sustaining itself, watching its self-determination falter, and reinventing itself for a new century.

Daniel, Helen and Hill are just a few of the people you will meet in this work. Because of the size of the industry, even confined to western North Carolina, telling the stories of all who contributed is still absolutely impossible. Many exited the scene without ever considering the legacy they left, the moment they occupied, the ways in which they took the business of furniture-making forward. This is understandable as those that came first lived in an uncertain world. Would the work they undertook turn into something substantial or would they be just an industrial blip? When the first factories were not successful, those initial workers probably subscribed to the latter notion.

In keeping with the popular old adage; 'if at first you don't succeed, try, try again', furniture entrepreneurs did not give up. Irregular, spasmodic, even convulsive was the venture of making furniture. Much like a complicated birth, the start was not pretty, but it was incessant. Tenacity explains much of the continued effort. People living not exactly in the mountains, but in the foothills, with enough of a mountaineer mindset to conquer, while being less isolated, saw the growing society around them as ready for a product they could produce. The pioneers of Western North Carolina furniture manufacturing took an age old commodity and turned it into a regional specialty, something they could do well, a logical extension of their time amongst the trees.

For these leaders though, the inherent sense of furniture making remained a wary proposition. Could they make it? Would consumers buy it? After all, the price tag was not cheap. Even when a dining room table could be bought for $15, the average industrial worker made less than 22 cents per hour. Stepping out in faith was what largely brought their parents and grandparents to the region in the first place. Life was not an easy affair. So it was up to them to take on the next challenge. Here's the story of how they did it.

Nobody said it better from an insiders perspective than Ed Harmon.

"The furniture business, to me, it's one of the greatest businesses in the world. From the standpoint that you're dealing with something artistic. You're making something that people enjoy, that people use, that has a beauty surrounding it, that has a certain amount of the human element that has to go into making it, like an artist, whether you're a Van Gogh or you're this or that. You're making a product that people use and appreciate. And it affords you the opportunity to be the artist. You're helping to create, helping to make. And it enables you to travel anywhere you want to go in the world and write it off."

Richard Eller
Hickory, NC
November 2022

—⊶⧓⊶—

Williams Wood Carving

Chapter One
THE UNEXPECTED TURN

The company had been in business for 46 years. And now it was closing.

Tony Williams recalled he was "nauseated to have to tell the people that spent a lot of their lives there and were very instrumental to the success of the company" that Williams Wood Carving, Inc. was shutting its doors. As Tony characterized it, "I guess politicians decided it's better to have it done somewhere else than here." [1]

Since age 11, Tony had been part of the workforce at his family's company. He walked a mile each day from his school, Sweetwater Elementary, to attempt any job his father thought his years and abilities could handle. "Basically, I would walk there, and I'd work until my dad got ready to go home, which varied from time to time." He started with simple tasks like sweeping the floor or fetching boxes for the shipment of finished pieces of carved wood, chair legs, to furniture manufacturers in western North Carolina and beyond. When Tony graduated from high school, he went to work full-time, and business was good. [2]

Tony's dad, Dan Williams started in the furniture industry at 18, the same age as when his son Tony committed fully to the family business. Along the way, Dan worked for several firms, including Century and Highland Furniture, before taking a job at Viewmont Wood Carving. The operation was very small, with just two employees. When the owner could no longer continue because of ill health, he offered to sell the business to Dan. In 1963, the name changed to Williams Wood Carving. "My dad bought his equipment out and went to the customers, and they allowed him to continue," said Tony, adding "he was the one doing the work anyway." [3]

It came as no real surprise that Dan recruited his children to become the future of his company. Of his five kids, Tony and his sister Joyce pitched in to help run the firm. Both got their hands dirty, absorbing details of the operation as they worked. "She dealt a lot with customers over the phone," her brother remembered. Tony went to see them "in person when it was required." Together, they became the second generation of Williams in the profession of woodcarving.[4]

By the 1980s, growth took the shop floor through two expansions, ultimately from 5,000 square feet to four times that. They needed the space because the company had contracts with a host of large manufacturers like Kincaid, Cochrane, A.Broyhill, and Kimball, a piano maker in Indiana. Regularly, Williams Wood Carving turned out over 8,000 pieces a week. One contract with Broyhill featured a line sold to retailer J.C. Penney. The order required "somewhere in the neighborhood of half a million to 750,000 of the same chair leg," Tony recalled, all made by his family's firm.[5]

The business of supplying carved work to the big boys could be tough. Dan Williams was an exacting employer. In a profile of the company by a national trade magazine, the banner quote from the owner said, "a miscalculation of one-sixteenth of an inch in the set-up of an automatic carver can cost us several hundred dollars - that's why we're super cautious in what we do." Dan made sure his children knew how much a mistake could hurt the company, not only in dollars but in the trust manufacturers placed in those chair legs being identical to specifications, each one exactly like all the others.[6]

To meet the demand, Dan bought carving machines that could churn out multiple copies. Williams Wood Carving utilized three machines that cut 24 legs at a time, one that handled 36, and two at 40. To get the legs as the manufacturer ordered them, some needed up to 35 separate operations performed before they were ready. Plus, these machines were not computerized. Most operated from a master copy. Wooden masters tended to wear down over time, so large orders required masters made from aluminum castings to maintain accuracy.[7]

A savvy businessman, Dan Williams used a creative practice that served him well to settle any argument a customer might voice about an order. When a furniture decision maker agreed that the example in front of them was the one they wanted, Dan required the buyer to sign the actual wooden prototype. If a disagreement emerged later about style, wood choice, dimensions, or any other faulty recollection of the deal, Dan presented the leg as irrefutable evidence. The father taught the practice to his son, requiring that each order include a signature on the wood. "We'd keep them where we

The multiple carving machine in use at Williams Wood Carving. The devices made exact copies from the original. During peak times the carvers were in operation for as much as 20 hours a day with some requiring up to 35 separate operations before they were ready for clients. (Image courtesy of Tony Williams)

kept all our patterns," Tony said, "and if there was an issue, that was what we were going to go back to."[8]

To meet demand, the Williams clan kept machines going for as long as 20 hours a day. When the situation required overtime, both Tony and Joyce pitched in. Occasionally, Tony saved time by carving the legs without a guide. Once, Dan asked his son, "how'd you run it?" Tony's reply, "I free handed it." Amazed, his father responded, "I looked at them, and they're all the same." Tony took some satisfaction by reminding his dad, "well, that's the idea." By that point, Tony's "muscle memory" had become so exacting that he could create an intricately carved leg copy with confidence.[9]

In 1985, Dan Williams decided to retire, at least officially. He turned Williams Wood Carving, Inc. over to his son and daughter, with Joyce Williams Hunsucker serving as president and plant manager and Tony Williams as vice-president and foreman. The parents travelled regularly, but Dan kept abreast of what was going on with the company, coming in daily when he was home.

Tony made sure he followed the practices his father had taught. For example, the firm seldom went into debt, waiting until they could pay for a piece of equipment before buying it. Also, they never purchased a new machine when it first came out on the market. Tony adhered to his dad's rule of "let's wait till they get a lot of the bugs worked out of it." The Williams clan maintained a consistent approach to business from one generation to the next.[10]

Throughout his time at the helm, Dan Williams always made sure he took care of his employees. Whether it was sponsoring youth baseball teams where the roster included the children of his staff or donations to churches and charities close to the heart of the workers, Dan Williams and subsequently his children were generous. Recognized as a leader in giving, the Hickory Better Business Bureau recognized the public-spirited work of Williams Wood Carving with its 1998 Community Excellence Award.[11]

Even with an effectively run business, slowly but steadily, business dwindled. The Williams' began to notice a loss of orders that totaled around 15% each year, starting in 1999, "when one of the trade deals was signed," said Tony. "We didn't lose a single customer to another American company; it was all China." All their work was leaving. From a friend, Tony found out that retailers "could buy a finished piece from another country cheaper than I could buy the wood before I ever started on it." The downward spiral continued each year until the family decided to cease operations. By that point, Williams Wood Carving was down to ten people. [12]

Even in the last days of the company, the owners made sure they went to whatever lengths necessary to take care of their people. Concerned that everyone losing their jobs would have something to fall back upon, Tony and Joyce appealed to their congressional representative for help with employee retraining through trade

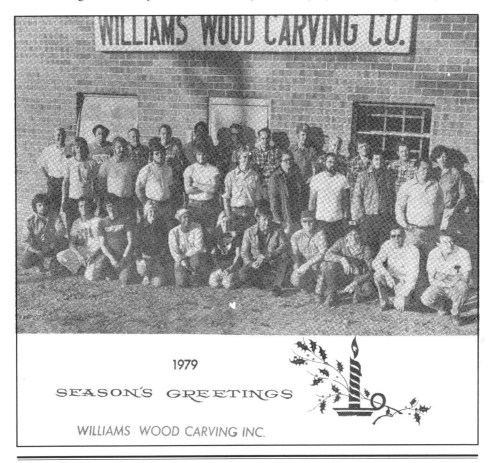

Dan Williams believed strongly in supporting his workers. In addition to the Christmas greetings sent out to friends and customers, Williams Wood Carving supported the community by sponsoring Little League teams and other philanthropy to show appreciation. (Image from Tony Williams)

adjustment legislation. They got the paperwork "where it needed to go in Washington." In fact, Tony also took classes at Catawba Valley Community College as part of the retraining effort for the skills necessary to finish out his career once the family business had ended.[13]

The wrenching experience of ending their family business punched Tony Williams right in the gut, as it did the entire family. Starting with the days he walked from elementary school to the factory, Tony gave 34 years of his life helping to build the company his father started. Now he was forced to let go, which tragically included saying goodbye to his father. In October of 2004, Tony and Joyce had known the end was coming; so did Dan. They agreed that what customers they had left needed to be notified. After filling current orders, they bid farewell to their loyal clients, directing them to look for another vendor. Before the reduced operation could complete those last carving contracts, Dan Williams died of a heart attack. [14]

Recalling the anguish that Dan faced with the loss of their business, Tony could see the stress it caused his father, who "didn't take that (the closing) very well. He was angry about it." So was Tony. "It bothered me for a long time," he said. From the perspective of 2021, he admitted "won't say it don't still." Time blunted a portion of the anxiety, but the wound remained. "I had to get to the point where I don't dwell because it was too harmful to my health. I had to let it go, but angry about the situation, that would be an understatement."[15]

Almost as painful as seeing the company destroyed by foreign competition was the indignity of watching the machinery that Williams Wood Carving owned be auctioned off for a small fraction of its worth. Tony and his fellow carvers always took immaculate care of those carving machines. They were the life blood of the firm, implements that turned blocks of oak, ash, cherry, and mahogany into pieces adorning furniture in homes across the country. All he could do was stand by as he witnessed buyers carelessly handling the devices as they attempted their removal. For the previous owner, it was too much. "I couldn't watch; I had to leave," remembered Tony as he turned out the lights.[16]

The fate of Williams Wood Carving illustrates the pain suffered by almost everyone in western North Carolina who looked to the furniture industry for their income. The generation who took control in the late 20th century trusted that the system would follow the same course it had for their elders, a fluctuating but stable

18

profession that they could rely upon until it was time for their children to take over. Furniture making had been a staple of life in the foothills of the Tarheel state since before their grandparents could remember. Why would it ever change?

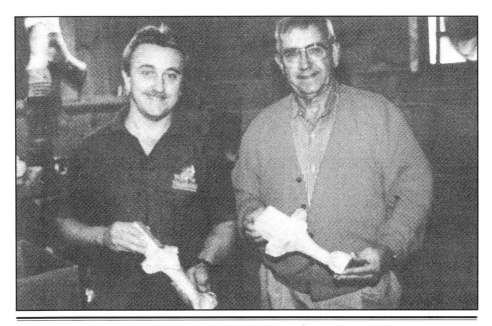

Son and father pose with their creation, chair legs which were integral to the furniture industry. Tony could amaze his father by free handing the carving of legs that met the exacting specifications of manufacturers throughout western North Carolina. (Image from Tony Williams)

Pioneers to western North Carolina relied on their own ingenuity to build the necessary furniture for their cabins when they began arriving in the later 18th century. This reconstruction of pioneer home includes examples of tables and chairs found in early area homes. (Author's Collection)

Chapter 2
Workmanship of Wood, Chisel and Awl

When English and German speaking pioneers crossed the Yadkin and Catawba Rivers into the backcountry to begin their settlement of western North Carolina, they brought with them the essentials to begin their new life. Furniture, for the most part, was not among those items. The trip was arduous enough without hauling cabinets for storage, tables for gathering, chairs for seating, and bedsteads for sleeping. Aside from a chest or trunk which contained all their worldly possessions, everything they needed for stockpiling and comfort in a settled household could be crafted from wood, the one thing the area had in abundance. Those settlers were much like every other group who migrated west to lay claim to middle North America in what became the United States. They squatted on land they saw as free and available, with all the natural growth of their future furniture upon it.[17]

Arriving in waves, ready to lay down roots, the first order of business was shelter; then came furnishings. Both were driven by necessity. But for these people, if their 'mother of invention' dictated what they would need, luckily for them, the father, named 'proximity,' provided a multitude of handy choices. These migrants had wandered into a land rich in a variety of wood. When first settled, trees could sometimes be more of a hinderance than a blessing to building a productive economy. The fruit of the forest, while perfect for erecting a cabin, needed to be thinned out to establish cultivated fields for food. Some planted around the stumps just to expedite a crop, but land was abundant so most of the acreage claimed in the 18th century went uncleared and left room for future expansion.

Adam Sherrill is credited as the first European settler to cross the Catawba River in 1747 with a clear intent to homestead. He brought with him a family and enslaved persons, who under his direction, turned wilderness into real estate. Spanish conquistador Juan Pardo had been through the area two centuries earlier, but in the name of exploration, not settlement. Sherrill and others like Heinrich Weidner (anglicized as Whitener) were all part of

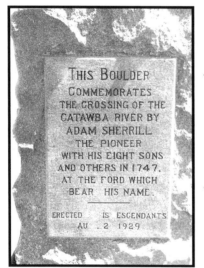

Just up from the ford in the Catawba River where the Adam Sherrill party crossed into the western wilderness stands a marker to commemorate the arrival. Sherrill and the families that followed began a woodworking tradition in a land with plenty of raw materials. (Author's collection)

a group that included "sturdy English Quakers, serious hard working Scots-Irish (Scots that migrated from Ireland) and frugal Germans who trekked down from the valleys of Pennsylvania to the Carolina foothills," as one account described the lot from the perspective of 1933. These groups formed the basis of a growing population in the Catawba Valley. Once they got there, they began to build what they needed to sustain life.[18]

With survival being the first order of business, useful but not absolutely necessary items would have to wait. Once a roof was over their heads, consideration could be given to units for everything else. Beds, tables, and chairs quickly became important to these families since they were of everyday use. The earliest settlers built what they needed themselves. Noted one observer, "tables and benches were generally only split logs. Legs were placed in bored holes. The product was dressed smooth by hand," a summation of the process of taking trees and turning them into useful articles. But ingenuity, a tool always in the shed of early settlers, helped them create more specialized furniture. It wasn't long before a stream of water within a property line was used to power a wood lathe. At that point, the poles of young trees could be turned into four poster beds, chair legs and cradle rails. Slowly, the process of crafting items for storage and relaxation developed.[19]

Settlers took what the wood gave. "The pioneer's work was gross, for his tools were few and rudimentary," said a Burke County historian, adding that "almost every early settler knew how to use the axe, the glut and the maul." The hardships of settling in the untamed region were many. Those first settlers trod into a land that presented harsh challenges with never-ending chores. They may have looked up to the high peaks of the North Carolina Appalachians thankful they did not have to traverse the gaps as they made their claims below. While family members craved the finery enjoyed down toward the flatlands of the coast, the basics of day-to-day life took precedent. It was, however, always their intention to bring order to the wilderness. When they came, items like family Bibles spoke to an adherence of a civilized, even polite world with a distinct ethic. What they could not attain upon arrival, they aspired to as the years of occupancy passed. Those desires revealed themselves in their evolving surroundings. Houses lost their dirt floors in favor of wood puncheons, windows were crafted of real glass, and mattresses were filled with feathers instead of straw, once they could afford such. Furniture followed suit.[20]

Along with the appearance of the house itself, the furniture inside denoted status. The head of a household never shied away from boosting his standing in the community. It was in the best interest of owners to shed crude tables, chairs, and cupboards made by them or their elders in favor of pieces crafted by artisans as soon as they reached the financial ability to redecorate. Wealthy homeowners could import finely produced items from England. If they did so, the new furniture would finally arrive by ship to Charleston, SC, and have to be hauled "over rough, often muddy trails, a trip that required several weeks." Those who could not afford the expense might instead imitate the style of their social 'betters' by improvising.[21]

The hard work of family and enslaved members of the household over a span of multiple growing seasons allowed accumulated affluence to build. As the 19th century dawned, finer and more aesthetically pleasing clapboard houses needed better furniture to match. Outside, stumps rotted or were dug up to add to the aesthetic. Meanwhile the progeny of the first settlers continued to shrink forests as they too built, creating their own homesteads and fields. As part of that landscape, households kept woodlots for firewood and future building needs. Even with this development, the southern highlands retained vast amounts of forested land, most of it fairly new growth, thanks to the clearing practices of the land's previous inhabitants, the Catawba and Cherokee Indians. If migrants to the Catawba Valley came for the land they could claim, sustainable life required the use of its trees, too.[22]

Family wealth dictated ever improving ornamentation to let neighbors see their emerging power within the community. They knew what finer furniture looked like, but living in the backcountry, they had little means to acquire items like sideboards (used as serving stations for family meals) and cupboards (for storage of dishes). They could, at great expense, import those large items from the homeland, even as this newer land had become home for successive generations of upwardly mobile colonists. An 1894 article from the St. Louis Globe-Democrat, remembering the world of 100 years earlier, declared that "almost all the furniture was imported from England." While such may have been true for ultra-wealthy homes around New York and Boston, procuring finely crafted pieces ordered from across the Atlantic proved both expensive and time consuming for the Western North Carolina residents. Those primitive roads up from Charleston or down the Great Wagon Road from Philadelphia were unkind to the merchandise. Settlers in western North Carolina took a more pragmatic approach.[23]

As the population grew, sprinkled among the skills of new arrivals was carpentry. Patrons who wanted sturdy, if not the most ornately crafted furniture, tapped them to adapt their abilities. It didn't take long for carpenters to advance their versatility and build anything a homeowner wanted. These craftsmen offered their services as itinerant cabinetmakers, traveling to where the work was. The surrounding forests featured a vast variety of hardwoods from which both buyer and builder could choose. Once a handshake deal was struck, the woodworker applied his expertise. The tree was chopped down, planks cut and dried so construction could commence. The more seasoned and flashy artisans brought miniature samples of their work to impress and inspire the head of the household as to the look of the finished product. Often, homeowners boarded the cabinetmaker for as long as it took to build the items. An unknown artisan who made a house full of appliances for Colonel William Davenport at his home, "The Fountain," stayed on the premise for three years. These journeymen fabricators were not always alone. Some brought their assistants with them, while others employed whoever was handy around the house, sons and daughters, or even the enslaved of the buyer, especially for tasks like felling trees.[24]

Those cabinet makers offered an additional service that is seen today as a separate job, that of an interior decorator. When contracted to craft a piece for an affluent homeowner, the carpenter "knew where each piece would stand and knew the owner's personality," which explains why many of those creations stood for centuries in the same space, never being replaced, as much a permanent part of the home as the walls.[25]

Skill and the imaginative eye of the area's first furniture makers remained an inspiration that carried down through the years. Periodically, mechanized manufacturers went back to the look of those hand-crafted pieces for inspiration. Acknowledging the beauty and strength of wardrobes, tables, and dressers built individually to 18th/19th-century tastes, those designs proved incredibly popular among buyers of later years. 'Early American' lines remained solid sellers in the 20th and 21st centuries.[26]

The education of itinerant furniture makers came from a wide variety of sources. Some received training from the prominent cabinetmakers of the day, a few as far away as England and Germany, but mostly from within the colonies. They carried those acquired skills into the settled wilderness to make a living, creating objects that would first satisfy the needs of the buyer but later be passed down to succeeding generations for use and pleasure.

The mysteries contained in the workmanship of wood, chisel, and awl have remained very real since their creation. For example, one secret drawer held the answer to an interstate dispute, finally settled after more than a century in the cabinetry of Colonel Davenport, at his home in upper Caldwell County. As Maude Minish Sutton reported,

> It was a large piece built of walnut with beautiful inlay and carving. It was made on the place (Davenport's home, 'The Fountain') in 1807 by a journeyman cabinetmaker from wood selected by Colonel Davenport. It was a typical Sheraton piece and isstrikingly handsome. Its chief interest, however, is historic. A few years ago the official survey of the boundary between North Carolina and Tennessee was lost. A great-granddaughter of Colonel Davenport, Miss Lillie Jones, the present owner of the sideboard found Colonel Davenport's notes of the original survey in a secret drawer of the old sideboard and let the Governor have them to reconstruct the original survey.[27]

The treasures of Davenport's desk demonstrated the intricacy and importance of crafted pieces to the lives of those who commissioned the work.

When the job was done, the maker would occasionally sign his work in an inconspicuous place, a reminder of who created the piece as well as a calling card for posterity, or at least the next job. One estimate suggested there were "hundreds of small cabinet shops" that dotted the landscape of the Piedmont region of North Carolina before the Civil War. While some left their mark on finished merchandise, others remained anonymous. Since furniture was then, as it is now, a large ticket item, pieces were not easily discarded. Many early homes did not include closets (a curse of taxation which declared them another room and therefore taxable), so a wardrobe was an essential to early generations. Only demolition might force removal of a piece too large to get through a doorway. Luckily, the majority of crafted items remained where they were originally placed, which allowed them to be treasured as family heirlooms and preserved for study. Their cherished existence proved their value, not only to the original owners, but to the sons and daughters who inherited them.[28]

The names of early cabinetmakers that did not sign their creations are sadly lost to history. Only conjecture relating to the styles and workmanship employed leave any clue to their identity. One craftsman, Henry Payne, came to be known for his carvings which could be found in his construction of walnut chests for patrons in the upper Catawba Valley. Payne learned how to inlay pieces of maple and holly into his work, taught by a Lincolnton cabinet maker named Houser, who, in turn apprenticed the trade in southern Germany. Payne lived "near the mouth of Little River" in what is today Caldwell County. The items he fashioned serve as a good example of the ability of a skilled craftsman at the end of the pre-industrial age. He trained his son Abner to carry on the tradition (and the business) of making custom furniture, furthering a family tradition in the art of building furniture as an honorable pursuit in North Carolina's back country.[29]

Some post-Civil War artisans used the new communication medium of newspapers to advertise their skills, thus leaving a more permanent record of their existence. One example is William Seaver. He made furniture in Marion and served as the town's mortician (he made coffins too). Seaver advertised his products as far away as Lenoir where he placed an advert for his work in the *Caldwell Messenger* in 1875.[30]

The work of these craftsmen matched the pragmatic lifestyle of the colonists. William Stevens, in his book on the Broyhill family's rise in the furniture business, offered ideas about the styles adopted by early "carpenters, joiners and sawyers." He asserted that beyond the limited skills early furniture makers possessed, which kept their product simple, the styles that reflected the world from which settlers came served as a "nostalgic" comfort to families far away from their origins. Stevens likened the early furniture crafters as a

One of the earliest ways customers could buy production line, though not machine made furniture. This 1875 advertisement from Lenoir's Caldwell Messenger appeared as the cabinet maker's shop began to face completion. (Image from the *Caldwell Messenger*)

type of Michelangelo, working in wood instead of marble, "with chisels driven not by hammers but, for maximum delicacy and precision, with the butt of a hand." Most of the true artists found work and renown in the cities of colonial America. In the sparsely settled foothills, their skill would have been less precise, with more craftsmen like William Seaver making furniture in plain styles. When the home furnishings business lagged, they made a living by other means.[31]

Statewide, hand crafters of furniture were all men and overwhelmingly white, but there were significant exceptions to this rule. Within households where enslaved persons handled the manual labor along with skilled work, some African-Americans became well versed in woodworking. The record of enslaved men who developed such abilities has largely gone unrecorded as craftsmen of furniture in western North Carolina for two reasons. First, the population of enslaved persons in the region grew significantly smaller as the land became more hilly. The largest landowner in what became Catawba County counted something near seventy-seven enslaved persons as a plantation workforce on the southern end where cotton was grown. This number would only count as a small plantation compared to estates down east. Secondly, if an enslaved person did show talent as a furniture maker, that fact would not be celebrated and passed down through history due to attitudes of the era. Where an owner might rent out such services, the fame of the skill would rest with the white owner who controlled such ability even though he did not have the talent himself.[32]

The expertise of an African-American man in building furniture, therefore, is uniquely found as a person who was never a slave but demonstrated such care with his handiwork that he has been called "one of the fathers of the North Carolina furniture industry." Thomas Day did not build any furniture in the Catawba Valley, though the Historical Association of Catawba County retains one of his chairs in its collection. Thomas Day does, however, represent the epitome of woodworking excellence, prized by all who came after. He is now considered the best known "master craftsman" of the pre-Civil War era. The fact that Day had to negotiate the prejudices of the era to develop and be appreciated for the furniture he made elevates his stature as even more astounding.[33]

Thomas Day's workshop, in the upper central North Carolina town of Milton, employed over a dozen workers, including some enslaved persons, though we can only guess at the relationship between the two. Day innovated the process of making furniture on a production scale by use of the era's best power source, steam. Day and his workforce turned out both furniture and moldings for interiors throughout central North Carolina. His style, described as "exuberant" was sought after by many affluent homeowners in the state. Today, Thomas Day's work can be seen gracing the campus of UNC-Chapel Hill and the governor's mansion in Raleigh. A cross-section of his pieces have been displayed at the North Carolina Museum of History, as well as the Renwick Gallery at the Smithsonian American Art Museum. Thomas Day demonstrated the levels to which a carpenter could rise if his designs were popular enough to draw a broad range of customers.[34]

Western North Carolina did produce an artisan of color who was regarded for his work. Born just a few years before Thomas Day died, Philo Gaither Harbison left scant information about his work and his life. He made a living as a woodworker, but his products were not celebrated in ways like those of Day. Harbison was born a slave in 1856 and grew up in Morganton. Upon his death 101 years later, he was hailed as once owning "the only furniture making plant in Morganton." Other than that, little is known about Harbison's work. To make ends meet, Harbison also worked as a carpenter. His house in downtown Morganton, later demolished, was noted as a prime sample of his abilities. Thankfully, a second example, Gaston Chapel A.M.E. Church, a "gothic revival" church he helped construct still stands near downtown Morganton.[35]

Even within the Jim Crow era, Philo Harbison was appreciated for his talent. On a trip he made to San Francisco, the Morganton paper was sorry to see him go, saying in the racist tone of the time that he was "a very industrious darkey." None of Harbison's pieces have survived, but a few descriptions document his design and craftsmanship. During a 1998 exhibit at the Old Burke County Courthouse, home of the Historic Burke Foundation, the historical organization highlighted Harbison, noting how he "designed and built custom made furniture" from his shop "on the corner of Sterling and Erwin Streets." Only a few pictures and stories told by the family Philo left behind preserve any understanding of the once prominent furniture maker.[36]

The Historic Burke Foundation presented one piece that spoke for an untold number of craftsmen whose work did not survive. In the exhibit was a handmade cradle. Over the years, the rockers were removed after an accident where the sister of a baby being rocked plunged the infant onto the floor. The builder was thought to have been an enslaved person of the John Perkins

Philo Harbison was one of Morganton's most famous crafters of furniture. Although none of his work survives, the African-American artisan was hailed for his carpentry, as well as furniture making skills in the era that began to move from individual craftsmen to machine made pieces. (Image from *Charlotte Observer*)

family, who lived on the banks of John's River in Burke County. With modest appreciation and no fanfare, carpenters who built pieces like the cradle have become invisible, their artistic fame forgotten by time. Items like the cradle that did survive are the only evidence left. The artifacts offer few details about how they were made and by whom, an unfortunate reflection of the times.[37]

As with a painter or an architect of the period prior to mechanization, the work of a skilled builder of furniture was considered important to the stature of the person who owned it. Burke historian Edward Phifer, Jr. maintained that carpenters and cabinet makers were second only to blacksmiths in possessing the most important skill necessary to any community. In its own way, a well-designed piece of furniture compared to paintings. In fact, pieces of built furniture were often displayed alongside framed artwork with both appreciated for their beauty. But like the design of a structure, the usefulness of a piece of furniture was also a consideration. In its function as well as its form, furniture straddled the two worlds requiring an armoire or desk to be both handsome and practical. The piece needed to be beautiful enough to be showcased while also doing duty as a sturdy appliance able to withstand the punishment dealt to it in regular use.[38]

With a few masterpieces under his belt, the ingenuity of the crafter came to be highly regarded in the cabinet shop era by his contemporaries as shown by the work of William Wiseman. He stowed away to the New World from London. When Wiseman arrived in Boston, he apprenticed to a furniture maker who carved feet to look like a claw holding a ball. Wiseman took the innovation one step further, making the ball within the clawfoot roll. No longer an apprentice, he took his skill to North Carolina, where he became a master craftsman.[39]

Before Caldwell was its own county, Thomas Sumter gained a reputation as a notable cabinet maker where he lived near Patterson. In the 1820 census, his shop hired six workers, and every year he and his crew went through "two thousand feet of walnut, cherry and pine," building custom pieces for families in the area. That year, he estimated sales at "approximately $1,200." Furniture makers like Wiseman and Sumter, along with others, were highly regarded for their abilities to envision lumber as decorative and useful furnishings, then turned that wood into crafted pieces.[40]

Mechanized furniture factories would one day overshadow the cabinet shops that preceded them. One state historian defined the rise of the furniture industry as a "recent" phenomenon (from the perspective of the 1960s), unable to see the thread that led from one generation of woodworker to the next with the contrast between handmade and machine-crafted furniture seemingly too diverse for connection. But as another observer pointed out in the 1930s, which likely remained true until the end of the century, "in every one of the furniture factories of the town there are descendants of the old craftsmen who made the fine old pieces." An example is "one early manufacturer, Henry Payne, who operated a furniture factory at the mouth of the Little River in Caldwell county before the Revolutionary war, has descendants in the factories of Lenoir, Hickory, and Statesville." The strong tradition of furniture made by hand paved the way for all that would come after.[41]

North Carolina found itself in a unique position before its attempted exit from the Union in 1861. The Old North State was a reluctant secession partner and harbored the largest region of Union loyalty in the South. These loyalists were scattered throughout the western mountains. Beyond that fact, Tarheels attempted to adopt the ways of industrialism much earlier than their southern counterparts. In her research on the advent of the furniture industry, historian Michelle Kilbourne noted, "as confirmation of the economic advantage, entrepreneurship, and fortune-hunting of the gentry, as well as skills of the state's small group of middle class artisans and mechanics, North Carolina claimed 3,689 manufactories on the eve of the Civil War, making it one of the most industrialized states in the South." Whether they realized it or not, the foundation was laid. Manufactories, in those days, represented any shop where a product was made. Some used horse power to turn lathes and the like, while a few that could afford small steam engines substituted human muscle with the power it provided. The number of such factories in the foothills was limited to one small textile plant in Patterson before the war.[42]

Some of those old workshop journeymen perhaps never knew exactly what they had spawned. Azor Shell was a carpenter in Caldwell County's earliest days, handling the interior woodwork of the first courthouse while his brick mason partner, Uriah Cloyd, constructed the exterior. But more importantly, Shell apprenticed a number of young men who would one day take the skill of crafting wood to new heights. Both George F. Ivey (Southern Desk) and Abram Kent, father of A.A. Kent (Kent-Coffey Furniture), studied under the old master, elevating wood-turning into a much larger affair when their time came.[43]

The rise of an industry that took the tools of the carpenter/joiner/sawyer and developed them into electric bandsaws, edgers, and varnish sprayers, adapted the tradition into the technology of a new day and created furniture for an ever-widening market. As a 1919 history of North Carolina, written during the era when those innovations were firmly taking hold, explained,

> *"The manufacture of furniture is an industry that has been developed from crude beginnings, as public taste and desire for greater comfort has grown. In the very early days, when careful, laborious, patient handwork, had to go into every piece, beginning with the tree in the forest and through long drawn out stages to its final completion in the cabinet makers' shop, comparatively few could own as many specimens of handsome, serviceable furniture as they desired, or even needed. Machinery has brought about wonderful changes."*[44]

Chapter 3
The Pivot

Out of the ashes of the American Civil War came fertile ground for industry and western North Carolina furniture production. Until the war upset the lives of southerners, farming served as the predominant occupation for most in the region. It wasn't the end of slavery that created substantial disruption in the foothills as share-cropping filled the void of a labor shortage brought on by the 13th Amendment and outcome of the war. Many small-scale farms relied more on family labor than from enslaved persons in the hillier climes. As ex-Confederates returned home to rebuild their lives and their farms, they had a tougher job ahead than they knew. Crop prices fluctuated constantly, usually downward and the ability to feed a family with the proceeds of each harvest became a constant worry. The generation learning at the knee of their returning fathers began to question if their chance of attaining wealth by farming would ever match that of their grandfathers or even their pre-war fathers.

For many survivors of the war in the foothills of North Carolina, the real destruction was not in the battles fought. 'Fire and sword' barely touched the western end of the state. In fact, the strongest support for the Union and against the Confederacy centered there. Only in the final days of the conflict did federal troops come to pillage. Failed cavalry commander General George Stoneman looked to restore his reputation after a disastrous miscalculation earlier in the war by leading a raid from east Tennessee. His primary objectives were Salisbury, North Carolina where a Confederate prison housed Union captives, then Saltville, Virginia, which had a lot of the staple for which it was named. His troops then foraged into Hickory and Newton to destroy the commissary supplies held in warehouses for the Confederate army. Along the way, he or some contingent of his command brought a short but terror-filled sweep through Boone, Wilkesboro, Lenoir, Asheville, and Taylorsville in 1865.[45]

More devastating than the raids to western North Carolina was the reduction in manpower that marched away or were later drafted to fight in conflicts far from their farms. Newly-clad-soldiers had left the business of agriculture to the care of their wives and children. Some heads of the household attempted to maintain control over planting and sowing decisions with instructive letters back home or visits when they could get a furlough. A portion of those men did not return, dying mostly of disease but also battlefield wounds. Those that did return brought with them the scars of the fight. Men from Catawba, Burke, Caldwell, McDowell, Iredell, and Alexander counties served in bloody campaigns on both sides of the Appalachians. What many came back to were farms less promising than what they left. Ultimately, trying to rebuild a pre-war life in a post-war world presented immense challenges beyond their capacity to control.

The biggest change brought about by the Civil War was the economic landscape to Western North Carolina. The next generation of southerners, those coming of age in the aftermath, sensed that the path to future prosperity was much different from what they saw and were trained to follow as they grew up. The sons of those returning Confederate veterans realized that the game had changed. The difference was a rising interdependent economy, where one prospered by making some item needed by the masses. This new thrust upstaged the self-sufficiency model of generations past. A southern revival would need a revised strategy to be successful.

Recognizing that a reconsideration was taking place, it became apparent that no longer could a man bring his experience and ingenuity to a piece of land and expect it to yield sufficiently for a lucrative lifetime. The outcome of the war signified that the future of doing business had a greater connection with industry than agriculture, no matter how much un-repentant veterans cursed the America they now lived in. Young men who understood that the word Reconstruction was code for assimilation to the already established northern model began to study what new outcomes were possible in the old, wrecked system. They needed to look for more instead of relying on the productivity of the ground to present them with a bountiful crop, only to see the market punish them for that productivity with lower prices for their goods when a glut occurred. As best they could, they determined to balance their heritage with their future, retaining a respect for the land instilled in them by their fathers, but also considering the power of new markets in the later 19th century.[46]

The first wave of mechanization to overtake the South was textile production. Two generations earlier, the North began to invigorate its economy with cotton mills, fed by southern bolls of 'white gold' as Confederates termed the fiber, thinking it was their secret weapon to winning independence. When defeat revealed otherwise, southerners and northern carpetbaggers agreed that bringing the mills to the land where the raw material grew could enhance profits while helping the region reinvent itself. Catawba County lay at the very northern end of the cotton belt. While Newton offered a cotton gin, mill locations for turning cotton into cloth were better situated farther south. A few were built in the foothills, but only because local leaders grasped for something, anything to mechanize business in their towns.

Families like this one populated the region in the years before and during mechanization. Their lives were dominated by agriculture and the skilled crafts. The Suddreths (pictured here) were stone masons, unacquainted with the industrial era at the time of this photograph in 1895. (Author's collection)

The pace of life began to quicken in the 1870s. Towns sprang up and down. Migration in western North Carolina became more fluid than ever before. The town of Morganton had a head start of a hundred years, dating its origin back to the period of the American Revolution. However, its neighbor to the east grew more quickly, from a solitary tavern before the Civil War to an enclave bursting with possibilities. The Western North Carolina Railroad passed through Hickory first, making the place attractive to those pursuing some entrepreneurial scheme. It's almost inexplicable how newcomers from as far away as Michigan ended up in Hickory ready to try an idea, but they did. Tobacco warehouses, race tracks, even an opera house were presented as viable money-making ventures. Some of these businessmen were Confederate veterans who saw the writing on the wall and could adapt to the changing economy. Others were that enterprising next generation, seeing a future built more on interdependency than the solitary work of a farmstead. Hickory, on the northwest corner of Catawba County, prospered while the towns of

Keeverville to the south and Eavesville to the east failed. Those populations were absorbed into Hickory and other towns of the region.[47]

Catawba County fostered numerous commercial centers, each trying to match the right combination of business, investment, and labor to create prosperity. Directly south, comfortably within the northern boundary of the cotton belt, the town of Maiden witnessed the rise of several successful textile mills. Newton, the county seat, relied more on government and tradition to fuel its success. When laid out in 1843, the town sought to be the geographic center of the new county. However, no one took into consideration that a ridge to the north would be the path of the coming railroad, so when trains came in the late 1850s, the tracks and the prosperity that came with them bypassed Newton. A spur to serve Newton only helped to create another competitive business district, Conover. The municipal structures within Catawba County differed significantly from counties that surrounded it. In Caldwell County, all roads led to Lenoir. Alexander County offered much the same model with Taylorsville in the center. So did McDowell County, with its headquarters in the town of Marion. Likewise, Morganton dominated as Burke County's commercial center.[48]

Firmly in the piedmont, Statesville too was at the center of Iredell County. It began as a military post. In 1755, Fort Dobbs was as far as the colonial government of North Carolina was willing to go to protect its western citizens. During the French and Indian War and subsequent clashes with the Cherokee, a stockade in the area protected settlers under attack. In the early years of the new republic, Statesville grew. Tobacco as a cash crop predominated. Up through and beyond the Civil War, the town remained the most prosperous of cities west of Salisbury. In 1860, the per capita wealth of Iredell County exceeded any other to the west. In the years following Reconstruction however, Statesville struggled to maintain its superiority due to the competitive rise of places like Hickory.[49]

The town of Morganton, named for Revolutionary War genius Daniel Morgan, had one unique advantage in the post-war era, the notice of state government. Established prior to the republic, at one time Burke County covered the entirety of western North Carolina and included all of Tennessee. Historically aware citizens of 'old Burke' liked to joke that the county's western border was once the Mississippi River. So important was Morganton as the last stop of civilization that state officials recognized the town as a 'mini-capital' in the west, establishing a variety of institutions that remain to this day. A branch of the state asylum (1883), and a school for the deaf (1894), were both located in Morganton. With an elevation nearing 1200 feet above sea level, similar to Hickory's, both towns became accessible summer refuges for affluent travelers trying to escape the heat. However, Morganton fell behind Hickory as a center of commerce because the railroad line that ran through Hickory just barely failed to reach the Burke County town before the Civil War. What Morganton lacked in entrepreneurs, it more than made up for with government officials. Like any municipality seeking to build its reputation, Morganton wanted economic activity to go with its prestige. Every town did.

It fell to local newspapers to generate enthusiasm for the future and to promote opportunities for expansion. All over the South, the call went out for towns to find their niche and develop their own economic identity. Atlanta journalist Henry Grady coined the term "The New South" as a signifier of post-war rebirth. He was by no means the only proponent, but he may have been the most effective, given the growth of the town he promoted. Grady was one of those sons of a Confederate veteran who realized the need for change to put the region back at the forefront of the American economy. Too young to serve in the war, he and his generation were left to answer how the South would pick up the pieces and craft a new trajectory. As it turned out, the South failed to gain any ground on the industrial Northeast for another hundred years, but at least they kept pace. The call for industrialism and the communities that answered did expand after Grady's journalistic boosterism appeared in newsprint. Industrialism became the new battle cry for southerners, at war again with the North over the future, an economic war that once again found them at a disadvantage. Southerners carefully considered the industries at which they could excel, seeking to help their region shake off defeat and malaise.[50]

In the summer of 1880, a letter came into the Morganton office of the *Blue Ridge Blade* from a "Friend To Burke". In a recent visit, the writer observed that "there seems to be a melancholy depression over everything. The streets are as quiet as if each day of the week were Sunday." He believed that the town "lacked enterprise" and needed help. "I say wake up, keep up with the world, or you will lose the race entirely and be left to die." [51]

Over the next few years, others began to notice the same thing. Undoubtedly, many made mention of the sluggish pace of activity, but it fell to the newspaper editor W. C. Ervin from a rival paper, the *Carolina Mountaineer* to make a lively case to his fellow citizens. "Our great want is the establishment of factories to work up our raw materials, to give our farmers a home market for their supplies, and to employ our unemployed population, thus changing a large percentage of our population from consumers to producers of wealth." With his 'Henry Grady-like' editorial persuasion, Ervin exhorted Morganton to become something more than a government town. He wanted industry. Ervin took the stark evaluation of the "Friend To Burke" to heart, saying, "no other branch of industry yields a better per cent on the capital invested or inaugurates such general prosperity as manufacturing. Not only does it benefit those actually engaged in it as laborers or capitalists, but it quickens the public pulse and gives new life to every other industry." W.C. Ervin voiced the reason every southern town should rise from its agrarian slumber and get to work modernizing, i.e. *industrializing* its activities. The only questions that remained were the type of product to be manufactured and the source of the capital to build factories. [52]

Ervin was on the right track, but his solution needed a bit more thought. "To come down to the practical, our town and our county need more cotton and tobacco factories. Situated as we are in the edge of the great cotton belt and in the very centre of the finest tobacco producing lands in the world, our advantages are unequalled," he reasoned. In a rather conventional way, Ervin came to the same conclusions that every other town in the region was reaching. By 1883 at the time of the editorial, Hickory already had two tobacco warehouses, and the Carpenter family of Maiden was in the process of expanding their textile operation in the southern Catawba County town. Yet the solution was there; Ervin just needed to determine what his city specifically could offer. As part of his declaration, the newspaper editor pointed out how "our water power is unlimited, fuel for the steam engine, both wood and coal, are cheap, the cost of living is small and wages, consequently, low - the very conditions necessary to a thriving manufacturing community." Wood, merely a source of energy in Ervin's mind, had far more to offer than he initially conceived. It would take another couple of years, but the idea that the cheap power he bragged about in the editorial had the potential to serve a more central purpose than he first imagined. What was just a raw material for Ervin could spark an economic boom in Morganton. Very quickly, the idea materialized within a small group of enterprising and energetic young men who had the imagination to make something happen.[53]

The hope of creating a mechanized factory to produce furniture was not new, but it was indeed risky. Sandwiched between the towns of Hickory and Morganton, the tiny community of Icard was home to three men braving the attempt. "Messrs. Lackey Bros. and Warlick are doing a large mercantile business in connection with which they have added a furniture shop and are also manufacturing first class furniture." About the time the "Friend To Burke" noticed the lethargy of Morganton, the combo of Lackey, Lackey and Warlick grabbed the idea that with wood all around, the ability to craft useful pieces of furniture could serve a local market quite well. Their chances of success might have been enhanced if they had stopped there, focusing on one business at a time. Instead, a story on the Lackeys and Warlick went on to report, "they also expect to establish a tobacco factory next spring." While W.C. Ervin pined for something to occupy the men of Morganton in 1880, about 10 miles to the east, the Icard entrepreneurs had the opposite problem, too many business enterprises in which to engage and likely too little manpower to get the job of any one of them done.[54]

Burgeoning interest in developing the wood market popped up here and there. When the first steam sawmill came to downtown Lenoir, "residents watch(ed) spellbound," reported historian Nancy Alexander. Pointing out that the operation used a vertical blade instead of a circular one, Alexander gave credit to Noah Spainhour as the first operator. His was an improvement over the "water-powered planing mill and cabinet shop" of Azor Shell, she said. Before he was usurped by Spainhour's newer technology, Shell held a lot of power in the country crossroads of Lenoir. In addition to constructing some of the town's earliest buildings, he dictated when the dead could be buried as the town's premier coffin-maker.[55]

Venturing forth to produce furniture in a mechanized way held promise, but also some drawbacks. Certainly, western North Carolina had the raw material in abundance. The question at hand was who had the resources and the skill to develop it? Southerners who went back to the land for their work after the war did not have the disposable income to put down cash to start local factories. Men like the Icard's Lackey Brothers and Warlick ultimately did not have the ongoing capital to sustain their furniture operation (or that of the planned tobacco business either). The early post-Civil War years found southerners much poorer than when they left to take up arms.

The only thing left under their own control was their labor and craftsmanship. One historian asserted that these farmers "primarily sold their handicrafts to persons of wealth," exhausting much of their own entrepreneurial drive. Those who returned to the plow for a subsistence life "fashioned their own crudely made benches and tables or traded commodities for the woodworking skills of the local carpenter," just like the early settlers. An investment in mechanized production was well beyond the means of most. Few had the funds to finance a coming industrial wave, even if they saw it coming. [56]

Conditions remained unfavorable for any kind of capitalized operation in the western foothills and mountains after the war. Only Morganton had a bank, a branch of a state institution. Other towns aspired to their own money-lending operations, but most lacked the necessary resources. Thus, any business venture would more likely come more from "northern industrialists in the southern marketplace" than a hometown effort. The majority of returning Confederates hated that idea. As they saw it, the interdependency of factory work and the loss of independence that came with it was too much for the man who still believed in the honor of providing for his family by his own hand. A considerable proportion of veterans looked down on factory work as means of livelihood, considering it servile and unmanly. After all, they had waged war against many northern 'pasty-faced mechanics' in battle after battle. Losing the war was enough. The least they could do was resist the idea of mimicking the victors any more than they had to. Diehards embraced the old lifestyle as a snub to the Yankees even as the times revealed that a return to the plow meant working harder, not smarter.[57]

Marketing to the world would take vision, connections, and a lot of ingenuity. Besides, the base of operations for the furniture industry was already established elsewhere. Boston, New York, and more recently, Grand Rapids, Michigan, had become the source for production of medium and moderately priced furnishings. Homes throughout the region that could afford it bought their bedroom suites and dining room tables from Grand Rapids (via mail order through catalogs) and had them shipped south. Increasingly, wood from North Carolina became a part of the raw material that ended up being crafted over 700 miles away in Michigan. Railroads allowed raw lumber to make the trip north, then value could be added and the finished product returned to the land from where the wood grew.

The initial step toward furniture making in western North Carolina came with the timber business. Technology in the last third of the 19th century had improved to the point that portable sawmills were in popular use. No longer would a large tree have to be brought down and the entire trunk hauled to a sawmill site. Instead, the sawmill could be brought to the tree. Steam engines were key, powering the turning blade that sawed up board feet of lumber into planks which proved much easier to transport. In addition, small, temporary railroad lines were laid specifically for the purpose of carrying the boards out of the forest to established lumber yards. The engines, called shays, pulled the makeshift train lines wherever they needed to go to retrieve lumber. The rails and cars were not held to any kind of standard like passenger railroads of the day since they carried a non-human cargo. Shays and the rickety rolling stock (railroad cars) on which they ran could go wherever timber cutters needed and could be moved in short order. The job was neither easy, nor cheap, but it was relatively quick, much more so than previous methods. The new system solved the problem of getting lumber to market. Demand and the prices it brought made the work economical enough to be worth the effort.

"Headquarters for lumber, dressed and in the rough" was the banner of sawmill owner Hamilton Erwin's advertisement for his operation. He offered everything at every stage. "Green, air or kiln-dried" was sold at his mill on John's River, two miles from Morganton. "Pine, walnut, cherry, poplar or white-oak" was on the menu. He provided lots of choices at any quantity and, as he claimed, "reasonable prices." In and around Morganton, Erwin's business had grown to proportions large enough that he could afford the luxury of advertising. For proprietors like Erwin, the inventory amassed from the portable steam-powered sawmills, sometimes called peckerwood mills, was plentiful. With proximity to vast forests and enough capital to bring the trees down, the sale of timber became a business that southerners could use to make money. Wood was a renewable resource, so cutting it down and shipping it to northern factories seemed like middle ground in the national push to industrialize. If trees were seen as a harvestable product, just like cotton (though with a much longer growing season), the wealth gained from it could provide a livable income for those committed to the land and resistant to factory life.[58]

Timber became a popular investment as the 1880s progressed in western North Carolina. Even if furniture making never came to the foothills, the extractive business of bringing the wood out of the mountains would be important to the regional economy. In Caldwell County, mountainous boomtowns like Mortimer and Grandin installed large operations for the purpose. Higher and higher prices for land that was once seen as worthless, got both attention and dollars from those who could estimate the rate of return. And quite a return it proved to be. "Valuable Land Sale" headings

An early example of the "peckerwood mills." Beginning in the 1880s, entrepreneurs like Tom Broyhill dragged these sawmills through the woods of western North Carolina to saw up the trees where they fell. Broyhill would parlay his steam-powered setup into factory ownership. (Courtesy of the Caldwell Heritage Museum)

began to show up in newspaper ads with greater frequency. Strangely, most of the announcements giving notice of public auction used, of all things, trees to delineate the boundaries of the tracts. One section, for example, described a line running "20 poles to an apple tree, then north 6 poles to a stake, then North 69 W., to a stake in the Dickson line, then east with said line 54 poles to a large white oak."[59]

When not enough land was in play, another business, that of broker sprung up. Just waiting to see who chose to sell did not feed the market fast enough. Newspaperman W.C. Ervin found spurring activity appealing. He turned from editor of the Morganton paper to manager of the Morganton Land and Improvement Company. His advertisements got right to the point. "Do you Want to Sell Your Farm?" He explained to potential sellers that he was in contact with various "real estate agencies in the North and Northwest" (presumably Grand Rapids) and that if an owner was willing to accept a reasonable price, his company could "find a purchaser for you." Offering this service at no cost to the landowner, the profit must have come from the bounties of agencies seeking to acquire property.[60]

The business of sawmilling was recognizable to both pre- and post-war North Carolinians. Prior to the conflict, the antebellum plantation economy included such operations, though with less portable equipment. When the cutting resumed after 1865, "thousands of former slaves and poor whites," some in service as the result of peonage (debt servitude), toiled in lumber camps throughout the region. Their output would keep the mills of Grand Rapids and other furniture producing states busy until local folks began to claim the raw material for their own.[61]

The Old South shed more than slavery in the Civil War. The days of hand-crafted, wooden appliances were numbered. The pace of commerce had quickened, driven by the example of northern factories that mechanized products for mass consumption. Some southerners hung on to the old ways, but the young men of the New South saw what it took to get ahead, and instead of burying their heads in Lost Cause rhetoric, they moved forward, looking to connect the human and natural resources of their native land to an accelerating business climate.

Throughout its progress, the question of how a circle of cities (Statesville, Hickory, Morganton, Marion, Lenoir) could build a furniture industry caused some to dream, others to guffaw at the possibility. The area was thought to be a backwater portion of a backwater state. North Carolina initially excelled as an industrializer, but by 1880 the state languished in the lower middle of the pack of southern states when it came to manufacturing per capita. Only Texas, Alabama, Arkansas, and Mississippi were in worse shape. However, in that lethargy lay the seeds of future success. [62]

Without a strong planter class in the region to rule and revise the Old South mainstay of agriculture, western North Carolina was free to improvise on the cotton mill model. Furniture would always live in the shadow of textiles as an economic driver within the state, but as the mountain west grew more formidable in its age-old battles with eastern North Carolina, activities in the hills announced a willingness to innovate. For accumulating wealth, rivals to agriculture sprang up. The promise of progress put manufacturing on the lips of every concerned citizen looking to advance their town. If the foothills were too far north to accommodate cotton mills (even though every town had one), the ability to take wood and craft it into a serviceable product could serve as an intriguing factory substitute.

Lumber entrepreneurs knew the value of the gold they had growing in the mountains of western North Carolina. They kept tabs by measuring important benchmarks like the circumference of trees and the height to the first limb, a show of maturity. After marching into the westernmost woods, the commissioner of measurements in 1878 reported finding white oak at "13 ft,, 4 in in circumference 50 feet to the first limb." The chestnut was even bigger at 18 feet, 6 inches around, while poplar measured "11 ft, 9 inches in circumference, 70 feet to the first limb." Yellow locust, hickory, shingle oak and black gum were all noted, ready for harvest. The intention was to bring those mighty giants of the forest down to fuel an economic resurgence of the land where they grew.

The rail line that ran from Chester, South Carolina, through Hickory to Lenoir. Once the narrow gauge line was established, industry could commence in the foothills town, named for General William Lenoir of Revolutionary War fame and home to Confederate Major, G.W.F. Harper. (Courtesy of the Caldwell Heritage Museum)

After reaching Lenoir, the Chester and Lenoir Narrow Gauge extended farther into the mountains. This image demonstrates how vital wood was to both the construction and payload of the venture, with carload after carload hauling lumber from Edgemont, in upper Caldwell Co. (Courtesy of the Caldwell Heritage Museum)

Chapter 4
Stepping Out In Faith

Even before the post-Civil War Reconstruction period was over and the South was allowed to set its own course for the future, D.A. Smith of Charlotte, NC, developed an idea. In early 1875, he took over the entire stock of a furniture store on East Trade Street. Next, he incorporated furniture sales in his mercantile store in Wilmington. As his retail chain grew, so did his purpose. He had been a retailer for twenty years, but now he wanted something more. Instead of stocking his stores with furniture made elsewhere, he conceived a plan to manufacture the product, selling it through his own outlets. Just to the northwest of Charlotte grew the raw material he would need. Smith reasoned that building his own factory there for the production of furniture had great potential. With the use of southern labor, he could reap the rewards of forests in the western North Carolina mountains, creating a product that might be larger than even his own stores could handle. If the new American economy wanted industry, he vowed to build it.[63]

Smith would not give in to those feelings of despair voiced by the "Friend from Burke" in Morganton. Throughout Reconstruction, southerners suffered for their armed insurrection. The end of Reconstruction brought new hope for those enterprising enough to see it. Businessmen like Smith rejected the idea that the South had no role to play in driving the national economy. Uniquely, he planned to take matters into his own hands. Around him everywhere remained the defeated. All most could do was vent their frustrations over poverty they felt had been inflicted upon them. The *Morganton Star* spoke for many when it printed the following lament.

> For years Morganton has been content with her merchants selling
> dry goods, groceries, farming implements and even bacon and hay to
> our farmers, and in the fall the farmers would haul their little crop of
> corn to town, pay the merchants and the proceeds would have to go
> North to pay the debts, and then the merchants and farmers were left
> - if not poorer men - barely even.[64]

At a place where the mountains of North Carolina grew so tall that the railroads could barely surmount them, D.A. Smith decided to build a furniture factory. Instead of locating in his hometown, or Wilmington where his non-furniture interests shipped products with ease, he decided instead to go where "walnut lumber is very plentiful," in a location thirty miles beyond Morganton, in Old Fort, North Carolina. Smith found the farthest west a rail line would go to cut the trees he sought. By the winter of 1878, the D.A. Smith Company already had buildings constructed and saws running. Incorporated as "Furniture Manufacturing Company" with $10,000 stock on March 14, 1879, by the General Assembly of North Carolina, Smith got a jump on many of his fellow-Southerners by advancing the New South doctrine of renewed self-sustainability.[65]

Around the same time as D.A. Smith's move, Henry Reicherdt extended an invitation. "I beg leave to announce to the citizens of this and adjoining counties that (I) have opened at Powelltown, near Lenoir, (a) First-Class Furniture Factory." He offered "Bedsteads, Bureaus, Tables, Lounges, &c. In fact, any and everything manufactured in a first-class furniture factory." In the days before production lines became standard, Reicherdt's "factory" was

An 1878 ad for a factory that was still a carpenter's workshop. Henry Reichert made furniture by hand, a proto-industrial enterprise that offered items for the household as well as coffins. The company, located on the eastern end of Lenoir, only did business for a few years. (Image from the *Lenoir Topic* via newspapers. com)

more a workshop where the majority of labor was by hand, very much in the old artisan way of the ante-bellum South, just on a grander scale. Everything he sold was "all of my own manufacture." So sure was he of his product that he invited "people of this section to call at my factory and see for themselves, and I will convince them they will find it to their interest to give me their orders." Unfortunately, best estimates are that the establishment did not last. Advertisements ceased to invite patrons by the end of the year. Reicherdt was out of business but Smith's enterprise in Old Fort continued to expand.[66]

D.A. Smith and his superintendent, William J. Calais oversaw a real mechanized affair. Boasting of "a large supply of the best native woods, walnut, ash, poplar, maple, oak and pine" the emphasis centered on the fact that buyers were getting standardized pieces, straight off the production line. "The outfit is so complete that all the work necessary to the manufacture of a set of furniture is done by machinery, save the putting together and giving the finishing touches." In its construction, customers were getting something seldom before available —machine crafted items— the very opposite of homemade pieces that served many houses in the region. Production-line furniture was offered from the factories of Grand Rapids, "the furniture here manufactured in style and finish is equal to that of any Northern establishment, while in point of solidity and durability vastly superior," said Smith, indicating that the output of the Old Fort factory topped its competitors, who at this point were exclusively in the North. Smith did not mince words. His furniture, either because it was from local trees or crafted under the watchful eye of southerners was a much better buy, a strong selling point, he believed. It didn't end there. The advantage of proximity to the wood meant quality, "for timber being plenty there is no stint in its use, and everything is just what it pretends to be, solid and substantial, no patch work or veneering." In an age when the idea of 'store bought' appealed to consumers for the conformity of style and sturdiness it brought, Smith argued that southerners could get every bit the value available from a Grand Rapids manufacturer, only locally.[67]

In case there was any question about the factory's output, the best way to judge was a comparison with the old way of doing things. D.A. Smith estimated his enterprise as "equal to the capacity of fifty or sixty cabinet makers without the aid of machinery." The popularity of Smith's initiative proved to be an early show of success. It dictated that he plan for expansion of the facility, which seemed sound. He believed his factory would never run out of wood to put through his saws, and with southern labor looking for work, pieces would continue to roll off the line well after he had turned the factory over to younger hands. [68]

Within a few years, calls went out from major cities in the region to make use of the trees waiting in such abundance in the mountains. Charlotte, then Wilmington; even Charleston, SC, recognized the brilliance of adding value to the lumber they saw passing through their towns. By one 1870 estimate, "manufactured furniture fetched nearly three times as much as the materials cost." Everyone wanted to replicate D.A. Smith's idea. Smith had stepped out in faith and found a positive result. If he was going to load anything on a railcar for transport, it was going to be a finished product. Geologists were now telling everyone what D.A. Smith also already knew: "the native woods of North Carolina are not surpassed in quality and variety in this country." Some observers even characterized taking the raw material out on railroad cars without further effort as theft. "We sell our magnificent cherry and walnut logs, worth $50 and $100 when cut into boards, for $5 or it may be $10. Our birth right for a mess of pottage!" ranted the *Greensboro Daily Patriot* in 1885 about the exchange. [69]

Smith developed a jewel of an operation. Advertisement of his Old Fort factory ran regularly in the Raleigh paper, proudly naming the location of the manufactory. Competitors tried to denigrate his product, or at least elevate theirs, but fellow North Carolinians came to Smith's defense, saying "the best black walnut does not grow in Michigan as claimed by an advertiser of this city. The black walnut of western North Carolina is unsurpassed by any in the world and such is an undisputed fact by all furniture manufacturers of this country." The defender went on to note that the factory at Old Fort turned out "first class work, finer indeed than the tawdry stuff of the North-Western houses." [70]

It didn't take long for money to come knocking at the Old Fort factory

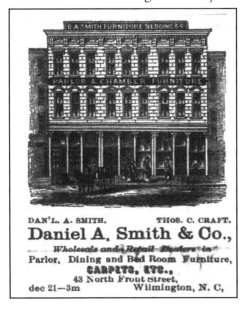

The first to mechanize the process of furniture, Daniel A. Smith brought his experience from owning retail outlets in Wilmington (pictured) and Charlotte to begin the furniture industry in McDowell's County Old Fort, where wood was found in abundance. His factory was the first. (Image from the *The Southern Home*)

door, and D.A. Smith got an offer he could not refuse. It came from none other than the chief engineer and former president of the Western North Carolina Railroad (WNCRR), Major J.W. Wilson. After the sale of the railroad to a "New York syndicate," Wilson "and other capitalists of Morganton have bought the Old Fort Furniture Factory and will move it to Morganton, and there run it on an extensive scale," read one notice. In reality, Major Wilson invested in furniture for the benefit of his son and several other young men of Morganton, all of them well connected.[71]

Wilson and his young management team embraced the New South ethic of industrialism started by and purchased from D.A. Smith. By 1886, activity had so changed in the Old South that for some, the new landscape was unrecognizable. In the pages of the *Morganton Star*, editor T.G. Cobb printed a statement (of which Henry Grady would have been proud). Cobb bragged on his town by writing, "who will deny that Morganton is on the high road to prosperity when they know that in the last two years she has built over sixty new dwelling and business houses and a number are on the way now; besides that, one furniture and one door, sash and blind factory, and last but not least, good prospects for a new railroad."[72]

Cobb liked what he saw Morganton becoming. The Wilson factory stood at the center of Morganton's industrial hopes and a perfect example of the entrepreneurial spirit forward-thinking people of the time were seeking. Outsiders could barely conceal their bewilderment. As far as the growth of its business activities, they wanted to know, "What is going on all Around Us?" *The Manufacturers' Record*, a business trade paper based in Baltimore asked the question. Keeping tabs on the South's post-Civil War economic activity, the April 1885 edition looked to see what kind of businesses were gaining capital investment. Their snapshot showed wide diversification throughout the formerly seceded states but especially in North Carolina. The largest investment of all was in the western part of the state where a $200,000 copper mine started. On the coast, Wilmington got a new 10-ton ice plant while Goldsboro sported a $20,000 foundry and machine shop. In that single quarter, the business journal tallied investment in the war torn South totaled some 21 million new dollars.[73]

Moving west in the Old North State, woodworking companies began popping up to augment the diversity reported by the *Manufacturers' Record*. The city of Winston (before its golden hyphen with Salem) built a new planing mill, but surprisingly at that time no new tobacco factory, a commodity for which it would one day be known around the world. Greensboro and High Point added tobacco companies, but those start ups competed for workers with the Greensboro Sash and Blind Company which in turn competed for raw materials with the W.H. Snow Company and Snow and Cox, both out of High Point. The two High Point enterprises made spokes for wheels while one also made handles, the other, spindles for textile mills. Wood as a central focus of manufacturing was beginning to find a variety of outputs.[74]

The only specific mention of furniture in the news came with the inclusion of the Morganton Furniture Company. Even before recognition in the *Manufacturers' Record*, the factory was up and running. Located near the town's depot, the building housed a dozen or more pieces of machinery for the workforce of 35 mechanics.[75]

In partnership with the Major, ownership of the Morganton factory was in the hands of H.R. Hicks, a former machinist and engineer at the State Asylum in Morganton, along with E.F. Reid and Major Wilson's son, Alexander Wilson. It appears that W.W. Avery, who would later go on to run his own furniture company, also had some financial stake in the company. From the announcement of the company to its start of operations, expectations and output for the operation grew quickly. By September, the monthly payroll hit one thousand dollars. "Substantially and rapidly this excellent enterprise is growing, and promises soon to be one of the largest establishments in the country," opined the *Asheville Citizen* about the furniture factory down the mountain.[76]

The new establishment took every opportunity to craft any essential family need. The *Morganton Star* energetically reported that "two of the neatest coffins we have seen for years were made at the Morganton Furniture Factory for Mr. W.S. Sudderth and Mrs. Girtrude McCall. Price twenty-five and forty-five dollars." Showing off everything they made, the owners gave a full-fledged tour to the editor of the *Carolina Watchman*, a regional paper from Salisbury. J.J. Bruner described the plant as "splendid" with "all the necessary improved modern machinery for manufacturing any kind of furniture or house decorations." He also noted the types of wood available. "They make walnut, ash, cherry, and oak suits and keep a large force constantly employed on the cheaper grades of furniture. They turn out immense lots of the latter and sell at figures that defy competition."[77]

Throughout its first year in operation, the future looked very bright for Morganton to lead the way in the new industry of furniture making. Planning for a catalog of their inventory, the company hired Lenoir photographer L.A. Ramsour to relocate in order to take "pictures of furniture for the Morganton Furniture Company." Business opportunities catapulted themselves at the factory. Just after opening in May of 1885, Alex Wilson got a visit from D.C. Pearson who asked for the building of a baby crib. Estimates were that if Mr. Pearson proved to be a satisfied customer, a market in cribs awaited sales. Proprietors Wilson and Reid left no stone unturned to meet market demand while squeezing every penny's profit. They even bartered raw materials. In an advertisement in the *Morganton Star*, the following request came. "Now is the time for the farmers of Burke County to furnish their homes with furniture made from our native wood. We will exchange furniture for walnut, maple, cherry and poplar lumber."[78]

Growth was not without risk as a few occupational hazards made headlines also. In April of 1886, an employee, Mr. S.S. Lane accidentally had "the misfortune to get two of his fingers sawed off by a circular saw." Another slight interruption occurred when one of the boilers broke down, giving the "hands" of the factory "a rest of a few days." By June, Alex Wilson and E.F. Reid built on, adding "to their already large furniture factory building."[79]

In addition to using wood for furniture, across town the duo of Messrs. Ross and Foster, described as "two energetic men" started a sash and blind factory. The company vowed to "furnish anything required to build a house in first class order at short notice." In their steam powered facility the company could supply the finishing woodwork needed, including bannisters, doors, and moldings. Demand for wood intensified as another pair, Winters and McCurry entered the manufacturing market, making mattresses, brooms and more importantly, chairs. Applauded in the press in early 1886, the two were noted to be "blind boys." The pitch for commerce was sympathetic, but essential the same. "We hope our people will patronize these worthy, unfortunate young men, who are trying to make an honest living."[80]

From these beginnings, boosters and observers alike hoped the efforts would place Morganton on the map as an industrial town, earning it even more prominence in the western part of the state. Wilson and Reid's Morganton Furniture Company became an emblem of the New South's boosterism energy. *Morganton Star* editor T.G. Cobb wrote about walking through the factory in early 1886 and noticing the caliber of worker he saw. Impressed by the sweat of young men whose families he knew personally, Cobb lionized their efforts as "the right step in the right direction." He challenged the old Confederates who still eschewed the value of industrialization and affirmed the northern work psyche as superior to that of the South. He declared, "the great secret of the North being heretofore so far ahead of the South in all kinds of manufacturing, was, everybody from the lowest to the highest, engaged in some useful employment, consequently labor was to be respected, while in the South, especially during the ante-bellum days, labor was to be ostracized." Cobb had put his finger on the turnabout necessary for southerners to compete. Admitting that one did not have the financial means to own enslaved persons to do the work for them was thought to be shameful, an acknowledgement of one's inferiority in the Old South's social pecking order. Cobb argued that the opposite had now become true. Industry and the pride that comes from its beneficial application, as in the usefulness of each man's craftsmanship created a more dynamic (and profitable) society than the patriarchy that envied idle plantation life. Without slavery in the North it was necessary for a breadwinner to demonstrate a contribution to society. The same had now become true below the Mason-Dixon Line.[81]

By February of 1886, the Morganton Furniture Company "closed contracts for the Waynesville White Sulphur Springs Co. to furnish their magnificent hotel with all the necessary furniture," indicating public acceptance of factory output. Folks in Morganton lauded their new industry as "the largest furniture manufactory in the State," noting its power source of steam, its working crew of between 30 and 40 men and the fact that orders have kept the company running at capacity.[82]

Then tragedy came to the entire organization. In mid-January of 1887, "while the hands were mostly at dinner," the Morganton Furniture Company "caught afire and was soon burned to the ground." The culprit of the blaze was judged to be a defective flue, its spread made worse by "the wind being very high. The fire spread rapidly and before help could arrive, the whole establishment was in flames." Due to its close proximity, the blaze threatened the train station. "For a while it was thought that it would be impossible to save the depot and its contents were being carried out. It caught fire several times, but with much effort was saved. Fortunately, two trains were passing and furnished a good supply of water."[83]

With a "moderate insurance," the estimated loss was $60,000. Other

THE MORGANTON STAR.

FRIDAY, JANUARY 21, 1887.

Local News.

—Miss Sadie Erwin, of Morganton, is conducting a flourishing school at Old Fort.

—A dog was burned to death in the commissary of the furniture factory during the fire.

—Rufus Avery has re-opened the old market-house and will keep

TUESDAY'S FIRE.

THE MORGANTON FURNITURE FACTORY BURNED.

Great Destruction of Property—A number of Person's Thrown Out of Employment—Nothing Saved—Loss About $20,000—No Insurance.

On last Tuesday, between 12 and 1 o'clock the alarm of fire was given and found to be at the large furniture factory of Messrs. A. W. Wilson & Bro., near the depot.

The notice from the hometown paper of the devastating fire that set production of furniture back by a dozen years. In the reporting came an additional notice that a dog had been a casualty of the blaze that started during the dinner hour. (Image from the Morganton Star)

reports asserted that Alex Wilson had no insurance at all. He vowed to rebuild in even grander style than before. Under the declaration "He Has Not Given Up", the *Morganton Star* reported that Alex Wilson "has gone to work to organize a company to establish a door, sash and blind factory on the same grounds where the furniture factory was burned." But by March, an excess of lumber caused Wilson to look for a quick sale. He advertised in the *Asheville Citizen-Times*, "Lumber! Lumber! I am prepared to furnish lumber for building purposes of all kinds at short notice and in any quantity. Before purchasing elsewhere write and get my prices. Alex W. Wilson, Morganton, NC."[84]

At the same time, Alex Wilson attempted to repair the engine that ran the furniture factory but to little benefit. It seemed the desire to continue making furniture was not in Wilson's interest. Part of the change may have been in the effort to develop other money-making pursuits since the younger Wilson ran a farm in neighboring McDowell County and a buggy works in Morganton. Also, he could have been trying to keep up with his early business partner, H.R. Hicks, who seemed luckier than most. After leaving Morganton,

Hicks went on to win a share of the Louisiana State Lottery. Alex Wilson left the area too, working with his father as a surveyor for railroad interests which grew into a myriad of other projects.[85]

With the exit of the young entrepreneurs, rebuilding efforts in Morganton floundered. Over the next three years a group of local businessmen tried to take up the Wilson family mantle, but any attempt to reestablish the half-acre works at its former location were out of the question. The property became popular, not for the industry it could house, but the avenues to which it would lead. "The State is building an excellent road from the depot to the W.N.C. Asylum. It will cross the branch just below the old furniture factory site on the bridge and thence will lead to the Asylum grounds crossing over the dam of Wilson's mill pond," reported the *Morganton Herald* in 1890. In addition, the land proved useful for the railroad too, given its proximity to the depot. "The railroad company is filling in the old site of the Wilson furniture factory with a view of extending the side track of the south side of the depot to make a connection with the main track."[86]

Two years after the devastating fire reduced the company to cinders, leaving the owners nothing of value except the land, another effort was made. In papers throughout the area came the announcement. "The Board of Directors of the Morganton Furniture Manufacturing Company are negotiating for a location upon which to erect the furniture factory. The secretary will at once open correspondence with parties for the purchase of suitable machinery to be used in the enterprise and all the work is to be pushed forward to an early completion." By May of 1889, a new company under the title of Morganton Furniture Manufacturing Company presented its notice of incorporation to the Clerk of Superior Court in Burke County for registration. Twelve principal owners were listed. Neither Alex Wilson nor any of the other original owners were among them. The initial stock for the company totaled $20,000 divided into 200 shares. The declaration allowed for the possibility of offering additional stock up to $100,000. The corporation signed on for a duration of 30 years. However, a year later the enterprise had not materialized.[87]

Also in 1890, the Robertson Sash, Door and Blind Factory in Morganton was forced into liquidation and sold at public auction. Reopened later as the Morganton Manufacturing and Trading Company, Major Wilson returned to Morganton's business world along with J.A. Dickson. The memory of the fire might have driven the Major to a new pursuit. The operation found an alternative specialty, making bricks. By 1892, the company doubled its capacity and became one of the prominently mentioned businesses by Raleigh's *News & Observer* in a tourism article on the town of Morganton. Nowhere mentioned was a resurrected furniture factory.[88]

The momentum for a furniture making enterprise in Morganton had passed. Selling furniture was another story. Retailing in home furnishings escalated. E.B. Claywell and his brothers' general mercantile store expanded into the sale of furniture with prominent advertisements in the local papers. With Claywell's name connected to the promised rebirth of a factory in town, his store looked to position itself as an outlet for wholesale prices. For a while his adverts featured the statement, "Not cheap furniture, furniture cheap." But competition lurked. E. Breese, a self-declared "leader in low prices" looked for an opportunity to best Claywell. When the Morganton Furniture Manufacturing Company failed to materialize in the 1890s, Breese funded a notice headlined, "Talk Is Cheap." He claimed to have brought retail furniture prices down by the very establishment of his store, but that was not enough. Breese made a big announcement that sought to beat Claywell at his own game. The notice read, "I have just closed a trade for a fourth interest in a Furniture factory which will enable me to get goods much lower than ever." As the furniture war waged, Breese just kept rubbing it in. "If you will call I will show you as large and fine a stock of goods as you ever saw in Morganton, and at prices that will surprise you as well as competition." No mention was made of the supplier or the manufacturing company's whereabouts.[89]

With no new factory to flaunt, E.B. Claywell looked as though he had been beaten. Undeterred, he played one last card. In a listing of the town's priorities in May of 1889, a furniture company rated second only to a new depot as the most pressing needs for Morgantonians. Claywell, who called himself "the poor man's friend," offered to take the lead in drumming up business for his company seeking subscriptions to pay for construction of a new furniture maker. The pitch went as follows: "the small amount that you have to pay per week on the plan suggested by Mr. E.B. Claywell puts it within the reach of every man in the county." Like the reorganization effort, the subscription scheme failed to produce the capital necessary to build.[90]

Up through the end of the century, Morganton continued to try some way to make woodworking pay. In a lull for textile mill establishment, a Chicago newspaper article looking for new and unique attempts to drive industry offered a notice touting "a sawmill to manufacture bee hives, washboards, etc., at Morganton, NC."[91]

Meanwhile, in the midst of trying to get a Morganton operation going again, several Morganton residents had been doing quite well with a furniture factory in Asheville. Receiving town approval in November of 1885, the company promised capitalization of at least $30,000. The first phase proved successful. The *Morganton Star* reported in February of 1889, "Messrs. Avery & Erwin will enlarge their furniture factory at Asheville." W.W. Avery had been associated with the Morganton furniture operation in its early days of operation. The party in Asheville didn't last long. Two years later, Avery and Company were dissatisfied with their locale and just like in Morganton were ready to move on. The *Morganton Herald* reported, "Mr. W.W. Avery, of the Asheville Furniture Company, was here this week making arrangements to get a force of hands to go to Lenoir, Tennessee, to which point the furniture plant is to be moved as soon as the necessary buildings can be (e)rected."[92]

The western portion of North Carolina had tried and failed to establish furniture production as a viable industry, but down east they enviously read about success. "The business of the furniture factory at High Point is so large that they are always five or six car loads behind in filling their orders, and will have to enlarge their buildings in order to meet the increasing demand for goods." Such a story could have been written about Morganton, if it had not been for one, fatal fire. Instead, a Morganton editorial returned to the drawing board, prodding locals to get back on the industrial horse that Major Wilson rode in on, encouraging them to try again. "Our citizens are now ripe for this enterprise, but if we let the time for harvesting the grain pass by, this opportunity may not return again for years."[93]

The grand experiment first spearheaded by D.A. Smith in Old Fort and its subsequent move to Morganton had promised but failed to sustain a furniture factory, despite the fact that whole mountains of forests surrounding it still offered their growth for the taking. The defeat brought reassessments on how, under slightly altered circumstances, such an experiment might succeed. Interesting seeds had been sown. Shop owner Claywell's retail idea to get community members to chip in for a factory had merit, even if the attempt did not. Maybe another community could make it work. As it turned out, communities in western North Carolina were not done trying.

---∞---

After reaching Lenoir, the Chester and Lenoir Narrow Gauge extended farther into the mountains. This image demonstrates how vital wood was to both the construction and payload of the venture, with carload after carload hauling lumber from Edgemont, in upper Caldwell Co. (Courtesy of the Caldwell Heritage Museum)

Chapter 5
Talk Factory

It started rather simply. One citizen openly asked two entwined but pointed questions. "Why does not Lenoir grow? Why don't we have factories, etc.?" Believing "the worth of a town is the worth of the individuals composing the town," Penrose Baldwin, a local pharmacist, offered his own answer to the question why his hometown refused to embrace the New South and its opportunities. He candidly admitted, "because we either don't want them, or we are lacking in the necessary energy to get them." With finger pointed, he spelled out a brutal evaluation of at least a portion of his fellow citizens. "In other words, we ourselves are to blame for our own standstill position. All are agreed that something ought to be done; but all are not agreed as to what is the proper thing to do."[94]

Penrose Baldwin ramped up the rhetoric. While others had been bewildered by inaction, apothecary Baldwin seemed downright mad, and he didn't mind going on the record to say so. He didn't have the capital to start his own factory like Old Fort's D.A. Smith, but he wanted action nonetheless. Many business people in small towns throughout the South shared the view to one degree or another. They wanted their homeplace to carve out for itself some distinction, unwilling to let the prevailing winds decide if their community was to grow or fail. Just like an untended crop, Baldwin believed initiative had to be taken, a plan conceived. Then, of course, he wanted to follow up with the execution of the plan. Only by sowing, Baldwin believed, could a harvest of industrial capacity be reaped. That bounty could serve not only Penrose Baldwin but his children, his grandchildren, and likely his progeny for a hundred years, but it had to see a practical start. The druggist made one more statement about the Lenoir of his time that pinpointed the dilemma. "Some want a tobacco factory or a furniture factory, and some don't." A third question, unasked by Baldwin, was, who would decide?[95]

W.W. Scott, Jr., editor and publisher of the *Lenoir Topic*, could not have agreed more with Penrose Baldwin. For years, he noted the establishment of one manufactory after another. Unfortunately, each was in a town other than his. "Winston is to have a broom factory." Next door, Alexander County had a cotton mill in action. But even as he reported, "a good deal of dogwood and persimmon (wood) is being piled up at the depot preparatory for shipment to Newton, being engaged for a shuttle factory there," he persisted in pointing out Lenoir's lack of alacrity, needling his fellow citizens. "Why can we not have such an enterprise here?" His question echoed Baldwin's, his reasoning following in line with New South philosophy. "The nearer such a factory is to the timber, the cheaper it can be run." That same logic had served D.A. Smith well in Old Fort a decade earlier.[96]

Even in his own county of Caldwell, of which Lenoir served as the county seat, factories hummed in towns like Granite Falls to the south and Patterson to the north. Even though both featured textile mills, Lenoir had none. With envy, Scott noted how the Granite Falls manufacturing company earned a "profit of 15 percent on the money invested." In Patterson, which Lenoir tried to claim as their own by saying "for what is Patterson's factory but a delightful suburb of Lenoir" because the train went through there, Scott reported that the business had "made great improvements lately in the texture and coloring of the cassimeres (cashmeres) made by them. These goods now compare with almost any foreign stuffs and are very popular." Try as they might, neither pharmacist Penrose Baldwin nor newspaperman W.W. Scott could put his finger on the exact reason why Lenoir attracted no industry. As a defacto spokesman for the town, Scott remained optimistic that some sort of large-scale business would sweep into Lenoir and employ his readers. He printed every rumor. "A bent wood and chair factory could be established at small cost and Charleston capitalists are looking favorably to Lenoir in this matter." "It seems to be settled that a canning factory will be established in Lenoir in time for this year's fruit crop." Both were just talk as none materialized.[97]

No industry in Lenoir could have been possible without a railroad line to carry the product of the factory to market. Trains arrived in the summer of 1884 with the completion of the Chester and Lenoir Narrow Gauge Line. The ride to get there had been long, ten years in the making. In the early post-Civil War era, narrow gauge railroads were popular. Construction, equipment, and operation were all cheaper than standard gauge railroads. The reason was size. Everything was smaller on a narrow-gauge line. Instead of rails being 4 feet, 8.5 inches apart, a narrow-gauge-line measured only three feet wide. Directors thought the savings would allow them to reach Lenoir within budget. But construction stalled as the line from the upstate South Carolina town of Chester reached Lincolnton and the company ran out of money. The directors appealed to the Charlotte, Columbia, and Augusta line, trading a lease for the last 37 miles of track to Lenoir. After the Richmond and Danville Railroad took over the Charlotte line, the railroad conglomerate agreed to honor the deal. Once the railroad came to town, industry could too.[98]

During a small housing boom in Lenoir, editor W.W. Scott wondered what would happen to the economy when construction labor ended. Again, like Penrose Baldwin, he had an answer at the ready, a much more hopeful one. "When the present astonishing demand for carpenters in the dwelling business line ceases there ought to be at once more work to keep them busy in another line. We ought to have some kind of factory business going in Lenoir. The town must have it to amount to anything. We do not see why we have not had one before now, and not one but two, three, a half dozen." The campaign for Lenoir to reinvent itself in the image of the New South had begun.[99]

The ache became more palpable with each new edition of W.W. Scott's paper. Every business story of another town's success invited comparison with Lenoir's failure. In addition to being editor of the *Lenoir Topic*, W.W. Scott practiced law in town as an attorney. Advertisements for his practice showed up regularly. It was with the precision of a legal argument that Scott made his case to the readers of Lenoir. When news spread of the Asheville Furniture Factory receiving an order "for forty thousand dollars," the pages of his paper rang out with frustration, declaring, "for the life of us we can't see why a furniture factory would not pay in Lenoir." He litigated incessantly, wasting no opportunity to sway the court of public opinion. Lenoir's citizens needed a nudge to inspire potential investors among them to put their money in some 'to be determined' industrial outlet. And like a good lawyer, taking the temperature of those he attempted to sway, W.W. Scott begged forgiveness when he realized his tone might seem too stern and overbearing. He admitted, "perhaps some of our readers will get tired of our talking about factories so much, but we can't help it. We know that Lenoir needs some kind of factory and we are going to talk until something is done." His client was the town, and he felt that nothing less than Lenoir's very existence hung in the balance.[100]

Finally, the town listened. But would the talk be just that, another promise unfulfilled or an idle boast by someone with the means but not the drive to follow through? In a frenzied conversation from within his own head, W.W. Scott declared, "We are going to have it. What? A furniture factory." He could not stop talking about it. A few notices down from the announcement, he began to obsess. "Where will the furniture factory be located? is a question now that bothers us." His editorial pelted questions at "the businessmen of Lenoir." Have you been in earnest in saying you wanted your town to prosper and grow? Have you been sincere when you said that a furniture factory would pay a good dividend to stockholders and put two dollars in circulation where now we have one? Were you talking business on the square or were you just talking for Buncombe (a 19th century epithet)?" After all his harangues, his pleading, his well-reasoned arguments, W.W. Scott could not be sure if the news was true and if it would lead to something tangible. Still badgering his contemporaries with more questions, he asked, "What is your own public spirit worth in cold, hard cash?" If the investors of Lenoir relented and contributed, the editor questioned the sufficiency of their commitment. "You have subscribed a few hundred dollars, it may be. Why not make it a thousand or two? Don't say you can't do it." His words were pointed, unforgiving, and evangelical in their fervor. He rested his case by laying the guilt of a rumored but unfulfilled factory at the feet of his fellow Lenoir-ites.[101]

> If you don't do something handsome now it will be just because you don't want to, and you will have to stop croaking and grumbling and growling in the future, and blame yourself if the town do(es)n't prosper and your real estate depreciates in value, and your business houses become "like banquet halls deserted." If the town dies you may have the satisfaction of knowing you killed it, and its departed spirit will dog your footsteps at night, and hiss into your ear when you toss on your sleepless pillow in the darkness-if it serves you right. What are you going to do about it?[102]

The scathing editorial ultimately did its job with the jury coming around to W.W. Scott's point of view, the verdict in his favor. With a majority now in agreement that a factory fitted tomorrow, the town saw for itself that making furniture seemed the most logical for production. Scott soon turned from doubtful to impatient. He asked, "how long will it be till we hear the whistle of the furniture factory?" Then he reverted to his earlier boosterism as he implored his readers to simply, "Talk factory." Immediately, he followed that with a new slogan, "keep the boom booming." Woe be it to any naysayers who whispered against the venture. When someone did, "that local was afraid to go out on the streets for fear of being lynched," reported the editor and lawyer.

The uproar was such that it demonstrated little toleration for a less than rosy attitude about the 'can do' spirit of Lenoir. "Peace has been restored and we are glad to say that 'they' predicted wrong," Scott wrote about the negative rumor. Presumably, the identity of "they" was kept secret for security, even with the public shame. Just in case someone agreed with "they," W.W. Scott was quick to assure everyone "that the prospects for the factory are bright and encouraging, as the subscription list is increasing." "Let the good work go on," decreed W.W. Scott in his role as Lenoir's advocate. Anticipation built.[103]

The long-awaited hour for furniture in Lenoir came at 2 pm on Thursday, March 28, 1889. Investors couldn't forget because the *Lenoir Topic* repeatedly reminded them. W.W. Scott admonished, "If you are a stockholder, be in the courthouse at that hour." A week prior, a gathering of local business leaders met to talk seriously about the particulars of creating a factory for the production of furniture. Speeches, one after the other, extolled the brilliance of such a plan. The crowd appointed a committee of two, J. M. Houck as chairman and none other than W.W. Scott as secretary. The ferocity of his printed grandiloquence demanded a central position for him. After all, who was more publicly enthusiastic? Before the meeting, investors laid down $3,300 in cash for subscriptions. They needed $5,000. The oratory rambled on and on. A thousand dollars more hit the books before the meeting released a tired business community to go home for a night's sleep. At least their slumber would not be the dogged one W.W. Scott prophesied in his editorial.[104]

It was with great satisfaction and a little revisionism that W.W. Scott summarized the zeitgeist of his town when he printed his rather self-satisfied editorial, "The Furniture Factory." He began by writing with irony, "the *Topic* has never been accused of 'blowing' about Lenoir." Portraying the city as "too modest to sound its praises," he tried to walk the line between promotion and objectivity. Scott perhaps felt he had stood by as an analytical observer of Lenoir's strengths and weaknesses. At times he harped on each. But the events

Cover of the minutes from the first meeting of the Lenoir Furniture Factory in 1889. The grouping of investors and their organization mark the first time a town came together to create a factory. The company sputtered until purchased by the Harpers ten years later. (Courtesy of the Caldwell Heritage Museum)

from the previous week signaled a transition for Scott. Citing the creation of a Building and Loan the previous year, he began to see this next step of a factory as proof that Lenoir had a sunny future. That next step, however, demanded unanimity of purpose. Scott admonished, "let there be no grumblers, no fault-finders. Speak cheerfully, approvingly of the new company and if you cannot speak so hold your tongue. Leave criticism to the officers in charge." He instructed readers, "it is now the duty of every true son of the town and county to make the new factory his especial pride and hobby."[105]

W.W. Scott, as both cheerleader for the town and the new factory, saw the latter as the prime means to support the former. He wasted no time splashing more ink in the *Lenoir Topic*, getting down to the business of factory creation now that the establishment of industry had been settled. Groping for guidance, he published a piece of instruction for factory directors entitled "How to Build Factories." The effort showed just how little anyone knew about the business they were getting into. The article liberally quoted Daniel Augustus Tompkins, the man credited with building the textile industry in Charlotte. In fact, only the first and last paragraph are anything other than Tompkins' words. D.A. Tompkins was a newspaperman like W.W. Scott, who tirelessly championed industrialism as the savior of the South throughout his career, a cross between Atlanta's Henry Grady and W.W. Scott. In life, as in his article, Tompkins dealt only with textile mills, but Scott used the guide as a reference. Perhaps the Lenoir editor reprinted the story from an earlier article in the *Manufacturers' Record* of Baltimore, less as a tutorial and more of a pique to heighten investor interest. Using two mills in Charlotte and one in Rock Hill, SC, Tompkins gave a financial accounting of payback for investors. "About four years is required to pay the stock in full," asserted the sage of Carolina manufacturing, giving those thinking about buying shares in the new Lenoir company some positive indication of when they could expect a return on investment.[106]

Lenoir's success would ultimately not rely on men from Charlotte like D.A. Tompkins but on the community's own crop of home-grown leaders. One was an obvious choice, the second his protege. Like many towns in the South, masters of the postbellum period originated mostly from those Confederates who returned from the war to rebuild their world in the wake of defeat. In Lenoir's case, the devastation came late. Easter of 1865 marked the date when the town endured an occupation by George Stoneman's raiders. The damage was nowhere near as significant as other places ravaged by battle, but citizens never forgot the work of the Yankees, so when Major George Washington Finley Harper returned to his hometown at war's end from service to the Confederacy, he was an instant hero to the local population. Some also saw him as a savior in the day of rebuilding.

The Harper family had been prominent before the war. Major Harper's father, James Harper opened the first mercantile store in Lenoir, making the family one of the town's earliest inhabitants, as well as one of the most prominent. In the second summer of the war, G.W.F. enlisted at the age of 28 as a private in the 58th N.C. Infantry. The unit fought mostly in the western theatre, and during that time, Harper quickly rose to the rank of major. Just over a year after joining, Major Harper ended up leading his men in battle at Chickamauga, the two-day contest that saw a rare victory for the Confederate Army of Tennessee. Pushed back into northwest Georgia by Federal commander William T. Sherman the following spring, Harper sustained a serious leg wound at the Battle of Resaca. He convalesced at home in Lenoir while his unit suffered humiliating losses for the control of Atlanta. He recovered sufficiently to rejoin the 58th in time for the November 1864 Battle of Franklin, a bloody clash that saw the Confederate Army make 13 unsuccessful charges. The Confederate leadership entrusted Major Harper to transport 1,700 captured Union troops from the fight at Franklin to Corinth, Mississippi. He then rejoined his unit in time for the Army of Tennessee's last engagement, which happened to occur in North Carolina, the Battle of Bentonville in March of 1865. Major Harper came back to Lenoir as both a venerated veteran and a budding entrepreneur.[107]

Major Harper began to build his wealth after the war in a number of ways. Never one to let the grudges of the conflict cloud his vision for the future, the Major sought to learn from the experience, pick up the pieces of defeat and rebuild. Railroads always interested the Major even before the

George Washington Finley Harper during his days in service to the 58th North Carolina Infantry as part of the Confederate Army (left) and as the elder statesman of business in Lenoir (right) before his death in 1921. At both times he was known as Major Harper. (Courtesy of the Caldwell Heritage Museum)

G.W.F. Harper served as the patriarch of Lenoir, upon his return from the Civil War. Recognizing talent in the generation that followed, he shared his mercantile business with the Bernhardt brothers, J.M. and G.L. before Harper and the Bernhardts plunged into furniture making. (Courtesy of the Caldwell Heritage Museum)

war, but following it he lobbied for rail service to his hometown. Meanwhile, he also sought investment in other railroad lines. By the mid-1870s, Harper served Lenoir as a town commissioner and owner of a store that boasted $10,000 in staple goods and cash. He cemented his leadership by securing completion of the Chester and Lenoir Narrow Gauge Railroad, for which he was named president of the line. Touted as a man "of enterprise," Harper became a controlling figure in Lenoir. Nothing of substance could be accomplished without his support. When organization for the Lenoir Furniture Factory came five years after rail service, Major Harper's support for the enterprise was essential. G.W.F. led the list of names elected to the five-member board, along with J.L. Nelson (for whom the Caldwell County town of Whitnel is half-named, P.J. Johnson, W.C. Ervin, (a former law partner of W.W. Scott and one time editor of the Morganton paper) and S.J. Sherrill.[108]

When Major Harper's favorable gaze fell upon the furniture factory initiative, he enlisted an up-and-coming young man who demonstrated the necessary energy and intelligence to get the job done: John Mathias Bernhardt. Born in Caldwell County in 1860, as a teenager, Bernhardt worked for the Major at the Harper store. The same year he graduated from local Finley High School in 1877, his father Mathias A. Bernhardt died. With a small inheritance, young Bernhardt moved to Concord, North Caolina but by 1881, he was back. The *Lenoir Topic* welcomed him home. "We are happy to announce the return to his old home of Mr. John M. Bernhardt. 'Barny' (a nickname) is clerking for Major Harper."[109]

J.M. Bernhardt's relationship with his old employer in Lenoir had not faltered during their time apart. While working for Major Harper, J.M. took on a trusted role, traveling to places like New York, Boston, and Baltimore, buying goods for sale in the store. The energetic protege also dabbled in cattle, with a herd near mountainous Blowing Rock, in Watauga County. J.M. Bernhardt looked up to the elder Harper, and obviously the Major was impressed with the vigor of the young man. In 1883, 'Barny' decided to continue his education. He chose the alma mater of Major Harper, Davidson College, north of Charlotte. Barny went off to school a companion of the Major's son, George Finley Harper. Within a year, the Major offered to go into business with his protege and Bernhardt's brother George Lynn Bernhardt. In Lenoir, the Harper general merchandise store had been in business since 1829. January 1884 saw the name changed to Harper, Bernhardt & Co. After another year, J.M. Bernhardt quit Davidson, but apparently not so he could devote all his energy to the mercantile business. Instead, he landed a job as a land agent for the federal government. The work took him as far as Oregon, where he attempted to protect huge sections of forested area from unlawful cutting. He never really enjoyed the work of catching and prosecuting those illegally logging government land. "I must confess that a special agent is not very popular with a large class out here," he revealed in a letter back home. It didn't take long for the young J.M. Bernhardt to return once more to the town he knew.[110]

John Mathias Bernhardt, who in his earlier days around town was known as 'Barny.' His intelligence and energy attracted the mentorship of Major Harper to go into several businesses with him, including Lenoir's first furniture factory. Barny also married the Major's daughter. (Courtesy of the Caldwell Heritage Museum)

Back in his high school days, John Mathias Bernhardt was known as a prominent young man about town. Often, Barny found his name in the paper, teased about his status as Lenoir's most eligible bachelor. The respect and devotion he had for Major Harper included another factor, the Major's daughter. As he established himself as a vital part of Lenoir's leadership, he also courted Ellen Douglas Harper. The couple married in 1894. The standing room only ceremony offered the town, in the words of the *Hickory Press*, "a sense of a perfect fit and harmony" as a result of the union. The *Lenoir Topic* called it "one of the most beautiful marriages ever witnessed by the people of Lenoir."[111]

The mixing of the Bernhardt and Harper names offered great promise. If there were two men in Lenoir who could make the new foray into industrialism work, it would be Barny and the Major. All the goading of druggist Penrose Baldwin and newspaperman/lawyer W.W. Scott aside, the team of Major Harper and John Mathias Bernhardt had the power to set an agenda and see it through. Their partnership demonstrated to what new heights a town in the defeated South could rise if the generations worked together with both looking to advance the economic cause of their community. As the nucleus of the town, it would be their job to turn an aspiration into an industry.

The Lenoir Furniture Factory went quickly to work, securing all it needed for turning trees into bureaus, tables, and bedsteads. Immediately, the committee that formed the Board of Directors with Major Harper as head selected John Mathias Bernhardt as president of the company. "Mr. J.M. Bernhardt left Monday for Northern cities, where he goes to see about the machinery to be used in the furniture factory," reported the *Lenoir Topic*. In addition, the company commissioned the casting of 200,000 bricks with which to build the new factory. Meanwhile, factory officials purchased the Weisenfield timber yard at the railroad depot as a site for the plant. One primary attraction of the property was the existence of a side track that was already in place. "Three buildings have been decided upon, a main building of brick, 120 x 50 feet, a two-story finishing house, and an engine house." Those were among the construction plans reported to the public by Bernhardt. There was little time to waste since announcements of furniture factories were also in the planning stages in Linville (40 miles to the northwest) and Morganton (15 miles southwest).[112]

Until arrival of the first furniture factory, most breadwinners in the region followed the pattern of these men, producing commodities on the farm & bringing them to market for sale. Hickory's Union Square & Lenoir's Hog Waller offered trading space to sell turkeys, as seen here. (Courtesy of the Caldwell Heritage Museum)

For a while, John Mathias Bernhardt channeled his interest away from making furniture and into the harvesting of the raw material. In the vast woodlands of western North Carolina, sawmills cut planks near where the trees once stood for companies like Bernhardt's. (Courtesy of the Caldwell Heritage Museum)

Chapter 6
Sweet Music

Upon J.M. Bernhardt's return, the new president sat down for an interview with newspaper editor W.W. Scott to discuss the direction of the Lenoir Furniture Factory. Bernhardt's answers revealed the turmoil and uncertainty that surrounded the risk of a community embarking on such a colossal effort. Scott reported Bernhardt's fear that when he left, he felt he might "come home with the blues and feeling there was no chance for a small concern like ours to compete." Following his excursion up north, Bernhardt took a different view. Among the places he ventured to were Cincinnati and Columbus, Ohio; Louisville, Kentucky; and Knoxville, Tennessee. After further consideration, he concluded, "I do not feel so at all. I am very much encouraged about the enterprise and believe it will be the best paying business in the country." His reason for optimism centered around costs. He figured labor for the factory in Lenoir would be half that of the larger, more established cities to the southeast, while lumber, thanks to its overwhelming abundance, would also cost half of what it would in the foothills. Also analyzing activity in Asheville, NC where a furniture operation was up and running, Bernhardt surmised that "Asheville pays more for labor than we will have to because living is much more expensive." But maybe the clincher for the traveling president of the Lenoir Furniture Factory was the money to be made in the furniture business for a facility at full production. "One new factory in Columbus, Ohio, paid a dividend of 17 1/2 per cent the first year," he discovered. With Lenoir's comparative advantages to the factory in central Ohio, Bernhardt felt he could do better, much better. [113]

The real fear lay not in managing the output but in the capital needed to sustain the operation. W.W. Scott put the question to J.M. Bernhardt directly. "Have you enough money to start on?" Bernhardt's answer revealed uncertainty. Responding to the popular view that everyone believed the firm was fully capitalized, he countered by saying, "this is a mistake." The need for funds was evident as he revealed, "we have never thought we had enough and have known all the time we would have to have more." Bernhardt added, "our reason for starting on such small capital was that we would save time." He planned to use the money raised to purchase equipment but hoped to stretch the cash as far as he could, believing that the company "will be all right if we can get our buildings put up without paying cash." More would be absolutely necessary for the enterprise by the time it opened for production. "We will have to have about $2,000 more stock," he confided. Then, with a salesman-like entreaty to invest, Bernhardt reminded Lenoir readers, "our subscription books are open."[114]

Plans called for the Lenoir Furniture Factory to acquire wood in a unique way. J.M. Bernhardt arranged for the company to finance several portable sawmills. "My plan to give the farmers (the) most benefit for their timber is for us to furnish good sawmills to move wherever they get 300 or 400 logs together and do the sawing for them," making it as advantageous and hassle-free as possible for the landowners with woods aplenty. Bernhardt needed every tree they could bring down and had experienced teams ready to saw them. He figured 20,000 board feet of lumber would be required each week, exceeding earlier expectations. Saying, "the business always pays when it is well managed," J.M. Bernhardt had every reason to believe that within a short time of the factory's completion, his efforts would propel the operation forward, rivaling any plant he saw on his northwestern journey.[115]

Lenoir remained all atwitter over the coming of the new world that J.M. Bernhardt envisioned and planned to create. However, the hard numbers of capitalization revealed how the enterprise stood next to other manufacturers across North Carolina who also pumped out furniture and would compete with Lenoir for sales. *The Manufacturers Record* acknowledged Lenoir's creation with capital of $15,000, but also noted the establishment of the furniture factory in Asheville had ten times the available cash. Bernhardt struggled against the problem of undercapitalization, hoping to get the company started while adding resources as needed. Questions arose surrounding such an underdog. Would the business draw enough additional subscriptions to fuel a rise to profitability? New South boosterism, Lenoir-style, banked on it. [116]

When the announcement of official incorporation was made, the company upped the price for its operation. Hoping to eventually have $25,000 in subscriptions (1000 shares at $25 each), the factory would still be dwarfed in size by other manufacturers. However, the new company had an enthusiastic supporting community, all the surrounding raw material a manufacturer could ask for and a reasonably sound organizational structure that publicly announced its intention to operate for the next thirty years. Several options remained for pulling in the cash they needed. Before issuing additional stock, the company could call for more of the pledged money. At the time of purchase, investors were not required to pay their full share. Instead, they could provide a percentage, with the rest to come when management called for it. The summons wasn't long in coming. By July, 1887, officials announced it was time. "The Board of Directors of the Lenoir Furniture Factory have issued a call for another installment of 25 per cent on the stock in the company to be paid in." Requests were announced with some rapidity, all in order to keep the

In the excitement to build a furniture factory in Lenoir, volunteers gathered to usher a new boiler to the factory site. At the head of the procession was John Mathias Bernhardt, president of the new company, eager to put machinery into place and begin production. (Courtesy of the Caldwell Heritage Museum)

momentum going. Two months later, another 25 percent was required.[117]

Ironically, as the *Lenoir Topic's* W.W. Scott announced the next stock call (he was a prominent investor himself), he inadvertently followed that notice with one right from the days when no one even imagined a factory was necessary to produce furniture. The next item in his column of May 8th harkened back to a handmade ancestor, an example of the very craftsmanship that the new factory would undoubtedly replace. Scott seemed wistful as he observed, "a thing of beauty and quite costly piece of furniture is the handsome new walnut desk in Clerk of Court Shell's office. It is a fine piece of work and was made by Mr. Shell's father, Azor Shell, Esq." For readers the juxtaposition of the two write-ups signaled a turning point in the pace of life in Lenoir, one in which some may have been uncomfortable, even wary. The days of master artisans taking their time to craft an individual piece for those that needed and could afford furniture was coming to an end. If the Lenoir Furniture Factory proved successful, their machine-driven output would soon replace workshops scattered in the area. One might have asked if Lenoir's new furniture making apparatus would ever produce anything as sturdy and pleasing as the hand-crafted desk about which Scott wrote. Unintentionally, the industrial age clashed with its predecessor in the pages of the *Lenoir Topic*.[118]

A groundbreaking on May 27, 1889 kicked off a summer of construction. Rain slowed both the digging of the foundation and the making of bricks onsite. Summer rains washed away the clay blocks "before they could be fired in the kiln." By July, activity picked up. Equipment began to arrive. A heavy planer stood idle in a temporary shed, awaiting completion of the building. Ever the organizer, J.M. Bernhardt scoped around Lenoir for someone to store a 16,000-pound engine until the factory floor was ready. By fall, the walls were up, just waiting for a roof and flooring.[119]

Across the state, news reached readers regarding Lenoir's new furniture effort. If the pressure to turn dreams into reality was not enough to drive J.M. Bernhardt, Major Harper, and the other investors, an item from the next town over certainly spurred them. After years of talk about replacing the burned Morganton factory, an editorial in the pages of the *Morganton Star* invoked rhetoric from the Bible, claiming the time had come to rebuild. Quoting both Solomon "there is a time for all things" and the Apostle Paul "be diligent in business," editor T.G. Cobb declared, "now was the time to build a furniture factory at Morganton." Without ever mentioning what was going on 15 miles northeast in Lenoir, Cobb called any further delay "hazardous." Seemingly, the momentum had slipped from the hands of the Morganton investors given the lapse of more than two years since their last published efforts. Cobb tried to get the endeavor back on track, calling for "vim and direction." He seemed to think those two ingredients were the only things missing that would allow Burke County to best Caldwell. However, the talk was only that,e talk. Another 14 years would pass before investors from Burke county actually created a furniture operation, and even then, the factory would not be centered in

Morganton.[120]

A feeling of anticipation was palpable as the factory lumbered into operation. W.W. Scott could not contain himself in the pages of his newspaper. He exalted the mere presence of the factory for which he had been lobbying such a long time. It filled all his senses. He liked the smell of fresh lumber hitting the noses of those who came within a short distance of the brand new facility. The activity was a feast to the eyes for Scott, but he chose to ruminate on the sound of a factory in his town. Writing, "the furniture factory whistle makes sweet music to the ears of all the friends of progress in town," he sent another caution to grumblers of the enterprise. The *Lenoir Topic* editor wanted them to get on the positive side of business development. He reminded readers that he had already "paid the factory a visit" and planned a much more detailed account so that he could further publicize Lenoir's accomplishment.[121]

On the heels of ringing in the new year of 1890, stockholders held their first annual meeting of the company in January. A need for capital remained quite apparent. After an accounting that listed $7,500 in "paid up stock," officials voted for an issuance of $3,000 in new stock. As usual, predictions were that the new "preferred" stock would go quickly. In fact, the announcement bragged that much of it "has already been taken." To entice investment, the new offering came with a guarantee "to pay a dividend of 8 per cent." The funds were cited as necessary for "a surplus of cash with which to purchase material" and "more machinery" to begin production. At this point, the building was complete with additional the machinery awaiting placement. Approximately $900 worth of lumber (mostly poplar) was on hand. Board membership remained steady except for W.C. Ervin, a former law partner of W.W. Scott's who moved to Morganton to publish his own paper. Investors re-elected J.M. Bernhardt to continue as president of the company.[122]

Evidently, the offer was not quite as appealing as current backers had hoped. Two months later came the issuance of more preferred stock with the

Downtown Lenoir in 1895. The courthouse to the right was located in the center of town, near where Main and Harper Avenue now intersect. During this period, the town's only manufacturing outlet, Lenoir Furniture Factory was in a struggle to survive. (Courtesy of the Caldwell Heritage Museum)

same "8 per cent" guarantee. Leaders of the meeting emphasized that it would "take precedence of common stock until the preferred stock and interest, shall be satisfied." The meeting whipped up interest with attendees committing to $1,000 worth in addition to another $900 sold, leaving "only $1,600 to make up." With the same positive attitude of the earlier offering predictions were that "it is probable that before a fortnight (two weeks) all of the remainder will be taken." However, this time, the offer came as a veiled threat. "As soon as this money is collected the machinery will be put in and the work of making furniture will commence," read the last line of the story, suggesting that the operation would not go into production without all stock being purchased.[123]

Word got out that Bernhardt and company were looking for financial backing, in part to purchase quality lumber. Quickly, the race started to procure large amounts as inexpensively as possible to feed the factory. Interest spread throughout and beyond Caldwell County. To the east in the Yadkin River Valley, timber men approached a multitude of farmers in search of trees ready for harvest. "Persons are buying up all the chestnut oak, water oak, and dogwood timber on the Yadkin, to be floated down and to be caught in a boom at Wilkesboro. From there, it will be shipped by rail." Though Wilkesboro stood only a day's ride by horseback from Lenoir (approximately 20 miles), timber had to take a much more circuitous route. No direct rail line existed between the two towns at the time, so the cargo had to travel east to Winston to access the main line, then back west. Once arriving in Hickory, the lumber would be offloaded to narrow gauge rolling stock for travel across the Catawba River to Lenoir.[124]

Motivated landowners with expanses of trees moved quick to supply the factory, no matter how much work delivery took. Forested land in western North Carolina predominated the landscape. By one account, almost 58% of all North Carolina was uninhabited woods, a near record in the southeast at the time. Of that percentage, the major proportion grew in the western foothills and mountains. Estimates concluded that hardwoods would supply the needs of industry for the next 50 years. Poplar stood in the greatest proportion, but oak, hickory, black walnut, ash, cherry, locust, pine, and other types of wood could be found all over the region.[125]

The flowering of summer brought the factory to fuller bloom. "The furniture factory has received 19 machines, and there are 5 more on the way. The Superintendent is expected to be in Lenoir this week. When the machinery, all of which has to be paid for, is set down, work will commence. A fine lot of logs has been piled up at the factory, and more are daily added," read an update. Anticipation grew to the point that W.W. Scott could no longer wait for completion. The newspaperman decided to take a sneak peek at the activity going on. He admitted being out of his depth when he recounted, "we went to see the new machinery at the Furniture factory last week and got so tangled up in the buzz-saws and other mysterious contraptions that we can give no intelligible account of them." Impressed nonetheless, Scott took account of the necessary support systems under construction along with the machinery proper. "A big cistern or reservoir, holding several thousand gallons, has been built on the hill above the factory, and water is to be forced into it from the well and then conducted to the factory through pipes, making an almost absolute protection against fire." His reporting of the factory's progress kept everyone in Lenoir informed, including potential stockholders.[126]

With completion in sight, a raft of ancillary businesses in support of the main factory began to form. From the beginning, the Lenoir Furniture Factory included wood products for the home, like doors and window sashes. Just down the track, another such operation also prepared to open. "Messrs. Stone and Kays have ordered a big planing mill with a capacity of 10,000 feet a day. They will erect a building for the machinery of the Cloyd and Nelson lot near the furniture factory and will also build a large patent dry kiln. This is an extensive enterprise and will dress thousands of feet of wainscoting and all kinds of lumber." The craft of turning wood for profit in Lenoir got quickly crowded. [127]

As president, J.M. Bernhardt handled issues necessary to the establishment of the company, but did not plan to oversee day-to-day operations. For that he sought a person of experience to serve as superintendent for the factory. First, Bernhardt hired Albert Kenyan, a man with credentials that included years in the furniture-making mecca of the United States, Grand Rapids, Michigan. Bernhardt needed an old hand at machine-based furniture making to avoid the rookie mistakes that would cost the new company time and money, neither of which it could afford to spend frivolously. For reasons never disclosed, Kenyan failed to arrive in Lenoir. Instead, a man from the not-nearly-so prestigious furniture-making town of Connersville, Indiana, accepted the position and actually showed up. E.T. Wheland arrived in early June and went to work immediately. A diligent taskmaster, Wheland was reported to be "pushing the work right along" a week after his arrival.[128]

Two weeks after Wheland got production going, one hundred pieces were ready for purchase. The dream of Lenoir realizing its destiny found fulfillment in those items. The first of those hundred pieces was ceremoniously claimed by George Lynn Bernhardt, the president's brother. He bought "a handsome cherry and walnut bookcase to cost $25." The other 99, however, did not move as quickly. In late August, the Topic announced, "Mr. (J.M.) Bernhardt will take to the road in a few days to clean up a large stock now on hand," in the effort to reduce his inventory. The Harpers and Bernhardts, both manufacturers and retailers, took out advertisements for local purchase to push sales. Harper, Bernhardt & Co. labeled themselves as "sole agent," appealing to the loyalty of readers by admonishing local folks that "there is not a home in Caldwell, Watauga, or Wilkes that should be without some of this furniture." At the same time, the manufacturer posted a notice that "we have made an arrangement with Harper, Bernhardt & Co., for the sale of our furniture. A complete line can be seen in their furniture rooms, which they will offer at factory prices." These advertisements fell somewhat short, however as most everyone in Lenoir realized the manufacturer and retailer were one and the same.[129]

The hoopla that marked creation of the company in the spring of 1889 was not matched when the company actually began producing in the summer 1890. In newspapers of the era, pages were rife with stories about various things happening in the next town over. Events that might seem trivial, especially the affairs of business, were of deep comparative concern in the press of the late nineteenth century. So it seems odd that the story of Lenoir actually turning out furniture for purchase in fulfillment of a year-long effort, brought so little attention. Hickory made no mention of it at all. In Morganton, almost as a swipe at Lenoir, the paper commented on the volume of furniture being turned out in High Point. By contrast, when Harper, Bernhardt & Co. shipped 180,000 lbs. of dried fruit as a milestone in their retail mercantile business, the story ran in papers all across North Carolina from Wilmington to Asheville. Perhaps the Lenoir factory already had its day in the sun when the venture was announced, but the actual, verifiable debut of an enterprise was all the more significant given that many other businesses never materialized. Community jealousy might explain the absence of coverage or perhaps Lenoir's western North Carolina neighbors chose a 'wait and see' attitude about the viability of operations in Caldwell County. Indications were not long in coming.[130]

George Washington Finley Harper guided the development of Lenoir after his return as Major in the 58th NC for the CSA. As an elderly man, seated left, he turned furniture making over in Lenoir to his son-in-law J.M. Bernhardt, standing, to build upon Lenoir's early effort. (Courtesy of the Caldwell Heritage Museum)

Prior to the 1889 creation of the Lenoir Furniture Factory, the county seat of Caldwell was a rustic, sleepy little village with the courthouse firmly situated in the town square. Citizens clamored for a quicker pace of commerce; the kind brought by industrialization. (Courtesy of the Caldwell Heritage Museum)

Chapter 7
Score One More for Lenoir

The furniture factory that had taken over a year to build from the ground up, one that had been discussed and conjectured for even longer, now had finished products rolling off the assembly line. Revenue from sales beginning to come in, yet stability remained elusive. Changes started at the top. With a little more than four months of operation under his belt, suddenly J.M. Bernhardt was out as president. Even more staggering was the decision to lease the company to Major Harper and his son, George F. Harper, who took over as president of the company. No reason was given for the change, but the ongoing issue of "the limited capital of the company" may have been a substantial factor as it appeared to be the unrelenting problem. The announcement only stated that "Mr. J.M. Bernhardt, the President and Superintendent of the old company, retires from the business." It seems that stock offerings from earlier in the year were not enough to sustain the Lenoir Furniture Factory.[131]

The announcement came with immediate plans for enlargement as a way to assure stockholders of a new vision. Word also arrived that the new operators "will push the business and enlarge the buildings." There seemed to be no problem with demand. W.W. Scott reported, "the Furniture Factory

After John Mathias Bernhardt left as president of the Lenoir Furniture Factory, he stayed close to the business as a lumber dealer. He considered staying in that business to the exclusion of furniture but returned with a box, then chair company to become firmly established in Lenoir. (Courtesy of the Caldwell Heritage Museum)

is booming and has orders away ahead of its capacity to turn out furniture." Apparently, if the Harpers were going to put money into the plant, they demanded serious changes which included closer control of the operation.[132]

It might be easy to conjecture that the new arrangement sprang from some disagreement between J.M. Bernhardt and the Harpers. If true, then subsequent events would have shown a sharp distancing between the two parties, but such was not the case. It is true that a year earlier, Bernhardt, ever the entrepreneur, purchased a farm in which he saw great potential, not as an agricultural outlet but for luxury tourism. Making the purchase with A.G. Benizer of Charlotte, Bernhardt's development of the property demonstrated his vision. Located "right at the turnpike gap," the site was situated adjacent to the easiest entrance into the mountain village of Blowing Rock, some 2,400 feet higher than that of Lenoir. A new hotel offered a respite for travelers as they climbed into what is today called 'the high country.' J.M. Bernhardt envisioned a summer destination for those seeking escape from the heat of the lowlands and with it, a financial reward for catering to their needs. By the 1890s, wealthier travelers sought respite in the upper climates of the North Carolina mountains. Some had become discontented with having to settle for Morganton, Hickory, or Lenoir, at around 1,200 feet above sea level. Better transportation allowed visits to a cooler environment as long as folks could afford the trip that included their baggage and entourage for extended stays to lavish retreats. Seeing the coming trend, Bernhardt felt an elegant hotel (still operating today as the Green Park Inn) could do well.[133]

Maybe J.M. Bernhardt's development of his resort deflected his attention over the ongoing and persistent capitalization problem for the furniture factory. It may have been that his enthusiasm for the new resort project signaled to Major Harper that a change was necessary, which freed up the junior associate to follow his more immediate passion. The same summer that the factory kicked into gear, Bernhardt spent time arranging for a sawmill to be brought to the Blowing Rock property "for the purpose of getting lumber for a 25 room boarding house." So the release from directing the furniture factory may have been a relief for Bernhardt, too, instead of a rebuke.[134]

Two further events demonstrate that the relationship between Major Harper and J.M. Bernhardt remained closer than might be expected following the change. First, less than two months after the "retirement," a terrible accident occurred at the factory. "Everett Monday, an engineer at the Furniture Factory, was quite severely scalded, Monday, by a whiff of steam and boiling oil that blew from a cylinder cap that was not securely fastened." To keep the facility running, a quick assessment was taken. "No serious damage will result. Mr. John M. Bernhardt at once took the engineer's place." For Bernhardt to fill in so readily demonstrated support for the success of the factory, unimaginable if the earlier split had been rancorous. Second, as Bernhardt prepared his hotel for occupancy, he needed furniture for each of the 25 rooms he constructed. Some of the furniture he purchased for his hotel came from his old mentor and his old company, now called Harper and Son Furniture. Even further, the relationship was so close that the Major helped Bernhardt by picking out what the new hotel needed but could not get from the limited product line coming out of the Lenoir factory. "Major Harper has just brought in New York carpets and other fine furniture for Green Park Hotel that the Lenoir Furniture Factory did not furnish. The furniture furnished by the latter is being conveyed to Blowing Rock. Messrs. G.L. and J.M. Bernhardt are both at Green Park." The reciprocity of gestures demonstrate a friendly relationship between Harper and Bernhardt, making the split over the factory seem less than bitter.[135]

To be sure, the loss of J.M. Bernhardt dealt a blow to the company. For months, Bernhardt had been canvasing the southeast for furniture sales and, by all accounts, his order book kept the factory running "to its utmost capacity." Reporting that "he found the sales easy," his strongest interests at the time may have been as a salesman and not an administrator. After all, Bernhardt's subsequent success in a number of future ventures would later showcase his talents more as a visionary than a supervisor.[136]

In attempting to fill the sales gap, the Harpers didn't have to look far for a reasonable substitute. They simply found another Bernhardt. "Mr. G.L. Bernhardt, who has been missed for several weeks, put in his appearance Saturday night, bringing a pair of Burnsides with him (a reference to his whiskers). He has been in the South, traveling in the interest of the Lenoir Furniture Co." Always a team player and apparently as good filling an order book as his brother, George Lynn Bernhardt, called Lynn or Linn, was heralded as "an accomplished salesman." He prviously had worked for the Shuford Cotton Mill in Hickory and participated in local government as a Lenoir town commissioner. Even before the arrival of the furniture factory, the Bernhardt brothers served as directors, with Lynn as treasurer of "The Caldwell and Watauga Land and Timber Company," a lumber business listing

$20,000 in operating capital. Once situated with Harper Furniture, G.L. Bernhardt proved his worth by getting a contract to furnish a hotel in Mount Airy, beating out "over six competitors." The association of the Harpers and the new Bernhardt remained close. When the town wanted a bank several years later, the "Bank of Lenoir" organized with Major Harper as president and G.L. Bernhardt as vice-president.[137]

Relationships must have remained cordial between the Major and the two Bernhardts, awkward though it might have been to now find G.L. in the middle. The end of 1890 saw the "closing out" of the retail partnership of Harper, Bernhardt and Company. Each would reopen or join a hardware concern later but under their own names. Bernhardt's reentry into the woodworking world and his creation of a furniture empire under his own name in Lenoir suggest a friendly competition with the Harper interests, maybe even a mutual respect between the two entities. More so, the 1894 marriage of J.M. Bernhardt into the Harper family signaled a rewarming of whatever drove Bernhardt from the company, but the conflict was never aired publicly, and if speculation about the rift ever floated around town, no one put it into print, and all principal parties carried any disagreement to their graves.[138]

The change of management signaled a new day for Lenoir's only furniture company. Immediately, Major Harper and his son, G.F. Harper got to work beefing up the operation, to some minds, a bit precipitously. "Harper and Son, who have leased the furniture factory, are having the new machinery put in and will build an extensive addition to the building to accommodate it. They are rushing things," opined one report. The expansion revealed at least some of the issue the Harpers had with the progress of the old company. Evidently, Major Harper believed the real danger lay in spending too little money too slowly for the factory's growth, so they proposed to spend more, a lot more. They quickly pumped a significant amount of additional resources into furniture making in Lenoir. Their plan centered around generating

"$50,000 worth of business during the next year." In order to make the goal, the operation changed in three important ways. First, the new lessees brought in additional equipment like a 75 horsepower engine and boiler to power faster operations. Second, with such expansion came a need for more labor. Hands at the factory grew to 45 with a weekly payroll exceeding $200. The third part of the plan called for a streamlining of output. For 1891, the only products offered by Harper Furniture would be "bureaus, bedsteads, and washstands." As the operation planned to make fewer products, the new directive called for making each in greater quantity.[139]

Observers of Lenoir's attempt to put itself onto the South's industrial map liked what progress they saw, concluding that the company had found its way. Everything was growing, even the number of buildings within the operation. It seemed justified. "When the buildings were first constructed, it was predicted that they were too large, but now they are cramped for room, especially in the storage and packing departments," offered one assessment. Other accounts of activity noted that "as fast as the furniture can be packed up, it is loaded on the (railroad) cars." Yet, a worrisome observation was also made. The boxcars may have filled quickly, but somehow, "the storage department is always full." Company officials boasted that the product line "meets with a ready sale, nearly every merchant who makes a trial purchase becoming a regular customer," while also modestly mentioning, "the stock has not yet been pushed upon the market." If all of those assertions were true, the factory was overproducing.[140]

As the size of the plant continued to grow, so did the infrastructure needed to support it. Water filled a critical need, both to fuel the boilers and as a line of first defense in case of a fire. To help, workmen dammed up the nearby branch for a readily available source. Only four years before, fire had ended Morganton's hopes of having such a factory in its midst. A furniture factory with a copious amount of sawdust increased the risk of going up in smoke. Also, firefighting in the era remained primitive. If a blaze broke out, damage would be much more likely to be minimized if the company had its own water at hand. Even though piped water was part of the construction plan, it never flowed inside the facility. Access remained only as close as the water tower.

Among the new workers to the plant was J.A. Bush, who constructed a sawmill on the property to prepare the wood for fashioning into useful pieces for the homes of consumers. When Bush came to Lenoir, he brought his family with him. It was only a few years later that the factory hired Bush's son Belk to come to work there at age 13. Following Belk Bush's retirement from the furniture industry, almost 70 years later in 1964, he remembered the jobs he was hired to do. "I carried the mail and also the water. There weren't any water systems or plumbing around here then. I had to carry the water shop workers drank from, a spring about a quarter of a mile away." For his efforts, Belk Bush added twenty cents a day to the family pocketbook with that first job.[141]

Even with the expansion, the factory steered a turbulent course during an up and down year. One of the high points was the order from past president J.M. Bernhardt for his new hotel. "The Furniture Factory is at work on a big order of furniture for the Green Park Hotel in Blowing Rock." Then came another. "Messrs. H.W. Connelly and W.C. Coughenour of Connelly Springs, were in Lenoir, Thursday. They have built an addition to the popular hotel at that place and came to buy furniture for it from the Lenoir Furniture Factory." But it wasn't enough. Notices of inactivity competed with the heralding of orders. "The Furniture Factory, which has been closed for several weeks for lack of material, is to begin today, Tuesday," read one announcement from July. Instability in leadership continued as a "new boss", J.A. Underdown took over daily operations at the plant. Another accident, this one mortal took the life of a worker. Charles Coffey, "a young workman at the factory, had been caught up by a pulley" and as a result "his right arm was torn off about 3 inches below the shoulder." Several bones were also broken. He died the next day.[142]

Maybe the most revealing view of where the factory stood within its community came in a small notice in the paper. It read, "10 shares in Lenoir Furniture Co. for sale. Apply to Dr. Spainhour." The momentum, which had such promise in its early days, as W.W. Scott asked his fellow citizens to imagine Lenoir as an industrial center, cajoling them to invest their money in a project that would only be successful with widespread support, now had investors looking for a way out. Dr. J.M. Spainhour was a dentist who gained recognition as an amateur archeologist. He raided numerous Indian burial mounds north of Lenoir for relics that went to the Smithsonian Institution. Around town, he speculated in land, dabbled in politics and business as a man of considerable influence. He was even a fellow director with the Bernhardts in the Caldwell and Watauga Land and Timber Company. The stock sale notice in the paper revealed his defection and signaled a retreat from great expectation.[143]

The Harpers did not share the view that the factory might not be successful. They couldn't, especially with the money and time they had poured

Dr. James Mason Spainhour overlooks the landscape of Lenoir as he invests in the first permanent furniture factory in western North Carolina. He was also the first to sell his stock in the company. Dr. Spainhour had many interests including collecting Native American artifacts. (Courtesy of the Caldwell Heritage Museum)

into it. When the gauntlet of the enterprise fell in the fall of 1890, they picked it up, ready to move forward. Sale of stock, injury and layoffs would not deter them. Looking for distinction, the Harpers had been at work trying to find a new line that would catch the furniture shopping public's eye. Less than a year after their takeover, they unveiled their designs. In the hometown paper came the announcement that "the Lenoir Furniture Company (Harper & Son) are getting out (debuting) a style of antique furniture, called the 'Sixteenth Century' set, that is the subject of universal admiration and will make a decided hit. It is made of polished quarter oak and is the most elegant furniture on the market. It was visited and admired by crowds last week."[144]

The dwindling fortunes of the furniture factory had to be turned around. To show all of Lenoir a different story about the company, the Harpers threw a lavish party on New Year's night, hoping to begin 1892 as a positive year for their fortunes. Described as "an elegant banquet at the Merchants' Hotel" in Lenoir, "employees of the Furniture Factory, and a few other guests" were treated to a meal and congratulatory speeches from a number of men, including J.M. Bernhardt. Major Harper wrapped up the night when he "spoke of the past, present and future of the factory and gave such a happy augury for the prospective success of Lenoir's leading manufacturing institution that the company was put in good spirits in anticipation of it." The pep talk did little good. Five days later, after a called assembly of the stockholders "failed to meet," meaning a quorum of stockholders did not care enough to attend, expectations that operations might quicken its pace beyond the same limping path as the year before faltered.[145]

Despite the lackluster sentiment following the stockholders' meeting, announcements for new orders came in from across the state over the next year. Judson College in Hendersonville, NC, State Normal and Industrial School in Greensboro, and Normal Collegiate Institute in Asheville all bought furniture made in Lenoir. So did the Oak Hill Hotel in Mt. Airy, NC. Reports from early in the year revealed that the factory was "running on full time." Sales seemed to be looking up a bit for the beleaguered operation, so much so that the next year when a called meeting of the stockholders was announced, it actually occurred. Once again, change took place. G.F. Harper gave up his seat as president of the company. Instead, newcomer R.R. Wakefield took over, with G.F. Harper as a member of the board. However, the Major dropped out of the management structure. Dr. Spainhour, even though he tried to divest himself of stock in the company earlier, also took a seat on the board. The most surprising addition was that of J.M. Bernhardt, back again, this time serving as secretary for the company. The major topic of business after electing the new slate of officers was the choice to lease the company to Harper and Son for another year. The group voted to continue with the arrangement.[146]

The deal did not last long. Before summer, a new set of players arrived in Lenoir with plenty of money and big plans. The duo of William S. Harvey and Colonel Charles N. Wire were spied the summer before sniffing around Caldwell County for timber. They didn't need to look far. The tree rich region north of Lenoir provided thousands of acres for harvest. If W.S. Harvey didn't know it already, he certainly saw what the landscape offered when he climbed to the crest of Hibriten Mountain, a peak near Lenoir that towered almost 1,000 feet above the surrounding terrain. "He pronounced the view one of the most beautiful he ever saw." His plan would see wide swaths of that beauty turned from green leaves into greenbacks.[147]

For W.S. Harvey, as for all the budding industrialists who sought to make money on the natural resource of wood, the game was the same. How to economically extract the timber and haul it to market was the objective. The portable mills of the era solved the first issue. In the fall of 1892, Harvey and Wire created the Caldwell Land and Timber Company (different from the Bernhardt brothers operation). Quickly, Harvey went to work putting a whopping $400,000 of capital to work solving the problem of transport. Step by step, Harvey and his "Philadelphia Syndicate," which included over a dozen other men "well known in the financial circles of Philadelphia," proceeded to build a vertically integrated empire for making money by turning trees into furniture.[148]

The first objective of the Caldwell Land and Timber Company was to acquire property. W.S. Harvey purchased the "Wilson Creek lands," 40,000 acres of virgin timber in the hills north of Lenoir. Inaccessible, but with a glut of trees, the purchase made news across the state. "It is the largest combination of capital to be brought into North Carolina in many years," noted the *Asheville Citizen-Times*, likely the largest into the northwestern portion of the state ever. Harvey's objectives loomed just as large.[149]

Among those "objectives are the buying up of lands, sale of timber, the building of railroads and the establishment of factories." Getting the predicted 60,000 board feet of lumber daily out of the remote area with any kind of efficiency required a substantial railroad, not a makeshift operation with shays. W.S. Harvey got to work immediately, first gaining a charter for the Caldwell and Northern Railroad (C&N), then letting a contract for grading the narrow-gauge railroad in the direction of timber rich Wilson's Creek.[150]

Stretching 20 miles north, hopes extended beyond even the territory of the Caldwell Land and Timber Company. With treacherous hills and valleys across which to lay a railroad line a very tall order, many believed the route could (and should) extend into the most remote sections of the North Carolina mountains. Once it got beyond places like Linville, Cranberry, and Elk Park, some dreamed that this rail line could eventually push into Tennessee and create a bridge across the Appalachian Mountains. If that could happen, the Caldwell and Northern Railroad would become a very popular commodity indeed. Such a line could explode commerce in the area because a lot more than wood would travel its rails. Splitting the Appalachians offered a pathway through the mountain wall that had kept explorers tied up in hills and valleys ever since it was traversed by the first settlers to the area in the 18th century. It would not be until 1918, when the East Tennessee and Western North Carolina Railroad bridged the gap that rail service found its way across the Appalachians and then from the Tennessee side, never making the trek down the eastern slopes of the Blue Ridge beyond Boone.[151]

The Caldwell and Northern Railroad focused on the more immediate goals of getting to the timber, with larger plans left to the future. By fall, the line extended eight miles north of Lenoir to the little village of Collettsville. The line had been graded two more miles, but crossing Mulberry Creek required the construction of a substantial bridge, which slowed progress. The other hinderance along the line came from citizens of Caldwell County. Colonel Wire, general manager of the line swore that "he is unwilling to put another dollar into an enterprise that meets with so much opposition from the people." The obstacles included vandalism and assault on both him and his workers. Wire claimed local law enforcement turned a blind eye to violations of law. Wire's railroad found itself also tied up in court with suits totaling $20,000 outstanding against the Caldwell and Northern. [152]

The reason for the opposition remained hazy. It is possible that the local population resented the intrusion of northerners coming in and taking over. Caldwell County men fought a war over similar concerns a generation earlier. If the wider goals of the C&N were to eventually be attained, Caldwell citizens stood to benefit handsomely from being situated at a new departure point to the west. In reality, the people who moved to the mountains above Lenoir did so for a reason, and if the ultimate goal for the C&N Railroad came to fruition, their rural lifestyle might turn urban very soon.[153]

The spring of 1894 brought enough completion of the railroad to begin daily trips between the Wilson Creek gorge and Lenoir. Cargos of wood along the narrow gauge began to roll down the line with only a few mishaps along the way. A notice went out to landowners up and down the line, presumably even some of those citizens who showed their lack of support with violence, that the Caldwell Land and Timber Company was buying "white pine, oak, poplar and chestnut" for cash. Were the techniques of W.S. Harvey and Colonel Wire so onerous as to spark resistance by the local population? While reasons remained hidden, actions did not as vandalism continued.[154]

Compared to building a railroad, the "establishment of factories" to hone the wood into a "value added product" turned out to be easy. W.S. Harvey and company pivoted from railroad building to manufacturing, subleasing the already leased Lenoir Furniture Factory. Soon after the announcement of the Caldwell and Northern, in the spring of 1893, Harvey paid $1,100 for a three-year lease on the furniture factory. Now the Philadelphia Syndicate had the trifecta, wood in abundance, a transportation system to deliver it, and the factory to turn raw material into a finished product. The switchover from the Harpers to Harvey took place at the beginning of July with great expectations for the new operator, the third in less than five years.[155]

Meanwhile, Harper and Son scurried to wrap up their tenure in the business by finishing orders. However, several items remained overstocked. Given the fact that the retailers controlled the manufacturing process, the Harpers used the switchover to drum up sales. Their advertisement from late May read in part, "Having given up our lease on the Lenoir Furniture Factory, the stock on hand consisting of Bed Room Suits, Bedsteads, Bureaus, Tables, etc., will be sold at reduced prices until the 1st of July, at which time we will vacate the premises. The Furniture, which is the first class of its kind, must be sold." The ad ran for the next year and a half.[156]

With each new version of the Lenoir factory, hopes rose again for the facility to reach its full potential and begin a furniture-making empire. The W.S. Harvey incarnation brought another round of fantastic pronouncements. The factory, it was reported, was "to be put upon a basis of usefulness and will do an amount of work that it has been not heretofore been able to accomplish."

In addition, the "plant" was expected "to flourish like a green bay tree and will be the nucleus of wood-working establishments to be built up around Lenoir." Along with great expectations for the furniture industry came the accompanying dreams for the rail line. "Would it not be a great achievement to have a line of cars running from Lenoir to Johnson City, Tenn., with the prospect of making one or more Southern connection?" a reference to the dream of a trans-Appalachian line.[157]

Not since the days of the first factory campaign to build furniture in Lenoir had such boosterism been seen. The only difference this time came with most unexpected partners, especially for a southern town, that of 'yankees' Harvey and Wire. "Let us roll up our sleeves and pitch in and help these co-workers from the North build up our country, and by our energy and public spirit, enable ourselves to share the good fortune," exhorted *Lenoir Topic* editor W.W. Scott. If those ex-Confederates held any animosity toward the Philadelphia Syndicate robbing their forests of wood, they did not publicly voice opposition. Much of the ill will demonstrated along the rail line in Collettsville evaporated quickly once Harvey and company put Lenoir citizens to work in the factory via their lease. It would not be the last time an outsider would come to Lenoir, taking over the process with promises they would not keep.[158]

Despite high hopes, the factory sputtered yet again. In May of 1894 came a rumor "that it is probable that the furniture factory will be started up again in June. There is too much money in this enterprise for it to be idle. It should be running on full time, and we hope this rumor is correct." The uncertainty of the factory remained a topic of discussion all summer. In a subsequent article, the question became direct. "When will the furniture factory begin operations?" No answer came from the new owners, who faced the same reality as the old ones. Harvey and his syndicate did not seem to spend a lot of time trying to make the factory pay. The three-year lease had not even seen the end of the calendar year before the railroad owners faced the fact that they did not have the proper experience to run a furniture factory. However, they soon found a party that did. The Wrenn Brothers, Thomas F. and M.J. had just lost their own factory in High Point to fire when they came to Lenoir, inspected the site, and sub-leased it. Ordering another round of new machinery for the facility, the Wrenns expected to employ up to 75 hands in their new version of the old factory.[159]

At this point, the Lenoir Furniture Factory took on the characteristics of an orphan, being passed from hand to hand. Each time, the lessees came from farther and farther away even if W.S. Harvey could be considered a somewhat naturalized local. After a little over a year of operation, the Wrenns gave up their lease in favor of a new set of brothers, the Kritz Brothers of South Bend, Indiana, the fifth group of operators in less than seven years. Frank Kritz had experience in the furniture business, leaving a similar position with Elliott Furniture in Charlotte to take the helm on the shop floor as superintendent in Lenoir.[160]

Within months, folks began to notice that the quality of furniture coming out of the factory was greatly improved. "A thing of beauty is a joy forever," opined *Lenoir Topic* editor W.W. Scott, quoting Keats concerning the "desks, bedsteads, and other furniture now finished at the furniture factory," calling the output "elegant." Giving his seal of approval, Scott said, "the lessee, Mr. Frank Kritz, knows what he is doing." Not long after, the *Morganton Herald* concurred, reporting the factory was "running on full time" because of demand. "The reputation of their work is such that they cannot begin to fill all the orders." The printed remark was no small accolade. With a vague competition that existed between the two towns, the Morganton paper acknowledging success was a triumph in Lenoir when they read the *Morganton Herald*'s banner, "Score one more for Lenoir."[161]

At the end of the first year's lease, it looked as though Frank Kritz might be the secret ingredient the Lenoir factory needed for success. Kritz leased for another year and reported turning out "about $2,500 work per month." Even with demand outpacing production, Kritz curiously shut down operations for a day to allow his entire force to pick "blackberries to make wine," no doubt winning the admiration of his hands for a day off.[162]

Even though the Lenoir Furniture Factory's output maintained a high level of appreciation, its product described as "beautiful" and Kritz's management called "clever," within two years, sales flagged. Production once again exceeded orders, and the factory reverted to its old routine of periodic shutdowns. The enterprise, so wanted and so heralded ten years earlier had spent a decade trying to get on its feet. It never could. Despite periods of promise and full production, sustaining the operation proved elusive. Neither J.M. Bernhardt, nor the Harpers, W.S. Harvey, the Wrenn Brothers, or Frank Kritz and company had a long-term answer to the intractable problem that plagued the Lenoir operation throughout the 1890s.[163]

What ultimately unlocked the key to success rested in a coalition of

An early gathering of workers from the Harper Furniture Company. This plant was the original factory in Lenoir, but hard times compelled Major G.W.F. Harper and his son to take over the plant and run it until they sold to the Broyhills. (Courtesy of the Caldwell Heritage Museum)

previous players at the site to unite and make the Lenoir furniture operation a winner. In February of 1900 came word that "the Harper Furniture Co., comprised of G.L. Bernhardt, J.M. Bernhardt, and G.F. Harper, will run the furniture factory. Mr. G.F. Harper will be general manager and Mr. A.F. Kritz, superintendent." At that point, the stop and start nature of the factory in Lenoir ceased and continuous production commenced. The road to establishing a sustainable enterprise finally got off the ground and until Harper Furniture merged with another local entity in 1930, the company enjoyed steady production.[164]

Profitability for industrial furniture production took a lengthy period to establish itself, a decade in fact. However, the long awaited success of the Lenoir Furniture Factory may have been the key trial through which furniture manufacturing had to pass if it was ever going to dominate the economy and the character of western North Carolina. Given the eventual concentration of companies that sprouted in Lenoir, it is arguable that none of those might ever have been started if this first effort fizzled.[165]

Maturation takes time. Just as investors united for common cause to fund the company back in 1889, managing the operation required a similar collective. Each new lessee thought they had the right skills to run the place. As it turned out they were half right. The company did need what they offered, but other contributions were also necessary. Once they began putting their heads together, this experiment in New South industry found its proper stride. As much as the dollars invested, the perseverance they demonstrated in repeated attempts shows uncommon dedication to the idea. They would not give up. Adding a perceptive ingenuity to learn from what did not work the last time, each group edged closer to a winning formula. Considering the point from which they started, ten years really wasn't that long at all.

---⊗∽---

Letterhead for Statesville's Key Furniture Company (below). Once an outlet for spiritous liquor (above), the Key family changed their output to a less controversial product. The family had direct ties to the author of the Star Spangled Banner, Francis Scott Key. (From the Statesville Photographic Collection. Courtesy of Steve Hill)

Chapter 8
New Players

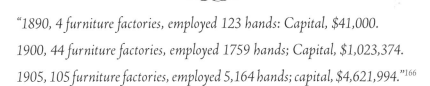

---❦---

"1890, 4 furniture factories, employed 123 hands: Capital, $41,000.

1900, 44 furniture factories, employed 1759 hands; Capital, $1,023,374.

1905, 105 furniture factories, employed 5,164 hands; capital, $4,621,994."[166]

Wood-Working Exhibit Great

Much Progress Shown in This Line

A Leading Industry

The North Carolina Furniture Exhibit at the Jamestown Exposition, 1907

---❦---

The natural advantage of wood in abundance to the economies of both Morganton and Lenoir initially eluded Hickory. While much of both Burke (Morganton) and Caldwell (Lenoir) Counties included large harvests of trees in their mountainous northern portions, Catawba (Hickory, Newton) was situated farther south with no wilderness forests to claim and no stockpile of timber to access for any new company. And yet, Hickory proved to be a much more stable environment for the furniture industry.

Within two miles of town ran the mighty Catawba River. It flowed out of the mountainous region that was part of the rich bounty of wood.

The river itself provided an avenue of transportation from the forests to a town that did not fumble with business. In fact, the first non-furniture wood-working business in the region sprang from the banks of the Catawba near Hickory. In 1878, George Bonniwell and Andrew Ramseur began a small wagon making firm on the Hickory side of the river using logs floated down the Catawba. Business grew to the point that the company, Piedmont Wagon, moved its operation to a factory complex on the west end of Hickory. For the next 50 years, the company reigned as the region's largest employer, with product going to farms and factories up and down the Eastern Seaboard and to Europe during World War I.[167]

The success of Piedmont Wagon also demonstrated another advantage of doing business in Hickory. When the wagon maker came to town, its industrial campus was located at the confluence of two railroad lines, the standard gauge Western North Carolina Rail Road (WNCRR) and the Chester and Lenoir Narrow Gauge (C&LNGRR). The WNCRR turned Hickory from a one tavern crossroad in 1859 to Major Player just a generation later. The rail line continued to lay track west after the Civil War in the effort to connect both ends of a geographically diverse state. Hickory's growth became so explosive that city leaders contemplated renaming the town Piedmont City to boast of its preeminent status in western North Carolina. The Chester & Lenoir Narrow Gauge Railroad, later renamed the Carolina and Northwestern, took both passengers and goods from upstate South Carolina through Hickory to the very same mountains from which the Lenoir factory harvested its lumber. As a travel alternative to the Catawba River, the C&LNGRR offered faster, more secure passage for the raw material of wood (especially once the Philadelphia Syndicate's W.S. Harvey funded an extension beyond Lenoir). Equally important, the WNCRR could take finished product to markets all over the wider railroad network of the United States.

Hickory at the turn of the 20th century. George Hall from a storefront on the right looked across the thoroughfare to the left (where the depot was situated) and got the idea to start a furniture factory to keep the lumber he saw leaving on the railroad and to make money locally. (Image courtesy Ann Goodman Collection)

The third advantage to locating a furniture factory in Hickory was the business climate spawned by the railroad and all who came as a result. Unlike mnay other southern towns where social acceptance came only with a longstanding family name, Hickory proved friendly to anyone from anywhere who brought with them the entrepreneurial spirit, a solid business plan, and a strong work ethic. The town's registry of companies exemplified diversity, with several cotton mills, tobacco factories, and planing mills, plus the highly successful Piedmont Wagon scattered within the business district. The desire to diversify further was evident in a point made by the local paper in the summer of 1893. The *Hickory Press* remarked in its pages, "there ought to be a North Carolina furniture factory to every ten acres of pine in the state." The other Catawba County paper, the *Newton Enterprise*, was more specific. "The short cut to the enrichment in Catawba County lies in filling Newton with furniture factories and other wood-working establishments." And while smaller municipalities in the region like Morganton and Lenoir had both started operations prior to that date, neither could claim a resoundingly successful, continuous operation within their borders at the time. The acumen of leaders in Hickory soon proved they could."[168]

The arrival of industrial furniture making in Hickory may have come after considerable evaluation, watching what didn't work in other towns, or it may have come with a blinding epiphany. The later scenario was the one linked to Hickory's creation of furniture so often, it gained currency as fact. As the story goes, George Whiting Hall, a prime example of the businessmen Hickory attracted, watched a load of lumber fall from a train passing through Union Square (called Park Place then) in Hickory. The accident caused him to ask why were other cities gaining the advantage of turning that wood into furniture when it could be done much closer to home and to the benefit of Hickory. Variations of the story purport no accident but Hall having his vision just the same. In many ways the thought replicated the one D.A. Smith of Old Fort had a quarter of a century earlier. Charles Preslar, writer of the first comprehensive volume of Catawba County history cites George W. Hall as "the man who pioneered in furniture-making in Catawba County." Whether by inspiration or analytical investigation, he announced his plans in the summer of 1901.[169]

"Hickory's New Furniture Factory" splashed across the headlines of papers from as far away as Charlotte. The announcement heralded that a new "enterprise will fill a long felt want among our wood manufacturers, who have been unable to utilize to advantage the beautiful hard woods which are daily shipped from this market to other sections of the country to manufacturers of fine furniture." If George Hall had such a striking vision, he must have conveyed it to everyone within earshot, thus the news coverage. But once he did, the new business, called "Hickory Furniture Company" coalesced its operational plan quickly. Knowing neither exactly what it would make or at what price point, Hall and company left those choices to be decided as construction of the plant began. "Whether medium or fine grades of furniture will be manufactured has not been definitely decided upon," reported the *Charlotte Observer*. It took a few months before the decision reached the public. The answer came succinctly with the statement, "it will make chamber suits," meaning bedsteads, dressers and washstands, i.e. bedroom suites, would be the focus of the operation.[170]

As the new century dawned in Hickory, so did a new generation of businessmen. Citing George Hall as "promoter" of the new factory as well as "one of the head officers," he also received the accolade of being "one of Hickory's progressive young business men." Unlike many who came to 'Piedmont City' upon hearing of opportunity there, George Hall already had an anchor. Both his father, P.C., and especially his uncle, J.G. Hall were part of Hickory's enclave of leaders. In fact, J.G. Hall wore a lot of hats in Hickory. Among his many activities, he served as president of Piedmont Wagon, a term or two as mayor, a partner in a tobacco firm, and as a member of the board of directors for the First National Bank of Hickory. Since 1872, the Hall Brothers ran a dry goods store in downtown Hickory offering everything from syrups to soaps. Any advice J.G. gave to George concerning the timber market in and around Hickory was likely one of 'carpe diem' (seize the day) and may have figured in the younger Hall's calculations to move forward with his new company. However, wagons and furniture were not the only consumers of wood in the Hickory business community.[171]

Two other companies already vied with Piedmont Wagon for the best lumber coming out of the northwest mountains. Since the early 1880s, Hickory Manufacturing honed wood into building materials for many of the homes and hotels around Hickory and beyond. Specializing in internal wood products such as moldings, stairs, hand railings, mantels, doors, wainscoting, blinds, as well as pews and pulpits for churches, the company offered custom work and complete satisfaction. Hickory Manufacturing was started by George Bonniwell, one of the original creators of Piedmont Wagon. In 1890, the Hickory Novelty Wood Works opened with much the same offerings as the earlier Hickory Manufacturing. Within a few years, a portion of the company was sold to interests outside Hickory but continued to offer interior finishing materials to builders throughout the region.[172]

In this period, the furniture business, while promising, still took a back seat to other manufactories in the region. Within the larger realm of Catawba County, industrialists looked more to textiles in the late 19th century for economic growth than furniture. While wood stood waiting to be harvested to the north, the annual crop of cotton lay south. Part of Catawba County's strength may have been natural diversity within its borders. Hickory sported roller mills and tobacco warehouses, while farther south in the county, cotton mills abounded. By 1885, the firm of Carpenter and Sons in Maiden had enlarged their operation to the tune of $28,000, one of the larger capitalizations of the period. Other Catawba towns followed Maiden's lead with mills in Conover, Newton, Brookford, and ultimately, Hickory.[173]

As soon as the announcement of a furniture company in Hickory came, a flurry of activity commenced. The paperwork to file the state charter for Hickory Furniture had already been submitted, and approval was announced within days. Quickly, George Hall selected a location and secured the land. "The site for the Hickory Furniture plant has been purchased from Capt. A.Y. Sigmon in the eastern part of the city on the line of the two railroads" reported several newspapers. "Dirt was broken yesterday, and the buildings will be erected as soon as possible." Horace Abee was contracted to construct those buildings while Hall headquartered at the Hickory Inn. Hall used the town's most upscale hotel, to welcome "representatives of a number of the large manufacturers of hard wood machinery" to demonstrate the most advanced and profitable equipment available to outfit his factory, which was a stone's throw away from Hickory's Lenoir College.[174]

George Hall had the confidence to move fast because the company could count on almost $20,000 in subscribed stock with assurances of more. He followed his alacritous execution of plant construction with a pursuit of personnel. Hickory Furniture welcomed both "a practical manufacturer and an artistic designer" to begin the process of building furniture as soon as they could move in. The speed at which the operation got on its feet was staggering (especially in comparison to the Lenoir operation of a decade earlier). A newspaper update in November read, "The Hickory Furniture Company will soon be ready to start." By February, the factory was in gear. "All kinds of saws and machinery for such work were running at full speed," reported a visitor from the *Hickory Democrat*, the local paper. The writer noted, "the class of work is very high. The boiler room and engine room are models of their kind." He concluded, "the enterprising promoters have erected and are operating a first class furniture factory, of which Hickory should be proud." The tour guide was George W. Hall.[175]

George Hall's capacity for showing the reporter everything from the dry house to the finishing room was not in his capacity as president of the new organization. After the announcement, Hall stepped into the position of secretary and treasurer for the company, a job originally slated for A.S. Ellison, who by February had himself stepped over to general manager duties. The office of president went to K.C. Menzies, a longtime banker in Hickory. He had previously worked as the assistant cashier during the town's first banking attempt, the Bank of Hickory. When it failed in 1890, Menzies' experience (and honesty) suited him to take the helm of the First National Bank of Hickory when it opened its doors the following year. However, George Hall knew the company inside and out. In addition to his tour guiding abilities, he kept account of $18,000 in actual capital as the factory started up with the rest of the "authorized capital stock of $100,000" still to come.[176]

If good ideas come in multiples, then furniture in Hickory must have been a genius move. No sooner had the announcement come for the Hickory Furniture Company than word of another factory reached the public. Thomas J. Martin, a successful lawyer and merchant from upstate South Carolina, followed the railroad line of the C&LNGRR that ran to Hickory. He also followed George Hall and the local contingent of investors who visualized profit in all those trees harvested in the mountains of Caldwell, Wilkes, Burke, and McDowell Counties. In the mind of the press and public, and ultimately the ownership, the two companies became intertwined. "The capital stock of the concern (Martin Furniture) is $25,000, and Mr. K.C. Menzies, its president, and George W. Hall, its secretary and treasurer, are two of Hickory's most successful young business men. The Martin Furniture Company is owned and will be managed by Mr. T.J. Martin, a man of means and experience who has recently moved here from Chester, S.C. His plant will represent about $20,000 and will manufacture sideboards, tables, and other dining room furniture." Menzies and Hall saw no conflict with being

Hickory Furniture Company was Hickory's first. Located in Highland, next door to Martin Furniture, which would soon follow, they shared a sidetrack of the Western NC RR. Employees included young boys and one woman, who was office staff in this circa 1902 photo. (Courtesy of Hickory Landmarks Society)

associated with both entities."[177]

The two firms shared much, including access to the larger world. "Hickory's second furniture factory, which will be owned and operated by Thomas J. Martin is now a certainty. The location adjoins that of the Hickory Furniture Factory company, in the eastern portion of the town, where sidetracks are accessible for both lines of railroad," reported the *Charlotte Observer*. Hickory folks didn't know whether to call their new citizen Thomas, John, or T.J. Martin, but they followed his every step as he proved furniture making in Hickory was no fluke. The city now housed two side-by-side factories. "Mr. John Martin, one of South Carolina's capitalists, was here yesterday looking over the ground with the view of locating the second furniture factory. He also wants to add a chair department, as there is an abundance of timber in this section suitable for the manufacture of chairs." [178]

The choice of producing chairs offered another example of the complimentary nature of the Martin and Hickory firms. With George Hall and company producing bedroom case goods, the newer concern expanded the offering. Plus, the output of both operations could be shipped out simultaneously, thanks to proximity and planning. "An engineer of the Southern Railway is here locating the sidetracks of the Hickory Furniture Company," read one newspaper account while another announced T.J. Martin's intentions. "The location adjoins that of the Hickory Furniture Company, in the eastern portion of the town, where side tracks are accessible from both lines of railroad."[179]

Hickory offered diverse employment opportunities and as the twentieth century dawned, both enterprises scoured the landscape for good, dependable talent to work the wood. T.J. Martin's design planned employment for "40 to 50 skilled men." The question for Martin, as well as George Hall at Hickory Furniture, was, from where would they come? Skill would have to be developed, but workmen from a wide variety of occupations were wooed to begin a career in furniture. These people were called upon to bet their livelihoods on the choice of an untested industry as a good living, just as Martin and Hall had with their investments. One notice demonstrated just how wide the net of employment needed to be cast for a full complement of workers. "Mr. Julius Ramsay has given up his position at the (Hickory) Inn to accept work at the Hickory furniture factory." For Ramsay, the bet paid off. The job of furniture maker lasted much longer than that of being a downtown hotel clerk.[180]

Workers came from many areas to fill the Hickory factories. Dallas G. Fox was himself a builder of furniture by his own hand. He crafted pieces using the methods of the old workshops while also farming. He made a good living with income from both ventures. However, once his wife "became terminally ill with cancer," Dallas Fox could only pay the medical bills by selling the family farm. Without a workshop to continue his trade, he leveraged his know-how by going to work in the factory."[181]

Quickly, the furniture men of Hickory took their place among the ranks of manufacturers populating the New South at a time when the industry began to come together. The fledgling Southern Furniture Manufacturers Association (SFMA) convened in Charlotte, its genesis described as a way to "establish a more cordial relationship" among these new companies, according to Wilber Jones, secretary of the group. Membership included both new Hickory companies. The SFMA promoted the idea that furniture making as a business held potential to become among industries, "one of the strongest in the South." The new trade organization sought to evangelize that fact as well as guard the interests of its members." The geographic array of companies from New Orleans to North Carolina demonstrated that George Hall and T.J. Martin's idea had caught fire elsewhere. After some fitful starts, mechanized furniture had finally reached critical mass, demonstrating its viability in a region that looked for redemption and purpose since its way of life had been catastrophically disrupted in the rebellion, euphemistically known as the War Between the States. The association showed intent on the part of New South industrialists to find their way in the aftermath of agriculture as a chief means of support. With 26 companies attending, including the two Hickory outlets and three from Statesville, the lineup welcomed cooperation amid competition.[182]

The year before the establishment of furniture as an industry in Hickory, to the east in adjacent Iredell County, along the same Western North Carolina railroad line, the idea bloomed in a somewhat different way. A man from the High Point factories with superintendent experience came to Statesville to establish not one but three furniture companies. E.M. Purdy's arrival, as well as the able-bodied workers he brought with him, advanced suggestions that Statesville "is likely to become the leading town in furniture manufacturing in the South within the next few years." It was unclear how much equity Purdy held in each company, but by year's end, he represented all three at the SFMA meeting in Charlotte. The sequence of companies began with Key & Company. Issuing an order for over 10 million feet of lumber, a gargantuan amount, Key was described as "one of the largest and best-equipped (factories) in the State." Statesville Furniture and Kincaid Furniture companies came into operation by the end of 1901, also associated with Purdy's experienced eye.[183]

E.M. Purdy's employment at Key & Company in late 1900 brought with it something of a sea change. The Key family, (a name most known for Francis Scott Key who wrote the lyrics to the Star Spangled Banner) headed by grand-nephew P.B. Key were longtime members of the Statesville business community as "Wholesale Liquor Dealers." Over an almost twenty-year span, the "distillers and jobbers" of "pure North Carolina corn whiskey" as well as "apple and peach brandy" found themselves under scrutiny of state and federal "revenue men." In most cases, the Keys avoided prosecution and continued to grow to the point of incorporation, adding tobacco to their enterprises along the way. Following their success came pains that only dealing in alcohol could offer. The Key family got it coming and going. From one direction, the federal government continually examined the company's books, looking for unpaid taxes, while on the other end, employee thefts implicated the company to the point that P.B. Key was reportedly ill, perhaps from just such headaches. Five years after incorporation, Key was dead. So it may have been no surprise that the family eventually chose to trade its manufacture of spirits for furniture.[184]

"Key & Co. to Discontinue the Wholesale Liquor Business" announced the company's entry into the new venture of furniture. To begin production, the firm sought talented workmen wherever they could find them. In addition to the men E.M. Purdy brought from High Point, the papers were full of announcements of new people coming to Statesville, all for one objective, to work for Key Furniture. "The Mocksville papers say Charles F. Graves left Tuesday evening for Statesville, at which place he will make his home for some time. Mr. Graves is with the Key Furniture Co.," read one post. In the same edition of the paper came word that "E.G. Hunt, of Lenoir has moved here to work for the Key Furniture Co." As the men filled the ranks, so did the raw materials they would need to make furniture. Purdy, through the Key Company, sought "pine wood" for his factory wherever he could get it. While navigating the success of Key Furniture, Purdy also found himself rising to the heights of the executive committee of the SFMA.[185]

With a fine newly constructed home on Elm Street, E.M. Purdy guided the Key operation for its first two years of business. His prominence in the community signaled that he might be willing to explore newer and better prospects for his furniture talents, leading him to more lucrative opportunities. In 1903, Purdy gave over the job of superintendent to a Michigan man, George Brown, to pursue new challenges. Be it ambition or conflict that caused his departure, the time had come for Purdy to invest his skill and acumen in a business that allowed him some ownership. Upon leaving, the Statesville

Record and Landmark suggested that Purdy "will probably engage in another line of manufacturing here." Within a week came word of just such a plan, a fourth furniture company in Statesville being planned with E.M. Purdy as one of the principal investors. In addition to Purdy, D.A. Miller, W.A. Thompson, and State Senator R.B. McLauchlin announced their cooperative venture with a capitalization of $30,000.[186]

If a traveling superstar in the early furniture industry existed, it was E.M. Purdy. Earl Milo Purdy was born in Factoryville, PA, five years prior to the Civil War. After earning a degree from Bucknell University and reading for the law, he decided that factory life was his calling. Purdy gained the notice of future employers. He was also a prudent judge of talent, often taking men along with every move. Returning to High Point, the local paper spotted Purdy, conjecturing that he was again poaching workers for a new enterprise. "After more inspiration, we suppose!" was their commentary. But with it came a compliment that Purdy must have heard a lot in those days. They pleaded, "why don't you come back to the fountain, brother," suggesting that High Point would welcome him back with open arms and keep away further startup competition. A month later, Purdy was back in Statesville, participating in the incorporation of the Imperial Furniture Company. In addition to the earlier announcement of the company's impending formation, investors J.C. Steele, Isador Wallace, Eugene Morrison, and W.D. Turner constituted the ownership group.[187]

As far as the other two furniture companies E.M. Purdy represented at the first SFMA meeting, Statesville and Kincaid Furniture, only cursory association with Purdy seems likely. They remained his competition, not his conquests. The duo of W.A. Thomas and J.G. Shelton ran Statesville Furniture as president and secretary/treasurer, respectively. The Kincaid enterprise was owned by two brothers, William T. and Henry Lee Kincaid. In 1912, the two interests merged. At the time of their union, Statesville Furniture shipped out approximately 350 train carloads of bedroom suites per year. The Kincaid company sold slightly less, filling "about 275" boxcar loads annually. Both exhibited their product at the Chicago market, with each shipping much of their product to the upper Midwest, where the company did a combined business of $400,000 a year. In doing so, they competed directly with their furniture elders, the factories of Grand Rapids, Michigan.[188]

Either out of boredom or always looking to greener pasture elsewhere, E.M. Purdy could not stay still. While in Statesville, he and fellow investors diversified their furniture factories, helping to start a glass factory in 1906. Within two years though, Purdy was again on the move, this time to Lenoir. Leaving Imperial Furniture, he took a leap, "elected secretary and treasurer of the Moore Furniture Co., of Lenoir," presumably for more control and more money. The local folks recognized the loss in Purdy signing with another company. The sentiment was that "Mr. Purdy is a furniture man of known abilities, and his resignation is a loss to the Imperial Furniture Company." However, after three years in Lenoir, the furniture pastures looked still greener down east. "The friends of Mr. E.M. Purdy will be glad to learn of his election as secretary, treasurer, and general manager of the Albemarle Furniture Co. at Albemarle, N.C. Mrs. Purdy will continue to make her home in Statesville at present." It seems E.M.'s wife was right to wait in Statesville because in 1919 her husband boomeranged back to help start another furniture operation, Statesville Wood Products. A modestly-sized compared to many of the other companies for which Purdy worked, the new enterprise "will give employment to 40 or 50 men. The authorized capital stock is $125,000, but the business starts off with $25,000 paid, which may increase later. The plant will be under the supervision of Mr. E.M. Purdy, an experienced manufacturer, and will, for the present manufacture parlor frames exclusively. The charter gives the privilege of engaging in the manufacture of any and all kinds of furniture." No matter where Purdy hopped, the move made news.[189]

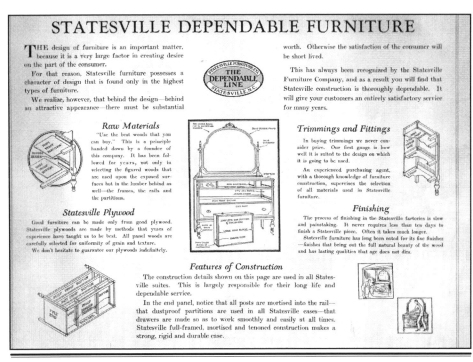

STATESVILLE DEPENDABLE FURNITURE

THE design of furniture is an important matter, because it is a very large factor in creating desire on the part of the consumer.

For that reason, Statesville furniture possesses a character of design that is found only in the highest types of furniture.

We realize, however, that behind the design—behind an attractive appearance—there must be substantial worth. Otherwise the satisfaction of the consumer will be short lived.

This has always been recognized by the Statesville Furniture Company, and as a result you will find that Statesville construction is thoroughly dependable. It will give your customers an entirely satisfactory service for many years.

Raw Materials

"Use the best woods that you can buy." This is a principle handed down by a founder of this company. It has been followed for years, not only in selecting the figured woods that are used upon the exposed surfaces but in the lumber behind as well—the frames, the rails and the partitions.

Statesville Plywood

Good furniture can be made only from good plywood. Statesville plywoods are made by methods that years of experience have taught us to be best. All panel woods are carefully selected for uniformity of grain and texture. We don't hesitate to guarantee our plywoods indefinitely.

Trimmings and Fittings

In buying trimmings we never consider price. Our first gauge is how well it is suited to the design on which it is going to be used.

An experienced purchasing agent, with a thorough knowledge of furniture construction, supervises the selection of all materials used in Statesville furniture.

Finishing

The process of finishing in the Statesville factories is slow and painstaking. It never requires less than ten days to finish a Statesville piece. Often it takes much longer.

Statesville furniture has long been noted for its fine finishes—finishes that bring out the full natural beauty of the wood and has lasting qualities that age does not dim.

Features of Construction

The construction details shown on this page are used in all Statesville suites. This is largely responsible for their long life and dependable service.

In the end panel, notice that all posts are mortised into the rail—that dustproof partitions are used in all Statesville cases—that drawers are made so as to work smoothly and easily at all times. Statesville full-framed, mortised and tenoned construction makes a strong, rigid and durable case.

Instructional page from the catalog of Statesville Furniture, showing why their furniture was named *The Dependable Line*. Salesmen used the tutorial to explain the advantages of the company over other furniture. (Author's collection)

E.M. Purdy's new operation competed with his old, as Imperial Furniture of Statesville continued the momentum he started. Not long after he left, Imperial crowed about the extent of its sales, shipping a carload (boxcar) of sideboards to Mexico City. Their reach spanned the oceans too as readers of the *Statesville Daily Record* found out in 1904. "Yesterday, the company shipped some sideboards to South Africa. Goods manufactured in Statesville go all over the world." Its wide distribution became one of Imperial's proudest claims. "The Imperial line is sold through commission only, and the main distribution is in the states east of the Mississippi River, practically every one of which is represented by orders in various volumes of the company's books."[190]

The various activities of E.M. Purdy demonstrated the erratic nature of manufacturing furniture in western North Carolina in its early days. Opportunity existed everywhere, and Purdy was quicker than most to jump when the time came. Many men at the investor level envisioned a longer game to be played, looking to establish themselves and their companies within a community and sticking around for generations to reap the rewards of stability. These operational geniuses like Purdy were consequential to setting the pace. Along with the guiding hand of men like George Hall and his Hickory contemporaries, the industry found equilibrium. Conversely, even with the capital and early success of Key Furniture when it jumped from whiskey to furniture making, the company went bankrupt three years after losing Purdy.[191]

Statesville, with or without E.M. Purdy was gaining stature as a furniture-making town. Looking for a specialty product, T.M. Crowell began crafting "show cases" (crafted display furniture for stores to display their wares). Quickly, the Statesville Show Case Company branched out to make bank furniture as well, placing pieces throughout the region and as far away as West Virginia and Tennessee. Later would come several veneer operations, including Armfield Veneer, Statesville Veneer and Panel, and Kennedy Veneer Company. Another enterprise also entered the arena, making living room furniture with a name that harkened back to an earlier time. The Carolina Parlor Furniture Company made "overstuffed and cane" sofas and chairs.[192]

South of Statesville and Hickory, in the small but older town of Lincolnton, the unique partnership of a husband and wife duo tried to put their company on the furniture map as well. In 1905, John Elam Cochrane and Emma McCoy Cochrane began (similar to T.M. Crowell in Statesville) "building display cases used widely in area department and grocery stores, their first factory nothing more than a small building on North Oak Street." According to family lore, the practice of furniture making went even further back to J.E. Cochran's father who made church furniture. By the 1930s, with their sons now part of the business, the family incorporated. The Cochrane family diversified products to include fireplace mantels, but their mainstay was household furnishings out of "pine, oak, and maple." The company prospered and continued to expand, making the Cochrane the largest furniture concern in Lincolnton.[193]

Back in Hickory, T.J. Martin soon lost interest and sold his investment in Martin Furniture, though it retained his name until a merger with Hickory Furniture years later. The *Charlotte Observer* reported that "Mr. Martin returns to South Carolina, where he is largely interested in cotton farming." The news bid farewell to the entrepreneur from the southern end of the narrow-gauge railroad line while western North Carolina continued to build its reputation as an emerging industrial power. Even if Martin no longer believed in the prospect, it was obvious that capable Hickory men (and at least one woman like Emma McCoy Cochrane) eagerly filled the gap. Purchasing Martin's shares were town luminaries A.A. Shuford, E.B. Cline, the Hutton Brothers (of the Hutton and Bourbonnais Lumber Co.), and K.C. Menzies, president of both Hickory and Martin Furniture. Operation of the Martin plant would eventually pass on to the husband and wife team of Colonel Marcellus Eugene Thornton and Elizabeth C. Thornton for a while, he as president, she as treasurer. Col. Thornton brought to the job his experience as a newspaper man and novelist, while his wife had amassed a tidy fortune prior to their marriage, thus her role as treasurer. Her business acumen was revealed in, of all things, her marriage to Colonel Thornton. She forced him to sign a prenuptial agreement, a canny act for a woman in those days.[194]

The emergence of furniture making by machine continued its long and winding trek to success, with a few failures along the way as cautionary tales. Unlike Morganton and Lenoir, where continual, stable operation remained elusive, Hickory proved to be richer ground for planting and growth. Even when T.J. Martin dropped the ownership ball, other financiers and managers picked it up to keep the enterprise prospering. In Statesville, even without E.M. Purdy, Imperial Furniture and the combined Statesville/Kincaid operation continued to ship boxcar loads to a wide array of customers, keeping themselves in the game. However, neither Morganton nor Lenoir would give up, and from those satellites to Hickory would come an atom of energy, as well as output that rivaled any other furniture town.

The Martin Furniture Company's beginning and end. The factory built by T.J. Martin in 1902 stood next to Hickory Furniture in northeast Hickory, sharing a railroad spur. Inset, a calamity that befell many companies. Fire brought the building down in 1926. (Courtesy of the City of Hickory)

Chapter 9
A Mighty Behemoth

In the industrial era, furniture startups were risky bets. Would the market accept another group trying to make its name as a sturdy, dependable and innovative producer of furniture? After all, furniture was not a cheap investment. Pitfalls may have frightened others, but New South entrepreneurs were made of stronger stuff. November 10, 1903 marked the date of another such attempt. In the countryside of Burke County, not far from Morganton, NC, came another group of investors betting on the promise of furniture. Facing not only the usual adversities but extraordinary ones as well, they navigated the uncertainty of the fledgling industry with prudence and grit. Agreeing to carve out 750 shares at $100 each, A.M. Kistler, Samuel Huffman, D.B. Mull, J.S. Abernethy, J.D. Boger, P.W. Patton, and an investor in earlier furniture enterprises, W.C. Ervin provided enough capital to get the company they called "Drexel" started.[195]

The name was unique. It did not reflect anything in the area. Instead, Sam Huffman looked for something to call both his company and what would become the surrounding town that would set it apart from other early players. When the firm told its story in a 1963 book, the creators supposedly asked for list of prospective names from the superintendent of the Southern Railroad line that would service the stopover." Among the names he (the superintendent) submitted was that of a Philadelphia family with large railroad holdings." The Drexel family supported the creation of a university that bore its name about a decade prior to Sam Huffman's appropriation of the moniker. He liked it

The choice of location began some years before when D.B. Mull and Sam Huffman (sometimes spelled Hoffman) started a sawmill in the wilderness along the Southern Railway line between Hickory and Morganton, calling it the Hoffman Manufacturing Company. They made "corncrib boards (used to build granaries)." Soon, they began fashioning dressed lumber into doors, sashes, and blinds. Adjacent to this factory, Huffman and Mull added a "flour mill with a forty-barrel daily capacity" while fellow investors initiated a "hosiery mill for the manufacture of women's and children's stockings." The creation of a furniture company added one more reason for people to move to the widening community, not yet a town but growing. To help expand this circle of workplaces into an inviting town, Huffman and Mull started a retail outlet for their wares; the building was first made of wood, then replaced by "a handsome brick store 28 x 100 feet" where the second floor was designated for use by the local lodge. Soon came a hotel along the railroad line where the hands and their families could reside as they worked. In short order, cottages began to spring up, including a company-built one for the new superintendent.

Drexel leadership knew the risk they took. In Burke County, the Colonel Wilson factory of 15 years earlier had come to naught. Since then, a national depression (the Panic of 1893) came and went, but the remnants of financial hardship hung on in Morganton. The 1897 failure of a bank in town, with "capital assets of $40,000" left local businessmen poorer. If Drexel wanted a regional return on their assets, they would have to rely on their own efforts. Since "business was slower than molasses" in Morganton, the "Huffman-Mull venture" interested investors and workers alike, if for nothing else than its audacity.

The land surrounding the site of the first factory was perfect. All around the railroad line a forest grew, filled with oak, poplar, chestnut, walnut, and maple, ready for conversion into items for the home. Son of the founder Sam Huffman and eventual president of the company, R.O. Huffman remembered the terrain as sparse, saying, "in 1903, there was not a mile of good road in Burke County," as the area was more wilderness than settled territory. Many Morgantonians resisted progress. For example, few welcomed the automobile into their midst. Gasoline was only obtainable from "drug stores." Taking Burke County from an agrarian identity to an industrial one would take time, requiring deft leadership to bring the local population along. However, the rewards of harvesting the vast timber resources of the region were too great to be ignored. As Huffman recalled, "the first furniture made by Drexel was a suite of native Oak, comprising a bureau, wash-stand, and double bed at $14.50." If those products found a market, a prosperous, new way of life in modernizing American awaited.[196]

The big problem for the company early on, like similar issues in neighboring towns of Hickory and Lenoir was its workforce. No one knew how to make furniture. Drexel repeatedly recruited men and boys in a five-mile radius of the the new factory. "Employees skilled in the manufacturing of furniture (were) almost impossible to obtain," recalled R.O. Huffman about the first workers his father recruited. Management in his opinion was equally scarce. Together and without experience both management and labor would have to learn the business from scratch. The weekday morning whistle at 7:00 am beckoned a new day of training for Drexel Furniture that went on until 6:00 pm each evening with only an hour break daily for lunch.[197]

Chief among the Drexel employees was A.W. Harris, the factory's superintendent. Like E.M. Purdy in Statesville, he brought much needed experience to the shop floor. "He got his training at High Point and is specially skilled at the trade," which made him essential to early operations. Harris oversaw the initial output of "about fifty articles per day" and handled the productivity of the workforce, which totaled a monthly payroll of $30,000, and included local young men like Mortimer Rhyne, a "capable engineer." Soon after getting down to work, Harris directed activities to fill an order for "five hundred oak chiffoniers" from Sears, Roebuck & Co., the national mail-order company. Local observers of the output called the workmanship "of high order," adding that the finished pieces are "of the very best." The company worked hard to get its line in front of national retailers, which garnered the Sears order. Investor J.S. Abernethy took on the role of salesman, traveling to the national furniture exposition in Chicago, order pad in hand, to challenge the manufacturers of Grand Rapids and begin to put southern makers on the map.[198]

Momentum began to carry Drexel forward, a solid bet as southern furniture became a legitimate choice. Unfortunately, adversity in the form of fire plagued Drexel just as it did the Morganton company. In September of 1905, a frame building owned by Huffman and Mull that housed a significant amount of the factory's output awaiting shipment burned to the ground. Contents were valued at "between $3,000 and $4,000 worth of furniture." The building was insured for $200, but there was no insurance on the furniture. "Rats and matches" were listed as suspects in the cause of the early Sunday morning fire.[199]

The blaze and its damage brought up a controversy about the new factory and its location outside the city of Morganton. One local observer suggested that by building the factory in the wilderness of eastern Burke County, the owners may have saved some tax money, but an event like the fire cost them much more. The lost inventory far outweighed being a part of the municipality of Morganton because without the town's services, in this case a fire department, the Drexel leadership was penny wise and pound foolish in placing their company so far away.[200]

No matter the criticism, in the aftermath of the fire the company chose to remain at its original location and rebuild at their little flag stop along the rail line. In its second incarnation, Drexel expanded operations, adding a "finishing and packing room which will increase the capacity of the factory by one-fourth. They are also preparing to build another large building for a store room and office." Adequate capital allowed Drexel the luxury to rebuild. They rebounded from the experience but more lessons awaited.[201]

A little over a year after the first fire came a much larger and more destructive blaze. Reporters surmised that the fire "was caused by the bursting of the blow-off pipe to the boiler in the engine room." Once it got to the shavings and sawdust, attempts to extinguish the inferno were futile, given the still inadequate firefighting resources of the company. This time the losses were much greater, since instead of just taking the inventory of the factory, everything was wrecked. "Beside the loss of the building and machinery, between $15,000 and $20,000 worth of finished furniture and about 150,000 feet of lumber were destroyed." Damages totaled near $50,000, with only about half of the loss insured. Once the flames subsided, the president of the company, A.M. Kistler, along with Sam Huffman, D.B. Mull, as well as other listed stockholders T.F. Wrenn, M.F. Scaife, and J.T. Brittain debated the option of rebuilding. They knew that if they committed to continuing, the task would be an enormous one. But one week later, the group was sure. Drexel would be constructed a third time from the ground up, better and more up to date than ever.[202]

The winter of 1907 witnessed the Drexel 'phoenix' arising from ashes once again. By the end of January two of the three main buildings were in place, with a third framed up. Hopes of a quick return to productivity were high for both investors and labor. "If the machinery companies are able to make deliveries, the shops will run on full time in six weeks," conjectured the *Morganton News-Herald*.[203]

Drexel enjoyed and benefitted from a loyal and stable workforce, right down to its beasts of burden. For over two decades, a horse named Frank hauled materials from place to place. He was named for Sam Huffman's oldest son, the father instructing supervisors the horse was to be used for as long as he lived. The amazing thing about Frank (the horse) was that he needed no supervision. His routine, carrying wagons of "finished furniture to the railroad station for shipment" was a repetitive, daily activity that Frank handled on his own. The task became Frank's specialty. The use of horse-drawn conveyances like Frank demonstrated a solid link to the agrarian past, even as the mechanical age took hold.[204]

Following the lead of the Drexel investors, another nearby contingent put together a plan to revive Morganton Furniture Company, connected to the earlier venture in name only. A charter from the North Carolina Secretary of State recognized a new company with "authorized capital of $125,000, of which $27,000 is paid in." That money came from organizers J. MacNaughton and N. H. Hall of Marion, and Frank P. Tate and W.E. Walton from Morganton. The new firm planned activities well beyond the making of furniture, though some might support its crafting of wood, like "very extensive privileges including the operation of mines and all sorts of plants, including those for electric lights and power." The factory located along the Southern line within the city limits of Morganton, making them better corporate citizens in the eyes of some than Drexel. MacNaughton and Hall were experienced timber men who decided to go full force into the burgeoning furniture industry. They sold their lumber business in Marion, taking their capital to the new venture.[205]

Shortly after the start of the Morganton operation and the rebuilding of Drexel came a slowdown in furniture buying that caused layoffs at both places. Preceding the national 'Panic of 1907' by several months, "Morganton Furniture Co. will shut down its shops for two weeks. This is a dull season with furniture manufacturers," came the suggestion that furniture, like agriculture before it, took on a seasonal quality. Besides, "the offices of this company want to attend the Jamestown exposition," a tricentennial celebration of the first successful English colony in North America, taking place in Virginia. Actually, the business suffered from more than one annual slowdown. During the winter of 1908, and with this time the Panic of 1907 in full flower, both Burke County furniture operations furloughed their employees, as well as supplier Piedmont Lumber Company. The shutdown put several hundred men out of work for weeks, causing concern for working families who depended on paychecks to survive. Operations got back to full employment in mid-February.[206]

For both Morganton and Drexel, as it was for all furniture employers, the workforce remained fluid. Because of temporary layoffs during their slow times, workers looked for and found other opportunities. E.T. Jarrett left Drexel shortly after the new, rebuilt factory started churning out pieces again to take a position in Sam Huffman's other woodworking business, Huffman & Mull's sash and blind factory. That same day, W.S. Johnson announced he "had decided to make a change." Instead of looking for more industrial work, Mr. Johnson revealed a hidden talent in announcing his intention to establish a "first-class bakery on Union Street." The loss of Mr. Johnson was a real one for Morganton in that he came from High Point with previous experience in the manufacturing business. As workers left, so too did they come. Drexel lured away George W. Poteet from a furniture factory in Toccoa, Georgia, to take over supervision of its shipping department.[207]

The competition between the two companies for employees and preeminence in the community was real and substantial. When the Burke Poultry Show came, and prizes were needed for the best in show, Drexel contributed a "twenty-five dollar quartered-oak dresser" while Morganton Furniture offered a "twenty dollar chiffonier." Either in cooperation or contention, both firms represented themselves so as not to be forgotten in the mind of the local furniture buying and furniture making public.[208]

While the Drexel operation was much larger than Morganton Furniture, the latter company had one advantage, it made furniture within the town limits, and though it paid taxes for the privilege, the municipal government of Morganton provided infrastructure, the kind Drexel could have used during both fires. In unincorporated Drexel, the kind of services Morgantonians took for granted did not exist. By 1915, the citizens of Drexel (the community) felt the omission and called for a graded school to teach their children. They initiated action, first calling for "an election to vote for a special tax" to fund the effort. Even with child labor an unfortunate growing aspect of the factory workforce, leaders at Drexel (the company) saw a school in its midst as a step toward respectability. On the day of the election, Drexel Furniture "suspended work" at noon so that its employees could go out and vote for the measure. In fact, two of the furniture company's prominent leaders campaigned for the tax to build Drexel's first permanent school. "Mr. F.O. Huffman (oldest son of founder Sam Huffman), secretary and treasurer, and Mr. D.J. Watkins, superintendent, remained on the election ground the rest of the day and with earnest determination worked for the success of the school." A citizen who reported the event using the name "patron" called it "one of the best days in the history of Drexel."[209]

A decade passed before those living around the factory decided to incorporate as a city. Until then some defined the community as Baker or Baker's Crossing as it had once been called. Of the 50 families documented in the 1910 census, over 80% of those living there were employed by the furniture company or the railroad. In 1913, the North Carolina General Assembly officially chartered Drexel the town that included Drexel the factory.[210]

As Drexel charted a path for continued growth of both company and community, the ownership group shifted. D.B. Mull, one of the original organizers in 1903, sold his share of the company to several fellow investors, S.R. Collett, A.M. Kistler, and F.O. Huffman, son of Sam Huffman. The men bought Mull out so that he could invest with a contingent from Connelly Springs (down the rail line east of Drexel toward Hickory) to start a hosiery mill there. In Mull's ten-year tenure with Drexel, he had seen both feast and famine. With each setback, Drexel came back stronger, weathering challenges,

The only company that could claim it spawned its own town, the factory complex rebounded from several fires to become the largest at one time in western North Carolina. This image from across the railroad tracks is the factory in 1908 after the second fire. (Image submitted by R. Douglas Walker, Jr. to Picture Burke, a digital photograph preservation project of the Burke County Public Library. Courtesy of Picture Burke)

both during Mull's period of investment and after to become a major operation in the Catawba Valley, as the region would come to be known.[211]

Issues beyond the control of investors sometimes embroiled the company in strife. The biggest scandal connected to both the town and company of Drexel involved a resident and employee, whose untimely death made headlines. Will H. Caps left work on a Tuesday afternoon and walked to his room at the local boarding house. There he picked up a shotgun and a cane, went into the garden, apparently intending to take his own life. Using the cane to trigger the gun, he sent "a load of shot into his left side." Fellow guests of the boarding house heard the blast and the groans of Caps. They rushed to his assistance, carried him back into the boarding house and called for the doctor. Through the night, Caps lingered, saying he wanted to die. Sadly, at 9:00 am the next morning, he did. At only age 22 and unmarried, no one understood the rationale for suicide until it was revealed that he had carried on "a love affair with his aunt, a sister of his mother." Even though the company had no specific involvement with its worker and his bloody decision, Will Caps was always tagged as "an employee of the Drexel Furniture Co." just as surely as other hires of the company in announcements of marriage, births, and other less, gruesome deaths. In the tight-knit community of workers the shocking loss resonated through the ranks.[212]

After many losses in both plant and personnel, up and downs marked Drexel's in the years before World War I. The company bought 4,970 acres of land in Rutherford County with the promise of over 20 million feet of extractable lumber. Paying $46,000 for the real estate from a Greensboro lumber company, the purchase solidified Drexel as a major player in the furniture game for some time to come. After the first two disastrous fires robbed the company of its inventory and work space, another blaze broke out at Drexel. The furniture factory was again reported to be engulfed in flames, though actually it was not the entire facility. Instead, the damage befell a nearby roller mill, along with Sam Huffman's separate woodworking operation, which sustained over $25,000 in damages. The furniture operation "was saved because of the fact that the wind was blowing in the opposite direction from the wood-working plant where the fire originated," a lucky break.[213]

The example set by Drexel reverberated throughout the region. Despite setbacks, everyone saw the success and sought to get in on the action. In 1921, a pharmacist in town recognized potential in the market and decided to put his time and energy into creating yet another furniture factory. William A. Leslie, in his retirement, pulled together a few investors to take over the assets of the old Morganton Manufacturing and Trading Company and create the new Morganton Manufacturing Company. It would be W.A. Leslie's last business venture. A year into the new enterprise, the retired pharmacist turned entrepreneur died, leaving the company in disarray. More a building supply concern than furniture producer, the company made "doors, sashes, mantles, flooring, ceiling, moulding and other building materials." In actuality, the firm was more important for its future potential than its past. Within three years, the Table Rock Furniture Company took over the space and ran operations from there for the next quarter century. In 1951, Drexel "purchased all of the outstanding stock of Table Rock and it became an operating part of that company."[214]

The mighty behemoth of Drexel prospered, thanks to the dedication of everyone who was a part of the team, both management and workers. R.O. Huffman, a son of Sam Huffman the originator, remembered his father "would get up every day at 5 a.m., feed and curry his horse and leave for Drexel, 6 1/2 miles away, in an open buggy at 6 a.m. - many times over roads that were mud up to the buggy axles. He got to the plant at 7." There, the elder Huffman watched over a plant of similarly dedicated employees. Bruce Hildebrand started there as a ten-year-old boy. He worked for three cents per hour as a "moulder helper" in 1907. By the age of 12 he got a raise. Now a "moulder operator," he earned four cents an hour. As Hildebrand recalled, the increase was "not much, but good for a boy my age." By 1920, Bruce had grown up in a workforce that totaled "100 high class operatives," as the company defined their employees, cranking out about 4,000 bedroom suites each year.[215]

Bruce Hildebrand personified a core constituency for not only Drexel but also of the furniture industry in the early twentieth century as an employee who devoted his entire work life to the business. Hildebrand spent 55 years as a furniture worker. When he finally retired in 1962, he joined a quartet of colleagues who had collectively supplied over 200 years of service to the manufacturer. Starting together as children, Hildebran and his fellow retirees grew up watching the first generation of men at their machines' create a world that they would follow. Learning from and fitting in to this new factory culture, Hildebrand found purpose in his contribution and never left. In that respect, the shop floor offered its own training program, as child labor did in many companies, developing loyal, trained, and generally contented workers. Boys

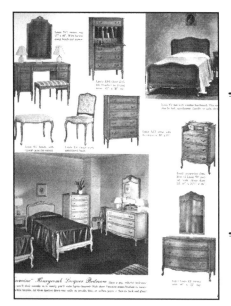

Before there was even a town of the same name, Drexel Furniture established itself along the railroad line just east of Morganton. Two fires tested the resolve of investors to stay in the furniture business, but the company endured, eventually becoming an innovator in the industry. (Courtesy of Hickory Landmarks Society)

marked their path to manhood moving up in the hierarchy of jobs, taking on more responsibility as they matured. About the time men like Hildebrand could be counted as an adult, the average wage totaled thirteen cents per hour, with foremen making twice that amount. The training ground provided by factory work for youngsters would one day also serve to train the sons and daughters of lifetime employees like Bruce Hildebrand.[216]

The use of child labor was not singular to Drexel. Every furniture company, as well as every industrial outlet including cotton mills (that were the first), took on youthful employees, sometimes as young as eight. However, the practice began to lose favor in a nation hopeful that education would provide the next generation with the kind of higher order thinking that could benefit the entire society. When the leadership campaigned for a school in Drexel, they must have known they were sacrificing some portion of their future workforce.

It is ironic that child labor, as a concern, came to national attention thanks to Drexel Furniture. The U.S. Congress had already tried to stem the use of children as workers in factories with a law that forbid any product made where child labor was used to be shipped across state lines. The Supreme Court struck down the law as unconstitutional in 1918. So Congress tried again. The following year they passed the Child Labor Tax Law, designed to impose a ten percent penalty on all profits that came from the use of labor by citizens under 14. The forerunner of the IRS, the Bureau of Internal Revenue, taxed Drexel $6,312.79 for its continued use of underage employees. The company paid the tax under protest and requested a refund. Denied, Drexel sued for it. Courts up the line sided with Drexel, but the government continued to appeal all the way to the Supreme Court.

An 8-1 decision settled the matter. Chief Justice William Howard Taft (the former 27th president of the United States) wrote the opinion which noted previous congressional attempts to eliminate child labor were an over-reach. His last sentence stated, "here the so-called tax is a penalty to coerce people of a state to act as Congress wishes them to act in respect of a matter completely the business of the state government under the federal Constitution." Taft believed that the Tenth Amendment reverted those kinds of decisions back to individual states. The proper place to debate the minimum age of Drexel's employees' was the North Carolina legislature. It took ten years of wrangling, but ultimately the General Assembly enacted a law forbidding anyone under 16 from earning a full-time wage. The law allowed a few exceptions. In extreme cases for boys (not girls) who were the sole breadwinner of the family, they could work full-time at age 14. But for the most part, boys from age 12 (girls from 14) could only work when school was not in session. Slowly, the practice began to die out even through hard times like the Great Depression made family revenue critical. However, given that jobs were scarce, the disuse of child labor opened more slots for adults, which was actually a benefit to some families.[217]

The Supreme Court decision affirmed Drexel's right to run its factory as it saw best, even if, on occasion, those choices were counterproductive. About the time North Carolina banned child labor, the president of the company, F.O. Huffman, was driving to a Drexel plant in Marion. He saw a company truck parked at a gas station. Stopping to scrutinize the problem, he found the driver "enjoying a bottle of beer." So angered by the nonchalance, Huffman fired Pat Poteat on the spot. Poteat was then "paid off in cash" for wages due him. Huffman took off toward Marion but soon realized his mistake. Who would drive the furniture on to its destination? Huffman turned around, rehired Poteat to drive the cargo to Marion and "fired him again," once the task had been completed. But nobody at the Marion plant could "work the truck's gear shift." Huffman rehired Poteat yet again. Back in Morganton, the president severed the employee for a third time. The story became a company joke for years because Pat Poteat was eventually rehired by Drexel. He even went on to serve a term as mayor for the town of Drexel. Talk circulated that the experience convinced Poteat to become a teetotaler from that point on. Meanwhile, Poteat and Huffman enjoyed the story for years with each retelling, but the incident demonstrated the complicated nature of the employer-employee relationship, one that required much more consideration than it was often given.[218]

Internally, the aftermath of the Supreme Court case was a tumultuous period for Drexel Furniture, despite its victory. Starting in 1930, the company went through four presidents in a five year period. First, A.M. Kistler died, leaving S.R. Collett to take over. Collett "served less than a year" before he too passed. The company then went to the second generation of the investment group when the board selected Frank O. Huffman, Sam Huffman's oldest son to take the helm. Frank Huffman lived less than three years after his ascendancy. The job next went to Robert Obediah Huffman, Samuel's second son and Frank's younger brother. Once R.O. accepted the position, a sense of stability returned as he guided the company for the next thirty years.[219]

Unlike his predecessors though, R.O. Huffman took chances. He changed the character of Drexel as soon as he took over. While the company had made fabulous profits selling "a cheaper line of furniture," Huffman wanted a different image for Drexel. It was the height of the Great Depression when Huffman insisted that Drexel walked away from "the policy of selling the basic needs of people to that of creating a desire for new types of furniture." In other words, Huffman was not going to cater to the masses (which bought their furniture in the large chain stores); he was going to lead. He reorganized his sales staff, modernized the factory, and positioned Drexel as an innovator. Huffman made sure the name of Drexel became synonymous with upscale furniture with newer, sleeker lines appearing in home furnishing magazines by 1937. The re-crafting of Drexel's product, as well as image carried the company through the rest of the century.[220]

The firm that spawned a town and did more than its share to instigate an industry for western North Carolina kept looking for ways to innovate and grow under R.O. Huffman. During World War II, the company created a new branch (Trans Air) to make the wooden parts necessary for Fairchild Aircraft's new trainer, the AT-21. The effort supported an important wartime need to train pilots, an absolute necessity for winning the war. The use of small aircraft like the AT-21 allowed trainees to rack up flight hours on their way to piloting more sophisticated planes in theaters of war over Europe and the Pacific. Drexel also produced "15 million tent stakes, millions of square feet of Marine plywood for boats and accessories," as well as 4,000 bedroom suites for families at the atomic development site at Oak Ridge, Tennessee, along with over 50,000 government desks, including a custom made one for General Douglas MacArthur, "handcrafted and funded by employees." Workers had also inlaid the general's name on the desktop, an exquisite detail, personalizing the desk for the commander.[221]

Despite repeated setbacks, fortune smiled on Drexel Furniture. Success eclipsed anything its founding investors might have dreamed of when they assembled to incorporate the company in 1903. Once again, the proximity of wood and an able workforce helped the region dent the reputation of places like Grand Rapids, Michigan as the mecca of furniture production.

Increasingly, local entrepreneurs looking to jump into the business took their cue from Sam Huffman in Drexel, George Hall in Hickory, and Major Harper in Lenoir, as models to study and emulate. None of the new breed of local entrepreneurs had been old-style crafters of household chairs and chests and they knew little about the handmade tradition. They were New South capitalists looking for a business from which they could profit, all the while providing jobs and products for their neighbors, as well as pride for their communities. Those intrepid enough to follow the lead of Huffman, Hall and Harper (and there were many) had a trail blazed for them.

As the century turned from the 19th to the 20th, most families in western North Carolina lived a rural existence. From these ranks, mostly farmers were recruited to learn the life of factory work, which gave them regular hours governed by the whistle and weekly paychecks. (Author's Collection)

Chapter 10
A Buxom Mountain Queen

The dawn of the twentieth century brought with it a regional collective consciousness. Independently, economic interests in the towns of North Carolina's foothills began to align behind the idea of creating their own culture, united around the effort to craft furniture for a national market. Each did it in different ways. Statesville reinvested its capital to spawn a variety of makers. Old Fort was first to the bar but sold out to Morganton where tragedy temporarily overwhelmed rebuilding efforts. Drexel took the opposite approach, building the factory first, then welcoming a city to surround and support it. Lenoir fumbled with a community-backed factory that resisted efforts to find a managerial structure that worked. Hickory hummed with twin factories on the eastern end of town. Undoubtedly, each subsequent enterprise learned from the mistakes and successes of those that went before.

No matter how they did it, the region recognized a sound idea and put it into practice, each in its own way as circumstances allowed. Together, they formed a nucleus of production, strangely stronger even with competition because of the unifying identity they were forging together. The years of groping in the darkness for some kind of economic distinction had paid off. These communities found their niche. Recognizing it, they would challenge all other regions of the country for dominance, both inside the Tarheel state and beyond. Western North Carolina was emerging as a furniture-making powerhouse, even if the output required producing items other than the

Workers young and old pose for a photograph while on a break from furniture making in Lenoir. These employees worked for Hibriten Furniture and exemplify what making a living in the factory looked like in the early 20th century. (Courtesy Caldwell Heritage Museum)

traditional bedroom suite.

"A charter is issued for the Kent Furniture and Coffin Co., of Lenoir. Capital, $50,000 authorized; $20,000 subscribed; by A.A. Kent, A.V. Miller and others," read the news in April of 1905. Six months later, the business was in operation. With approximately 40 hands, the shop was described as "one of the busiest places in our town" orders loaded up on boxcars for shipment to Chicago. In fact, the Windy City came to Lenoir. "Mr. Andrew McAnse, of Chicago has been in Lenoir for a few days looking over the furniture industries of the town. Mr. McAnse is of the firm of McAnse, Duger & Co., who handles the output of the Kent Furniture Co. and the Lenoir Table Works. He would like to contract for the output of at least two more factories at this place if he can." The activity of the region began to attract outside attention as men like McAnse recognized the profitability of presenting Lenoir's output nationwide.[222]

Almost immediately, Kent Furniture needed more space. They

"found it necessary to build an addition to the already large storage room at the factory." But the goods were not staying warehoused long. Orders poured in. San Francisco sought nine boxcar loads, while St. Louis ordered eight. Furniture from Kent was also going to New York City, thanks to reps like Andrew McAnse.[223]

In the early days of the industry, the term 'furniture' denoted a wide range of items made for consumers but not all of them for the home. When Dr. A.A. Kent built his 1905 company, explicitly in the name was a unique wood product, later handled by undertakers, coffins. Until the professionalization of the funeral industry, coffins were available in furniture stores. One might pick one out, much like selecting a chest of drawers, although for a much different purpose. As the six-sided box that defined a "coffin" gave way to caskets, furniture manufacturers eventually discontinued their production, but in the early days, anything that could be made of wood and sold to the public, was.[224]

With growth came the usual ups and downs for furniture companies of the era. Kent Furniture lured James Booth away from his position as foreman at Imperial Furniture in Statesville to a job as superintendent. Regrettably, industrial accidents also became part of the landscape for furniture factories. One notice read, "A young man named Smith who works at the Kent Furniture and Coffin factory had his hand badly cut by a cove saw yesterday." If the accident proved fatal, Kent had an appliance for Smith's final rest.[225]

Even with the mishaps, it didn't take long for new enterprises to join the growing number of firms. One came in the form of another furniture company by the same entrepreneur, this one a partnership called the Kent-Coffey Manufacturing Company. A.A. Kent was a prominent doctor in Lenoir who harbored intentions of getting into the business world. He had invested in Lenoir's 1889 factory before becoming the first to publicly pull his support from the venture by selling his stock. Now with his own independent concern going so successfully, he decided to go into partnership with Finley H. Coffey.

Incorporating the company to the tune of $32,500, with the doctor claiming 50 shares while Coffey bought 100. The other 170 shares went to investors in the community.[226]

The times were right for getting into business in the New South. Two major changes aided profitability. It took the remainder of the 19th century for the region to rebound after the Civil War, but by 1900, the agricultural market rebounded, adding a new vitality to communities all over the former Confederacy. Also, a new source of power offered a cheaper, more streamlined alternative to steam in running the machinery. Local power companies (often using dynamos to generate electricity) were consolidating under James B. Duke's Southern Power Company to offer electricity for industrial outlets, as well as homes. Not long after Southern Power came to the Catawba Valley, companies like Hickory Furniture eagerly switched from steam power to keep plants operating on schedule.[227]

With newly created companies also came casualties. Looking for space to locate their factory, the Kent-Coffey Furniture Company found it at the old Gwyn Veneer plant. Within a year of incorporation, the company started by R.L. Gwyn closed. He had begun with subscribed capital of $20,000 as the Gwyn Veneer and Panel Company, making strips applicable to finished pieces that needed dressing up into fancier finished products. Gwyn recruited John W. Coffey (no direct relationship to Finley of the Kent-Coffey partnership), originally from Lenoir but living in Raleigh, to return to "take charge." Nearing its first anniversary of operation, the plant sold out to the Kent interests.[228]

The pairing of Finley H. Coffey and Dr. Alfred A. Kent might have seemed unlikely for entry into the furniture business. While Coffey took off to Kansas for 15 years to farm after growing up in the mountainous Caldwell County community of Collettsville, Kent spent most of his adult life as part of Lenoir society. As a young man, Kent got through UNC-Chapel Hill in just two years before studying medicine in Philadelphia. His first practice was

The Kent-Coffey factory as the company would have customers see it. Every early firm had drawn images like this that proudly presented their sprawling complex even though in reality many were less pristine than the image portrayed. (Courtesy Caldwell Heritage Museum)

for the Cranberry Iron Works in nearby Avery County before putting out his shingle in his native Lenoir. Neither had credentials that would recommend them as manufacturing executives. Under the surface though the two men held great similarities. Both were successful at their diverse interests. Coffey's lineage could be traced back to Daniel Boone, and the fathers of both men served in the Confederate Army during the Civil War. Finley Coffey's father Drury was a member of the 58th North Carolina, the regiment commanded by Major G.W.F. Harper. So it is likely that Kent and Coffey knew each other well and upon the latter's return to Lenoir, decided to unite in business. Since Kent already had one successful operation, another mainly managed by Coffey looked to be a safe bet.[229]

No sooner had the good doctor and his partner cranked up their furniture factory than three family members came out of the mountains north of Lenoir with the same idea to start turning wood into wardrobes. William C. and his brother, F.P., along with F.P.'s son, Joe C. Moore "bought 12 or 15 acres of land just north of Lower Creek trestle on the C&NW Ry., about one mile from the centre of town and will build a furniture factory on the site at once." The arrival of the Moore family signified that making furniture had become a popular pursuit. Quickly, a number of other investors joined the party. H. Richard, J.P. Coffey, H.T. Newland, and several others pooled their resources with the Moore brothers to amass the capital requirement of $25,000. Building began immediately. By May of 1906 the company was in production, employing "about 100 hands, and its plant is equipped with the latest improved machinery." In terms of personnel, the Moore operation became the biggest in Lenoir. [230]

That equipment churned out "case work and tables" and, on one particularly horrific occasion, death. "This morning about 11 o'clock while Fred Pearson was running a moulder in the shops of the Moore Furniture Company he was caught in the belt and hurled to death in an instant. His right side was torn open, his jaw broken and his head badly crushed." What made the accident more tragic was the fact that Fred Pearson was 11 years old. The employment of children in factories was still common and, according to some, necessary. Just as children had been used to assist the running of family farms, so too were they deemed important to the continued financial interest of each family. Like the textile industry, workers came to the factories at a tender age. But unlike the cotton mills, the recruits were exclusively boys. Just as with Drexel and every other industrial employer, it took time to weigh how absolutely necessary child labor was to the process. [231]

Slowdowns in 1907 that kept workers idle in some places were not evident in Lenoir. Moore Furniture announced orders "that will keep them running until February 15th or longer. No signs of panic in transactions of that kind," assured the editor of the *Lenoir Topic* about the nation's financial crisis. But Joe, the next generation of the Moore's in furniture, decided to leave the company in favor of another furniture start up, Lenoir Chair. By the summer of 1908, Joe Moore's new enterprise was "one of the busiest places in this community." Along with T.J. Stone, his new partner, Lenoir Chair, was "turning out 350 to 400 chairs per day." With "46 hands employed," the company shipped out a variety of "medium and high-grade chairs and box seat dining chairs," most ready for use, but not all. "Some of these are finished complete and some are shipped 'white,' meaning before being varnished." The finished chairs, in "a variety of styles," came "in a number of popular shades, including weathered, Mission and Flemish oak."[232]

Within a year, the Lenoir Chair plant doubled its capacity, making up to 100 dozen chairs per day. Additionally, the company began manufacturing tables "and other lines of household furniture" to go along with its chairs. "The authorized capital is $50,000 with $15,000 paid in," read the notice for Lenoir's fastest-growing factory. To more effectively distribute the capital at hand and grow the business, the Moores and Stone recruited W.A. Shell away from the Bank of Lenoir, where he had been a bookkeeper for the last 15 years, to take on the role of secretary and treasurer for the company. Filling orders became a real challenge for the company, including one instance where "a (box) car load order having been recently cancelled because they could not fill it quick enough for their customer," was immediately sold elsewhere. In addition to W.A. Shell as their top money counter, the Moore Brothers and T.J. Stone became experts at finding talent and bringing it to their operation.[233]

Soon, the standout furniture superstar in Statesville also found it advantageous to bring his services to Lenoir Chair. E.M. Purdy arrived just in time to attend the Chicago furniture exhibition, ostensibly hawking the outfit's output but more likely he was surveilling the competition for talent and design ideas. As a supremely accomplished operator in his own right, Purdy paired with T.J. Stone to create quite a powerhouse in furniture production.

There has never been anyone in the business like Tilden Joseph Stone. Known for his exquisite carving that defied categorization, T.J. was born a Quaker in Thomasville, NC, where he was orphaned as a child. He fled to New York City, convincing a master woodcarver to take him in and train him as an apprentice. It was there he wrapped an overly fertile imagination around the skills he learned. He decided to return to North Carolina, ending up in Lenoir, to start a high-end manufacturing outfit with his brother Bert. For whatever reason, maybe the ornate styles or the high price of finished pieces, the operation did not prosper. From time to time T.J. Stone worked as a master designer for other companies, including Bernhardt, Broyhill and Fairfield Chair, but his fanciful, original work did not fit the conventional world of mass-produced furniture. Creations that have survived include pieces with adornments that range from animals to the steering wheels of ships as part of his work.[234]

T.J. Stone's handiwork fully reflected his experiences, even if the public failed to appreciate or could not afford his creativity. In the 1920s, during Prohibition, Stone crafted pieces that held secret compartments. Bottles of alcohol, sometimes even full bars, were all contained within his intricately crafted furniture that disguised the illicit contraband from discovery by casual observers and more importantly, law enforcement. In all likelihood, T.J. Stone qualified as a genius, discontent to merely copy the popular designs of his era. Artist Waitsel Smith chronicled the adventures of T.J. Stone, along with some of his most detailed and inventive furniture. After much evaluation, Waitsel decided that the work of the master carver completely defied any particular type of classification, given his use of so many different techniques. Smith's analysis of Stone's pieces noted that T.J. Stone was "never satisfied with copying any historical style, as most furniture makers did, and never venturing into modern styles, T.J. would use a historical style as a foundation, and then embellish it with his carving. Almost always, the carving would take a fanciful turn."[235]

Along with the fanciful, creations built by T.J. Stone contained practical elements. At one point, he received a "United States Patent Office" copyright for a set of bed rails he invented that effectively locked in the mattress to minimize "lost motion." It also prevented "spaces where vermin may collect." The patent was awarded just three years before his death in 1952.[236]

T.J. Stone's life was as wild as his art. Every year, he would deploy with the Merchant Marines for a four-month "stint" to Asia. There he observed the carvings of the region, including many of the motifs that showed up in his work. Always in stylish clothing and reportedly a ladies' man, Stone eventually married Rose Etta Triplett from Lenoir, giving her the married name of Rose Etta Stone; luckily, she went by Etta. One story demonstrated his temperamental nature as an artist of wood. The wife of James B. Duke sought a carved piece of furniture from Stone. When he delivered it, she made some disparaging remark about his work which prompted him to refuse sale to her.[237]

It wasn't just furniture that captured T.J. Stone's designing eye. After moving to Lincolnton at one point, he built a house that resembled a houseboat. Supposedly, he always wanted to live at sea, so he constructed the next best thing. Unfortunately, Etta refused to join him there in his houseboat on land. While in Lincolnton, he also crafted a playhouse for his niece that took on the look of a giant shoe to go with the 'Mother Hubbard' nursery rhyme. The landmark 'shoe' stood for many years on the western outskirts of Lincolnton as an example of his eccentric style.[238]

The early days of mechanized production included a broad spectrum of individuals who saw making furniture in different ways. Men like T.J. Stone were artists who found wood as an outlet for their creativity, honing inventive items for use in the home. His work has gone down in history as the most idiosyncratic of any furniture maker in western North Carolina ever. Since most of his creations could not be mass-produced economically, his artistry failed to be easily replicated for the public. But a dreamer like T.J. became another example of the community of crafters who would contribute to the budding industry. There would be others.

If 'restless' described the artistry of T.J. Stone, the word also adequately reflects the entrepreneurship of Joe Moore. At Lenoir Chair, Moore, the son of F.P. Moore and nephew of W.C. Moore, took charge of the rough end, where he brought wood into the shop for refining, but the job was apparently not enough to keep him interested. Less than two years after Lenoir Chair went into operation, Joe Moore sold all his shares in the previous company so he and partner T.J. (also called Joe by his friends) Stone could set up the Moore-Stone Chair Company. The site he located for his new operation was just across the tracks from the original company that Joe Moore and his elders started four years earlier. He planned to make the same thing at his new company that he had made in all his previous endeavors, chairs. He also remained ambitious, expanding his capacity to produce up to 100 dozen per day. It seems Joe Moore proved himself to be adept at raising a furniture factory from the ground up but regularly regarded the ongoing operation a chore, a daily drudgery that failed to capture his imagination.[239]

The loss of Joe Moore at Lenoir Chair did not hurt the company. One estimate pictured the chairs made by the company "placed side by side in a single row, to reach more than fifty miles. Fifty miles of chairs." The output of approximately 200 per day soared to over 180,000 per year. To reach such a capacity, the company expanded its facilities by fifty percent. The retail price range for a chair at the factory stood between $1.50 and $4.50, and "orders poured in in a way that made the general manager, Mr. W.A. Shell (promoted from Secretary/Treasurer) smile broadly when he acknowledged the prosperity of the company." One of the reasons Shell could grin was the addition of almost 14,000 square feet of floor space for the next 50 miles of chairs.[240]

Unfortunately, many of those chairs would end up as charred ruins. On a Saturday night in November of 1910, the night watchman was off duty. In his place was a new man, who checked the factory around 11:00 pm. Noticing nothing of suspicion, he went to get a drink of water. When he returned, flames had engulfed the wood frame building. He raised the alarm, but by the time

An example of a chair Made by the Moore Stone Company in 1910. Factories all over western North Carolina turned out multitudes of these chairs that sold well across the United States. Though they were fanciful than some of T.J. Stone's other creations, they were serviceable. (Image from Charlotte Observer)

firefighters arrived, it was too late. Superintendent of the factory, Bert Stone (T.J. Stone's brother) was at the depot cafe when he "recognized the alarm whistle and ran out on his way to the factory. As he started down the steps, he fell and broke his leg," rendering his effort of relief to the company moot. The estimated loss for Lenoir Chair came to between $70,000 and $80,000 with about only one-third of that amount covered by insurance. The single saving grace of the catastrophe was the containment of damage. Flames did not spread to the Moore Furniture plant across the C&N tracks. The *Raleigh Times* called the loss of the chair factory "a heavy blow to Lenoir and vicinity. Eighty-nine men have been thrown out of employment."[241]

Like Drexel before it and many other factories destroyed by fire, Lenoir Chair vowed a rebirth. Within a month, President W.A. Shell announced that new machinery was on the way. He planned to have the operation back on its feet, producing chairs within three months. He also hoped to have more men than ever in his employ, figuring that as many as 110 would be on the payroll by February of 1911.[242]

During the fateful month after the fire, the cause of the blaze came to light. It was arson. "Two boys were tried here yesterday afternoon before

Squire J.A. Bush, charged with burning the Lenoir Chair Company's plant, which was destroyed by fire." Luther Bowman and Richard Shumake(r), two white juveniles, were found guilty of the crime, as well as robbing a hardware store the same night. A watchman at the Kent-Coffey plant testified that the boys "stayed about an hour" at his location then left. Forty-five minutes later, he saw the flames. Others told how they noticed three boys running from the flames as everyone else ran toward them. "It was given on the authority of at least one witness that one of the boys said he was going to leave this town and with an oath said he intended to leave some ashes behind when he left." At the time of the arrest, guns stolen from the hardware store were in the perpetrators' possession. In court, the two pled guilty and were sentenced to two years in state prison. The identity of the third assailant was never discovered.[243]

Upon rebuilding, Lenoir Chair chose to incorporate. The size of the its new incarnation totaled $20,000, with another $15,000 promised. The listing of investors was also interesting. In addition to W.A. Shell, the rebuilt Lenoir Chair included some familiar furniture names. George F. Harper, son of the Major who already had Harper Furniture in operation, was a stockholder. So was his brother-in-law, John Mathias Bernhardt. By that point, both were known for their extensive furniture experience as a part of Lenoir's first furniture outing, which had occurred over twenty years earlier. S.S. Jennings, Bert Stone (the superintendent who broke his leg at the fire), cotton mill investor J.L. Nelson, J.H. Beall, and C.L. Robbins constituted the rest of the ownership team. For Bert Stone, it was an especially auspicious time to celebrate. He reveled in two beginnings: the rebirth his company and his coming nuptials. Just after Christmas he married "the efficient stenographer of the Lenoir Chair Company," Miss Ethel Kerley.[244]

Woodworking in Lenoir had become a trendy endeavor. Under the banner of "New Enterprises," the *Weekly News* boasted, "Lenoir can show more new manufacturing enterprises projected within the last six or twelve months than any town of its size in the country." Touting Kent Furniture and Coffin Company, Gwyn Vaneers (Veneers) and Panel Works, Lenoir Vaneering (Veneering), Builders's Supply Co., Coffey Wagon Manufacturing Co., Moore Furniture Manufacturing Co., and even the Conley Bobbin and Handle Works, were all examples of the growth Lenoir had seen in the first decade of the twentieth century. Those enterprises, coupled with the already established Harper Furniture and the ongoing business of J.M. Bernhardt made Lenoir ideal for even further expansion. Newspaper editor J.C. Martin hit the nail on the head when he asserted, "the raw materials are right here among us and the money paid for them is kept at home instead of being sent away as in the case of cotton mills." His observation of the homegrown furniture industry explained the reason such an effort had been undertaken by a growing number of New South men willing to put their capital at risk. He added, "the manufacturing industry is just in its infancy however in our town and if the town as a municipality will keep pace with the other features, within five years Lenoir will have a population of five thousand." It would take another twenty-five years before the town actually reached that milestone, but the increase was impressive, nonetheless. By the time of the 1910 census, the emerging furniture city saw a rise of over 150% in population.[245]

Given the activity in Lenoir, it took no time at all for the town to gain attention statewide. The *Raleigh News and Observer* sent a journalist to investigate all the action. In his printed reply, Raleigh's reporter described the town as a "beautiful and buxom 'Mountain Queen'." Harper Furniture, the vestige of Lenoir's first furniture manufacturing attempt now loomed as a grandfather to all the new companies popping up. The Raleigh paper's inventory of the number of woodworking-related plants stood at 14, which included lumber yards, box makers, and veneer operations.[246]

The creators of Lenoir's original factory had finally proven their point. Even if the first company did not survive as originally planned, a climate for making furniture profitably had indeed shown its viability. With a variety of personalities trying their hand at producing furnishings for the home, the lure beckoned even more. They refused to let the hazard of fire (a constant threat), rain (a future threat) and fluctuations of business deter them from turning a fledgling industry into a powerhouse that would define the region in the future, and make them money, now.

Just down the road, Hickory was already blessed with two stable companies, each making items for different rooms in the home. Something was missing, however, town leaders sensed they were coming in third in the region's furniture making race, behind a flurry of firms in Lenoir and Burke County's dominating enterprise of Drexel. They vowed to catch up. Business leaders got together and amassed their capital, offering it to anyone who would come to Hickory and establish a successful chair factory. Word soon spread beyond the hills of western North Carolina. George Bailey heard about the proposition and inquired. His Surry Chair Company could use a boost. Located to the north in Elkin, not far from the Virginia border, the promise of up to $200,000 in capital was too much to keep him anchored. He willingly relocated.[247]

The *Hickory Democrat* characterized George Bailey as "a man of push and enterprise, and was quick to jump at the opportunity to move the plant to Hickory." The attraction was mutual. According to the *Democrat*, "Hickory gobbled up the fine Elkin enterprise like a wild turkey (would) a fat, red chestnut." Business was not bad in Elkin. Bailey brought to Hickory with him a number of outstanding orders for the "old Surry Chair Co.," to demonstrate demand for his work and assure his new neighbors that they had made a sound choice. Competition for the deal had been extreme, with Hickory investors dangling their offer for "some time" before Bailey came through with a viable plan for a favorable partnership. The business solidified the area's interest as then new firm was rightfully named Hickory Chair Manufacturing

Company.[248]

It was almost inevitable where the new company would be located. Given the cozy proximity of Hickory's existing furniture factories, the new chair maker would easily fit right next to them. The railroad's sidetrack could now serve a third operation, and the "six grades of chair" slated to be manufactured by Hickory Chair complemented the output of both Martin and Hickory Furniture. Reports differed on the actual capitalization of the Hickory Chair Manufacturing Company, the amount somewhere between $100,000 and $150,000. Bailey's reborn factory kept all options open. In addition to chairs, Hickory's newest factory retained authorization to also manufacture "wagons, buggies, etc." suggesting it might seek to compete with Piedmont Wagon. However, Hickory Chair stuck to its namesake product after George Bailey arrived. Within a year of startup, advertisements seeking oak for their machines signaled a focus on furniture.[249]

In the summer of 1912, when Hickory Chair was just getting on its feet, producing its first products, Hickory booster and sometimes business reporter, Dr. R. Wood Brown, toured the Martin plant. He offered to readers of the *Times-Mercury* his thoughts on what was going on in furniture manufacturing. He credited the machines in operation at the factory as being "able to do everything but think and talk." He marveled that "a beautiful piece of furniture handsomely oak finished" had gone "from the lumber pile to the shipping room" in only five hours. As a result, the visit left Dr. Brown to conclude of his time, "we live in a rapid age."[250]

Brown's article spelled out for readers how the art of manufacturing worked. "Rapidity of manufacture lessens the cost," he instructed, "therefore useful articles which can be manufactured the most rapidly, cost the least to put on the market and consequently give more profit to the manufacturer." The sentiment defined the business plan of not only Martin but every furniture enterprise in the region. To drum up local business, he asked his readers specifically, "do you want a washstand or a bed?" He took civic pride in saying that Martin Furniture in his hometown of Hickory "makes 125 of each every working day." Dr. Brown wanted everyone of his fellow citizens to know how industrialization worked and what it meant to them, even if they had no direct connection to the job of furniture making.[251]

The quickened pace Hickory experienced with its new industrial sector unsettled some. Dr. Brown sought to remind those who wanted to go back to the old days that such a return came with a heavy price. The viability of manufacturing was twofold. As population in the United States grew, so did need. Workshop crafted furniture by hand would not meet that need. Industrially produced product could keep up with the masses. "If everything we used were hand made," he argued, "we would be where our forefathers were in comfort and convenience." He went on to explain that we enjoy through "the inventive genius of the American people, conveniences and comforts which in some foreign countries, would be luxuries almost Utopian." Though life now included the relentless buzzing of saws, folks in Hickory were participating in a grand national pageant of improvement, complete with machinery doing the work for them, allowing them more time to do the only things the machines could not do, think and talk. As they did both, conversations on furniture manufacturing created unique value and stature for those building it, boosting Hickory (along with the rest of the area) as smart and enterprising partners in progress.[252]

Competition began to heat up, between towns, between companies. Collectively, the factories turning out crafted wood products in the western part of North Carolina were gaining notice and sales. With Drexel leading the way, the assemblage of factories demonstrated the furniture industry was viable and profitable enough to sustain itself into the future. Burke, Caldwell, Catawba, Iredell, and McDowell Counties showed viability, able to compete with High Point in the central part of North Carolina as a center for the burgeoning furniture industry. There would be challenges to the claim, but at last, the foothills economy had found its purpose.

An old photograph of the workforce at Hickory Furniture in the 1913. This image projects the prosperity of the era with everyone dressed for the picture and not for work. Only two women were in the shot. (Courtesy of Hickory Landmarks Society)

Young people were part of the industrial workforce since its inception. Thought to be more valuable to parents for their wages than their productivity on the farm many were sent to the factories. These were cotton mill workers which competed with furniture for hands. (Courtesy of Hickory Landmarks Society)

Chapter 11
Heirs to the Major

Even though J.M. Bernhardt bowed out of what became Harper Furniture in the 1890s, he remained close to the burgeoning industry through the years, seemingly looking for an opportunity to get back in. In 1896, he returned to the fray. By 1899, his box factory and planing mill enlarged to the point of needing "another boiler." His factory handled some "35,000 feet of lumber a week and (was) unable to keep up with their orders," thus the addition. Within a few years he added a forty-foot smoke stack to the operation. During that time, he traveled extensively as a major buyer of timber, most notably connecting himself with lumber operations like Giant Lumber of Wilkesboro. In this endeavor, capitalized at a whopping (for the time) $125,000, Bernhardt partnered with E.P. Wharton of Greensboro, W.J. Palmer, and Bernhardt's brother-in-law G.F. Harper. J.M. Bernhardt took on the role of president of the company. The following year, Bernhardt joined forces with the Moore brothers, Joe, T.P. and W.C., to start the Globe Lumber Company, with stock similar to his Wilkesboro venture. [253]

J.M. Bernhardt's interests varied far and wide. Among the public improvements he championed was Appalachian State Teachers College in

Boone, extension of the Carolina and Northwestern railroad line north from Lenoir to the growing lumber town of Mortimer, and a water works for Lenoir. He also spearheaded an effort for a new turnpike to be built up the mountain from Lenoir to Blowing Rock. For the latter, he was accused of supporting projects that benefitted his interests. A better road into the mountains assured his vast timber interests access to Lenoir factories for both he and his partners. When roadwork construction began, Bernhardt personally joined the work crew as surveyor. It also was no coincidence that his luxury hotel, the Green Park Inn was situated along the route, so he stood to gain on several fronts. [254]

At times, J.M. Bernhardt mixed his business, his pleasure, and his vision. His participation in the creation of the Mountain Home Club, a retreat for the affluent, allowed him to associate with industrial notables like Daniel Augustus Tompkins, the cotton mill magnate from Charlotte, along with many of his other furniture contemporaries in the Catawba Valley area. The club sought to turn the higher elevations of western North Carolina into a place of respite for those who could afford the cost to enjoy the coolness and the views. He owned vast amounts of land in the area, eyeing the harvests of timber it could bring. But he also saw the potential for a vacation getaway, primarily for he and his ilk. His first foray into luxury stays in the mountains had come with the Green Park Inn at the entrance to Blowing Rock. Now he sought an even more remote, exclusive, and "popular resort with people of the best class." The club was a members-only organization with a clubhouse located in Edgemont, some 16 miles farther into the wilderness than Blowing Rock, far more remote than the Green Park Inn. As a member of the club's board of governors, Bernhardt could see that transportation and wealth allowed his friends a place to get away for extended stays.[255]

The reentry of John Mathias Bernhardt into the furniture-making business came with the floundering of another company. The Moore Brothers, minus Joe, had weathered competition, a nearby fire, and the loss of some of its own, only to find their fortunes fading. A connection to Bernhardt with the Globe Lumber Company gave T.P. and W.C. Moore someone to take over their operation. Early in 1911, "at a special meeting of the directors," the factory and all its equipment were sold to Bernhardt. This move put Bernhardt back into furniture making for good.[256]

For the Moore family, it was the first step toward their complete removal from the furniture business. After Moore Furniture became Bernhardt Manufacturing, there remained the Moore-Stone Chair company, created by Joe Moore and T.J. "Joe" Stone. In 1913, the 'Joe and Joe show' moved all their chair-making equipment to Greeneville, Tennessee. Their plans to make "regular furniture" in the building they left behind in Lenoir never produced a single piece under their own name again. Instead, Moore-Stone was reported to be merging with the Lenoir Furniture Corporation but was instead bought by several new players in the industry, including L.E. Rabb as president, J. Russell Powell, secretary, and O.P. Lutz, general manager. They named their new enterprise Royal Furniture Company.[257]

The kaleidoscope of changes continued with the transition of another local company. The Lenoir Furniture Corporation was created from the sale of the original Kent factory to another new name to the game, but one that would build a strong legacy in the years to come. "Messrs. T.H. Broyhill and R.L. Steele closed a deal last week for the Kent Furniture Company's plant. Under the new organization, Mr. T.H. Broyhill is president and general manager, Mr. W.L. Minish, secretary and treasurer, and Mr. R.L. Steele, vice-president." Subsequently, the name was changed to the National Furniture company; however, they soon found out the designation conflicted with an already established firm in Mt. Airy. Tom Broyhill then decided the name should be the Lenoir Furniture Corporation.[258]

The Broyhill entry into furniture manufacturing is illustrative and significant. Thomas H. Broyhill was member of the New South generation

The oldest and youngest sons of Isaac and Margaret Parsons Broyhill, Tom ventured first into the business of saw milling before finding himself a partial owner of a factory. Once he owned one, he welcomed Ed into the fold, who took furniture production to new heights. (Courtesy of the Caldwell Heritage Museum)

who sought opportunity in manufacturing instead of farming, leaving his father Isaac's land in Boomer, near the Caldwell-Wilkes County line. Tom, the oldest of five sons, worked his steam-powered saws up and down the tree-lined hills, making connections with the first generation of furniture makers in Lenoir as he supplied their wood. At the same time, he amassed enough revenue from the work of his sawmill to be able to buy into their operations when they began to flounder. In the case of the Kent company, Tom supplied timber to the operation and when the company could not pay outright for the wood, Broyhill took "a 4 percent" interest in the company as payment. Dr. Kent's company gave Broyhill just the opportunity he needed. Over the next few decades, Tom Broyhill managed to pull several dying or underperforming factories into his orbit, creating an ever-enlarging empire that would for a time dominate furniture making in Lenoir and North Carolina. His reach in the business exemplified his approach, slow and steady.[259]

Tom Broyhill's understanding of wood products was vast and far reaching. About the time he gained a financial stake in the Kent factory, he also helped start a veneer plant. With a total of $8,000 ($40,000 authorized), Tom allied with G.N. Hutton and A. Bourbonnais (of Hickory's Hutton and Bourbonnais wood manufacturing company) to start Lenoir Veneer. Virgil D. Guire was also part of the team and he ran the operation most of his life. Manufacturers needed veneer to dress up inferior lumber and give finished pieces a more refined look. Rotary cut machines shaved thin strips from logs for application to a wide variety of furniture. A company in town that could supply sheets of veneer to other operators helped facilitate output and served a useful function as a supplier to the finished product.[260]

Lenoir Veneer crafted more veneer than it needed for hometown makers, a lot more. By some reports, half of the company's output went to furniture makers in other states, including Grand Rapids, Michigan, the center of the nation's industry. H.L. Doty, the factory's superintendent, himself a native of Ohio, could spur production to the point of turning out 14,000 square feet of veneer per day. Using "steam vats and drying racks," Doty and his crew rolled out thin layers of wood to adorn the fronts of a variety of pieces from other plants in 72 x 52 inch sheets. The output was called "first-class," and the plant took in up to 4,000 oak and poplar logs daily for its work, using the most advanced equipment of its day.[261]

The Broyhill and Bernhardt names started a slow but steady rise to

Veneer adorned the fronts of many finished pieces that came out of furniture factories. Lenoir Veneer was an early supplier to the larger furniture industry in Lenoir. Tom Broyhill was one of the originating investors. (Courtesy of the Caldwell Heritage Museum)

establish themselves as future furniture empires. J.M. Bernhardt, with his extensive experience in many operations readied himself for the future success he and his company attained. For Tom Broyhill, a prudent approach with measured growth helped the climb of his family name to the top. Both were, in a sense, hometown boys grown into businessmen who knew the region and never tried to push it beyond what it could give. Their pluck and luck proved to be a winning formula. To an outsider, success may have looked easy. Others tried with their own companies, falling away every year. It turned out they did not have what the Bernhardts and Broyhills had, staying power. Others rose fast but fell even faster.

Of those who started a company or two, the arc of J.M. Chiles across the early furniture landscape might best be described as something of a meteor. "Mr. J.M. Chiles, of Greenville, S.C. has been here several days this week. He is a furniture dealer and is the man through whom the Kent Furniture and Coffin Co. and the Lenoir Table Co., Builders' Supply Co., sell their products." Though the name might not imply it was a furniture concern, Builders Supply Co. made tables to go along with the hundreds of chairs being produced in Lenoir by a variety of companies in 1906. That year a fire swept through Builders Supply. Losses totaled over $20,000 as the company's inventory went up in flames along with that of the Coffey Wagon Company. But the setback did not deter Chiles. He came to town with ambitions as big as the number of companies he started. Earlier that same year, Chiles partnered with the father and son duo of Edmund Jones, Sr. and Jr. to create the Chiles-Jones Furniture Company. The combination, however, wasn't right. Before the year was out, the company name had changed to Chiles-McCall, with his colleague from Builders Supply, J.V. McCall. J.M. Chiles business partner from Builders Supply was brought into the operation, which caused a switch of names on the door.[262]

J.M. Chiles demonstrated talents as a pied piper, bringing a number of others into his business schemes. Before Chiles-Jones underwent the name change, Andrew McAnse of Chicago, a furniture rep, was enticed into an ownership stake in the company. Even though the Jones name lost prominence as Edmund Jones, Sr. watched his name removed from the marquee, both he and McAnse remained with Chiles and his company as investors.[263]

James Madison Chiles, or Jake as he was called, may have originated from South Carolina, but as an adult, he made his home in Asheville. He was known there for creating the neighborhood of Kenilworth and not as a furniture man at all. He always had grand ideas, and his plans for real estate development at the time were characterized as "stubborn and delusional," but later evaluation credits him as visionary. He brought much of that same colorful exuberance to Lenoir. Previously dabbling in furniture as a silent investor in the Martin company in Hickory, Chiles took on several wide-ranging partners to create a huge company, if not in reality, at least in imagined scope. Chiles gathered Charles Hipp of New Hampshire and Elmer Gray of Boston to establish the United States Furniture Corporation with an unheard of capitalization of $250,000.[264]

The United States Furniture Corporation headquartered in Lenoir, perhaps a recognition of the town as a center of furniture making activity. However, much of the operational aspects would occur in J.M. (Jake) Chiles' hometown of Asheville, where he was building his grand neighborhood. There he constructed a Spanish Revival Villa for his personal use. Some of the cash reserve amassed by United States Furniture went toward the purchase of land adjacent to the Vanderbilt estate near Asheville. With "four and one half acres of land along the railroad at Biltmore," Chiles and his partners planned a factory complex down the mountain that "takes furniture in the white, (meaning rough pieces), finishes and assembles it and sells the product all over the South and East." It was an ambitious plan, in keeping with the way Jake Chiles approached everything he did. It also met with the same contemporary

One of the multitude of furniture making operations of J.M. Chiles, this one started in 1901. A player in the early furniture game, Chiles created several companies including the United States Furniture Corporation, based in Lenoir. His showplace home in Asheville is still a showplace. (Courtesy of Hickory Landmarks Society)

acceptance of his Kenilworth neighborhood.[265]

It didn't.

Within a few years of creation, the United States Furniture Corporation was the subject of a lawsuit that went all the way to the North Carolina Supreme Court. In the suit, Jake Chiles was the plaintiff, suing his own company. As the grand plan began to fail, Chiles felt he did more than Hipp and Gray to keep the company afloat, serving as a salesman for the company he also managed. He argued that he should be paid for his additional role and sought supplementary company wages, totaling $500 per month. The other investors thought the idea preposterous. Jake chose to take his partners to court. They countered that as a partial owner of the company, they had no reason to compensate him. Ultimately, the court ruled in Jake's favor, ordering his now former company to pay him back wages. The acrimony of the court case ended his status of popular partner and he retreated to Asheville to pursue his housing plan.[266]

The fall of Chiles-McCall created opportunities for others. "A deal was put through last Monday that will mean much for Lenoir. A company of nine of our best business men bought out and assumed control of the Chiles-

McCall Furniture Factory and will make all necessary improvements in the plan and resume work at once," reported the *Charlotte Evening Chronicle*. The paper went on to say, "the plant has been idle for several weeks. Mr. L.E. Rabb is manager of the new enterprise." With a host of nine men taking over, several names were or would become prominent. Among the group was W.J. Lenoir, descendent of William Lenoir, Revolutionary War patriot and namesake of the town. L.E. Rabb was joined by J.P. Rabb, whose son would one day bring his era's technological advance to Lenoir in the form of a radio station, WJRI (a fabled distilling of the phrase "Watch John Rabb Improve" or "We Just Rolled In," take your pick). J.V. McCall was back as an investor from his previous association with Jake Chiles. Lenoir businessman O.P. Lutz returned as an investor in Royal Furniture and later became Lenoir's most popular furniture retailer. But most important to the future success of the operation was Tom Broyhill, selected as vice president of the company.[267]

Within Lenoir, a game of roulette began. Unlike the first or second factory, which took a long time to build and operate, those wanting to start a company only had to wait for someone to go out of business. They could sweep up the assets at fire-sale prices and go back into operation, often with the same worker group of the earlier, failed company. Each successive owner believed they had the right stuff to make a go of it, only to fall into the same pits as their predecessors. It would take a while before those adept at moving an enterprise forward would rise to the top, take over the failed factories, and bring stability to the industry.

In the period when the world was at war, but the United States had yet to join, the last of the early furniture operations cranked up in Lenoir. In the summer of 1915, Bert Stone, the manager who broke his leg trying to get to the fire at his former company, Lenoir Chair, moved to create Ethel Chair, named after his wife. Ambitions were great for the new maker, even if working capital was not. "The Ethel Chair Company of Lenoir was chartered today with $100,000 authorized and $500 subscribed." Stone and his brother L.E. Stone went in with B.F. Smith to create the company designed for "chair and general furniture manufacturing." Bert Stone expected to make "a box seat dining chair which finds a ready sale on the New York and Chicago markets." Within a year, Joe Moore came to the firm, representing Ethel Chair at those national markets. Prospects were good for Ethel. Before 1916 was gone, the company expanded, its second addition since inception.[268]

The promise of Ethel Chair was built on the failure of an earlier, equally promising venture. In 1907, a group of Lenoir investors got together. Perhaps they thought of furniture as too confining an application of woodworking, as their idea was to create a company that would mold wood for a variety of industries, including but not exclusively furniture. The Blue Ridge Bending Corporation crafted "rims for wagon and buggy wheels" but also made table rims, spokes, and handles. Within a few years, they expanded their repertoire to include washboards. After another year passed, they stepped into the furniture market proper, "building an addition to the plant with a view of adding the manufacture of tables to the already long list of articles made by the concern."[269]

As the western North Carolina foothills geared up for furniture making, so too did the western North Carolina mountains to harvest the wood. With a company name as big as their ambitions, J.M. Bernhardt teamed up with W.J. Palmer and F.G. Harper of Caldwell County and E.P. Wharton of Greensboro to start Giant Lumber. From its base in North Wilkesboro, the lumbermen devised a "24-mile" flume that brought logs down from the remote depths of 10,000 acres buried in the mountainous wilderness. The flume got its water from the nearby Reddies River and carried "the equivalent of 150 wagonloads of logs a day" for shipment. Not all of it went to local furniture makers. Estimates of the time said about half the output was transported by rail to firms as far away as Michigan. Built in 1909, the Wilkesboro flume was not the first; but while it lasted, it was the longest, carrying logs down a two percent grade, just enough to keep them moving.[270]

With more companies came an increasing output of furniture, going to more homes throughout the South and beyond. Production required a steady flow of timber, much of it from the mountains located just north of the factories. Entire towns like Mortimer and Grandin sprang up around the lumber mills, vying to supply the raw material. The abundance of trees in the southern Appalachian chain seemed endless. Companies like Ritter Lumber in Mortimer and W.J. Grandin's operation between Lenoir and Wilkesboro profited handsomely from the largesse of nature.

But just as Mother Nature gave, she also took. In the summer of 1916, two hurricanes swept over western North Carolina in a ten-day period. Near Grandfather Mountain, over 22 inches of rain fell in a 24-hour period. Western North Carolinians experienced devastation, unlike anything they had seen before or since.[271]

Towns surrounding the core furniture makers suffered the most. To the west in Asheville, the rains inflicted over $1 million in damage of the total $22 million caused in the catastrophe. In Elkin to the north along the Yadkin River (from where Hickory Chair had come), an entire warehouse washed away. The giant flume of the Giant Lumber Company washed away completely. Instead of building it back, Bernhardt and company sold their interests in the land and the flume, choosing to look elsewhere for prime timber. To the south, a rescue effort to save the railroad trestle over the Catawba River at Belmont took the lives of ten men when the bridge collapsed.[272]

In the foothills, the destruction was somewhat less pronounced, but the catastrophe took a toll. Every bridge over the Catawba River was destroyed. In the Burke County community of Bridgewater, two boxcars, one filled with furniture, the other timber, were washed away. In the factories themselves, the rains had caused relatively minor damage, company officials reported. After the flood paralyzed the region, factory production shut down. In Lenoir, the reason centered around companies "not having any shipping facilities to get their output to market." Perhaps the headline of the *Lenoir News* expressed it best for the town and others throughout the area when it reported, "Lenoir Isolated From Outer World." "Scarcely a mile of railroad track between Asheville and Salisbury" avoided damage, along with the loss of all telegraph lines. The storm "marooned" citizens until transportation and communication were restored weeks later.[273]

While the furniture business was only temporarily disrupted by the calamitous event, it bore a measure of responsibility for the scale of the destruction. Since the first companies were established, a mad rush had consumed entrepreneurs in their effort to support and profit from the emergence of furniture making. Lumber companies raced to fill orders from the factories and, as a result, cared little about the erosion they caused. The blight on the land was a minor concern as they cut down every tree they could get their saws on. Industrialism in the South had tempted entrepreneurs by offering a release from the poverty that gripped the region since the Civil War. Those goals stood paramount as the trees fell. In fact, such motivation was the impetus for Lenoir's first factory. A quarter-century later while business was good, there was no time to consider environmental concerns, until the rains came, that is.

In the aftermath of the flood, the "intensive logging" that fed the factories was recognized as a reason the waters came as fast and as furious as they did. The trend of increased flooding in the region started before the 1916 event, but as reports of lumber and logs floating down the Catawba left reminders of how completely timber interests had mined the landscape, lawmakers sprang into action. The same year as the flood, the federal government purchased land to protect against a future tragedy. The acquisition stemmed from a 1911 initiative. The Weeks Act, authorized the U.S. Forest Service to acquire

500,000 acres for preservation, calling the new reserve Pisgah National Forest. This protected land would serve as a hedge against the onslaught of portable mills serving the furniture industry and would require factory owners to search elsewhere for their principal raw material.[274]

The year following the Flood of 1916 brought more trouble in Lenoir to all furniture operations, this one man-made. The union came to town. On March 14, Ethel Chair shut down at noon and "paid off all men associated with the union." Caldwell Furniture did the same. The rest of the factories in town followed suit. The popular thought of the day (and later) was that unionism was responsible for driving northern manufacturers south as labor costs rose, thanks to collective bargaining agreements. Southern owners wanted to deal with their employees on an individual basis, not as a group, which meant they could control their workforce better and keep costs lower. So it was no surprise that efforts to unionize factory workers in Lenoir were met with stern resistance by the owners. "For several weeks the labor union has been agitated, and a few days ago, a national organizer was secured by the local men to help them out with their organization. In the meantime, the owners and managers of the plants gave the men notice that no union men would be employed by them - that to join the union meant loss of their jobs," reported the *Lenoir News-Topic*. In all, 157 men were fired as the Stones, Broyhills and Bernhardts were determined to "nip in the bud the effort of the men to organize a labor union."[275]

Management and some employees saw labor unionism as a threat to success. Workers like Ralph Bowman, who would one day rise to the top of the industry, believed "unions ruined the factories in Michigan and upper New York." He fought against unionism establishing a foothold. In Bowman's estimation, northern factory owners "couldn't get anything out of their help. They couldn't control them." Owners were within their rights to lock down the factories and weed out the organizers, in Bowman's opinion. With this tactic, furniture management blunted labor organizing. Even talk of unions became a dangerous, job-threatening proposition. Some employees felt they had enough threats to their jobs from layoffs and fires keeping them out of work. The benefits they might receive from union representation were outweighed by management's hostility toward organization.[276]

Attempts to unionize became the talk of Lenoir, despite repeated failures. Ethel Chair though, had bigger problems. By 1921, keeping the company profitable proved impossible. The operation fell into receivership. Kent-Coffey sought the property, but another group outbid them and took possession. They reorganized operations and branded the new effort as Fairfield Chair. The old headquarters of Ethel Chair served as home base for Fairfield, situated as it was along the railroad line to create. The new company was an instantly formidable manufacturing operation. In fact, several failing operations were merged to create Fairfield, including Hudson Veneer from the neighboring town of the same name. W.J. Lenoir, E.F. Allen, and J. Harper Beall (pronounced "Bell" in Lenoir), were the incorporators. The latter was was a nephew of Major Harper. The name Fairfield came from the home of the Harper's, marking another example of the family's influence in Lenoir's furniture culture.[277]

As the 1920s dawned, a sunset came for Lenoir's most influential citizen. Major George Washington Finley Harper passed away in Lenoir at the age of 86. His hand had been a guide to start Lenoir and put much of the Catawba Valley on the road to industrialization. His wisdom and wealth had gone a long way into making furniture production viable. He offered a blueprint for all around him to emulate. Although the Harper name became less synonymous with furniture in the way Broyhill or Bernhardt later would in Lenoir, his rank was apt for the role he played. G.W.F. Harper, called the "Last of the Founders," served as a guiding hand in the establishment of an industry that would eventually employ most of Lenoir's population. The

Major's retirement in his later years and his ultimate departure from the business community of Lenoir required the next generation to pick up the banner and carry it forward. As far away as Charlotte, observers noticed how well the junior partners were doing. They wrote, "the Lenoir furniture factories all report that they have all they can do-kept busy to the limit. That sounds good among these groans of hard times we hear in some other places."[278]

Lenoir was fortunate. Even with the loss of the Major, a crop of apt pupils, some who had observed Harper's philosophy at his side, were taking over. They had learned the value of vision, persistence, and optimism that Major G.W.F. Harper demonstrated throughout his life. Even the Confederate Army's ultimate defeat did not deter Major Harper from parlaying his family's influence into productive business for his hometown. He bet on them with his family's wealth, even when the dream of Lenoir's first factory seemed like a nightmare. His steady presence navigated the town through uncertain years when he could have just as easily quit. He chose otherwise, and the sons of furniture-making that came along after, owed a debt of thanks to the Major for his tenacity. They learned well.

⁓

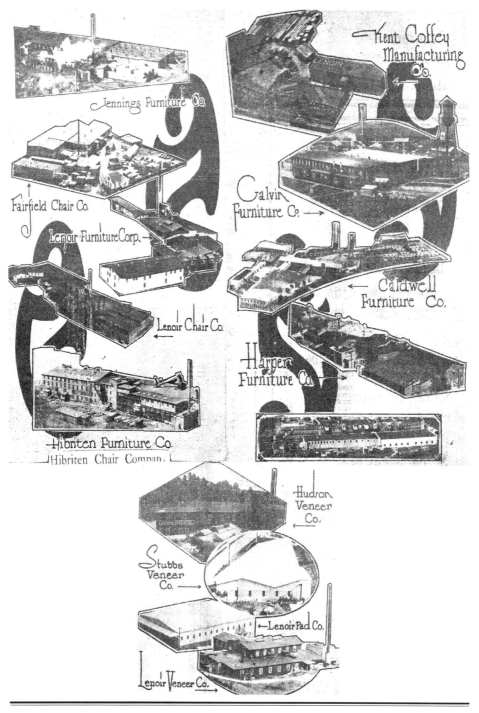

Jennings Furniture Co.

Kent Coffey Manufacturing Co.

Fairfield Chair Co.

Calvin Furniture Co.

Lenoir Furniture Corp.

Caldwell Furniture Co.

Lenoir Chair Co.

Harper Furniture Co.

Hibriten Furniture Co.

Hibriten Chair Company

Hudson Veneer Co.

Stubbs Veneer Co.

Lenoir Pad Co.

Lenoir Veneer Co.

An early 1920s newspaper advertisement featuring the different furniture industry factories in and around Lenoir. The variety of facilities, including veneer makers, had come together along with ventures in adjacent counties to bring the center of American furniture making south. (Courtesy of the Caldwell Heritage Museum)

Chapter 12
A Hustling Business

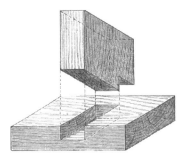

Just before the First World War, western North Carolina furniture manufacturing saw incredible growth. In 1916, the number of companies statewide more than doubled, with capital doing the same. Most of the employees were hourly workers, spending an average of almost ten hours per day on the job to fuel this productivity. Before the American call to arms in 1917, companies grouped, regrouped, fell by the wayside, and started again as the business of making furniture developed to its next stage. It offered a level of production that could be called an industry.[279]

The furniture companies began to realize more fully the scope of

All of the early factories were powered by steam, which meant that each machine was driven by one large engine. Individual machines would be powered by a belt that connected each to the power system, as seen here, requiring a worker to engage the machine for use. (Courtesy of the Caldwell Heritage Museum)

markets beyond their region, with abounding sales possibilities. Firms hired salesmen to hawk their wares, often with miniature pieces to show the style of the lines they represented in a three-dimensional way that drawings or even photographs could not, just like the cabinet makers of old. Often these traveling salesmen promoted more than one manufacturer. H.C. Chaffee lived in Clinton, Iowa, but traveled "for several of the furniture factories of Lenoir." He visited the Caldwell County town on occasion, but his work, which kept the machines humming, spanned both coasts. In a meeting of the Southern Furniture Manufacturers Association (SFMA) that convened in Hickory, the discussion even included the South American market. Of the forty members present, a vote to send W.A. Thomas of Statesville to drum up business there was approved. Like Chaffee, Thomas represented "different manufacturers with a view of building up trade on that continent." The move showed that furniture makers were beginning to think globally, with destinations far and wide for their local labor and wood.[280]

By the time of the Hickory meeting, the SFMA had been around for fifteen years. Created as a consortium of owners, its officers were dominated by High Point concerns. Hickory, as indicated by the setting of the summer 1914 meeting, was represented, as were like companies in Lenoir, Morganton, and Marion, but the choice of a Statesville man to introduce North Carolina to Latin American homes demonstrated that the western manufacturers definitely had a role to play in the Tarheel industry. Thomas' destination was vague, and under the heading of "South America Will Be Invaded," there seemed to be some confusion over exactly what lay ahead in that direction. When the meeting selected W.A. Thomas to go, the *Statesville Sentinel* declared, "he will go to South America at once. He will make a thorough investigation of furniture trade conditions in that country," hopefully using the term as synonymous with territory instead of being unaware that the continent held more than one nation.[281]

The worldwide appeal of furniture made in the foothills of NC was confirmed with a letter. As October of 1916 began, the Lincoln Furniture Factory in Lincolnton received "a request" from Sluis, Holland. It read, "Please send me your illustrated catalogue. After war, I'll write you for a price list." The letter was signed "Walter Van Robays, merchant." The notification of the letter spoke directly to the popularity of the product and the name western North Carolina was making for itself. Crowed the *Lincoln County News*, "here is a foreign merchant in a foreign land, who anticipates a business boom after the war ends and trade relations are resumed." Word had gotten out that something significant was being manufactured in the backcountry.[282]

The inquiry from Holland came at an interesting time for furniture making in Lincolnton. Lincoln County lies directly south of Catawba County. Back in 1842, Catawba seceded from Lincoln in a contentious separation that took years and several votes by the North Carolina legislature to settle. Seventy years later, the Lincoln Furniture Company began in 1914, an effort of Lenoir entrepreneur M.W. Shook and several other investors, including Daniel E. Rhyne, the chief benefactor of Lenoir College (Hickory's institution of higher education). The college would eventually adopt his name, too, becoming Lenoir-Rhyne College, later University. Reports said that Shook planned to "take charge" of the operation once completed, but investors elected Rhyne to the post of president of the new company. The plant went up in about six months, located adjacent to the railroad, with a plan to make several grades of furniture. After another six months, the operation started to come apart from the inside. First, a lumber supplier started "litigation with reference to a quantity of lumber and in which the sum of about $500 is involved." Then, a little over a year later, Daniel Rhyne sued Lincoln Furniture, a move that threw the company into bankruptcy. When the factory came to public auction that summer, Rhyne bought the entire plant for $15,000. He tried to restart the company as DER Furniture (his initials) but less than a year later sold it to the Lenoir interests of M.L. Cornwell and B.L. Stone.[283]

Wood and labor were homegrown, the two chief ingredients in spawning the industry that found its footing in the early days of the twentieth century. However, one material of increasing popularity needed in the manufacture of coordinated suites was mirrors. Most glass had to be imported from western Pennsylvania and Ohio. Getting the commodity shipped kept prices high for ensembles that included items like mirrored-backed dressers. In 1913, the Interstate Commerce Commission ruled that those companies selling to furniture makers did so at "unreasonable rates." By then, Lenoir had solved the problem in much the same way the furniture industry began. They would produce mirrors themselves. The previous year, a manufacturer from the other furniture community in North Carolina (High Point) made a deal with the Kent-Coffey company to build a new plant next door to their furniture factory. Lenoir Mirror Company started with capital of $20,000 to supply a furniture amenity that consumers had come to expect as part of their bedroom suites. Lenoir Mirror kept the process of self-sustained manufacturing going.[284]

Another sign that the elements of the furniture industry were taking root could be found in the move from wood-framed workshops to brick and mortar buildings. Late in 1916, Southern Desk's George Ivey decided he wanted more permanence. At the site of his old structure west of Hickory, he awarded a contract to a local builder "for the foundation of a brick foundry, 75 (feet) by 160 for the Southern Desk Company." The *Hickory Daily Record* reported that "all the wooden buildings used in the manufacture of picker sticks will be torn down when the brick buildings, which are being erected in sections so as to be occupied as soon as finished." Ivey planned a foundry for his new brick structure "to make castings for school desks and furniture." As the European war loomed on the national landscape and participation would one day threaten the availability of workers, Hickory took pride that the expanded Southern Desk Company would "make quite an addition to the manufacturing industry in this city."[285]

George Ivey took the idea of furniture manufacturing and added his own unique twist. Instead of furniture for the home, he focused on the institutional market. Where some companies had been enlisted to craft odd items like church pews and desks on occasion, Ivey went from picker sticks for textile plants (a necessary device for retrieving broken strands of yarn in spinning machines) to building sturdy pieces for churches, schools, governmental buildings, and business on a full-time basis. Specialization gave Ivey and his company a niche that separated his operation from the pack of firms producing home furnishings. Though the company's output appealed to a smaller market, Southern Desk offered unique product lines, allowing it regional exclusivity in the market.

Before the First World War took many workers from the factories to the battlefields, the machines hummed. Statesville Furniture paid a 10 percent dividend to stockholders in January of 1916 with word that the company "is now prosperous and running overtime." The work was so good that High Point companies raided western North Carolina factories for talent. One example was C.S. Van, "who has been connected with the finishing department of the Bernhardt Manufacturing Company for the past several months, has moved to High Point where he has a similar position with a furniture factory there." E.A. Argo was a "machinery foreman with a High Point furniture factory." He reportedly came to Hickory, where he had lived previously. Under the guise of returning to renew old friendships, "he is also looking for workmen" to take back with him to High Point. It appeared that western North Carolina produced superior labor for the furniture industry. Other enterprises sought the foothills workforce for their plants. Beyond High Point companies recruiting them personally, workers found opportunities in the classified section of their local paper. "Wanted - Experienced Cabinet men for furniture factory. Steady work. Give references, experience, state wages desired. White Furniture Co., Mebane, N.C." read the *Lenoir News* as one example.[286]

The prosperity of the industry and the popularity of jobs in it hid the fact that working in a factory could be dangerous. In the days when government at all levels looked the other way, working belt-driven, steam-powered machinery, much of it with saws, led to periodic injury, even fatalities. Vance Jenkins, a young employee of the Diamond Furniture Company, was struck by a flying piece of timber at the factory this morning and seriously injured," read the *Charlotte Observer* on February 16, 1916. Operating a ripsaw, Jenkins loaded a piece of wood into the cutter. Instead of paring down the wood as the saw had done multiple times, the timber bucked and "struck Mr. Jenkins over the stomach rendering him unconscious for 30 minutes." Vance Jenkins was fortunate. Instead of killing him as those around the man feared might be the result during that fateful half hour, he woke up and recovered. Several weeks earlier, Russell Houser felt a blow while working at a Lincolnton furniture factory. This time "a knife flying from a plane in one of the machines" hit Houser. He, too, recovered. Unfortunately, Bard Williams was not so lucky. A "fireman" for the McDowell Furniture Company, Williams was gathering scraps from the machines as fuel to heat the boilers. As he reached for "materials from one of the machines," he "came in contact with the saw, which cut his body and arm. The cut on the body went through his entrails and cut them in three or four places." Several doctors were summoned, but the damage proved too destructive to save Williams.[287]

Danger in the factories was not always the result of interactions with machines. During the First World War, a labor shortage was acute. Many draft-age young men reported for duty with the military. As a result, companies like Hickory Chair struggled to keep production going. Almost a year into the nation's declaration of war with Germany, white factory workers objected to the pay they received for their work. Their objections came once they found out African-Americans also working there received the same wage. A group of white employees met to strategize after an altercation between "a white man and a negro." They demanded that the company either fire its black workers or give all whites a ten percent increase. With Jim Crow laws in full force throughout the South at the time, the "50 or 60 employe(e)s" petitioned management for their answer to the workers' ultimatum. Company leaders refused. The leadership reasoned that with wartime labor shortages being acute, "it is a condition they cannot help. It is being done elsewhere (according to Hickory Chair management) in furniture factories as a matter of necessity." Since the two groups did not work together directly, the fight likely revealed the parity in pay. Hickory Chair officials were more concerned about losing the labor of African-Americans in this instance than the white workers, thus their stand. Everyone went back to their jobs without any further disruption.[288]

The entry of the United States into world war depleted the ranks of male workers, not just in the furniture industry but across the industrial spectrum. Women came into the factories en masse for the first time. The *Hickory Daily Record* considered women in furniture jobs previously held by men a "demonstration in applied patriotism." Employed primarily as "upholsterers, weavers of cane bottom chairs, finishers and sanders," women kept production going during the war. Men who observed the influx of women noted that many were called upon to do the heavy work too. Running machines like band saws, panel sizers, and tailing machines, women performed whatever job was needed. "Management treated them no differently than their male counterparts," as the war effort continued.[289]

As the war raged for global stakes, the government sent a shock wave through the furniture industry. The War Industries Board handed down an edict that "declared no more bedroom product could be produced after January 1, 1919." The agency had been set up to make just such decisions, guiding the use of raw materials (in this case, wood) by factories that would contribute most effectively for the war effort. The Washington, DC oversight board, making such a determination, called for the shutdown of factories throughout the foothills. In the end, only one thing kept the ban from taking effect, the end of the war. With the surrender of Germany in late 1918, the emphasis shifted back to a peacetime economy, which would surely need new bedroom suites for returning soldiers and others. The ban was recalled before it started.[290]

The experiment that D.A. Smith conducted in Marion 40 years earlier, surmising that furniture production could prove viable in the land where the wood grew, had been a fortuitous idea. He was right, as were many of those who followed in his footsteps. The use of indigenous materials using local craftsmen to make products for markets beyond the borders of North Carolina had hit its stride. Reports listed the Tarheel state as using more wood than any other state in the South, the vast majority of it coming from its own forests. In doing so, NC factories undercut the average of the top ten furniture-making states, coming in at seven dollars per thousand feet of lumber. In the South, North Carolina was king among industrial employers. Lumping its three top industries of which furniture was a substantial part, along with cotton and tobacco, the report concluded that the value of raw materials was tripled by value-added manufacture.[291]

Every operator made the best use of the wood, right down to the last splinter. What didn't go into the actual pieces sold to customers found several other uses. Larger scraps were used for crating shipments. Often, companies were their own best customers, burning leftover chips and sawdust to heat their boilers since, in the early days, most factories operated by steam. What couldn't be used could be sold. The Catawba Furniture Company ran a classified advertisement reminding McDowell County folks that "now is the time to buy your winter's supply of dry stove wood. Oak factory blocks at $1.00 a load."[292]

The principal reason furniture factories looked to sell their leftovers instead of using them to fire their own furnaces came with the ever-increasing mechanization found on the factory floor. McDowell Furniture, a rival to Catawba, both located in Marion, invested in a "Monarch heater" to keep their workers and machinery warm. In doing so, the company saw its bottom line improve dramatically. "We have not had to purchase a stick of wood, whereas, formerly we used all the waste from our factory and in addition one a car of wood per week," crowed the company. They went further by asserting, "We figure that it saves us half the fuel we formerly used, besides giving far better results in our dry kiln. It has already saved us many times its cost." The continued sophistication of machinery spurred companies like McDowell Furniture to minimize the hazard of open flame in fire-prone factories.[293]

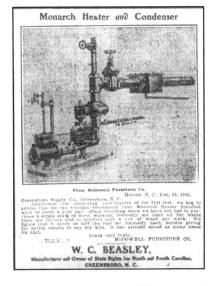

Labor saving devices like a Monarch heater were being added to factories as operations became more stable and financially solvent. From humble beginnings, McDowell Furniture, like many of its contemporaries improved working conditions for employees as it went. (Image from the *Greensboro Daily News*)

The danger of fire had long stood out in every mind, especially in McDowell County seat of Marion, a few miles east of Old Fort. In 1894, citizens felt the flames as the entire city was almost "swept from the map" by an intense blaze. On a November Sunday morning around 11am, "an old dilapidated building" caught fire. Since the structure was "old and dry and burned like tinder," the rest of the town went up with it. One report noted "the wind was terrible and the fire spread like lightning." The town had "no fire company or water works." The charred ruins left only one store, a brick structure, habitable. The devastation resulted in over $200,000 in losses for citizens (3.2 million in 21st century money), but more importantly to the coming furniture industry, just about every future investor in area factories suffered almost total loss in the fire, most with no insurance. The devastation made the rebuilding of Marion all the more significant.[294]

When town businessmen rebuilt, their plans included a rush of furniture factories. McDowell County lay on the western fringe of the foothills, and within it, Old Fort, slightly farther to the west at the foot of Black Mountain than the country seat of Marion. The D.A. Smith experiment of the 1870s to produce furniture from the wood that grew nearby remained an inspiration in their effort to rise from the ashes. Many recognized the value of a factory in town. Three years after the fire, the county seat's paper, The *Messenger*, echoed Smith's theory by extolling Marion's advantage. "Marion is especially adapted for all kinds of woodworking factories, on account of the cheap timber and good railroad facilities." In addition to the east-west line of the WNCRR (later Southern Railway), Marion was the "northern terminus of the Ohio River & Charleston Railroad." Town leaders hoped the line would continue to the Ohio River by getting over the mountains to Johnson City, Tennessee. With or without the extension, products coming out of Marion still had a way to reach wider markets, however down the railroad line through Hickory. Others characterized Marion without blandishments, saying, "Marion's paths may not be all peace nor her ways pleasantness - because of her mud - yet her strides to the van as the High Point of the Blue Ridge indicates 'mighty good goin'." The comparisons between eastern and western spheres of furniture-making had already begun.[295]

With such advantages, a stream of factories emerged. For a while, a new one came along every few years, some of them short-lived. It started with Marion Furniture, opened in 1896 by Major William A. Conley, a Confederate veteran who also served as president of the First National Bank in Marion. Major Conley's financial acumen did not translate to furniture making. After about three years with regular capital increases, Conley leased the plant.

After that, Marion Furniture shut down, and the plant was sold at a public auction. Similarly, the Novelty Woodworking Company came along with big ambitions. Not a furniture company but an enterprise making products for home construction, Novelty started with grand intentions of marketing their products in Europe. However, when the factory burned in 1901, the owners did not rebuild.[296]

The surer bet on a stable, long-term enterprise came with Thomas F. Wrenn. In 1888, Wrenn and his brother Manleff joined other investors to organize High Point Furniture Company, the first in that city. He then joined Lenoir's struggling effort, and in 1895 began another startup there, but Blue Ridge Furniture closed the following year. Undaunted, Wrenn tried again. He situated the Catawba Furniture Company in Marion and partnered with a local, W.H. Frasier. Soon, Wrenn took over the entire company, personally moving to McDowell County to oversee his operation. The relocation brought a lot of expertise to the new company, given Wrenn's experience. Immediately, he began bringing seasoned people to his new factory. Ed Foy joined the operation early, coming over from Lenoir. With loyalty to T.J. Wrenn, Foy saw something in Marion that he did not see elsewhere, confidence and capital. Ed Foy and his fellow workers at Catawba came to their jobs ready to operate a full range of machinery. The list included a "swing cut-off saw, rip saw, glue jointer, band saw, hand jointer, planer, moulder, double cut off saw, shaper, dovetail, sander, tenon, and some half dozen smaller machines." Called "one of the best outfits in the state," workers built chiffoniers and odd dressers at first, soon graduating to full bedroom suites. Estimates of the time suggested that Catawba Furniture handled about 100,000 feet of lumber per month. Once those pieces had gone through the factory, boxcar loads of pieces left Marion for destinations like New York City. Some shipped as far as South Africa.[297]

As the century grew in years, furniture making became a popular investment in McDowell County. Thomas Wrenn started a second factory in

Marion. This time he joined with J.L. Morgan and Major Conley, investors in the defunct Marion Furniture to form Western Furniture. After Major Conley's death in 1914, the driving force seemed to leave the operation. Two years later, the plant went up for sale.[298]

Western incorporator J.L. Morgan helped to also start a factory under that same name as Wrenn's unsuccessful attempt in Lenoir, Blue Ridge Furniture. Morgan's partners in the new Blue Ridge were the Gilkey brothers, John Quince and William Kelly Marvin. Operations continued at the company

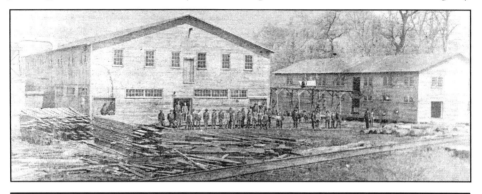

Western Furniture Company around 1912. This factory was the second of T.J. Wrenn's Marion efforts. The company went into receivership by 1916. Eventually, Drexel owned the grounds and would build the facility where Western Furniture once stood. (Image from the Warren Hobbs Memorial Photographic Collection

until the decision came to lease the factory during World War I to Drexel. Western Furniture lasted only until 1916 when Blue Ridge incorporator J.Q. Gilkey picked it up at auction.[299]

Acquiring lumber was always a necessary component of the furniture business. Some manufacturers looked to other companies to supply board feet, but the American industrial model, crafted by men like entrepreneur and steel magnate Andrew Carnegie emphasized the value of controlling all raw materials necessary to the production process. In the furniture-making business, Carnegie's theory of vertical integration favored direct control of the source of lumber instead of buying from others. Owning the supply chain provided steadier management of production costs since a supplier could always raise prices, leaving the manufacturer powerless. In short, they could pay the price or find another supplier. Ownership also streamlined the process to guarantee manufacturers of acceptable quality and ample supplies that they might not have when relying on others. In Lenoir, both Broyhill and Bernhardt understood the concept. In Marion, Thomas Wrenn, also an old hand at the most economical way to churn out pieces for customers, saw it as well. In 1909, he moved to vertically integrate his company by starting a lumber operation capitalized at $40,000 with several other investors, among them Ed Foy. Not every successful company owned its own lumber operation, but the ones that did more closely controlled their own destiny.[300]

Another Marion man did much the same. Dr. W.P. Jones augmented his medical practice with a lumber yard and its natural successor, a furniture manufacturing enterprise. McDowell Furniture began in the spate of new factories after the 1894 fire and grew to become one of the largest, but most importantly, longest-lasting businesses of its type in McDowell County. A 1903 article chronicling all afoot in Marion cited his plant as "immense," "covering 26,400 feet of floor space." Jones also got notice as "one of the largest lumber dealers in the city." Specializing in poplar wood, so robust was his enterprise that some of his output went well beyond McDowell Furniture, instead being "shipped to foreign countries."[301]

A representative of McDowell Furniture attended a 1906 meeting of the North Carolina Case Workers Association when, as a group, the manufacturers decided to collectively raise prices. The organization argued that they needed a ten percent hike to cover the escalating price of lumber. The secretary of the association said, "we have worked diligently over the matter, all day; we have discussed it from every standpoint, and we have concluded that our only salvation is to make an advance of ten per cent." The move occurred during a time when companies could form formal and informal 'trusts' to minimize outside competition. After 1911, the Supreme Court ruled the practice anti-competitive. The most vocal of those companies voting for the increase were ones not also in the timber business.[302]

Substantial growth at McDowell Furniture might have been attributable to the fact that Dr. Jones took on a partner who infused the operation with the capital to grow. D.N. Lonon "purchased an interest" in the company soon after it started. The *Morganton News Herald* described the new duo as "the leading spirits in that hustling enterprise, and it is doing a hustling business." One hustle involved taking on salesmen to hawk the wares of McDowell Furniture. J.P. Culp came on as the "traveling representative of McDowell Furniture Company." By train, he hit the road for new customers in Georgia, Florida, and Alabama. J.P. Martin also went to work traveling the country. Martin's career was short-lived. Checking into the Central Hotel in Savannah, Georgia, on a Monday afternoon in late June, he "was attacked by heat apoplexy," meaning he collapsed from heat stroke. Ironically, the desk clerk "thought him drunk, and had him arrested. At the barracks he was examined, and (police) ordered him taken to St. Joseph hospital. Fifteen minutes after arriving, Martin died."[303]

One curious career that came through Marion was that of D.R. Raper. Originally a superintendent at the Lenoir Furniture Factory, he was so important to the operation that his illness shut down operations. Once he left for good, his absence became one of many reasons the Lenoir company sputtered. Next, he took work at Marion Furniture in 1897 as general manager but did not stay long. After beating six other salesmen for a contract to supply the Round Knob Hotel, he bought out the stock of one investor, sold his shares, then started a new operation to make bookcases using power purchased from the Novelty Manufacturing Company before the year was out. Ten years later, Raper could be found in High Point, not as a player in the furniture industry but instead as proprietor of the High Point Marble Works, a business to which he devoted the rest of his career.[304]

McDowell Furniture weathered the World War nicely. By the 'Roaring Twenties' the plant had grown to cover "30,000 square feet of space and manufactures bedroom furniture of all kinds." $175,000 marked both the value of the property and the annual output of the company. Through the decade, the company profited from a flourishing economy, hampered only by a 1924 blaze "of unknown origin" that caused $35,000 in damage. The earlier addition of Monarch heaters to the shop floor did not ultimately protect the company from fire.[305]

The circle of cities supporting furniture manufacturing operations had grown, each of them built on trial and error. Collectively, they created an industrial base that stood ready to catch the wave of consumer culture that came during the decade that followed the Great War. Finally, they lucked into the right product at the right time.

Men unloading bark in McDowell County. Extracts from the bark went into the tanning of leather, a supporting component of the furniture industry. In the age before development of the highway system, rail and horses supplied most of the transportation needed. (Image from the Warren Hobbs Memorial Photographic Collection, McDowell County Historic Preservation Commission, 2002. Courtesy of the McDowell Historical Society)

Lumber men and their product. Every furniture factory had its own lumber yard. It was the rough end where the wood came in and was dried and stored for usage. These workers had the dirtiest jobs of any. (Courtesy of the Caldwell Heritage Museum)

Chapter 13
The Land of Scenery, Sunshine, and Prosperity

Southern furniture factories found themselves in an enviable position after the First World War. Thirty years of business had given them an incubation period to develop their lines and sell to a local, then wider audience. With life in the 1920s moving toward a consumer economy, the factories of western North Carolina found themselves ready to compete on a national scale. They needed to do so, having mostly saturated southern homes with their furniture. Upgrading the look of their pieces with new styles like Art Deco and extending their marketing efforts, these companies found their furniture competitive in style and price with every other product made in the United States. Southern manufacturers originally made furniture for the southern market, where most could only afford modestly priced pieces. But in a national context, enhancements offered more. Northern buyers tended to be a "more discriminating market," which required products to be of the highest quality. Southern manufacturers salivated over that market but knew that their offerings fitted a more modest product line, one they could easily supply. Southern furniture would soon come rolling off the line into boxcars bound for the Northeast and beyond, but the finer homes still preferred the product of Grand Rapids.[306]

The market for wood products and what constituted furniture expanded. The end of the World War (as it was called before a second one came along) reoriented the American economy toward a more consumerist culture. The technological feat that entranced the buying public in the 1920s was radio. Every family that could afford one bought a set. In its early days, a receiver was also easy enough for amateurs to assemble, buying parts through mail order and building their own. Advertisements in radio magazines sold everything from antennas to speakers. Furniture firms got in on the act by selling cabinets to house the wiring.

George F. Ivey followed up the success of his Southern Desk Company with a new venture, located adjacent to his factory in west Hickory. He conceived the Southern Toy Company, not as a maker of radio cabinets, but first as a manufacturer of a variety of wooden playthings to capture the imagination of children. The factory began turning out what it called "juvenile furniture," which included "shooflies (a child rocker), rocking horses, dolls, cars and similar products." The business stayed in the family, with George F. Ivey's brother E.C. Ivey tapped to run the business when it started in 1922. The times were made for an American toy manufacturer. Prior to the war, the best toys were known to be crafted in Germany, but the defeat of the Kaiser changed attitudes. Also, the burgeoning consumer economy created a more affluent market that could afford non-handmade playthings for children.[307]

One of the early best sellers for Southern Toy came from a design created by a Hickory man. Augustus Harper (nor relation to the Lenoir Harpers) "invented" a "clever merry-go-round toy which is appealing to kiddies in Carolina towns." The item sold for one dollar and sported "two gaily prancing horses and two real seats for dollies who may crave this sort of amusement," wrote one account of the new product. Stores in Charlotte, Lenoir, Statesville, and Hickory carried the item.[308]

In West Hickory, "the toy plant is getting more orders than they can fill," read a report on the Southern Toy Company after its first six months of operation. By that point, the enterprise had already expanded into the production of radio cabinets, something of a natural progression since building sets appeal to adolescent boys. Historian Bart Lee noted that of the three dozen or so manufacturers, Southern Toy's cabinets were the cheapest, with some as low as three dollars. Ads for the appliance appeared in several trade publications like Radio News and Radio World, alongside other components necessary for the building of a set. The walnut or mahogany boxes came with nameplates for each model that reflected the maker and the region. Names like the Iveyline, Piedmont, and Carolina gave young builders a choice of just how snazzy they wanted their creation to look. Ever proud of its origins, Southern Toy noted in its advertisements that the company was located in "Hickory, North Carolina…(the land of scenery, sunshine, and prosperity)."[309]

Celebrating its centennial in 2021, Fairfield Chair weathered the changes in the furniture industry. The company continues to make furniture in the area where most of Lenoir's early factories were located. (Courtesy of the Caldwell Heritage Museum)

The ancestry of the Harper family, in addition to spawning the remarkable career of Major Harper, went back even further to the very roots of Lenoir. Harper Beall's grandfather, James Harper (via his mother, Mary Harper Beall, sister of the Major), left the family home at Fairfield, a community near Gettysburg, Pennsylvania seeking warmer climates. Relatives in Wilkesboro partnered with Harper to establish a store that happened to sit at the intersection of two roads, one linking Wilkesboro and Morganton, the other Statesville and Watauga. James Harper prospered in business to the point that he donated a portion of the land around his store for the creation of

Lenoir. He funded the first cotton mill in the area (Patterson), spinning yarn for the consumer market. Among his other ventures were a tannery, "a smithy, a harness shop, a tailor's business and a carriage manufactory." He also took over the store partnership which had become a chain, extending from Tennessee to South Carolina under the name "Fairfield." The designation was also used also used for his family estate, so when Lenoir folks heard of the new furniture company, the name was a familiar one that clearly defined ownership.[310]

Fairfield Chair, with its combination of failed and struggling predecessors broke an emerging pattern in the manufacturing profession. So many companies that began with the greatest hopes and fanfare died torturous deaths with their facilities being auctioned off as failures for all to see. Hopeful aspirants picked up the pieces at bargain prices only to experience the same ends. J. Harper Beall served as an example of what it took to succeed. His business acumen and his resources charted a fortuitous course that energized Fairfield Chair. He also brought in experienced personnel, like V.D. Guire to oversee production and give furniture making in Lenoir the stability it needed.

In short order the community of manufacturers started to get crowded. In 1922, hoping to follow the Fairfield model through its reuse of the Ethel Chair site, A.G. Jonas, Dr. C.L. Robbins, and R.C. Robbins invested $75,000, with expectations to raise another $125,000 for a company they called Star Furniture, a recycling of the Moore-Stone company that started in 1906. J. Harper Beall sold the new company, land and facility that was once the Royal Furniture Company for $40,000. The sale exemplified the spirit of the industry in Lenoir. They competed but also cooperated when deals were mutually beneficial, creating a brotherhood of sorts among manufacturers. At the very least, they understood each others problems and refrained from cut-throat tactics that might sink them all. [311]

For the Robbins brothers, the 1920s beckoned them to get into furniture manufacturing in a big way. Again, taking a second old factory, this time a working one, and turning it into a new company offered a track record to build upon. They also knew skillful management was a must. "Robbins Buy Local Lenoir Chair Plant" read the headline in the *Lenoir News-Topic*. They changed the name to Hibriten Furniture (the name of the mountain east of town) and planned a total revamp of the operation with some new machinery and a new product, "a line of walnut furniture." R.C. Robbins said he would not give up his investment in Star Furniture, but would "assume the duties with the new concern and manage both plants."[312]

It would not take long before one of the Robbins companies was reduced to ashes. The summer of 1925 had been a hot one in Lenoir. When a fire started on the afternoon of July 13th at the Star factory, it only took ten minutes for flames to consume the building. The fire department arrived around that time and fought the blaze as much as they could but witnessed the destruction of the entire building. The flames damaged the nearby railroad trestle enough to disrupt service to Lenoir for several days. Bernhardt Chair Company stood next door. Fire threatened it too but as luck would have it, the wind kept the fire from spreading in that direction, protecting it from harm. Unfortunately for Star Furniture, the inferno spread so quickly that even though the plant had a sprinkler system with most of the valves working, the rush of water was not enough to save the buildings. Insurance covered only about two-thirds of the loss. Since the Robbins brothers owned Hibriten Furniture too, many of the orders were moved over in an effort to salvage something from the devastation. Hands at Hibriten worked double shifts to handle the overload.[313]

From the ruins of Star Furniture came a rebuilding effort, but it didn't take long for the Robbins brothers to abandon the firm in favor of their other firm, Hibriten Furniture. Co-investor A.G. (Adolphe Gustave) Jonas took over Star, re-christening it Jonas Furniture. Jonas started in 1928 by manning the helm of his namesake operation, announcing big plans to expand. By then, he and his son A. Garland Jonas were on their way to Chicago to present their new product to the furniture market, "a high grade line of medium-priced bedroom furniture and odd dressers."[314]

A.G. Jonas was no stranger to the furniture industry. Having dabbled in manufacturing with Star Furniture, he believed he knew what it took to be successful in the Lenoir market. Ten years earlier, Lenoir furniture manufacturers brought Jonas to town to start Lenoir Mirror. As manager of Lexington Mirror, he guided that operation to substantial profits (they declared a ten percent dividend in 1910); his operation adroitly fed furniture makers the silvered glass they needed to complete a well-appointed bedroom suite as consumers began demanding the amenity. Quickly, he joined his furniture operation with that of Lenoir Mirror to form Jonas Manufacturing.[315]

A look at tax revenue coming in all across North Carolina revealed that Lenoir had become the center of furniture production in the western part of the state. When the "Collector of Internal Revenue," Gilliam Grissom, reported corporations assessed over $100 in taxes to Tarheel state coffers, the snapshot revealed where furniture production was entrenched. At the time, Morganton listed no company qualifying, while Marion reported only one. Drexel was a big contributor of taxes to the state, located within the bounds of its own town. Hickory, with four companies, offered substantial revenue to North Carolina's treasury collectively, though not as much as Drexel's payment, but still substantial. Statesville eclipsed Hickory with five furniture companies contributing, but the king of concentrated manufacturing was Lenoir. With close to $30,000 in taxes paid, compared to Drexel's solitary company at $25,000, Lenoir had clearly demonstrated its collective dominance as an industrial base. While Hickory businesses remained well-diversified, with just one/sixth of its firms specializing in furniture, Lenoir's ratio was well over half, by far the greatest concentration of woodworking companies in the state per capita.[316]

By mid-decade, the grove of factories in Lenoir appeared thicker than the surrounding forests. In addition to all the other enterprises, Stanley S. Jennings started Jennings Furniture in 1926, making maple bedroom sets. Nothing in S.S. Jennings' background suggested that he might ever succeed as a factory owner. Coming from Pennsylvania, Jennings was at one time a builder, bank cashier, baker, auditor, fruit store operator, Republican candidate for Register of Deeds, and Wilson Lumber Company representative before investing in Moore Furniture. He was then part of the group that started Lenoir Chair three years later. Jennings traveled extensively, often attending furniture markets in Chicago and New York, so his move to create his own company was no shock to his associates, despite a varied career. When he retired from active involvement in his companies, S.S. Jennings accepted a management position at Stubbs Veneer Company.[317]

When activity in Lenoir got crowded, budding entrepreneurs spilled out into adjacent towns. Some started small, which required less capital, allowing owners to grow at their own pace. In the fall of 1925, Table Rock Furniture began operations, taking its name from the stone crowned mountain that overlooked Morganton. C.A. Spencer of Morganton joined with N.O. Pitts and J.H. Giles of the nearby community of Glen Alpine as owners. Spencer shared an old manufacturing plant with his new partners to get the company going. Table Rock started with a "truck, boiler, dry kiln and office equipment" to facilitate its operation. Soon, they added additional space, and by the end of the decade, Table Rock gained a reputation for "an unusually high grade of bed room suites and specializing in an all walnut group of exceptional beauty." Attempting to rival Drexel and Morganton Furniture as Burke County's largest employer, Spencer elevated activity, expanding the workforce to over 250, production having doubled its output in its first five years. Eventually, despite its success, Table Rock sold out to Drexel.[318]

In one way or another, the collective of furniture-makers, now an

This crew of furniture workers comes from an unknown era but the attitude they convey is eternal. Solemn and resolute, by the 1920s they found themselves part of an industry making a name for itself nationwide. The foreman/manager is likely the one in the suit. (Courtesy of the Caldwell Heritage Museum)

industry, drew a wide variety of individuals to its ranks. Farmers abandoned the land to take day-shift jobs in the factories. Young men looking for a regular wage joined them. Management recruited from anywhere they could get hands. For many who spent their youth behind a plow, the opportunity to work inside was a welcome change. Hill Baker toiled in several plants around Catawba County, including Conover Furniture. Given the choice, he opted for the regular wages and the steady schedule of shop life. "That or farm work?" he said, considering the choice, "I'd rather work in a factory. It's not hot in the factory exactly like it is on a farm."[319]

Both Hill Baker and his brother worked in the furniture industry. They were a part of a small group of African-American men who made their living doing the "dirtiest, heaviest, least desirable, and lowest-paying jobs, such as furnace tenders, dock loaders, and sweepers." The Baker brothers performed each of those tasks at one time or another. During his career on the shop floor, Frank Gilbert (a white man) who worked with the Bakers, observed that "there was some work over there (Conover Furniture) that most white men wouldn't do, and (the black men) never did mind doing it, it didn't seem like.

202

I believe they had a will to work."[320]

A first job in a furniture company often led to a lifelong career in the industry, even if a worker went from factory to factory. Many of them did. The skills learned in woodworking were more specialized than the cloth trade which meant a better paycheck. Flake Meyers worked in both and was convinced that furniture "paid a little better than the cotton mill. It did." For a working man like Flake, "that was about the best paying job," he recalled. Frank Gilbert also recognized a good deal when he had it. He chose furniture because the alternative was tougher. "It was a hard life in those cotton mills," he said.[321]

Still, a furniture job was not easy. Hill Baker remembered working from 5 a.m. until 6 p.m. each weekday and 5 a.m. to 4 p.m. on Saturdays during his time at Conover Furniture. He admitted it didn't leave time for much else. "There was nothing I could do because of the long hours and the time I went to work." By that point though, it was his life's work. He started as a child. "When I was a kid way back then, there was not too much that I could do. I'd go with my daddy to carry water, maybe, to a few of the hands or something like that. But when it come down to read hard work, I couldn't do that until I got up thirteen or fourteen." At one point, he was a sweeper, earning 40 cents per day, but he never saw any of that money. Recalling payday, he said, "minors like me, you could draw your money, but your daddy would collect it. In place of me getting it, he'd get it. And what I needed, he'd get it for me."[322]

To be fair, not every factory worked their employees for as long as Conover Furniture did Hill Baker. Just after the First World War, "Bernhardt Chair, Ethel Chair and Kent-Coffey instituted an eight-hour day." They were ahead of many other manufacturers who still operated on a 10-hour day. It would take the New Deal of Franklin Roosevelt to institute a mandated eight-hour-day for the other companies to change their schedule.[323]

Factories offered their own kind of vocational education for the next generation. Hill Baker got the on-the-job training that prepared him for his career as a young boy. Some blamed company owners for the exploitation. George Hutton held a different view. As a stockholder in a factory that employed children, he accused "rapacious parents" of taking advantage of the situation, saying that the extra income from children padded the family income. Employment in western North Carolina furniture factories came during a transitionary period when fewer and fewer sons wanted to take up their father's line of work, especially in the fields as farmers. Some were eager to learn the ways of industry as an alternative. In all likelihood Hill Baker didn't fret too much about the wages he earned going into the family coffer. The routine was widespread, even expected in families. A father might ask how was the practice any different from employing a child on the farm to handle tasks. By one estimation, a child in the factory could earn a quarter of the wage his father commanded, about half of what his mother earned. Families lived easier lives thanks to the contributions of children; the more, the better.[324]

A few companies offered perks purported to improve a family's lot, especially if more than one member were employed. Taking a page from life in a cotton mill, Conover Furniture rented homes to workers. Ralph Simmons paid $5 per month for a house but said he would never buy it because the ceilings were too high. He argued that the structure was hard to heat and the draft it caused in winter led to sickness in his family. "They build some of them kind of rough," he remembered. Both Drexel and Conover Furniture engaged in a similar experiment, building homes near their respective factories for workers. Like with cotton mills, management believed that proximity to the factory curtailed thoughts of playing hooky. However, unlike mill villages, furniture owners sold the homes instead of renting them. Since the company held the lien on the house, the practice tied the family even more strongly to the job they had to keep in order to make the payments. Largely, constructing living quarters for workers remained an uncommon practice in the furniture game.[325]

For those who could move from factory to factory in search of a better wage, they did. Flake Meyers started at Hickory Chair in 1915. Eventually, he became an assistant foreman there. He then took a job running a planer at Highland Furniture in Conover. By then he was married so the couple enjoyed the fact that, "Flake would not have to take the bus from Hickory," according to his wife. From there, he switched over to Conover Furniture to run a band saw but after a while he went to Newton Furniture for more money and as a position as assistant foreman. Still unsatisfied, Meyers went to work for Southern Desk as a tenon machine operator, then back to Conover Furniture and back again to Southern Desk where he worked as a "set up man for an automatic shaper." Though some stayed with one company, Flake Meyer's experience was typical of workers in the furniture industry who would leave one shop for another, gaining a few cents more per hour with each jump.[326]

Perhaps the most widely traveled of all workers was a man born in Illinois, who spent time in the gold fields of Deadwood, then trained horses on the plains of South Dakota before trying his hand at growing oranges and raising turkeys in California. When each of those attempts failed, he settled in Caldwell County on land his wife inherited. What brought Olborn Clapp to Lenoir in the first place was a 'lonely hearts club' courtship with Addie Swanson. At age 41, Clapp came east to marry a woman he had never laid eyes on before. He whisked her away to his ranch in South Dakota. There they began a family but partially due to his wife's inability to handle the cold weather, they migrated to California, buying an orange grove sight unseen. The Clapps arrived to find the orchard barren. After fire obliterated a turkey farm Clapp tried as an alternative, Addie Clapp put her foot down and the family moved to Lenoir in 1909.[327]

After a career of adventure that took him to South Dakota, then California, Olborn Clapp settled in the hometown of his wife and went to work for Bernhardt Furniture. In February 1926, a freak accident mortally wounded him. Both his sons would one day work in the industry as well.
(Image courtesy of Betty Laws)

Due to Addie's connections, the easiest job to find was in furniture so Clapp went to work at Bernhardt Chair. For sixteen years, he worked alongside men half his age in the factory. One night in February 1926, he left the plant, ducking under railcars to make his way home. "Evidently he thought the cars would remain stationary, left there for loading and unloading. Being too old to climb over the boxcars, he attempted to duck under them," suggested one report. Just at the moment he shinnied under the path of the wheels, the yard engine bumped against the boxcar he was navigating. The jolt pinned him between the wheels and the track. In excruciating pain, he waited for the railroad doctor who attended him only long enough to get the 64-year-old father of three back to his home. His wife saw his condition and decided to take him to a hospital in Catawba County.

The delay in treatment and the cold ambulance ride allowed pneumonia to set in. Two days later, Olborn Clapp died, an inadvertent casualty of life in the furniture business. Despite the accident, both his sons ultimately found careers in furniture, one down east in High Point, the other in Lenoir.[328]

Amid pitfalls, injuries, and death (of both companies and individuals), the foothills of western North Carolina now had an industry worthy of the designation, a collective way for communities to demonstrate their best work to an American public interested in buying machine made furniture. The region began to define itself by the industry it had spawned. Slowly but surely, manufacturers found a solid footing upon which to build their companies. They employed successive generations of foothills families who began their training at an early age and looked to the factories for a stable career. Challenges awaited for both owners and laborers who increasingly found their handiwork in homes well beyond the South, their means of support determined by a national economy.

᚛᚛᚛

Built in 1905 as the Catawba Tannery & Extraction Works, leather from the tannery supplied furniture companies in the region. Prior to World War I, it was bought by U.S. Leather Company. The facility employed over 400, but a series of fires closed the facility by the 1930s. (Image from the Warren Hobbs Memorial Photographic Collection, McDowell County Historic Preservation Commission, 2002. Courtesy of the McDowell Historical Society)

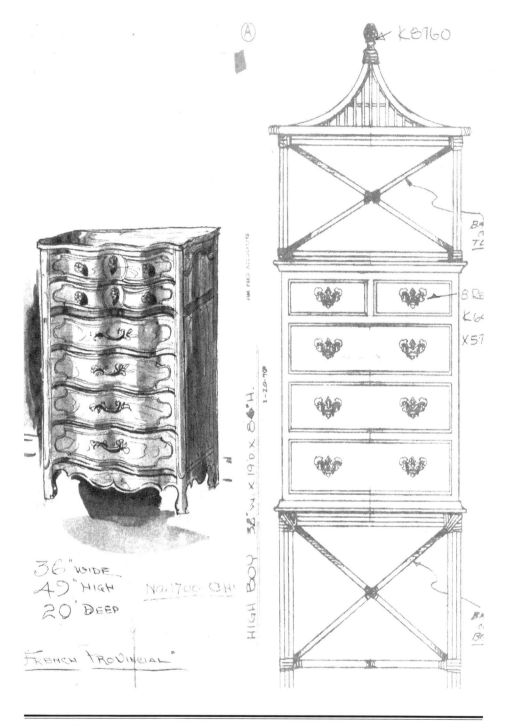

Sketches of furniture before the pieces were made. Salesmen often sold from these drawings, some lining them out right on the spot where they got the order as store owners explained what they were looking for. Others were done by designers as the business sophisticated. (Courtesy of the Hickory Landmarks Society)

Chapter 14
Family Ties

In Lenoir, J.M. Bernhardt had already established himself as a founding father of furniture production, even if he took a rather circuitous route to establishing a company that would one day bear his name. After leaving Lenoir's first company, which was eventually managed by his in-laws, Bernhardt explored a number of business opportunities before he went back into the wood business, opening a planing mill and box factory in 1896.[329]

For several years, the Bernhardt Planing Mill and Box Factory occupied its owner. J.M. Bernhardt' company supplied those who made the finished product. His workers took boards straight out of the sawmills and refined them for use in furniture construction. His company also furnished crating to protect finished furniture during shipping. Along the way, Bernhardt upgraded his facility regularly, once to the amusement of B.S. Blair, the editor of the *Lenoir Topic* who noted the factory made "a very unusual noise." Residents were cautioned the blast was not "Gabriel's horn," but an "80 horse (power) boiler" that furnished power.[330]

The location of the box factory was a highly coveted industrial space located along the Carolina and Northwestern rail line, adjacent to Lenoir's depot. The building and grounds were substantial. J.M. Bernhardt owned a complex that covered over three and one-half acres of ground. The lot was so large that in the spring of 1917, when a carnival came to town, Bernhardt offered the troupe temporary space on the site. A description of the main facility noted, "the building, which was erected in 1904 is 100x160 feet, two stories high with an 11-foot basement." Made of brick with an adjoining "power and boiler room," Bernhardt had constructed a factory that was capable of much more than that for which it was being used.[331]

In 1917 J.M. Bernhardt sold the box factory to start his own furniture company. The buyer was an astute judge of good factory space, Tom Broyhill.

John Mathias Bernhardt helped drive the campaign for the first Lenoir furniture factory. After striking out on his own with a box factory, he made the decision to get back into furniture production. He built a new, streamlined facility to compete with the other companies in town. (Courtesy of the Caldwell Heritage Museum)

At the time of the announcement, Broyhill could not respond adequately to questions about his future plans for the site, "but it is known that he is interested in the hosiery mill project." Instead of hosiery, in making the jump to actual furniture, Bernhardt returned once and for all to the product that would define his career, just down the tracks from the original 1889 factory. Incorporated with a planned total of $50,000 (with varying amounts reported as subscribed), he created Bernhardt Chair Company where he envisioned "a chair factory and general woodworking working business," with partners B.L. Stone and M.L. Cornwell listed as fellow incorporators.[332]

In reality, Bernhardt had never been away from the world of furniture for very long. Since 1906, he had been a part of the Moore Furniture Company as an investor. Largely, the Moore operation morphed into the Bernhardt Company a decade later, with J.M. Bernhardt returning to the helm. The interim gave him the time to refine his skills and determine a path for future success. With the Moore Furniture Company, Bernhardt had a dress rehearsal to develop the techniques needed for a prosperous company that would ultimately be under his full control as well as his name.[333]

For its first decade, Bernhardt Chair specialized in "a splendid line of high-grade dining room suites, finished in shaded walnut." Additionally, the company made "chairs to match bedroom suites for several of the local furniture plants, and these are finished in walnut, shaded ivory and gray." Much like the parallel convergence of the Broyhill brothers, Bernhardt Chair was becoming a family operation. Son George Harper Bernhardt was now a part of the business, taking "active charge of the office." The job of sales, however, was left to the father.[334]

John Mathias Bernhardt saw great advances for 1926. At the beginning of the year, he showed his company's wares for the first time at the Chicago Furniture Market. That summer, he announced plans to build a spectacular addition to his existing factory. The new portion was designed to encompass three stories to augment the four-story building already in place. In his new plant, he wanted finishing rooms on the second and third floor with "the very latest machines and most modern equipment." In this addition, he planned to use the first floor for "packing and shipping, and will have three places for loading." It was a grand vision. Bernhardt believed the new building would double the output. He considered every option to create a spectacular facility, even evaluating the model of cotton mills that provided housing for their workers. He ultimately did not adopt the notion, but designed an impressive workspace for employees. With "approximately 100,000 square feet of floor space," the Bernhardt factory would be "easily one of the largest furniture plants in Lenoir."[335]

In less than six months, the work of Bernhardt's dream of creating Lenoir's premier furniture factory suffered a fate that sooner or later disrupted the plans of many furniture operators, fire. On November 30, 1926, a huge blaze swept through the plant, burning the entire facility to the ground. At the time 172 men were working in the new Bernhardt factory. It was about 5:15 that morning when "a short circuit in one of the paint spray machines" caused an explosion that engulfed the finishing department in flames. Several of the men working there "were forced to jump from windows" four stories high. It took less than an hour and a half for the entire plant to burn completely down. With approximately $260,000 insurance on the factory, the damage was estimated at $325,000. The greatest loss was one of the factory's workers. In the aftermath of the event, no one could find Joe King. A day later, his "charred body" was discovered in the rubble. Nine other employees were injured, two seriously. Most of Lenoir came out to see the gruesome inferno. The fire was witnessed "by several thousand persons who gathered on the hillsides above the plant." Reports called the catastrophe "rapid and spectacular."[336]

The fire left J.M. Bernhardt uncertain about his future, according to his youngest son, John Christian Bernhardt. At the time, John Christian was finishing up at his father's alma mater, Davidson College. The son planned a return to Lenoir to work for the family firm. As he confided, "everybody worked for their daddy in those days." When the fire came and J.M. Bernhardt was informed of the losses, John Christian remembered that "for a while, they weren't sure if they were going to rebuild or not." As an alternative "they thought they might concentrate solely on lumber rather than furniture."[337]

It took nine months, but by the summer of 1927, J.M. Bernhardt was ready to give it another try. He broke ground on a rebuild, hoping to produce furniture ready for market by the new year. New construction allowed Bernhardt to replace the steam system, so vulnerable to fire in the past, with a

On a cold December morning in 1926 the state-of-the-art factory J.M. Bernhardt planned to operate as his reentry into the furniture business went up in smoke. The blaze cost one worker his life. Bernhardt debated rebuilding, but a year later he did. (Image from *Charlotte Observer*)

new, more modern model. Press inquiries revealed that machinery "was being bought with the idea of giving the greatest production possible. All of it will be electrically driven by individual motors" instead of belt-driven. At that point, the name of the company changed from Bernhardt Chair to Bernhardt Furniture.[338]

In the three decades since Lenoir's first factory, the business of furniture making had solidified. Workers and management alike acclimated to factory life as both gained an education that equipped them to better handle the pitfalls of operation. It seemed Lenoir, as well as the rest of western North Carolina, had found its signature industry. Back in late 1920, the *Lenoir News-Topic* offered an extra section of its paper to promote the state of the local economy. The banner headline read, "Second Largest Furniture Center in the South." The claim came from the local chamber of commerce, who crowed that the county indeed ranked second in the output of chairs nationally and third in "all kinds of furniture," behind High Point in the South and Grand Rapids, Michigan, nationwide. The statement put Lenoir at the forefront of furniture manufacturing.[339]

In subsequent editions, the *News-Topic* highlighted the companies that landed Caldwell County in its position of prominence. Among them were Harper Furniture ("walnut and mahogany bedroom furniture"), Caldwell Furniture ("dressers, buffets, chiffoniers, and kitchen cabinets"), Kent-Coffey Manufacturing ("chiffoniers, wash stands, buffets, beds, sideboards, dressers, also building materials, sashes, doors, windows, etc."), Hudson Veneer and Lenoir Veneer ("rotary cut veneers from native woods"), Ethel Chair (before takeover by Fairfield), Lenoir Chair, Bernhardt Chair, and Lenoir Mirror.[340]

The final entry in the special section belonged to the Lenoir Furniture Corporation. With sales throughout North America, the company boasted showrooms in New York and Grand Rapids. Lenoir Furniture proclaimed its use of local lumber and its one hundred employees who turned that wood into "a high class of bedroom furniture and buffets." Those workers were also touted as "a high class of home owning native Carolinians, who are loyal and highly efficient." No doubt those homes contained some furniture from their own factory. In the first seven months of 1920 alone, the output of these workers produced over a half million dollars in inventory.[341]

The path of the Lenoir Furniture Corporation epitomized the short and roundabout tenure of industrial furniture making in Lenoir. The company evolved from an earlier furniture operation (Kent Furniture and Coffin), but much of its growth came from the entry of Tom Broyhill to the furniture-making business proper. With his stake in the company, he gave Lenoir Furniture a means to procure a steady stream of wood, given his background in sawmill activities. In addition to his burgeoning career as a furniture executive, Tom maintained a portable mill that could cut ten thousand board feet of lumber daily. Keeping as many aspects of the business "in house" as possible helped control the process, from growing trees right down to finished case goods. As it turned out, Tom Broyhill and furniture making was a match made in heaven. Originally a sawmill operator, he parlayed supplying furniture companies with the wood they needed into partial, then majority ownership. Hardworking and conservative in his business moves, Broyhill brought the Lenoir Furniture Corporation into prominence as Lenoir's largest.[342]

Individually, the emerging group of manufacturers in Lenoir aspired to balance the job of making furniture with the job of selling furniture, keeping both in proportion so that they could attain the overall objective of staying in business. Challenges came from everywhere. Lumber, labor, capital for expansion, and national buying trends constantly worried management. Curve balls like fire meant owners had to keep a keen eye on their operations. Individually, they worked out their problems on a daily basis as they competed for business. Together, they were an industry. On occasion, they collaborated.

In the summer of 1921, Tom Broyhill and J.M. Bernhardt joined together in "an experiment with the local factories" to produce several suites of bedroom furniture "in the period and semi-period styles." Broyhill made the main pieces (dresser, chiffonier, bed, and vanity table), while Bernhardt contributed the accompanying chairs. Daughter of Harper Furniture head and granddaughter of the Major, Miss Margaret Harper (niece of Bernhardt's wife), "painted on the designs on each piece for photographing, and also for the samples" due to the short turnaround before the "July market." The set, finished in white ivory, was enough of a hit with consumers that the alliance continued for another five years with Bernhardt making a rocker, chair and bench for Lenoir Furniture's bedroom suites. Additionally, Broyhill and Bernhardt pooled their resources in the hiring of salesmen to hawk their wares in distant markets.[343]

About the time the furniture collaboration in Lenoir was taking shape, so was another union. For several years, Tom Broyhill had employed his brother, James Edgar Broyhill as an assistant. Ed was Tom's junior, both in age (he was 12 years younger) and furniture industry experience. However,

Ed Broyhill had a kind of knowledge his older brother did not. He spent three years finishing high school at Appalachian State Teachers College and then served the American cause in the Great War (WWI). His typing ability, plus his energy and intelligence impressed the leadership of Lenoir Furniture Corporation enough to allow the sibling to move right into the front office, despite Tom's intention to show no favors to his little brother. According to Ed's grandson, Edgar Broyhill II, his grandfather was expected to earn his way in what was becoming a family company.[344]

When Ed returned to Lenoir, Tom treated him, as well as two older brothers, just like anyone else seeking employment. Luckily, when he was in the line of applicants looking for a job, the question of "do you have a skillset?" had a ready answer from Ed Broyhill. "Well, I know how to type," he said. The reply might just have changed the course of the furniture industry. When Ed heard the words, "OK, you go to the main office," he happily complied, even as two of his older brothers headed to the lumber yard. Because of an illness that landed Ed in Walter Reed Hospital in Washington, DC, the Red Cross taught him the skill of typing during his convalescence and gave him the break that would later demonstrate his abilities as well as set him on a path for success.[345]

At Lenoir Furniture, Ed Broyhill proved himself. "When he went into the front office as a typist, he was able to immerse himself in customer service issues in the furniture business," noted grandson Ed Broyhill II. "He also learned how to do bookkeeping since he was reliable." The hands-on education Tom's younger brother received augmented everything he was taught at Appalachian State. Ed handled whatever Tom and/or the company needed. It seems the Broyhill brothers had an understanding that might seem unusual today, but at the time suited them both. For the opportunity to develop his own skills, Ed never received a regular salary. Instead, at the end of the first year, Tom gave his younger brother a bonus of $1800, which Ed used to buy stock in his brother's company.[346]

After a few years as "a young business man," Ed Broyhill felt comfortable enough in his job with the Lenoir Furniture Corporation to put down several sets of roots. First, he planned to get married. On a Saturday afternoon in June 1921, Ed Broyhill wed Satie Hunt at Lenoir's First Baptist Church. The new Mrs. Broyhill and her family were already part of a prominent social order connected to the furniture industry. Satie's father, Hartley Hunt had been timber manager for a sawmill operation roughly halfway between Lenoir and Wilkesboro, the area from which the Broyhill clan had come.[347]

Hartley Hunt came to western North Carolina in the employ of W.J. Grandin, a Pennsylvanian who saw the value of timber in the area. Grandin purchased 50,000 acres of forested land, then built a sawmill along with a railroad to haul the wood to Wilkesboro. The Watauga and Yadkin River Railroad also carried passengers. Grandin's plan called for extension of the line to Lenoir where he could deliver both people and wood for the growing local furniture industry.[348]

Grandin started his operation about ten years before the nuptials of Ed and Satie. While the trees were plentiful and the first leg of the rail line was being established, old timers in the area warned Grandin that the upper Yadkin River was subject to flooding and placing a rail line along its banks might be unwise. The Pennsylvanian scoffed that he could "stop the waters with the heel of his boot" and went forward with construction. He completed the line to Wilkesboro by 1912. Four years later, he paid the price. The summer of 1916 brought rains that massively flooded the entire area, washing away Grandin's rail line, but not his hopes. He vowed to rebuild, but a smaller flood in 1918 dashed his capital, as well as his ambition. During the heyday of the town of Grandin, Satie Hunt was a resident and caught the eye of Tom's younger brother.[349]

Ed Broyhill knew of Hartley Hunt before he knew that Mr. Hunt had an eligible daughter. As a teen, Ed hauled wood for the Grandin operation, then worked as a barber, a sideline job while at Appalachian. Ed Broyhill gave Hartley Hunt one of the best shaves in his life while hearing that Hunt planned to send his oldest daughter to Appalachian. There, Ed began to court Satie. Through college and his war service, they kindled a relationship that culminated with their exchange of vows at Lenoir's First Baptist Church.[350]

The role of a younger brother joining a furniture operation might have been a footnote in Broyhill family history, except for the fact that Ed had ambitions and talents that his older brother Tom could only admire. As Ed's grandson characterized it, "my grandfather had the ability to promote and sell which my Uncle Tom did not have." Five years after his marriage and seven after coming to work at Lenoir Furniture, Ed made a fateful decision. He settled on a plan to start his own company.[351]

With the one-hundred-fifty dollar per month salary he now earned at Lenoir Furniture and selling insurance on the side, Ed Broyhill amassed enough capital to start the Lenoir Chair Company. He also "mortgaged his house for $5,000" to fund the operation. His idea was to supply chairs for Lenoir Furniture. The move accidentally coincided with the fire at the Bernhardt plant that produced chairs, so Ed Broyhill's timing was inadvertent but opportune.[352]

Lenoir Chair began in the basement of Ed Broyhill's home on East College Avenue in Lenoir, the one he mortgaged to start the company. He intended to set up upholstery operations there, but when an old buggy shop next to the Carolina and Northwestern Railroad depot became available, Ed switched production to the new site, renting the space for fifteen dollars per month. Within six months, he was expanding in both square footage and personnel.[353]

The new company started as a complement to Tom's, not a competitor. It helped that the two men were brothers. Since each was making something that paired with the other, both companies promoted the same product. Ed sold Tom's case goods, while Tom's sales force offered Ed's upholstery. According to family member William Stevens in his landmark book, *Anvil of Adversity: Biography of a Furniture Pioneer*, the relationship between the older Tom Broyhill and his younger brother was very close, lacking any hint of competition or suspicion. Ed Broyhill remembered their 35-year business relationship existed "without a cross word" between them. Observer Ted Broyhill, Tom's son, characterized them as "the greatest team I have ever known. They worked together like two greased bearings."[354]

The name Lenoir Chair was already familiar to the community of furniture makers in the town from which it got its name. Less than two years before Ed Broyhill started his company, S.S. Jennings sold Lenoir Chair Manufacturing Company to the Robbins Brothers, Dr. C.L. and R.C. They preferred the name Hibriten Furniture Company. The Robbins sought to shift the plant "from the manufacture of chairs to the manufacture of case goods." At the time, R.C. Robbins was already the head of Star Furniture in Lenoir. With the old company chartered under the new name, "Lenoir Chair" as a moniker became available. Even with some financial investment from Tom Broyhill and Emory McCall (a friend of Ed's), Lenoir Chair Company remained undercapitalized in its infancy. Ed and a few loyal employees worked twelve-hour days to fill orders and seek new ones the best they could.[355]

In just over a year, Ed Broyhill expanded his company and influence. He added "98,000 square feet of floor space," building a two-story addition to a factory he had purchased. Ed was quoted as saying the space was "necessary to balance all departments of the manufacturing plant to bring production up to standard." In his facility, Ed continued to make "a line of overstuffed living room furniture (upholstery) and odd chairs" while conceding that the additional space would be utilized when growth allowed "an increase in the production of the plant." Orders came quickly. By the end of its first year,

The output of Lenoir Chair under the leadership of J.E. Broyhill quickly outgrew his basement. When this old blacksmith's shop along the railroad line in Lenoir became available, Broyhill rented it and moved in. The location housed offices and factory with an expansion. (Courtesy of the Caldwell Heritage Museum)

the company "did between $150,000 and $200,000 worth of business," as Ed himself remembered. Also, because of his demonstrated sales ability, Ed "controlled the sales force" for Tom's company too.[356]

Ed Broyhill possessed a multitude of strengths. He worked hard, inspiring the loyalty of those who worked with and for him. He recognized talent in others. He remained even-tempered in stressful times. He was a quick study but always willing to consider advice, especially from his bother Tom. But perhaps his greatest attribute was his technique with customers. Until he started his own company, Ed drove sales for Tom's Lenoir Furniture Corporation as sales manager, doing most of the selling himself. His ability was quantifiable in the volume of business his fledgling Lenoir Chair conducted from the start. Remembering the rise of Lenoir Chair, Ed remarked "the next year we did a good deal better and in 1929 we did better still."[357]

In his later years, Ed Broyhill passed down a few stories of those early days to his grandson and namesake, Edgar Broyhill II, with whom he had grown extremely close. The younger Ed recalled his grandfather telling him about "an epiphany" he had during those first years as a salesman.

"He walked into a downtown Detroit retailer and asked to meet the owner. And when he met him, the man looked at him and my grandfather of course had a Southern accent. He made fun of granddad's accent. They looked at

my grandfather's design and said, 'how does a Southerner country boy from Appalachia know a damn thing about what sells here in Detroit? There's nothing here I want to buy.' And so he rejected and turned my grandfather away.

"From what he told me, he was very depressed, enough so that he stopped for the day and took a tour of Henry Ford's automobile factory. He saw how Ford was making cars with an assembly line. He was at the end of his rope, but he said, 'I can do that. I can make furniture like that.' So he had an epiphany.

"The next day, he walked back over to that retail store and asked for the owner. The man said, 'I thought I told you yesterday, there's nothing you can sell me?' My grandfather said, 'I have another proposition that I'm sure that you'll take.' So the man asked him what it was. Grandad said, 'show me the best-selling dining room suite you have here in your retail store.' He showed him what was in the window. My grandfather said to him, 'If I make that collection, and it looks exactly like that, will you buy a carload of it, which was a train car at half price?' The man said, 'If you can make that to my satisfaction, to look just like that, I'll buy five carloads.'

"So my granddad borrowed the collection. He didn't have enough money to even buy the furniture collection. He sent it back to Lenoir with the train with him. He threw away his designs when he left the store, and he got up with his people in Lenoir and told them what they needed to do. To basically Xerox (copy) this and to make it exactly like this, and that they had to sell it at half price.

"He had some ingenious people in the furniture factory in that day. A man who specifically comes to mind was Clarence Beach. He truly was my grandfather's right-hand guy. My grandfather was a promoter and the salesman, and Clarence Beach knew how to make it. He knew how to get blue collar folks to work for him and work overtime. Henceforth, when Broyhill began to grow, it was always based upon the assembly line that Clarence Beach played a role in *designing.*

"When it came to presenting a product to a retailer, the idea was you've got to sell a carload, you don't sell onesies and twosies. You will sell them anything they want. Broyhill was known for variety. When you went into a furniture showroom, that was a Broyhill showroom, whether it be in San Francisco, Atlanta, New York, Chicago, or Lenoir. You would see acres of furniture with a variety of price points. It would be designs from French to contemporary and it would always be either a knockoff or a lookalike, to whatever the best sellers were in America. So that led of course then, to being able to satisfy the needs of larger merchants. That was the bottom line and it all came from that trip in Detroit. And I think every business man who's successful, at one time or another, has an epiphany, and that makes change."[358]

The Detroit encounter revolutionized Ed Broyhill's entire factory. Once he installed an "overhead monorail finishing conveyer," productivity increased, and he could claim one of the first streamlined furniture manufacturing facilities in the South. In his eyes, failure opened the door for success. As a result, the pivotal encounter became the point where Ed stepped out from his brother's shadow and into his own destiny as a leader in the furniture industry. The story also reflects a belief that Ed related to his grandson more succinctly. "Change only occurs when there is a crisis," Ed told his namesake. As the younger Ed Broyhill explained, "he wanted you to experience failure" for the wisdom it taught. Tenacity, humility, and a competitiveness that forces ingenuity were all lessons that Ed Broyhill learned in Detroit. As he built his company during turbulent times ahead, he would draw upon each one of those tools.[359]

The 1920s came to a spectacular close in Lenoir, not with the oncoming of the Great Depression but instead with the sale of one giant furniture manufacturer to another. George F. Harper had been right alongside his father, Major G.W.F. Harper, when the family took over Lenoir's first factory.

However, G.F. was much more interested in banking than manufacturing. He continued to have a hard time finding the right person to take over Harper Furniture. World War I compounded those problems. Before the war, G.F. looked to his son, James C. Harper or perhaps his nephew, James A. Marshall, to step up as the next generation's furniture leaders. When the call for troops came in the spring of 1917, Marshall and the younger Harper enlisted, taking them from Lenoir to the battlefields of France. Both survived the war and returned to Lenoir in 1919. Ideally, G.F. Harper wanted his son to take over Harper Furniture, but James C., now known as Captain Harper from his wartime rank, had other ideas.[360]

Captain Harper loved music. When he came back to the United States, he took a job at a bank in New York, seemingly a good move for the use of the master's degree in business he received from the University of North Carolina before the war. Restless, he moved to Winston-Salem for a similar job with Wachovia. There he met his future wife, but Harper had a big problem. He hated working in business, which threatened his father's intentions. As Captain Harper later confided, "it soon became apparent that furniture manufacturing was just not my cup of tea." He gave it his best effort, moving back to Lenoir, and working at Harper Furniture. Recognizing the difficulty, Captain Harper noticed that "while my father was mechanically inclined, as are some of my children, I simply was not." Captain Harper escaped his dilemma temporarily by doing the thing he loved. He formed a jazz band, which ultimately compounded the problem. He discovered that he enjoyed music so much that he yearned to make it his life's work. When the band folded, he gave the instruments to Lenoir High School, offering to teach for free. The school took him up on the offer, and for a while, Captain Harper held down two jobs, director of the band and a part of the management team at Harper Furniture. Eventually, Captain Harper could no longer hide from a decision. He chose the band over furniture. Under his leadership the Lenoir

High Band rose to dizzying heights with one of the greatest high school band programs in the nation. Some graduates went on to music careers, others profoundly affected by the lessons they learned. From the 1920s until his retirement forty years later, Captain Harper conducted band concerts and parades all the way to Washington, DC. Without his son to take over, G.F. Harper opted to divest himself of his interest in furniture.[361]

It was no surprised that when Harper Furniture came up for sale, the Broyhill brothers were keenly interested. Up to that point, Tom and Ed operated their companies separately, but the purchase of G.F. Harper's factory would mark the first time the two enterprises officially joined forces in one company. James Marshall, who owned half of the old Harper organization, "remain(ed) with the factory under its new organization." In buying Harper, Tom and Ed Broyhill took over what had been Lenoir's first furniture factory, built 40 years earlier. G.F Harper and his father, the Major, had guided the original firm through ups and downs to create a stable company. The Broyhills took over that mantle, continuing to consolidate operations into what would eventually become a Broyhill empire.[362]

The team of Broyhill and Broyhill began to dominate. Like a passing of the baton from runner to runner, the twelve-year age difference in age between siblings may have held the key to their success. In 1926, the year Ed started his chair company, Tom's interest widened to include more sporting pursuits. That was the year he built Lenoir's first and only golf course. Due to a heart condition, Tom began to slow down just as Ed was speeding up. With Tom's experience and their trust in one another, the combination accelerated their mutual goals. The duo was adept and diversified enough to handle the opportunities that would surely come their way as hard-working businessmen, each mindful of the strengths of their own operations as well as their collective synergy.[363]

In the public's mind, they were already one company. A year after the

Harper purchase, an article lumped them together as the "Broyhill interests." In totem, they employed over 600 people and made furniture for almost every room in the house (except bathrooms and kitchens). Bedroom, dining room, living room, as well as desks and secretaries, were all produced by the Broyhills in one factory or another. By that point, the industry was beginning to recognize the contribution of western North Carolina to furniture production with the Broyhills leading the way. "The furniture industry is at the very heart of the trend of industry at large to move southward, and the North Carolina factories represent the nucleus of development yet undreamed of, according to national prophets," proclaimed the *Charlotte Observer*.[364]

The prosperity of the twenties gave companies a wider market and more sales, along with time to build their efforts into stable, profitable firms. They were now strong enough to weather tragedies like fires that destroyed factories and lives. With some consolidation, manufacturers grew larger and found that they could compete effectively in a national market. While they rivaled each other for purchase orders, they occasionally cooperated when the situation was right. In Lenoir, furniture had become a family affair with the arrival of the Broyhill brothers and the second generation of Bernhardts and Harpers (including James Marshall and J. Harper Beall), even if Captain Harper chose to bow out. Down on the shop floor, younger brothers and sons followed their elders into jobs that offered gainful employment, creating ties to each other and the wood they worked. Their identity expanded to the point that the companies themselves became siblings, a kinship of operations, where each knew the other well. They shared the same forests, the same styles, and sometimes even the same workers. Together, they proclaimed themselves a force to be reckoned with in the making and selling of furniture.

Hauling chairs in the early motorized days for a local market. Henry Murdock delivered as many as he could pack for Troutman Chair Company, a small community in southern Iredell County, just south of Statesville. (From the Statesville Photographic Collection. Courtesy of Steve Hill)

Chapter 15
The Western North Carolina Furniture Club

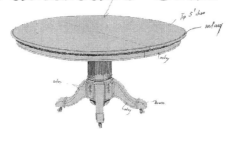

--- ✦ ---

Hold Furniture Exposition, High Point in June

"*The board of directors of the Southern Furniture Exposition building met at High Point last week and voted to hold a furniture exposition in High Point from June 20 to July 2. The exposition is expected to attract buyers from all sections of the United States. The exposition will be held in the new ten-story building now being erected. It will mark the first time in history of High Point that such an exposition was held there.*"[365]

--- ✦ ---

The notice in the *Lenoir News-Topic* cast a shadow that furniture manufacturers in the western part of the state would always live under. High Point, along with its own circle of cities, formed the counterpart to Hickory/Morganton/Lenoir/Marion (with Statesville the connecting portion of the figure eight) as enclaves of furniture making in North Carolina. The move in 1921 to establish a showcase event for manufacturers was indeed a step forward. High Point took the lead as the city where the most furniture was being produced. The precedent however, forever set the two regions in opposition, as the cities of the west were regarded as subordinate in the eyes of the nation seeking to

227

define a center for North Carolina's woodworking industry.

Still, the exposition was a boon to western North Carolina manufacturers. By 1923, Drexel had sold all of its inventory and did not show a single sample in High Point. Company officials were too busy with expansion plans to bother. Meanwhile, enterprises in Hickory, Marion, Lenoir, and Morganton exhibited with abandon. Martin Furniture in Hickory presented a line of dining room furniture with a finish that was "two-tone walnut and mahogany, in different patterns." Conscious of the buying market the set was categorized to be "in a medium priced" range. Hickory Furniture complemented Martin's offering with "medium and high grade bedroom furniture," featuring finishes in "walnut, mahogany, ivory and French gray." Hickory Chair offered "a line of dining and bedroom chairs, with tapestry and leather bottoms," while Statesville's Imperial Furniture displayed "a splendid line of bedroom furniture" including "suite No. 115, a handsome duo-tone four-piece suite which is one of the company's most popular numbers."[366]

If a 'rising tide floats all boats,' the western manufacturing circle benefitted from the High Point trade fair. Lenoir men like J.M. Bernhardt, Tom Broyhill, and G.F. Harper (the Major's son) voted for the exposition. They, along with their counterparts, had been looking for ten years to attract national notice of their factory output. While each may not have been enthusiastic about showrooms so far from their own plants, they were excited to sell their lines closer to home than other market shows. The new venue meant "southern furniture was being shipped northward, reversing a flow of a century or more." Additionally, a furniture market in High Point took some of the air out of Chicago, the nation's established showplace for display.[367]

Along with the larger family firms came a spate of smaller ones. Family ties like those in Lenoir were also consequential to the south of Caldwell County where a transportation company germinated a spinoff. The lineage of Southern Furniture Company began with the Bolick Buggy Works in

Conover, a small Catawba County town to the east of Hickory on the railroad line. In the early 1880s, Jerome Bolick developed his skills as a wheelwright to create what was described as a "perfect steel-spring wheel." The design proved to be sturdy and more comfortable than its competition, allowing Bolick to specialize in building buggies to transport people in the days before the advent of motorized transportation. Bolick gained four patents as he honed his reinvention of the wheel to the point that one day Henry Ford came to Conover. He purchased the Bolick "steel wire hub with spoke wheels" for the Ford Motor Company's 1928 Model A, a noteworthy day in the history of Catawba County.[368]

One aspect of buggy making was the upholstered seating, which son Oscar W. Bolick specialized in, building them for his father's product. By the 1920s, the buggy company transitioned into making frames for motorized buses and trucks. With other sons to carry on the buggy works in a mechanized world, Oscar's interest did not follow the new direction of the company and in 1926, adjacent to the family factory, he began Southern Furniture Company. One observation said that diversification of the Bolick family from "buggies and busses to upholstery and casegoods was a fluid one." Originally dwarfed by the family's larger transportation business, Oscar started "in a 50x60-foot corrugated metal building with two employees," Bruce Bost Burris (grandfather of future furniture entrepreneur G. Leroy Lail) and Hubert Dellinger. The early days of Southern Furniture were simple in offerings too. The company only made a "two-piece living room suite" for customers to purchase. Oscar's son, named Jerome for his grandfather, eventually took over the company. He told of how his father, along with Burris and Dellinger would "make a couple pieces of furniture and then go out and sell them in the community. Then they would come back and make a couple more."[369]

Southern Furniture expanded slowly, from humble beginnings, but up the railroad line in Morganton, Drexel experienced dramatic growth. The

When Jerome Bolick's son Oscar learned the skill of upholstering seats for Bolick's buggy works, it was the genesis to his entry into the world of furniture making. Southern Furniture began in 1928 adjacent to this workshop, even bigger than the manufactory it came from.(Author's collection)

company never abandoned the town it created that also carried its name, but when the time came to build a new factory, it looked to the city it had once shunned for a spot."Plant No. 3, Located at Morganton, is Now in Operation," read the headline announcing the creation of another factory under the Drexel banner, this one strictly for the production of dining room furniture. Like many an expansion, Drexel did not build from the ground up. Instead, they enlarged the old Morganton Manufacturing and Trading Company's facility. The new factory measured three hundred feet long and boasted of "the raw material starting at one end and coming out at the other as a finished project." The improved facility needed 150 men to run it and was touted as the "big thing for Morganton, adding much to the industrial life of the town."[370]

The boom of the 1920s did not anticipate the bust of the 1930s. When it came, companies would have to deal with the downturn, but while the sun shone on the advent of mass consumerization, collars both blue and white vowed to labor in the service of turning trees into seating and storage comfort for the home. News filled the papers (as well as countless speculations between businessmen) that creating furniture could pay. Southeast of Hickory in the Catawba County seat of Newton, a new factory joined an old one. Newton already had a cotton mill, but as the future looked toward lumber to the north, investors recognized an opportunity. "We are delighted to carry the news that about $120,000 has been subscribed for a new furniture factory in the town of Newton - and if more money is needed, the men who are interested have it and will put it into business to make it go," extolled the *Catawba News-Enterprise.* "The stockholders met at the courthouse yesterday and authorized W.C. Feimster and W.B. Gaither to prepare the charter. The name of the new corporation will be the Newton Furniture Company." Capitalization was always a bragging point with ventures, a signifier of just how big the plans of the creators were. With ready capital of $120,000, Feimster and Gaither let the region know they meant business.[371]

Every bit as grand as the Newton operation in terms of output was a plan to launch a new table factory in Hickory. The High Point salesman duo of J.W. Yeager and his younger brother Mason put forth a plan to amass $125,000 in capital to build the company just east of Hickory in the Highland section, a community that would soon be annexed as part of greater Hickory. Located in proximity to Hickory's other furniture-producing companies like Hickory Chair and the Highland Cordage Company, the Yeager Brothers gained the attention (and the backing) of such experienced manufacturers as Southern Desk's George F. Ivey. The board of directors included town merchants George Bisanar, L.F. Abernethy, and George Lyerly. They planned to produce as many as 400 tables per week with a workforce of 35-40 men. The Yeager Manufacturing Company offered one product, advertising that "we specialize in popular priced oak extension tables," 'popular priced' being a euphemism for cheaper. After some weather delays, the company was up and running by April, with equipment bought from a failed attempt just up the road in Granite Falls. By the following year, the company had expanded its capacity and was displaying its output at the High Point Furniture Exposition. Within five years, Yeager tables were sold in "nearly every state in the Union." The original 15,000 square feet of factory space expanded to 85,000 in that same period. According to one press account, "the manufacture of every piece is supervised by Mr. J.W. Yeager or Mr. Mason Yeager, and nothing is allowed to leave the plant that is not one hundred per cent perfect in every detail."[372]

One of Hickory's biggest and most memorable events of 1923 concerned Hickory Chair. Just before midnight on June 25, fire broke out. The Hickory Fire Department rushed to the scene and placed five streams of water on the blaze, which took three freight cars of finished furniture as part of a total loss of "around $125,000." No cause of the fire was determined, but the work of the firemen, concentrating on saving the machine room, proved to be "effective work." The effort served as a start for Hickory Chair's resurrection.[373]

The 200 workers thrown out of a job by the mishap were soon recalled. The company grabbed every spare space it could to continue filling orders. Within two months, manager George Bailey supervised the clearing of debris, the rebuilding of the factory (with an extra fire wall), and pulled back together his workforce, which had been scattered in "at least four different buildings since the fire." The new Hickory Chair included a "large electric generator and (a) unit drive system" to power machinery, which was intended to make the shop floor less vulnerable to a blaze. It was hard to say which event was more spectacular, the fire that destroyed a large portion of Hickory Chair or the frenzy of activity that got the company back on its feet in such short order.[374]

Two and a half years later, Hickory Chair's neighbor, Martin Furniture, met the same calamity. Its finishing and shipping rooms were also destroyed. Efforts to save the Martin factory were hampered by sub-zero temperatures in the waning days of December that caused the water needed to subdue the inferno to freeze until the fire was in full flame. "Nearly 200 finished suites were destroyed" in the morning event that saw firefighters put out a "slight blaze" on the first floor, unaware that a larger catastrophe was growing on the second. When the fire department returned, the entire wooden structure was engulfed in flames. Again, following the model of Hickory Chair, Martin vowed to rebuild. The decision wasn't as independent as it might seem since George Hutton and K.C. Menzies headed both companies. It took Martin just over two months to return to full production, another speedy rebuild.[375]

Like the return of Hickory Chair and Martin Furniture, factories started popping up regularly. In 1924, W.C. Feimster (who previously invested in Newton Furniture) started Maiden Chair, in the town 10 miles south of Newton. Touted to be Catawba County's largest factory for making furniture outside of Hickory, the company suffered the same ups and downs as other companies. Taking over an older factory, the payroll grew to 120 within a year, as the shop turned out 1,000 chairs per day. Floor space grew to 65,000 square feet to accommodate expansion. One unique aspect of Maiden Chair was the way the firm treated its employees. Annually, between Christmas and New Years' Eve, management threw a big party for workers, offering them a banquet with entertainment and recognition for everyone. The gathering at City Hall in Maiden was so big that local ministers were also invited to attend.[376]

Those were the ups. The downs came in a variety of ways. Just over a month after the stock market crash, Maiden Chair was being auctioned off. The twelve-acre site was under receivership with enticements of sprinklers, "modern machinery," and predictions that the "plant has capacity of approximately one million dollars annually." Along with the location of the factory along the rail line, the workers (even though they were presumably out of a job) were hailed right along with the equipment as an asset. "Abundant supply of good labor" read the auction announcement as a lure for prospective buyers.[377]

Indeed, the facility returned from its shutdown to produce more furniture. Under the name of its previous plant manager, the J. Smith Campbell Furniture company cranked up operations again. Unfortunately, in the summer of 1932, the entire factory burned to the ground, a loss estimated at over $200,000. Campbell had only $35,000 to cover the total loss. Once again, the workforce estimated somewhere between 100 (working at the time) and 250 (full capacity) was thrown out of a job.[378]

For a third time, Maiden Chair came back. Several lawsuits, however, irrevocably did the company in. The thrust of the legal action was unclear, but according to press reports, there were many "judgements rendered against Maiden Chair company, et. al.," some dating back to the time of the first shutdown. Before its last breath, Maiden Chair had competed successfully with a town known more for its cotton mills as "one of the largest manufacturing concerns in the town of Maiden."[379]

Just before the onslaught of the Great Depression, manufacturers realized their commonality and organized. They called themselves The Western North Carolina Furniture Club and met regularly in the cities where their factories were located. Members included company heads from

The gathering of workers at Maiden Chair. The company started a decade earlier only to be hampered by a bankruptcy, a fire, and lawsuits. When times were good, employees were treated to annual banquets. (Image courtesy of the Historical Association of Catawba County

as far away as Waynesville (west of Asheville) with discussions including items and obstacles common to their concerns. At one meeting in March of 1929, "around forty" members sat through a formal program, as well as "freely discussed" problems they encountered. Though they competed with each other for customers, the gathering showed them also to be cooperative.[380]

The coalitions they put together had an impact on the business as a whole. The western club joined a fight by the Southern Furniture Manufacturers Association, headed by F.H. Coffey of Lenoir, to challenge another association on the way hardwood was classified. The National Hardwood Lumber Association "proposed to change the grades on hardwood lumber." The result would have been an additional "$6 a thousand on the price of all hardwood lumber that goes into the manufacture of furniture." Coffey, along with W.A. Thomas of Statesville and J.R. Blair of Thomasville, trekked to Chicago for the lumber association's annual meeting. There, they made their case. In a vote so tight that it had to be counted twice, the two associations agreed the hike was out of line, saving southern furniture makers "$75,000 per month on hardwood lumber purchases," a demonstration of just how much wood was needed in the growing factories of the South, as well as the growing clout of leaders like Finley Coffey.[381]

Since companies around the region often faced the same problems, the shop talk in which the club engaged served as a 'think tank' for solutions. One prominent example centered around "safety standards." Leadership could not always agree on how to deal with employees hurt on the job. Together, they sought the help of North Carolina's government to set a benchmark for dealing with accidents. The group welcomed clarifying regulations to guide their actions following injuries on the shop floor. Since other states (like Tennessee and Georgia) had such laws, the western furniture companies believed North Carolina needed to define what was "just and fair to all concerned" when an incapacitating event occurred. Firms welcomed a law to which they could point as a way to overcome "discord and unrest" that sometimes popped up when workers felt the company was insensitive to mishaps. A statute made plain what should and should not be done when injuries took place on the job.[382]

The Western North Carolina Furniture Club did a good job of working closely together. Some said too close. Across the country, several companies were accused of price-fixing. In 1927, the federal government charged "72 furniture manufacturing concerns and 57 individuals" with violating federal anti-trust laws for "fixing and maintaining prices for bedroom furniture." In the action, no North Carolina companies were named, showing the conversations at the club did not reach the level of collusion in the foothills[383].

F.H. Coffey was very active in industry associations of the 1920s. In addition to his leadership of the Western North Carolina Furniture Club, his participation in the Southern Furniture Manufacturers Association (SFMA) helped local companies combat a number of issues that confronted them all. When "the high prices of plate glass and mirrors" aroused the concern of furniture makers, it was Coffey who brought the issue to the attention of the SMFA, seeking an investigation. He joined a committee to study the idea of the "state A. and E. (agriculture and engineering) College (N.C. State), to investigate the feasibility of establishing a "furniture department" on campus. Coffey liked the idea of educating the next generation of management. "It was thought that an educated boy or man," in the increasingly complex industry, "could take hold of a department and make a success of it, whereas at present an employe(e) has to work from the bottom up to a certain place of responsibility."[384]

Just before the Depression, F.H. Coffey was interviewed about his business. "What of the furniture trade?" the reporter asked in 1929. Coffey believed that the industry had "undergone a revolution in the last five years," as he described it from his perch as a company owner. Coffey believed the focus of buyers had shifted from price to design, a step up for furniture makers looking to elevate their reputation in the national market. Referring to his and his colleagues' firms, Coffey said, "they would buy the most wood and glass for the least price." He argued that the emphasis had changed. He contended that "quality and style and individuality are what sell furniture. Price is secondary." The demand required "modern machinery," Coffey declared, unwilling to concede that tough times might be ahead for Kent-Coffey and all of his fellow furniture firms.

F.H. Coffey made his remarks just a month after the stock market's first announcement of the Great Depression, Black Tuesday (October 29, 1929). While historians regard the day as the trumpet that sounded the coming of the Great Depression, most point out that the drop did not cause the economic calamity. It had been brewing for some time. Despite the sentiment, Coffey remained bullish. Strangely, during the interview a rather ironic mishap took place. One reporter chronicled, "as Mr. Coffey was talking, the back panel of a chair in which he was sitting slipped out and fell on the floor." The manufacturing boss picked up the wood, "examined it carefully and then with a dexterity foreign to the average man put it back in the chair." When complimented on what he knew about the construction of a chair, he "smiled." It's hard to say what spoke louder, the chair coming apart as an example of the furniture made in western North Carolina or the metaphor of the crumbling chair as a sign of things to come. One might also read meaning into the pragmatic confidence of a furniture maker simply using his know-how to rebuild whatever was broken as a bulwark against the bad times on the horizon.[385]

A reason for Finley Coffey's optimism was his faith in technology. One machine, in particular, he felt, heralded the future direction of furniture production. Components were arranged so that when a skilled craftsman carved "one post, there are nineteen others carved just like it. This is a mass

Though Dr. A.A. Kent and Finley Coffey began as partners, as president of Kent-Coffey Furniture, F.H. Coffey charted the firm's direction. He crusaded for his own company and fellow manufacturers, representing them in industry organizations. (Courtesy of the Caldwell Heritage Museum)

production of high-grade hand-carved stuff, and what becomes profitable in lots of twenty would be unprofitable if done one at a time." If machinery like the one the head of Kent-Coffey furniture described could extend the labor force twentyfold, he felt success was guaranteed.[386]

The Roaring Twenties were a heady time for furniture making in the area. The advent of a mass culture, offering advertising opportunities through national magazines and the new medium of commercial radio meant word could spread the names of furniture makers rapidly. Falling farm prices continued to force workers into the factories, which itself generated customers with money in their pockets at the end of every week to buy furniture for their homes. The growth of western North Carolina furniture had been steady, expanding to the point of seeing the entire community of working men join in for substantial, collective output. Would they be able to sustain the advance in the coming decade once the crushing economic downturn reared its ugly head? The strength of the industry's foundation in the foothills and mountains of the Tarheel state would be tested, with ultimately an answer revealed.

Chapter 16
Borax and Depression

---❈---

The tumult of the Great Depression was not good for any business, but western North Carolina furniture makers made the best of it. Despite the downturn, Ed Broyhill asserted "our sales increased every year during the 1930s." One reason was the type of furniture he and his fellow factory owners offered. In a word, it was "borax." The term referred to the type of pieces sold. Like calling lines "promotional," Borax was code for inexpensive furniture, characterized as "cheap, flashy and poorly made," and described as "bulging with waterfalls, swirling with synthetic inlays, slopped up with shading and gopped up with gingerbread hardware." Some critics described the pieces as "cheap, poorly constructed southern case goods." In many respects, these overly ornate copies of more expensive furniture were made for the times. With a quarter of the nation's workforce unemployed, those who still had jobs needed furniture they could afford, so the price of the product found a waiting market.[387]

Southern manufacturers took a lot of abuse about their offerings. Maybe the most insulting joke that illustrated the low esteem felt for borax furniture concerned a furniture store dealer who wired the factory with a question. "Bedroom suite just arrived, but don't know whether to set up the suite or the crate. Advise." A wry response instructed, "Set 'em both up, put 'em in your window and reorder whichever one sells."[388]

Another story about the reputation of furniture makers in the western end of the state involved a purchase made by a woman from Hickory. She reportedly bought furniture from the Sears and Roebuck catalog. When it arrived direct from the manufacturer, she was appalled to discover that it had been made in her hometown. She would not accept the delivery. Responding, "I ordered it from Sears, not you," she refused the furniture because she believed that locally produced merchandise was inferior. As it turned out, she would rather have nothing than the products her neighbors were crafting in local shops.[389]

According to one furniture expert, the term borax gained currency in the Depression to describe the cheapest of cheap furniture. The use of the term began with another consumer product, seemingly unrelated to home furnishings. Borax was a type of laundry detergent and included within the box were coupons redeemable for furniture, thus the association. "Inferior wood" like poplar or gum was often painted to disguise the shoddiness of a finished piece. Knowing what they were offering, manufacturers used a router "to produce an engraved appearance." Sometimes a layer of veneer was also applied to conceal deficiencies.[390]

Retailers tried to make the purchase of borax furniture easy. Consumers who didn't get their furniture with soap coupons had another option. Some were so poor they would have to buy even cheap furniture on credit, using an "installment plan." If those schemes weren't enough to move pieces, some retailers tried sleight-of-hand methods called 'bait and switch' schemes. Unsuspecting customers were lured into shops with advertisements for "ridiculously low priced" furniture that had just coincidentally sold out.

They would then be offered substitutes, i.e., cheap lines at higher prices.[391]

The slur rankled some furniture industry veterans of the era, but they knew that at least a portion of the reputation was true. Ralph Bowman, retired president of Hickory Chair, once conceded, "a bedroom suite then (1924), like most of the small furniture stores sold was made out of gum and poplar lumber and, if it lasted ten years, that was doing well. If you happened to drop a chest or a large dresser it would just about collapse." Bowman admitted that "the predominant thought across the nation was that the South produced lower grade furniture than the established factories in Michigan, New England, Pennsylvania and other areas of the country." The stigma dogged western North Carolina companies for decades.[392]

Some of the criticism stemmed from a general attitude about the South held by the rest of the nation. The stereotype of the lazy hillbilly extended to their work. The choice to make furniture that drew the borax epithet actually rested with management, who decided upon the styles to be produced. As far back as 1909, the *Southern Furniture Journal* reported that "the labor available, as a general proposition in the South, is not equal to the production of higher grades of furniture," a rather unfair characterization of the skills of southerners. The view of the time was that companies producing the best (and most expensive pieces) were located above the Mason-Dixon Line and crafted by immigrant labor from Europe, another stereotype.[393]

In fairness, one of the major factors in the cost/value relationship of furniture made in western North Carolina had nothing to do with the workers, the styles, or even the wood used. Exorbitantly high railroad transportation costs drove up the price to the point that many customers felt the product was "unreasonably priced for its quality." Since the early part of the century, freight rates for products coming out of the South were excessive. Try as they might, furniture companies could not persuade the Interstate Commerce Commission (ICC) to recognize the situation. Not until the creation of an alternative transportation method with the advent of trucking in the early 1930s did the ICC relent. By then, the reputation of many southern furniture companies and the workers who made the goods had already been ruined.[394]

Some companies did employ a tactic that would be used much later with devastating effect, which was with the offshoring that would eventually take place. Both Drexel and Caldwell Furniture worked around the high shipping rates by sending unassembled pieces as far away as Kansas for final construction. Rates in the north were lower, and even though it meant that components had to be shipped twice before reaching a final destination, "companies enjoyed considerable savings" compared to them being hauled from Drexel or Lenoir in completed form. For the first time, furniture carrying the name of a western North Carolina manufacturer but (partially) made elsewhere would be a company strategy in the effort to economize.[395]

Some dealers tried to counteract the connotation of shoddiness by asserting, "Good Furniture is Not Expensive Furniture," suggesting that price

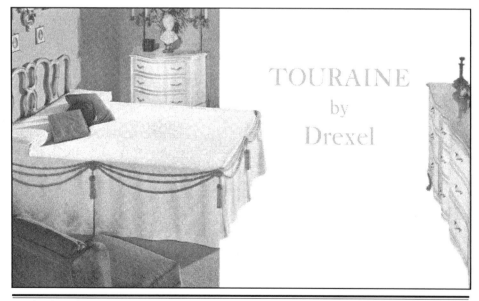

A brochure for a new Depression-era line that challenged the borax label given to many southern manufacturers. The 1930s saw Drexel successfully upscale its products and its reputation as a maker of fine furniture. (Courtesy of the Hickory Landmarks Society)

did not determine quality. The argument did not gain currency in the 1920s, but when the economy tumbled, cheaper furniture quickly became popular as families tightened their belts during the Great Depression. The strategy almost guaranteed sales, thus Ed Broyhill's claim of profitability during the 1930s. Most companies followed the trend, selling what they could at whatever price point the consumer would buy. A firm that diverted from the plan would either find a new, underserved market or go bankrupt.[396]

Amid the "schmaltzy plunder" of standard furniture offerings of the 1930s, Drexel made a counterintuitive decision. The company revamped its lines, moving into a "simply detailed, tastefully designed French Provincial suite in a grade of cabinetry heretofore unknown in the South." The new style was named *Touraine* and it was soon augmented by another grouping called *Travis Court*, described as an "18th century mahogany series and one of the first truly complete ensembles ever shown on a retail furniture floor." In the midst of the Great Depression, Drexel went against the grain, anticipating a return to prosperity. The effort made Drexel a furniture-producing innovator, which was exceedingly risky for such economic times. In addition, Drexel even added another feature that further upped the ante. The Burke County company was now designing compatible furniture lines not to complete just one room but an entire coordinated home. *Wishmaker House* offered a way for "even the most inexperienced decorator" to "plan her own home decorations with assurance of complete harmony with every combination." The idea "got underway slowly, but eventually became the selling sensation of the industry." While still in the South, Drexel hiked its reputation to compete with its northern counterparts.[397]

The rest of the western North Carolina furniture makers continued to churn out the same kind of furniture they had all along, selling as much of it as the financial downturn allowed. The example of Hibriten Furniture, organized in 1930 from the merger of Star Furniture and Stubbs Veneer, demonstrated the need to consolidate where possible to assure survival. When the *Lenoir News-Topic* touted Hibriten's owner, R.C. Robbins as "one of Lenoir's oldest and most experienced furniture men," it was lauding a person who had weathered the early days of the industry to create a solid company. Robbins and his brother navigated uncertainty with Stubbs and Star, craftily weaving them together for maximum efficiency and consistent output. They knew that, even in hard times, there was money to be made selling consumers what they could afford. The Robbins brothers survived the Depression with moderately priced lines. During World War II, they would go on to also take over Jennings Furniture, gathering them all under the banner of Hibriten Chair. The move demonstrated that unprofitable enterprises could improve under the right management making the right product. [398]

The Robbins brothers were an unlikely pair in the furniture business. While both were born in Caldwell County, R.C. (Robey Columbus) graduated from Mendota College in Illinois. Eight years after graduation, he served as its dean for another six years before returning to Lenoir. C.L. (Colbert Leroy) began his career as a dentist with a degree from the University of Maryland before getting into furniture. He also served on the Lenoir City Council. The Robbins brothers, unprepared though they were for the world of business (given their previous careers), nonetheless found making inexpensive furniture as a better path to success than dentistry and academia. The Great Depression gave them a market of buyers looking for cheaper home furnishing alternatives. [399]

When FDR initiated programs under the New Deal banner to cope with the Depression, he attempted to standardize the workforce by "installing the 44-hour week with a minimum wage of $12 (per week)." Instantly, eleven of Lenoir's furniture companies signed on. A coalition that included every furniture company in town sent a telegram. They wired Washington D.C. that, "effective August 1, the entire furniture industry of Lenoir, employing approximately 2,500 men will begin operating, at the request of the President, under the industrial recovery agreement." Many factory owners grumbled behind closed doors that FDR was ballooning their labor costs. With times tight and orders hard to come by, paying workers more put an additional squeeze on their bottom lines, which they felt threatened their very existence. However, none of them could afford to look unpatriotic during and at a time of severe economic crisis, their public faces grinned and bore the costs.[400]

A 'tightening of the belt' spurred by the Depression caused the three major companies in Hickory to join forces. Stockholders from Hickory Chair, Martin Furniture, and Hickory Furniture met on a Saturday afternoon in March of 1931 to vote on consolidating their efforts to get through the financial crisis. The vote culminated negotiations which had been going on for a while between the heads of each company. Since its earliest days at the turn of the century, Hickory and Martin made bedroom and dining room furniture to which Hickory Chair, the 1911 transplant operation from Elkin, added

During the Great Depression Hickory Chair consolidated with Martin and Hickory Furniture to form a single company. These workers were from the Sewing Room, photographed in August, 1935. The boss of the crew was Spurgeon Phillips, who would go on to start his own company. (Courtesy of the Historical Association of Catawba County)

upholstery. All three companies came to a logical conclusion that the times called for working together more directly. The trio became one, now known as Hickory Chair Manufacturing Company. The move did indeed shepherd them through the New Deal era. Collectively, they survived the Depression, and kept the Hickory labor force on the job and off the bread lines. When World War II hit, they found themselves in a good position, ready to make whatever the war effort needed. Since the three businesses were located next to each other, along the railroad line in east Hickory, the 1931 merger made sense. Streamlining their operations with new "authorized capital stock of one million dollars," unification kept Hickory productive during the national economic calamity. Within a year of the merger, "approximately 150 men went back to work."[401]

The union of Hickory Furniture, Martin, and Hickory Chair might have been a cozier arrangement than the circumstances of the Great Depression would indicate. Furniture historian John Bray, in his research of the merger, revealed a common management group and ownership between the three companies. On the board of directors for each were the Hutton brothers, A.B. and G. Norman, as well as K.C. Menzies, who was "president of all three firms" at the time of the convergence. Certainly, the financial straits of the economy led to the move, but in no way were the three companies strangers to each other or driven only by necessity. Hickory Furniture and Martin began in the early days of the 20th century with a complementary relationship. So too was Hickory Chair when it came to town. Their subsequent performance would validate the combination as a prudent measure to take. Since they were located next door to each other, and each made items in tandem with their neighbor's product, the three were as well suited for consolidation as any ever in the history of the western end of the furniture business. By previous design, they were a perfect combination, especially once hard times hit.[402]

Though the Depression might seem like the worst moment to expand a furniture company, the timing proved right for Hickory's H.D. Fry, Sr. In the 1920s, he had been "a farmer, a justice of the peace and a small-time furniture maker who built piano stools and parlor chairs in his barn." Realizing that the nearby railroad was his avenue to customers, Fry traded "a portion of his apple-tree orchard for a building he would use to manufacture quality furniture." Sending "a line of boudoir chairs" to brokers and department stores in the "northeast," his company, Hickory-Fry, grew steadily and solidly each year, eventually allowing his son and daughter to take over in the post-WWII era. Certainly, the Depression reduced the volume that companies had done in the Roaring Twenties, but as Fry proved, a quality product always had an opportunity to find a market.[403]

The fragile economy caused a variety of companies to come and go. While Statesville Chair reported "running full time with a full force of men that includes an increased number over last year (1930)," a host of other companies failed. They were either sold or slipped into receivership. Statesville's K & L

Ed Broyhill added to the blacksmith shop, creating a factory complex that expanded during the Great Depression. The operation eventually included factories in Catawba and McDowell Counties. This shop, in Lenoir, remained the center of Lenoir Chair for many years. (Courtesy of the Caldwell Heritage Museum)

Panel Company took over the defunct Kincaid Veneer Plant in 1930, only to struggle for a decade before also going under. From company to company, the managers who succeeded and those who didn't possessed many of the same skills. The difference was the calculations each made in determining how much furniture they should produce against the labor and material savings of cutting back. They all hustled to find markets for their products, but often success went to the ones who were lucky enough to attract customers and develop distribution networks that could move their products without overextending themselves.[404]

After the stock market crash of October 1929, the Great Depression emerged, reducing business and increasing inventory. The downturn inspired merchandisers in the Tarheel state to swing into action to combat lowering sales, thus helping the manufacturers. Efird's Department Store in Charlotte staged a "Made-In-Carolinas Sales Exposition" in February 1930. All the major producers (except Drexel) brought their lines to showcase Carolina workmanship. The exposition took its cue from the governor of North Carolina, who initiated a "program of 'living at home'," which included the admonition that "all Carolina homes should be completely furnished with products of Carolina manufacturers."[405]

Every promotion of the day attempted to bolster orders and keep factories operating. All the while, management simultaneously sought to economize, looking for more efficient ways to make each piece. No one was more aware of his company's bottom line than Ed Broyhill. In establishing his chair works, the younger Broyhill brother was nimble and always looking for ways to improve operations, which sometimes required expansion. Just after he started his own upholstery company, Broyhill rented a space across the street to build frames, then went in with his brother Tom to purchase Harper Furniture. When the full force of an economic slowdown swept the country, Ed Broyhill grappled with ideas of growth, now exponentially riskier than they had been a decade before. During the Twenties, everyone, it seemed was getting into furniture. Unfortunately, not all worked out. The Catawba County investors who had started the Newton Furniture Company with much fanfare, were casualties. Just before Ed decided to go into business for himself, Newton Furniture broke ground on an entire complex of four buildings near the Southern Railway line. Sadly, bankruptcy closed the factory, and fire finished off any intent of reopening.[406]

The loss of the Newton Furniture Company promised gain for Ed Broyhill. In 1932, he sought to expand outside of Caldwell County, wanting to buy the Newton plant, which totaled 50,000 square feet of factory space. Inducing his brother Tom and a few others to make the $12,500 purchase, fellow investors expected to flip the property at some profit. Ed wanted instead to start the facility back up. His vision was to follow the pattern of the former operators, making "a low-priced line of bedroom furniture." In the middle of an economic slowdown, the younger Broyhill saw the new line as "compatible" with the "medium-priced range" output that Ed was selling everywhere he went.[407]

Once again, Ed Broyhill employed an exceptional sales ability, along with an entrepreneurial spirit to envision where he could expand his operation. However, he confided to his son-in-law that the capacity to convince others did not come naturally. He remembered how "it took a considerable amount of bucking up my courage for me to go in and make a sales call, particularly a cold call." Several factors helped Ed. Though "naturally shy," he was always a hard worker. For a time when he needed capital for his company, he sold insurance on the side. More than anything, he believed in his product. He worked long hours, and was always serious about the furniture business. Perhaps those he met could sense the earnestness with which he presented his products, just like with the reluctant Detroit retailer, who initially spurned Ed Broyhill's sales pitch. To a great extent, he cracked the code on selling. Much of Ed's success came from his tenacity in showing up, thinking on his feet, and forcing himself to ask for the order.[408]

Since his days in brother Tom's company, Ed traveled extensively. His wife Satie Broyhill lamented, "so many times I watched him back out of the driveway and wave good-bye for a week or two or three at a time." With his own company he had the latitude to hire salesmen to do the selling for him, although he still went on the road regularly. He immediately built a sales force that could promote his wares and drive production back in Lenoir. Now he turned his attention to selling Tom on the idea of branching out in an unpredictable economy. In his vision for the Newton plant, Ed played salesman to Tom, trying to get his older brother to see the potential.[409]

It took almost two years, but the patient and persistent sales pitch worked. In January 1935, Ed convinced his fellow investors to restart the Newton operation as Lenoir Chair No. 2. With it, the Broyhill interests stepped outside Caldwell County for the first time, finding serviceable facilities to build more so they could sell more. It would not be their last such move. Seven years later, Ed negotiated a plan to buy not one but two more defunct plants. In Conover, next to Newton and Marion, old factories took on a new name, Broyhill.[410]

Ed Broyhill gambled and bet on his ability to sell furniture in bad times. During the Great Depression his grandson described him differently, joking that his grandfather became a 'counterfeiter'. During all the expansion, there were times when cash flow got tight. At that point, all Ed had was the good name of Broyhill to draw upon to get him over the next hump. When he couldn't meet payroll, he issued a form of IOU. According to grandson Ed, "he printed it up to look like a dollar bill. It was small, it was scrip." Knowing that his employees would spend their money around town, Ed went to the merchants and offered to redeem his promissory notes at the end of the month. "He was actually serving as the federal reserve, the local federal reserve, issuing

250

currency," said Ed's grandson. "In this day and time, that would be illegal," but it worked for Ed Broyhill.[411]

The Broyhill name was rock solid in Lenoir. If not, Ed would never have gotten away with issuing his own money. People trusted Tom and Ed to make good on their promises. Before and after the Depression, the Broyhill name was attached to a myriad of projects that benefitted the citizens of Lenoir. Tom Broyhill brought the first power plant to Lenoir, providing electricity to homes and businesses. The first generation of Broyhills were responsible for a number of civic improvements, including roads and pools, during times when no public funds were allocated to build such. The paternalism of the Broyhills and the tangible benefits they provided to the community brought respect, even reverence by the people of Lenoir including those who worked at a Broyhill plant as well as those who did not.[412]

Just before World War II, Ed and Tom Broyhill pooled their interests permanently, which had been intertwined for years. In 1941, six factories were merged into one company. The Broyhill Furniture Factories (later called Broyhill Furniture Industries) were established. In the late 1930s, a heart attack convinced 60-year-old Tom to consolidate the Broyhill names into one and let his younger brother take over. Tom's son Otis was also a part of the family business, and the convergence created an enormous company with operations from the piedmont to the mountains. The new company had a tremendous track record upon which to build. As William Stevens pointed out, "during the 1930's the Broyhill plants made an astonishing record. Despite the Depression, the group of companies not only showed a profit every year, but continued to grow in size." Much of that growth could be attributed to the vigor of Ed Broyhill.[413]

The Broyhills also collected and traded several outfits that were either bankrupt or ready to get out of the furniture business. By 1936, the Jonas conglomerate of furniture, glass, and mirrors had run its course. As was the case throughout the region, the adventure of the Twenties became the caution of the Thirties. Tom Broyhill found himself somewhere in between. As soon as he bought Jonas Furniture, he sold it to a former stockholder in his own company, Jack Galvin. Tom made a sizable profit on the deal, almost doubling his money, but Ed wanted to keep "the old Jonas plant." Unfortunately, Ed was out of the loop, in the hospital at the time for an appendectomy. Twenty years later, Ed paid a quarter of a million dollars for the Jonas factory in a bankruptcy sale.[414]

The economic downturn of the 1930s kept workers wondering if they could feed their families. Many companies shut down, which scared workers still on the job to remain where they were without making waves, no matter the working conditions, just to keep a paycheck coming. As Dorth Reichard remembered it, "not many people owned cars during the 20s and 30s." He and many of his fellow employees "had to walk several miles to hitch a ride." Dorth was lucky. Others had no ride whatsoever and walked all the way and back each day, a trip that could be "six or seven miles" each way. Then, they put in "9 or 10 hours on the job," five days a week. Fellow worker Lemuel McCall had much the same routine. He awoke early enough each morning to be on the job "at 7 a.m." He recalled that "sometimes we waded through snow over our boots and sometimes we had to go through mud that was almost up to our knees." What bothered Lemuel the most was never seeing sunshine during winter weeks. "It was dark when we walked home." Some got inventive. One co-worker hated to walk, so "he took to riding a mule to the shop." To keep his ride sheltered, the man "hauled some lumber and tin over there and built a shed to keep that mule in while he worked." Given the ethic of the time, he no doubt constructed the makeshift barn when he was not on the clock.[415]

Both Dorth Reichard and Lemuel McCall shared a positive opinion of their employers. Reichard recalled making only "20 to 30 cents an hour," but said when the company started to crawl out of the Great Depression and business got better, so did their wages. McCall pointed out that "the plant owners did show compassion toward employees who were seeing rough times," adding, "I feel like I was always treated pretty good." Sometimes that treatment included inviting preachers in to talk to them while they worked. McCall explained, "the factory owners were good Christian people who knew the value of having honest Christian employees," perhaps to help encourage workers on the straight-and-narrow, either as a caring act or a coercive technique, maybe some of both.

One thing the two old veterans of the shops, whose work life totaled a century, could agree upon was the quality of the furniture they made. Unwilling to accept the jokes about the borax furniture they supposedly churned out, both called the output "excellent." "A lot of the quality came from the fact that the same people were involved with the product from the forest to the shipping room," said Dorth Reichard. "And a lot of the quality came from a sense of pride each worker had in the piece he was building."[416]

One of them didn't make it through the Depression unscathed. During the 1930s, while Dorth Reichard was building a house for his family, he got laid off. "The shop didn't operate for 13 straight weeks," he remembered. Undeterred, he tightened his belt and struggled to get through it. One thing that helped him and many of his fellow workers was their experience in agriculture. "People knew how to farm back then," he said. So Dorth reverted to the way his ancestors had gotten along for centuries before the factories came. He lived off the land. Reichard recalled how "families pulled together and helped one another." Positive about the experience, he looked back on that time and said, "we shared and got by, and we were better for it. I guess it made us appreciate the blessings we did have."[417]

It took a national economic crisis to turn management and labor against each other. Unrest brought on by the Great Depression eventually spilled over into the furniture industry, creating a renewed opportunity for unionism, despite the fear of layoffs. After a mass meeting, three hundred workers walked off the shop floor of Caldwell Furniture demanding a "40-hour week and 40 cents per hour minimum pay." The company shut down the plant and at first refused to negotiate. Organizers claimed "that all but twenty-seven of the mill force are affiliated with the American Federation of Labor." Despite the initial deadlock, the two sides got busy and after two weeks, workers returned. The company called the resolution "very satisfactory to both parties." Management refused to say how the matter was handled, but obviously the leadership at Caldwell Furniture finally got serious at the bargaining table, enticing the return of its workforce while keeping the union from being recognized.[418]

Generally, an owner looked upon his workforce with a father's eye. Labor returned the favor, accepting whatever they got from their employer. Ralph Simmons remembered how approachable Jerome Bolick (son of the founder), the owner of Southern Furniture, was each time he had a problem. "I went to him numbers of times for something that I thought we needed or could use to do better, and he never anytime, ever let on as if he owned the place a bit more than I did," said Simmons about the owner. Likewise, Ralph Simmons never complained about his pay. He was philosophical about the fact that he never "got no big salary," believing that "if they had given me more, I might not have what I got." He reasoned that "I may have been careless with it. I got so little I had to be close." The cozy relationship didn't stop Simmons from employment elsewhere. When he worked at Southern Desk, Simmons enjoyed a bonus of one percent of his annual wages, which came to "right at two hundred dollars," he figured. During his time at Conover Furniture in the middle of the Great Depression, owner C.R. Brady would not deduct rent from Simmons pay (he lived in company housing), though his hours had been cut. Said the employee of his employer, "he was nice to us in that way."[419]

Some hands were even stoic about injuries. Frank Gilbert thought fellow worker Dewey Little was potentially careless when he got his hand cut off by a saw, saying the accident was "mostly his (Little's) fault." When he lost a portion of one finger in a joiner Gilbert admonished that "any machine is dangerous, if you don't watch it." The way Frank saw it, responsibility belonged to the operator, not the operation.[420]

Gifts from the owners to their workers became more common as time passed and relationships grew stronger. Christmas was a big season for giving, with baskets of hams, fruit, staples, even blankets and dinnerware sets handed out, in addition to cash bonuses. Some even got more special treatment. George Hall, the father of furniture in Hickory, reportedly paid for the wedding of Jim Jones, a ten-year employee of Hickory Furniture. A ceremony was held for the nuptials of Jones and his bride in "the grove in front of the Hickory Furniture Company." The gesture also spoke well of the racial climate of Hickory. Hall's paying for the ceremony of a black couple, showed that he, and others like him, appreciated workers for their loyalty, no matter what the Jim Crow era tried to impose.[421]

On occasion, the relationship between management and labor could get contentious. One man who worked for Martin Furniture quit over a cigarette break. It seems the hand went out to the lumberyard daily for a smoke during his break. A foreman informed the employee that he would have to put the cigarette out. Angered, the hand launched into a tirade, saying, "What time do you think a man is going to smoke? You don't get but one little break, then minutes to eat a sandwich and smoke a cigarette." Unmoved, the foreman replied, "Well, I can't help that. You ain't supposed to smoke out here." The rule stirred the employee's independent streak. He shot back, "I smoked when I wanted to before I come here, and if that's what it takes to hold a job, why I'll give it to you." Taking two of his friends with him, all three quit. They took their talents up the road to Hutton and Bourbonnais, where they got jobs immediately.[422]

Companies kept a careful eye on how far they could push the workforce in the effort of greater productivity. Efficiency experts were contracted to "help" employees maximize their energy during the workday. However, the laborers did not take kindly to the surveillance. In Lenoir, when Kent-Coffey tried "a wage incentive plan," workers walked out. Finley Coffey claimed his crew misunderstood the intention of the program. Leaders in the walkout sat down with H.C. Lucas, the efficiency expert known to them as a "minute man," to explain the program. Ralph Simmons worked as a foreman at Conover Furniture and noted that his company considered a similar plan only to scrap the proposal because "management had figured that it could cause more trouble than it was worth," just as it had at Kent-Coffey. Simmons defined a "minute man" as an observer who would "watch over you and time you to see how long it'd take to do a certain job." For many, the scrutiny felt like a devaluation to the status of a machine.[423]

At times during the Great Depression, it was the company at odds with the federal government. "Walker Lyerly, of the Hy-Lan Furniture Company, and E.M. Fennel of the Hickory Chair Manufacturing company" were part of a meeting of the Southern Furniture Manufacturing Association meeting in Winston-Salem that passed a "resolution opposing government regulation of business." At issue was a requirement that the company deduct social security taxes from employee paychecks, required by the new Social Security Act. When companies took their argument to court, they lost. The politics of the New Deal Era required employers to take the extra step of withholding earnings for retirement, just as they did for state and federal taxes.[424]

Employer/employee relations were often tenuous, but the economic downturn of the 1930s proved to be especially difficult times to navigate. It would seem to have been the wrong time for workers to strike for more money, but that's exactly what approximately 100 hands at Conover Furniture did in late May of 1933. With hard times being felt by all, workers refused an offer by C.R. Brady, owner of the company, for an increase, saying the raise was not enough. Conover Furniture was already in pseudo-bankruptcy when the strike occurred, operating "under a sort of receivership with agreement with creditors." Labor unrest did not help the situation, and though the walkout seemed counterintuitive, many workers felt their honor was at stake, which meant more to them than money.[425]

The Depression Era, with reduced factory output and constant job insecurity, altered the factory culture. Shorter hours and threats of layoffs loomed making workers careful about spending money, especially considering how hard it was to earn. Anywhere a few cents could be saved, workers thought the effort was worth it. Under those circumstances, Lucille Winkler and Jessie West seized opportunity. They assembled "discarded sheets of corrugated tin and used crating lumber salvaged from trash piles behind various factories, stores and warehouses" to build a makeshift restaurant. Known by workers as "the Stand," Winkler and West offered hot dogs at a nickel, "hamburgers a dime, sandwiches and cakes and pies, 5, 10, and 15 cents. Soda pop, tea, milk, and coffee were 5 cents, with unlimited refills on tea and coffee."[426]

For two decades after the Depression, "the Stand" remained a popular eatery for furniture workers. In the winter, a pot-belied stove heated workers; fans cooled them in summer. There was no dining room; the deal was grab-it-and-go. One intimate feature of the eatery was payment. They used only a cigar box since "there were very few cash transactions," remembered Jim Church, who, as a teenager, worked at the Stand. Owner Jessie West "would stand there with a tablet and pencil and as the customers walked by in single file, they would either pay her or tell her how much to charge to their accounts." The Stand became a popular hangout, sometimes a bit too inviting. The lumberyard foreman for Hibriten Furniture spent entire days overseeing his workers while jawing at the Stand's counter. Since the Stand was next door to the lumberyard, "on cold or rainy days," the foreman would "sit beside a window and sip hot coffee and laugh and joke with Aunt Lou and Jessie" while theoretically doing his job.[427]

The hard times of the Great Depression ended on December 7, 1941. That day the United States entered an even harder time when the Japanese attack at Pearl Harbor pulled the nation into an already raging world war. Like a generation earlier, men left their jobs to serve their country, leaving their wives and sweethearts, little brothers, actually anyone available, to fill in. Ironically, the tragedy of World War II brought back full production to the factories as the federal government geared up to fight. Wood became a war materiel, and orders put the industry on a full-time schedule once again.

The generosity offered by factory owners, especially at Christmas, was always a treat for the workers. During the Great Depression, the goodies were welcomed as many in the labor force experienced layoffs, and/ or shorter hours. Every worker worried about it happening to them. (From the Statesville Photographic Collection. Courtesy of Steve Hill)

Chapter 17
War Relieves Depression

Life in a furniture factory included a culture all its own. Practical jokes were rampant, and so were flirtations and romances. And like the Stand, so was food. Near every factory, restaurants and stores sold whatever workers needed at breaks (if they were quick enough to get there and back) and their half-hour lunches. With time at a premium, hands waited for the whistle like a starting gun to be the first to get in line for eats. While the fare was whatever the store or diner offered, many counted on soft drinks as a lunchtime pick-me-up. Caffeinated drinks became one of the little pleasures of life in which workers could regularly indulge. In the foothills, Sun Drop reigned as a primary choice. As historian Tom Hanchett suggested, it was no coincidence that caffeine drinks gained popularity in southern factories, saying "that machinery keeps at you." Employees needed to keep up.[428]

The lemon-lime taste of Sun Drop was a staple of the work day. Hailed to be "as refreshing as a cup of coffee," the drink was tailor-made for industrial workers. Coffee was too hot to be practical on a spring or summer day and was never packaged for easy consumption like a bottled drink. Both Coca-Cola and Pepsi had their devotees, but Sun Drop was unique, not found everywhere, and thus, special. During morning and afternoon breaks, some factories welcomed food trucks that were also called "dope wagons," offering a treat. Carbonated beverages like Sun Drops were called "dopes" because of the reputation of Coke, which at one point reportedly used cocaine as a stimulant. By the time workers began to swill down Sun Drop, caffeine had become the "kick" that gave workers more energy for their furniture-making duties. The textile industry also embraced soft drinks as a way to keep their hands alert on the job and was likely where the practice originated. In furniture, it was the same story. Between the sugar and caffeine in each bottle, the jolt kept the production line active for work as well as horseplay.[429]

Jokes, practical and otherwise, helped pass the day and assured the factory floor remained a lively place. Frowned upon by supervisors, mischievous workers looked for ways to tease their counterparts, often to the dismay of those being pranked. Cutting off the pants legs of someone on their birthday was a common occurrence, as was the usual everyday banter that included insults and razzing. New employees were the most vulnerable. If one let it be known that a taunt got under their skin, the jeers persisted until either the victim quit reacting or the jokers got tired of the gag and moved on.

When the war came, many left the factory floor with its jokes and light moments for more serious work, that of defending their country. Men, and some women, volunteered in unprecedented numbers following Pearl

A candid moment as employees leave their jobs for a break. Either a short respite at mid-morning, mid-afternoon or a half-hour lunch, workers created their own entertainment and drama on the shop floor, fueled by coffee and/or soft drinks that kept them going. (Courtesy of the Caldwell Heritage Museum)

Harbor. Those who were left made factory work something of a patriotic duty. Employees from both Broyhill and Drexel pledged to work overtime to raise funds for war related causes. Companies paid time and a half to workers, who then turned over their extra pay to the American Red Cross War Relief Fund. The push in early January 1942 centered around efforts to "celebrate" the Japanese new year. Combined, over 2000 workers raised $3250 in Marion for the cause in one week.[430]

With the progression of the war, more left for service, leaving substantial gaps in factory workforces. As with the First World War, women walked back onto the factory floor in large numbers to help out. The industry found time to evaluate the change in mid-1943 with a panel discussion at a state-wide industrial safety conference. Representatives from Drexel and Hickory Chair were among the companies that found "women workers are proving to be most capable" in their capacity as replacements for G.I.s.[431]

World War II brought the opposite problem furniture factories had experienced throughout the previous decade. No longer were orders scarce with an overabundance of labor. Now, both manpower and raw materials proved hard to come by, but demand flourished. Reported one paper, "the furniture factories are at full capacity for one shift of workers, with some overtime work being done." Otis Broyhill (son of Tom) who became president of the Marion operation, pointed out, "the difficulty in getting glue, hardware, and rubber used in the production of bedroom suites has forced the plant to operate on a 'hand to mouth' basis."[432]

The Allied War effort was just getting started when seven area furniture companies ruefully found themselves at odds with the federal government. The Elkins Act was an early twentieth-century Progressive reform that disallowed the use of rebates by railroad companies for hauling manufacturers' goods. No matter the volume a manufacturer consigned to a transportation company, and in those days it was mostly hauled by rail, companies could not negotiate for a better rate. Drexel, Bernhardt, Kent-Coffey, Morganton, Hibriten, and Lenoir Furniture skirted the rule, negotiating a better deal with the railroad. Along with the furniture makers, Southern Railway and the Carolina and Northwestern Railway lines were cited in charges filed in federal court. The prosecution stemmed from the companies paying for shorter boxcars while getting larger ones, thus allowing them to ship more, in this case twenty percent more. Fines for violations totaled $56,000, which all the companies paid without complaint. Similar to their public stand on paying workers during the Great Depression, manufacturers could ill afford to look unpatriotic during another time of national emergency.[433]

In Hickory, the combined Hickory Chair Manufacturing Company was also in trouble with the government. The National Labor Relations Board (NLRB) heard a case in March of 1942 brought by the American Federation of Labor (AFL). Three former employees contended Hickory Chair fired them because of their "union activities." The company appealed, alleging "there was not even any evidence to prove that anyone in a supervisory capacity connected with the Hickory Chair Manufacturing company knew of the existence of a labor union in their organization." After hearing the case, the NLRB sided with the union, ordering Hickory Chair to "stop discouraging membership in the A.F.L.'s Furniture Workers Local 869, United Brotherhood of Carpenters and Joiner of America, or any other labor organization of its employe(e)s." The company was ordered to reinstate the fired workers. They did, but the union never represented the employee base at Hickory Chair or any other company in the latest wave of unionism in western North Carolina, even after elections were held.[434]

The black eye of suppressing union activity at Hickory Chair was counterbalanced by its support of the war effort. Just a few months after the NLRB order, the company held an afternoon of speeches where the firm raised "a blue-and-white treasury Minute Man flag" over its facility, "signifying that 90 per cent of the 600 workers there are buying war bonds through the payroll savings plan." The show of support was not unusual. Many businesses were a part of community efforts to sell bonds to fund the war. Before the war was over, Hickory would conduct five successful drives. At the same time, Hickory Chair was also lauded for its participation in a "scrap metal campaign" that brought in over 20,000 pounds of scrap for the war effort.[435]

Not long after Hickory Chair clashed with unionization, the company that was part of consolidation in the early days of the Depression broke apart. Near the end of the war, a group headed by "Coleman Harris and associates of Cincinnati, Ohio," bought the chair manufacturing portion of the operation to augment output they were producing elsewhere. The purchase split up the once combined furniture companies of Hickory. In the deal Hickory Furniture was sold too, but the purchase proved too much for local folks to stomach. Two months after Harris' purchase, a group of local businessmen, including the mayor of Hickory, Walker Lyerly, bought the companies back, boasting "the plants will continue to operate exclusively with local employe(es) and local management."[436]

Joe Moretz was part of the team that put Hickory furniture manufacturing back in Hickory's hands. Told by Alex Shuford, Jr. that the "syndicate from Cincinnati" would sell, the local team pulled together several pots of money to buy and reestablish Hickory Chair and Hickory Manufacturing as a hometown concern. Moretz remembered the Cincinnati buyers coming down for negotiations. After dining at Hotel Hickory, talks got down to business the next day. When the deal making was done, Hickory Manufacturing sold for $200,000 while Hickory Chair went for $50,000.[437]

It was clear that local investors recognized the value of the production lines they built. Banking on the clamor for orders to keep factories humming, Hickory Chair filled the furniture needs of the United States Navy producing not only chairs but also cushions. The firm also shipped desks to the Treasury

Department and sold lumber intended for constructing truck bodies. Federal government orders rivaled the largest retail purchases during the war, which assured that lights on the factory floor would stay on, workers would continue to draw a paycheck, while companies returned their ledgers to the black.[438]

The war activity allowed several new furniture concerns to open their doors. Three men walked out of Hickory Chair, taking what they had learned with them, and started their own operation. Western Carolina Furniture debuted in 1942 with T.F. Digh, H.D. Rhoney, and J.S. Phillips as principle owners. Supposedly, the trio got the name from "the old outlaw textile league circuit," a baseball league that several of the founders had played in before the war. Among the important items the new company got from the old was contacts. Salesman Jack White knew who to approach at the Chicago American Furniture Mart to get Western Carolina's Early American line in front of the buying public.[439]

Hickory Chair served as an incubator for several enterprises beyond Western North Carolina Furniture. Builders of post-war companies like Sherrill Upholstery, North Hickory, Hickory Tavern, and others got their training at the established firm and then ventured out to start their own. Predominately, the new companies gravitated toward upholstery making. Little did they know it at the time, but their products were just what the nation's homeowners were looking for in the years after WWII. Across the tracks from Hickory Chair, at Hickory Manufacturing, Joe Moretz noticed an emerging trend. With the advent of television, Americans did away with their formal dining rooms in favor of television rooms, also called "rumpus rooms, game rooms or playrooms." To make space in existing homes, even some bedrooms were converted. With the shift, fewer dining suites were sold. Instead, families wanted cushioned seating to watch their favorite TV shows. As Moretz put it, "this was hard on case goods and a field day for upholstered furniture people." Either through vision or luck, the new, small ventures making sofas and chairs had the right furniture for the new world order.[440]

Retooling after the war presented a challenge for furniture makers in what was increasingly described as a modern lifestyle. When Joe Moretz and his fellow investors took over Hickory Manufacturing, they owned a factory in serious need of renovation. From old quirky boilers to overloaded power lines, the plant required an infusion of funds not seen since the days before the Great Depression. Joe Moretz went to work securing loans for the overhaul. He used the capital to implement a conveyor system on the rough end, reducing labor and speeding up production. The process assured boards were sawed quickly and were ready for the process of turning them into useable and attractive furniture. Through the 1940s, Hickory Manufacturing showed substantial profits, with 1948 a banner year, unmatched before or since. By the end of the 1950s, their fortunes withered. In 1961, post-war startup Maxwell-Royal Furniture pursued the Hickory Manufacturing site and paid half a million dollars to get it. All over the region, companies were either reaching new heights or falling to those who did.[441]

At the close of the Second World War the Broyhill family claimed not just a collection of factories but a furniture empire, enveloping Lenoir and many of the surrounding towns as well. Ed Broyhill and his nephew Otis (Tom's son) acknowledged that the number of factories owned by the family had grown to the point of confusion with "far too many names for the dealers to contend with." Instead of Lenoir Chair (1 and 2), Conover Furniture, Lenoir Furniture, Newton Furniture, and Otis L. Broyhill Furniture (in Marion), Ed and Otis agreed to "establish a selling agency for all six plants." The Broyhills had managed to come through the Great Depression and into the war years stronger than ever. Their timing matched perfectly with a return to prosperity brought on by the war and its aftermath. This resurgence catapulted Broyhill product into homes across the nation with dizzying speed. The ingenuity of the brothers along with a lot of hard work by both themselves and their team of employees earned Broyhill a spot at the head of the pack of North Carolina furniture producers.[442]

The combined enterprise placed Ed Broyhill at the center as president of the company. It was a grand undertaking for the younger Broyhill brother. In the twenty years he had been involved in furniture, Ed developed an unparalleled acumen for reading the market, then producing for it. Learning as he went, the man who "sold several (train) carloads of furniture from only a sketch" improvised when he had to, just like during the Depression when he had paid employees in scrip due to bank closures. Broyhill handled every curve ball thrown his way. By 1941, he had risen to the top and would stay there for the rest of his career. With plaudits galore, he was named "Furniture Man of the Year" by the American Furniture Mart right after the war ended.[443]

The war years proved to be a pivotal time for western manufacturers. In essence, it allowed the region's furniture makers a stage upon which to shine in the national crisis. Early on, as Britain and France fought Germany, the United States remained neutral but served as an "arsenal of democracy" for the Allies before joining the war effort directly. After coming through the turmoil of the nation's largest economic downturn, Hickory Chair bet that the wages gained by factory workers pumping out war materiel would be spent on designs that the ancestors of those workers would recognize. In 1941, the furniture maker sought to copy the furnishings of the founding fathers by licensing duplicates of furniture found in the old plantations around the colonial capital of Williamsburg, Virginia. Reproductions of 18th century pieces were called the *James River Collection*. Unfortunately, plans for the debut of the line were slowed by the nation's entry into the war, hampering a sales rebound. World War II also kept Hickory Chair from getting materials like mahogany, which delayed pieces rolling out of the factory until 1943 because of wartime restrictions. Even with the issues, those buying furniture in the war years appreciated a return to the classic early styling. The collection became a tremendous seller for Hickory Chair. Twenty years later, the company reissued the *James River Collection* again, demonstrating its enduring popularity. Other companies also prioritized their own *Early American* lines, a perennial seller.[444]

The war changed the products offered by companies, but it also altered the cultural dynamic of the factories for good. When women filled roles previously unavailable to them (except during World War I), they once again showed supervisors, to paraphrase the words of Rosie the Riveter, "they could do it." Women had worked clerical jobs in the factories since the early days, but necessity brought them to the shop floor, putting saws and varnish in their hands. The war allowed them to prove again that their labor was every bit as competent as any man. Women committed to doing their patriotic best, juggling child-rearing with factory hours. They also laid the groundwork for better times, stockpiling their wages so that upon the return of their husband's and the return to a peacetime economy, they could spend that money on bigger houses. Those homes that might even include some of the furniture they made. However, something curious occurred when the war ended. Unlike the days of 1919, women in great number stayed on the job, creating two income families throughout western North Carolina. With increased demand thanks to a robust post-war economy, companies kept many of them on.

In addition to office work, women had become skilled at just about all aspects of manufacturing. It was a steep learning curve for some like Ruth Church. She began her working career in 1942, when she got a job at Kent-Coffey Furniture in Lenoir. She was 16 years-old. Her first job was on the sanding line, but soon she found her specialty. "They brought us the backs," she recalled, referring to the board that covered the back side of "wardrobes, nightstands, dressers, everything." Her task required that she "put the nails in them and then, put them on the cases." The nightstands kept her the busiest because "they were fast." She remembered that she could keep up most of the time, but every now and then she would get behind, mostly because "the backs

Ruth Church during her days as a nail setter, applying backs to a variety of case goods. The work was challenging for the teenager, but with occasional help from male supervisors, she met the challenge of the production line ably. (Image courtesy of Ruth and Romey Church)

were heavy." One of her supervisors helped her catch up when a backlog piled up.[445]

By the time Ruth started in the early days of World War II, a job in furniture had become a family tradition. Her father worked for Kent-Coffey and asked if they had a place for his daughter. She remembered her days setting nails fondly but eventually quit and went to a hosiery mill. Of the two, she preferred furniture, saying, "I liked furniture better than I did stockings." Eventually, she went back, taking jobs at "Kincaid, Singer, Bernhardt, and then back to Singer." Her son continued the tradition, following his mother into the factory just as she had with her father.

Ruth Church's experience typifies the life that many women lived as contributors to the labor force. The bosses in her department were men. There was no real chance for advancement and she conceded that she did not expect any. Despite the lack of opportunity and the effort it took to try to keep up with the wardrobes and nightstands, Church enjoyed the work enough to be there every day. Remembering the pace that she had to keep, the diminutively sized woman said, "they came through there flying, but I was right there every day. I never laid out a day." Like her female coworkers, she felt adequately paid for her labor and reveled in being part of the factory world.

Women joined in the furniture industry but took a backseat to the men creating companies. Though they contributed mightily to the industry's development, news coverage of the day muted the role women played. Only occasionally would a woman have a larger impact. At age 16, Mary Miot Buys came to Lenoir to attend Davenport College. She traveled from Belhaven, in upper Cleveland County, to go to the all-female school. A poet by nature, Mary put forth her work in several contests and received honorable mentions mostly. One of her poems was printed in the pages of the *Asheville Citizen-Times*. It was called "Apparition."

"The golden flower, the moon, has gone, leaving my meadow bare,
Except for a few small shining stars to gather and put in my hair. Then
I'll wrap around me a soft trailing cloud and go to where you sleep.
I'll hope you'll awaken and think me fair
With my cloak that's a cloud and stars in my hair."

Mary Miot Buys
North Carolina"[446]

After graduating from Davenport in 1930, Mary stayed in Lenoir as an avid participant in the local social scene. She took part in the marriages of all her friends as the thirties progressed. In mid-decade, she landed "a responsible position" with Kent-Coffey Manufacturing as "secretary to the president." There she met a varnish salesman from Kentucky.[447]

Hamilton Bruce was just one of many who inundated decision makers at furniture factories across the region with a product they was sure the operation could not do without. Thirty-nine-year-old Ham, as he was nicknamed by friends, came to make his pitch. To company officials, he asserted that Reliance Varnish was superior to any other product being used by Kent-Coffey. If by some chance his varnish did not impress, he also represented Central Glass Company. Using every tool in his box, Ham Bruce finagled to get the executive in charge to agree with him so that he could write up an order.[448]

Once Ham met Mary, their lives and their names entwined. Ham came to Lenoir as a widower with two children. In his high school yearbook, classmates jokingly called Ham "Reverend" and described him as "a 'choice' actor who is in a 'class' by himself." It may have been theatre that drew Ham and Mary together. Miss Buys had acted in at least one production of the Lenoir Women's League before Ham got to town. Whatever the attraction, the two became an item. By August of 1942, the couple wed.[449]

Just over a year later, Ham and Mary embarked on yet another partnership. In an alley in downtown Lenoir, the couple rented factory space for $15 per month, hired a couple of workers, and started their own furniture company. They called their new enterprise Hammary, a convergence of their first names. Ham made the rounds selling while Mary ran the office as "secretary of the corporation," skills each developed in their previous occupations. The

Kent-Coffey operated at full scale during WWII, producing for both the consumer market and the military. It was at Kent-Coffey that Ruth Church began her career and salesman Hamilton Bruce met Mary Biot, the two joining in marriage, as well as a new company, Hammary. (Courtesy of the Caldwell Heritage Museum)

first product to carry the Hammary name was "canvas covered lawn chairs." Ham's goal was to produce 24 chairs per day.[450]

When the war ended, Hammary incorporated. By that point, the repertoire of products had expanded. With only $300 subscribed of a total of $100,000 authorized for the new corporation, Hammary planned "to manufacture and deal in chairs, toys, furniture and supplies for homes." The expansion showed how intent the couple was to be successful in the furniture business. Uncomfortable with relying on one item to make money, they searched for other wood products that diversified their little factory. In the post-war world, a new innovation in lawn furniture was the use of metal frames with webbing. Suddenly, the kind of "rockerless rocker" made by Hammary was out of style, so their nimbleness became an asset.[451]

Ham went on the road in late 1947 to present Hammary's newest creation, occasional tables. Heading to the "Eastern retail furniture outlets," he sold them on an idea. Either a testament to his salesmanship or his vision (probably both), potential buyers only saw sketches since his factory had not made one table at that point. Retailers bought, and Ham returned to Lenoir with enough confidence to invest in a twelve-acre site along the railroad tracks where he built his own grand factory to produce the tables he promised. Using mahogany and gum wood, Hammary crafted tops in both leather and mahogany originally, "shifting the next year to leather tops exclusively with all genuine Honduras mahogany." With Mary back in Lenoir to operate the factory and get the tables in production, Ham Bruce could exercise his gift as a salesman and designer to great effect and substantial profit.[452]

The boom spawned by the Second World War and the trajectory it set for post-war prosperity fit foothills furniture makers like a glove. The Great Depression had been hard on companies and their workforce. Plants that did not close still suffered the consequences of an economic slowdown. The best run of those firms hung on, some even growing, especially after wartime orders flowed. The furniture industry came out of the war era invigorated, ready to meet the demand of the veterans who were returning home. Those G.I.s came back eager to start families, who would need household furnishings. Broyhill, Bernhardt, Drexel, Hickory Chair and all the other firms aimed to supply them with whatever they wanted. In an ever widening variety of styles and price ranges, workers crafted pieces for those homes, fueling a substantial period of national prosperity which included furniture jobs for all.

Inside Kent-Coffey in Lenoir with a group of shop hands, around the same time as the latest edition of the Factory Whistle, the monthly bulletin. During World War II, the machines hummed as government contracts exceeded consumer demand for furniture made in the foothills. (Courtesy of the Caldwell Heritage Museum)

Chapter 18
Bright Spots and Bitter Battles

The Broyhill family had been preparing Ed's oldest son Paul for a life in the furniture industry since he was a boy. The waters were inviting. While Hamilton and Mary Bruce jumped in right before the conclusion of the Second World War, others waited, like Paul. Regardless, when they all took the plunge, it made quite a splash.

"I did not pick a very good time to enter the furniture business," said Paul Broyhill about his full entry into the family business in 1948. During World War II, factories hummed, making anything the war effort needed, then supplied returning servicemen with as much furniture as production allotments would allow. After the initial boom came another downturn. It was short but intense. Paul Broyhill called it a "severe readjustment period" when "production caught up with demand." The lag caused the Broyhill workforce of approximately 850 to work on a three-day week periodically, as warehouses bulged.[453]

The next generation of furniture men were entering the fray, and like the choices for consumers, business got crowded. Not only did the nation switch its buying habits from war to peacetime, which favored furniture, but a glut of young men were also looking for jobs to feed the new families. For a year and a half in the late forties, fortunes for furniture companies took a 180 degree turn. During the war, everything they cranked out sold. For a short period after initial demand was met, warehouses overflowed.

For Paul Broyhill, a career in furniture was pre-ordained. The first son of Ed Broyhill was expected to step into a leadership role and guide the company's future. His mother believed the family vacations marked him. In 1933, Ed Broyhill took his family to Chicago to see the World's Fair but also attended the semi-annual furniture market there, as he had been doing since it first opened in 1924. Satie Hunt Broyhill, the family matriarch, commented, "it was then that the boys (including his younger brother Jim) began getting some of the furniture business rubbed off on them." Paul was nine and enjoyed a playful repartee with the salesmen in Chicago.[454]

In the same way Ed Broyhill learned from his older brother Tom, Paul

The next generation of Broyhill leadership, Paul was the oldest son of Ed. He joined full time, right after publication of the June 1947 edition of the Broyhill Bugle, a monthly newsletter that kept employees informed on the all facets of the company and its workforce. (Courtesy of the Caldwell Heritage Museum)

would do so from his father. Call it a burgeoning "family tradition." When Paul, as a youngster, came to the company, he began part-time work at the shop with no specifically assigned job. The younger Broyhill was expected to observe as he learned all facets of the business, in some ways a parallel of how his father had been introduced to furniture production when he joined his big brother's operation. The process began in earnest when Paul was ten-years old. Licking stamps, stuffing envelopes, and running errands were all in a day's work. He even operated the company's telephone switchboard on occasion, explaining, "it was at this job that I got my first regular pay." His knowledge of the company deepened with every task he undertook.[455]

As he grew older, Paul gravitated to more manual jobs. The work of handling wood as it came into the lumberyard was so "backbreaking and grimy" that his mother made him eat lunch on the back porch when he came home at noon. The hard work prepared him to step into his father's shoes. Interrupted by a college education, which was interrupted by the war, Paul served in the U.S. Army before finishing a degree in business; he returned to Lenoir in late 1947. A few years after the first son's arrival at the family company came the second, when Paul's brother Jim joined the company in 1950. Jim stayed for a little over a decade until the lure of political office beckoned. In 1962, he won the first of 11 elections to the United States House of Representatives as a Republican in what became the 10th Congressional District, which included Lenoir.[456]

The world of furniture making in the western corridor was moving from its adolescence to adulthood with its new prominence as national best seller. Learning the practical aspects from his father, Paul Broyhill brought a more worldly awareness of trends and ideas, thanks partly to his education. Paul's brother-in-law Bill Stevens, part of the Broyhill management structure and enough of an observer to pen a history of the family's growing furniture empire, called Paul "not exactly a chip off the old block." Stevens characterized

Paul Broyhill as "an innovation all his own." Admiring him for his "cool, assured, in perfect self-control" demeanor, Stevens noted that Paul "made his presence known" in any room into which he walked, a persona that gave him all the command he needed to assume a leadership role at the family business. Within seven years of officially joining Broyhill Furniture Industries, Paul took on the role of general manager. He was president of the company within a dozen years and chairman of the board by the time he was 52.[457]

Americans who observed both world wars were ready to predict an economic boom coming out of the second one that would eclipse the first. While it took a few years for the country to recalibrate from wartime to peacetime footing after the boys came home from France the first time, a consumer culture the likes of which manufacturers had never seen, loomed as a salivating possibility. The aftermath of the second round of world war, by all measures, stood ready to welcome home soldiers, eager to marry and start a family with all the products they would ever need. With only an occasional hiccup, times were ripe for expansion.

On the heels of war's end, four Morganton businessmen decided to start their own furniture empire. Taking a page from Ham and Mary Bruce's nomenclature choice, they titled their new company Henredon (Hen-re-don), reflecting aspects of the names of the founders (though Sterling Collett seems to have been left out). T. Henry Wilson, Ralph Edwards, Donnell Van Noppen, and Sterling Collett had already begun construction of a factory in Morganton when they announced the new venture. Their goal was to begin shipping their "quality line of wooden furniture" by the spring of 1946. To do that, they envisioned a plant of 112,000 square feet that employed "approximately 300 persons." Henredon thought big. With a huge factory built using operating capital of $1million, the new company rivaled Drexel's operation, well above many of its competitors who formed around the same time.[458]

All four men had been "formerly connected with the Drexel Furniture

Company," and as refugees from Burke County's largest furniture maker, they looked to challenge the dominance that the Huffman family had established. Within two years, Henredon took its place alongside Drexel as a "nationally known manufacturer." Soon, the Henredon name began appearing in furniture store advertisements from New Jersey to California. Unwilling to start without experienced personnel, Henredon poached employees from other furniture companies, a common practice between shops. M.C. Talley was perhaps the most visible of new management to come to Morganton. He left Statesville Chair Company as superintendent to take an equivalent position with Henredon.[459]

The Henredon product line began small, but their approach to furniture production differed from any other in the western region. They built three different types of chests, insisting on quality over quantity. In fact, Henredon consciously did things differently than other manufacturers. The Morganton company teamed up with High Point's Heritage Furniture to jointly place advertisements for their lines. While western North Carolina ventures cooperated and displayed their wares at the High Point Exposition building every April and October, never had such a close relationship been forged between an eastern and western North Carolina enterprise. "The two companies have pooled their advertising appropriations," announced Elliott Wood, head of Heritage, a move that showcased the furniture lines of both companies in the pages of *Better Homes and Gardens* and *House Beautiful* magazines.[460]

Another way Henredon demonstrated its unique approach to marketing itself was in the selection of a woman, Helen Kelly, as its "merchandising coordinator." Miss Kelly handled the "joint-sales and advertising campaigns" for the two companies, the placement of which may have been her idea since she came from *House and Garden* magazine to take over advertising for Henredon. Her counterpart at Heritage was a man, but the move to value a female's

With the end of World War II came an influx of personalities to shape the business of furniture making. Helen Kelly was prominent for her plain-spoken assessment of southern furniture. She also advocated for the empowerment of women, since they were often making buying choices. (Image from the Charlotte Observer)

point of view about home furnishings was a remarkable break from accepted practice. In their selection of Helen Kelly, Henredon chose a juggernaut.[461]

Helen was brutally honest about the furniture business, and since she was a writer, she made her case in print. Soon after taking the position in Morganton, she penned an article that acknowledged and sought to break down stereotypes about furniture made below the Mason-Dixon Line, and about the South itself. Her approach might have raised the eyebrows of her employers, but she insisted on being blunt, writing, "we heard of Southern hospitality and famed Southern cooking and found food in southern restaurants and hotels the worst we'd ever tasted." Helen admitted that she was a newcomer to the region. She was "born and educated in the Midwest" but found her way South. She acknowledged her perception of the region to be "a contradictory phenomenon." Incendiary as her views may have sounded at first, there was method to her madness.

With an eye toward the national market, she called out the South as "a stage with a backdrop of beautiful women in romantic gowns, courtly gentlemen who played and worked hard, white pillared plantation houses, velvety green lawns, magnificent magnolia trees, and gardens riotous with color. Sharp and bitter against that backdrop set the shabby shanties which mark the North-South highways." She confessed to the national market that everything they heard about the South was true, both good and bad. Admitting the borax tradition of southern furniture, she agreed that "in the majority of Southern stores we found only the cheapest kind of bad design crowded together so closely that you couldn't see quite how bad it really was." Perhaps part of the reason she could get away with such criticism was the attitude of men at the time. Chivalry, an old, cherished southern trait, demanded that women were pedestalized and not subject to the same rebuke a man would receive for the those kinds of fighting words. However, since she was one of the first women to make such statements, her words carried a different weight than anyone before her. [462]

Accepting the reputation that furniture makers from the South would not be the first choice of those who saw their homes needing the finest, Kelly reached back for the image of an earlier South, using the Henredon line as an example. "But...there are bright spots, very bright spots that stand out like an oasis in the desert," she reported. Helen Kelly walked a fine line in her unvarnished but ingenious sales pitch. While touting the quality found in the furniture lines she promoted, she also was unwilling to price anyone out of the market, asserting Henredon-Heritage pieces were "furniture such as the Old South would have been proud to put in its great plantation houses, furniture within the budgets of the pretty brides and brides-to-be." While she was candid, she was not suicidal. Her critique offered her companies' lines as a solution to the gauche output she saw from other manufacturers.[463]

Specifically, Helen Kelly pinpointed her audience, the homemaker. Gender attitudes of the first half of the twentieth century meant that men still controlled the purse strings in households, even though women often made the choices of styles and patterns. It was true that many advertisements for furniture regularly used the feminine pronoun when talking about selection, but husbands determined what was purchased. As future retail entrepreneur Leroy Lail noted, "furniture follows fashion," and in the home, decor choices were generally conceded to women; that's why, beyond price, females controlled many buying decisions. Kelly recognized that fact, and her words served as a guide to women concerning their options, all the while assuring them that Henredon furniture would not cause conflict with their husbands, who only looked at the price tag. The settlement may not have been true, but it sounded good.[464]

Helen Kelly led the way in promoting furniture selection as a lifestyle choice. She made appearances as a "furniture expert," giving "home decorating fashion show" presentations entitled "Live As Well As You Look." Indications are that she did not stay long with Henredon, but during her tenure, she opened the door not only for Henredon's image to be considered tasteful above the others, but also for women to play an important part in how home furnishings should be marketed.[465]

The insular nature of the western North Carolina furniture fraternity was exposed by the arrival of Helen Kelly. Never before had an outsider joined a local firm and made such a name for herself and the company she represented. Her rise seemed almost accidental. In an article about her move, she admitted that in her first profession, as a teacher, she was "bored" and took a summer job with a department store. That's where she found out about salesmen who offered their wholesale goods to the store for retail sale. "I thought I wanted to be a buyer," she recalled, but quickly acknowledged, "it looked more glamorous than it really is."[466]

A department store worker with a college background was an oddity. During a coworker's lunch break in the furniture department, Helen Kelly took over, and "after a short time, he asked me to join his department," she said, referring to her male boss. She embraced the new horizon with verve, despite admitting that she knew "nothing about furniture, woods or fabrics, I

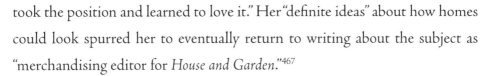

took the position and learned to love it." Her "definite ideas" about how homes could look spurred her to eventually return to writing about the subject as "merchandising editor for *House and Garden*."[467]

Never one to let her opinions go unvoiced, she became a spokesperson for the new age. "Despite the fact there is a lot of bad modern furniture," Helen told reporter Frances de Wolf, "it is time we turned from the 18th Century to 20th Century pieces," a shot at the mass of Early American lines rolling off assembly lines throughout North Carolina furniture factories. Her viewpoint was unrelenting, declaring that "our lives have changed. A truly creative person, you know, designs things for his time and life and people." She aimed to revolutionize what she might have called the dreary designs of furniture conceived by her predecessors into more vibrant choices, an alternative to the same old product put out by her heretofore, male colleagues.[468]

Despite her drubbing of what the furniture industry offered, Helen Kelly offered practical advice on how to make buying choices "for the housewife of today," a nod to the fact that she knew who really made decisions in the early post-war period. She advised that furniture buyers make two studies. First, home furnishing magazines, like her previous and future employer, was a good place to start. More importantly though was one's own household. She told women (and men too) to look for what would serve "the needs of each member of the family." She suggested buying "furniture which will do double duty, and which will make entertaining at home easy and enjoyable."[469]

Goading her colleagues toward breaking new ground in furniture design, Helen Kelly believed the time was right for taking southern furniture production to the next level. She asserted, "we have the top designers in the world which combined with our mechanical efficiency, and coupled with American know-how, should make us world leaders in the furniture field." The keen sense of style possessed by Helen Kelly created new possibilities for the western North Carolina furniture industry to become trendsetters for the coming, burgeoning market. Several manufacturers, like her own Henredon and Kent-Coffey jumped on the bandwagon of modernist designs. The field, however, had grown to such large proportions that there was room for a wide array of styles within the industry, something Kelly might call the good with the bad.[470]

The early post-war era also saw a whole new crop of traditionalists seeking to develop a proven style for those not as avant-garde as Helen Kelly. Lenoir's Joseph Wade Kincaid was born into the furniture industry. His father, George, hauled lumber as a young man, which was where he met J. Wade's mother. George went to work for Tom Broyhill's Caldwell Furniture, living near the plant when, in 1910, his first son, whom everyone called Wade, was born. George eventually became a foreman for Broyhill. Wade grew up, spending his years going to school for six months and working in the factory for six months. By the tenth grade, he went into the factory full time as a "drawer boy," which meant he would make drawers, then give them to case-fitters for inclusion into chests and dressers. As an ambitious young man, Wade left furniture for a time, opening a grocery store in Tennessee. He even began a "sideline" business of making "liver pudding," but he left those pursuits to return to the seemingly more stable furniture environment during the Depression, sometimes working under his father.[471]

After a plant fire in Mocksville left him jobless, Wade teamed up with the machine room foreman, the also unemployed Mutt Revis, to start building cedar chests in an old gas station. Wade bought a load of dried cedar and hauled it to Hudson, just south of Lenoir, and started his own factory. His father George matched Wade's investment of $4,900, and with a $200 contribution from his sister Ruth, the three began Kincaid Furniture Company. Cedar chests led to larger wardrobes, with a daily output of twenty per day.[472]

Two years into the business, fire swept through his shop, almost killing Wade. In the effort to save his business, he suffered "serious but not critical burns." The fire destroyed the plant and $5,000 of inventory. It only took firemen two hours to put out the blaze, but Wade was hospitalized for almost six months. During his convalescence, Wade's father found another building to rent on the site of Kincaid's factory, along the railroad line just north of Hudson, in Caldwell County. The family picked up the pieces and started again.[473]

One of the advantages the Kincaid family had was the uniqueness of their product. With the sales help of Adolph Frutchter in Philadelphia, cedar wardrobes proved popular with families living in old houses built with no closets. In those early days Wade called it "our best market." Other salesmen assisted the effort and with Wade's return and a new factory to build cedar chests and wardrobes, the company found a good niche. The firm remained small. In the summer, their workforce of about 25 or so would haul pieces outside to dry them in the sun. On one occasion, J.J. Miller stopped by to look. He offered to sell the drying output for them and became another salesman for the company.[474]

After a few years making cedar furniture, Wade was beckoned to Roanoke, Virginia. The owner of a retail store there wanted to see if Kincaid could duplicate a mahogany bedroom suite he owned. Intrigued, Wade went on the hunt for the wood, finding an ample supply that Drexel Furniture was willing to sell. Just like he had done earlier with cedar chests and wardrobes, Kincaid Furniture built to order, this time a 5-piece suite. For a year and a half, until the stacks of mahogany ran out, Wade and his workers cranked out approximately 2,000 sets. The move put the company into the business of bedroom furniture. Once the mahogany ran out, they transitioned to the use of pine and maple for their offerings.[475]

The salesman who brokered the mahogany deal for Wade Kincaid was Grover C. Robbins, Jr. The stacks of mahogany were thin, "3/4 to 5/8 inches in thickness," according to Wade, and thought worthless by Drexel. As

J. Wade Kincaid started out making cedar chests just after the war ended. Thirty years later his company had expanded to a sprawling complex along Highway 321-A, just south of Lenoir. At the top of the picture (along the rail line) is Hammary's factory campus, along with Singer. (Courtesy of the Caldwell Heritage Museum)

Wade said, "I got it awfully cheap." Grover Robbins demonstrated masterful skill in evaluating the lumber and handling the negotiations. Just a few years after his work with Kincaid Furniture, Grover and his brother Harry founded a novel tourist attraction, North Carolina's first theme park. The brothers brought back a steam engine to the mountains, one that had once regularly traveled from Boone to Johnson City, Tennessee. As young boys, the Robbins brothers had ridden that line. America's fascination with the Wild West in the 1950s, thanks to television and movies, prompted Grover and Harry Robbins to turn "Tweetsie," the noise made by the whistle of the East Tennessee and Western North Carolina Railroad, into an amusement park. The train ride took passengers through cowboy bandit, and Indian raids. Grover Robbins used the proceeds to develop two more tourist attractions, ski resorts in the western North Carolina mountains.[476]

For many, however a life in furniture proved irresistible. Like Wade

284

Kincaid's endeavor, the trend of starting a furniture company became a popular one in the post-World War II era. Roger B. Triplett created Blowing Rock Furniture in 1946, the same year that W.J. Spainhour got into the business with a furniture company that took his name. Consumers were already familiar with the family. Spainhour's Department Store sold women's clothing in several towns in western North Carolina, including Hickory and Lenoir. In twenty years, both would sell out to Magnavox, known for its manufacture of televisions.[477]

The times and the industry welcomed returning veterans too. A flood of men coming back to civilian life were expected to take up jobs at the factories after their discharge from active service. Just like the days following World War I, women who faithfully filled the slots and kept production going worried that they might be out of work if the male workforce returned with a vengeance. It did not work out that way. Some servicemen had bigger ideas than to come back as hourly workers, leaving spots for women who wanted to continue to draw a paycheck on their own. A new company that started in Statesville served as a good example of the boom. Captain Nathan McElwee and Major Addison Long got together to create Ross Furniture. The two grew up in Statesville, with Major Long receiving a degree from Davidson. Both the captain and the major joined the military before the war, Captain McElwee serving as an engineer in the Pacific Theatre for two years, while Major Long was part of the Ninth Air Force in Europe. No sooner had the new year of 1946 dawned than the two servicemen announced their intention to start "Ross Furniture Manufacturing Company, with Captain McElwee as president and Major Long as secretary." Both were investors in the new operation, along with the captain's father, Dr. Ross McElwee, a Statesville dentist and source of the new company's name.[478]

The biggest startup of the period was Century Furniture. The Shuford family had a long and influential history in Hickory. They owned the largest group of textile factories in Catawba and surrounding counties. It wasn't until Harley Shuford, Sr. bought out his brother's interests in a weaving plant did the move into furniture begin. After taking control of Valdese Weavers in the middle of the Depression, Shuford began to think about upholstery. With fabric scarce in the post-war world, he placed a portion of his output with several frame shops around Hickory. He then began "a furniture sales agency, which he called Century Furniture," according to his son Harley, Jr. The way it worked, Harley Shuford, Sr., bought the finished pieces from as many as a dozen small upholstery companies, created a showroom, and sold the finished products.[479]

In 1947, upholstered furniture using Valdese Weavers' fabric sold under the Century Furniture name. The pieces were popular and well received. Harley, Sr., became convinced that he could take over the entire chair making process in his own factory, adding case goods to the product line as well. Buying Longview Furniture Company in the nearby locale of the same name, Century began making its own upholstery. A year later, completed factory construction brought a branch of the Shuford family into the general furniture business.[480]

Even though the war had ended, government contracts were still a good source of revenue for furniture makers. In May 1949, Century landed an order from the "army's Chicago quartermaster" for "4,291 bureaus at $47.97 each; and 17,992 chiffoniers at $39.69 each." That same year Harley Shuford followed the Henredon-Heritage model by aligning with Morgan Furniture of Asheville. The partnership created a vice-president, shared by the two companies. The new VP, Leonard S. Walworth, "maintain(ed) headquarters in Chicago" as a representative for both companies.[481]

As lucrative as it might seem to make furniture for the federal government, Spainhour Furniture got burned over just such a contract. Before the Korean War, the federal government needed a lot of desks. Officials contracted Spainhour to provide them with 4,442 at $37.74 each.

The company went to work producing a sturdy desk made of knotty pine that could withstand daily use. The finish was extremely important as Spainhour experimented with coatings that "would not show anything less violent than a cigarette burn" to supply serviceable use.[482]

When the conflict in Korea broke out, "prices of lumber and other materials skyrocketed." Spainhour's management went back to the Army, explaining the situation and asking to renegotiate the price per desk at $55.87. The government refused. In typical bureaucratic fashion, the Army said, "it would get the desks from another company." They did so but paid for the privilege. In buying the additional desks, the federal government paid over $64 for them, $8 above Spainhour's revised price. It was bad enough for the Lenoir Furniture company to lose the contract, but to rub salt into the wound, the federal government sued Spainhour for the sum of $119,405, claiming breach of contract.[483]

A further irony to the impasse came with the Truman Administration. During World War II, Harry Truman made his name as a Missouri senator investigating and exposing government waste in factories across American that supplied war materiel to the government. In fact, many attribute his rise to the vice-presidency on those efforts. When Franklin Roosevelt died just a month into his fourth term and Truman became president in 1945, he vowed to continue the initiative to make common sense contracts between the government and small business. Spainhour Furniture fell into that category of a small American business.[484]

Numerous politicos recognized the unchecked bureaucracy of the Army's position. North Carolina's senate delegation introduced a bill to relieve Spainhour of the debt. "The bill states that the corporation was unable to complete i(t)s performance of the contract by reason of increased costs of production attributable to the enactment of the Fair Labor Standards Amendment in 1949," reported one newspaper. The legislation never saw passage. The court case did.[485]

Three years later, a hearing on the complaint was convened in federal court in Statesville. In their brief, the federal government pointed out that the first 1,875 desks were delivered. However, the contract had already been amended, "hiking cost per desk by $0.40." The "Quartermaster Purchasing Office, Department of the Army, Chicago, Ill.," the government entity seeking the desks, was forced to buy the remaining 3,020 desks from another Lenoir furniture manufacturer at an "additional cost of $80,875.60 and suffered 'liquidating' damages of $36,618.31," a reference to the delay incurred over the contract. While the company had insurance to cover a portion of the money sought (less than $40,000), Spainhour was on the hook for the rest. The jury returned a quick verdict, siding with the Army, saying "the government was entitled to recover the damages." Spainhour did not appeal the decision.[486]

The same year Spainhour received its contract, Century was awarded another order for a large job. The Army's quartermaster, the same one who sued Spainhour, announced contracts to purchase bureaus and chiffoniers from Century, a deal that totaled $928,163.91. Century fulfilled the order without incident, demonstrating better luck than Spainhour in supplying the United States Army.[487]

Meanwhile, Century was getting into other kinds of trouble with the government. The National Woodworkers of America union, affiliated with the Congress of Industrial Organizations (CIO), charged that Century fired one of its employees for organizing activity. As well as terminating the employment of O.J. Love, the union alleged "that the company in other ways interfered with the rights of its employees." The union also charged Hibriten Furniture in Lenoir with conducting similar practices.[488]

The moment looked ripe for unionization. The South had taken a giant step toward becoming an industrial region in the first half of the twentieth century. Furniture production was part of that movement, and with factory workers uniting came attempts at collective bargaining. The first unions established themselves in the Northeast before the Civil War when that region was the nation's only industrial sector. Organizers had long seen potential in filling their ranks below the Mason-Dixon line, but after the Second World War, opportunities looked especially promising. By then, the competition had developed for the organized southern worker. The American Federation of Labor (AFL) was the nation's oldest union, begun as a haven for skilled workers. During the Great Depression, though, some organizers wanted to throw a wider net over American labor. They broke from the AFL, organizing the CIO. Both groups wanted to represent southern furniture workers.

In unionizing efforts, the AFL came first. Trying to organize both the Drexel and Broyhill plants in Marion, union officials described opposition to their efforts as a "reign of terror." The Upholsterers International Union of America (affiliated with the AFL) petitioned for an election with the National Labor Relations Board at Broyhill. A late January 1950 vote swept the union into the Morgan Furniture Company at Woodfin, near Asheville, suggesting momentum for the Marion effort. In Woodfin, the two AFL unions fought each other for the right to take on factory management. The Upholsterers' International Union lost to the United Brotherhood of Carpenters and Joiners, 62-17. Only two employees voted "no union." Two months later, 75 workers walked off the job after contract negotiations broke down. The thirteen-day strike ended when both parties signed a new contract in Woodfin.[489]

The CIO began its campaign in furniture with a winning streak in other North Carolina industries. From fertilizer workers in Wilmington to a hardwood company in the state's northeast corner of Edenton, the union added 500 workers to its ranks with election outcomes. It sought to keep up its streak in furniture. The momentum ended when by a 2-1 margin employees at Galvin Furniture in Lenoir rejected the union in a National Labor Relations

Board-supervised election.[490]

The union movement had some currency in the Catawba Valley. The United Furniture Workers, another CIO backed union, filed a petition to allow "300 production and maintenance workers at Century Furniture" to vote on union representation. The CIO convinced some workers from Longview Furniture to go out on strike, even though the plant continued to operate. During the walkout, tensions rose to the point of violence. The local constable "arrested 12 persons on assault charges following a flare-up at the plant" in mid-November 1950. A few weeks later, Bill Cauble, Jr., a container sales rep, crossed the picket line as he entered the Longview plant. Warned that when he returned, "they would get him," three strikers followed Cauble's car to Century Furniture. Instead of being allowed to make his next call, the three attacked. Cauble sustained a gash to the head, severe enough to require stitches from the local hospital. The day after, a truck driver for the company threatened strikers with a gun (which was unloaded) if they did not let him pass through the picket line. Each side filed charges against the other for various types of threats.[491]

Petitions were filed to hold elections at a number of Hickory plants, including "Hyland Furniture company, Century Furniture company, Hutton and Bourbonnais (who made finished wood products for the home), Hickory Springs Manufacturing Company (a firm that made cushions and springs for upholstery), Longview Furniture company, Conover Furniture company," and a cabinet maker in Lenoir. With times as flush as they were and orders coming in regularly, union organizers acted as though they had management over a barrel, since operations could ill afford to slow down over labor disruptions.[492]

Intense campaigning and bitter battles marked the effort to organize furniture workers. In Hickory, in the fall of 1950, a national director in the CIO invited wood workers to the city's auditorium so he could explain the benefits of unionism. His remarks were bold as he informed his audience that employers had "bled their employe(e)s to the tune of $60,000,000 last year (1949)." He declared that workers could double their pay if they were union members. Another address on radio in Lenoir compared the pay of furniture workers in that town to other markets. By the estimate of Franz E. Daniel, the NC director of the CIO, wage rates were "about $172,000 a week under what they would be in other furniture centers. With published labor figures, Daniel told the local market what they were making, about "$39.60 for a 40-hour week," contrasted sharply with paychecks on the west coast, which totaled some $17 more per week for the same work. Union leaders also pointed out how unfair the harassment had been on the part of the companies to keep workers from organizing, with owners receiving no penalty for their behavior.[493]

When elections were held at area furniture plants, the union lost heavily. Despite the union funding last-minute appeals on local radio stations as employees headed to the plant for their vote, Southern Desk, the largest furniture employer in Hickory, emphatically withstood organizing attempts. Workers there rejected union representation by more than 2-1. The count at Hyland Furniture was even more decisive. In their tally, the margin was 3-1. Down in Newton at the Broyhill plant (Lenoir Chair No. 2), the margin was thinner, but the company still won, 132-91 (69%). When Hibriten Chair's Lenoir workforce decided, the "no" vote won with 64 percent of ballots cast.[494]

As unionism came and went, so did a gaggle of furniture companies. T.F. Digh carried his expertise from Western Carolina Furniture to the new enterprise of North Hickory Furniture in 1950. So did J. Spurgeon Phillips, a salesman who brought substantial business to the former company, along with H.D. Rhoney. In doing so, they partnered with Shorty Ennis (who started Ennis Chair Company in 1945) to create North Hickory Furniture. Even though it came after the wave of post-war unionism, North Hickory still had its own union fight. In the spring of 1966, by just 18 votes, the management of North Hickory Furniture survived an attempt by the Woodworkers of America, AFL-CIO, to represent the employees.[495]

The maturing of industrial furniture manufacturing was exhibiting growing pains. Bright, enterprising workers who felt they had more to contribute were restless. Some no longer felt they were getting an equitable share of the earnings for their contributions. Both management and labor liked the ride of an economic spurt that would keep both at their jobs full time for the next two decades but the relationship between white and blue collar workers frayed. The people who actually put their hands to the wood thought themselves underpaid, while a growing number of ambitious young men felt stagnated in the hierarchy of established companies, seeking instead to start their own. They were willing to accept the risk of going out on their own. As it had always been, time would validate the winners and force the losers into bankruptcy. These issues were the price western North Carolina paid for a maturing industrial community. Internally, they maneuvered to settle their differences while showing the buying public a different face, one that had come of age, ready to supply the world with what it needed to furnish the home.

Always a company to celebrate its history and its expansion, Drexel took the opportunity of its 50th anniversary to display growth. Factories in western NC were highlighted. The Marion plant was one of 5 Drexel operated at the time. (Courtesy of the McDowell County Public)

Chapter 19
Upholsterers and Upstarts

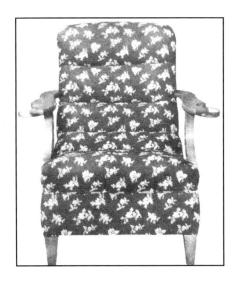

Upholsterers and the companies they created sprang up as quickly as the eight-way-hand-tie method they used for support springs in the product they made. Hickory Tavern in Conover (1955) and Bruington Furniture in Hickory (1958) were part of an explosion of companies that included J.R. Jones, Jr., president of the former and a vice-president in the latter. In addition to common leadership, not an uncommon occurrence in new firms, the fate of these two companies would be tied together even further when both were purchased in 1969 by the Lane Company of Altavista, Virginia. The same circumstance would also befall Hickory Chair. Lane's purchase of the two companies demonstrated the dicey nature of existence in the furniture business in the boom of the 1950s and 60s.[496]

At times, it seemed a scorecard was needed to track the number of

Chairs like this one from a manufacturers catalog were efficiently made by almost every furniture company in the region. In fact, many firms were started from humble beginnings making upholstered chairs, some in the shed behind a budding entrepreneurs house.. (Courtesy of Hickory Landmarks Society)

companies that came along, started by one ambitious individual or another. On the heels of World War II, Harvey and Robert LeFon joined with Joel Miller to create Hickory Cabinet and Furniture. Hoping to raise $100,000 to fund the company, they started with the smaller sum of $10,000. Ten years later, after the first venture folded, Harvey tried again, this time calling his company Crestline. He located in Hickory and named himself as president. Quickly, the grass appeared greener in Burke County. Harvey Lefon moved the operation to Valdese, a small town between Drexel and Hickory, but within two years, something soured. Lauded as a "veteran salesman," he quizzically took a step down to the role of sales manager and vice president before resigning in 1957. No reason was given for the split, but Harvey announced a plan to start yet another company after his departure.[497]

Like a growing family, one generation of furniture company set the stage for the next. As a salesman, designer or manager gained experience from their job, he (and almost exclusively, it was a 'he') often parlayed those lessons into his own enterprise. Joe Moretz took the experience he gained at Hickory Chair to the creation of Maxwell Royal Chair. Phil Bracewell learned the business as sales manager for Maxwell, carrying his expertise into the Haupt Furniture Company (1947), where it became Bracewell-Haupt in 1962. In reality it didn't take much in the way of financial backing to start an upholstery business. Custom Craft Furniture in Hickory started with just $300. So did Sherrill Upholstering.[498]

The parade of new companies was so plentiful that many began with no fanfare or even a written announcement and often closed with the same lack of notice. The name of these companies turned up in furniture store advertisements but little more. Firms like Hickory Tavern and Bruington, though they were established companies, still chose to remain obscure about their origins. To that list could be added King Hickory (1956), the ubiquitously named Quality Upholstery (1958), and Highland House (1959) in Hickory, plus Cutrite Furniture in Claremont. Among those companies that might have provided fascinating stories about their creation but instead chose to remain silent was Kay-Mar Furniture. It was a rarity. Margaret Newton Shumate started the company in 1976 and ran the operation for 30 years as chief operating officer.[499]

Founders like Margaret Shumate might have characterized their debut as uneventful. Often, factory leadership was too busy worrying about how to meet payroll and procure raw materials than to explore the luxury of marketing. Some preferred to let their product speak for them. Since many companies from the era began in sheds behind the house, perhaps the originators felt that where the furniture was made should be concealed. The emphasis would instead be focused on what they made. The surroundings were not important, only the finished product was. Until those companies could sport larger, more impressive factories, like some of their competitors, it would be best to hide the circumstances of production. In that respect, they were not unlike the first cabinet makers in western North Carolina, who might exalt the finished product while the shop location was deemed superfluous.

One of the new companies to crank up in the post-war period and become a hugely successful operation was Laine Upholstering in 1958. Clarence E. Roseman, Sr., had run a dry cleaning business in Hickory for 25 years. Approached by a group of friends and fellow businessmen to get into furniture, the senior Roseman was looking for a business that might interest his son, C.E. Jr., known as Sonny. "I guess he felt sorry for me. He didn't know what was going to happen to me," said Sonny Roseman about the creation of Laine Upholstering. Starting in "the old general store in Brookford," a cotton mill community south of Hickory, the younger Roseman returned from college to help his father run the company named for his sister Elaine. For the first eight years or so, his father handled the manufacturing side while his mother kept the books, but when his father had a stroke, Sonny Roseman stepped up to take over the operation. With an original company workforce of "about 10," he admitted that "we struggled for a while, and I had an awful lot to learn." But slowly, the company found its footing and began to prosper.[500]

Laine Upholstering started with a "goose-neck rocker, which goes back a long way." As Sonny pointed out, "if you look at our catalog today (2021) and look at it, say 30 years ago, you'd never know it was the same company." An ever-increasing product line matched an ever-increasing group of highly valued employees. As they grew, the company moved into larger spaces along Highway 70 in Hickory. Uncertain times and spurts of tremendous growth accompanied a near-constant stream of buyout offers. In 1990, Sonny Roseman changed the name of his company to C.R. Laine, executed to avoid confusion with The Lane Furniture Company, an outside enterprise which had bought a number of operations in the area.[501]

Along the way, C.R. Laine gained a sterling reputation in the furniture business. Through it all, Sonny Roseman credited his success to something he got from his father - tenacity. "I inherited a lot of my dad's determination," he said, revealing that quitting was not an option. "I think it's what 75% of

The post-war era saw factories pumping out furniture in great quantity. These men were part of the logging and saw milling of wood that were the life blood of factories. Pictured lower right is Ed Tolbert, a one-time farmer who brought his son, Gene (behind, in back) into the business. (Courtesy of Lois Tolbert Ward)

success is. It's what you want to make out of what you have," he added, seeking to explain the overriding philosophy that kept C.R. Laine a healthy company. A key component of his staying power was constant recognition of the need to change. Saying there was "no question" about it, "we've really had to adjust to circumstances as they developed." C.R. Laine became one of the success stories of the era, maintaining its independence while growing both its inventory and its customer base.[502]

Companies started, merged, and folded rapidly during the post-war years. Those that remained and grew eventually became proud of their origins and wanted to tell their stories, if for no other reason than to highlight their longevity. One company that went into business in that era serves to illustrate the point. Sherrill Upholstering incorporated in 1947, with Oscar T. Sherrill, Theodore Cummings, and Ailene McGuire at the helm. While the company never announced any changes in operation like Drexel would often do, Sherrill products were featured exclusively in advertisements for stores like Ivey-Taylor's in Raleigh. Over the years, the company continued to grow and eventually son H.W. "Buddy" Sherrill took over. One statement about Buddy Sherrill exemplified the attitude to shun company origin stories. "He's a holdover from an era of manufacturers who didn't seek acclaim," explained the observer.[503]

Some furniture companies became more famous locally for activities beyond the factory than the furniture they produced, good and bad. Crestline Furniture falls into both categories. After Harvey LeFon left, the company tried to keep the focus on its output, creating the "biggest stuffed chair in the world" during an exhibit seen by North Carolina's governor. However, Crestline gained more notice in the papers for the performance of its baseball team that played to sizable crowds and won district championships in games across western North Carolina. When the Federal Highway Administration cracked down on commercial drivers, Crestline found itself gaining notoriety again, the wrong kind. The company received a $750 fine for "permitting its truck drivers to maintain false daily records," in order to drive farther and make more stops. The effort, sanctioned or inadvertent, sought to improve efficiency for the company at the expense of driver fatigue. They paid up and ended the practice.[504]

The allure of the area served as a calling card, not just for individuals who were looking to start a company but corporations too. Some outside manufacturers just bought out existing companies. Others liked the region and sought to establish themselves independently. Kewaunee Manufacturing had "long been a leader in the scientific laboratory equipment field." The federal government used their products in "atom bomb laboratories," including the Manhattan Project, as well as hospitals and science facilities across the nation. With some fanfare, the company announced the creation of a furniture division, locating in Statesville.[505]

Kewaunee Technical Furniture offered furniture for the institutional market. Before arriving in western North Carolina, the secretary for Kewaunee, Paul Meech, noted that "all our products are custom made." "After a nine-state search," the company decided to locate in Statesville, noting that "both natural resources and experienced woodworking labor influenced the choice." "Eager cooperation" with property owners and the city of Statesville sealed the deal.[506]

From its beginning in the early 1920s, the Michigan-based company had grown into an operation with $8 million in lab equipment sales. Kewaunee's expansion into lab furniture proved to be a brilliant decision when it came to Statesville in 1954. Five years after they got to town, Paul Meech claimed that the furniture division rivaled the parent company, saying, "Technical Furniture, Inc. has expanded continuously to the point where its sales during the present year (1959) may well exceed those of Kewaunee Manufacturing Company." With that kind of business, a 30,000 square-foot warehouse to go along with its 47,000 square-foot factory was needed. Additions mounted and Kewaunee established a substantial presence in west Statesville.[507]

Just up the road from Statesville stood Kewaunee's biggest competitor. By the 1950s, Southern Desk had three plants, its original factory in West Hickory with expansions in Longview and Hildebran. Kewaunee and Southern Desk competed head to head on sales of institutional furniture for any kind of public facility that needed seating and tables. Schools and colleges were an important market for both. Often, they went head-to-head, submitting bids for the same contract. One example saw Kewaunee winning the right to outfit a junior high school in Indiana, while Southern Desk got the contract at Western Michigan University. One Michigan paper lamented the awarding of that contract when it noted how both Kewaunee and Southern Desk beat the bid of a Grand Rapids company. The headline, "Southern Firm May Win WMU Bid, Cost State Jobs" warned Michigan readers that "they would have to lay off people if they don't get the contract."[508]

The routine of awarding the bid to southern manufacturers like Southern Desk caused an uproar in Michigan. Letting go of $221,123 for furnishing equipment for the university, especially to a firm from North Carolina, was unthinkable. Dissatisfied with the process, Michigan politicians called for a new round of bidding to take place. To their chagrin, Southern Deck came in with an even lower bid, theoretically sealing its first place position. The head of the state building division, A.N. Languis did not know what to do. State policy "has always been to give the job to the lowest bidder, whether from Michigan or out of state," said Languis, grimacing that "we know they can bid lower because their wage scale down there is lower." After some research he found that state law did not require awarding the bid to Southern, but "the long standing policy" was in his estimation, "in the public good." The building committee did not follow through on the protectionist threat and five years later bought more from Southern Desk with again, the lowest bid.[509]

Bruce Nelson started his career in furniture at Southern Desk in 1964.

He remembered how competitively his firm worked to win bids. The company "had an estimating department" intently focused on those proposals. Southern Desk had a group that "would bid on jobs, just like a general contractor would," with architectural specifications to help them envision product placement and cost. Bruce's job was in the credit office where he secured payment for contracts. "You had progress payments" as the work was being done with "payment and performance bonds," to keep everyone on track. For Southern Desk, an extra step in the process was an installation department that came to sites and made sure their product would fit the institutional space to the customer's satisfaction.[510]

One market into which Southern Desk ventured that Kewauwnee did not was church furniture. Estimates number over 20,000 houses of worship were outfitted by the company, with workers taking great care and pride in creating each one. In carefully crafting "chancellery" furniture, Ed Walker pointed out how Southern Desk employees were not like most furniture workers. "They were generally educated people because that's what it took," recalled Walker, who was one time head of the chancellery department. He pointed out that the work "required a certain amount of engineering knowledge and you just had to learn it." Southern Desk maintained an employee base that was up to the task as Walker saw it. He observed that "we had young people who wanted to learn it and wanted to move up."[511]

The atmosphere at Southern Desk was remarkable for its cohesion and unity. Employees commonly used the term "family" to describe the environment they shared. Company nurse Fay Abernathy commented on just how close they were by saying, "you couldn't get a job at Southern Desk until somebody died." Plant manager Fred Cochran concurred. He recalled a ten year period where he only hired five people, noting that "guys would come in half sick because they didn't want anyone to run their machine." As Ned Armstrong put it, "we looked forward to going to work in the morning."[512]

Maybe it was because their work was going into a house of worship or how they viewed the product as an extension of themselves, but whatever the reason, employees made a strong effort to ensure their handiwork was as perfect as possible. Southern Desk employee Foy Huss believed that "people took pride in making a good piece of furniture back then." For he and his colleagues, "nothing would do but the best." Word of the quality spread. Sales of seating for stadiums and auditoriums, libraries, and schools, often came from recommendations. "The name was usually out there in some way, amongst the public," said Ed Walker. While some congregations might not immediately consider Southern Desk to outfit their church, given the specialty in their name, previous service offered a calling card. Walker remembered the "times we would be called into a church job because the school superintendent had said, 'look, I buy school desks form this company and they are qualified to do this sort of thing." In that way, one division helped the other, thanks to satisfied customers.[513]

Southern Desk even had a spinoff company that supplied other furniture firms. Behind its main plant in Longview, the subsidiary Southern Dowel Company made its namesake product for companies in western North Carolina and beyond. Factories used dowels in the production of household furniture. When hardwoods became hard to find, the company moved production north in 1956, to New Hampshire, in search of adequate supplies of the raw material. The reason for the migration was simple: "New Hampshire forests have more extensive hardwood resources."[514]

The business attracted a wide variety of companies and individuals, including some not normally associated with furniture. The Jarrett family lived in rural Catawba County, closer to Newton than Hickory. Ned Jarrett, and later his son, Dale became famous for their success as stock car drivers on the NASCAR circuit. Going back a generation, the family actually had an earlier association with the furniture business through the Jarrett Lumber Company,

Furniture makers used veneer to dress up their product, either to disguise less attractive wood or enhance designs for a more cosmopolitan look. This machine shows the latest mid-century technology in carving thin layers for application to a variety of pieces. (Courtesy of the Caldwell Heritage Museum)

started by Ned's father, Homer Keith Jarrett, known to many as H.K. The company was a family affair with H.K.'s sons and grandsons working for and with him to bring down timber and saw it up for the industry.[515]

The oldest of Ned Jarrett's sons went to work for Jarrett Lumber at age thirteen. "We cut hardwoods and pine," recalled Glenn Jarrett. He worked summers loading cut wood from portable "peckerwood sawmills" in the woods of upper South Carolina and hauling it back up to the foothills. "We'd take all that stuff to the local furniture factories around the area." Every morning he and his cousin Wayne would "get in the truck with the truck driver. He lived not far from where my granddad did and we'd ride down there in that bumpy truck. It was just a straight-bed Ford truck." For the "monstrous sum of $5 a day," Glenn stacked freshly sawed boards anywhere from 8 to 12 feet in length on that straight-bed truck until they had a full load, then head back to the foothills for delivery.[516]

For Glenn, the job was an education as well as a source of income. The first morning, "I noticed when we got out of the truck, Wayne put on a pair of those big, heavy work gloves." Glenn wondered why they were necessary. When he asked if it was because of the splinters, Wayne just said, "you'll see." All that day they loaded "raw oak boards" and when they got through, young Jarrett had no splinters to speak of, but he did find that "both the palms and fingers of my hands were as black as a lump of coal and it would not come off. There was something in a green oak board that if you get it on your skin, you have to wear it out." He tried everything he could imagine, including Clorox to clean his hands but nothing worked. That next day he spent his first five dollars on a pair of gloves.[517]

For several summers, Glenn Jarrett labored in the business. It was only later that he would take up the other family pursuits, like racing, after he enjoyed a collegiate career in baseball. Following high school he went to the University of North Carolina at Chapel Hill where he got a business degree, then returned to the foothills in May of 1972. At that point, his father was running Hickory Motor Speedway (HMS). In adjacent offices at the legendary short track, Glenn rejoined Jarrett Lumber, this time managing the business side of the company. He had been accepted to Wake Forest University's Law School but decided against it in favor of getting back into what he knew. "I inherited from my dad a pretty good head for figures and for record-keeping," said Glenn about his return, "so it served me well."[518]

His days working out of "the racetrack" witnessed even greater ventures for the Jarretts' lumber business. In addition to expanding operations, a decision within the family led to further growth by buying and selling wood from other sawmills. Jarrett Lumber Sales combed the region to develop deals for handling the output of smaller operators, while employing the considerable connections Glenn, his uncle and his grandfather made within the circle of furniture companies in Lenoir, Hickory, Morganton and Marion. It all went back to the first days when H.K. Jarrett offered lumber by the truckload, building "good relationships" with factory buyers. A man with an imposing presence, (he stood well over six feet tall and in the range of 250 pounds) he became a trustworthy supplier throughout the region. "His word was his bond," said grandson Glenn. When he called an associate in the furniture business and said "we got this," an honest assessment of the type and quality of lumber he had on the back of the truck, companies were always ready to take delivery.[519]

At HMS, Jarrett Lumber handled so much wood that they used land behind the back straightaway to repackage and trim stacks of lumber for delivery, in addition to another "concentration yard" over near the original sawmill at Propst Crossroads (southern Catawba County). "Sometimes we'd buy four or five, six, seven trailer loads of lumber a week," recollected Glenn. In addition to sales and accounting, Jarrett also got his hands dirty occasionally handling the wood, although not as filthy as his first day. He recalled, "me, and believe it or not, my brother Dale Jarrett, the Winston Cup Champion in 1999, we would be out there and we handled each load of lumber, every single board, 7,500 to 10,000 board feet, by hand because we had to grade it, separate it out."[520]

Engaging in such work allowed Glenn Jarrett to become an expert in the process of grading lumber. In order to meet specifications, "most of your bigger companies like a Broyhill or a Henredon or one of those, they wanted graded lumber," meaning inspected so as to meet an industry standard. For a while, Jarrett Lumber Sales paid a National Hardwood Lumber Association certified inspector to verify the product. As they examined, Glenn studied how the process worked and posed questions about the classification criteria. After getting a feel for the method, when an inspector came to a different conclusion about a particular board, Glenn would say, "time out, tell me why." With the help of a mentor like Blake Watson, Jarrett learned what to look for and developed his skill. Soon, companies trusted his word as much as they had his grandfather's.[521]

By 1975, the Jarrett family sold their lumber firm and moved on to other business opportunities. For a few years after Glenn kept his hand in activities including an operation attached to Appalachian coal mining interests in the area where Kentucky, Virginia and West Virginia meet. Before a mountain could be strip-mined, Glenn Jarrett put his abilities to work harvesting the timber. Complications with the plan, like the ever closer blasts of the coal companies caused several close calls from flying boulders, finally concluded the partnership.[522]

In addition to his contribution to furniture making, H.K. Jarrett and his lumber company could rightly be acknowledged to have spawned the racing career of not one but two champions. Ned worked for his father before surreptitiously launching into his phenomenal career as a NASCAR driver. Chauffeuring his family to church since the age of nine, Ned loved cars. He got his drivers license at 14 after he bluffed his way through the process with NC Department of Motor Vehicles personnel. Like his father, he was big for his age. On one auspicious Saturday night at Hickory Motor Speedway, Ned eagerly took over a car from another driver who could not finish the race and went from last to first, winning the contest, though it was announced under the name of the starter, not the finisher. It just so happened that on that very day his father had concluded a deal for the sale of lumber to a furniture company from Virginia. The visitors wanted to see a stock car race, despite the fact that Ned's mother informed the men that "the only thing going on over there is a bunch of drinking and fighting and cussing." They persisted and persuaded H.K. to take them to HMS.[523]

Ned Jarrett showed talent as a driver and expressed interest in racing, but his father discouraged participation, forbidding him to compete. He shared the same views about the sport as his wife. When H.K. Jarrett and the furniture men got to the track, the father discovered his son driving to victory under an assumed name. It turned out to be an odd beginning to a stellar racing career. Angry, somewhat bewildered by the use of an alias, but collected, H.K. delivered quintessential guidance to his son after the Virginia visitors departed. He said it "doesn't matter what you do with this life of yours. It's yours to do with what you please. But you do not do it, good, bad or indifferent. You do not do it hiding behind someone else's name. Do you understand me, boy?" Relieved, Ned nodded in agreement.[524]

The moment proved pivotal. H.K. Jarrett's involvement in the furniture industry, his sale of lumber and the trip to HMS that night created a tense scene that brought a fateful delivery of values from one generation to the next. More importantly, the success of Jarrett Lumber as a supplier to furniture makers provided prosperity to the Jarrett household. It was enough for a young man like Ned to impetuously try a dangerous profession that ultimately made him a star, and in turn led to the same achievement of his son, Dale, in later years.[525]

Like the Jarretts, untold numbers of careers were sparked by the presence of furniture making in western North Carolina. Carl Rullman was one man who came to the area with little to indicate that he, too, would associate himself with the industry. Trained in Chicago as a teacher, Rullman traveled to Conover, ready to take on a classroom at Concordia Lutheran School. When the Great Depression hit the congregation, they told Carl that they could not pay him. Needing a job, he went to Oscar Bolick's Southern Furniture and got work. Carl Rullman ran the factory while Oscar went on the road to sell the pieces that he and his workers had recently built. As soon as Carl could get back into teaching, he did, with a position in the public system at Oxford Elementary School. As Carl's son Hank Rullman remembered, "that's how he got a taste of the furniture business."[526]

For years, Carl Rullman taught school and served as an administrator for Catawba County and Hickory City Public Schools. He coached and was a principal, all the while marrying and starting a family. Carl's teaching career even included a principalship at Lail School in the St. Stephen's area of Catawba County. That school was donated by and named for the grandfather of Leroy Lail, who would one day become a close friend of Hank Rullman and the dominant player in both Hickory's wholesale and retail furniture markets. It didn't take long before the Rullman clan grew to nine children and Carl realized he needed more than a teacher's salary to support five boys and four girls. He went to the bank, got a loan, outfitted a small factory behind his house and started Rullman Incorporated, employing a few sewers and upholsterers, putting to use the skills he learned at Southern Furniture.[527]

Carl Rullman followed the footsteps of his one-time employer, Oscar Bolick in many ways. Beginning small, he periodically left the shop floor to go out and sell, then came back and helped build the furniture he sold. Carl banked on the prosperity of the early post-World War II period to be a good time to start a company. However, he struggled, selling to retailers who defaulted. The unpaid bills forced Rullman Incorporated out of business, and with it, killed Carl Rullman's dreams of owning his own furniture manufacturing company. As his son, Hank observed, "it was difficult to run the operation and be on the road at the same time." All the while, Carl may have unknowingly guided his son into a career in furniture. Hank remembered his chores as a boy, which included starting the morning fire in the furnace before the workers arrived, so the shop would be warm. It was the younger Rullman's "first taste" of life in the furniture business.[528]

Since the very beginning, the failure of one company often paved the way for the success of another in the furniture industry. While Rullman Incorporated did not soar to the heights its founder envisioned, it did sow seeds for future success. Another area furniture business that started around the same time heard of Carl Rullman's ability as a salesman. Scales Furniture of Claremont (in Catawba County), a forerunner of Montclair Furniture, sought out Carl for his sales prowess. "They had heard about him and how proficient he was in selling," said son Hank, "hiring him (Carl) as their first representative." The elder Rullman's territory included everywhere "from New York to Miami." When making calls, Carl brought a few of his sons along, including young Hank, who got his second, and most important impression of the business.[529]

On one of those trips came a fateful moment. During a call on a retail store, Hank watched his father guide the store owners in their purchase of a line of furniture. As they left, Hank posed a question. "How much commission did you make on that particular sale?" His father's answer was simple.

"Sixty dollars." As Hank remembered, "right then and there, I knew. I knew because at that time I knew guys would work all week in the factories making $30 a week." Saying to himself, "that sounds almost too good to be true," Hank Rullman marked that moment as the beginning of his long, profitable career in furniture sales.[530]

After a stint in the Marine Corps, a college education at Lenoir-Rhyne, and a six-year period of working under his father, Hank Rullman went on to sell a variety of lines, some made in the Catawba Valley, some not. Carolina Table, Comfort Chair, Hickory Leather, and Herman Chairs were all enterprises he represented in Florida. Working with the Babcock retail chain, Hank's territory centered in the sunshine state, where he sold until his retirement. "I love the selling," Hank confided, adding that once after a big sale, "I did a flip on the floor after they walked out the door. It was such a big order."[531]

The longevity of the Rullman family epitomizes the way the furniture industry developed in the years after World War II. Seeing the money to be made, some jumped in after careers in other fields, adding a diverse skill set, like Carl Rullman and finding a place where they could contribute. The plunge into the furniture business aided the lives of those who worked in it, while the industry benefitted from the involvement. Carl Rullman went on to serve as a state representative in the North Carolina General Assembly and was honored by the International Lutheran Layman's League. While part of the furniture business, he lent his talents and his fortitude to building a stronger industry that included training his son Hank for a career. The younger Rullman explained his path by saying, "it's a great feeling when you have something that you know the dealers can sell and make money on and are happy with it, and when you walk into their store, they're happy to see you. They're smiling, you're smiling, everybody's smiling. It's just a very warm feeling."[532]

Investing in new furniture was generally a positive transaction for both the buyer and the seller. Purchases were made in greater numbers every day, which intrigued author Cameron Hawley enough to want to write about the other end of the business in a novel he called *Executive Suite*. The story centered around the purchase of a furniture company. Granted, the intrigue that went along with controlling the path of a large manufacturing company might not be interesting to some, but the author used furniture as a backdrop to examine the levels to which people will stoop for power in a profitable company. The fictional factory location in the book was Pennsylvania, but it could have been anywhere, especially western North Carolina. The story found its way into a Hollywood movie, raising the profile and nationwide interest in the business. Some began to see the furniture production as an economic high-roller. Cameron Hawley had spent most of his career at Armstrong Cork, a Pennsylvania company that would one day acquire a North Carolina furniture concern. His writing and the film predated the 'muscling in' of larger corporations. That phenomenon would arrive about the time the film hit the late show on television.[533]

Two sides of upholstery. On the left is the eight-way-hand-tie procedure as another chair is being created. On the right, Howard Smith, Jr. demonstrates the process via a cutaway model of a chair during the semi-annual furniture market. (Courtesy of the Caldwell Heritage Museum)

Chapter 20
New Markets

By 1961, the furniture industry employed more workers in North Carolina than any other state in the union. The Tarheel state topped all others at 12 percent of the nation's workforce, with New York second at 9.1, followed by California and Illinois. The former home of furniture, Michigan ranked seventh.[534]

The superpower status of the United States and the incessant ringing of the cash register in the 1950s convinced many Americans that they were living in a golden era. Southern furniture makers pivoted successfully toward modernist designs created to fill homes and satisfy the tastes of the World War II generation who were now having families. Successfully weathering the days of borax ridicule when their product was seen as no better than the crate it was shipped in, factories hummed with whatever the market wanted. To add to the utility of furniture when designers sought to imagine what the future might hold in the space age, Raymond Sobota had an answer.

Born and raised in the city that used to claim the title of furniture capital of the United States, Ray Sobota grew up in an earlier tradition that sought to create beauty and utility in every piece of furniture crafted. His uncle, Karl Schmidt, was an "eminent furniture designer in Grand Rapids, Michigan." Ray called him "his idol" and got first hand experience by working under the tutelage of Uncle Karl, after earning a degree from the Kendall

School of Design in Grand Rapids. Once Sobota's education was fully complete, he struck out on his own as a "free-lance furniture designer." When he did, he made a tremendous splash with a headboard.[535]

Ray Sobota took a standard piece of wood and turned it into something of a command center. His newly envisioned headboard did not just hold up a pillow top of the bed, it also contained a bookcase for storage and an attached nightstand. Remarked one description, "the bed at once looks like a seating piece and the bedroom looks like a bed-sitting room." Made from walnut, the bed went on display during the fall 1952 show at Chicago's Merchandising Mart. A modern multi-use piece of furniture, Ray Sobota's product became so popular, advertisements for it carried his name as the designer.[536]

In creating furniture, Ray Sobota explored many styles. He used "Spanish and Mexican motifs," and his *Janus* collection was described as the "subtle influence of the Orient meets the contemporary sweep of Scandinavian design." His work was called "brilliantly imaginative," and collections made by him were showcased in high-end furniture stores from Boston to Los Angeles. With the marvelous approach Sobota brought to what a piece of furniture could do if reimagined and the agile way southern manufacturers were giving the public what they wanted, it seemed destined for the two to come together.[537]

In the mid-50s, Century Furniture stumbled upon Ray Sobota. Hearing about a great designer in Grand Rapids, Harley Shuford, Sr. went there to find the guy. The designer turned Shuford down, instead recommending Sobota, whom Harley hired the same day. Harley Shuford, Jr., known as Buck, son of the founder, credited that partnership with making Century Furniture distinctive to the buying public. "He pulled Century out of the pack," said Buck. Harley Sr. and Ray were ambitious. They built a huge collection, "encompassing bedroom, dining room, living room, occasional," recalled Buck about the *Citation* project. "I remember Dad saying that he was going to find out whether the Lord intended him to be in the furniture business," Buck remembered about taking a chance on Ray Sobota's vision. "He went ahead and put in a big cutting before the market and fortunately, *Citation* was a big hit."[538]

When the *Citation* group debuted in the mid-1950s, an Italian Provincial style "with a definite contemporary air," it was called "striking" by furniture critics. Described as "beautifully sealed in clean graceful lines," the huge collection featured over 70 pieces. The reason for the size was to create a group that could tie every room in the house together. *Citation* catapulted Century as a leader in the retail market. The contemporary styling offered a fresh approach to home furnishings, especially for a western North Carolina manufacturer. However, neither Ray nor Century intended to rest on their laurels.[539]

On the heels of his triumph with modernist designs, Ray Sobota sensed change. As the fifties were morphing into the sixties, an ironic twist occurred. "It has been fantastic," Ray was quoted as saying about the resurgence of traditional furniture in the buying selections of Americans. Just when the space age took off, Sobota noticed that people wanted something more grounded, more rooted in the past than the future. Always a keen observer of consumer buying practices, Ray offered an answer as to why. He opined that "people are looking for security in the middle of this cold war, space flight, unsettled age." Ray returned to his drawing board ready to add his flare to a old style.[540]

As a freelancer, Ray Sobota had the luxury of following his own path in the furniture he envisioned, then offering it to a variety of companies. For his embrace of traditional forms, R. & E. Gordon Manufacturing in Asheville (of which Harley Shuford, Sr. was associated) leapt at the opportunity to produce the pieces Ray created. He sketched a whole grouping that, like Century's *Citation*, included, "every room in the home." Harley, Sr. saw an advantage for Century and commissioned Sobota for more.[541]

For this project, Ray went to where he could find the greatest gathering of artifacts, the Henry Ford Museum and Greenfield Village in Dearborn, Michigan. After Ford secured his wealth as an automaker, he turned his attention to preserving the America of his youth, building an entire town to reflect an earlier era that did not, ironically enough, revolve around the automobile. An authentic collection of furniture contained ideas from which Ray would draw inspiration. Sketching designs from the earlier era, he commented, "I had a ball." Ray developed the *Henry Ford Museum Collection* by setting up his "drawing board in the middle of the village and they brought the pieces to me," adding, "I never had so much fun in my life."[542]

Designers like Ray Sobota brought the larger world of what home furnishings could be to the western North Carolina furniture industry. Manufacturers certainly wanted everyone to see their wares but had been somewhat hampered by the fact that when buyers came to the semi-annual market, makers in the Catawba Valley were constricted by conventional thought and ended up playing second fiddle to their eastern furniture-making cousins. The moment had come to step out of the shadows and cease carting their new creations down an unfinished Interstate 40 to High Point. If retail store reps could come to North Carolina, why couldn't they trek across the Catawba River to see where foothills manufacturers made their magic.

The Hickory Community Center (a latter-day YMCA) served as a gathering spot for the city's numerous civic organizations and citizens. Spacious and versatile, it provided an excellent venue for manufacturers of the area to exhibit their output in a communal location. In the spring of 1951, as the show went on in High Point, seventeen companies displayed their lines at the first Hickory Community Furniture Market. By the next market that fall, it wasn't only local producers. Several makers from Virginia joined the Catawba Valley companies to offer an alternative to the showrooms of High Point. The cooperative effort did not end the practice of larger companies maintaining their own showrooms, but Hickory began an event that was to grow over the coming years. Meanwhile, hotel accommodations in places like Lenoir, Hickory, and Morganton became scarce during the spring and fall markets as furniture buyers looked upon their visits as something of a vacation, many bringing their wives. Some even stayed as far away as the Green Park Hotel in Blowing Rock, created by J.M. Bernhardt and now owned by the Broyhills. Buyers could enjoy a mountain spring or the vivid fall colors as they drove down to showrooms in Lenoir, a feature not found in High Point. The scenery (and the furniture) brought buyers from places as far away as Boston, Milwaukee, New York, and Texas.[543]

The early days of the multi-vendor Hickory furniture market demonstrated what a makeshift affair it was. Furniture salesman Hank Rullman looked back at the displays with incredulous amazement. He sold lines by Comfort Chair and Herman Chair, remembering those were about the size of companies (smaller in output) that showed at the community center in Hickory in those early years. Normally, the complex included "a bowling alley downstairs and a gym for upstairs where they played basketball," but all that was covered over to make way for showroom space as Hank described it. As far as the display area for furniture makers, "they had sheets hung up," he said, "with lines, wires dividing the different showrooms on the floor there on the basketball court." He met customers who strolled through to see if offerings in Hickory could match what they saw in High Point. From the perspective of grandeur, it could not. Nonetheless, the idea of a market showroom that gave smaller companies a chance to introduce themselves to a buying audience began to catch on. Every fall and spring, seeing all that was new in furniture manufacturing included a ride to Hickory.[544]

A more intense rivalry with High Point had begun. From its inception, the market in the west drew "thousands of visitors," and manufacturers reported "fine returns" on their investment. Each year, the number of participants,

The first multi-manufacturer furniture market in Hickory was staged at the Hickory Foundation Center. For makers who could not afford their own space, this annual event beginning in 1951 became a tradition, outgrowing the gym floor where collections were separated by sheets. (Author's collection)

both sellers and buyers, increased. Everyone in and around Hickory noticed the economic boost of those two weeks each April and October. Trade even became competitive within the Hickory showrooms, themselves.[545]

Before the Hickory market celebrated its first decade of operation, a hotel operator on the east end of town opened his own 6,000-square-foot space for more retailers. Since the end of the war, J.P. Mull had been developing a growing complex of attractions along Hickory's newly constructed Highway 64/70 bypass. Starting with a gas station and restaurant, he added a drive-in theater and motor court, but in 1959, tore down the old eatery to make way for a new 220-seat facility, Mull's Restaurant. In the basement, he created Hickory Furniture Mart.[546]

For a few years, Mull's competed with the Foundation Center, both having similar space limitations. Hickory's city leaders then upped the ante.

They announced plans for a new, grand building on Highway 321, the road that ran through the northwestern section of town on its way to Lenoir. The Hickory Home Furnishings Mart debuted in 1963 as an 86,000-square-foot facility that cost $700,000 to construct. The two-story showroom included "conference rooms and a dining facility" that "made it really easy for manufacturers and buyers to get together." The imposing structure, situated on a hill just south of the Catawba River, was a massive investment in the wholesale furniture display market and quickly caught the attention of High Point officials.[547]

While Hickory Home Furnishings Mart and Hickory Furniture Mart were independent organizations that worked with both local and out-of-the-area furniture producers to attract retail merchants, they were also part of the Furniture Factory Marketing Association, which meant they were expected to abide by rules set in High Point. Try as they might to regulate opening dates for the market, the association never could corral Hickory. Both western furniture marts always let buyers in a day or two early, ostensibly to accommodate the schedules of those trying to hit both cities, but in reality to get a jump on what the High Point companies were doing. As furniture market reporter Robert Marks noted from High Point, "furniture is a competitive business, Southern furniture manufacturers will tell you. So it is when it comes to the business of selling furniture."[548]

By the time the Hickory Home Furnishings Mart opened its doors, plans to expand Mulls were already in motion. J.P. Mull tapped his son-in-law, G. Leroy Lail, to take over Hickory Furniture Mart and see if he could grow the venture. At the time, Leroy was just leaving service in the United States Navy as an officer. A cryptographer (code writer) during the Cuban Missile Crisis of 1962, he had been part of the most threatening nuclear confrontation of the Cold War. Once the crisis had been averted, he chose to begin his business career back in his hometown. Lieutenant Lail and his wife, Lynn

Mull Lail, returned to Hickory to help her parents with the business. Lail brimmed with ideas to improve the furniture mart to bring in more furniture makers, which meant more visiting buyers. Some were local companies, but Leroy also attracted manufacturers from as far away as Mississippi to show their products during the now established markets each April and October. Not long after Leroy Lail took over, he planned expansion.

Within four years of assuming control of Hickory Furniture Mart, even with a new, competing operation across town, Leroy Lail drew more presenters than his in-town rivals. One account of the 1967 show revealed that "more than 4,000 furniture dealers are expected in Hickory today for the opening of the fall Furniture Market. There will be 38 exhibits at the Home Furnishings Mart, 52 at the Hickory Furniture Mart, and 10 other showrooms in Hickory operated by the manufacturers themselves." Leroy's vision for furniture showrooms quickly outgrew his father-in-law's basement setup, and construction never seemed to stop as expansion took place between each market. "I had a tiny place attempting to compete," admitted Leroy, a reference to those early years, but as a truly unique entrepreneur, he had two strong impulses. "I love to build, and I love to promote," he said. During his career, he would do both with alacrity.[549]

The establishment of the two furniture showrooms put Hickory on the map, not just as an appendage of High Point but in its own right. Even though Lenoir put out more furniture, and Drexel was a larger company than any in Catawba County, the central location of Hickory as the nexus of the western companies made logistical sense. Locating furniture showrooms in Hickory was seen as a strategic move for the Catawba Valley furniture economy. Soon, the markets were two city affairs. To see all the industry offered in North Carolina, just visiting High Point was not good enough. A car ride to western North Carolina was essential for buyers to make their choices. The term that came to describe the route was the "Furniture Figure 8." With Statesville as a convergence point, a map of furniture showrooms resembled the numeral 'eight' lying on its side. The western circle wove through Taylorsville, Lenoir, Marion, Morganton, Drexel, Hickory, Newton, and Conover, while the eastern one traveled between Mocksville, Winston-Salem, High Point, Thomasville, Lexington, and Salisbury before closing up back in Statesville. Broyhill biographer Bill Stevens likened it to the "symbol for infinity." Though other towns in the region were home to furniture factories too, the figure-eight defined the core of manufacturing for the state. With High Point and Hickory hosting their own showrooms, each side of the 'eight' had a focal point.[550]

Of all the towns on the western end, Hickory presented the most varied array of furniture. One snapshot in 1959 reported, "Catawba County includes such diverse plants as Century Furniture, young and expanding; Jones Chairs, which makes chairs only, Maxwell Royal featuring rockers, and Hickory Chair Company, which does chairs and many other pieces; Southern Desk Company, whose weekly production of pulpits and pews alone is enough to fill nine churches." The description also singled out another company, not because of its output but its leadership.[551]

William Cox started his own furniture factory in 1932, just as the Great Depression was reaching the industry in western North Carolina. What seemed like bad timing was just the opposite. Three years into operation, a newspaper quoted the owner saying, "this place is almost like a madhouse," a reference to the speed at which his workers had to perform to keep up with the influx of orders they received. Among the hard workers was Nelle Burns. She worked as William Cox's assistant since the beginning as a secretary, but more accurately, his 'Girl Friday,' a gender specific slang term for right-hand-man. The phrase was celebrated in a 1940 Rosalind Russell/Cary Grant movie, *His Girl Friday*, about how important the position was to the smooth running of an operation, in the case of Cary Grant, a newspaper, in the case of William Cox, a furniture factory. Nelle had become an essential part of the success of the company. When her boss died unexpectedly in 1951, she, her sister Frankie, and an investor from Chicago bought the business, putting Nelle in charge as president.[552]

"The Burns Girls," as they were called, continued the company product line of "chaise lounges and boudoir chairs." Nelle and Frankie took the company forward, with nationwide sales. By the time she sold Cox Manufacturing twenty years after buying it, Nell could proudly proclaim that her chairs were a part of the decor of the White House. Not one but two First Ladies bought from Nelle. Mamie Eisenhower and Claudia "Lady Bird" Johnson purchased Cox Manufacturing chairs made in Hickory.[553]

The work of the Burns sisters proved that furniture was not just a job for men. Women could, and did, successfully steer companies. However, few got the chance. During the 1960s, a plethora of factories started, all by men. For example, in 1960, the Teague family in Alexander County founded Clayton Marcus, named for one of the originators. They had little practical experience in operating a furniture factory at the time but did not let that

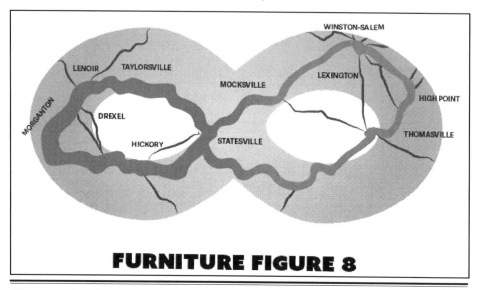

FURNITURE FIGURE 8

The two circles of furniture making in North Carolina includes conjoining spheres, one headquartered in High Point in the east and the other, the western furniture makers with their centerpiece in Hickory. They cooperated but also competed. (Image by Jennifer Pegg, Author's Collection)

deter their "entrepreneurial spirit." The operation revolved around Clayton Marcus Teague. His nephew Hurshel Teague explained, "Joe (Clayton's son) and I decided that we wanted to get something going in the furniture business and Dan (Clayton's son) and Clayton wanted to go into it too." In Bethlehem, just across the Catawba River from Hickory, the Teagues began manufacturing in a "300-square-foot building." When it came time to name the business, after using ACME Furniture for a bit, they chose the first and middle name of the group's senior, calling it Clayton Marcus Furniture. For the next 25 years, the company grew three factories, two in Hickory with a distribution warehouse in Bethlehem. In 1984, the company was bought out by "LADD Furniture Inc. of High Point." The sale came just when Clayton Teague reached retirement age. Asked about the takeover, Hurshel Teague believed it would be good for the firm, saying, "a company can't stand still, and we felt our potential for growth would be better if we merged." Characterizing LADD as "not a real tight-reigned conglomerate," Teague held the opinion that their new owner would "allow each division the autonomy it needs."[554]

After almost a century of production pitted against other furniture making areas in the United States, then toiling in the shadow of High Point, the output of factories located in western North Carolina were starting to gain recognition. Outsiders arrived, in the form of corporations looking to invest in existing firms and new enterprises that liked what they saw in the region. The reputation of the area as "a source of both materials and skilled labor for fine furniture" had spread far and wide. A trio of firms even generated a new wood-based product that reached beyond the scope of most manufacturers and until it became obsolete, harnessed the celebrated resources to make beautiful music.[555]

In 1954, Kohler and Campbell Piano Company came for the wood and the workers. Among piano buyers, Kohler and Campbell commanded a gigantic share of the market as one of the nation's largest. Started in 1896

A pioneer in furniture company ownership, Nelle Burns worked for Cox Manufacturing from its early days, When owner William Cox died, she took over in 1952 the business with her sister Frankie. She sold boudoir chairs to First Ladies Mamie Eisenhower and Lady Bird Johnson. (Image courtesy of Hickory Daily Record Archives)

by machinist J.C. Campbell and businessman Charles Kohler, the two were famous for buying up other piano makers, some with roots back to 1789. Kohler and Campbell made uprights and grands but specialized in player pianos, instruments with mechanisms to play note-perfect songs without help from a human. The device that made songs automatically flow from the piano was known as the "action." Kohler and Campbell sold 50,000 actions per year.[556]

Since its inception, Kohler and Campbell built pianos in New York City. Then, in 1954 they moved all of their production to 12 acres near the small town of Granite Falls, located along the rail line between Lenoir and Hickory. "The site was carefully picked for its skilled woodworkers and its proximity to the heart of the Appalachian hardwood lumber producing area," reported a company history. A cramped, multi-story facility in the Bronx prompted them to build a "single-story straight-line" facility down south, giving the firm a modern factory with room for growth. At the time of the relocation, son-in-law of the founder, Julius White, sought "to keep the cost of each unit down to the average family's budget in an era of skyrocketing production costs." He oversaw the move just as he neared retirement. Once in Granite Falls, he tapped his son Charles Kohler White to take over as president.[557]

Charles Kohler White assumed the role of Kohler and Campbell's new head, but his time in the job only lasted 6 months. He moved to Hildebran, a community between Hickory and Morganton, to be near the new factory with his wife and two children. During a trip to Chicago, he inexplicably "plunged" from the open window of his room on the 13th floor of the Conrad Hilton Hotel. Press reports of the incident noted that "identification of the nude body that landed on an inside court roof at the fourth floor level was made from a wedding ring bearing White's initials and those of his wife." No one could explain what happened. When asked, his father could only say that "Charles was in good health and spirits when he left home." No note was left, only a small "grip" (suitcase) in his room. Company accounts of the 32-year-old's death refer to the mishap as an accident.[558]

Leadership of the firm passed to non-family member Charles Clayton. He ran the operation successfully in place of Charles Kohler White for as long as the firm produced pianos in the United States. The factory shipped out some 16,000 pianos in 1979, their best year. After that, the company began a decline that saw sales drop by 61% over five years. Clayton and "two New York stockholders" sold Kohler and Campbell to a California company who in turn sold it to Samick Music Corporation in South Korea. By the summer of 1985, the plant was shut down and the 200 remaining workers were let go. The once modern factory fell into ruin as efforts to sell the plant to Kincaid Furniture faltered after the discovery of a contaminated well on the site, leaving the facility abandoned with no hope of a new operator.[559]

Years before Kohler and Campbell arrived in Granite Falls, Sam Westbrook started a small piano factory in Marion. By 1968, Westbrook Piano had grown to the point of opening a "new factory outlet showroom and sales office." Two years later, it all burned down. By that time, International Musical Instruments was the owner. The plant was rebuilt, but two years after the fire,

Kaman Corporation bought the company for $1.5 million. Kaman originated as a maker of helicopters, but the Bloomfield, Connecticut company branched out to musical instruments, buying Ovation Guitars before its Marion purchase.[560]

The company, now called Currier Pianos, had a secret weapon, "a native genius in woodworking." Born in Drexel, Thad Poteat was quoted as saying, "I've always been fascinated by wood." His study included business school and a short stint in a furniture factory where he gained an education in wood. He teamed up with Phil Johnson, who became president of the company. Johnson called Thad Poteat "one of the last modern craftsmen" for his multiple innovations in piano design and construction. Thad, as executive vice-president and general manager, "earned Currier the coveted *Parents Magazine* Seal of Approval" for his work. A few years after the Kaman acquisition, Thad oversaw an operation that employed 125 and "an annual payroll of just over half a million dollars."[561]

Business was so good that by 1978, Currier broke ground on a new plant allowing production to double. The popularity of pianos flying out of the warehouse was again attributable to Thad Poteat. Collaborating with a chemical company he developed a finish for the wood called "Curriercote." Scratch, scar and stain resistant, Poteat would run his hand over the surface and liken it to a "baby's bottom." Phil Johnson declared, "Curriercote gives us a dramatic, competitive advantage," noting that dealer demand for their pianos had "in some cases" doubled.[562]

But like the fortunes of Kohler and Campbell, the sales highs of the 1970s would come crashing down in the 1980s. A similar decline in sales caused management to say, "people's habits are changing." Evaluating the reason, one executive candidly asserted that "the piano represents discipline, and discipline is not what it used to be." He laid much of the blame at the feet of the era's newest creation, video games. "We're in an instant-gratification society, with TV, Pac-

Man and all that, and Pac-Man is eating the piano business," quipped the exec. The game wasn't the only culprit. Competition from overseas, a bad economy, and interest rates at an all-time high contributed. By 1982, the writing was on the factory wall. Workers were not out of a job immediately, though. Kaman attempted to keep production going by moving its other musical instrument, Ovation Guitars, to Marion, keeping most of the workforce of 200 on the job. The solution only lasted a few years, with the guitar factory unfortunately closing, just like piano production before it.[563]

Morganton's entry into the piano manufacturing business came later but shared significant similarities with its other western North Carolina makers. Joe Kincaid knew nothing about pianos. He could not play one, much less construct one. His background was in furniture. A part of the Kincaid Furniture family, Joe took up the challenge of building a piano that would undercut Japanese competition in the market. In 1961, he started Grand Piano Company in Morganton, named after the retail company that originally posed the notion to Joe. "We started with a price first and had to build a piano to fit that price range," he recalled. It took months of intensive research. Joe assembled a crew that first built a sample, then began turning out two or three pianos a day. Within a few years, he pushed the number up to 30. Even though the name suggested Kincaid and company included grand pianos in their line, they didn't. What they did make was a full-size upright piano that retailed for $399, "about $100 lower than any other American piano. The model competed favorably against Japanese-made alternatives. A Japanese instrument at the same price could only provide a shorter keyboard, while Kincaid's offered the "full 88."[564]

At the height of piano sales, Marantz bought Joe Kincaid's company with ideas other than focusing on a low-cost alternative for the market. With them came technology to turn the instrument into "the world's only computerized player piano." Somewhat like the Kohler and Campbell models of old, Marantz used over a dozen patents to create a piano that played itself. Instead of the old paper rolls that directed keystrokes, updated technology used a "digitally encoded tape cassette that looks just like the latest Barry Manilow tape," reported one observer. Unlike the guiding force that first drove Joe Kincaid, the price of the "Pianocorder" was not cheap. Models ranged from "$2,000 to $4,000," which priced Kincaid's previous customers right out of the market.

A whirl of hoopla came with the introduction of the unique musical instrument. Celebrities like "Barbra Streisand, Neil Diamond, Stevie Wonder and Liberace" all bought one of the 2,000 sold after its introduction in 1978. The *New York Times* and the *Wall Street Journal* both wrote about the innovation. NBC's *Tomorrow* show demonstrated its capabilities. Marantz developed a coin-operated version that sold to "restaurants and lounges." Company Executive Vice-President Anthony Blazina expected even bigger things for the musical wonder. "What I'd like to see in 10 years' time," he dreamed, gazing into the future, "is no pianos built without this product included as a needed accessory." By that time, the home musical landscape had changed.[565]

Even with its self-playing ability, which needed no self-discipline on the part of the owner, Marantz suffered a down market just like Kohler and Campbell and Currier. By 1989, the Morganton facility closed. Joe Kincaid thought he had a deal to buy back the plant from Marantz. He wanted no more of the piano market, opting instead to make home furnishings in keeping with the family tradition. Kincaid and his newly formed company, Kincaid, Inc., sought to buy the factory, an offer that Marantz accepted. Until the deal was done, Joe and company rented the facility. As the closing date approached, Joe Kincaid found out that the plant was "listed by the State of North Carolina and the Environmental Protection Agency as a hazardous waste site," a fact that endangered financing. The closing date came and went without action. The renter and would-be owner remained in the building. Marantz sued. The court verdict handed down found that Marantz failed to adequately notify Kincaid, Inc. of its intent to cancel the sales agreement. Eventually, Joe Kincaid left the Marantz property without buying it, and much like the Kohler and Campbell site, as of 2022, it remained unoccupied and for sale.[566]

The piano business could not match the larger furniture industry for longevity. Arriving for both the wood and the labor, all three companies failed to sustain their operations over the long haul. As attractive as making pianos in the foothills looked when they began, none of them would have predicted such a change in American behavior that their product would become outmoded in just a few decades. General home furnishings had a broader appeal, a more established history, and a better ability to adapt to changing tastes and lifestyles. Those advantages would not guarantee security; however, it did offer some protection. Even if fewer people had the time to learn how to play a piano, they still wanted a place to sit.

From a Broyhill Training Manual. These individuals were part of the management team in the 1950s. Most opportunities at supervision were afforded to men, but of the dozen from this page, two women are listed, though the term "floorlady" seems ambiguous. (Courtesy of the Caldwell Heritage Museum)

The 1960s brought mammoth change to the western NC furniture industry. In addition to new corporate owners, processes like this mainframe computer at Broyhill gathered, collated, & dispensed information so that orders could go out faster to customers, nationwide. (Courtesy of the Caldwell Heritage Museum)

Chapter 21
Buyers Guide

With growth came new opportunities. No longer was there a question of survival, unless the enterprise was a startup. Established firms controlled the heftiest resources ever. By the 1950s, these western NC companies competed on a global scale for customers. Providing for the market and employing hundreds, sometimes thousands of employees, required that they conduct business in a manner far different from when they started.

Eventually, buyouts of local companies signaled a change in the industry but also a recognition of what local entrepreneurs had built. The first move in the larger corporatization of the industry came from within the region. In 1959, Drexel Furniture began to look into the possibility of merging its various furniture operations into one corporate structure. A study of the idea proved positive and the following year Robert O. Huffman announced the creation of Drexel Enterprises, Inc. The parent company would reportedly oversee but not interfere with what had been separate companies owned by Drexel. With over $25 million in assets and business of $40 million annually the three companies, now one, were the largest in the foothills of North Carolina.[567]

The new corporate structure included Heritage Furniture Company

The largest furniture company in western North Carolina maintained a sprawling complex in both Drexel and Morganton. By 1960, Drexel also owned Heritage Furniture in High Point and Southern Desk in Hickory. It would in turn be bought by Champion Paper/U.S. Plywood. (Image courtesy of the Burke Historical Museum)

in High Point, and Morganton Furniture, as part of the Drexel empire. At that point, Drexel operated six sites under its name with the original site in the town that bore its name, three in Morganton where the company housed its "research and engineering center," a factory in Marion, and a "veneer operation at Kingstree, S.C." Morganton Furniture consisted of one plant in Morganton while Heritage operated both in High Point and Mocksville, NC. Each operation would become a division of the larger corporation and the output would continue to be shipped under the same names, as they did before the restructure.[568]

The change streamlined operations. Drexel even used its new clout to go on a buying spree. The company took a 7.5 percent increase in sales to fund the purchase of Southern Desk, the company that George F. Ivey started in 1911, which was run by his son Leon at the time of acquisition. The younger

Ivey took a seat on the board of the directors at Drexel Enterprises, Inc. When sold, Southern Desk was "the world's largest manufacturer of church furniture, and a big name in school, library and dormitory furniture." A few years later, Drexel bought the old Morgan Furniture plant in Woodfin (near Asheville), a 360,000 square-foot facility that had been owned by the R. and E. Gordon Furniture Company. In 1966, Drexel opened its checkbook again, buying another plant, a factory that had been idle for 15 months in the mountain community of Whittier, North Carolina.[569]

Before another year was out, Drexel planned a public stock offering, issuing an additional 1.7 million shares to go with the 800,000 shares among the ownership group. They also sought a listing on the New York Stock Exchange. In addition, the company built a new plant that stretched 6.5 miles in length. Already huge, Drexel Enterprises added to its size to become the largest of the furniture giants in western North Carolina, in a strata by itself.[570]

The real advance for Drexel began in the 1950s. Between 1954 and 1963, the company went from $19 million in sales to $61 million. Industry observers and management at Drexel credited the rise to a selectively aggressive approach to the market. Advertising led the way. Full color layouts with Drexel's latest were a part of almost every women's and home furnishings magazine. One spread went on for 24 consecutive pages. Instead of the industry trend of saturating the market, management sought to place "its products in the prime stores of an area rather than going for multiple or mass exposure." Drexel burnished its reputation as a maker of high-end furniture by outfitting hotels like the San Francisco Hilton, site of the 1964 Republican National Convention. If that wasn't enough, the firm also worked key deals to furnish the cabinets for Motorola televisions and Baldwin organs.[571]

Times were good at Drexel. With sales increasing every year, management doled out more than $1.5 million in bonuses for workers, just in time for Christmas 1965. There was reason for jubilation. That year sales hit a record $74 million. Stockholders benefitted too with a dividend of forty cents per share paid out in early 1966. Before the end of the decade Drexel tried to merge with Stanley Furniture, a Virginia company about half the size of Drexel. The move was characterized as a "wedding of two giants in the furniture industry." The nuptials were never consummated, however. Negotiations between the two companies broke down when neither could propose a plan suitable to the other.[572]

After the demise of the Stanley deal, things went awry at Drexel. While they still continued to make money, not every idea that came from them proved to be sound. One example was a notion to create a line of furniture for teenagers. Certainly, the concept had merit since the teen market was making itself felt in the 1960s with its size and growing power as purchasers of items like records and clothing. At Drexel, designers conceived the unique idea of making a line that would "last as long as young people are teen-agers." The concept proposed the use of "disposable cardboard" as the raw material. One Drexel designer called the plan "great," saying, "there's no teen-age furniture offered today, because there is no furniture (of that kind) manufactured as far as I know." With an eye toward planned obsolescence, he added, "about the time the teens grew up, the furniture would disappear. After the teen-agers are gone, the adults could go buy guest room furniture instead of making the teen-ager compromise." The scheme for a line of teen, cardboard furniture never hit the market.[573]

If cardboard furniture for teenagers wasn't strange enough, Drexel plunged ahead with an even odder concoction for the 1966 market, "furry fabric." Observers joked that it brought out the caveman instinct with one designer quipping, "every time I walk by it, I want to throw it a bone." The grouping, called *Connotation* featured fabric in three shade choices, "blue, orangey-red or green." Another description of *Connotation* cracked, "it would add a massive look to anyone's home, with wild fibers looking like someone who doesn't use hair tonic." Drexel made the most of the weird approach in outfitting a room with the design. A press release suggested one could "sit on it nude after a bath." In the public square, however, the company took a beating for its attempt to appeal to the "non-conformist" market. A reviewer called a chair in the *Connotation* line, "too much icing on a cake. The covering here was wide-wale corduroy."[574]

Before the decade came to an end, Drexel turned from the acquirer of companies to the acquired. U.S. Plywood-Champion Paper spent $100 million on Drexel, who was at the time the third largest furniture manufacturer in the nation. Drexel became part of a large conglomerate, U.S. Plywood-Champion Paper ranking as the 98th largest company in the nation with over $1 billion in sales. The move brought on more interest in larger non-furniture companies looking to diversify, and with all the local firms still largely owned by the families who started them, the furniture tree was ripe for picking.[575]

Change occurred fast and furiously during the 1960s at Drexel. Before the U.S. Plywood-Champion Paper deal, Robert O. Huffman stepped down from daily charge of the company to chairman of the board. A long time lieutenant stepped up as G. Maurice Hill took over as president. The company employed approximately 6,000 workers by the end of its purchases, commanding the output in twenty factories across the state. Drexel, under U.S. Plywood-Champion Paper had become so big and attractive to union organizers that the Southern Council of Lumber and Plywood Workers of the United Brotherhood of Carpenters and Joiners made an attempt to unionize the employee base. The union had its work cut out for it. Given the profit sharing plan Drexel offered, along with regular bonuses that came like clockwork each July and December, winning over workers ended up beyond the persuasive powers of organized labor. Employees voted representation down the representation bid with the "no vote", carrying 68% of the ballots cast.[576]

Technically, the furniture makers of the western portion of NC competed with each other. Many made lines that vied for customer notice, but occasionally, in their mutual best interest, they cooperated. The market for furniture had grown so wide that suites made in Hickory, Morganton, and Lenoir could be found anywhere on the planet. In 1965 two of the biggest in the area, Drexel and Broyhill announced a "joint venture." The two giants pledged to "share the same sales organization in Europe, offering an across-the-board price package" to attract purchases from consumers on what was regarded as a lucrative market. The leadership, as well as the employees of both companies, were proud to see the popularity of their output spreading far and wide, believing like many in the era, the bigger the better.[577]

The purchase of Drexel served as one example of how popular furniture enterprises had become to companies elsewhere. The more well managed and profitable they were the juicier the targets became for takeover. Southern Virginia also had a furniture tradition that never spawned quite the number of companies that the North Carolina foothills had, but like Drexel, their footprint had grown very large. Their size gave them lots of profits to spend as they saw fit. In 1963, Bassett Furniture of Martinsville came looking for a Tarheel concern to call their own. They found it in the factory of Rome Jones, a World War II veteran who returned from action to start Prestige Furniture in North Newton, an industrial corridor between the Catawba County seat of Newton and Conover to the north.[578]

Rome Jones grew up in Newton, taking a full advantage of what the town offered in industrial capacity. Prior to the war, he worked as "sales manager of the Conover Chair Company." Upon his return he prepared himself for broader horizons with a course of study at Newton Business School, a beacon for "entrepreneurial young men." In 1949, he and Glenn Yount started Prestige Chair with four other investors. Within five years, the business expanded into new facilities, enlarging the company payroll by 50%. The upholstery company did good business, employing upwards of 250 hands. When Bob Spilman at Bassett wanted to get into the upholstery business and went looking for an already established company, he found Rome Jones' operation in North Newton. Basset paid $3 million for the operation Rome Jones built. The move gave Bassett an upholstery wing to go along with its case goods production back in Virginia, diversifying its furniture offerings. Spilman convinced Rome Jones to stay on for a while after cashing Bassett's check.[579]

In the deal, Bassett got much more than just a furniture company. Unknowingly, they got a seventeen-year-old kid coming out of high school, who would become an invaluable asset. Looking back, the kid recalled how lucky he felt to have the job of "tailing a ripsaw and other odd jobs in the frame department." Like his boss, Glenn Hunsucker never wasted an opportunity to better himself. At the urging of Rome Jones, Hunsucker took a "mail order course" in drafting. He put those skills to good use for the company by laying out a "flow of the product" which included a conveyor system for a 1954 expansion. Hunsucker regularly put in 60 hour weeks trying to figure out better work flows for the upholstery coming off the line. "I enjoyed what I was doing, mostly," he said. He worked hard because he needed the job.[580]

In coming to Prestige, Glenn Hunsucker did not stray far from his Catawba County roots. "I was a poor boy and I got out of high school and had no money," he remembered. "My father died when I was 11 and I knew I had to go to work. I had to do something," The bright young man applied himself to any task he was given, which distinguished him in the eyes of Rome Jones. By the time he celebrated ten years with the company, Hunsucker "was put in charge of manufacturing and product development."[581]

Supported by his boss and unafraid of change, Glenn Hunsucker oversaw some big adjustments in the production process. He found himself managing employees much older than him who wasted no time in telling him that his ideas were "crazy." Routinely, their answer was "that's not the way we do it." Undaunted, he replied, "well it is now. We've changed." One of the biggest came when he ended the time honored tradition of "spitting tacks." The technique had been around since furniture was made in workshops. Upholsterers kept a reservoir of tacks in their mouth, spitting them out as they nailed fabric to the frame, Glenn replaced the process with staple guns. "I had quite a few of them to quit," remembered the young department head on the Monday of the changeover. The process was entirely new he remembered, saying "nobody else in the industry had used them." After the fallout, he had to find replacements for those that walked off the job, then train them, "even though I'd never been an upholsterer," he admitted.[582]

Glenn Hunsucker saw a lot that needed innovation at Prestige and he instituted new measures one after the other. The use of "regular lumber" for chair and sofa frames presented a "major problem." It would split, warp and twist. Hunsucker helped introduce plywood as a substitute. This time, it wasn't the workers he had to convince of the change, but the retailers. Companies like Sears and J.C. Penney were skeptical and needed assurance of the product's quality. At the time, sales total about $70 million with the major retailers and Prestige could not afford to lose the business. The change, like the staple gun, ultimately demonstrated its value and built quite a reputation for its architect.[583]

In the days after the sale, Bassett continued to expand in the region. In 1969, the Virginia manufacturer picked up Taylorcraft, another upholstery shop in Hiddenite, located between Taylorsville and Statesville. They would go on to buy Impact Furniture in Hildebran as well. Bassett's presence in the area expanded during a period when the relationship between Virginia and North Carolina leadership had rough patches. Glenn Hunsucker characterized Rome Jones as "very opinionated, but he wanted to do it right." When it came to agreement on the best path ahead, Rome and Bassett management "had a hard time getting along." After a while, the solution called for a change. Rome

Jones left and Glenn Hunsucker was promoted, eventually all the way up to president and chief operating officer of Bassett Furniture, a position he held for a decade, until his retirement in 1997.[584]

Despite the fact that Rome Jones could be "a very demanding person" to work for, he mentored the careers of numerous furniture leaders. Designer and executive Ed Harmon gained tremendously from his time learning and watching Rome Jones. "You never called him Rome," Harmon recalled. "It was always Mr. Jones, and you didn't argue with him because you weren't going to win." Mr. Jones taught Harmon and many others "the fundamentals," which included a systematic way to organize production, making him in Ed's eyes "one of the smartest people I ever met in the business." Compared to the chaotic way in which some factories operated, Prestige ran efficiently, thanks to the original vision of Rome Jones and the assistance of men like Ed Harmon and Glenn Hunsucker. At one time Ed Harmon oversaw product development while Glenn Hunsucker handled all aspects of manufacturing. Both met with Rome Jones every morning to iron out problems. "He didn't believe in a lot of conversation," said Harmon, recollecting the way they addressed problems. Everything was so organized that problems were handled by "change requests" that pinpointed bottlenecks. Rome Jones handed them out every morning and expected the problems fixed promptly. The orderliness of the operation made Prestige a plum when Bassett came calling.[585]

Just like every manufacturing whiz making furniture, men like Rome Jones were always looking for better, more streamlined ways to produce their product. So did the budding next generation of leaders. One day, Ed Harmon suggested there needed to be a better way to set springs in upholstery. Instead of the time-consuming chore of using nails, he suggested the idea of creating a clip with its own point that could be hammered in place directly. A supplier had no clip to fit the bill. According to Harmon, "Rome was ticked." However, the frustration found a solution when Rome Jones designed, built and patented what became known as the Rome Jones Short Spring. For a while all those springs were stamped "RJS" until other companies knocked off the idea. Once Bassett took over, they decided that prosecuting copyright infringers was not worth the cost and abandoned defense of the patent. Throughout the life of the RJS clip, Ed Harmon never received a dime for his idea.[586]

Like Bassett before it, the Lane Co. Inc. was also one of the many Virginia manufacturers looking for a western North Carolina furniture outfit. Lane had grown to gigantic proportions the way firms in the Catawba Valley did, slowly but surely. Looking for an investment, unlike U.S. Plywood-Champion Paper that was looking to diversify, Lane bought into the business it knew: furniture. Lane acquired Hickory Chair, Hickory Tavern, and Bruington, a move that gave another Virginia company a substantial footprint to compete not only with its intra-state rival of Bassett, but also enterprises in the Old North State.[587]

NO. 2120 - PECAN VENEERS AND OTHER SELECTED HARDWOODS

No. 2124-588 Dresser Mirror
14 x 41½ in. - Framed - Gold Finish

No. 2120-576 Dresser Base
19 x 72 - Ht. 31½ in.
5 drawers, 2 doors, 6 trays

Like the Borax of old, furniture stylings of the 1960s had gotten more ornate. This page from a Kent-Coffey catalog shows the Mediterranean influence that was a part of the varied offering of manufacturers, trying to guesstimate the tastes of the furniture buying public. (Courtesy of the Caldwell Heritage Museum)

One company buying another was not new to the furniture industry, but buyers from well outside the region were. The new wave was larger, more rapid and motives more suspect than anything manufacturers had seen since outsiders tried to buy Hickory Chair (and locals bought it back) in 1944. The first to succumb was Superior Chair. Just after the Second World War, Harley Shuford, who was cranking up Century Furniture in Hickory, teamed with A.C. Black and Y.M. Smith to start Superior Chair in 1946. The company opened its doors in Maiden, south of Newton. In 1958, Connecticut manufacturer Ethan Allen came calling with a wish to fully possess the company, renaming it Baumritter Chair for a while before revealing the true owner. In fact, Ethan Allen had already been a part of Superior Chair since 1948, when it invested as a minority owner, before buying the factory lock, stock, and barrel for its very own, ten years later.[588]

The 1960s witnessed an increase in the number of buyouts, but during that time a plethora of new furniture enterprises also emerged. With little fanfare and mostly private money, companies set up shop all across the region. They included Marlow, located in Hildebran (1960), a community between Hickory and Morganton, Stylecraft of Hickory (1960), DeVille of Hickory (1961), Laurel Furniture (1961), Customair Furniture (1962), Old Hickory Tannery (1963) specializing in leather furniture, Temple Furniture in Maiden (1962), south of Hickory, and Leathercraft Furniture (1968).[589]

Just as some were rising, some were sinking too. Hy-Lan Furniture, an outfit that came along during the Depression, was owned by the town's one-time mayor, Walker Lyerly, Sr. who also had interests in textiles. Weathering a union vote, the death of the mayor, and a plane crash that took the life of Walker Lyerly, Jr., adversity slowed Hy-Lan's momentum to the point that the company was sold at public auction on the steps of the Catawba County Courthouse. Picked up by Titian Research and Development Corp., workers continued to build its signature dining room suites until the factory went to

Welbilt Corp., an appliance maker, a few years later for an undisclosed amount.

For an ambitious and experienced furniture player, it was easy to start a new company, sometimes several. Tom Shores cranked up Classic Leather in Hickory in 1966. As the name suggested, the company dealt exclusively in leather upholstery. A few years into production, Shores began to look beyond the leather market. At this point, he found a young Marine veteran from the Vietnam War who had decided upon a career in furniture. John Bray began with Highland House Furniture in Hickory as credit manager but within a few years met Tom Shores. Bray noticed that Shores "was having difficulties hiring salesmen and creating enough products for his sales representatives to be successful." Observing that "velvet fabrics were starting to sell with his customers," Tom created a new company, Vanguard Furniture with John Bray leaving Highland House to lead the enterprise.[590]

Keeping a full stock of velvets to cover its chairs and sofas, Vanguard could "manufacture and ship orders in two weeks," according to John Bray, who was one of the first eight employees. He called their efforts "upholstery customization" and characterized their approach as being in something akin to the "fashion business." "Our model was to design and make products for the higher end or fashion part of the industry," Bray said. "We were constantly looking for ways to differentiate ourselves from companies who made similar products." The market had saturated to the point that if a company was going to make its mark, it had distinguish itself in the eye of the customer.[591]

Over the years Vanguard expanded well beyond velvet but early on they created new companies to build different items for different markets. In 1973, St. Timothy Chair was born "to make vinyl furniture for the contract industry." The move gave Vanguard another arena in which to compete, the institutional market. After that, Craftwork Guild combined the styles made by Classic Leather, Vanguard, and St. Timothy, producing furniture that would comply with California's "new flammability requirements." Eventually, the various

TIMELESS ELEGANCE . . . Here is a chair that is basic. It is a chair certain to complement your decor — fulfill your practical needs. The ageless beauty of simple lines, extreme comfort and superb craftsmanship mean many years of prideful ownership. For free brochure and name of nearest dealer, write Dept. HG 2, North Hickory Furniture Co.

NH

Chair No. 715

NORTH HICKORY
FURNITURE COMPANY
P. O. BOX 785, HICKORY, NORTH CAROLINA

The stylings of North Hickory Furniture always gravitated toward Early American, a consistent seller in any era. About the time of this advertisement, the company built its own showroom, requiring furniture market buyers to make another stop in their sojourn to Hickory. (Author's collection)

operations were combined. In fact, to assure the look of their furniture in showrooms across the nation, Classic Leather and Vanguard also got into the case goods business. Instead of making pieces themselves, they commissioned production of items to go along with their upholstery. The companies wanted to make sure that the ancillary pieces they displayed, properly accented the main product. As John Bray confided, "we were fearful that our beautiful velvet sofa would not be shown in vignette with attractive case goods and also that when case goods pieces were sold off the floor, they would be replaced by a truly incompatible piece - like a low-end colonial cocktail table." In order to create the right atmosphere which spurred sales, they "started creating case goods that complemented our upholstery and could be used to enhance the display for our products at retail."[592]

As the sixties progressed with its buyouts, competition with High Point also heated up. During the spring 1966 furniture market, a group of fifteen furniture manufacturers sought to throw a party like no other, something no buyer anywhere would ever forget. The Lenoir Country Club was "invaded" by superheroes, with Batman (a popular television series at the time) showing up along with other comic book characters, ranging from Wonder Woman and Cat Woman to Superman. "The mood was camp and pop art all the way," reported one attendee. The event sought to create an artistic, "must see" atmosphere in the west to distinguish itself from the stodgy parties down east, bringing together "company presidents, tired market goers and editors." With a giant ice bat spreading its "frozen wings over the buffet," the crowd of over 100 guests rose the next morning with a unique, but understandable refrain that signified a successful party. "Holy Headache!"[593]

The trend of expanding showrooms with more lavish spaces accelerated as each group of companies sought to lure furniture buyers. Both east and west, display space grew with companies enlarging to show their wares. For the fall market of 1967, North Hickory Furniture followed the lead of other top producers and built its own space. As long as they could entice buyers to visit, North Hickory could show off its "11,000 square feet of decorated showroom space at its factory." The expansion made room for North Hickory to display all of its designs, "227 pieces of Early American, Colonial, contemporary and traditional furniture." In addition, "over 225 fabrics with thousands of color combinations and designs are also on display."[594]

Both North Carolina markets were vying with each other, as well as outside locations in places like Dallas, Texas, and Atlanta, Georgia, for the attention of retail buyers throughout the United States. Ideally, the Hickory and High Point groups of companies worked in general cooperation with each other, but with High Point always seeing larger numbers of visitors. If the east was the dog, the west wagged as the tail. In fact, some companies, especially those in the west continued setting up displays in High Point in case market visitors could not or would not to make the drive up the newly constructed Interstate 40 for a look see. A definite line existed between the two camps, but it began to blur when the High Point circle of companies reached into the Hickory market for ownership. In 1966, Thomasville Furniture bought

Western Carolina Furniture. Over the next decade, more and more local enterprises cashed out with offers too good to turn down.[595]

By 1968, the choice of furniture styles exploded too. No longer defined by a definite trend the way modernist design took stage in the 1950s, or the Early American resurgence of the early 60s, companies offered 'anything and everything' to customers. French, Mediterranean, Spanish, Asian (called "Oriental" at the time), Italian and styles with "a crisp military influence" were all part of the offerings. Also, wood was no longer the exclusive material in the new looks. The list included "cane, simulated slate, plexiglass, burls (irregular grain patterns in wood), smoked glass, bamboo, parquetry, inlaid wood, leather straps," even chrome and "simulated concrete." Upholstery was just as wide ranging with chenille, vinyl, needlepoint, velvet and suede all part of new creations. Home furnishings editor Mamie Zillman wrote "new designs run the gamut at furniture companies sprinkled between Drexel and Hickory."[596]

The late sixties just might just have been the pinnacle for the furniture business in western North Carolina. Business was stellar, and the area recognized itself with the moniker "Furniture Capital of the South," a direct swipe at High Point. Trucks leaving every day with pieces rolling off the production line had the phrase emblazoned on the back door of their forty-foot trailers to tell everyone who got behind the vehicle, as well as those retailers who swung the doors open for their next delivery, that furniture made within a twenty-mile radius of Hickory was the leader. Whether it was from real conviction or hopeful thinking, western North Carolina announced itself as the furniture epicenter of the world. The assertion boasted a handy, if not completely accurate way to place the western manufacturers on the forefront of furniture production. The ground they claimed would be difficult to defend, but with an ever-growing number of companies making a little bit of everything, and with a track record of overcoming numerous obstacles to establish itself, the slogan had a viable shot at becoming reality.

A 1966 Buyers Guide for the Hickory Home Furnishings Mart listed a glut of furniture companies, by the community from which they originated.

In Claremont:

Clairmont Chair Co.

Montclair Furniture Co.

Scales Furniture Co., Inc.

In Conover:

The Accent Line

Carrousel Furniture Corp.

Conover Chair Co., Inc.

Hallcraft, Inc.

Nandel, Inc.

Southern Furniture Co. of Conover, Inc.

Timmerman Mag. Co.

In Drexel:

Drexel Furniture Co.

Knob Creek of Morganton (lighting company)

In Granite Falls:

Dakin Chair Co., Inc.

In Hickory:

Ashley Furniture Co.

Americana Furniture Co.

Beau-Hill Furniture Co., Inc.

Bolick Bros. Chair Co.

Bruington Furniture, Inc.

Carolina Comfort Furniture Co.

Cegan Furniture Co.

Century Furniture Co.

Charvelle Furniture Co.

Clayton-Marcus Furniture Co.

Comfort Chair Co.

Cox Manufacturing Co.

Custom Craft Furniture Co.

Decor Furniture

De Ville Furniture Co.

Fashion Furniture Co.

Granline Corp.

Herman Chairs

Hickory Chair Co.

Hickory Colonial, Inc.

Hickory Foliage Co.

Hickory-Fry Furniture Co.

Hickory-Hill Furniture Co.

Hickory Manufacturing Co.

Hickory Parlor Furniture

Hickory Tavern Furniture, Inc.

Hickory Upholstering Co.

Highland House of Hickory, Inc.

Hylan Furniture Co.

Kaymar Furniture Co.

Keith Manufacturing Co., Inc.

King Hickory Furniture Co.

Laine Upholstering Co.

Markay Furniture Co.

Marlow Furniture Co.

Maxwell Royal Chair Co.

North Hickory Furniture Co.

P & G Chair Co.

Pioneer Cabinet and Speciality Co.

Posture Built of North Carolina, Inc.

Sherrill Upholstering Co.

Style Craft Furniture Co., Inc.

Style Upholstering Co.

Suggs & Hardin Upholstering Co.

Terrytown Importing and Mfg.

Trend Line, Inc.

Western Carolina Furniture Co.

Whites Chairs

In Lenoir:

Bernhardt Industries

Blowing Rock Furniture Industries

Brandon Furniture Co.

Broyhill Furniture Factories, Inc.

Caldwell Furniture Co.

Fairfield Furniture Co.

Flair, Inc.

Hammary Manufacturing Co.

Hibriten Chair Co.

Hibriten Furniture Co.

Kent-Coffey Manufacturing Co.

Kincaid Furniture (Hudson)

Maehill Chair Co.

In Lincolnton:

Burris Manufacturing Co., Inc.

Cochrane Furniture Co., Inc.

Lincoln Furniture Co.

In Maiden:

Temple Furniture Mfg. Co.

In Newton:

Bracewell Furniture Co.

Newton Manufacturing Co.

Prestige Furniture Corp.

In Statesville:

Builtright Chair Co.

Bylo Furniture Co.

Carolina Crafts Co.

Dixie Seating Co.

Gilliam Furniture, Inc.

Home Made Chair Co.

North Carolina Furniture Co.

Ross Furniture Co.

Royal Danish Corp.

A.L. Shaver & Son

Shaver Stool & Novelty Co.

Sherrill Furniture Co.

Statesville Chair Co.

Statesville Manufacturing Co.

Troutman Chair Co.

In Valdese:

Crestline Furniture Co.[597]

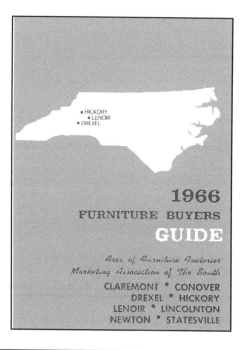

Three pages from the 1966 Buyers Guide, including advertisements for the largest venues in the region for retailers, the Hickory Home Furnishings Mart and the Hickory Furniture Mart. The guide also included ads for suppliers, furniture companies, shippers and area amenities. (Author's collection)

Chapter 22
Flights of Fortune

"Little by little, almost unnoticed by the general public, the furniture business has been sprouting wings as its operations have expanded in scope and magnitude," conveyed Russell Christensen, vice president in charge of sales for Bernhardt Industries in a 1966 article. His analysis made two points about the furniture industry. First, the business at large and his company in particular, were on the move. In the space of a few years, Bernhardt had started an upholstery division (Flair, Inc. in 1958), added a second 200,000 square-foot-factory, bought controlling interest in Hibriten Furniture and would soon buy out several small Statesville upholstery shops, Sherrill Furniture and Orbit Industries. The furniture industry, and Bernhardt within it, were on the move.[598]

An equally important point Christensen was making with his statement was the pace at which the world of furniture production was increasing. Not only was Russell Christensen an executive with Bernhardt, but he was also a pilot, a skill he employed regularly with the company. As columnist and historian Nancy Alexander described it, "impelled by rapid growth and swift development, furniture industry officials are taking to the air to keep abreast of complex markets." Christensen revealed that Bernhardt had acquired two planes to transport management staff to the vast number of appointments

The 1960s marked the apex of furniture making on the western end. Manufacturers 'knocked off' the designs of each other, creating a homogenous look that magazines like *Fortune* criticized roundly, all the while alerting corporations of furniture profitability. (Courtesy of the Caldwell Heritage Museum)

that required more than a car ride. He flew one of the planes in his duties with Bernhardt.[599]

From humble beginnings, the industry had matured. Whether by natural progression or the influx of corporate owners, the 1960s saw the furniture making business become a fast-paced, big time industry in western North Carolina. Of the four largest producers in the United States, two of them were in the foothills, Broyhill third, Drexel fourth. Additionally, the second largest producer Bassett, held a presence with ownership of Prestige in Newton. In the late 60s the production lines on the western end of the furniture "figure eight" hummed with activity. Each year more workers were needed to keep up with increased demand. Periodic labor shortages reminded management of just how important a hand was to the process. On occasion, foremen looked the other way when employees pulled practical jokes on their fellow workers. The shenanigans were just part of the furniture culture. As long as acceptable product got made and orders were filled, everyone was content, even as serious change loomed.[600]

The late 60s might well have been the ultimate era of the mountain/foothills furniture business. A plethora of factories had made Lenoir a one-industry town. Morganton had state institutions like the School for the Deaf and Broughton State Hospital to balance employment, but furniture captured the rest of the town's workforce. Hickory remained somewhat diversified with textiles/hosiery balancing out its employment landscape, but as in Statesville and Marion, furniture came to be the product for which they were known. The region embraced the distinction.

Local manufacturers were proud of their accomplishments. They marketed a product that sold well throughout the United States and felt they offered a fair day's wage for a fair day's work. They had kept out unions with their own benevolence and rhetoric. Families like the Shufords in Hickory, the Huffmans in Morganton, and the Broyhills and Bernhardts in Lenoir were looked upon with esteem for the job-creating enterprises they ran and the philanthropy they dealt out. Despite the growth, the world of business took a less charitable view of the southern enterprises. The February 1967 issue of *Fortune* magazine thought rather less of them, calling the lot "a group of mountain hicks." As one observer saw it, the "beautiful swans" furniture makers saw themselves as, woke up one day to be called "ugly ducklings" by observers all over the country. And while the condemnation hurt, it came with a silver lining, sort of. The article pointed out just how lucrative the business of furniture production was. Maybe after reading the entire article, those local "hicks" who read *Fortune* didn't think themselves so ugly after all.[601]

The article was unkind to furniture makers across the country, not just Tarheels. Author Thomas O'Hanlon called most of the 5,350 companies operating as of 1967, "insignificant in size, inbred in management, inefficient in production, and inherently opposed to technological change." As he surmised, "an air of earnest amateurism pervades the industry." Since "two-thirds of all furniture makers employ fewer than twenty employees," prevailing thought in that era strongly suggested the industry was prime for takeover, the corporate giants more knowledgable in how operations should be run. O'Hanlon even went as far as to say that the way things were run, was a "disservice to the consumer." Some of the blame rested with retailers, the magazine writer said. Asserting store owners were not "consumer-oriented," he charged that retailers simply bought whatever they perceived to be a "good value," which made the whole process for the customer "a frustrating experience."[602]

These criticisms aside, one great attribute of the furniture industry was that it made money, lots of it. In eight years, firms had gone from $2.7 million in sales to $4 million. O'Hanlon attributed the rise more to "an elementary need for millions of people that buy new homes," and "less from shrewd management." The Bureau of Labor Statistics reported that the average urban consumer spent more on color televisions than it they did on furniture, which for O'Hanlon pointed to unrealized potential. In an era, where room, and even home coordination was in vogue, pairing furniture with carpet and every other element of decor stood out as a trend the furniture companies of 1967 were missing.[603]

Luckily for western North Carolina, O'Hanlon zeroed in on the one-industry town of Bassett, Virginia. There he reported on the sole employer with its Bassett school, Bassett houses, Bassett-built baptist church, Bassett Bank, and a Bassett community center. Within the article Lenoir showed up, as well. According to O'Hanlon, 23 of the top 30 furniture companies were located in close proximity. Here's how he described the lot. "With the exception of Drexel Enterprises (which had just recently been acquired), the southern companies are controlled or managed by the men who founded them or by their offspring. All of them have a paternalistic approach to their employees." Like a father trying to keep his children at home, the owners have a "fierce animosity toward labor unions," to keep other opinions about their work life silent. Operationally, he added that company ownership had also erred over the years inadvertently building "a Rube Goldberg assembly-line technique that breaks down the construction of any piece of furniture into scores of simple individual assembly operations." In the eyes of *Fortune*, the industry could do little that was seen as competent.[604]

The biggest criticism of the furniture industry O'Hanlon voiced centered around the industry's quality control efforts, or lack thereof. One foothills manufacturer was singled out for not having any at all. Reminiscent of the jokes about borax furniture, the article detailed how the National Retail Merchants Association was forced to articulate minimum standards of quality for the furniture it received. One rule stipulated that "all screws must be turned and not hammered in." Another stated, "pieces should be steady and free from wobble in normal use." The rules seemed to only reflect common manufacturing sense, but O'Hanlon quoted Paul Broyhill as saying "we can't inspect for quality," questioning the worth of everything that came out with a Broyhill label. With firms asserting that "structural defects are inherent in low-priced, mass-produced furniture," the criticism made it look as though the local manufacturers were either inept or too greedy to hire inspectors before the pieces went out the door.[605]

The article cast southern manufacturers as the yokels and rubes of the borax days, perpetuating the stereotype of workers as too lazy to craft a fine piece of furniture. In attempting to humiliate leaders like Paul Broyhill, O'Hanlon forgot (or never bothered to notice) what companies like Broyhill were actually creating. In his autobiography, *This Is Broyhill*, Paul explained the ingenuity that went into growth. He recognized the need for modernization and when it came time to expand, he spent a lot of money to do so. When he joined his father's company he noticed that all work in the machine room was done by hand. "We made changes first by automating the lumber cutting

Inspired by the design of a General Electric plant in Kentucky, Paul Broyhill designed the Broyhill Industrial Complex in the same way with a central warehouse. The plant covered 1.5 million square feet of workspace, not exactly the hometown enterprise *Fortune* portrayed. (Image courtesy of Bill Tate & Kay Stableton via Wikimedia Commons, photo by L.R. Bernhardt)

department," Broyhill noted. "Then, instead of manhandling each board up to the machine, the boards were laid on a roller conveyor and automatically pushed along. Gradually, we added roller conveyors throughout the machine area and eliminated the need for factory (hand drawn) trucks." Efforts like those were never investigated in favor of the 'hammered screw' story that connoted a sloppy assembly effort.[606]

Companies like Broyhill wrestled with how to modernize when the tried-and-true ways their workforce knew continued to produce. Like a magician pulling out a tablecloth and leaving the dishes intact, Paul Broyhill tasked his company's construction crew to "tear down a plant a little at a time and keep production going. We could not afford to let production stop, so we built roofs over tops of roofs, floors over tops of floors, moved machinery from one side to the other side, and somewhere were able to keep factories running and producing while we tore out old roofs, walls, and floors all around them."

Innovation, under its own terms, kept production going.[607]

Broyhill management of the 1960s sought better ways to craft its lines. Paul Broyhill went so far as to load up his management staff, and flying them to Europe on several occasions to see the newest equipment available for furniture production. In Germany, they saw their first chip-core machine, which mixed wood chips with resin for a sturdy underbody that could be disguised by veneered pieces. They bought four machines. The later innovation of particle board so impressed Paul that he wrote a check for one even though "it was by far the largest machinery purchase we had ever made." The effort to innovate was there, despite Thomas O'Hanlon's characterization.[608]

As prudent traditionalists, most operators conducted business in much the same way they always had, sometimes all the way back to the firm's creation. For those methods, companies were depicted as living in their own bubble. As with any snapshot, change within each company depended largely on the age and vision of who was in charge. The old-timers were not like Paul Broyhill who was willing to spend money for the latest idea. Industry in the 1960s was only beginning to understand the value of computers as a tool that could spur productivity. A Thomasville Furniture executive was excited at the prospect, believing that furniture manufacturing would benefit from technology and that future production could be "rationalized by setting goals based on market forecasts, restructuring the flow of materials, and most important, by introducing mechanization." The article pointed to a brave new world, but the older players resisted change. Outside observers characterized manufacturers as backward, goading them to wake up and see what was going on all around them.[609]

Under the heading "The Outsiders Move In," *Fortune* pointed out to its readers how a handsomely profitable company like Drexel, which made piles of money, had already been scooped up in a buyout, equating profitability with outside management. Magnavox Corporation had bought three smaller factories in Lenoir and was also held up as an example of what was waiting in the foothills for corporate interests. Thomas O'Hanlon exalted Colin Capri, a thirty-five-year-old management consultant who began buying up furniture companies with an eye toward consolidation. The article quoted Capri exclaiming that he was "dumbfounded" by his inquiry into furniture, saying, "here was a mammoth industry that was almost dormant and yet it had tremendous potential."[610]

Fortune magazine painted its picture with a distinct agenda. On the side of growth and change were perceived visionaries like Colin Capri. On the other were the current owners of companies who believed their conservative approach ensured the stability of the business as an ongoing enterprise, lasting much longer than the time it took to buy a factory. Locals "scorned" the intruders. One "North Carolina executive" scoffed at newcomer interest, saying "you can't understand furniture, until you have your pockets filled with sawdust and your mouth full of tobacco juice." Sure, O'Hanlon flattered the owners with accounts of their profitability, but intoned that they were too dumb to develop the industry further.[611]

The compliment of profitability resonated with more than the furniture makers themselves. The acknowledgment beckoned a number of larger companies to come calling. Bassett's president and executive VP of the Southern Furniture Manufacturers Association noticed that after the article appeared, "big companies started to bombard the association with calls. They were looking for furniture companies to buy." Joking that the wave brought a "merger of the week" as acquisition ramped up quickly, it became harder to stay independent. While some enjoyed and benefitted from "the advertising money, merchandising muscle and vaunted managerial experience of the big Northern companies," others saw mergers as a trap.[612]

Bernhardt Industries was intent upon retaining its independence. Alex Bernhardt, grandson of the founder put it succinctly, "We don't let them in the door." While some had chosen to cash out on all their fathers or grandfathers had built, the Bernhardts stood firm. They prized their own decision-making in a heavily splintered market where even companies like Bassett, one of the largest in the nation, only had three percent of total sales. As Alex Bernhardt pointed out, "if we want to do something, we can do it. We don't have to call a meeting or write New York for permission." He and his father John Christian Bernhardt knew that in a nation with thousands of companies, and no dominant player to dictate direction, Bernhardt Furniture could maintain its niche within the industry, and planned to continue to do so without outside meddling. Bernhardt's stance did not stop inquiries, though. "We have at least one call a week from someone who wants to buy," said Alex, but he remained confident that his company would move forward under its own steam.[613]

Phone calls to Bernhardt coincided with an internal and extensive plan of expansion. Second and third generation owners John Christian and Alex Bernhardt stepped outside their native Caldwell County for the first time when they bought Sherrill Furniture in Statesville, not to be confused with Catawba County's Sherrill Upholstering. The firm bought by the Bernhardts began as the Sherrill-Green Furniture Company, a maker of "bedroom furniture and occasional tables" that was a part of the 1920s wave of manufacturing. The company had a spotty history, struggling through the Great Depression, then reopening as Sherrill Furniture before Bernhardt bought the operation in 1969. Two years later, the Lenoir-based manufacturer added Sechrest Veneer, also in Statesville. Immediately, Bernhardt launched expansion projects at the two factories, as well as construction of a $5 million, 400,000 square-foot facility on the southern end of Iredell County near the small town of Troutman. Completed and dedicated in 1974, the factory was hailed as a "completely modern, fully-automated, furniture manufacturing operation." What made the "new concept" unique was air conditioning.[614]

In an effort to take the lead in better working conditions for more efficient operation, Bernhardt designed and built their new factory a long way from their base in Lenoir. "The Troutman plant has a unique ecological system that is completely new in the industry," asserted one account of its creation. Using a "closed system of continuous air reclamation and recovery" throughout the plant instead of "spot cooling," Bernhardt sought to create a workspace that better accommodated employees, in character with its view of being a "people oriented" company. President of Operation, Wes Collins had thought it all out, crafting an intelligent approach to furniture making. With this new plant, he wanted space for growth, good working conditions and management that operated "on the principle of trying to have the people on hand before the need becomes pressing."

As a hedge against productivity declines that might slow down Bernhardt and negatively impact the bottom line, Wes Collins shrewdly anticipated problems. Since coming to Bernhardt in the 1950s, he had shepherded Bernhardt's upholstery line Flair, with growth of over 20% every year, a phenomenal record. At Troutman, he continued to demonstrate a well-reasoned approach to meet the needs of the company as it met the needs of the buying public. Before the facility opened, Collins had already lined up training through "several area educational facilities, such as Catawba Valley Technical Institute" in Hickory to prepare workers for what was expected of them. As many as 500 students flocked to the training. To stay as far away as they could from any tempting merger offers Bernhardt, with Wes Collins directing activity, took a well-considered approach to running their business.

Most companies of the era equated bigger with better. Western tarheel manufacturers always reached for growth like the kind Wes Collins achieved at Bernhardt. Nationally, conglomerates embraced a belief that "in diversity is strength," which put furniture companies in play as acquisitions. At about the time of the *Fortune* article, the practice of diversifying portfolios in large corporations came into vogue and since many neither owned nor understood furniture making, North Carolina manufacturers became ripe opportunities for broadening their horizons. However, the trend went both ways.

By 1967, growth had turned Thomasville Chair into Thomasville Furniture Industries. The company began "in the wilderness between High Point and Lexington" as a chair factory. Much like Tom Broyhill's entry into the business, the Finch brothers supplied lumber and when the company could not pay them, T.J. and C.F. took stock. In less than a year, they took over. This mushrooming manufacturer from the eastern sphere grew substantially with a series of record profits that allowed management to buy a number of smaller firms. Reaching into the west, Thomasville started with a chair plant in the mountain community of West Jefferson, located north of Boone. Purchase of Phenix Chair in 1964 brought Thomasville back to its roots, since Phenix built chairs exclusively. Two years later, Thomasville bought out upholstery maker, Western Carolina Furniture in Hickory. Thirteen months after that, Thomasville reached once more, this time to Lenoir where it bought Caldwell Furniture. For Thomasville, the purchase diversified their line since Caldwell's output was characterized as selling "price brackets below Thomasville products."[615]

As Thomasville purchased, so was it bought. "Armstrong Cork, of Lancaster, Pa., diversified maker of flooring and carpets" swapped stock with the publicly traded company in 1968. The deal rivaled the Drexel-Champion Paper union for size, placing a company of gigantic proportions, now owned by an outsider, in the eastern and the western portions of the state. The only furniture executive to officially address the merger trend (and the O'Hanlon article) was Thomasville's president, grandson of early owner T.J. Finch. Speaking to the New York Society of Security Analysts, Tom Finch sought to set Thomasville and Drexel apart from other manufacturers, noting that "the six largest U.S. furniture companies (which include both Thomasville and Drexel) account for just 12 per cent of industry sales but have been growing at the rate of about 10 per cent a year, twice the industry average." His analysis suggested that superior performance made furniture companies the ripest of plums, ready for takeover, an accolade in his eyes.[616]

Tom Finch also saw mergers (which were really buyouts) as the inevitable outcome for most sizable furniture manufacturers in the world of American business in the 1960s. When asked, he "suggested many mergers were prompted by lack of management depth in small, family-owned businesses, (and) tax problems as firms are inherited and the inability of smaller companies to finance the new machinery needed for efficient operation." While Finch saw the business he just sold as well run in his estimation, many of his competitors were not, especially those brands that carried family names. He agreed with O'Hanlon's thesis that succession from father to son, once an accepted practice (and one from which he benefitted) had become too risky to be accepted as prudent.[617]

Thomas O'Hanlon would likely have had a field day with a Statesville company as a testament to his thesis that hometown companies were backward, badly run, and a relic of western NC's furniture past. The name of the company might have gained his attention, had he noticed. The same year as his article came another in the *Statesville Record and Landmark* that the assets of the Home-Made Chair Company were being sold in U.S. District Court after bankruptcy. Opened during the Roaring 20s, the firm incorporated in 1935, during the depths of the Great Depression, "to manufacture, build and rebuild furniture, novelties and etc." The company weathered fires, workplace injuries, wood shortages, the death of its founder, and encroachment by state highway officials to improve traffic flow in west Statesville before sinking into insolvency in 1967. Apparently, Home-Made Chair was not an attractive acquisition. Instead, they simply faded from the furniture roster.[618]

To many of the workers, progress was a scary thought. They wanted stability, not the uncertainty of corporate deals. Life in the shop could mean daily drudgery, often with repetitive tasks for eight hours. Folks on the shop floor jockeyed for as much as they could get, but given the available jobs, they didn't have much leverage since they were considered 'unskilled.' Some moved from plant to plant for a higher wage but the difference was often only a nickel or a dime more per hour. In the old days an employee took comfort in knowing the owner, even if the interaction was infrequent and superficial. Conversely, Tom Finch's view argued that system had become antiquated. Decisions directly affecting the workforce would be better if they were more impersonal, not less. Changes would be good for the health of the company (i.e. stockholders), not the workers. The new structure left hourly employees with no one of consequence to consult concerning their livelihood with their performance secondary to corporate needs.

Mildred Church toiled at hourly jobs throughout her working life. As she grew older she eventually gravitated to various furniture factory positions. Along the way, she made jumps from one plant to another seeking pay increases with each move. Writing to her oldest daughter, June, in 1968, she detailed one effort she made with her other daughter, Dottie, also a furniture worker. "We went up to Lenoir Furniture Saturday morning," Church wrote. "He talked real good but I told him I would not come for less than $1.85 and I would not work in the finishing room." She realized the conditions she laid down might be a deal breaker, adding, "he probably will not call me and I don't care. I did not like the place anyway." The issue of real consequence was not the money, it was her workmate daughter. She went on to write, "I hope they don't call Dottie either. I would be lonesome without her." At the time of Mildred Church's letter the national hourly minimum wage stood at $1.60, while in North Carolina, the rate was $1.00.[619]

Workers sought something beyond a paycheck to get them through the day. Those that didn't have a family member to share their experiences with looked for other ways to pass the time. Some resorted to mischief. Antics could be offhand like sneaking up on a fellow worker and scaring them by a flick of the ear or a tug of the hair. Verbal jousts such as name calling, put downs, and jokes at the expense of others were constant, sometimes cruel and often unconscious attempts to establish a pecking order within the department. Workers vied to see who was tough enough to "take a ragging," a slang term for being able to withstand the abuse. When the injured party lashed out, the joke became all the funnier to everyone except the victim.

The mundanity of the job gave employees time to think of tricks they could play. Following the lead of his mother Ruth into the industry, Romey Church (no relation to Mildred) went to work for Singer Furniture Plant 4. He was bored by the work of handling veneer, so he came up with a string of practical jokes, saying it was "the way I got through the day." Some were simple. A water fountain had been installed and when he found the cutoff valve for it, he would wait for a colleague to get a drink. When they bent down to sip the water, Romey turned the valve off, waited for the reaction and tried to stifle his laughter. "I did that a long time before I got caught," he said admitting, "that's pretty silly, but it was a lot of fun in the factory."[620]

Romey Church engaged in a lot of practical jokes while he ran a hot press that glued boards together. Many followed the model of the water fountain trick with unsuspecting folks left scratching their heads when something did not work according to plan. His most elaborate stunt involved a man who brought his lunch every day. Before the noon hour whistle, the worker set out a can of beanie-weenies or pork and beans on a pipe that as Church described it, "would get super hot." Every day the man followed the same routine, opening the can a little, set it on the pipe and came back about 20 minutes later for his heated lunch. "I got to watching him," remembered Romey Church about conjuring up his plan. "As soon as he walked around the corner, I'd get his can and set it in the window. In the wintertime, it's pulling cold air and it'd be ice cold, freezing." As Church watched the man start back, he returned the can to where the unsuspecting man left it, only to find the can cold to the touch even though the pipe was "radiating heat." The stunt went on "for years," as the practical joker looked back. The duped man tried everything including increasing heating time up to an hour, all to no avail. "He looks at it, he shakes it, he looks at it," all the time drawing never-ending laughs from Church. "Finally somebody caught me," confessed the prankster, "so the game was up."[621]

Workers down on the shop floor, at least some of them, weren't the only ones who enjoyed a good practical joke. The furniture market was a time when salesmen came back to town to greet the retailers they serviced during the year. Of all the furniture company owners, DeVille's Bill Mosteller was the most likely to play a good practical joke. One night during the market in Hickory, one of DeVille's salesmen drank too much. Bill decided to have some fun. He got a Highway Patrol officer to take the inebriated salesman

During the era of local ownership, affairs like this Christmas party were part of a fringe benefit package workers expected each year. Once mergers and acquisitions took place, many annual events were curtailed or dropped as management/workforce relations became impersonal. (Courtesy of the Caldwell Heritage Museum)

back to his room. Meanwhile, Bill convinced "one of the guys that worked in the plant there that had got a pig" to bring it to the salesman's room. Along the way, a veterinarian friend of Bill's gave the pig a sedative. Both the pig and the salesman ended up in the bed. The pig woke up first, thrashing about the room and scaring the salesman "half to death." Reportedly, Bill Mosteller and everyone who knew about the hoax, got "a big laugh out of it."[622]

Practical jokes helped relieve the tedium of a job, be it among salesmen or on the shop floor. However, the reliability of of a job in the industry was no laughing matter. The work was steady and seemed secure, but the warning signs were there. With a national magazine announcing that highly profitable western tarheel companies were ripe for the picking, and some already snapped up, the future would not be as rosy as it once was. Workers, powerless though they were, stayed on the job and hoped for the best. Meanwhile, management fielded calls from interested buyers and weighed their options. A new day was dawning in the foothills of western North Carolina.

Chapter 23
An Odd Cat

Furniture, as an industry found itself at a crossroads as the 1960s ended. Now a major player in the statewide and national economy, the question became what kind of presence would it continue to be. The answer was conjectured widely with answers as vast as the number of companies that existed. Startups, expansions, buy-outs, bankruptcies, all happened regularly, just as they had since furniture production started in the region. Mostly though, decisions about the progress of local factories were made locally. With the influx of new owners, a turn was shaping up.

The crossroads called for an account of how the industry was situated as it moved forward. *Hickory Daily Record* (*HDR*) reporter Paul Fogleman surveyed the landscape in a 1970 report, reprinted statewide. His analysis signaled new directions for a product reaching a century of existence. A reckoning for both workers and the region seemed close at hand.[623]

Likening furniture as important to the area as cotton was to the South before the Civil War, Fogleman began counting the number of operations that now had new owners. These parent companies had no real interest in furniture, except as investments. They bought only to diversify their holdings as a hedge against a changing economy. With the Unifour (a four county grouping of Alexander, Caldwell, Burke and Catawba counties that the *HDR* covered) having "hitched its wagon to the future," in this case a corporate structure, how would the new furniture boss differ from the old boss?[624]

Trying to put the best face on it, Paul Fogleman pointed out that many of the latest outside owners chose local people to run their new divisions. "The Lane Company named a Hickory man president of Hickory Chair Co., which was acquired in the fall of 1967," served as a hopeful example. Fogleman took inventory of the old companies, noticing that many of the new owners still referred to plants by their original names. "Old habits die hard," the reporter observed. What once was Spainhour, Blowing Rock, and Kent-Coffey now belonged to an aptly (but generically) named Consolidated Furniture Industries, while the Western Carolina Furniture plant and Caldwell Furniture were the property of a conglomerate called Armstrong Cork via its purchase of Thomasville Industries.[625]

Thomasville's reach into the western circle of companies encompassed the largest collection of any buyer. Not only did Thomasville take control of plants in Lenoir and Hickory, the eastern North Carolina manufacturer bought Gilliam Furniture in Statesville. Started in 1919 by L.S. Gilliam upon

A happy attendee to the Hickory Furniture Market during its heyday. The two young ladies represent the local hospitality that accompanied the April and October, ten-day events every year. The markets brought a boost to the western North Carolina economy. (Image courtesy of Hickory Furniture Mart)

his return from the First World War, with the original name of Carolina Parlor Furniture Company, the business stood for 33 years before the next generation of Gilliam's (sons and daughter of the founder) joined. The Gilliam family decided the name change gave the firm individuality, which was retired in 1986 when Thomasville took over.[626]

The number of factories now operating under the control of another company became significant. Hammary sold out to U.S. Industries. Fashion Furniture was bought by Stanley, which in turn had been purchased by the Mead Paper Corp. At the same time, Mead also snapped up Hickory Tavern and Bruington Furniture. Additionally, National Service Industries in Atlanta went on a buying spree in the Hickory area, grabbing DeVille Furniture, Hall Mark Furniture, Colony Frame Company, as well as DeVille's trucking company that carried its product to market.[627]

As troubling as the list was, Paul Fogleman did not set out to write an obituary for the regional furniture industry. He chronicled a second list of companies that, as of his writing in 1970, had remained "independent." Century, North Hickory, Sherrill Upholstering, Bernhardt, Fairfield, Kincaid, and Comfort Chair were all cited as stalwarts, resisting the temptation to cash out. However, eventually all but Sherrill, Century, and Bernhardt would one day migrate to the other list. Still trying to put a positive spin on an alarming trend, the *Hickory Daily Record* reporter offered "confidence in the capitalistic system" as a reason that the future of furniture companies would always include homegrown folks. He maintained that "there are numerous cases of plant owners who started out on their own and failed several times before reaching success." After a century of crafting, furniture seemed to be in the blood of western North Carolinians. They knew how to make it just as their daddies and mommas did in an earlier era, who were in turn taught by their grandparents. Thus, furniture would always have a hometown flavor, or so they thought.[628]

"Blessed be the tie that bind," sang the Unifour economic congregation, fully aware that their fates were incresingly bound together, regardless of the changes. The fates of labor and management might still be intertwined despite numerous changes. Downtown store owners and the people who worked for those businesses found themselves dependent on the success of furniture manufacturing to keep them going. In various ways, factory money trickled down into everyone else's paycheck, allowing everyone to share. While pay in the industry was meager for the workforce, it was enough to keep the cycle going. What owners did not pay in wages, they gave by funding projects designed not only to benefit the community but also enhance the company image. Once decision making shifted elsewhere, concern about the generosity of the new overlords weighed on the minds of those who had previously benefitted. Others simply went to work and expressed appreciation for the fact that they still had a job.[629]

Furniture had become enormously important to the region and not just the concern of the manufacturers and the workers themselves. Each April and October, hotels, rental car companies, restaurants, nightclubs and even home owners who rented out their houses, benefitted from the influx of buyers, making money each time the furniture market convened. It became all the more important for Hickory and its satellites to keep visitors happy as they added to the local coffers. With good economic time to be enjoyed by all, the region had a reason to cheer furniture's ongoing success. Hopefully, outside leadership recognized how well the industry functioned and would not interfere. At least, that was their belief.

Every spring and fall, the region kept tabs on the semi-annual furniture market as a barometer of times ahead. The local grapevine crackled with daily details on the levels of activity. Good reports assured full production for another six months while downturns left them in jeopardy. Word spread about the number of attendees and the amount of business being done so that summative conclusions could be drawn. The livelihood of most everyone throughout the region depended on a positive market. Statewide, the focus always centered on High Point, but Tarheels from the uplands paid particular attention to what was going on around Hickory, the core of the western market. In reports, Hickory was lumped in with a list of other "showroom cities" that buyers frequently sought out. Western reporters tickled out the numbers to see if they matched what was going on down east or what they heard during the market. The reach of the furniture market even extended into towns that had no furniture factories at all. Blowing Rock, in the mountains, for example, offered available luxury space, especially in the spring when there were no leaf watchers to compete with furniture buyers. In March of 1973, a landslide closed the main road and shut off rooms in the resort town which made accommodations down the mountain all the tighter and Blowing Rock's merchants all the poorer.[630]

Around that same time, a national emergency threatened the mobility of buyers between High Point and Hickory. The "gas crisis," brought on by the OPEC nations, reduced petroleum supplies across the country, causing visitors to wonder if they could get from one showroom to another for the Spring 1974 market. Organizers went all out to assure that no buyer would have to wait in line for gas. Estimating that "3,000 rental cars in the market area" might be needed for travel, the Furniture Factory Manufacturing Association of the South guaranteed visitors that gas would be readily available for them, even if it wasn't for the locals. They made deals that supplied an extra 1,000 rental cars, just in case. The Association offered bus transportation during the market too, acknowledging that almost all of the 3,000 people they expected to peruse showrooms in High Point and Thomasville would also want to see the same in Hickory.[631]

Not every retailer who came to North Carolina ventured west to see what manufacturers were building and that created a problem. For the state as a whole, estimates concluded that 85% of buyers nationally came to North Carolina for the furniture market, proof of the event's dominant power. Some still regarded Hickory as a sideshow to the big show in High Point. Western companies worked overtime to lure customers to see their wares. Established clients could be counted upon to rent a car and head west, but with the substantial exhibits in and around High Point, some buyers left what was going on toward the mountains off their list. Competition for the attention of furniture retailers intensified in the 1970s.[632]

After the hoopla was over, local curiosity about the offerings of the market remained. Most were too busy either making furniture, attending to the buyers needs or supporting those who did, to see how the latest lines were being displayed and sold at the various venues. Besides, they were not allowed to crowd the aisles anyway as the market was open to retailers. Hickory Furniture Mart's Leroy Lail recognized an untapped opportunity. He began to schedule "after-market" showings for people to see what the buyers saw. Following the Spring Market of 1974, the public got to see what all the fuss was about. The event served two purposes. It lengthened the excitement of market time while also allowing companies to sell off their display models at good prices.[633]

Getting furniture to the masses had always been a hit-or-miss effort. Customers in Omaha, Nebraska for example, could only see what the buyers from their local furniture stores purchased at market. Eventually, the entire industry sought to overcome the problem and make its presence felt with an annual event that blanketed the entire nation. The inaugural effort was called *Debut '72* and it sought to "revolutionize the home furnishings industry," according to John Hubbell of the Home Furnishings Council (HFC), when first staged during the Spring 1971 market. He believed recent declines in buying was the result of the public not knowing about all the available offerings. The campaign drew immense press coverage. National advertisements lured the buying public, its goal to boost sales. The HFC urged retailers to outfit their showrooms in much the same way as the furniture markets, with coordinated displays that looked more like real living, dining, and bedroom spaces, and less like the warehouse where inventory was kept. The number went up by year (*Debut* '73, '74, etc…) as visibility and expected participation grew. Surprisingly, subsequent campaigns lost steam. The second year was perhaps the apex for the program as a house was given away (although without furniture strangely enough). Seven second prizes were rooms of furniture, but after that, enthusiasm dissipated. The program tried, but failed to bring the nation's consumers to an appreciation of the furniture industry as a whole. Even though everyone needed furniture, they were not willing to buy at what seemed to be an annual nationwide retail furniture market. A nationwide attempt to promote a wide array of makers, including those from the foothills, died.[634]

Undaunted, individual companies promoted new styles and functions for furniture, all coming from a fresh crop of creators. Michigan State graduate David Zagaroli started at Drexel, "where he began at the bottom and worked to the top of the design department." As his ideas about what functions furniture could serve expanded, so did his reputation in the industry. Designs and materials stretched far afield with the introduction of his *Impact Collection*, a grouping of 60 pieces including "selected paldao veneers and elm solids. Paldao was found in the East Indies, the Philippines and Indochina." For a long time the trees of western North Carolina had been used. With a wider palette from which to choose, the reach for materials became global.[635]

It didn't take long for David Zagaroli and his concept of decor to impact the market. Encouraged by the popularity of his work, he soon ventured out on his own. In many ways a very different type of visionary with thoughts that leaned toward the eclectic and away from matching furniture, Zagaroli championed the needs of the individual and created accordingly. In that, he was at the front of an emerging trend in the industry. Unlike many contemporaries who presented what they thought the market wanted, Zagaroli stepped forward to show the market how the right pieces could enhance their lives. Ironically in doing so, he also embodied some very traditional thoughts on the accepted utility of furniture. He once said, "the idea of obsolescence is becoming obsolete," indicating that 'throw-away' furniture alienated buyers and would not serve the long term reputation of his craft. He made his point by suggesting that just about everything else bought by a family was temporal, using clothing and cars as an example. For the most part he exempted home furnishings, putting them in a different category. "Furniture is an odd cat in a way," Zagaroli conjectured in a 1970 interview. "It is total warmth, security, looks and function. Home is where the family is brought up, where minds are formed, where impressions are made," he theorized, arguing that a more intimate and long lasting relationship with the buyer existed and thus a different purchasing calculation had to be made. "It is the family circle," Zagaroli liked to say.[636]

The trick of luring consumers to rethink the feel and use of their home furnishings had been a snare that entangled the industry for a long time. Since its earliest days, manufacturers saw that once a family bought a sofa and chairs, they were loath to replace them. Despite changes in style, some kept purchased pieces long after the look was fashionable. In the 1920s, the Southern Furniture Manufacturers Association first sought to push consumers into a more esthetic reason to replace their old sofas and chairs than just choosing pieces for their durability. The trade organization sponsored billboards for the burgeoning motorcar traffic that filled the roads after WWI. The message asked them "would you drive an automobile as old as your parlor sofa?" A slight variation for women wanted to know, "would you wear a gown as out-of-date as your dining room table?" The association reasoned that to get households to think about the age of their furniture would drive consumers to update their home furnishings, even if their current furniture was still serviceable. Furniture makers wanted to be thought of as fashion leaders, enticing customers to buy for look, which meant periodic replacement as styles changed.[637]

The convictions of David Zagaroli came as a blend of new designs and old values. "Consumers are hungry for ideas," he said, "and we are trying to show them how they can use furniture in a room so that it becomes more exciting." The assertive, inventive furniture designer with boundless energy wanted his industry to exhibit that vigor, suggesting that showrooms should display the same pieces in different settings "to show the versatility." When asked how he decorated his own home, Zagaroli admitted to a certain eclectic blend. "We have many things found in junk stores that I think are very good-looking," he confessed, characterizing his home as a mixture of "traditional, modern and contemporary things." Some of those choices demonstrated the ethic he brought to his work.[638]

Debate waged in furniture circles about what companies should promote: sturdy value or inspirational design. For many years, manufacturers, especially those selling high-end pieces, had promoted their wares as future heirlooms. In the mid-priced and promotional lines, volume was the key. Keeping a dresser or sofa for generations was not a way to promote quarterly profits. To get product out the door, companies felt they needed to capitalize on whatever styles tickled the fancies of consumers at the moment. If one company produced something innovative that sold well, every other maker crafted their own version by the next market. The practice was known as "knock-offs" and almost every manufacturer practiced the art of imitation as the sincerest way to ring the cash register. In his lengthy career, furniture salesman Hank Rullman saw a lot of knock-offs. "If they (furniture companies) saw something good that somebody else was making, if they felt they could make it cheaper and make money, they would knock it off," he said. At one point he remembered, while selling a rather unique group, "I was about the only one selling that particular line." It didn't take long for the copies to follow, Hank asserting that "it (the practice) was no secret. They all did it, especially the medium to lower guys." With no copyright on furniture design, innovation was open for just such flattery (or theft).[639]

One sign that furniture had taken its place as a major industry in North Carolina came with educational outlets wanting to offer students entry into the manufacturing process. In 1953, N.C. State University created an entire program concerning management of the furniture business. The program struggled for the better part of two decades to become a viable area of study. Still, "fully 60 per cent of our students haven't heard of our program when they get to college," conceded Dr. Anco Prak in 1970, head of a "three-man furniture program, a subsidiary of State's industrial engineering curriculum." By that time, the program had quietly placed its enrollees in a number of high level positions in the industry. By Dr. Prak's estimation, of "275 graduates, 5 are company presidents and 27 are vice presidents." Alumni usually started in middle-management and moved up the ranks which helped validate the program. Dr. Prak characterized the program as "unique in the South and probably the only one of its type in the country."[640]

Closer to home, Hickory's Industrial Education Center also involved itself in training for the furniture industry, though at the other end of a company's organizational chart. Recognizing that "approximately 25 per cent of the total employed labor force in Catawba County has jobs in the furniture industry," the institution that would one day become Catawba Valley Community College developed classes to train skills necessary for the furniture industry's front line workers. Courses in upholstery sewing began an ongoing effort that firms needed to advance productivity. Students could "make progress with their work from the simple to the more advanced types of operations," under the tutelage of "top personnel from the furniture industry," who included a mix of professionals from the industry.[641]

The popularity of furniture classes for students seeking to improve their upward mobility led the local community college to increase its offerings. Catawba Valley Technical Institute (CVTI), as the Industrial Education Center was later known, started an entire furniture program, teaching "such things as furniture styling, supervision, lumber characteristics, construction techniques, assembly methods, cost analysis, production scheduling, quality control, finishing, machine room methods and many other things to provide a proper foundation for initial employment and future advancement." CVTI president Robert Paap assured prospective students, "the furniture production program was designed cooperatively by industry and education." As developed, the initiative utilized a "work and study" concept. After a morning of labor at a furniture company, students attended class for five hours every afternoon, Monday through Friday. The two-year program was described as "the only one of its kind in the southeast," graduating the first class in the spring of 1970.[642]

Not every furniture company thought the idea of a formal post-secondary education dovetailing with a career in furniture was sound for their future. Some companies were suspect of schools, wondering if they might one

Graduating its first students in 1962, the Industrial Education Center grew into Catawba Valley Technical Institute at the time of this demonstration of the furniture program in 1964. The program worked with local factories to train key personnel for skilled positions in the industry. (Image courtesy of Catawba Valley Community College)

day steal away the labor force. In Hickory Manufacturing's company newsletter, called the *HMC New Round-Up*, regular contributor Lloyd H. Hyder wrote on the subject. He voiced a concern. "Can we go on and give everybody a higher education and expect some of them to fill all the places in our plants and factories?" If college was now in reach for practically everyone, he wondered where would tomorrow's workforce come from? In a world where college (increasingly even the community college) offered alternatives to factory work, Hyder saw his employer losing some of the brightest and best prospects to other, better paying occupations, ones that required a college education.[643]

Lloyd Hyder begrudged no one an education. He believed that "everyone should seek as high a level as possible." However, he saw higher learning through the lens of his industry. As a proponent of the old school, he believed that "young people ought to start to work and learn on any machine that suits their interest level" as a way to find their niche. He preferred the vocational opportunities at Catawba Valley Technical Institute over a liberal arts, general education but remained suspicious of formalized education beyond high school. The best and brightest in western North Carolina now had choices about their career path, the first generation to be afforded such luxury, and their trek had the potential, in Hyder's eyes, to wreck the workforce. In an era when a greater number of students from the region were seeking higher degrees, the risk of losing a traditional employees endangered companies like Hickory Manufacturing, who one day might find themselves devoid of hands.[644]

Formalized instruction developed as one of many new trends transforming furniture operations. So did public money to fund factories. In January of 1970, Cochrane Furniture of Lincolnton "went public." The company started in 1928 by J.E., A.B., T.E., and P.C. Cochrane with a total of $16,000. A little over forty years later the business received over $1.1 million for shares of its stock, initially valued at $8 each. The firm used the proceeds to build a plant in the eastern part of North Carolina, needed because, as President T.E. Cochrane related, "our plants are now operating at capacity and our backlog of orders is substantial."[645]

A shift in the paradigm of how things were done in furniture factories had come. No longer was it a strictly local, or in the case of western North Carolina, a regional concern. The wider world had taken notice. From finance to formal training, the 1970s signaled a more complex landscape to navigate than had been the case even 10 years earlier. The furniture industry had finally taken its place as a major force in the economy, one that echoed well beyond the Tarheel state. Companies of all sizes based themselves in western North Carolina. As the world bought their goods, the ways of the world infiltrated the work flows of those same firms. The communities who benefited welcomed the former, but may not have anticipated how devastating the latter might one day be.

Like many companies, Hickory Manufacturing communicated with and spotlighted employees through a regular newsletter. This edition touted the training offered by the company to improve the skills of workers. Lloyd Hyder's column also appeared in the newsletter. (Courtesy of Hickory Landmarks Society)

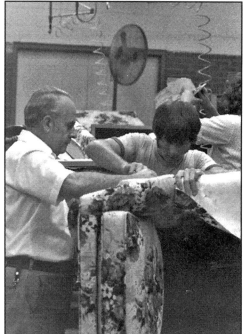

It looks like a furniture factory, but it is not. On the campus of Catawba Valley Technical Institute a state-of-the-art training facility was built to offer the industry a course of study on the practical side of furniture making. Inside, instructor Tom Winn oversees student learning. (Courtesy of Catawba Valley Community College)

Chapter 24
Plastic Soul

By the dawn of the 70s, every component in the making of a piece of furniture required reconsideration. One article on the phenomenon wondered "whatever happened to wooden chairs?" It was an apt question. Not only was wood being replaced by other materials, but the cloth used in upholstery was also changing. "New names like polyester, polyurethane and polystyrene are creeping into the language of Carolina furniture makers," reported one observer. Furniture manufacturers found themselves busier than ever trying to figure out what lay ahead for their industry.[646]

One good sign of success was the bottom line. Even as designers debated the use of components other than wood for their products, consumers around the country generally liked the innovations they saw from Tarheel manufacturers. As a result, the furniture market continued to grow. For the year 1969 furniture sales had risen to $4.4 billion, "up from $2.8 billion in 1964." Estimates were that the number would soar even higher in the years to come. If housing could keep pace with population growth, more rooms than ever awaited to be furnished. An estimate of new apartment construction in the nation for 1970 approached a million units, a 25% increase. Mobile home construction was also on the rise. It was good times for every one of "some 60,000 Tar Heel citizens," who were part of the furniture industry.[647]

"More is going to happen in the furniture industry in the next ten years, than has happened in the last ten million," asserted Dr. Anco Prak, head of North Carolina State's furniture education program. What he saw coming was a new wave of furniture, a reconsideration of how and why it was made.

In the old days "impoverished North Carolina mountain men discovered that people were actually interested in buying lumber and cheap wooden furniture." Those views had given way to an era when the latest technology defined what home furnishings could be to an increasingly sophisticated American consumer. Furniture makers looked to the future more than ever to drive sales. The past had become antiquated.[648]

So many changes were happening in furniture making that many in the industry would agree with Dr. Prak. In 1970, plastic was seen as an answer to an age old problem with furniture. Durable and scratch resistant, manufacturers embraced the new raw material, the bigger companies building plants to extrude the petrochemical into any shape they needed for their products. One headline screamed, "New Era In Furniture Replacing Days of Sawdust and Sweat," as an announcement that in that ten-year period to which Dr. Prak alluded, everyone would be sitting on chairs and sofas crafted out of entirely different materials from what they had previously known.

To prove the point, one furniture maker took pride in handing a two-by-four to customers, instructing them to whack one of his tables with all their might. They did, breaking the piece of wood but not the table they were hitting. The table was not even scratched. It was made of plastic. J. Wayne Burris just giggled as customers put all their might into destroying the plastic furniture only to find it more durable than the wood they used to wreck it. The stunt served as a calling card, not only to a coming change in furniture but also a new type of spokesman.[649]

Wayne Burris was born into the business of furniture. His father, J. Alonzo Burris opened the Goodin-Burris Furniture Company the year of his son's birth. It was actually more of a furniture repair store the elder Burris started with his father-in-law than an actual factory. When he incorporated the business ten years later, it was as both a retail and manufacturing outlet, although by that time, the company was well established as one of Lincolnton's premier furniture stores. Alonzo even opened his own home as a showcase for the furniture he sold. Pieces crafted by father Alonzo began to show up in other furniture venues, like Ivey's Department Store in Charlotte, completing the Burris family's transition from seller to maker.[650]

As Burris Furniture grew, so did Alonzo's son Wayne. He went to Harvard Business School, graduating with an MBA, then returned to Lincolnton, ready to spice up his father's company. "Most people think of furniture as dull stuff you have to have," opined Wayne on the business he planned to energize. "We try to make them think of it as something fun." Wayne brought a new mentality to the business of furniture making, something of the old entrepreneurs blended with a showmanship not seen before. His stunt of enticing customers to break his plastic table was only the beginning.[651]

It seemed Wayne Burris intended to be as imposing a figure within the industry as he was in real life. Standing almost 6 foot, 4 inches and 235 pounds, he stood out in group photos. His ideas did much the same. He once

A promoter of plastics, Wayne Burris welcomed a new era in furniture production. He took over Burris Industries, a company his father created to widen the possibilities of what furniture could be in the 1970s. He brought in European designs and with inventive promotion, prospered. (Image from the Charlotte News)

"upholstered a chair with 2,000 chinchilla skins, then had Wells Fargo men haul it all over the country." In keeping with his 'furniture is fun' philosophy, he promoted his father's company, ultimately as president himself, in ways no one ever thought about before. Intrigued by *Playboy* Playmate's, the models who posed for the men's magazine, Wayne ran a contest at his booth during a furniture show, with first prize being a date with a "Playmate of the Month." He also gained notoriety as "one of the few people ever to give the Playmate of the Year a chest (of drawers)."[652]

But it was as a furniture visionary that he had his greatest impact. By 1970, Wayne Burris developed the technology to extrude plastic to make a sofa frame as the basis to build upholstery. He characterized plastic as "indestructible." "When they dig up our civilization in two million years," Wayne chortled in a newspaper interview about his plastic furniture, "they won't find anything but a couple of these tables, some red tape and a handful of beer cans." Similar considerations were taking place at companies like Bernhardt and Broyhill. Like Wayne, a growing segment of the industry awakened to the possibility that wood might be part of their past, not their future.[653]

Burris Industries sought to revolutionize not only furniture, but housing as well. As an extension of his plastic dream, Wayne bought "Construct, Inc., a firm pioneering the use of plastic in the manufacture of modular housing." His plans were to put his plastic furniture in a plastic home, creating "packaged housing." The only drawback to the idea was the price. While old wood and brick homes of the era averaged around $25,000, the new Burris model sold for four times that amount. Wayne and his associates asserted that the plastic homes would be easy to heat and cool, allow for customization, but most importantly, relieve the housing shortage going on in the nation at the time. With a proper foundation laid, the homes could be built in a day, and with the factory turning out "five to 10 homes a day," the company stood on the forefront of a unique type of modular housing.[654]

The possibilities brought by petrochemicals captured the imagination of those looking to the future for what their lifestyle might be in twenty years, even if they had trouble discerning how any of it might be accomplished. Just as film director Mike Nichols was making fun of the fad in his movie *The Graduate*, furniture people were taking the idea seriously. National companies like 3M Corporation claimed they made "better 'wood' than nature." It was easy to see why Dr. Prak would make such a declaration turning the process of furniture making upside down.[655]

As a furniture man, Wayne Burris continued to innovate. Furniture reporter Edith Low of the *Charlotte News* remarked, "if you've ever seen a chair or sofa made by Burris Industries of Lincolnton, you won't forget it." Wayne took the ideas of his era and charged ahead. He said, "I believe the future of seating will be molded furniture," showing great faith in his polyester-boned upholstery. Exhibiting his line in High Point (not Hickory), he offered what Edith Low called "squashy" chairs. While the seating looked compact, she assured readers that sitting in them "invites you to unwind." Relaxing was a key aim of Wayne's furniture. Burris chairs reclined in a way that allowed the position of the chair to "sit flat against the wall," an innovation at the time.[656]

Wayne Burris epitomized all that was forward thinking about the industry in the early 1970's. Before jumping into plastics for furniture making, he spent time in Europe, learning the process, then guiding its application back in the states. While abroad, he met Henning Korch, a Danish designer who sold him on the 'squashy' style. In a sauna one day with Henning and German Elmer Terstappen, they joked about "how a big American and a small Japanese would look in the same chair." The trio began to design for the possibility. Henning proposed to Wayne that "too many people think of furniture just as their grandfathers and fathers did." Comparing Early American styled rocking chairs to "moon rockets and electronic kitchens," Henning "thought it was so funny" that people chose to outfit their homes with the appliances of the past.

Wayne Burris saw the world in similar terms and wanted to use Henning Korch's designs to teach consumers a better approach. Both believed in what was called "the thinking of tomorrow."[657]

The workforce of Burris Industries turned out to be as diverse as its product line. While it was his trips to Europe that introduced him to designers like Henning Korch, back home he gained one of Wayne's best salesmen by accident. Ellen Hamberg never thought she could be a salesperson for Burris until the death of her husband. He had traveled six states in New England for the Lincolnton manufacturer until his passing in 1960. Left with a nine-year-old daughter to raise, Ellen decided to take over her late husband's territory.[658]

Unsure if Ellen could handle the job, Wayne Burris employed her on a trial basis. Looking back on those first days as a salesman in her own right, she said, "I just ran like crazy." For the first six months she kept her head down and focused totally on sales. Eventually, she forgot about the trial period until, during a trip down south to the furniture market, Wayne called her into his office. She panicked, saying, "my God! It's about the trial period - they're going to fire me." Fearful, she met with Wayne Burris only to find that she had already met "87.5 per cent" of her quota for the year. The company planned to keep Ellen Hamberg on as one of their nationwide representatives. In fact, that year she surpassed any of her late husband's best years in sales. Burris Industries had a star.[659]

The company stumbled upon the same formula for success that Henredon did with Helen Kelly or Mary Bruce at Hammary. As a woman, she brought a unique perspective to the world of furniture. From the very beginning of her sales career, she touted the advantage. "I told my dealers from the very start," she said, reflecting on her efforts, "that the majority of their customers were women and that I could tell them what women want." Her observations and hard work served her well. During a long career with Burris, she remained one of their top sales agents. It wasn't easy. She admitted to encountering some difficult individuals along with a lot of genuinely nice and sympathetic folks in her travels, but she took the bad with the good in an optimistic manner, saying, "there may have been some nasty people, it's true, but think how they must have been to the men."[660]

For a while, the technology forward approach that Wayne Burris developed and Ellen Hamberg sold, captured the imagination of those looking to what furniture could be, instead of what it had been. A number of companies jumped on the bandwagon, but Burris Industries stayed ahead of the pack. The Furniture Council of the Society of the Plastics Industry awarded the Olympia chair, part of the *Burris Domani Collection*, as "best in show." Henning Korch designed the chair, which judges said, "represents new, almost boneless soft seating that plastics make possible." While some were intrigued by this 'brave new world' proposed by Wayne Burris and his company, traditionalists remained standoffish. They had enough problems without a total redesign of everything they made.[661]

Located in the western circle of furniture companies in Lincolnton, Wayne Burris did not look to Hickory and its furniture showrooms for display space. Instead, he took his unconventional line to High Point. That move signaled he was a different breed, just as High Point was trying to solidify itself as the capital of North Carolina furniture, a signature of its intent, even embedded in its sidewalk: "the heart of Furnitureland, U.S.A." Perhaps considering the foothills manufacturing group to be like "grandfathers" in the game, the Burris mind frame advocated enlightenment from such archaic thinking. Wayne may have felt like a fish out of water and judged High Point as a more accepting climate for his futuristic designs. Following a key market, "the 20-35 year old age group" (which comprised about a quarter of the U.S. population), Wayne banked on the young adult demographic as his core. They were the least tied to the old styles and as they grew in age, numbers and incomes, he planned to supply them with his furniture.[662]

Redefinition was everywhere in the 1960/70s. With new companies coming along almost weekly, older establishments were driven to revitalize. Bernhardt, for example, went through "a major remodernization project." It started with plants under the Bernhardt moniker and continued in their Hibriten Furniture facility in 1967. A formerly independent company, Bernhardt acquired the Lenoir factory to expand their product lines.[663]

The times promised innovation. The skill of cutting and carving wood was standard, even old news to those interested in the next great idea. Did a brave new world belong to furniture made with plastic instead of wood? About the same time as Wayne Burris took a 2 x 4 to a plastic table, one of the industry's grandfathers also began to experiment. Bernhardt's *Quinella* line replaced some wood parts with plastic, creating a cost savings, even though the company had to use an outside producer to extrude the shapes they needed for an "old-world-styled dining room and bedroom suite of furniture." Developers found it necessary to treat the plastic surface with a "barrier coat" to get "wood stains and finishes" to adhere to it the same as wood, but once applied, they felt sure customers would appreciate the innovation. Sales provided positive feedback for Bernhardt with the *Quinella* line selling out in 1967, leading third generation Alex Bernhardt to wonder "if the $3 million spent to renovate the wood plant at Hibriten might have been better used for plastic facilities."[664]

If the inherent problems in plastics could be worked out and the public didn't care what their home furnishings were made of as long as it was stylish, a new facet of furniture making had arrived. Ed Harmon wanted to make a one-piece chair/sofa arm and leg, but cutting it out of plywood only caused problems. One day he got an idea. "I want to mold this thing out of plastic," he said. Luckily for Ed, Charles Coley had started Projection Products, an injection molding plant in Newton, just up the road from his Maiden shop. Ed took the part over to Charles, asking if the new plastics plant could possibly "shoot" the part, referring to the injection of heated plastic pellets into a mold

Bernhardt Industries delved into plastic as a material for building furniture with its *Quinella* line in 1967. The line sold out in its first year, an encouraging sign for the future of non-wood materials. Other companies also jumped on the plastics bandwagon, for a while. (Image courtesy of the Caldwell Heritage Museum)

to make the arm/leg. Within six months, Charles Coley cranked up a new "hundred ton machine" capable of making the seven pound piece. Once Ed was convinced that the idea would work, he got busy making a model.[665]

The process of developing a part made from plastic was much more expensive than one from wood, but once in production, manufacturing was significantly cheaper. Ed's company operated on "a shoestring" as he recalled. The risk was great, but if it worked the reward would be greater. Once he got a model carved, he then found a company in Ohio that agreed to create a beryllium copper mold for $6,500, a major expense for his small company.[666]

Committed to the process, Ed Harmon bet it all that the chair side piece would work as an extruded piece of plastic. When the mold, that Ed surmised "weighed close to a ton" arrived back in Newton it was 1:00am. Ed got out of bed to see the first leg come out of the mold. After several heart-stopping mechanical setbacks, a finished piece emerged. When it was finished, "you swore it was wood," Ed recalled, examining his creation for the first time. It looked good but would it sell?[667]

The Spanish-style line named *Conquistador* made the cash registers ring better than anything Ed Harmon expected. "We were selling that thing like you would not believe," he remembered, calling it a "turnaround" for his little company. His bet paid off in multiple ways. He made a profit and the design also won an award. *Plastics World* magazine, the industry journal, bestowed Ed Harmon and his company, Dresden Lounge with the 1968 Major Market Award for his "innovation in furniture."[668]

The high risk expense of a mold to make furniture parts did not catch on with most manufacturers in the area. As Ed Harmon looked back on the experience, he admitted that the possibility of failure loomed. "You think something is going to be great and you make the mold and it doesn't sell, you're stuck with the mold." Harmon realized his daring innovation was just too risky for most established companies. Many looked at the initial investment and balked, preferring instead to make a chair arm in the old-fashioned way, out of wood. The choice, while safe, would only be considered a wise move after the novelty of plastic faded from public favor.[669]

The tremor that plastic sent through the industry, so promising in theory but so problematic in practice, took its toll on most companies. At

Ed Harmon took a real chance on an extruded plastic arm/leg for a Spanish styled line called *Conquistador*. The mold cost his small furniture company $6,500 to produce. The gamble paid off when it not only sold well but was cited by *Plastics World* magazine as an innovation. (Image courtesy of Ed Harmon)

Bassett's Prestige upholstery plant in Newton, Rome Jones got a bit carried away by the idea. He "spent a lot of money on a revolutionary idea of molded frames," remembered Glenn Hunsucker of his early days with the company. After a presentation in New York for substantial retailers like Macy's and Gimbel's, Rome sold the idea "before he knew what the cost was." Back in Newton, Glenn put pencil to paper and determined that "for every piece we shipped, material cost, not counting labor, was somewhere around 150%," meaning "every time we sold one, we lost more than 50%." Though "very successful for department stores," Bassett dropped the line as quick as they could.[670]

The early 1970s also saw the tradition of furniture making diverge about as far as it ever got from its product origins. Materials other than wood had become a trendy, if temporal, replacement. Manufacturers got so attuned to the possibilities that they explored niches with specialty products designed for individual user groups. One example was furniture made for children with "glossy plastic coatings in brilliant enamel colors," in an effort to be damage resistant. The need to anticipate every possible use for home furnishings caused manufacturers to reconsider the old adage of making furniture for the masses. Consensus on what the finely furnished home looked like was up for debate.[671]

The idea of diversity was not lost on the furniture makers themselves. Paul Broyhill aimed to make his father's company bigger than any in the region. He, like Bernhardt and Burris, got caught up in the plastics fad. The company bought a variety of extrusion machines, making molds for furniture but also other products, in essence diversifying its diversification. For a short while the firm devoted an entire plant to production of plastic components. However, Broyhill got in on the trend late, and when the gas crisis of 1973-74 came and the petroleum-based raw material was in short supply, Paul cast about to unload the plastics operation. By that time he had lost his enthusiasm for the look of plastic as a versatile adornment, saying "in looking at our furniture, I'm no longer proud of it. I have decided that we are going to get back into the furniture business and replace plastic with wood." He sold all the equipment to an Ohio company, getting "more or less our money out of it." Even though the great experiment in plastics did not work out, it did get Paul Broyhill thinking about manufacturing possibilities beyond furniture.[672]

If making home furnishings was profitable, it seemed that similar ventures might be as well. A local construction company that had built factories for Broyhill convinced Paul that the prefab housing market was a good bet. It was not the same as Wayne Burris' attempt with his plastic home, but a more conventional effort to bypass the delays that come with a 'stick built' structure. However, like Burris, Broyhill also reasoned that a new home needed good dependable furniture. In his mind, that meant Broyhill lines. Like the foray into plastics, the dream of supplying houses to be furnished by his own product was also short-lived. When the savings and loan crisis hit in the 1980s, a "housing slump" killed sales. The factory that once made plastic furniture components, then prefab housing, converted again, to Broyhill's core business of furniture.[673]

During his tenure at Broyhill Furniture Industries, Paul Broyhill made another, more conventional move to expand. This time, he stuck more closely to his roots. Commissioning a factory in both Texas and Louisiana, he intended to create new opportunities to spread the Broyhill name (and its product line) to a new part of the United States. However, Texans and Louisianans had already heard of Broyhill. At the very least many had seen *The Price Is Right*, a television network game show. It turned out that Broyhill furniture from Texas and Louisiana competed with its North Carolina counterpart. Locating a factory out of the area gave no advantage and eventually, the company saw no reason to base operations so far away and shut down production. However, they kept the idea in mind for a day when they could use it to their advantage.[674]

Chapter 25
History, Old and New

By 1970, the industry as a whole had greater problems than a plastic future. Transformation everywhere threatened to force every system developed in factories to accommodate new considerations. A housing slowdown caused a slump in furniture sales, "every house not built is a house not furnished" was the attitude. With the advent of the Environmental Protection Agency, big companies had to clean up their acts. Calls for the factory floor to be less noisy, so workers would not lose their hearing was gaining momentum, so were calls to be more cautious about disposal of waste. Outside conglomerates were increasingly calling the shots, leading some to refer to their new owners as "carpetbaggers." The new generation of management coming out of college instead of from the shop floor brought with them new ethics and new methods with which the older generation were not always comfortable. And wood, the substance that sparked the whole industry was up for debate as a smart

Hickory Manufacturing offered designs meant to please the widest number of potential buyers. This dining room set epitomized the look of furniture offered in the late 60s/early 70s. Innovators would challenge the ethic despite the fact that furniture like this sold well. (Courtesy of Hickory Landmarks Society)

raw material investment. Old timers in the business could only shake their heads at the disarray they saw all around them.[675]

Competition continued to increase the speed at which companies needed to operate. Some were advertising for the first time, an expense "once seen as an unnecessary distraction." A few of the larger companies were even hiring outside public relations firms to market their product. The trend of coordinating everything in a room caused substantial reconsideration. No one was selling just a dresser anymore. "Coordinated merchandising" now included everything in the entire room, even carpet. It all had to fit together, right down to the ashtray, a prominent accessory of the era. Long after Helen Kelly articulated the idea, coordination had become the standard approach to home decorating.[676]

The early 1970s welcomed a host of lively ideas coming from the emerging baby boomers, now adults and ready to take their place as both consumers and producers. One company that personified the energy of a wave of new design was Santi-Ross Furniture. The operation was a creation of a young New Yorker, pared with a graduate of Drexel High School. Dario Santi studied architecture in both Brooklyn and the Sorbonne in Paris before meeting Ken Ross. Both exhibited a starry-eyed exuberance about the future possibilities of furniture that led to their partnership. Ken Ross served as president of the new firm after gaining a furniture degree from N.C. State and experience in companies both local and far away. He sought to gain the notice of "young, professionally-oriented consumers, recently married," who "have a desire to move beyond the Mediterranean (his term) phase of home furnishings and start using something a little more dramatic. Striking might be a better word." That vision found its form in the designs of Dario Santi. Perhaps using the word, "cosmic" for the first time in any explanation of a new line of furniture, the company's design director prophesied, "the future in retrospect, will see this period as a time in which the human spirit moved manifestly toward a cosmic search for the candor of the extraordinary."[677]

The two young lions, with their grand vision for creating furniture were rooted in the economic dynamics of the market in one important way. They knew their creations had to be affordable. Even though they asserted their furniture was "the honest expression of technology and art," they still endeavored to build for an important customer sector. While they wanted "something truly pertinent to the changing tastes in the furniture field," it had to be "inexpensively priced." Ken Ross went to work finding "just the right kind of craftsmen who could produce these designs efficiently on a production basis." The unlikely pair heralded a new era in western North Carolina furniture.[678]

One reporter described the look of the *Santi-Ross collection* as "reminiscent of the contemporary Italian Milanese look." The maverick attitude of the new company embodied in its leaders overshadowed even the furniture itself. The presentation of their pieces were described as a "herd" of furniture. As Ronald Stockton wrote in an article about the new company, "the total effect is at once dramatic, humorous, and indeed, as this reporter sees it, a refreshing counterpoint to the generally commercial air of the more usual showrooms. Maybe wild is a better word."[679]

These two entrepreneurs hit the scene with a fresh approach that demanded attention be paid. Bravado in both design and marketing made sure the name of Santi-Ross would not be thought of as just another furniture maker. They located their showroom in Drexel, home of the giant. In their spare time they lent their expertise to Catawba Valley Technical Institute's furniture program, leading students out of the morass of traditional styling they felt needed to be replaced by their designs. Dario and Ken added their voice to a growing chorus of new professionals challenging the orthodoxy of the established furniture business and its tendency to accept and perpetuate the tried-and-true.[680]

Many of these new furniture makers had something in common. They wanted to built products that would attract the baby boomers. Whether it was Burris or Bernhardt's plastic pieces or Santi-Ross's unusual design, the largest demographical group the United States had ever seen was coming to the forefront as wage earners and consumers. These companies believed that the new consumer did not want to furnish their apartments and houses with the same kind of pieces that satisfied their parents. To interest and satisfy this group would be a sure fire avenue to establishing the next great furniture company. All the designers and builders had to do figure out what the boomers wanted. Nobody knew, but whatever it was, most figured it had to be different.

Dario Santi sits in one of his creations as a new generation of design hits the home furnishings market. New Yorker Santi, along with Burke County native Ken Ross teamed up to start a company to appeal to baby boomers and their tastes. (Image from the *Asheville Citizen Times*)

The furniture industry had been expanding for quite some time. It was an industry secret that the wood used in company offerings was no longer from trees in the area. Just how widespread the practice had become was revealed publicly in an article about Clarence Holden, a vice president at Broyhill. In late 1970, he recounted numerous oversea trips to procure wood for the company. He had been doing so for 35 years. Estimating that he had circled the globe at least twice in search of the best, most abundant wood for furniture production, Clarence pinpointed the Far East as the location where he made most of Broyhill's raw wood purchases. The article began by making a statement that shocked some consumers. It read, "chances are when a consumer buys one of those early American style captain's chairs he essentially is buying a Japanese import." *Charlotte Observer* Home Furnishings Editor Barbara Ingold revealed that the only effort Broyhill made in the production of the chairs was to assemble them when they arrived on shore.[681]

Strangely, a good portion of Broyhill's wood was coming from the same corner of the world where the sons of factory workers were serving the military as part of the Vietnam War effort. "He finds the Southeast Asia area from Thailand to Cambodia, even as far as New Guinea to be one of the fastest timber growing areas of the world because of the rainfall and hot temperatures," reported the *Observer* editor about Clarence Holden's experience. He had visited portions of Africa but found the Europeans had beat the American company to the punch. Holden even made some geopolitical observations, asserting that one major reason the "communists" wanted Southeast Asia was the growing seasons that allowed two crops of rice per year. "They need it to feed their people," he said.[682]

The article rather innocently introduced its readers to a practice that would become more significant to workers over time, the concept of offshore labor taking the process of furniture making away from local laborers. The signs were there. At around the same time as the article appeared, the industry was facing stagnation. Statewide, furniture workers were making an average of $104.48 per week, just shy of the $105.01 made by textile workers in the same year of 1970. That year had been a tough one for the hands. During the that time, 3,120 had lost their jobs due to a downturn in the economy. It would take another 30 years for the dots of foreign labor and the demise of the established factory way of life in western North Carolina to become dire, but the shift of labor was slowly beginning to turn away from the communities where the furniture companies got their start.[683]

Consequently, at the same time, industry observers began to notice two trends, both troubling in their own way for the furniture labor force. The first was development. One evaluation called "the furniture industry, one of the fastest growing industries in America," which on first look seemed positive. However, that expansion had caused management to look beyond the resources of their own community for labor, an ultimately problematic quandary for the hometown folks. Also, the communities themselves began to recognize how dependent their economy had become on the furniture industry. With textiles soon to depart the area, as something of a harbinger of things to come for furniture, Lenoir, Morganton, Drexel, Hickory, Newton, Lincolnton, Marion, and Statesville each began to see themselves as a "one-horse town." If that horse ever galloped away, their economies would be wrecked.[684]

The turmoil was enough to give pause to those in the shops witnessing all the reshuffling going on around them. The perceptive among them might have wondered if the changes taking place were the same as what furniture workers in New York or Michigan felt a century earlier as the business was coming south to establish, leaving them high and dry. Now the shoe found itself on the other foot.

Lessons were many for those reading the furniture tea leaves. Most however, were not looking that far into the future. They had more immediate concerns, like figuring out what would sell. It was an industry that looked forward to new markets but often backwards to designs. In Conover, Fred Preddy, Jr. started Venture Furniture in January of 1972. Before long, he was delving into past styles, like those of the 1890s. Espousing a "touch of romance" in his furniture designs, Fred and his wife Nancy found themselves vacationing up the mountain at the Green Park Inn, the resort hotel built by John Mathias Bernhardt in the late 19th century. The couple traveled extensively always taking inventory of the styles of furniture they encountered. As Fred recalled his epiphany, "for some time we had been gaga over the idea of white Victorian wicker." Staying at the Green Park Inn "added fuel to those flames." As he rode back down the mountain to Conover, Fred searched for some way to "manufacture it commercially," believing he would "find a winner," if he could.[685]

The new line was designed, built, and tested quickly. Then it went out to the market to see if the public fancied the same kind of unique furniture the Preddys did. The Green Park Inn line skyrocketed overnight to success. Selling over $3 million worth to retailers like "Belk in Charlotte, Marshall-Field in Chicago, the Haverty Furniture chain and Miller & Rhoads," the collection appealed to consumers who, like the Preddys valued "identity, (and) individuality." "People want to do their own thing as much as possible," said Fred Preddy, reflecting on his times. He intended to give them real choice, even it it was one based in history. Maybe everything old could be new again.[686]

The early 1970s fashioned itself as an era that leaped forward in design and materials, a break from the past. But as Venture Furniture demonstrated, the market still enjoyed looking to an earlier era for their home furnishing styles. None looked back farther than William Karslake. An Illinoian by birth, he came to Hickory just out of college to work for the G.C. Murphy Department Store chain, their only outlet in the Tarheel state. There he met his wife, Martha who was friends with the daughter of the head of Hickory Chair. The owner hired Bill Karslake as a salesman. He and his wife spent the next nine years in Boston representing Hickory Chair to New England retailers. Along the way, a funny thing happened.[687]

On the long trips he took twice a year from Boston to Hickory, Bill Karslake always made a side trip. "I decided that I needed to educate myself," he recalled, so on each outing he found a different museum to visit. He sought to better understand the history of furniture making, originally as way to excite customers about the upholstered 18th century lines Hickory Chair sold. He admitted, "I found myself enthralled with the styles of that period of time." As he studied, he soon found out that antique pieces "did not hold up well," because when a chair wore out a latter day craftsman "would remake the chair, which ruins it" for understanding the brilliance of the original builder. One of his stopovers found him at a museum in Wilmington, Delaware where Karslake determined that he had found "the mother of all museums in the United States."[688]

He visited often and his fascination of 18th century upholstery flourished. He described each trip to Wilmington as going "in with a different set of eyes." He developed a deep appreciation for the craftsmanship, ingenuity, and beauty of the museum artifacts. Not really sure what he might do with the wealth of knowledge he was gaining, he spent two years as sales manager back in Hickory before he put all the pieces into place.[689]

In 1973, Bill Karslake decided to start his own furniture company that sought to share his love of the kind of furniture George Washington would know and admire. He and a partner went into business as Southwood Reproductions. Karslake chose to keep the company in the South for two reasons. First, "all of the suppliers, cotton fabric, everything it takes to make a piece of furniture is in the Hickory area," he observed. Bill Karslake also admired the skill of southern workers. He did not accept the ridiculous stereotype of southerners as lazy. Instead, he believed "the opposite is true." A good upholsterer, Karslake asserted, "was the highest paid employee of all furniture makers" for a reason. He likened them to the craftsmen of the era he loved. At Southwood, he would watch an upholsterer "spitting tacks," as a piece of beautiful furniture was created right in front of his very eyes. Like an artist, "not everybody can be an upholsterer," Karslake asserted.[690]

Southwood Reproductions found an interesting niche in the furniture business. Never a product line for the masses, Bill Karslake and company always showed their lines in High Point, not Hickory. He felt that buyers who appreciated the products his company was making, "weren't coming to Hickory necessarily." Plus, to enhance his offerings to retailers, Southwood

Reproductions partnered with a company called Council Craftsmen that built pieces to complement Southwood's product line.

In his own way, Bill Karslake was reminiscent of the old masters, whose designs he held in high esteem. He wanted his company to "focus on quality. It has to be at every level," he declared. The ethic was exemplified in Southwood's advertising, which included the statement, "Excellence Still Exists," as a contrast to mass produced lines. He was even able to borrow a few of those pieces he studied as a visitor in museums up and down the East Coast, taking them back to Hickory to study and reproduce. In order to build them, Bill Karslake enlisted a 93-year old designer who understood 18th century furniture better than anyone. Fred Maddox "was the only designer I've ever seen that can take that pencil and draw a Cabriolet and get it right the first time." The attention to detail created a product different from much of the rest of the market, in both design and precision.[691]

The industry in furniture making had widened to the point that, in addition to the dominant, mainstream offerings, niche companies like Southwood Reproductions and Venture Furniture could specialize and succeed. There was a line of home furnishings for everyone, even those who

After a sales career with Hickory Chair, Bill Karslake became enthralled with 18th century furniture design. In 1973, he started Southwood Reproductions building chairs like this one for a market that shared his interest. (Author's collection, subject courtesy of Bill Karslake)

didn't mind plastic in their decor. A broader variety of styles than ever were coming out of factories as western North Carolina companies competed for sales, sometimes with similar product, sometimes altogether different, but all in a burgeoning national market that was going global. New players with fresh ideas took furniture forward, betting on the innovations they contributed, unaware that larger concerns would one day blunt the effort.

One more area where the furniture universe hung onto its old values in the face of great change was in giving help to help the needy in a time of crisis. In August of 1969, Hurricane Camille slammed across the Gulf Coast as a Category 5 storm with winds over 200 miles per hour. At the time, it was one of the deadliest and most costly major hurricanes to hit the United States. Over 250 died and looking back, one survivor said, "it was like World War III" in Mississippi, where it hit hardest. Many Americans felt compelled to provide assistance to the relief effort. One of those was Lenoir's Consolidated Furniture Industries. They donated furniture that on the retail market would total an estimated $20,000. Local trucking firm Caldwell Freight Lines chipped in by supplying a tractor-trailer and driver to haul the goods to Gulfport Mississippi. At the time Consolidated was the only furniture company reported to have given directly to such a degree, proving that if times grew hard enough, a helping hand could still be found in the factories of the foothills.[692]

Chapter 26
Ingrown Ideas

"Furniture Tradition to Tumble" read the headline in April. Added competition and a down year for the furniture business in 1970 caused a sacred practice to be abandoned in Lenoir. For the first time during a furniture market, a showroom would open its doors on Sunday morning. Up to that point, company leaders had exempted Sunday from the schedule, leaving buyers who might find themselves in town without much to do until the market resumed at 1pm, to attend church services, then join the Sunday lunch crowd. Burnett Tremlett thought the lag hindered sales. The papers quoted him, saying as much. "That's one of those old, ingrown ideas," he proclaimed. Then, he handed down the commandment that Consolidated Furniture showrooms reopen by 8am on the Sabbath.[693]

Burnett Tremlett, or "Burnie" as he was called, had come to Lenoir to shake things up. He felt he needed to. "We're trying to do business," he declared, making sure everyone knew he would leave no stone unturned to find orders, punctuating the point with "I don't care if it takes 24 hours a day." Burnie had been selected to take over Consolidated just a year earlier. A native New Yorker with experience in the appliance industry before coming south to furniture management, he looked at the practice of shutting down for church as archaic, a luxury the fast moving furniture buying world could no longer afford. "The churches are here," he announced, adding "they're available if they (the buyers) want to go."[694]

A perfect storm of sorts had hit Lenoir with the arrival of the Tremlett 'hurricane'. A trio of old companies, Blowing Rock Furniture, Spainhour Furniture, and Kent-Coffey Furniture found themselves under the control of a new owner, Magnavox. That corporation, known for making televisions acquired the three local furniture makers in 1967, wrapping them up together for the ultimate arrival of Burnie Tremlett to run. If the uncertainty of consolidation wasn't enough, local management teams now had to deal with a foreigner as their boss, what the hometown folks called a 'yankee,' some even a 'damn yankee.' While other takeovers left local management largely intact, Burnett Tremlett called all the shots, and loudly. Burnie could see the warehouses filling up as sales slumped, and he knew it was his job to do something about that. Given the personnel and the pressure, a change had to come.[695]

An outsider president leading an outsider corporation telling people who had been there all their lives that a tradition they held dear was expendable, spoke volumes to the small town population. To head off a backlash, Tremlett boasted he had "sent out letters telling people about it, and had no objections from anyone," but the decision still rankled. A lot of factory, even management people, who regarded Sunday mornings as a time set aside for personal church attendance felt the move was disrespectful, both of the Protestant faith many practiced but also the limits of business in the personal lives of the local furniture community. Burnie Tremlett knew the buyers were unlikely to attend church and as far as the people who manned the showroom, he did not care. So in a pragmatic, take charge way, the president of Consolidated (the name under which Magnavox operated), made the decision to maximize the time buyers were in Lenoir, no matter what feathers it ruffled. Speaking like the decision maker he was, he jabbed, "When things go sour (like last year) a lot of companies will draw in their horns." Not Burnett Tremlett and not Consolidated as long as he was at the helm. "We didn't do that. We got ready for the upsurge." After a few markets, the affront passed and so did Burnie. By 1974, he jumped to Bassett after a VP job with Broyhill in between.[696]

In reality, Burnett Tremlett was just another tremor in the earthquake of change for the workers at Consolidated. Burnie himself was a replacement president, a third in quick succession. When the buying spree started, Roger B. Triplett was the head, a local Lenoir furniture executive of long standing. After the various companies had been consolidated, he "requested retirement." Magnavox selected Robert D. Darden, Jr. as his replacement. He was fresh from a vice-president's chair at Heritage in Morganton, but after two years on the job, he decided he didn't want to be a furniture division president. He opted to become a "corporate dropout" instead, going to law school at Chapel Hill. When quizzed, he worded his decision tactfully, saying he found "the rewards of corporate life at that level just did not seem to us (presumably his family) to warrant the price."[697]

The veneer of hometown ownership was peeling away, along with local veneer companies. A few years after Magnavox came to town, setting up shop as Consolidated Furniture Industries, the soon-to-be-gone Robert Darden got together with Broyhill to buy National Veneer in Lenoir. Each owned 50 percent. Likewise, they split management between the two companies. Across town, the other veneer company also found itself under new ownership. Broyhill bought Lenoir Veneer outright. The shuffle kept employees wondering what was next. Surprised, but probably not shocked,

An unnamed employee sands down the top of a chest of drawers on the line at the Kent-Coffey factory in Lenoir. Workers in the 1970s became increasingly unsure of the permanence of their jobs as layoffs began. In the coming decades, joblessness was more common. (Courtesy of the Caldwell Heritage Museum)

they woke one morning to discover that Magnavox decided to get out of the furniture business entirely. The new owner was Singer, the sewing machine company, who bought out Magnavox for an undisclosed price. Times had gotten very chaotic in the furniture game.[698]

In the 1970s, everyone did anything possible to keep the momentum of production and sales going. The pressure was especially acute on company management. Bill Mosteller owned, at one time or another, four different furniture-making firms, selling each for a profit. Once he started his final company, Impact Furniture, he wanted potential buyers during the market to be the happiest of any. So he took a page from a blockbuster movie of the era. Or maybe he was the film's inspiration. Who did it first was unclear.[699]

During the era, the distribution of Coors beer was unlawful east of the Mississippi River. That made drinking it all the more exotic for those from the East Coast. Once during the furniture market, the Impact owner arranged for a driver to pick up a load on backhaul (the return trip after delivering furniture). The shipment was supposed to be delivered to the market showroom for consumption by furniture buyers. Unfortunately, law enforcement detected the contraband at a weigh station and held up the shipment. Phillip Mosteller, son of the owner remembered the incident well.[700]

"Of course the truck driver wasn't going to take the fall for 80,000 pounds of Coors beer in the back," said the younger Mosteller. When pressed, the driver referred officials to the elder Mosteller. The Highway Patrol reportedly told him, "we're going to let him through this time but don't ever think about doing it again." It was the one and only time attendees to the Hickory market cheered with clanking glasses of Coors, like they were a part of Smokey and the Bandit,whose theme centered on bootleg alcohol delivered by truckers.[701]

The most vulnerable in the ongoing epic of furniture making on the western end of North Carolina were the workers. In the mid-'70s the economy pulled back from the good times of the '60s to leave the business of manufacturing "uncertain." An unfortunate example was a couple who both labored in the industry. Winfred and Doris Wagner agreed that they made "a good living working in furniture," but also acknowledged the riskiness that came with it. He was an upholsterer for Orbit Industries, and she was a sewer for Montclair Furniture. Both had spent their working lives in the business. In 1974 however, each filed for unemployment for the first time. They typified the ups and downs of a labor force that had grown 32,000 strong in the Catawba Valley. This scene was repeated in a myriad of families as workers began to feel the punch of employment shifts.[702]

Everyone in the furniture business knew the pitfalls of the market. Changing tastes sent designers back to the drawing board often as one year Mediterranean lines were popular, then a quick shift to Early American the next season caught companies off guard. However, the underemployment of the Wagners was attributable to no such whims. The gas crisis of 1974 brought on a severe economic downturn that affected furniture purchases. It was, "the first thing a money-pressed consumer will do without," noted a furniture executive. When Mr. and Mrs. Wagner finally went back work full time two years later, they knew the rest of their employment life would be tied to the economy and a cycle of good and bad times. They remained "happy" about the choice they had made to work in the industry, but knew they needed to be frugal, in case another such recession should come and their hours shortened again. In their mid-50s, Winfred and Doris represented a vanishing breed in furniture, a couple who spent their entire lives rising through the ranks to skilled positions, only to see their expertise subject to forces over which they had no control.[703]

Coming to work regularly and delivering a conscientious day's work for their employer was becoming more rare. Part of the problem was the reputation of the industry for its low pay. By some estimates, skilled positions like upholsterers and sewers could earn somewhere near $20,000 per year, a very respectable income at the time. Many though were considered low skill and were paid less. With a minimum wage of $2.85 during the mid-'70s, it became more difficult for companies to find and keep workers. Downturns like the one that sidelined the Wagners, reduced jobs and the labor force. For a long while companies could take their pick from a pool larger than what they needed, but as college became feasible for young adults with upwardly mobility ambitions, the pool of high schoolers naturally moving from school to factory began to dwindle. Some rejected the fate of their fathers and mothers, leaving only those with fewer prospects to go into the factory, at minimum wage.[704]

One anonymous observer who worked in the industry blamed the companies. Characterizing their reliance on low-skilled labor "shortsightedness," this person argued that with competition increasing, factory management should get more involved with developing its workforce decades in advance. "Furniture companies are not training young people to develop skills and are not offering adequate work incentives," said the worker. Employees with both white and blue collars noticed the gap. Nan Bumgarner of Hickory's Granline Corp. posited that she went "through 50 interviews before you find someone who really wants to work." She had gotten tales from prospective laborers about how destitute their family was, only to find herself hiring a person who turned out to not want the job enough to actually show up. "I hire them and they work for one or two days and walk off." The relationship between employer and employed had become strained, each side lacking appreciation for what it took to get the job done.[705]

As in past eras, workers faced another decision in the seventies. Did they want to work in a union shop? In 1978, the United Brotherhood of Carpenters and Joiners thought that a majority might and came calling again, seeking to organize. Targeting fifteen plants in Lenoir owned by Singer and Broyhill, the National Labor Relations Board geared up for elections, testing if "at least 30 percent of the workers in all seven plants (Singer) supported the union." One interesting statistic stood in organized labor's favor. Of the 80,000 furniture workers in the state (which included those from High Point), the average per hour wage was only $3.88 compared to national manufacturing average of $5.36. The union, however, had an uphill climb. North Carolina was the least unionized state in the nation, with only 6.9 percent of workers belonging to one. The vast majority of furniture plants in the Tarheel state (600 total) were unrepresented (95%). That did not deter the Brotherhood of Carpenters from wanting to become part of a $1.5 billion per year industry in North Carolina.[706]

All eyes were on Broyhill's Harper plant in Lenoir since they held the first vote. Just before the election, the union charged that management had fired an employee for union activism. Harper plant manager Bill Berry called the charges "picayunish," but an investigation delayed the electon. Both sides propagandized the voters. The union handed out leaflets, while the company treated its hands to several films, "one about Broyhill Industries and two about the sometimes violent history of the American labor movement."[707]

Delay damaged the union's effort. Lamenting that "we had no choice but to withdraw the (election) petition," Mike Bracken, union organizer explained, "when we submitted them we had well over 30 percent. But we later found out that turnover had cost us over 200 cards." The withdrawal came after the union decided to drop attempts to organize all 15 plants and concentrate on Broyhill's Harper Plant, the oldest furniture factory in Lenoir. One of the Harper plant's youngest employees smelled doom for the union in the move. A sixteen-year-old worker called the choice a "big mistake," believing "the union is weak. A lot of people are saying the union won't get into Harper because of that." Chairman of Broyhill Industries, Paul Broyhill agreed with his worker, observing that the union seemed to be "vacillating." It didn't help the union's cause that they had decisively lost an earlier election in nearby

Hudson when the All-Wood Products Manufacturing Company's workforce rejected representation, 71-16.[708]

After an additional two months, the vote at Harper was finally held. Just like in all other attempts to organize workers in the furniture plants of western North Carolina, the union lost. The final tally was 247-99, the Carpenter's Union carrying less than 30% of the total. The vote ended a year-long campaign to organize the "largely nonunion furniture industry." Organizer H.L. Thomas could only say that "at least the people wanted their choice and they got it."[709]

A rival to the Brotherhood of Carpenter's, the United Furniture Workers of America (UFWA), an AFL-CIO affiliate made one last push in the region to organize a factory. The Phenix Chair Company dated back to 1935 when Robert Barr started making dining room chairs with three employees in the mountain town of West Jefferson in Ashe County. For years, Phenix Chair grew slowly, increasing their initial output of approximately "one hundred chairs per month," until Barr sold to Thomasville in 1964. Just on the heels of the Harper plant loss for the Carpenter's Union in Lenoir, the UFWA opened a four-month campaign to unionize Phenix.[710]

To everyone's shock, including the union's, the vote passed. By a slim majority, 267-223, workers invited the United Furniture Workers to collectively represent them in their dealings with the company. According to reports, "working conditions were a major point of the union campaign." As with the vote, the workforce was divided about the outcome. One older worker grimaced about how the election would bring trouble, saying "all unions ever do is cause confusion." A younger worker saw it differently. She delighted in how the UFWA was going to get "equal treatment" for her and her coworkers. "We'll be able to stand up for our rights now," she said. Union officials expected the vote to echo down the mountain to the other Thomasville plants. Company officials wanted no such outcome. "They won at Phenix," vice-president Robert Holladay snorted, "but that's just a small percentage of employees."[711]

The "breakthrough" of finally winning an election proved to be a bumpy ride for the union. Four months of contract negotiations produced nothing. The company went ahead and offered 25 cents per hour more in wages on average (roughly seven percent for most workers) and more vacation and paid sick time. It was the same increase the company had given to all its other plants earlier but withheld pending the union vote in West Jefferson. Union organizer Ted Davis called that move an attempt "to buy them off and forget about the union." Once the totals were in, Thomasville used the pay increase to show they cared more about their employees than the union did. Workers rejected the hike "unanimously," sending contract talks back to the square one. Executive vice-president Mike Bish said the move would be the "firm's final offer." It was not.[712]

The impasse took on additional meaning, considering all the rest of Thomasville's plants were not unionized. But workers were watching. It took well over a year for a final pact to be agreed upon but when it was, workers fared better than Thomasville's earlier offer. Average pay increases totaled 37.7 cents in the one-year deal. As the union hoped, future votes would also go their way. Following Phenix, two plants in Tennessee and one in North Carolina voted in the union. All was not rosy in West Jefferson, though. Four years after welcoming unionization, many of the same employees who chose the United Furniture Workers as their representatives, voted to throw them out. In a 217-158 vote, Phenix ousted the UFWA in a move some attributed to the economic downturn across the nation. Teamster's president R.V. Durham put it clearly. "When you're going through this type of (economic) period, workers are more interested in trying to hang onto their jobs, rather than trying to improve them."[713]

While the union was in West Jefferson, Thomasville Furniture's president, L.E. Bish denied that a collective bargaining organization like the United Furniture Workers helped any worker, claiming "the contract at West Jefferson doesn't call for anything more than we have at the other factories. This just goes to show you that unions don't necessarily mean higher wages and benefits." The UFWA begged to differ and prior to their exit from Phenix in 1982, they planned to organize the rest of Thomasville's labor force as an entrance to the rest of the industry. Union officials later revealed the reason for their choice. Thomasville was the only division of Armstrong Cork, the parent company, that was not organized.[714]

Despite the efforts of union organizers to raise wages, and the refusal of workers to accept representation as a solution, everyone in the industry knew the furniture business could not shake its impoverished image. Workers still made some of the lowest wages of any industrial job in the nation. Most were listed as "unskilled" which meant they could be paid minimum wage. Few got more than a dollar above that line which totaled well below wages for manufacturing at large. State Labor Commissioner John C. Brooks struggled to explain why workers in furniture made so little, citing factors like the cost of living in the non-urban areas where the factories were located. The disparity haunted companies looking for good employees, unable to employ them if an offer in another line of work was on the table.[715]

Even though the industry was in flux, one promising trend of the seventies had run its course. By the end of the decade, plastic was out as a furniture component. A spokesman for the Southern Furniture Manufacturers Association noted, "consumers are returning to natural styles, with oak and pine becoming the most popular wood species for furniture products." The attempt to augment wood with "decorative plastics," even some attempts to fully replace wood with an extruded petrochemical frame had come and gone as the fad it turned out to be. Frenzied belief in technology remaking the way furniture was made reverted back to a more traditional view. Plastic, once viewed as the savior of the industry, was ultimately seen as artificial and cheap. Consumers instead wanted something they felt they could rely upon.[716]

Toward the end of the 1970s, two curious trends in the furniture industry found observers sad and happy at the same time. First, sales were down. Fewer people were spending their "disposable incomes" on furniture. By some estimates, declines totaled as much as 15% nationwide, while at the same time, employment in the North Carolina furniture industry was going up, way up. Over the decade, the Tarheel state increased its share of the manufacturing sector, which accounted for a rise in workers. The growth offset falling nationwide retail sales. One other quirk of economics helped sustain the purchase of home furnishings in the era. While inflation shot up prices for other goods by as much as 72%, the price of furniture only climbed 40% in the era, leading buyers to the conclusion that they were getting fantastic deals. Anticipating the oncoming 1980s, industry watchers were salivating over the rise of the baby-boomers moving into the 30-44 age demographic, prime time for home buying, family-raising and consequently, furniture purchasing.[717]

Analysis of the industry revealed trends, both worrisome and promising as the decades switched. One of the biggest called attention to the foothills. It seemed that while interest in furniture was growing across the state, it was specifically growing in and around Hickory. Talk had been rampant that the furniture market might actually leave NC, thanks to new markets commencing in places like Dallas, Texas, and Atlanta, Georgia. Though both cities drew retailers, the manufacturing home of furniture remained strong. Of the state's growth, "the western end of the market has experienced the most dramatic growth during the '70s," as revealed by the Furniture Factories' Marketing Association of the South. One reason cited was the increased number of companies concentrated there, but some felt the opening of the interstate highway (Interstate 40) between Winston-Salem and Hickory was the reason more buyers made sure to make a trip. High Point never lost its crown as the primary location for wholesale shoppers during the furniture market, but those in and around Hickory began to question the dominance of the eastern sphere. Could Hickory become the new High Point? Locally, the answer was, 'why not?'[718]

Western companies were feeling good about their growing power, sure that the best kept manufacturing secret, hidden up in the foothills and mountains of North Carolina was becoming known. By the mid-1970s, major companies like Broyhill began to explore an intriguing idea, "self assembly" furniture. A concept that Swedish manufacturer IKEA had already developed and would market successfully in the United States later, the intent was to offer furniture at a lower price with the customer handling the process of putting the pieces together. Wes Collins, president at Broyhill promoted the idea with the market-risky quote, "we have tried to make it idiot proof." Saying that it could all be put together with a screwdriver, "and we include a screwdriver in every box," Broyhill was the first to introduce the idea with a line of "dining room, living room and bedroom furniture" that was shipped to stores nationwide.[719]

Broyhill acknowledged the concept wasn't for everybody. Only about two percent of their offerings were what they called "knock-down" furniture (meaning it could be disassembled in case it needed to be moved). Sales Manager Pete Steib conceded that it was unique, but he pointed out that "this concept is only new in the States," adding that in English homes about one-third of the furniture is self-assembled. "We don't say this replaces conventional furniture," Steib admitted. "It doesn't. It's an alternative." The main attraction was the price. A $190 fully assembled dresser would cost $160 if the store delivered it in a box. If the customer carried the box out of the store, the price dropped to $148. Some retailers balked at the "lower markup," but Broyhill saw promising increases in sales, enough to devote one factory to making the new type of furniture. Perhaps it was the factory that was no longer devoted to producing plastic parts. Broyhill, like many other companies was never forthcoming about failures, only cheering its new initiatives.[720]

About the same time, Broyhill also led the way in the concept of rental furniture. As a hedge against a deteriorating economy, the company opened a number of "rental operations" in the Southeast. Harry Morgan, manager of the Broyhill store in Charlotte wasted no time in acknowledging "when the economy goes bad, we generally do better," a nod to the need to reduce initial outlay for the cost-conscious furniture buyer. His example involved a grouping that might cost $3,000. Companies generally required a 20% down payment ($600) on credit purchases with the rest payable over time. A rental alternative sent customers out of the store with the same furniture for $200. Putting its toe in the rental market, Broyhill continued to look for lucrative options to sell (or rent) its own product. Some questioned if Broyhill was selling furniture or credit.[721]

The new ventures at Broyhill were certainly the most experimental of any furniture operation in western North Carolina. They were the largest family-owned furniture maker in the nation. With Ed Broyhill's retirement from the board of directors, son Paul had taken over first as president of the company, then chairman of the board. For a short period he reassumed the office of president when Wes Collins resigned in 1980, but it wouldn't matter for much longer.

In the summer of 1980, word leaked that the company was being sold. Broyhill officials denied that talks were underway with the International Shoe Company, known then as Interco, Inc., which had diversified from its footwear origins. Without doubt the most successful of the Lenoir companies, with plants extending to Marion, Newton, Conover, Rutherfordton, and Statesville, Broyhill had become the biggest name in furniture, not only in the west but also among all North Carolina manufacturers. Paul gained invaluable name recognition for the company in the 1970s when suites of Broyhill furniture turned up as prizes on the CBS game show, *The Price Is Right*. Now, the company that Paul, his father, and his uncle Tom, had built was passing into other hands.[722]

The shock was seismic in Lenoir. Buyouts had occurred previously, so the concept was not new. However, Broyhill was more than a furniture company. It was an institution. The year before it sold, the company tallied sales at $265 million. The 7,500 workers employed by Broyhill in their twenty plants would now answer to a corporate headquarters in St. Louis, Missouri. The Broyhill labor force became step siblings with Ethan Allen, the company Interco bought the previous year for $66 million. This time the buyer shelled out $151.5 million to approximately "300 Broyhill shareholders." Interco could afford the purchase, having raked in over $2 billion in sales the previous fiscal year. Instantly, Interco became the largest furniture manufacturer in the country. Company officials insisted that "Broyhill will operate autonomously under its present management." The complexion of the business was beginning to reflect outside interests, not the hometown atmosphere it had always cultivated since its creation. First Kent-Coffey, Spainhour, Blowing Rock, and now Broyhill had sold out. It seemed like large portions of Lenoir had begun to cash out from the only real business it had ever known.[723]

Takeover fever had begun again. Not since the "merger of the week" era of the late 1960s had outsiders come looking to diversify their holdings so fervently. That same summer textile giant Carolina Mills in Maiden (southern Catawba County) got into the mix, buying Null Manufacturing, just down the street for much the same purpose. They did not want to live or die with the future of textiles, so they got into the furniture business. The purchase gave Null the capital to build a new $8.5 million plant to consolidate operations. Null and Broyhill found themselves part of a new acquisition trend, just two of a dozen furniture companies subsumed into a larger entity.[724]

Just as a big tree fell in Lenoir, so too did one in Hickory. Out of

Furniture workers from the 1960s forward might have needed a scorecard to keep up with who owned what furniture company. Hickory Furniture, the city's first, had consolidated, then split, then got bought out, all quite possibly during some long-standing worker's tenure. (Courtesy of Hickory Landmarks Society)

Chicago came the Technical Equipment Leasing Corp., known as Telco, looking for variety. They found it with 77-year-old Hickory Furniture and its 1,300 workers. Telco specialized in "leasing sophisticated medical equipment to hospitals and other health care facilities." The buyout was smaller, Telco buying 540,000 shares of the company for a reported $8.1 million. In its last fiscal year which ended in July 1980, Hickory Furniture had done $40 million in sales. While the Interco deal indicated that Broyhill owned a plant in Louisiana and a recently purchased one in Texas, Telco was getting a factory in Grand Rapids, Michigan, (previous home of the furniture capital of the U.S.) to go along with three plants in High Point and two in Hickory. The official word from both parent companies assured the workforce that they planned to treat their acquisitions "as an investment," and not take an active role in their operations.[725]

Buyout fever came at an ironic time, just as interest rates were up and factory orders shaky. With the prime interest rate headed for 20 percent, industry insiders expected a drop off in sales for 1981. L.E. Bish, president of Thomasville was honest when he exclaimed, "we're scared to death." With the exception of the Great Depression, future success for the furniture industry had never been so unpredictable. One industry newspaper pointed out that interest rates "have begun to choke off some retail furniture sales and spur cancellations of manufacturers' orders." With no credit available, most consumers could not buy the bigger ticket items like home furnishings, which left companies to either fill their warehouses or lay off workers.[726]

The desperation of the times spurred more knockoffs than ever. Wild tales from the interactions that came during furniture markets could probably fill its own book. Among those stories was a the invention of a new product sold by Sherrill Upholstery. A successful, but opinionated owner/operator, Buddy Sherrill favored traditional styles. A conversation between Ed Harmon, who worked for Sherrill at the time, and a young designer resulted in the creation of a sofa of modern design. Buddy saw the piece and said, "you're not putting something like that in there (the showroom)," according to Ed Harmon. When "some of the salesmen come in for market," they saw the innovation and said, "man, that's fantastic. We've been needing something like that. This is great." Buddy Sherrill had been backed into a corner. He hated

These sewers manned their machines faithfully to turn out an ample supply of upholstery fabric, ready to be spread over cushions and onto frames. During the '70s some companies experimented with plastic frames, but ultimately consumers demanded a return to wood. (Courtesy of the Caldwell Heritage Museum)

the look of the sofa, believing it did not reflect the image of his company, but his salesmen enthusiastically believed it could sell. As Ed remembered, Buddy took a middle path, saying, "we can put it in the show but it has to go in the break room. You're not going to put it in the showroom proper." Ed humorously recalled that market as one in which "we probably did more business in the break room than we did on the showroom floor." To combat the bad economy, management found themselves forced to stretch beyond their comfort zone, a trait which had served them well in the past.[727]

Exiting a turbulent seventies, the 1980s offered some hope of stability, until it arrived. With buyouts and a generally bad economy, the furniture business was either in for a temporary rough patch or the beginning of the industry's precipitous decline. It turned out that the answer was actually a 'yes' to both scenarios.

Women were always a part of the furniture workforce. Initially, they held jobs in the office but especially after World War II, their labor was needed on the factory floor. These two, carrying chair legs reveal just how important their presence was to the repetitive tasks of manufacturing. (Courtesy of the Caldwell Heritage Museum)

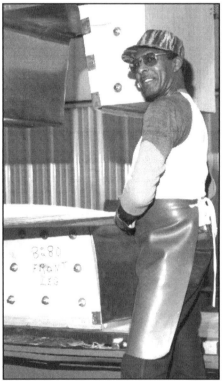

Two men at a Statesville furniture factory work with machinery in the furniture making process. African-Americans constituted a minority of western North Carolina workers (proportional to population numbers). They were largely excluded from management positions. (From the Statesville Photographic Collection. Courtesy of Steve Hill)

Chapter 27
The Exodus

After a couple of tough years in the American economy, sales in furniture began to rebound. Oddly, that's when the real trouble began for the western end of North Carolina's furniture world. The 1980s began as a continuation of the '70s for furniture production. Sales slumps led to sporadic shutdowns, which rippled through the entire local economy. Out of work furniture hands meant no new car sales, fewer folks coming through the door at restaurants on Friday and Saturday nights, and most assuredly families holding on to their older home furnishings, even if many locals could buy at wholesale from the factory. Apprehension plagued the populace.

It all came back to the consumer. Store owners listened closely to the needs of shoppers. Retailers relayed what they heard to manufacturers who tried to overcome objections by crafting products that they thought would fulfill those needs. A furniture store owner in Caldwell County came to Hickory's spring market in 1983 with an eye toward what he thought his customers would buy. He postulated that "people want their money's worth. They're buying something that's going to have to last them a long time." In his opinion, the economy had beaten down the buying public. "In the boom period, we could sell just about anything on the floor," he said. "But since the recession, people have gotten more quality-conscious."[728]

Buyers headed to showrooms still ready to choose, but sometimes the new hesitancy showed. Store owners mimicked what they had seen customers do time and again in their own stores, plop down on sofas and chairs, run their fingers across the lines of case goods, and evaluate collections in the decorative settings provided by companies. Each retailer knew he or she was taking a

419

calculated risk. Would shoppers shell out their hard earned money at the local furniture business, the same stuff store owners traveled to Hickory and High Point to buy? In good times, the process had been hard enough, but for the past decade, wave after wave of bad times had fatigued all concerned in the journey of a chair from factory to home.

The economy and its retreat from the bountiful era of the '60s tempered the desire for new furniture. Several factors were at play. The economy had damaged the credit of some who walked into furniture stores, making "on time"

Since Hickory began its own biannual furniture market in 1951, there had been intense competition with High Point for the eyes and orders of retail buyers. Venues in the west staged lavish parties and perks to lure market attendees. (Courtesy of Hickory Furniture Mart)

payments riskier than ever before. The buying power of the American public could also be seen in the size of the houses they bought. Floor plans for new construction shrunk. Thus, grander pieces like large sofas were not a good bet to move off the showroom floor in most furniture stores. Downsizing also caused home owners to look at furniture in a new way. "Consumers are going to smaller rooms and smaller houses," suggested a Caldwell County retailer, requiring him to "take into consideration the size of the furniture suites."[729]

The spring market of 1983 looked to many like furniture was finally turning the corner back toward good times. Salesmen geared up for the rush of buyers with order books in hand, although they knew only "10%-20% of the total industry's orders are made during market." Manufacturers began upping the perks in an effort to get retailers to say yes. One example was $3,000 worth of prime rib. At the back of DeVille Furniture's display area, buyers were treated to free prime rib lunches as just one of many expenses incurred by companies to keep their clientele happy. The game had gotten expensive for companies to entice potential buyers.[730]

Ancillary expenses associated with exhibiting furniture had gone up over the years. Broyhill spent "about $75,000 a year on just artwork in its showrooms and another $50,000 on showroom wallpaper." Another company paid a local florist $12,000 for plants to adorn their displays. The expense was seen as necessary to gain the attention of buyers as they walked through presentations. With the market so important to not only the company but also the local economy, manufacturers could take no chances.[731]

Another issue caused by all the expenses meant that many smaller firms could not afford to show at the spring and fall furniture markets in and around Hickory. While 85% of the nation's furniture retailers made the trek to North Carolina for the markets, many little companies shied away because of the overhead and chose to stay at home. Paul Bollinger started Startown Furniture Manufacturing Company in Catawba County back in the early 1960s. He began his operation limited in scope and stayed that way, remembering that he never had over 15 employees working for him at one time, ever. Most times it was closer to 10. His philosophy and his success were simple. "I get my business from word of mouth - we don't advertise, and we don't show," he said, emphatically. According to his calculations it would cost him "around $10,000 a year to show and the cost is too high for the small manufacturer."[732]

Instead of buying into the promotional scheme, Paul Bollinger decided to keep his company lean. He felt that was how he stayed in business. By watching his overhead closely, he posted continuous profitability. Producing "an average of two truckloads of furniture a week," he took pride in saying, "I don't know of one week we actually lost money." His was a different business model than the "big boys," a company much more akin to the way furniture was first made in the early days than what his competitors were doing in the 1980s. His story mirrored how almost every competitor began. A one-time farmer, Paul had "worked in his youth in a furniture factory." He started making upholstery as a hobby. Demand for his output convinced him to incorporate, but he purposely kept the enterprise from getting too large.[733]

Startown Furniture was a "mom-and-pop outfit" by Paul Bollinger's own admission. He took pride in adding, "and we cater to mom-and-pop stores." He delivered some of his product in either a furniture van or a pickup truck to stores in North Carolina, South Carolina, and Georgia. Customers from a wider range (Florida, New Jersey and Ohio) had to pick up their purchases themselves. Bollinger estimated that he had "between 60 and 70 loyal customers and about that many occasional buyers." Over the years, he expanded his workspace from 1,200 square feet to around 10,000, with most of the equipment coming from bankruptcy sales. Paul Bollinger's Startown Furniture demonstrated that a company could sustain itself without growing too large, if they chose to do so and were content with what they made.[734]

Bigger markets and bigger profits lured other companies to participate in rituals like the spring and autumn markets. Even then, displaying was often not enough. From the heyday of the market in Hickory, a slide had begun toward High Point. In the late '70s, the western end of the furniture figure eight offered some 225 exhibitors. Seven years later it was down to 130. Some argued the change did not reflect the amount of furniture moving but was a result of the market itself. It was though, cause for concern. A shock came when Hammary, then western anchor Bernhardt moved their entire showroom to

High Point. The shift signaled a change in attitude about a divided furniture market.[735]

Much of the decision was based on the kind of overhead companies were shelling out just to "lure" buyers to the west. For Alex Bernhardt, president of his family's company, the equation was simple. High Point offered "a dramatic increase in traffic," he admitted. Instead of the "lavish cocktail parties, lunches and renovated showrooms" in Lenoir, the Bernhardt company felt their promotional money was better spent in a location where they would increase the number of buyers by "10% to 20%." The move was not cheap. Reports indicated that the transfer would cost the company somewhere near a half million dollars, an expense they hoped to pay for in the extra sales generated in High Point.[736]

During the spring 1984 market, talk centered around the departure. "Would the west survive?" was a common question, quite a humiliation after some sought to eclipse High Point just a few years earlier. As Alex Bernhardt pointed out, "High Point has always been the center of the market." He was right, but that didn't allay the fears of most everyone else in the western industry. The Hickory Home Furnishings Mart, the city's showroom for area manufacturers changed its name to the Home Resource Center, an attempt to diversify its displays to include accessory items like "lamps, stereos, telephones, outdoor furniture, crafts," really anything that related to home decor, but was not exclusively furniture. It may have been too little, too late. That year about one-sixth of the facility's floor space went unused. Said general manager Robert Triplett, "we did attempt to diversify even before the exodus started." The effort did not save the facility from closing. Two years later the building was sold to Siecor and retrofitted as their corporate headquarters.[737]

Across town at Hickory Furniture Mart, Leroy Lail had kept his eye on the deteriorating situation for some time. He reasoned it was time to rebrand Hickory and its furniture market. He and his Hickory Furniture Mart had gone to great lengths to promote a niche within the larger furniture market. One billboard that lined Interstate 40, the main highway between Hickory and High Point, proclaimed, "Hickory Builds the Upholstery Market." Another touted Hickory as the "Nation's Upholstery Center." Witnessing the exit of furniture showrooms to the east, the owner of Hickory Furniture Mart said he felt he "needed to tell the story of the marketplace." In that, Leroy Lail and Richard Barentine, executive director of the Furniture Factories' Marketing Association of the South were in complete agreement, but their focus was completely different.[738]

Ever since its rise, the furniture makers of western North Carolina were known for the cheap, "borax" furniture they made. While the description was unflattering, the industry had come up with a code word, "promotional." Along the way, some companies, like Drexel and Bernhardt enhanced their output to attract a more affluent buyer, moving into higher-priced lines. Those firms were extremely proud of their products and rushed to High Point to show them off, leaving promotional furniture the domain of other western manufacturers. Richard Barentine began advocating Hickory embrace the cheaper product as a lifeline to continue the sojourn of furniture buyers to the west. Keeping some portion of the market in Hickory became a last ditch effort, one Hickory was now clearly losing. "If the western area is going to evolve as the promotional end of the market," said Barentine, "they are going to have to promote." The question of pushing Hickory as the capital of cheap furniture versus an upholstery center could only have been an argument between an outsider to the area like Richard Barentine and a veteran of the west's long tradition of furniture sales like Leroy Lail.[739]

Leroy Lail and his Hickory Furniture Mart (HFM) had gone into overdrive to promote Hickory and its furniture market. At his direction, HFM marketing manager Burr Thompson made sure that the Mart contacted over 500 retailers personally, first with a letter followed up by a phone call, to keep the

As a way to brand itself in the era of the furniture market's departure from the west, Hickory Furniture Mart developed a campaign based on Leroy Lail's contention that "furniture follows fashion." This young woman presents the idea in the first of a series of posters. (Courtesy of Hickory Furniture Mart)

relationship strong. In addition, Hickory Furniture Mart launched a national campaign, using the upholstery theme to bolster support for Hickory to still be a destination for the wholesale furniture buyer. Lail acknowledged the controversy by admitting, "there has been so much negativity said of the western market, we must work together to create a better image." From his chair as president of HFM, he advocated publicly that he still saw Hickory as a "viable showcase."[740]

Other signs pointed to Hickory losing its hold on the bi-annual furniture market. One buyer, Dick Danner from a five-store chain in Illinois admitted that the way he visited discouraged him buying from the western manufacturers. "I see Hickory first," he said. Putting the west earliest on his itinerary worked against the area as he also admitted, "I don't make any commitment because I want to see the rest of the market." Once he got to High Point, he willingly conceded that what he saw in and around Hickory had become hazy in memory and instead of returning, which he regarded as "too expensive," he chose from what he could see in High Point. And with the anchor city of the eastern market continually building more luxurious showrooms, Danner's actions spelled more revenue for those that displayed there.[741]

By the following year, the handwriting was on the wall. No matter how many prime rib sandwiches were handed out, Hickory had lost the furniture market. Some of the region's biggest names had hung on, not wanting to be the one to collapse the local economy of the boom weeks each April and October, but eventually they had to go to High Point to remain competitive. Jerome Bolick's Southern Furniture and Broyhill were the last to leave.

A malaise engulfed the area as they saw furniture trucks still proclaiming the region as "furniture capital of the South," on the roads traveling out of the Catawba Valley. They sadly had to admit it was no longer true. Curiously, the move actually strengthened the position of furniture workers. Whether their company showed in Hickory or High Point did not matter, as long as retailers bought. Bernhardt, along with its workers, found the move prudent with more orders than ever. However, for motels and restaurants all over Hickory, Lenoir and Morganton, getting a room or a table in October 1985 was no problem. The same was true at Hickory Furniture Mart where only 30 manufacturers exhibited on a four-day, instead of the usual ten-day schedule demonstrating a devastating hit to the economy of the region.[742]

Already, Hickory Furniture Mart had filled its empty hall with events that attracted many of the same manufacturers who brought their furniture to sell during furniture market. Only this time the companies were buyers. Back in 1981, forward thinking Leroy Lail could already see the coming void created by the then, unthinkable loss of the market in Hickory. That year he began a suppliers show, where manufacturers could find anything they might need to build their product. "Nuts and bolts, screws and glues, glass and brass, spring and machines and foams and fillings" were all on display as the Mart offered "about 200,000 square feet" for the show. By 1986, the activity was much needed. One-hundred, fifty-three suppliers from across the country came, trying to impress companies like Broyhill and Bassett, who came to "compare prices and see new products." The show was a bright spot in what

The hole that had been left by the departure of a portion of the semi-annual furniture market in Hickory was partially filled by the Furniture Suppliers Expo. Manufacturers came to Hickory Furniture Mart, not as sellers, but buyers of the supplies they needed to make furniture. (Courtesy of Hickory Furniture Mart)

otherwise looked like a dismal future for the building that formerly bustled with activity at market time. The suppliers show was no replacement, but it showed Hickory was still aggressive.[743]

The furniture industry in the foothills had always been a "good ol' boy" network, thanks in part to the family nature of companies, where the oldest son took over control when the founders retired. Never did daughters fill those roles. The rare exception was when Alex Bernhardt, Sr. moved in to the president's chair at the family company and brought his wife Anne, into the organization. She eventually became president of a Bernhardt division.[744]

Largely, women and minorities were excluded from the management structure of the western NC companies. A 1984 study of the industry as a whole in North Carolina found that of almost 68,000 workers, just over half were white males. "Officials" and "managers" were overwhelmingly white men. Of companies reporting their gender and racial mix, 87.38 percent were "white male." The category left the remaining slots to be filled by women (8.95%), "minority male" (3.33%) and women of color, the least represented at .34%, though they represented 6.64 of the total workforce.[745]

In 1984, the word 'minority' meant African-American in the days before significant Hispanic migration. Since the furniture industry began, African-American men and women had been a part of the labor force. Since those early days coincided with the Jim Crow Era, jobs for people of color were relegated to the lowest paying and hardest working at every factory. For men, that usually meant handling lumber as it came into the plant, often called the 'rough end.' African-Americans worked in furniture at approximately the same ratio as their numbers in the general population, but even by the 1980s, they had made little headway toward better paying jobs. White women fared a bit better, but both lagged significantly behind their white, male counterparts.[746]

Down on the shop floor, both groups showed up more. Women, both white and black, filled 24% of craft, or skilled positions. African-American men accounted for almost 10%. The issue was another sore spot in the industry. "A can of worms" was how one "furniture industry observer" characterized discussions of "race and sex" among leadership, who, when they gathered for industry functions counted "few women - and virtually no blacks" in attendance. When it came to releasing numbers of minorities in leadership, some companies like Broyhill flatly refused, which clouded the picture for representation of how diverse management really was in the west. The implication of silence was obvious. As it had been since its beginning, while the labor force was mixed, its leadership was not.

North Carolina prided itself on not being part of the Deep South where racism was at its worst. Seen as one of the more progressive southern states, Tarheels liked to think of themselves as less brutal in the racial divide than, say Mississippi, which had also developed its own furniture industry. In the western hills, opportunity was only slightly better for African-Americans. No one dared explore the disparity. Over in the textile world, one spokesman said, "we just don't want to go on record on this topic in any way," indicating how touchy the subject had become. Regarding the hiring of women, one Tennessee furniture executive was more forthcoming. Speaking for some of his neighbors to the east, he believed the issue is tied up in the old southern tradition of "chivalry." He observed that the cause of women's under-representation came from the way southern men treated women. Claiming, "we just don't put our women down. But by the same token, we don't put them in business either." As the industry moved toward the new millennium, the "good ol' boys" maintained their dominance.[747]

Among those white males controlling furniture production, companies continued their churn of startups, mergers, and acquisitions. For a while, much of the ownership of furniture companies had been in the hands of a small circle of families or executives, who ran their operations in a relatively conservative manner, not wishing to be branded a 'maverick'. Webb Turner had different ideas. He was an outsider with enough money to buy into the manufacturing world and a brash belief that he could run a business about which he admittedly knew very little.

His business plan called for a shakeup of the way the industry operated. Turner believed that "most furniture firms are run by third-generation families steeped in traditions or by bureaucratic conglomerates that inhibit swift, aggressive decision-making." He intended to follow none of those rules. In the early 1980s he turned from "Wall Street financier" to furniture mogul, going on a buying spree of companies. By 1984, he got to Hickory and laid down money to purchase what had once been Bill Mosteller's DeVille Furniture, to go with Turner's growing number of companies.[748]

DeVille had been just one of the companies Bill Mosteller created. Starting as a salesman with Andre Teague, Mosteller got the hang of the furniture business quickly. He and Wilfred Sigmon opened Fashion Furniture in the early 60s, with the agreement that one could buy the other out. The factory made "cheap" upholstery. As Bill's son Phillip characterized his father's philosophy, "do you want to hit the market where everybody can buy or just a few can buy?" Calculating that upper-end upholstery would only attract 10 to 15% of the public, Fashion (and Mosteller's subsequent companies too) wanted to sell to "the masses." They did. After several years Mosteller bowed out, heading on to his next startups, Trendline and DeVille. Once he sold DeVille, he went on to yet another company, Impact.[749]

Immediately, Webb Turner raised eyebrows at DeVille. After also buying Burlington Furniture he laid off "80 middle-management employees," stoking fears he would do the same to DeVille's Hickory workforce. Alex Bernhardt, himself one of those "third-generation" furniture owners said he was "somewhat skeptical" of Webb Turner and his "potential for success in the industry," adding a dismissive, "I've never met him personally." The skepticism didn't seem to matter. Webb Turner intended to turn the way business was done upside down. He felt he had a clearer idea of profitability than any of his furniture counterparts.[750]

Turner relished being a maverick. His connections to North Carolina included earning an economics degree from Duke University. While in Durham, he worked for a "woodworking equipment manufacturer" which may have explained his interest in furniture. He married a member of the "S.H. Kress retailing family" and began a successful career working "as a consultant in productivity improvement and an investment banker specializing in mergers and acquisitions." His assessment of the furniture business, as it was run in the '80s was frank. He saw the industry as "fragmented, labor intensive, subject to imports" and "has a low return on investment and low return on sales." He concluded, "it's crying for change." He never objected to terms like "vulture" being associated with his style, and continually sought to be "brutally candid" about his goals.[751]

As the furniture industry zigged, Webb Turner zagged. He planned for his companies to step back from "the traditional rush to show lots of lines at the twice-yearly furniture markets." He wanted to instead concentrate on "fewer lines and confidently produce them early enough to give market buyers quick deliveries." He saw his competitors as bloated. "There's a reason companies lose money," Turner opined, noting the firms he bought "were overstaffed and most were poorly managed." His first moves were "initial decreases in employment" with the operations he bought, stating that he would add jobs back "as companies begin turning a profit." He also pulled back on "employee benefits" offering incentives for aggressive sales that he felt would "more than compensate." The Webb Turner philosophy differed completely from the corporate giants buying up other furniture companies in the area, who generally kept local management. With Turner, white collar workers were the first to go.[752]

Once in Hickory, he didn't stop with DeVille. The next year he bought Dunmore Furniture, his "ninth acquisition in 2 1/2 years." At Dunmore, Webb Turner discovered management he determined to be effective, so he kept them. In this case, he referred to Andre Teague as Dunmore's "resident genius." As in many of his other purchases, Turner planned to set overall policy and leave the daily operation up to his chief lieutenants. He looked to subordinates like Andre Teague to help him bring "fresh management techniques" to companies that might not appreciate the Turner style.[753]

All did not go as planned for Turner Furniture Industries. The dream empire Webb Turner built fell apart quicker than it came together. Down east, his companies closed their doors, filing for bankruptcy. Less than a year after the Dunmore purchase, the holdings were up for sale again. This time the highly touted managers were the buyers, and Turner himself was the seller. No doubt the sale provided validation to those managers who had so unceremoniously been cut by Turner. DeVille, Dunmore, and State of Newburgh Furniture, (a New York manufacturer that he relocated south), were all sold, bringing a sigh of relief to the more than 1,000 workers at the plants. These upholstery firms may have been the most profitable of all the Turner companies with annual sales topping $74 million. Terms of the deal left Andre Teague back where he began when he first met Webb Turner, as sole owner of Dunmore, the company he started.[754]

Some of the savvy of Andre Teague came from his background. He had grown up in the furniture business. His family started Comfort Chair in 1945, and his association with the company served as a launching pad for future endeavors. In the 1970s, known as much for his sponsorship of race cars as his furniture career, Teague took an old dilapidated furniture factory and transformed it into Dunmore Furniture. While on the outside it looked like something "that scared most people," on the inside "the internal structure of the building was as good as any in town," observed the new owner.[755]

Facility-wise, the new Dunmore Furniture was actually the old Maxwell-Royal Furniture Company. Andre Teague did not know much about the company he was replacing, and as one reporter conceded, "no one seems to keep written records on former furniture factories," but a canvas of furniture old-timers found a former employee who explained the legacy. Maxwell-Royal actually began as B&B Manufacturing in Viewmont (a section of Hickory). The name change came when the company incorporated just after World War II and went on to expand to a new building (the one that became Dunmore) garnering a "good reputation all over the country." Some time in the '70s, "the 135,000 square-foot manufacturing plant" closed, ceasing to make its signature Early American lines. An interim owner kept the factory going for a time before he too had to shut down.[756]

Now it was Andre Teague's turn. Despite the tempestuous time with Webb Turner, Dunmore prospered. The company grew so big that it ultimately engulfed another, much older enterprise. Kroehler Furniture dated its beginning a century before Dunmore's, but the new owner chose to take the name of the old. Shortly after his disentanglement from Turner, Andre Teague and Kroehler were cited as one of three furniture makers from the area to be named in an annual ranking of businesses, called the "*North Carolina 100*, a list of the top 100 privately owned companies in the state" (Classic Leather and Bernhardt were also included). By the time of the award, Dunmore/Kroehler operated plants in Hickory, Newton, and Maiden, as well as one in Newport, Tennessee. Later, he would go on to create another firm, the short-lived Jordan Alexander in Granite Falls.[757]

Kroehler Furniture found itself in good company in the *North Carolina 100*. Another entry, Classic Leather ranked even higher as a private company doing well in the environment of western North Carolina furniture operations. In 1986, Classic Leather bought Statesville Chair. Like Kroehler, Thomas Shores, chairman, decided to avail the newer company of the most prime resources of the old. Given the superiority of Statesville Chair's Conover location, Classic Leather moved into the facility it bought.

Furniture entrepreneurs continued to jockey for available acquisitions that complemented their holdings. In 1987, Westchester Leather of Hickory purchased Herman Chair. Company head W. Steve Ikerd commented on the sale, saying "basically this gives us another price point and helps us add more to our package," with the two brands being described as "moderately priced."[758]

Of all the startups Bill Mosteller established, his largest was his last. He built an enormous factory just west of the Burke County town of Hildebran. Instead of another upholstery company, which he swore anybody could start in their basement, Impact immersed itself in the world of case goods. Seeing a need and determined to fill it, Impact followed Bill Mosteller's philosophy of the earlier companies by producing affordable wood products for the homes of the masses. Once again, Mosteller's timing was right and he used an ingenious payment plan. Instead of his company having to collect late payments from furniture stores, credit lines were directed through banks, which meant they, not Mosteller had to cover the loss if non-payment became an issue.[759]

Impact Furniture was incredibly profitable throughout Mosteller's tenure with the company. As with his other enterprises, he eventually cultivated buyers, first looking across the ocean to Germany. When that did not work out, he decided to take the call of Bassett, who had been pursuing him for some time. Bill Mosteller's son, Phillip recalled people telling him that his dad "could sell ice cubes to the Eskimos." In 1984, he sold Impact to Bassett for an undisclosed amount. Bassett wanted Impact for its unique "laminated non-wood furniture." To keep the price down, Impact used a process of adhesive laying sheets that looked like wood over fiberboard. The product sold well. Bill Mosteller had some of those items in his house, even after he sold Impact. Thirteen years after buying it, Bassett found that they did not have Mosteller's genius and closed the plant.[760]

Be it companies buying out operations of like size, others selling to conglomerates, or some splitting off from the same, the furniture business had taken on a much more cosmopolitan air in the 1980s. Certainly, the loss of the semi-annual furniture market from Hickory hurt the local economy but not that of the furniture makers themselves. Many benefitted from the increase of sales that came with showing their lines exclusively in High Point. The shift was an adjustment to the west, but once Hickory and its neighbors accepted the realignment, folks got used to the new role as manufacturers, not presenters.

The western end of North Carolina furniture had indeed taken a hit. The 'second fiddle' status was a bitter pill, but not life threatening. There was no time to relax or catch a breath. A challenge to the very existence of the furniture makers was brewing, some companies even complicit in the next great challenge, emerging overseas.

Chapter 28
A Short Respite

The furniture market left Hickory by the spring of 1985. The loss devastated individuals, businesses, and cities alike. In its last days, those who had the most to lose tried everything to keep the business intact. Shuttle busses rotated throughout the day between Hickory and High Point to give buyers a day trip to see the new lines. If a day was all High Point visitors were willing to give to western manufacturers, they'd take it. It was not enough. Some tried to put a brave face on it. The manager of the local Ramada Inn said, "we don't live off eight days in April and eight days in October." However, most knew that the influx bolstered the economy of the Unifour (Catawba, Caldwell, Burke, Alexander counties) mightily. When the market moved east, everyone, including the hotels, felt it.[761]

The cascade of companies moving their showrooms to High Point deflated whatever hopes anyone had about keeping some portion of the market, even the cheaper lines, in Hickory. During the summer of 1984, Hickory-Fry (then Benchcraft) announced their departure. High Point crowed. "The bottom line is that they've come to the conclusion that this is where the action is," said the head of the High Point design center, referring to the rush of western manufacturers heading east. Hickory Leather's sales manager, Jerry Sherr expressed exasperation with the entire process. He described the whole furniture market show concept as one which was "drying up." Calling it a "rat race," he questioned the idea of "leasing showrooms that are used only twice a year," calling them "expensive." The ones who could afford the cost, moved out while those that found it a hardship, rethought the industry's business model of a showroom for use that only a small, but influential contingent visited twice a year.[762]

In the wake of the market leaving town, a new idea began to emerge. Leroy Lail pondered the exit of the wholesale crowd and considered what that meant for his ever expanding Hickory Furniture Mart (HFM), which had grown into the largest showroom space on the western end. During the abundant years of the '60s and '70s, the Mart never stopped growing. Between markets Lail would build an addition, completing it just in time for the next market. "We never built on speculation," he said, "we always had tenants ready to occupy." By 1985, HFM had more space than it needed, with many former companies showing in High Point. He too sought a new approach.[763]

Consumer interest in the furniture market in Hickory had always been there. Hickory Furniture Mart opened its doors in the wake of every bi-annual market to let anyone who wanted to see the displays of furniture, after retailers had made their selections. Leroy Lail began to realize that what was at one time an afterthought of the furniture market could emerge as the very thing that might save Hickory, the western furniture industry, and Hickory Furniture Mart. Along with several key manufacturers, Lail began to welcome folks interested in buying furnishings for their own homes. One key experimenter in the new business model was Jack Sheer at Hickory Leather, who, along with Leroy had questioned the old approach. He set up his displays for year round presentation, so that "consumers as well as professional buyers" could see the output of his factory, which was located in Vale (a small community in southern Catawba County).[764]

The head of Hickory Furniture Mart had long seen the potential in furniture as a custom business, even if for a long time he left those choices to the manufacturers. Now with his Mart empty, Leroy implemented a plan to develop the design choices that many homeowners were eager to make in their own decor. The time had come for Hickory Furniture Mart to repurpose itself. The building now sought to welcome a new clientele. The move was not as earthshaking as it might sound.

For years, Hickory Furniture Mart invited the public to see what the furniture buyers saw. The Mart held a myriad of shows and events created to keep the facility busy in between markets. Now Lail and his staff expanded the concept. He established the Hickory Furniture Mart Design Center to serve as a hub for companies seeking to become part of the new consumer-driven sales atmosphere. Establishing an "open year-round" center for "interior designers, architects and builders to shop for furniture, accessories and fabrics" the reimagined version of HFM broadened its appeal and created a new reason for anyone connected with furniture, or curious for that matter, to come to western North Carolina. The rebirth of Hickory as an outlet for the buying public made good sense. Lynn Lail, Leroy's wife, headed up the Design Center. Leroy also brought his sons Scott and Brad into the organization to make the new Hickory Furniture Mart a family affair.[765]

The emerging strategy in and around Hickory was no longer to gauge the health of the furniture industry by the buying practices that went on only during two markets in the year. That focus was now the concern of High Point. Instead, success was to be determined by a different yardstick. Before the move east, Hickory Furniture Mart's Vice-President, John Schenk acknowledged, even "if 25,000 people came through the door (during the Southern Furniture Market), we would still be a 360-day-a-year market." In a prophetic statement of vision and optimism, Leroy Lail said, "buyers would always visit the Hickory area because of the large concentration of furniture manufacturers in the area," a nod to what he planned.[766]

The old system that western North Carolina furniture manufacturers had followed for decades had changed. No longer an insular existence, companies gained enough stature to be scrutinized on a much wider scale than ever before, along with the image fostered by the industry. Furniture companies had long been tagged as a low-wage employer, but one that contributed to local business via the furniture market and the philanthropy it doled out to the community. Now company heads faced the dilemma of finding additional ways to engender good will.

Ever since the rise of the community college system in North Carolina, debate raged about how educated the workforce should be. Workers receiving too little training hindered companies who needed employees that could think and operate ever more sophisticated equipment; too much education often led to higher paying jobs which were not in furniture. To combat the stereotypes of furniture as a lowest common denominator profession, firms began to give the community college another look, especially if the schools could tailor learning opportunities to the workers and not interfere with productivity. Leadership began to believe that improving the education of employees would raise the stature of the local population and in turn, ready them for better service inside the factories. Generally speaking, few had completed high school. Most had not. Some chose work over school as early as 16, when they were legally able to do so. Those who dropped out of their last two years of high school opted for the steady paycheck of a factory job, instead of waiting for a high school diploma which they felt would do them little, if any good. Often out of necessity, they decided to get a head start on their wage earning career.

Bassett Furniture was the first to reach out and see what could be done. Glenn Hunsucker, Catawba County native and Bassett vice president wrote a letter to Catawba Valley Technical College asking if the school could offer workers instruction that would help them learn what they missed in high school. Bassett's personnel manager was enthusiastic about the project. Kathy

Eads knew about CVTC's high school equivalency diploma classes (GED) as part of its Adult Basic Education program (ABE). She believed "it would be a good idea" and once the plan came together, she sent out a memo to see if anyone would take part. A total of 54 interested employees came to the first meeting.[767]

CVTC staff explained that classes would be held in the company cafeteria just after the end of the workday. The training was free for the taking, with the community college providing the instruction and Bassett paying for textbooks and all other needed materials. Just like course offerings on campus, Bassett "students are started off on an individual level and get individual attention according to their needs," reported Claudia McLean, CVTC's ABE coordinator. Within a few years, the idea spread to other furniture companies including Century Furniture and Leathercraft, as well as textile plants like Shuford Mills and U.S. Hosiery.[768]

Leadership at Broyhill also recognized a gap between the educational skills their workers possessed and what they needed. The company approached Caldwell Community College and Technical Institute (CCC&TI) about training that would eventually allow their employees to get a high school diploma equivalency, with the possibility of extending their education even further. Pride in raising the education level of its people was one motivation. Preparing them for greater competencies on the job was a more immediate consideration. One worker admitted she avoided helping her children with their homework because of her embarrassment over her own skills. She was one of the first to take "twice weekly" classes in reading. Session by session, the instruction began to elevate her confidence and bring back an appreciation for education that she had once discounted.

The Adult Basic Literacy Education program (ABLE), had a stated "two-fold" purpose. Both Broyhill and CCC&TI saw the training as a "public service," to heighten the abilities of the local community and help dispel the image of an illiterate labor force. The program would also, "because of the increasingly sophisticated equipment being used in the furniture industry" prepare workers for their jobs in the future. Broyhill saw the curriculum as important, filling " a need for more employees to work with new technology that requires better reading skills." Employees manned computers on company time to increase their reading abilities in a neutral locale, not at the community college or anywhere near the shop floor, but in the less intimidating atmosphere of a local shopping mall. Observed one CCC&TI official, "people who are almost non-readers became so fascinated with the machine (computer) they come in and go right to work." The initiative, jointly funded by Broyhill Industries, Caldwell Community College, and the Appalachian Regional Commission was sorely needed. At that time in Caldwell County, approximately 56% of the population had "received less than a high school education." The number topped the state average of 45% and the national average of 33%. Broyhill was lauded for the effort, both by the state of North Carolina and the employees who benefitted, including the worker who could not help her kids. After taking the program, she confided, "now I can go to the grocery store and buy something without a picture on it." CCC&TI Continuing Education Dean, Gene Carpenter said he got "goose bumps on my arms" hearing her words.[769]

On the heels of the success in educating its labor force, Broyhill delved into education in another important way. In late 1987, the corporate headquarters was also home to the Broyhill Education Center. The company created the "training center" to teach students to "see firsthand how furniture is made." The idea was to offer classes to salesmen on the retail level, so they could use their acquired knowledge to help customers make better buying decisions. The initiative was touted as "the first of its kind run by a furniture manufacturing company." Trainers conducted "courses in refinishing and repair, sales and management to furniture retailers and Broyhill employees." In Broyhill's estimation, everyone needed to get smarter about furniture.[770]

One area where Broyhill still had something to learn was safety. Its largest facility in Lenoir, known locally as the "particle-board plant" was a sprawling complex on the western outskirts, in the town where the company first got its start. On a Sunday afternoon in November of 1994, a spark ignited wood dust that became an explosion that folks "felt for miles." The blast took the lives of two workers. Robert Richardson died instantly. Rescue workers airlifted James Anderson to the UNC burn center in Chapel Hill, but he succumbed to his injuries. Three other employees were injured but not critically. A State Bureau of Investigation report revealed two detonations, actually. The "initial explosion likely shook down dust that had collected on surfaces, causing a second explosion."[771]

Also disturbing about the industrial accident was the interval between inspections by the Occupational Health and Safety Administration. The last time that plant had been checked was following a 1975 incident that also produced a fatality. Local officials admitted that fires were "common and very dangerous." Most went unreported said one fire chief, if injuries were not life threatening. They did admit that wood dust could be "so fine that when it mixed with air or any kind of ignition source, it explodes with the same velocity as gunpowder."[772]

Factories had always been a potentially dangerous place for workers since the first ones in the late 19th century. Death was not new, but when fatalities came, they served as a reminder of the risk taken by the rank and file in their daily jobs. The industry had meant much to the communities that sent their citizens to work on their shop floors. Generations of workers had come and gone, thanks to the rise of an industrial outlet for their labors. As tragic as it was, both blue and white collar workers took the good with the bad, joyful in times of prosperity, stoic when incidents like the Broyhill fire occurred. If they could keep the gains ahead of the losses, they considered their lot positive. Many put their trust in management to guide the course of their company, accepting whatever answer they were given for reverses. The hierarchy had not changed much since the first wood ran through a factory saw.

Hope remained that the business of furniture would continue to blossom, despite occasional mishaps. The western manufactures attempted to rebound from the loss of a local furniture market, repositioning themselves for new and better opportunities. Going on the hunt to find new allies, the furniture community found it could still attract partners, especially considering the money it pulled in as a manufacturing hub. West German-based machinery company, Bottcher and Gessner recognized the business it could do among the still powerful companies of the foothills. They set up shop in Hickory's Piedmont Business Center, the same site that had once been the Hickory Merchandising Mart, one of the markets' display venues. Bottcher and Gessner made woodworking machinery, including "saws and finishing systems" and planned to expand their reach by new proximity to factories all around the area. While the company catered to a "nationwide network of dealers," it based operations in the heart of the western district.[773]

Bottcher and Gessner was in good company. It was perfectly placed to participate in the furniture suppliers showcase Leroy Lail created as one of the ways to replace the seasonal furniture market loss. By 1988, the Furniture Industry Exposition drew "more than 15,000 visitors" to Hickory for the two-day event. The show not only drew local manufacturers, but companies from "more than 30 states" came to see such innovations as a "zero-wall recliner mechanism, developed by local furniture supplier Hickory Springs Manufacturing. In size, the event was second only to one in Atlanta and another in Germany for generating furniture manufacturing interest. Some companies sent upwards of 50 or 60 representatives. The showcase helped western North Carolina discover a new niche within the furniture business. If they could not supply the retailers, they would instead supply the suppliers, while themselves continuing to operate as a key contributor to the state's industry.[774]

Companies like Hickory Springs Manufacturing (HSM) became an important asset to area furniture firms. Parks Underdown started Hickory Springs in 1944, seeking to supply area factories with essential non-wood items in the production process. As product lines widened and a greater array of components were utilized, HSM made getting them easier, even if they didn't make the piece themselves. Don Coleman joined the company in 1972 when vinyl had become a popular fabric for upholstery. Though HSM did not manufacture the covering, Coleman could offer a company that did, B.F. Goodrich, the Ohio tire maker. Of those days, he remembered, "we wanted to expand into non-manufactured products, that we could sell to our customers," to complement the springs, bedrails and polyurethane cushions that HSM produced itself.[775]

HSM solidified a niche by getting the outside parts a furniture manufacturer needed in the production process. "Our word was our bond," asserted Don Coleman about HSM's dedication to its furniture making customers. Sometimes, his salesmen were in the same factory "once, twice, three times a week." That trusted connection allowed manufacturers to be able to rely on HSM for competitive prices, but more importantly, high-quality service, to make sure a component was on-site when required. Buttons, castors, and zippers were all among the array of items Hickory Springs delivered.

"We were successful," remembered Don Coleman, who eventually became president of the company. "The other good thing is that most of those products, we warehoused them in Hickory, or wherever they were going to be sold, so that gave us an advantage." To be as responsive as possible to large companies, HSM situated its plants in close proximity. "In Hiddenite (between Taylorsville and Statesville), when Broyhill had their plant up there, we put a plant within two miles of where they were," said Coleman. By the end of the twentieth century, HSM had become "the nation's largest foam and metal component supplier to the furniture industry." Venturing into products that dovetailed nicely with furniture lines, like mattresses, Hickory Springs maintained its focus on serving its customers. As Coleman figured, "75 to 80%" of HSM's output supplied the furniture industry.[776]

Increased sales from the next several High Point-centered furniture markets also helped manufacturing on the western end to rebound from its loss in prestige. Unemployment fell to less than three percent in Caldwell County in late 1987, a nice showing given that fully one third of workers there were directly tied to the furniture industry. In Catawba County, the rate was similar, while Burke County posted a slightly higher jobless rate of 3.4%. Labor market watchers called the job market "tight." Company officials hoped the convulsive economy of the '70s and early '80s was over. Now they faced a good problem; "too many jobs and too few workers."[777]

All was not rosy with the workforce in those days, though. Broyhill, and every other furniture company needed employees, so each applicant was precious. The growing problem of drug use clouded the issue for employers. To combat the rise, Broyhill instituted a requirement for "all new employees to submit to a drug test before coming to work," which they knew would reduce the pool of applicants even more in the tight job market. Periodic tests for truck drivers and others "as deemed appropriate" were also instituted. Concern about those on the clock in a proper state of mind rose after an August 1988 raid by Broyhill security officers, the State Bureau of Investigation, and the Lenoir Police Department. The trio of law enforcement officials "conducted predawn drug raids that netted 49 suspects." The arrests in the year-long investigation involved the sale of "marijuana, cocaine and LSD." Productivity hampered by recreational drug use had concerned furniture manufacturers since it first showed up on the shop floor in the '70s. Some of those caught were Broyhill employees and transactions were thought to have occurred in Broyhill plants. The company pushed for testing, over the objections of groups like the

American Civil Liberties Union. Broyhill president Gene Gunter declared his company felt "an obligation to commit to a program that will help provide a work environment free from the problems associated with drug use."[778]

Companies dealing simultaneously with current problems like drugs and future issues like sales for the next quarter had little time for considering their past. Nevertheless, the communities in which they were located began to recognize and appreciate the historic contribution of the industry to the lives and lifestyle of its inhabitants. The Caldwell Arts Council put on a "Chair Fair" to "commemorate Caldwell County's history as a furniture manufacturing center," announced Liza Plaster, head of the Arts Council in 1987. The two-day event featured races, parades and vendors selling wood crafted items. At the same time the Catawba County Historical Association declared its intention to work with a history professor from Appalachian State University to produce a history of the furniture industry. The book was supposed to be an "oral-history style book" about the advent of the business in western North Carolina. The effort replicated an oral history volume crafted ten years earlier

Though the industry was changing with corporate ownership, market maneuvers, and looming foreign competition, workers in factories built product in much the same way their elders had, by hand. The intricate 8-way-hand-tie system of upholstery remained a coveted skill. (Courtesy of the Caldwell Heritage Museum)

by a Lenoir-Rhyne College history class under the direction of Dr. Carolyn Huff, called "Splinters." For unknown reasons, the historical association's effort never came to publication.[779]

After a short respite, the landscape for furniture workers changed again. Fewer orders again led to "downtime" with widespread layoffs. Unemployment shot up to five percent in Caldwell County, with surrounding counties also reporting increases. Bernhardt VP Dan Wortman got to the point by saying, "business in not good." The economy had taken yet another turn, flattening out to the point of denying consumers of the kind of disposable income that funded furniture purchases. As usual, the climate slowed down output tremendously. Bernhardt, with its ten plants (eight in Caldwell County, one in Statesville and one in Shelby) implemented "short-term temporary layoffs" to wait for a better economic environment. Hammary Furniture went to four-day weeks in order to "reduce inventory." Full employment days with overtime in the 1950s and '60s had been replaced by erratic schedules throughout the '70s, '80s, and now '90s.[780]

It was no longer as simple as waiting for the warehouses to empty before workers could go back to the job. In early 1991, Interco, the parent company of Broyhill announced it had filed for bankruptcy. The working lives of 6,900 employees, populating 18 factories spread out across western North Carolina were threatened by the news. For a short time, local banks would not cash the payroll checks of employees after hearing that all of Broyhill's assets had been frozen. In the ten years Broyhill Industries had been part of the Interco group (along with Converse and Florsheim shoes, and fellow furniture maker, the Lane Co.), workers had never felt a terrifying shock like this one. Gene Gunter, Broyhill president sought to allay fears of catastrophe. He told the press, "the company is stable, employees are being paid, and their benefits are in place." Most had no choice but to take management at their word. Those familiar with the workings of American business knew bankruptcy did not always mean total insolvency. "Bankruptcy court protection under Chapter 11" allowed Interco time to restructure in order to "ease the debt burden" that had been building and permit the company to continue much as it had before.[781]

New concerns occupied the minds of furniture workers as they kept seeing changes. However, one old occupational hazard remained. An employee at Thomasville's Lenoir plant was on his usual job of operating a tenon machine that "cuts huge pieces of wood." Either "because of human error or because (of) machinery malfunction," both of Billy Jones's hands were severed. He was flown to Duke Medical Center in Durham, along with his hands, that were packed in ice. Thanks to a quick response to the emergency, surgeons were able to reattach both hands. The 15-hour procedure was successful, but doctors took a wait-and-see attitude about how much use the patient might regain. Locally, medical personnel acknowledged that they saw between "30 to 50 patients a week" (none as severe as Billy Jones) who come in with industrial injuries. Most, according to Athel Wilcox of Caldwell Industrial Medicine, were more "repetitive motion-type injuries and back strains." Training and safety guards on machines like the one used by Billy Jones reduced accidents, a Caldwell Memorial Hospital nurse confided, but they still had "a lot of amputations of fingers and a lot of bad lacerations." Curiously, she said injuries often came in cycles with periods where "there'll be days without an injury, and then they'll pile up within hours."[782]

Increasingly, the community colleges began to play a larger role in the development of the furniture industry, including safety training. Catawba Valley Community College began its history as a training ground for furniture workers. By the mid-70s, the school expanded its offerings for furniture workers to the point of creating a Furniture Technologies Division, complete with a new regional training center that included "some $130,000 in renovations." The facility looked like a mini-factory with a "dry kiln, machining, assembly and finishing methods in case goods and upholstery furniture," to enhance

Students were part of a mini-furniture factory at Catawba Valley Community College. Pieces turned out were sold to support the program. When it looked like the end of furniture making in western N.C., the college shut the program down, repurposing the building. (Courtesy of CVCC)

learning for students. Like Caldwell County, the furniture workforce claimed a large (though not as large as Caldwell) portion of the population.[783]

The commitment of the community colleges were a hedge against the lean times the western end of the industry had hit upon, developing solutions that would provide a rebound. When computer-integrated technology became useful to furniture making, CVCC held a "two-day seminar for Microdynamics, a computer software supplier" that could assist in the production of upholstery. "Century Furniture, Conover Chair, Klausner, Sherrill Furniture, Southwood Reproductions, Thomasville, Vanguard, and La-Z-Boy" all attended.[784]

By the early 1990s another wave of buyouts had taken the control of furniture making out of the hands of local folks. DeVille Furniture of Hickory, after its disastrous tenure with Webb Turner, went on the auction block again, this time purchased by a group called Met Capital Corp. At the time of its purchase, DeVille needed an infusion of capital for its network of production facilities which included local factories in Hickory and Wilkesboro, as well as out-of-state facilities like Pontotoc, Mississippi, and Downey, California. Met

Capital, headquartered in Boca Raton, Florida, picked up DeVille, buying out a total of 20 stockholders and paying $3.75 million in the bargain. At the same time Met Capital took over DeVille, it was also taking over seven other furniture companies to give itself a larger presence in the industry.[785]

Perhaps the biggest roundup of companies came a few years earlier when La-Z-Boy came to town. "The nation's largest manufacturer of upholstered furniture" hailed from Michigan, the 19th-century furniture capital. Quickly, they snapped up Burris Industries in Lincolnton, Hammary in Hudson, and in a surprise move, Hammary's next door neighbor, Kincaid. The deal that brought the "merger" between Kincaid and La-Z-Boy came just as several other corporations vied for the company. Both Nortek and LADD Furniture offered on the family run business, but both were outbid. Just before La-Z-Boy entered the picture, Nortek, Inc. from Rhode Island got serious, buying up shares of Kincaid stock. In fact, the Rhode Island company already owned more stock (18.9%) than members of the Kincaid family (15.6%) when the winning offer from La-Z-Boy came in. Just like Broyhill before it, Kincaid, another Caldwell County manufacturing family had sold, leaving only Bernhardt as a lone Caldwell County family-owned holdout.[786]

The battle for Kincaid revealed a new era had come to the furniture business in western North Carolina. Once Kincaid became a publicly traded company in 1983, it was in play, as far as its ownership. An up-and-down balance sheet offered reasons for a takeover, attracting a lot of interest for outside companies. When Nortek began buying up shares, Kincaid had already given up majority control of the company to Forstmann, Little and Co. The earlier partnership resulted in Kincaid ceding 71% ownership to Forstmann in exchange for $17.6 million in capital to fund additional growth. Nortek was "acquisition minded" noted one industry observer when the bidding began, characterizing them as having "no qualms about taking you over, even if you don't want to be." It was an example of a hostile takeover, which had become a standard maneuver in American business.[787]

Kincaid spurned the Nortek offer. John Harwell, Kincaid Furniture's treasurer, took his company's measure of Nortek and concluded, "they're not a furniture company." He added a caution to both Kincaid's situation as well as any other ripe plum, saying "they have a history of buying and selling companies." The idea of Kincaid being owned by a group that might one day sell them off did not endear John Harwell's company to Nortek. Some within the Kincaid organization saw Nortek and its pursuit the reason for a dip in the company's performance. One analysis reported that "Kincaid blames much of the decline on expenses fighting takeover offers." A view of sales, which continued to go up versus a drop in earnings, tended to confirm the accusation.

To resist Nortek, Kincaid opened itself to other offers. High Point-based LADD Furniture already had a presence in the area. They bought Clayton-Marcus in 1984 and even earlier acquired American and Drew Furniture in North Wilkesboro, merging them into one division. High Point based, LADD was very interested in Kincaid, making an offer that rivaled the Nortek money. The bidding war got the attention of La-Z-Boy, who was a much more compatible owner for the Kincaid family. The match was so desirable that Kincaid risked $1.5 million in cash promised to La-Z-Boy if a merger failed. Part of the icing on the cake was assurances from Michigan that it would keep the management structure that now found Steven Kincaid, son of the founder, as president. The machinations that marked the long path to a deal showed that both companies had started from humble circumstances and were now playing in a much larger arena, a business climate that did not resemble the one in which Kincaid first entered the industry in 1946. Instead of a passion to make furniture and see how it sold, profitability became king.[788]

As Kincaid and DeVille were being taken over, a significant number of furniture workers bowed out of the business. The early '90s marked a time when many faithful hourly employees, some retired, began to fill the obituary columns of the newspaper. One notice about Verna Mae Campbell listed her as an "inspector in the furniture industry." She was part of a labor force who had spent their lives with filling the jobs that took wood from boards to dressers, their handiwork boxed up and sent around the world. Their hands-on work produced products that had made the hometowns in which they lived famous. In passing from the scene, these workers took with them experiences in a very different environment than the one emerging. During their heyday, a war for control of a company like Kincaid would never have been possible. When Campbell joined the ranks of furniture makers, a walk to see the 'head man' involved a few steps up to the main office, not a plane ride to a major metropolitan area. While more workers than ever were required to take the place of Verna Mae Campbell and her contemporaries, regard for the industrial worker of western North Carolina had changed. Furniture making involved more of a consideration of the corporate portfolio and very little about local identity.[789]

Survivability in furniture had gotten tough. Market forces were one thing, but the inability to control a factory's destiny from its local headquarters emerged in the 1990s as more of a fragile proposition than anyone could have conceived a generation earlier. Interco, the shoe company that bought Broyhill in 1980, went on another buying spree six years later, trying to snap up Virginia's Lane Company, which had already acquired Hickory Chair. By the time of Interco's interest, Lane also included Hickory Tavern, Highland House, Hickory Business Furniture, and Fred Preddy, Jr.'s. Venture Furniture. Just like with Kincaid, when Lane refused a "friendly merger" with Interco, the game became brutal, with plans launched for an all-out assault. The weak point was the people who owned stock in the company. Harvey Saligman spoke directly to them saying, "we value the relationship we have with our acquired companies and we think it is in the best interest of the (Lane) stockholders," an acknowledgement that 'shareholder capitalism' had taken over. At the time,

Interco had bought a little over four percent of Lane and telegraphed its intention to buy as much as it could to muscle its way in, if management at Lane did not respond favorably to its "attractive" offer. For the factory worker, things had gone completely awry. Now, two companies were vying for control of the products they made, neither in their home state. Their future had moved completely outside the realm of local control. Employees might have heard of the time when the idea of outside management at Hickory Chair so distasteful that local investors bought back the company at the end of World War II.[790]

No one outside the company could understand if Lane was being coy, or if they really wanted to survive a takeover attempt. Some regarded Lane as the perfect acquisition. Their "steady growth, cash on hand, and well-managed inventory" piqued the interest of investor groups looking to expand. Interco was already the largest manufacturer of furniture in the United States with Broyhill and Ethan Allen in their stable. With a $55 per share offer, at a time when the stock was trading for $58, the signs were unclear as to what game the Altavista company, with numerous ties to the foothills of North Carolina

Among the many companies to go through rounds of ownership change was Hickory Chair. It began as a transplant but became one of the largest firms in Hickory. As of 2021, the company remains in business, focusing on upholstery, an enduring product in western North Carolina. (Author's Collection)

was playing. Lane held their cards "close to the chest," observed one industry analyst.[791]

In the end, Interco's offer was too much for Lane to refuse. A stock swap brought all those companies Lane controlled in Hickory into a corporation with Broyhill and Ethan Allen. The final deal was estimated to cost Interco $522 million for Lane, making the combined enterprise the largest furniture making company in the world. Interco followed its practice of keeping the already-existing management structure, with Lane president Stuart Moore still in daily control. Furniture factories that dotted the landscape in the western end were systematically becoming part of large conglomerates.

At the same time Interco grabbed Lane, Ethan Allen showed up on the chopping block. The first foray Interco had made into furniture back in 1980 was now itself an expendable company. "Restructuring to avert a takeover," by Cardinal Acquisition Group, in Washington, DC., Interco looked for a buyer. Ethan Allen Furniture had been around since 1932, founded by Nathan Ancell and his brother-in-law Theodore Baumritter in New York City. Named for the Revolutionary War Patriot, the company moved to Danbury, Connecticut, in 1972. Eight years later, they sold to Interco. In another eight years, a group of "top managers" including founder Nathan Ancell wanted to buy the company back. Plants were located all across the country, including a factory in Maiden (Catawba County) and Old Fort (McDowell County). In addition, a new, $12 million veneer plant was under construction in Spruce Pine, (directly north of Marion) at the time of the sale.[792]

The takeover by Cardinal failed when Interco refused their offer. The change did not stop the spinoff of Ethan Allen, however. Interco needed money for restructuring so ultimately, a deal went through. Nathan Ancell and his team took back his company for $338 million.[793]

An unexpected casualty of corporatization came with the designs on display. Industry observers noted how the spate of acquisitions had changed what manufacturers offered. Interior decorator and furniture designer Vladimir Kagan remarked that companies under new ownership were "not as willing to take chances as the little companies do." The showroom floor reflected "fewer opportunities for creative design because firms have to be darn sure something will sell before they stick their neck out," was how Kagan described his design colleagues who found themselves working for conglomerates.[794]

Communities and the workforce within them historically had tried to emphasize the local pride that came with crafting furniture. Even if the companies no longer had a management structure that lived in the cities where the product was manufactured, workers still did their best to put a good face on a trend that had permeated the economy. After a century of independent existence, the realization of just being another cog in the wheel of corporate America dampened a lot of enthusiasm. The entrepreneurship that marked the establishment of the furniture industry in the area had been replaced by a despair when stockholders cashed out, leaving the local labor force to fend for themselves. In desperation, the hands hung on, most suspicious of the assertions of each new owner that their vision of a bright future would give them security. Most promises were never kept, leaving the rank-and-file to see just how desperate the furniture business might get.[795]

—◦◦◦—

Chapter 29
A Numbers Game

"Encouraged by favorable demographics and ample room for increased market share, the highly fractured furniture industry is becoming the latest to consolidate."

- Chicago Tribune

It was no secret, yet hugely ironic, that the industry was making more furniture than ever, while at the same time the number of organizations doing so were shrinking. The contraction in companies came largely, from large ones buying up smaller ones. In its heyday, furniture firms totaled over 5,000 nationwide. By the late '80s, the number had been cut in half. During that time, even with the reduction, industry watchers remained bullish on the prospects for furniture's future. Since no one brand ever came close to dominating the market, there were always opportunities, leading analysts to believe, "there's potential for growth from gaining market share." The optimism always had its "but," as in "but furniture is a large consumer purchase that's often deferrable." The industry had seen economic rough patches that coincided with downturns in the economy where people did indeed put off buying new furniture as their budget got tight. As a commodity, furniture sales held "potential," according to market watchers, but they were always quick to add, "it's a time to be cautious," which showed an eagerness to hedge their bets.[796]

One reason for optimism in furniture making as it moved into the '90s was the rise of the 25-44 age group. A new generation of Americans called the 'baby boomers' had come into their own as working adults. They were now buying homes and increasingly, "high-end furniture" to go inside, which is where this generation largely stayed. The phenomenon was called "cocoon"-ing, and it spelled good times for companies looking to outfit the lairs of these children of the World War II and Korean War veterans, who now had families of their own. In the foothills, a significant number of baby-boomers also found gainful employment in those very same factories.[797]

One baby-boomer had a better idea. Edgar Broyhill II's furniture pedigree showed in his very name. Born in 1954, he was the grandson of Ed Broyhill, who along with brother Tom, turned a sawmill into a furniture empire in the foothills. Now "Edgar B Furniture Plantation," as he came to call his company, wanted to revolutionize the industry again. While in his twenties, he started a "do-it-yourself home furnishings store in Winston-Salem." From a traditional retail perspective the store did not take off, but one aspect did. Trying to move his inventory, he took out a magazine ad and slashed his prices. A mail order business was born.[798]

The times were in his favor. "Between 1980 and 1985, one-third of the retail furniture industry died and the mail-order business grew fivefold," reported the *Chicago Tribune*. Edgar (Ed) published images and prices of the furniture he carried in a catalog and opened the phone lines (in the era before online sales), closing his storefronts and opening a direct market operation. For his brash new approach, some called him the "Benedict Arnold of the furniture industry." The younger Broyhill, in his effort to sell furniture directly to the consumer, offered prices substantially below that of furniture stores across the nation, thus the moniker of traitor. In one case, he sold a piece of Thomasville furniture for half of what a customer would pay in a retail store.[799]

Naturally, colleagues hated the move. Edgar B found the demographic that was "predominantly 35- to 50-year-old dual career couples with incomes of more than $70,000 a year" and with a "224-page color catalog" and a convenient toll-free 1-800-number, he made significant inroads in the traditional market. His firm garnered $18 million in sales in 1982 alone. One analyst applauded the innovation, asking, "what makes the furniture industry think they can keep on blindly merchandising the way they have for the last 100 years?" Edgar B had an answer, just like his granddad before him.[800]

Maybe it was because he grew up as an industry insider, but more likely he recognized the way the game had been played and could be improved. Either way, Edgar Broyhill the younger, saw opportunity. His prices exposed how high the markup of furniture had gotten. A marketing researcher estimated retail stores sold furniture "at cost plus 100 to 120 percent, adding that furniture stores were "afraid people will read the catalog and come in and tell them what a ripoff their prices are." Edgar B didn't care what retailers said about him. Out of a converted school house in Clemmons, NC, the third generation furniture Broyhill shipped "America's finest furniture, at deep-discount prices, direct from North Carolina." That's why some resorted to calling him "a Carolina bandit."[801]

Edgar Broyhill described himself differently. In his view, if "this industry is full of cowboys," he quipped, then "I'm the Butch Cassidy of the furniture industry." As a result of Edgar B Furniture Plantation's sales and a few others emulating the model, manufacturers tried to get furniture stores to "yank from the walls" their toll-free phone lines. He vowed to keep his ringing, saying, "Edgar B is the only retailer in the state that is not giving in to the huge manufacturers and conglomerate pressure." The battle lines had been drawn.[802]

It got ugly. Furniture producers forbade the marketing practices of this sort, which prompted the North Carolina General Assembly to consider a bill that would shut down such efforts. Discount retailers initially got on board with Edgar B early, but began to desert, first when court action against them emerged and then when the threat of legislation came. Ed's fellow discounters realized the adversarial relationship they might engender with the very manufacturers they needed for product. Ed Broyhill stood his ground, refusing to quit. Instead, he proposed "organizing a buying network that would guarantee huge orders to factories that can produce high-quality furniture comparable to name-brand products." It was a calculated way to lure companies with the one thing they wanted most, demand for their product.[803]

Ed Broyhill's innovative plan took flack from all sides. His imitators abandoned him. Furniture producers kept the pressure on, as did retailers. Plus, a recession in the early '90s caused him to comment, "it's not a very positive picture." By then, the newest generation of Broyhill had stepped fully into his grandfather's shoes.[804]

If Edgar B still saw himself as a cowboy, he could not have found a better partner than the man who redefined western films. It seems Edgar and Clint Eastwood had previously rubbed elbows, and now called each other friends. When the star of *Hang 'Em High* and *The Outlaw Josie Wales* needed home furnishings for the restoration of his Mission Ranch resort in Carmel, California, he turned to Ed, who designed and built a high-end collection for his celebrity buddy. Clint Eastwood likened Edgar B's work to his own profession, saying, "furnishings are much more comfortable if they are simply designed and sort of straight forward, with simple elegance. It's like simple drama sometimes is the most straight forward. It's the most honest." The film actor/director appreciated the engaging nature of the rooms Edgar B furnished for him. Further likening the world of the two, Clint told Ed that "some of the collections you have done in the past have that feeling. You walk in and you feel that it's inviting, it's comfortable and it's homey. The main thing is that it's its quality workmanship. In every profession you hope that people will strive to make the best product possible. If I'm making a movie I try to make the best I can." He clearly thought the furniture created by the third-generation furniture maker deserved an Academy Award.[805]

The association with Clint Eastwood propelled Ed Broyhill to demonstrate his new way to buy furniture. The shake up landed him on the nationally syndicated *Oprah Winfrey Show*. Using Clint's endorsement of Edgar B as her lead-in, Oprah primed the interview by touting the catalog put out by the Furniture Plantation. Her question was "how do we get that catalog?" The 800 number fluidly rolled off Ed's tongue. What she really wanted to know was "do the retailers get upset with you?" Quickly, Ed said, "sure they do." As the interview continued Oprah seemed to be at a loss as to why Edgar B would discount the price of the items in his catalog so heavily. His intro noted that buying through the 800 number could save consumers up to 50%. "Why did you decide to do it this way, because you could certainly make a whole lot more money?" she trailed off, with Ed Broyhill taking up the challenge.[806]

Edgar B had his facts at the ready. Citing "a half million people around the country are buying from us." The number of customers spoke to the lure of his retail alternative. Audience members probed him with questions about hidden costs, like shipping that could make the deal not so rosy, but he was ready. Since his headquarters were located not in the western sector, but on the western side of Winston-Salem, the Edgar B Furniture Plantation found itself right in the center of North Carolina's furniture industry, which also included High Point. "From Clemmons, North Carolina where 60% of all furniture is manufactured in the area, we can deliver it at a cheaper price than a palatial retail store in Chicago or New York," he informed his future furniture buying public, assuring them that his shipping costs still undercut retailers.[807]

Proximity to the factories was not his only advantage. He added that "to avoid brand name conflicts, we've actually compiled enough product under a private, signature collection. Over 40,000 different items are available." Oprah seemed incredulous over this new business model. Asking, "you did this what, because you just like folks or something?" He didn't take the bait, instead calling his approach "a significant business that is taking the country by storm." Audience members probed the only disadvantage to buying out of a catalog, not being able to sit on the furniture they might buy. One asked if they could go to a retail store, get the model number then call Edgar B and reap the discount. Another guest panelist on the show interrupted Oprah's guest to say, yes they could. Uncomfortable with the implication that might further antagonize furniture store owners he responded, "we don't encourage our customers to go shopping in local retail stores" trying to take the conversation back to his furniture guide. He declared that "our catalog and all the various pictorials and visuals that we offer show the items a lot more than what might be in the four walls of a retail store." Looking back on the interview, Ed thought Oprah "made me look like a typical North Carolina discounter." Even so, over 200,000 inquiries poured in after the episode aired.[808]

Sure that the retailers and manufacturers were violating anti-trust laws, Ed sought advice from his father. James T. Broyhill, who had long served the western foothills as United States Congressman from North Carolina's 10th district. In the late 1980s, the elder Broyhill was North Carolina's Secretary of Commerce. When the son explained the situation, the father recognized the problem but according to Ed, the Secretary advised him to "find another way." With the inescapable name of Broyhill, there was "no way he was going to sue the furniture industry," remembered Ed.[809]

Despite Ed Broyhill's best efforts, and the exposure he got from selling to Clint Eastwood, appearing on *Oprah*, having a father in politics, plus a new, innovative way to sell furniture, "Edgar B. Furniture Plantation" did not survive. The company filed for bankruptcy in 1995. Estimates were that Ed owed money to approximately 4,500 depositors. A federal judge approved "a $3 million settlement" to customers, refunding them up to $1800 each for deposits on furniture orders. The furniture industry was changing, but not in Ed Broyhill's direction. He saw manufacturers gravitating toward options like "galleries, sign(ing) franchise agreements (with retailers) or they all went under." Desperate to find a formula that would generate sales, the relationship between maker and seller was too great to allow an interloper to break the mold. "I'm not saying that the fact that they removed themselves from my catalog played a role in that," meaning bankruptcy, "but I bet it did," he opined. "Once they shut it down (Edgar B Furniture Plantation), they weren't getting the action that they thought they had earned," a reference to companies like Henredon and Drexel Heritage eventually going out of business.[810]

Eight years after the end of his company, Ed turned to the other family profession, politics. Like his father, the furniture entrepreneur ran for the House of Representatives himself. During that campaign, Edgar, now known to the public as Ed, needed to explain why his company went belly up. He did so by saying Edgar B was "a victim of poor economic times and a change in manufacturers' distribution policies, which forbade North Carolina retailers from discounting lines and conducting national marketing campaigns." His assertion was true in that furniture makers banded together with retailers to force mail-order companies like Ed's to quit selling furniture at such small markups. Pat Bowling, a spokeswoman for the National Home Furnishings Association pointed out that other direct sellers like "Furniture Land South, Rose, and Boyle, are still growing and expanding," in contrast to the demise of Ed Broyhill's company. She went on to say, "The Edgar B situation must have been precipitated by something else other than people not wanting to buy furniture." Court appointed trustee Joseph Burns could only say, "we don't know what went wrong with the company except they ran out of money." Quite possibly Ed Broyhill and his brash approach to the retail market was the 'canary in a coal mine.' His pioneering work announced a coming change to the way furniture was sold, that drew the ire of manufacturers, maybe even the company that bore his family name. He, being an early adopter of a furniture buying alternative, one without an extravagant markup, did not survive the furor it caused.[811]

Ed Broyhill lived on the opposite end of the spectrum from most people working in the furniture industry. He admitted, "sure, I was born with a silver spoon in my mouth; I just learned to feed myself with it," a far cry from the workers who built the products he sold for a while. The labor force knew a very different existence. Furniture workers at Morganton plants like Drexel-Heritage and Henredon, felt the turmoil of working for an international conglomerate. Champion Paper sold off Drexel to a New York holding company in 1977, who then sold to plumbing and hardware giant Masco (a corporation on par with Interco). The sale grouped both Drexel-Heritage and its cross-town rival Henredon together in 1986. Before that they looked upon each other as fierce competitors. Ten years later, Morgan Stanley Capital Partners, one of the nation's largest investment banking firms came knocking, offering $1.1 billion for Masco's furniture interests. The deal did not go through, but once again, the intrigue that went with the "will they? won't they?" reports spoke loudly and clearly to the workforce. The decisions made concerning their destiny would be out of their control, made in boardrooms far from western North Carolina.[812]

Buyouts had become a regular occurrence in furniture. No company was too small or too large to become the property of another, even if a buyer had no previous interest in furniture. Sometimes, those punching in for hourly work never knew the difference, other than an unfamiliar signature on their paychecks. In the same year of the failed Masco-Morgan Stanley deal, the peril of being a pawn in a corporate game came home to Caldwell County with shocking realism.

"A week before Christmas, Singer Furniture Co. told more than 700 employees Wednesday that they'll lose their jobs early next year." That's how a story began that illustrated the vagaries of working for a large corporation. Singer, a company still more known for its sewing machines than its furniture, decided to shut down all five of its plants in Caldwell County just as the new year of 1996 began. A generation of workers had come to accept the outside corporation as the issuer of their paychecks until the day came when the money stopped and the company chose to turn out the lights. By that point, Singer had been a player in the western North Carolina furniture industry for almost a quarter of a century. "Gosh, it was sudden," sniffled employee Annie Burch as she fought back tears. Her frightened bewilderment was a reminder of how precarious a job in the industry had become.[813]

Twenty-five years after Singer shut down its furniture operation, the factory still stands, somewhat worse from neglect. The row of buildings along Highway 321-A were early indicators of the downturn in furniture production that would accelerate following its 1996 closure. (Author's collection)

Singer had been around long enough to see the corporate logo fade on the plant's water tower, a sign of its perceived longevity. Ironically, many of those getting pink slips had been around even longer, like Annie Burch, remembering when Singer took over from Magnavox, another corporate overlord. Some went back ever further when outsiders first bought in to the local furniture company structure, days when Singer's plants operated under the original owners, Spainhour, Blowing Rock, and Kent-Coffey.[814]

Fortunately for most of the workers, they lost their jobs during a period when furniture orders were still on the rise. Caldwell County again boasted 2.8% unemployment. The return of a good economy seemed to assure workers that other plants would absorb the loss. Plus, Singer's workers had already experienced an uncertain year, an inkling of what was coming. In 1995, "Singer laid off several hundred Lenoir workers temporarily. The plants closed and reopened several times," leaving hands in an undependable situation over which, in a corporate America, workers had no control. The instability came from a battle of ownership between Semi-Tech International, which owned Singer, and investor Paul Bilzerian. They tangled "over ownership of Singer Furniture in the early 1990s." The courts sorted out the clash, but by the time the Hong-Kong based Semi-Tech won, "the damage was done," confided a vice-president for the company. The labor force bore the brunt of the calamity.[815]

Reverberations were felt across the state. North Carolina governor Jim Hunt sent "a team of state officials to Lenoir to see what could be done to find employees new jobs." Governor Hunt recognized the terrible timing, saying "this type of news is always bad, but it is especially difficult during the holiday season." He vowed assistance, adding, "we are going to do all we can to make sure these workers continue to receive a paycheck." By then, the wage earners were way ahead of the governor. Most had already put in applications for jobs at surrounding furniture companies. They were not happy about the disruption, some even bitter. Steve Greene could only stand back and watch. He worked at Singer for 21 years before quitting two years ahead of the shutdown. He called the announcement and its callous timing, "a tragedy." Greene summed up the discontent of his former fellow employees by commenting, "when they (the workers) put out for the company, they think the company should put out their hearts for them." Singer's bombshell announcement indicated to many that the company did not.[816]

Six months later came another closure, this time in the Burke County town of Hildebran. Impact Furniture specialized in low cost furniture made of particle board that was then overlaid with veneer. Bassett purchased Impact in 1984, but when competition from other low end manufacturers hurt sales, the company, which also had plants in Newton (Catawba County) and Hiddenite (Alexander County), chose to shut down the factory putting 400 out of work. Bassett offset the losses with some transfers to the other plants, making the move to combat an 8% loss of sales from its previous fiscal year. Still, the manufacturer stumbled with a 19% loss in earnings the same year as the closure. Like Caldwell County, Burke also sported a low unemployment rate (2.4%) signifying that it could absorb much of the loss.[817]

On the heels of the Impact shutdown came a similar announcement in Spruce Pine. Lexington Furniture, named for the city of its base in the High Point orbit announced the loss of 225 jobs. Lexington president Jeff Young went to the plant to tell workers of a plan to consolidate its two factories into one. The Lexington head expressed frustration over the predicament he and his colleagues in furniture found themselves in. He said, "the economy is so good, and the stock market is soaring. Yet our industry is mired in a recession the likes of which we haven't seen in some time." Jeff Young's feelings echoed across the industry. As in situations like the Spruce Pine announcement, some workers were little comforted by the president's announcement, knowing that at the end of the day he still had a job. They didn't.[818]

Perhaps the most surprising of reductions was at Cochrane Furniture. Several years after taking over the old Pem-Kay factory in Newton and less than a year after Indiana based Chromcraft Revington Inc. bought Cochrane for $27 million, company officials announced the closing of an upholstery facility that employed 125 people. Attributing the move to "consolidating," with some jobs moved to Cochrane's main plant in Lincolnton, "Jerry Cochrane, the company's former chief executive, referred comment on the shutdown to Steve Healy, the new firm's executive vice president." Healy could not be reached for a quote.[819]

Anemic bottom lines for retailers left them asking for someone, anyone, to "just please, please buy furniture." No one could understand the slump. While theories abounded, from consumers being "tapped out" to baby-boomers planning for retirement to uninspired designs by the companies themselves, no one had an adequate reason why business was so "poor." The slump meant fewer orders for producers and a general slowdown in the manufacturing ranks. For the time being, the answer was to reduce the amount being made in hopes of an upsurge that might be just as unexplainable as the slowdown had been.[820]

The layoffs did not cripple the furniture economy in the region, but they did hint at bad things to come. Furniture employment looked very different for those employed at the end of the twentieth century than it did fifty years earlier. Many of the factory names had not changed, but the dynamics of control certainly had. Workers operated in a corporate environment in which they had absolutely no agency. All they could do was go to work each day and plan to come back tomorrow. No matter how hard they worked, or how much pride they put into their efforts, they still faced the ongoing possibility that they would face a permanent layoff like the one at Singer. What would have been unthinkable just a few years earlier was starting to dawn on blue and white collar workers alike. The western North Carolina furniture industry had begun to contract.

One reason for a decrease in the foothills was expansion elsewhere. For a long while, western Tarheel furniture firms did not make all the goods that went out under their company names. Factories in faraway places like Mississippi, Virginia, and other Carolina locations were part of the manufacturing mix. A growing number of items also began to emerge from overseas as well, an ominous sign. Right about the time the Singer plant closed its doors, customs officials visited the Henredon plant in Morganton. They were looking for end tables. When they found them, workers were removing labels on the boxes that proclaimed the tables were "Made In Philippines," replacing the designation with "Made in U.S.A."

Henredon's president Mike Dugan claimed it all a misunderstanding, offering that "customs regulations aren't always clear-cut and can conflict with foreign rules, placing the company in the middle." A report quoted an employee who noted "as many as 50 boxes" were altered. Asking for guidance, the Henredon head acknowledged that "for as long as anyone can remember, our product line has included imported materials, components and products." He put forth, "there is no market advantage for us to label their products one way or another." The attitude about imports was ambivalent then, but that would soon change.[821]

The problem wasn't just with Henredon, and it wasn't in just the furniture industry. At a time when retailers like Wal-Mart built entire ad campaigns on the proud proclamation of goods "made with pride in the U.S.A.," the U.S. Customs Service looked at the offense as "a crime against the economy." Imports were a part of American business. Since the 1950s, when Japanese companies could make radio transistors less expensively than firms in the United States, the debate raged over cheaper prices for goods versus the loss of American jobs. Now the issue came to the furniture business.[822]

The times had once again caused the industry to regroup. Not only was the financial end of the business much different than when it began, American society continued to evolve. New habits and new needs demanded new types of furniture to accommodate. The advent of the personal computer meant home offices had begun to increase. During the Christmas buying season in 1995, "PCs outsold television sets in this country" for the first time, noted a furniture executive, a clear indicator that opportunity awaited. Companies like American Drew in North Wilkesboro quickly put out a line of "oak and cherry desks and other furniture for computer users." Though in its infancy, American Drew's Dave Ogren called the trend "a growing phenomenon," one that could be a savior to wood-working companies everywhere.[823]

Furniture makers began to hitch their wagons to the computer industry, which had become the fastest growing sector of the economy in the 1990s. The problem to be solved was how to craft desks for limited space. The first incarnation of PC use found machines located "in dens, bedrooms, living rooms - even kitchens." Furniture manufacturers began to bank on the idea that "the kitchen table plan was getting a little thin." Designers immediately went to work building an appliance that would fit in with the decor of the rest of the house but offer the functionality users wanted. "Power-surge suppressors, space for any kind of printer, pullout locking trays for more work surface, built in left- and right-handed mouse pads, rear-entry access and special drawers to store computer diskettes and CD-ROM discs" were all part of the reinvention of home work spaces for the new age. Companies like American Drew saw the home office trend growing to the point that, as Dave Ogren envisioned, "it could be a $100 million line," just in time to take manufacturers into a new century.[824]

The legacy of furniture in western North Carolina had been long. By the 1990s a few manufacturers could even claim centennial status. Sporadic attempts to document its value to the area came and went. By then, Hickory Furniture Mart (HFM) had reinvented itself as a destination for the consumer market. Turning its four stories into showrooms for sales directly to the public, it took the downfall of one market to create another. As a key part of its promotion was an event conceived by Leroy Lail. He had always been interested in the history of the industry and wanted to celebrate it. At one point, he outfitted a small museum at the Mart, to commemorate the tradition of furniture making. More importantly, he used his promotional abilities to inaugurate a festival that celebrated all things connected with furniture.

Along with ample food and entertainment, HFM welcomed a craft fair, centered around woodworking for one weekend each summer, calling the event, the "Furniture Festival." Members of the North Carolina Woodturners, "demonstrated the fine art of woodturning on Woodfast and Carbatec lathes." Restoration demonstrations were scheduled throughout to show enthusiasts and gawkers alike how the process was best handled. Leroy Lail invited the furniture production school from Catawba Valley Community College to demonstrate the process of eight-way-hand-tying for upholstery. During the festival, door prizes including a $1000 shopping spree were given away. All the while, tenants of Hickory Furniture Mart put on some of their best prices to attract shoppers. The furniture festival, starting with its debut in 1986, grew in scope every year. The event became a centerpiece of the HFM's promotional activities that made it "one of North Carolina's top visitor attractions."[825]

The retail aspect of Hickory Furniture Mart had grown to stellar proportions. Much larger than its days of welcoming furniture buyers, HFM became a nationally known location. Guests on the *Oprah Winfrey Show* hailed the selection and buys. Designers and decorators led full airplane loads of shoppers to Hickory, just to wander the halls and buy whole rooms of furniture for their own homes. Some wrote checks in the tens of thousands of dollars

One success in an otherwise troubled furniture landscape was Hickory Furniture Mart. Turning from a wholesale showroom twice-yearly to a retail outlet open all year, HFM became a nationally known destination for bargain hunting shoppers. It was even on the *Oprah* show. (Courtesy of Hickory Furniture Mart)

for suites they bought while there. Leroy Lail had taken the sourest of lemons with the loss of the Hickory furniture market, and turned it into the sweetest of lemonade. Hickory was now more famous than ever for its retail shops at HFM. The transformation marked one bright spot in an otherwise troubled environment.[826]

Many of the furniture factories located all around Hickory Furniture Mart had become pawns in a high-stakes game of corporate capitalism, driven by outside interests in their effort to maximize profits. Convergence started when multi-industry conglomerates began buying up furniture companies as an investment. Competitors found themselves lumped together in new corporate structures never dreamed of by their founders. It still shocked the local community when Drexel Heritage and Broyhill became siblings. Masco, which owned Drexel Heritage and Henredon had already spun off the two Morganton manufacturers only a few years after acquiring both in a deal with Furnishings International, soon to be renamed LifeStyle Furnishings International. The sale netted Masco $1.1 billion. LifeStyle tried to raise capital through an initial public offering of stock, but the effort was not enough. The corporate parent put a price tag on the former competitors plus Maitland-Smith (an out of the area manufacturer) that the old Interco, now known as Furniture Brands International bought for $275 million. Suddenly, two of the largest manufacturers in the region were now part of the same team. Some factory workers scratched their heads and wondered if one day they might all belong to the same entity.[827]

The shell game that went on with companies in the west obscured the more ominous fact. Jerry Epperson was the industry's leading analyst. He might later be called a prophet for his prescient analysis of where the 1997 slowdown ultimately took the sector. First, he focused on a generational shift, pointing out that "factories were built to service the 77 million boomers," which were being replaced by "only 45 million X-ers" (a reference to Generation X who followed them). In his view, many of those children of the baby-boomers were "sucker punched by having all these service jobs that don't pay very well," in sharp contrast to their parents. Granted, furniture didn't pay very well either, but for those who stuck with it, skilled jobs and the heightened hourly wages that came from long service somewhat compensated. A sliding economy threw prospects into doubt for Generation X-ers to afford the same level of financial security as their parents, or even their grandparents. For those who stayed in the furniture business, Jerry Epperson named an even bigger pitfall, one that no generation could combat; one with which no generation in the South ever had to deal - imports.[828]

A few analysts called out furniture companies for their expanding dependency on manufactured pieces from outside the United States while at the same time failing to expand the export of their products elsewhere. "Imports have gone from creeping up each year to growing at a double-digit pace with no signs of slowing," one said. Analyzing the dismal growth in exports, Jerry Epperson clocked the rise at barely one percent, while imports rose twelve percent in 1996. Instead of reducing the amount of non-American-made items, which companies were not likely to cut back on, given the savings on labor such practices produced, Epperson suggested companies needed "to claim more foreign sales." A consultant to the furniture industry, Ivan Cutler, put it in even harsher terms. He called it an "asteroid of foreign competition" heading to furniture company boardrooms everywhere. He explained, "fewer buyers, more imports - do the math, and the result is an industry with excess production capacity."[829]

Leaders looked for ways to combat the dire predictions. Since furniture occupied an odd strata between sturdy big ticket items and replaceable fashion accessories, marketing efforts walked a fine line. As a result, an industry consensus never developed. Some wanted furniture to be thought of like an automobile where "consumers expect to spend a lot of money" and accepted the fact that the car's value depreciated "the minute they drive off the showroom floor." In that way, furniture did the auto business one better by not needing regular gas, oil and maintenance. However, consumers looked at the two types of purchases far differently. One comparison noticed how "people will spend a far smaller amount of money on a bedroom suite and (will) be upset if it doesn't last a lifetime." Marketing furniture required a finesse that many firms did not possess. Most relied on retailers to do the work for them, a system that had begun to sag like an old mattress.[830]

Manufacturers vowed to do better. Mickey Holliman, head of Furniture Brands International (FBI), and by extension Drexel and Broyhill believed advertising was the solution. Asserting he had three of the most "outstanding...brand names in the business," he said it "don't mean a thing if consumers don't know the names." He proposed to spread the brands of Broyhill, Thomasville, and Lane (he left out Drexel Heritage) everywhere a potential customer might see it. In addition, FBI planned opening more retail outlets as a way to speak directly to the public.[831]

Furniture designers scrambled for a look that would get customers back into stores. One late century idea stemmed from name recognition. If the brands themselves were interchangeable, the public would likely instead perk up to names like Bill Blass, Ralph Lauren, and Eddie Bauer and other top names in the design world. Henredon signed both Lauren and Alexander Julian to design furniture that would bear their names as well as their look. Manufacturers took a page from the auto industry where Eddie Bauer and Nautica were already features of automobile interiors. A consumer, riding home in his or her Lincoln-Mercury minivan could continue the Nautica experience with a "150-piece collection for Lexington Furniture." Lane Furniture would allow the same thematic transfer from a Ford Bronco to their home with the *Eddie Bauer Collection*, an unadorned look that was described as "something between Shaker and Mission." Since clothing, then cars, had sported designer labels for years, with some popularity, furniture makers thought it was time to get in on the act.[832]

For some furniture makers, the idea went even further. Drexel Heritage based a line on the golfing tradition of Pinehurst. Not to be outdone, Century Furniture created "37 pieces of furniture based on the Italian Renaissance," in partnership with Save Venice, Inc. Like Century, crosstown manufacturer Hickory Chair looked to the past for a new collection, only this time it drew upon the 18th century American tradition in a grouping it called *Westminster Classics*. Maybe the most outlandish choice was Henredon who fielded a "flamboyant 30-piece *Carlyle* group (that) represents fantasies that might have 'graced the homes of royalty'." Firms were quick to promote these lines when they debuted, but hid the losses when some of these designs turned out to be stinkers.[833]

The relatively straight-forward idea of making a piece of furniture and selling it to the public had become a much more complicated calculation by the end of the 20th century. Workers in the foothills were still constructing

The furniture industry had always been predominately white, especially the management, but as this photo op shows, something approaching a quarter of the workforce was African-American. This exceeds the average of the industry throughout Western NC. (Courtesy of the Caldwell Heritage Museum)

piece after piece on the production line, and while the process remained the same labor intensive job it had always been, the entry of high finance, with a multitude of eyes on costs and the push to reduce expenses, drove many companies to decisions that would be to the detriment of the industry. Innovative avenues of sales challenged the old methods to get new chairs, beds, and tables in the homes of consumers. Designs no longer reflected regional tastes, they spanned oceans, looking for something to strike the fancy of shoppers. Globalization had come to the western North Carolina furniture industry and seismic disruption was on the way.

A glut of furniture. The downturn in furniture jobs came more from corporate decisions over profits than employee productivity in the early 21st century. The offshoring of case goods hurt the manufacturing base in western NC. Upholstering took a hit too but proved resilient. (From the Statesville Photographic Collection. Courtesy of Steve Hill)

Chapter 30
Slowly Killing the City

"I was looking for a job when I got this, and I'll be looking for a job when I leave," was how Larry Penley replied to notification that he was unemployed. He had heard rumors about cutbacks at Broyhill's Harper plant in Lenoir, but now company officials confirmed that the entire plant was scheduled to close. He took it stoically. Calling his layoff "just one of them things." He realized there was nothing he could do to change the outcome. He had worked twelve years as a boiler operator for Broyhill only to find himself caught up in a nasty industry reality.[834]

Both Broyhill and Thomasville, part of the same conglomerate, Furniture Brands International (FBI), delivered pink slips at the same time to some 1,200 employees in the summer of 2005. Broyhill announced it was consolidating operations by closing both Harper and Occasional No. 1 in Lenoir, while adding approximately 300 jobs at another Lenoir location. Those working for Thomasville had no such option. Mickey Holliman, head of FBI, spoke in corporate terms when he commented that the shutdowns would help the company "gain greater efficiencies in our domestic facilities." Most of that meant nothing to Larry Penley.[835]

Workers had been job scared since the late 1990s, when the process of downsizing began. Thomasville employed "about 7,000 workers" in the

The remnants of the Bernhardt Box Factory, on the west end of Lenoir, in the same area where many early furniture companies were located. On the National Register for Historic Places, the building has been adaptively reused numerous times, but in 2022, stands empty. (Author's Collection)

summer of 2000. The latest round of layoffs cut their labor force by half. The trend gave North Carolina the unwanted title of losing more industrial jobs of any state in the union, with 57,000 gone in five years. It wasn't just the furniture industry. The decline began with textiles a decade earlier. Over 13,000 fewer cotton mill jobs existed when furniture followed in its footsteps, losing 6,600 in ten years, but causing "deep concern" about the industry.[836]

Everyone knew the reason why. Economists traced the trend to the offshoring of production. The American embrace of globalism had eased import tariffs, piquing the interest of furniture makers to look beyond their own factories for cheaper labor. Accelerating the problem were Chinese manufacturers eagerly seeking to knock-off American furniture, selling it at drastically lower prices than what domestic companies could. Some of the savings stemmed from lower labor costs, some from Chinese government underwriting the effort to get a foothold in the American market. Both successfully undercut the American worker.[837]

In explaining its rationale behind the 2005 Broyhill and Thomasville layoffs, FBI senior vice-president and chief administrative officer Lynn Chipperfield tacitly admitted that production from Asia had torpedoed the American labor force. In the first quarter of 2005, 36% of FBI sales came from imports. In less than a year, he expected the number to "reach 40%." From a financial point of view, the layoffs were rationalized as necessary. In fact, Denise Ramos, FBI's CFO, treasurer, and senior VP said, "we haven't closed plants fast enough," focusing only on the financial sense of it all. Her priority was not the misery unemployment brought to workers. She worried more about the "less than 80% capacity" at which divisions like Broyhill and Thomasville were operating and pointed out how such performance "significantly hurt profit margins." Of the 60 American factories FBI operated three years earlier, they had "closed 21 case goods plants and six upholstery plants" in light of the inevitability of closures.[838]

Some towns took a double hit. In Newton, city officials announced not one but two closures. Within a month's time, the shutdown of a textile plant ended jobs for the last 125 workers there (the operation at one time employed 400), then Broyhill closed the factory Ed Broyhill bought during the Depression. After 66 years, making mostly bedroom furniture, 277 workers were let go. Newton City Manager Glenn Pattishall called the news, "very unsettling." Broyhill President Dennis Burgette said Broyhill was, like any company at the time, "taking a step back." He pointed to a slowing economy as the reason for the closure, but everyone knew the real reason lay elsewhere.[839]

The furniture workers of western North Carolina were being replaced by hands half a world away. With such incentives to cut costs and play on a much wider field of manufacture, FBI and its counterparts surmised they could only compete if their industry followed the cheaper labor market. One Thomasville executive predicted that "75% of its case goods" would be produced offshore before the end of 2005.[840]

To many displaced workers, management at FBI seemed like the bad guys. They were cutting jobs and making excuses. In reality, Mickey Holliman and his team were only repeating the cycle that brought furniture production to the foothills of the Tarheel state in the first place. When southern labor (and boosters like W.W. Scott) cried out for industrial jobs as a way to energize the desolate, war-torn South in the 1870s, men with capital at their disposal took notice, creating the first factories that gave former farmers what they wanted, a way to feed their families that sheltered them from falling crop prices with employment in factories. The loss of market share back in Michigan, where jobs were in decline meant nothing to the families of the Catawba Valley as the twentieth century dawned. They were more interested in putting themselves on the furniture map. It took a hundred years for a cheaper workforce to emerge, but once it did, the callous process repeated itself. Furniture Brands International was as good as its name. They headed to the Far East to find a cheaper way to make a chair. The move made them truly, international.

The day after the announcement of the closures, Lynn Chipperfield gave an interview. He carefully answered questions on the reasons for such draconian measures. His words revealed the overriding mindset of corporate management in the business of making furniture. *Charlotte Observer* reporter Kerry Hall pelted FBI's senior vice president and chief administrative officer with questions on many of the 'whys' associated with offshoring. Chipperfield gave solid, corporately controlled answers.[841]

One primary complaint of overseas production was the poor quality of products shipped back to the United States, prompting dissatisfaction by consumers. Chipperfield took on the question with an acknowledgement of the problem but assurances of improvement by saying, "we have found, frankly, that if you watch the quality and if you oversee production, quality is no longer an issue." While validating concerns that poorly made furniture had been shipped across the Pacific (further damaging the product), Chipperfield stressed that the Chinese were "getting better over the last several years," still not to the level of the American worker, but improving. He also threw in the fact that Chinese labor had improved beyond the point of making cheap furniture and was moving into production of pieces at "upper price points."[842]

The most shocking admission Lynn Chipperfield made was the margins involved in furniture made domestically versus the overseas product. Kerry Hall asked directly, "how much money does the company save by offshoring?" After describing the process, Chipperfield got to the bottom line. "You see anywhere from 3 to 5 percent better margins." Hall's followup revealed disbelief at the number. "That doesn't sound like a lot of money," the reporter replied. "What could be done to keep more furniture jobs in the U.S.?"[843]

That's where Chipperfield prevaricated. He cited "many problems," with the age of the industry used against it. "A lot of domestic production is working out of factories, some of which are 100 years old." He suggested new factories might be designed to make the process more efficient, but FBI was clearly not interested in constructing new plants just to save American jobs. In fact, Lynn Chipperfield could not think of when the last case goods factory had been built.[844]

Then, the Furniture Brands International representative turned his gaze toward the consumer, blaming buying trends for much of the shift. The attitudes of shoppers were the reason for the lack of sales, he asserted. He insisted that the furniture buying public was "focused on price," which in his estimation validated finding cheaper labor to build their dressers and tables. Even if a customer had money in their pockets, he argued, "consumer confidence" in the future was dismal, which Chipperfield argued was "not a good sign." He also added that buyers wanted no hassles, and were unwilling to accept the wait times of weeks and months that used to be an accepted practice of delivery.[845]

At that point in the interview, Lynn Chipperfield talked himself into something of a hole. Kerry Hall shot back, "why not make furniture closer to U.S. customers then?" Relying on the old vantage point that intimated there was a lot about the furniture industry the reporter did not understand, Chipperfield finished the interview with a blanket statement that said nothing and everything about how the corporate world looked at a product that local people had taken so much pride in producing, a responsibility that had been ripped from their hands. He said, "that's where the balancing act comes in. We have to worry as a company about a lot of things. And you can't just load up warehouses around the country with inventory because sooner or later you run out of cash." The statement instantly revealed the priorities at play.[846]

The damage done by the drive for profits at the expense of the infrastructure (which included workers), even if it only meant a few percentage points, harmed not just the company but all around it. Chris Byrd spoke for many of his fellow merchants when he characterized Lenoir's future by saying, "it just keeps going down and down and down." Looking back on it past, he said the furniture industry "built Lenoir," but saw what had become a more corporate world, was "now slowly killing the city." "I'm a used car dealer," he said, "and in the last three years it has killed me," a reference to dwindling sales to the very people whose livelihood the FBI decision ended.[847]

There seemed to be no way out of the twisting downturn to which Chris Byrd pointed. Corporate profit-making superseded the local paternalism that ruled the factories for so many years. Back then, workers hadn't made much money either, but at least they knew their company fathers would take care of them and assure both them and their children of a job. Lifelong loyalty in exchange for job security was no longer part of the deal. Those promises went out the door as the first out-of-town decision about a furniture company was made.

Workers in Lenoir were not unique, they were just ahead of the curve. All over the country, jobs in the furniture industry declined. In the six years that followed the devastating layoffs at Broyhill and Thomasville, a steep decrease in furniture jobs were lost to globalization. One estimate put national furniture employment at around 675,000 in 2000. By 2011, the number would plummet to right around 350,000, a 48% reduction.[848]

During the days of layoffs for Furniture Brands International, the last family-owned company in Lenoir proved it didn't need a corporate structure to gain press. Bernhardt landed several plums. Alex and company partnered with home merchandising mogul Martha Stewart to present a line that bore her name. It quickly became a top seller. As one Lenoir resident quipped, "she didn't really make it anyway, it was just her name on it." Demand for the line was so great that Bernhardt added pieces (for a total of 62), which they unveiled at the Furniture Market in High Point. Plans for a "fourth Stewart collection (were) in the works for 2005." Two years later, the Lenoir manufacturer announced it had developed "history-themed home furnishings" in connection with the Smithsonian Institution. Citing the coup, Bernhardt worked with the nation's premier museum in developing the line. Alex Bernhardt said, "the Smithsonian name is synonymous with quality, trust and prestige, and this furniture collection will deliver on all those expectations."[849]

Soon after, Bernhardt would go through a changing of the guard. In 2009, third-generation president Alex Bernhardt, Sr. stepped back from daily control of the firm to hand off the company to his son and his nephew, G. Alex Bernhardt, Jr. and J. Roundtree Collett, Jr. The younger Bernhardt took over the "residential division" while Collett became president of Bernhardt Ventures. Alex Sr., did not relinquish the reins totally, maintaining a hand in the direction of the company with his wife, Anne Bernhardt and Lewis Norman as a three-member "Chairman's Committee of the Board" of directors. At the time, the senior Bernhardt noted that the committee amassed over 100 years of service to the company but felt the moment had come "to recognize the achievements and talents of these fine young executives, doing all we can to support and help them to continue their successes."[850]

Across town at Broyhill, more trouble awaited, this time with its leadership. Only 15 months after taking the job as president of the company, Harvey Dondero resigned. The only explanation came in a Furniture Brands International press release that said, "in resigning, Harvey cited concerns regarding reporting responsibilities, authority and duties." Workers, industry analysts, and the public were allowed to read whatever they wanted into the statement, but it signified turmoil. During Dondero's tenure, the company shed another 2,000 jobs and closed five plants. One story about the departure said, "Dondero's time at Broyhill Furniture was not a positive period for the company."[851]

The top job at Broyhill had become an unsteady one. Following Dondero, Jeff Cook took the helm, setting an outlandish goal for the company to double in size in five years. Cook proclaimed the "bold statement" with a banner that hung outside Broyhill's corporate offices for all to see. He attempted to buck up the employee base by saying, "if we don't worry about jobs first, if we worry about being the very best and setting the standard instead of following, if we focus on setting the standard and being the best, I can promise you we will have one more job, not one less." By the time Jeff Cook made his declarative speech, worker suspicion was understandable. Many employees had done their very best for years, if not decades. No matter how hard they worked, the result was fewer, not more jobs.[852]

The spiral down continued for Broyhill, not the direction Jeff Cook wanted. Word leaked that Broyhill might just take its company elsewhere. Alarmed, both the City of Lenoir and Caldwell County governments sought to initiate emergency "last-minute incentives" to enable the employer to stay where it started. Four million dollars was set aside to "keep the company here," announced Jeff Cook. The question had been whether to relocate all "remaining domestic manufacturing and warehousing sites" to Mississippi "where a former Lane plant was ready and waiting." The state of North Carolina was part of a retention plan, adding $2 million "with the understanding that Broyhill would create 432 new jobs within the next three years." In order to accomplish the consolidation, the firm shut down a number of factories in other places, including Taylorsville and another facility in Lenoir. What Jeff Cook called a "mega upholstery plant" would pump out both cloth and leather sofas and chairs, so Broyhill could live up to the bargain.[853]

Not everyone was happy with "Operation Whirlwind," the five-week, intensive negotiation that brokered the deal. One Lenoir city councilman called it "blackmail," and in a letter to the editor opined, "in my eyes they have just become another low quality company from China." Citizens were resentful that Broyhill would dare to ask for such concessions, in light of the way it had treated employees since FBI took over.[854]

Jeff Cook endured the heat. The funding for Broyhill was a hot topic of debate around Lenoir as it was being ratified. Most looked upon the plan as desperate, but necessary to retain the furniture maker with a long-standing history in Lenoir to keep what jobs were left, where they had been for over a century. After the pact was approved though, reports surfaced that Cook was the recipient of $2.32 million in a payout by Furniture Brands International in 2009. The controversy reignited with local folks up in arms again, feeling they had been used. Two years later, Cook was out, leaving to take the president's job at A.R.T. Furniture, an importer and manufacturer of case goods. The new firm was "wholly owned by Markor," a Chinese manufacturer.[855]

Two years after Cook's departure, eight years after the massive layoffs, and a bailout in between, came what many in Lenoir felt like was a just fate. Furniture Brands International filed for bankruptcy. The *Lenoir News-Topic* took some glee in beginning the editorial that ran across the state with the line, "sewage flows downhill, a cleaned up version of the old saying goes," adding Furniture Brands International workers and retirees probably "have a renewed sense of why that saying endures." No one had forgotten the gut punch Lenoir suffered in the 2005 shutdowns or all the other indignities before and after. The local paper was not the only publication to jab in print at the downfall of FBI.

The spreadsheet of FBI noted a "$40 million dollar second-quarter loss" in 2013. The investment firm of Raymond James titled their report on the impending bankruptcy, "Oh My! Circling the Drain - Faster and Faster." It seemed no one took pity on FBI, many using the same analogy of a company circling the drain. All the digs and pokes highlighted the fact that the real ones left hanging were the workers and retirees of the firms within the conglomerate who watched proceedings with unease, since their pensions remained a very open question. A $200 million pension obligation by FBI was listed "among its unsecured debt." The *Lenoir News-Topic* pointed out in its condemnation that "not one resident of Caldwell County made a single choice or decision that contributed to Furniture Brands' financial problems, but hundreds of local residents have been suffering the consequences of bad decisions emanating from St. Louis, the company's headquarters." From a local paper that generally cheered the business community, the denunciation was scathing.[856]

Perhaps the best epitaph for the furniture industry was the headline that ran in the *Lenoir News-Topic* on October 28, 2018. It read, "What a great company it was," with emphasis on the past tense. Complete with a picture of then, 95-year-old Paul Broyhill, the article described how one employee was proud to tell anyone about Broyhill Furniture when she started in 1981. Thirty-seven years later, she saw it as "just a name to be licensed, not a manufacturer or employer." Robin Harshaw was only 19 she when joined the company, admitting "I loved it when I first started…We were proud of where we worked." She weathered two corporate bankruptcies, but when the third closed her plant, she said, "I felt betrayed."[857]

The best anyone could say about the sour ending was that at one time Broyhill was a great place to work. Jerry Church, a former chief financial officer remarked that "they (Broyhill) put a lot of food on a lot of tables." His career moved on from manufacturing, but he had fond memories of Broyhill, calling it a "family-type atmosphere." Melissa Bolick agreed. She noted how she made many friends during her tenure, but when the job cuts began in the 2000's and factories began to close, she "had to watch as friends who were more like family lost their jobs." The reduction, while damaging to the region, took a very personal toll on those displaced.[858]

The Broyhill bailout alerted other furniture companies that help, even if temporary, was available. Kincaid was next to the trough in Caldwell County, asking commissioners for half a million dollars. They sought the funds in an effort to consolidate some of the other La-Z-Boy companies like American Drew and Lea, that had come into the corporation's fold since Kincaid was acquired. The move promised only 30 additional jobs, but the county was much more worried about the ones they might lose if they didn't come to Kincaid's rescue.[859]

The local money bailouts had gotten desperate. T.J. Rohr, the Lenoir City Councilman who opposed Broyhill's package also lobbied the county commissioners to reject Kincaid's request. He reminded them that, following Broyhill's successful play for money, the company rewarded Jeff Cook with a huge bonus, making it look as though some of the municipal money was not as direly needed as the company made out. He also produced a letter from Kincaid executives opposing the earlier Broyhill deal. Now they wanted their own, which looked hypocritical. He also informed Caldwell County that they were competing with their neighbor to the north for the company. "You are being held hostage by a company that is making you compete county to county," he said, a reference to an entreaty made by Wilkes County for a new home for Kincaid. Strangely enough, it would have been a homecoming for American Drew, a firm that once was headquartered in North Wilkesboro. Just like Broyhill, Kincaid got their money.[860]

The deal lasted about five years. In 2014, Kincaid announced it would shut down much of its operation in Hudson. Earlier, management moved warehouses out of Wilkes County back to Hudson to utilize the property where the company began, but for most of the workers, it was the end. They took it hard. Donald Walker had been with the company in the cabinet room since 1992. Still recovering from a hand injury, he found out after a company meeting announced that the upholstery operation would be moved to Taylorsville. Offered a job there, he didn't want to go. He figured that "99 percent (of the folks he worked with) don't want to drive that far." He expected he would have to "find furniture work elsewhere," a riskier proposition given the shrinking furniture job market.[861]

The closure had ripples. Another disappointment rested with many of the ancillary businesses that served Donald Walker and his fellow employees. The Food Fare convenience store, just across 321-A from the main Kincaid plant was always packed at lunch. So was Donna's Cafe, about a mile down the road in Hudson. Both lamented that times were going to get tough with the end of Kincaid Furniture. Donna Greer regretted the loss of business, but also the disappearance of many friends who were also customers at her restaurant. "I'm really depressed a plant that been here so long would shut down," she said. Sad, but not surprised, she lamented, "we'll miss them all."[862]

The depression Donna Greer felt was shared all around the region. The last "12 percent of the company's wood-based furniture business" was handled at the Hudson plant at the time of its closure. Company officials reported that Kincaid would still produce those products, "but will be transitioned to all imported furniture," a way to avoid saying the goods would be coming from Asia.[863]

In the doom and gloom of the death of the furniture industry came an occasional bright spot. A Canadian company, Distinctive Designs, Inc. announced it would take over a 60,000 square-foot facility in Granite Falls (in southern Caldwell County) that had been vacated by Royal Hosiery. The expectation was that between 50 and 75 jobs would be available, not near those lost by earlier layoffs, but curiously, in keeping with the size of Caldwell County's first furniture operations, a century earlier.[864]

Jobs on the factory floor were drying up in the heat of globalism. So were positions at the top. At Hickory Chair, popular president Jay Reardon, who had been there 17 years, was let go as part of FBI's successor, Heritage Home Group's reorganization of their companies. At the same time Lane's president was also terminated. Hickory Chair's Vance Johnston, their senior vice-president and chief financial officer walked away too. When Fairfield brought in Dixon Mitchell as chief in 2017, they made no mention of who he replaced, which was Mark Craven. The media contact for Fairfield refused to clarify the reason for the change. Craven had worked for the company for 27 years, the last five as president. His father also had a long tenure with the company, some 52 years. It was apparent no one was safe from the turmoil.[865]

And turmoil had become a constant in the furniture world of the western foothills. Nothing could be counted on with certainty. The fates of everyone at Broyhill, Thomasville, and Drexel Heritage remained an open question. Once they became pawns in a larger corporate world, the stability of the days when they were ruled by their founders, or at least the founding family, disappeared. Each company had since been bounced around with more to come. Heritage Home Group, LLC (HHG), became the next firm seeking to bring furniture back to a secure existence. Instead, they dealt out more uncertainty.[866]

In fairness, the decline came from more than mismanagement from the top. At Drexel, Bruce Nelson noticed how "the marketplace became smaller." Efforts to assist retailers required investment that shrunk returns for large operations like Drexel Heritage. Prices had to go up which further weakened sales. Nelson asked the question, "how many people now appreciate great furniture?" Based on Drexel's sales, it seemed the number was plummeting.[867]

The new plan from Heritage Home Group proved fatal for Drexel Heritage. After closing a combined Drexel Heritage and Henredon plant in High Point during the FBI days, HHG put the final nail in the coffin in 2014. The last factory ceased operation in the summer of 2014 as Plant 60/63 in Morganton shut down. The mayor of Morganton, Mel Cohen offered his regrets saying he felt Drexel "never needed to leave this community." Calling the end of the Drexel era "sad," he blamed Drexel's decline on "poor decisions by top management." Reporter Sharon McBrayer reported the news to Cohen's constituents in the pages of the *Morganton News-Herald*. She made sure to note that Drexel's footprint in the market had grown steadily smaller in the 20 years leading up to its closure, while management increased its "pursuit of lower labor costs in Asia that have not contributed to increase sales." Not long after, the plant on Hogan Street was demolished. By the time it did, only 87 workers were displaced, a paltry sum compared to Drexel's once mighty workforce. Also contained in the story was a tally of the number of jobs lost in the new millennium, over 6,000, of which many were in western North Carolina.[868]

Discerning employees could see the last days were coming. As Bruce Nelson observed, "it evolved over time." Early retirements allowed some to exit as an option, others watched departments get smaller until only a skeleton crew was left. Nelson left before the actual shutdown but he remembered how "in the office, there were less and less employees." He noticed how with each successive change in leadership, "they were squeezing the cost side of the operation." Bruce Nelson would never have believed when he got into the furniture business that his last days would parallel the actual end of the company for which he worked. Like others, his 40 year career witnessed a peak for Drexel, followed by a long decline.[869]

Already, Drexel-Heritage had killed one of the companies it absorbed.

After incorporating Southern Desk into a division after the 1961 purchase, contracts for the once bustling manufacturer of stadium, school and church furniture began to dwindle. By 1974, Southern Desk factories started transitioning over to make household furnishings. Workers installed their last church pew in 1982. From that point on, the facilities became just another part of the Drexel chain of factories. That was bad enough but when the announcement came that the old Southern Desk plants would completely shut down, the anguish was obvious. Company nurse Faye Abernathy arrived early on the day management delivered the news. "When they announced that

The remains of Drexel's largest factories. On the left, a check-in box to the company parking lot remains in front of the factory that once was. The town of Drexel is just over the hill. On the right, a wall is slowly caving in at the Hogan Street site in Morganton. (Author's collection)

the Hickory plant would be closing, I saw men cry, a lot of men cry. That was the only place they had ever worked. They had never filled out an application. Some could not really write to fill out an application. And they wondered 'what will I do? Where will I work?'" Management had no answer to those questions.[870]

The furniture landscape had evolved, and not for the better. One big shock Caldwell County folks felt was at the Broyhill corporate office. Built in the 1960s as a showplace for the company to sport its prominence, the huge box of a building had weathered many storms over the years, much like the enterprise that first built it. Just before FBI's bankruptcy, Broyhill sold the building to a pharmaceutical company, Exela, an act unthinkable when the structure was built. The head of Caldwell County's Economic Development Commission, Deborah Murray pointed out at the time of the sale that the county was "focused on broadening its economic base beyond furniture, which is still its largest employer." Getting out from under the shadow of furniture in Lenoir remained a daunting proposition, but the county was prepared to try, one landmark at a time.[871]

The headquarters that once conveyed the power and prestige of Broyhill was gone. At one time it was so iconic to the company, that when William Stevens published the 1968 book on the life of Broyhill's founders, the image of the corporate office was a prominent part of the cover. Now, another corporation, a much smaller one, called the edifice home. Broyhill Furniture moved headquarter operations, under its new president Mark Stephens, to space adjacent to its Vision 1 plant in Lenoir. The price they put on the real estate was $4.5 million. "Getting out of that building was the responsible thing to do," said Stephens, remaining as upbeat as possible. He added, "we are pulling all of our resources together to be a more efficient company." [872]

Built in 1966, this building served as the headquarters for Broyhill Industries for 45 years. Paul Broyhill said of the structure at the time of its opening, "our building is a modern adaptation of the Parthenon, and not only is it striking in appearance but also is functionally efficient." (Author's Collection)

Soon, Heritage Home Group met the same fate at its predecessors. In 2018, the parent company filed for bankruptcy, too. The companies they controlled, now referred to as "brands" included some once important employers in the foothills. Henredon, Hickory Chair, Thomasville, and Broyhill, looked like orphans in search of adoption. Within the corporate structure, Heritage maintained the rights to the use of the Drexel name, which was still a valuable commodity, not in the furniture it produced as that had all ended, but in the reputation it kept alive, especially with baby-boomers.

Perhaps the most revealing account of how bad the furniture business had gotten was from one of its own. Michael K. Duggan helmed Henredon Furniture for 17 years, the culminating event to a 40-year career in the industry. In 2009, he released an honest, but devastating book on the inner workings of the business. In *The Furniture Wars: How America Lost a Fifty Billion Dollar Industry*, he looked back on the spree of buyouts by conglomerates who had no understanding of furniture, but took over anyway. The squabbling between what he called insiders and outsiders distracted management at a time when they should have been preparing themselves to fend off the real threat of globalization. Duggan ended his firsthand account of the decline of companies with a chapter called, "The Asian Invasion," detailing the process of offshoring. The book threw a bomb into the turbulent world of an industry on the retreat. For many, Michael Duggan (who became a professor at Hickory's Lenoir-Rhyne University) told an honest story of the furniture companies that became part of the vortex of acquisitions and detailed how mismanaged it all became. In many ways, the book served as an obituary of a once important industry, that had been ravaged by outside ownership and global competition.[873]

The decline of furniture, as an industry to be respected and supported by the community, was exemplified by a court case that to its defendant seemed so ridiculous that it should never have come to trial. Anyone of longstanding tenure in the furniture business might well agree that suing a furniture company over misleading claims about what kind of wood was in its furniture was as frivolous as lawsuit could get. And yet, David Good sued Broyhill over its *Cherry Hill Collection*, arguing that the name and the promotional materials describing the line constituted an "unfair competition/false adverting claim."[874]

In the case that came to trial in early 2001, "Good filed a complaint on behalf of himself and 'the general public of the State of California'" that alleged "Broyhill was misrepresenting to consumer in 'catalogs, brochures, newspaper layouts and the like,' as well as by the Cherry Hill name itself, that its Cherry Hill line of furniture was made of soldi cherry wood." In essence, the argument cited consumer protection laws created to prevent false claims. Good's side said that if furniture was called *Cherry Hill* and the website asserted the product was "classic 18th century designs available in Cherry," a buyer could expect the pieces to be made from cherry wood. Broyhill disputed that characterization. Instead, they pointed to the dictionary with the meaning of cherry having two possible definitions. Broyhill argued the word cherry, "could refer to the wood from which the furniture is constructed or to the stain used to finish the furniture."[875]

The ruling mostly favored Broyhill but a judge did take exception to the website. By the time of litigation in court the description had already been changed to verbiage that read "available in Cherry stain finish," a restatement that clarified the furniture was not made from cherry wood. Broyhill appealed. First, they challenged Good's standing to bring the suit, which the court shot down, while also arguing that no one was hurt by the characterization. This time judges agreed that Broyhill's advertising efforts "were not likely to deceive reasonable consumers."[876]

In reality, the issue over which Broyhill defended itself had been going on since mechanization began. Especially for promotional lines, firms had always used the most cost-effective material available, thus creating the need for veneer as an overlay. Criticized and lampooned for disguising its output during the borax era, once again a foothills manufacturer gave the public an impression that their purchase was something it was not. Instead of cherry wood, consumers got a reddish finish that was not what they assumed it to be. Customer confidence eroded just as employee loyalty had. The trick in this case was not that Broyhill's lawyers were able to litigate the accusation away, it's the ability of their public relations team to keep the story from the news media and Broyhill from getting another obvious black eye, which they could ill afford.

The public never heard that a case of such questions was even being considered. Other than the filing of the complaint and the decision, media did not cover the trial and/or its appeal. It may have been regarded as silly but in hindsight, the question demonstrated the depths to which one of the grand old companies of the western region had sunk. No longer guided by anyone named Broyhill, the brand had to defend itself from questions of legitimacy.

Collateral damage from the contraction of the furniture industry. For many years, Triplett Furniture Fashions stood as one of the many retail outlets along Furniture Row (Highway 321) in Caldwell County, offering lower markups which drew consumers to the region. (Author's Collection)

Anatomy of construction. These furniture professions at McCreary Modern demonstrate some of the work that goes into the crafting of a piece of furniture. The work produced is complex and requires great skill, a dedication appreciated by manufacturers in the 21st century. (Courtesy of McCreary Modern)

Chapter 31
Profit and Loss

Since the early 1960s, the name Highland House Furniture attracted customers. Traditional styling and quality workmanship built a reputation for its product that included case goods and upholstery, all made in Hickory. In 1986, the firm sold out to Interco, the same company that bought Broyhill.[877]

Much like all the other manufacturers looking to cut labor costs, the decision was made to transfer production of case goods to Chinese factories in the late 1990s while retaining the crafting of upholstery in already established factories. At Highland House, a new line named for the prestigious Harrod's Department Store of London was planned using that strategy, with the imported portion of the full 55-piece line brought to Hickory before shipping to retail outlets, worldwide.[878]

Robert Allen knew better than anyone how the product was faring in his position with the customer service department. He fielded calls "about pieces falling off" Highland House furniture and began to investigate the cause. The search brought him to the warehouse where he made a compelling discovery. Quickly, Allen phoned the president of the company, Tom Staats asking him to take a walk down to the warehouse. Once Staats got there, he wanted to know the reason. Robert Allen told the company head to "just be quiet for a minute and listen." Impatient, but interested, Staats and Allen stood waiting until they began to hear pops and cracks ring out in the cavernous storage facility.[879]

"What is it?" Tom Staats asked.[880]

Robert Allen's research and observations had a ready answer. "It is the wood contracting and the veneer popping off." During production, the case goods had not been "dried properly" and with more moisture during shipping, the veneer loudly disengaged from its base. Angrily, the head of Highland House "stormed off" looking for who might be responsible for the quality control issue that Allen had brought to Staats' attention. Two years after its introduction, parent company FBI closed Highland House and with it, the Harrods' Fine Furniture collection. "Not all that significant," was how one executive referred to discontinuance of the line. Mickey Holliman, chairman, president and CEO of FBI said, "the reality is, however, that this division of our company had not generated the financial returns our shareholders expect and deserve." Among the many out of a job was Robert Allen.[881]

With anecdotes like that, it was easy to conclude that the party was over. Furniture making, as an industry, was dead. The only satisfaction laid-off workers got was to share stories, like Robert Allen's, about how dissatisfied customers were with what came off the ships. Many former employees didn't know how they would fill out the rest of their work lives and make it to retirement, but they were sure it wouldn't be in furniture.

Just over the hill from the original Bernhardt factory, Bernhardt Design, Plant 3 still operates in Lenoir. The company after over a century of operation, remains (as of 2022) the last of the original family companies and still in business. (Author's Collection)

As industry jobs were going away, Caldwell County looked desperately to fill the gap. That's when Google came to town. Seeking concessions, not unlike Broyhill and Kincaid, but with a much higher price tag, county officials seized the opportunity to diversify. The move was controversial. Google paid better than the furniture industry, a comparison often made between the two. While the average job wage at the tech giant was almost twice that of factory work, the number of employees Google needed was drastically less. Lenoir mayor, David Barlow candidly, but hopefully said, "Lenoir needs a new identity. It's been known for furniture forever, and furniture has left us." It seemed that any substitute was worth a try.[882]

Under the banner of "diversification," not unlike the buzzword outside corporate giants used to justify their purchase of furniture companies starting back in the sixties, the City of Lenoir conceded much to get Google. Along with the county, the municipality "agreed to waive 100 percent of Google's business property taxes and 80 percent of real estate taxes for 30 years," all for the construction of a 215-acre data center, built partially on Bernhardt Furniture's old lumber yard. Some local merchants started to turn cartwheels at the prospect, others were not so sure. One skeptic put it baldly, saying "Caldwell County has lost hundreds of furniture industry jobs in recent years. Putting Google in front of local officials is akin to unveiling a swimming pool before a dehydrated traveler wandering the desert. Who cares if the water is only an inch deep?" Starved local governments grasped any lifeline available in what seemed like the aftermath of the furniture era.[883]

A lot of hand-wringing went on about what to do in furniture's wake. Lenoir-Rhyne University welcomed furniture executives to "The Future of Furniture Forum." At the 2007 conference, N.C. State University's Dr. Art Padilla (keynote speaker and professor of management, entrepreneurship and innovation) offered a fair, if somewhat skewed assessment. He told the crowd that "many furniture factories failed because they couldn't compete globally."

However, he believed that, in the "furniture failures" there were "opportunities for success." With a track record of good leadership and workers, furniture had a path to return as a "technology-savvy" business, proclaimed Mickey Holliman, at the time still head of Furniture Brands International. Dr. Padilla gave the brightest ray of hope, reminding "the audience that businesses in other industries, such as IBM and Motorola, 'looked death in the face' but now thrive because they reinvented themselves."[884]

For many, reinvention seemed impossible. Workers had been undercut by a cheaper workforce, a circumstance from which there seemed to be no turning back. To them, the reversal was so complete and so devastating that the only path forward was to forget what had gone before. The influence of the Far East was everywhere. FBI leader Mickey Holliman was quoted in an investors' conference in 2003, sharing an ill advised, but revealing Chinese proverb. Saying he had distilled the Furniture Brands philosophy into one sentence, he proclaimed, "he who rides the tiger can never dismount." As uncomfortable as it was, everyone could see the meaning of the metaphor. Once manufacturers began to reap the profits from offshore product, reverting back to American-made creations was unthinkable, or so they believed at the time. Holliman said it himself in his statement about the shutdown of Highland House. His duty was to shareholders who wanted maximized profits. Drastically lower labor costs abroad made it so that a return to the stateside production became unthinkable. Anyone who suggested otherwise was laughed at, then fired. Management knew it could not "dismount."[885]

Old models of operation no longer applied. Asian interests became a player, sometimes as partners with American firms, some even bolder. In 2007, several Chinese corporations with no connection to American firms arrived to show their lines at the High Point market, aiming for a portion of domestic sales with no U.S. partner to ease the blow. The only saving grace for Hickory was that it had lost the trade show business more than 20 years earlier so it did not directly witness the competition.[886]

'Offshoring' and 'China' became dirty words for folks in the area, the culprit of job losses that devastated the economy of the Catawba Valley. With unemployment in 2010 reaching past 10%, the words were spit out with disdain. But furniture workers, both unemployed and the smaller number still working, could see the trend from only one side of the world. Meanwhile, in Asia, the same fate that befell western North Carolina labor was coming to China, as manufacturers began to eye the labor force in Southeast Asia as a source for even lower hourly employees. Vietnam now took furniture jobs, giving China an unpleasant taste of its own medicine. The trend was cold comfort to those left behind in Hickory, Morganton, and Lenoir. They continued to wonder just what a post-furniture world would look like.[887]

By the early 2000s, numerous furniture entities scrambled for anything that would make money. Some explored retail possibilities. Manufacturers like Ethan Allen got into the arena in a big way, opening a chain of stores. Most other furniture makers did not go that far, but each at least opened outlets for the public. Among the stores along Highway 321's furniture row (between Hickory and Lenoir), Kincaid, Bernhardt and Broyhill offered shops for direct sales. Despite cheaper prices, one contributor to Forbes wrote, "the brand names may still remain, but they are shells of what they once were."[888]

The lesson gained from the perils of corporate control was not lost on one Hickory operator, who avoided losing power over its own destiny. Century Furniture, the post-war creation of Harley Shuford remained steadfastly under family control. Instead of selling out, the Shufords chose to create their own corporate parent, RHF Investments. The failure of Heritage Home Group allowed RHF to add to its portfolio of companies, which included Century, but also crosstown furniture maker Hancock & Moore. In 2018, they supplemented their roster, buying Hickory Chair (plus Maitland Smith and Pearson) for $17.45 million from the failed HHG. They

A rarity in western North Carolina furniture companies, this back entrance notes production of a type of product most companies have conceded to China in favor of upholstery. In more ways than one Century Furniture has remained much as it was built, bucking industry trends. (Author's collection)

even brought Highland House. Like the furniture companies of old, RHF Investments played their corporate structure close to the vest, divulging few details, and like those bygone management teams, they kept their business local and their people employed. Century took a gamble that in the long run, paid off. Avoiding offers to sell, either stateside or around the world, had value for firms with a solid business plan that served the market, including a local constituency.[889]

Keeping the manufacture of furniture at home made sense, even at times when experts decried the practice. The main reason was level of expertise. Those working in the furniture business knew what would work and what would not. Local control saved company leadership from the embarrassment felt by Tom Staats as he stood in the warehouse with Robert Allen listening to his product fall apart. Back in 1979, Hickory Chair engaged in an experiment to see if a "contract furnishings division" could prosper in a changing market. Hickory Business Furniture "shipped its first order of high-end business furnishings in 1981" with increasing success. A skilled group of designers and a contact list that included a number of Fortune 500 companies combined with management knowhow proved to be the key. Soon, Hickory Business Furniture (HBF) began to use its initials as its official name, as did a sister company, known as HBF Textiles. Hotels, banks, even the Australian embassy in Moscow offered seating made by Hickory's HBF, something of a higher end successor to Southern Desk. Professional sports teams including the National Football League's Carolina Panthers filled their exclusive spectator areas with HBF furniture. Sales grew substantially by the mid-1990s, as did its workforce. Starting with just 24 in 1981, HBF peaked at over 300 until required layoffs in 2012 proved that no business model was totally immune from cutbacks. That year 60 workers were cut from the rolls. HBF started life as a division of Hickory Chair, which was a division of The Lane Company. Thomasville, which was part of FBI, owned them for a while before Iowa based HNI Industries, Inc. bought HBF in 2008 for $75 million.[890]

Beyond Iowa, the relationship between furniture makers in western North Carolina and Asia remained an uneasy one. In the new millennium, Chinese interests in the furniture business extended well beyond the practice of supplying American companies. On occasion, domestic producers sold their company lock, stock and barrel to enterprises in China. For the most part, Chinese companies bought out manufacturers with the intention of moving production to their homeland and off American shores. Over time, however, the calculus changed. In 2019, to the surprise of many, Conover's Southern Furniture sold to Universal Furniture, a brand of Samson Holdings, from Dongguan, in southeast China. Third-generation owner of Southern, Jerome Bolick called the sale "good for his company," telling his employees they were "in good hands." Observers expected the plant to shut its doors.[891]

The news wasn't that another furniture family was leaving the game, it was the terms of the deal. Larger furniture companies buying up smaller ones was not new. Back in 1980, Jerome Bolick added to his family's company by acquiring Bracewell Furniture, which had itself had bought out the

Haupt Manufacturing Company twenty years earlier. One furniture maker buying out another had been around as long as the industry. Players beyond corporate America had long since ceased to be novel, though still a harder pill to swallow.[892]

When any new owner came to town, the speeches were always about being bigger and better. Furniture workers had heard those lines bandied about before. At the time, nobody knew that Universal was serious about following through. Both owners and labor celebrated the first anniversary of the new arrangement with notable followthrough of promises made. Universal's management stressed how "pleased" they were "with the work coming out of Conover." Improving efficiency by rearranging and adding new machinery to factory operations allowed general manager Dale Smith to assert that "all the changes and improvements have helped us make a lot of progress in a short time."[893]

What differentiated the Universal purchase of Southern from other buyouts was an attitude toward the workforce. The infusion of fringe benefits and improved working conditions happily surprised Southern's workers. Some had expected to be in the unemployment line by that first anniversary but in addition to a more productive workspace, the company instituted a "health-care insurance package," offering coverage for "medical, dental and vision and includes a flexible spending account." Perhaps the biggest advantage was the surety of work at Southern. Introducing new upholstery styles (some 200) and a swell of new upholstery accounts (topping 300), Universal required more people, a rare occurrence.[894]

Universal needed to go the extra mile to compete with the legacy of Southern. Newton historian Sylvia Ray commented that the sale "was a shock to the local business community." In repeated cases, four generations of the same family worked for the Bolicks. Some even remembered back to the Great Depression when Oscar Bolick kept the factory running, despite the dire economic times. As one employee mentioned, "the Bolicks were always close to the families they employed," an example of the old paternalism that guided the employer-employee relations for decades.[895]

Understandably, the community eyed Universal with suspicion when the news of the sale arrived. However, the new owner brought with it a different ethic, one much more in alignment with smaller companies in the region that had managed to survive. Instead of relying on cheaper labor elsewhere, Universal invested $500,000 in the former Southern plant to make the manufacturer the envy of the industry. The approach defied the logic that corporate America had spouted for years.[896]

Since purchasing the company in 2019, Universal installed "new technology...updated and rearranged" the facilities, introduced "thousands of new fabrics, furniture styles and offerings" to keep the company competitive and western North Carolina workers on the job. In a rare move, unheard of with some corporate owners, General Manager Dale Smith "improve(d) the workflow in the factory as well as the morale and culture of the plant." Some changes were subtle but important. Employees were encouraged to come to Smith with concerns and ideas, while the shop walls were painted white to freshen up the place and new floor coverings replaced some very dated green shag carpeting. Dale Smith and his team invested in such things as new sewing machines, equipping each station with electronic tablets for easy access to patterns. All the changes were a sign to employees that the company valued their efforts. Workflows were streamlined, to take out some of the 'Rube Goldberg' systems *Fortune* magazine decried a half century earlier.[897]

What gave local leadership the ability to make those changes was their productivity. As Universal's senior vice president, Sean O'Connor asserted, "we're financially stable enough to do it right." Dale Smith said that he had been wanting to make the changes, and "when I said I wanted to do it here, they said go for it." The venture was the kind of one that might have saved other factories if only American conglomerates thought like Universal. When Furniture Brands International cut jobs in Lenoir 14 years earlier, changes like those going on at Universal were the very initiatives that could have made the plants more productive, giving them an opportunity to survive. Unfortunately, business leaders chose a path that favored quick profit over longevity, perhaps a clue to long term intentions.

Certainly, workers had to adjust as well. With so many new things to learn, the environment at Universal/Southern required teaching some old hands new ways of making furniture. In its new incarnation, the company revived an old concern, one not seen for a very long time. They needed workers. As had so many others before it, the firm turned to the community college to find prospective employees, seeking those fresh out of high school, looking for a career with competitive wages. Suddenly, upholstery skills became popular once more. With a mix of newly trained young-bloods and an experienced corps of hands, the pride was back, at least at Southern. Much of the new attitude came from the ways in which management demonstrated that they valued labor. Neil MacKenzie, VP of marketing exuded optimism, saying he felt "good about where we're at." He went on to reveal, "to be in special-order upholstery we've had to train all our teams, and with all that has been taking place on Earth in the last year (a reference to the COVID-19 pandemic in 2020), we're happy with what we've seen."[898]

The success of the transition at Southern Furniture might not have been such a surprise to anyone in western North Carolina if they had been watching a little factory in Hiddenite. Over a decade earlier, the China-based conglomerate that bought Southern Furniture invested in another company, Craftmaster Furniture in neighboring Alexander County. Under the name of Lacquer Craft Manufacturing, which owned Universal, Craftmaster was much like the later purchase of Southern, a privately owned upholstery concern. For those at Craftmaster, China was not a four-letter-word.[899]

Craftmaster began as an alternative to the corporate furniture world. Jack Stokes worked as vice-president of manufacturing for DeVille Furniture, Bill Mosteller's company. When Mosteller sold DeVille to National Services Industries, the new corporate owners sought to expand into Mississippi to take advantage of lower labor costs. Jack got tired of spending so much time in Mississippi, telling his son-in-law, Steve Lackey, "I don't think I want to work for a big, huge company." Steve Lackey was also part of DeVille, at one of their satellite plants, Hallmark Furniture. Jack approached Steve about both of them leaving DeVille and starting their own operation.[900]

Jack Stokes, Steve Lackey, along with several DeVille salesmen and CPA Dick Boggs formed a plan. The father and son-in-law pair knew the furniture business well so in the summer of 1972 that they got down to business, leasing an old cotton mill in Taylorsville for their new company, Craftmaster Furniture. DeVille's refugee salesmen covered the southeast, drumming up the first round of orders. "We started with about five designs," said Steve Lackey on the initial offering. The product line included both a 90-inch and 100-inch sofa, skirted with pillow arms. Since the salesman had all come from DeVille which featured Early American styled furniture, it was a market with which they had experience and were comfortable selling. There was no discussion about what style Craftmaster would initially offer.[901]

Business was good from the very start, too good to remain in a converted cotton mill. Steve Lackey found land adjacent to the Bassett factory (bought from Taylorcraft) in Hiddenite, a small community between Taylorsville and Statesville. As soon as the 50,000 square-foot factory was built, they added a 40,000 square-foot addition. One reason for the early success was their responsiveness. If a retailer had a need, Craftmaster worked hard to fill it. Flexibility defined Craftmaster's approach to its customers and for that effort the company gained a "loyal following."[902]

One important way in which Craftmaster guaranteed the steady flow of income was the use of a 'factor'. In essence, the process required those buying from Craftmaster to work through a third party that handled payment and took the loss if remittance was not made on goods. Craftmaster paid a percentage of the money collected by the factor, but writing off bad debt was eliminated. "They took the paper, they took the risk," as Steve Lackey characterized the relationship. Often, Craftmaster worked with more than one factor so that if a customer could not get accepted by one, they could apply to another. He likened it to a credit card, where the card company accepts the risk of non-payment, not the company with the merchandise.[903]

Steve Lackey called his father-in-law Jack Stokes, "a father to me." In the absence of Steve's own father who died when Lackey was ten years old, Stokes mentored his son-in-law in many aspects of the business, even when it was time to let go of the company. "When the time is right, you'll know," Jack told Steve years earlier, adding, "if I'm not here, you sell. But you'll know." Jack Stokes saw well into the future. After he passed away, Steve made the hard decision to look for a buyer.[904]

From time to time, calls came in asking if Craftmaster was for sale. Similar to the use of a factor, Jack Stokes and Steve Lackey chose to filter any offers through an intermediary. "We had lots of offers," Steve remembered, but with ownership split between the two when Jack was an active member of the team, both agreed that the time was not right. After Jack Stokes died in 2003, Steve Lackey took control of the company. He began to see that with "China buying product and bringing it in," the business was going to need "a tremendous amount of investment." As he looked ahead, he came to a conclusion. "I just didn't see any future in it." In 2006, he called broker Tim Stump and said, "I'm ready to talk."[905]

Looking for the best deal, Stump and Company came back to Steve Lackey with two leading candidates, one American, the other Chinese. The U.S. firm had no real tie to upholstery. They were a case goods company.

However, Steve held strong reservations about selling to an overseas company. As the owner of Craftmaster who had put his sweat, toil and investment into building a profitable operation, Steve said, "I did not want (the Chinese) to buy the company and move everything to China." With assurances that Universal wanted an American presence and a total migration of operations to China would not happen, a conversation began.[906]

The art of putting buyers and sellers together required hard and soft skills. Tim Stump's father Ralph spent his career developing relationships, keeping abreast of changes within industries like furniture and used that knowledge to find good matches. He began in "the money business of factoring companies," the same lending system later used by Craftmaster.[907]

Ralph Stump started his own "advisory-based business" the same year Stokes and Lackey created their furniture company. Over the years, the elder Stump taught his son, Tim, the expertise necessary to put together deals. Tim Stump learned well, stepping into the role of handling mergers and acquisitions for Stump and Company. Meanwhile, Craftmaster and Stump nurtured an ongoing relationship. As Steve Lackey recalled, Ralph Stump "and his sons would always come to the showrooms or be traveling up in the area and call and come to the plant and sit down and talk." In those days, Lackey "never thought about selling."[908]

As Tim Stump characterized it, 2006 was "early in the Chinese invasion, if you will," but several aspects of a deal with Universal Furniture, owned by Samuel Kuo/Samson Holdings, encouraged him. First, the goals of each fit with the other. After negotiations began, Universal was willing to meet Lackey's price and conditions. Second, "the chemistry between the people was excellent," said Stump. Lastly, a solid transition plan came together that included Roy Calcagne, once a VP for Hickory's JoAnn Fabrics, who worked with Universal's owner, Samuel Kuo.[909]

When Steve Lackey expressed concerns, Roy Calcagne reassured him that instead of abandoning the Hiddenite plant, Universal planned the opposite. As Lackey remembered, Calcagne told him, "that's not going to happen." Pointing out that Universal wanted "an American presence," Samuel Kuo's intention was to grow the company from a $40 million company to $100 million, which ultimately meant expansion, not contraction. Initially though, Universal intended to shift as much as "40% of its U.S. production to China." The expected savings to be reaped on work done overseas dwindled though as transportation costs soared, leaving the management team to reconsider the proposition. Steve Lackey stayed on for a year after the sale to help ease the transition to Roy Calcagne, the new president of the company. As Calcagne told a reporter in 2008 about the altered business plan, "it's changed our whole equation for where we produce."[910]

Despite the original intent to partially migrate, ultimately, changing conditions in the business world and a need to protect newly acquired assets in the United States charted a direction that centered the company in Hiddenite. "They realized there are some things that have to be done in the U.S.," commented analyst Jerry Epperson. He observed that "it can't all be done overseas." Bringing back upholstery to Alexander County proved a benefit for everyone, including customers, workers and Craftmaster. The labor force took a 'wait and see' attitude about the situation. Roy Calcagne joked about the circumstance, saying "it was a real hurdle convincing people that a Chinese owned company with a Yankee running it was a good thing," a reference to his own status as a transplanted northerner.[911]

Three years into the deal, business hummed so loudly that it caught the attention of the *Wall Street Journal*. They came south to see why Craftmaster thrived in an otherwise bad economy. As had occurred so often, a new owner usually brought disruption to an operation. Roy Calcagne found himself on the cover of the paper explaining how the Great Recession had forced a number of his competitors to fold, helping his firm to gain market share, an

508

Craftmaster Furniture headquarters in Hiddenite. Started by Jack Stokes and Steve Lackey in 1972, the company was purchased by a Chinese firm in 2006. Since then, the operation has doubled its output, size and workforce. (Author's Collection)

opportunity Craftmaster might not have had without the secure financial backing of the now-not-so-new Chinese owner. Calcagne told the Wall Street Journal reporter that their success came from "taking advantage of what China offered," which meant investment in furniture manufacturing and the local people who made it work.[912]

Improvements within the company popped up everywhere, beginning with worker benefits. Craftmaster increased its contributions to the 401k plan. Management upgraded facilities. Worries over job security began to ease as the number of employees increased, almost doubling, as did plant square footage. It paid off with Craftmaster becoming one of Universal/Samson Holding's most profitable companies.[913]

Another round of significant expansion moved forward as 2020 began. In Lenoir, an old abandoned factory found life again as Craftmaster's home for "cutting and assembling" frames. The company sought to relieve supply chain problems by taking a job in-house that had been outsourced for a long time. When upholstery frames failed to arrive on time, disrupting the entire operation, Craftmaster bought an old Broyhill facility and adapted it for its needs. The firm paid $1.5 million for it, but figured to save around $10 per sofa as a result. The company expected a profit from the move within three years.[914]

The key to success for the harmonious marriage of a western North Carolina manufacturer and a Chinese owner was the relationship forged between the two. Roy Calcagne described it by saying, "we're still run like a family business." In contrast to how American conglomerates handled their acquisitions, Calcagne observed about Samson Holdings, "they don't micromanage." Samuel Kuo receives "a regular monthly report on the financials and a couple of paragraphs on what's happening in the business" along with quarterly reviews to keep the owner informed, but does not direct the day-to-day activities of Craftmaster. That job is left to Roy who is trusted to make prudent decisions on behalf of the company. One example of the autonomy Craftmaster management has enjoyed was a local decision to handle more of its own shipping. Because of demand, other carriers could not get Craftmaster's furniture to market fast enough. So Calcagne and his staff bought a few used trucks and began hauling their product to retailers "within five or six hours" of the plant. "I didn't tell him about it. He'll find out," said Roy about the move, referring to his overseas boss. "He'll know it's OK because we are doing it for a reason." The same trust invested in Craftmaster would also be found at Southern Furniture in keeping with the management style of Universal/Samson Holdings. "They let us do our thing."[915]

Everyone in the foothills furniture industry could rightly claim that they had seen more than their share of curve balls thrown at them as first corporatization, then globalization rummaged through the business. Those left with jobs could rightly describe themselves as survivors. Many more were not so lucky, brought down in a wave of mismanaged cuts and mergers. A half century after economist Milton Friedman hailed shareholder profit as the only driver of American business, the wheel had turned, looking in its rearview mirror to see the devastation it caused. Furniture workers were one of the casualties, with the factories they once inhabited looking like war-torn battlefields. Companies like Drexel, that were once a king in the furniture world were soon to be wiped from the face of the earth. Others had been reduced to nameplate status with no real identity besides what history might suggest.

In an ironic twist, *Fortune* magazine, the same one that alerted the world to the immense profitability of those little furniture companies in western North Carolina back in 1967, said, "half a century later, it is clear that this narrow, stockholder-centered view of corporations has cost society severely." If the magazine sought to redeem itself from its earlier stance, the apology came too late. Abandoned factories and displaced workers showed the cost of their earlier folly.[916]

Inside Hickory Furniture Mart a vast array of furniture went on display during the heyday of the local furniture market, every April & October until the mid-1980s. Outside, the expansive complex instead caters to retail (instead of wholesale) consumers 360 days a year. (Courtesy Hickory Furniture Mart)

Instead of presenting furniture in a manner consistent of an earlier era, Mitchell Gold + Bob Williams created edgier, sexier advertisements to highlight the work of their Alexander County factories. (Courtesy Mitchell Gold + Bob Williams)

Chapter 32
One Comfortable Place

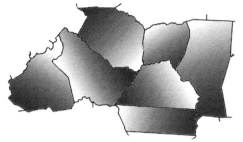

Municipalities became desperate to figure out how they could reinvent themselves after their manufacturing tenants left town, early in the 21st century. Lenoir pinned many of its hopes on Google. Morganton altered its image to attract millennials with a revitalized downtown atmosphere and successful efforts to increase a sector already in its wheelhouse, a branch of state government, the NC School for Science and Math. In and around Hickory, the solution, while also including development of amenities, had a more familiar ring.

Sutter Street Manufacturing, a subsidiary of furniture retailer Williams-Sonoma, showed interest in crafting upholstery in the heart of the once dominant furniture territory. Offering its own package of tax breaks and incentives, totaling upwards of $11 million, Catawba County attracted the California company to the small town of Claremont, east of Conover in 2008. The enterprise announced plans to hire 820 people over a five-year period. Wages were expected to be good, very good, for the area. Annual salaries were listed at $42,000 per year, well above the Catawba County average wage of $33,000. Catawba County beat out competition for the manufacturer in places like Virginia, New Jersey, and dreaded Mississippi (home of its own furniture industry and the threatened landing-place for Broyhill when they tried to exit Lenoir).[917]

The establishment of companies new to western North Carolina who sought to locate in Catawba County to be near where expert craftsmen lived, was a both an acknowledgement of the tradition and a shot in the arm to the ongoing furniture making economy. (Author's Collection)

Sutter Street didn't reach the 820-job threshold, but it did do something else remarkable. It stayed. Almost ten years after announcing its intention to come to Claremont, the company reported the addition of 72 more jobs as part of a $1.9 million expansion, to go with the 583 jobs it had already produced. North Carolina Governor Roy Cooper hailed the news of the increase, saying, "it's that talent that keeps furniture manufacturers here, and this expansion is a testament to the health of the furniture industry in North Carolina." The governor may have been overstating furniture's "health," but it was a sign, showing resilience. The statement emphasized the area's best untapped resource, the accumulated experience of unemployed and under-employed furniture workers.[918]

The Sutter Street connection fostered a new company, with a leader who knew and appreciated the area. Eric Fulcher, former president of Sutter Street, announced a new enterprise called Design Foundry. Locating in Hickory, the firm planned to invest $3.1 million in the project. Fulcher and his furniture venture got some help from Governor Cooper's office, a 12-year grant totaling $1.5 million, demonstrating how the game was now played. By the time the grant was fulfilled, state officials estimated that Design Foundry would pump some $320 million into the economy. One way was the salaries it paid. Design Foundry planned to offer pay at an average of almost $58,000 per year, again well above the Catawba County average, which had grown to $41,531 by 2019.[919]

The future of furniture was looking up. Fulcher liked the educational climate of the area, pointing out how the county's investments in STEM (Science, Technology, Engineering, Math) had "played a role in the decision to pick Hickory." Catawba County Economic Development head Scott Millar delightedly shared how "the high-end furniture" business was still the top employer in the county, even with the job losses in the first part of the 21st century. He said, "we're trying to grow the employment pool in the county." It wasn't where it had once been, but a rebound was in progress.[920]

Of all the new companies that popped up in the territory of the western manufacturers, Mitchell Gold's firm might have seemed the most unlikely. He had enjoyed a prolific career as a furniture buyer for Bloomingdale's department store and later, as part of one of the nation's largest manufacturers. But in 1989, Mitchell Gold decided to build his own line, joining with his life partner, who had never been in the furniture business before. Bob Williams previously worked as an art designer for Seventeen Magazine. The entrepreneurs recognized that the offerings of traditional furniture makers differed, sometimes widely from what customers actually wanted.[921]

In its early years, industry analysts observed that Mitchell Gold's company "flew under the radar, despite the fact that it was quietly revolutionizing the furniture industry." Observers noted that Mitchell and Bob's designs were imaginative, yet comfortable. Together, Gold and Williams formulated a unique approach based on instinct rather than convention. "When we did the slip cover sofas, there wasn't an enormous amount of market research on it," said Mitchell about the offering, "but we felt we knew a lot of people that were having young children, pets, and the one thing we noticed is you go to their homes and they're constantly saying to their child, 'don't do this'." The need to rethink how people lived with their furniture was obvious to the visionaries.[922]

In subtle, but vital ways, Mitchell and Bob offered the market what it really wanted, style and convenience. By 2006, the professional partnership prompted Mitchell Gold to add "+ Bob Williams" to the company name giving it the name Mitchell Gold and Bob Williams (MG+BW) a recognition of the value Bob's collaboration brought to the firm. With fabric slip covers to protect pieces and interesting designs that were sold by companies like "Crate & Barrel, Pottery Barn, Restoration Warehouse and Williams Sonoma Home and Storehouse," MG+BW altered the look of home decor nationwide. Their impact locally changed norms too, especially the way they ran their factory.[923]

Manufacturing began in 1989. The first facility opened in rural Alexander County, just north of Hickory and Catawba County. Workers there had seen firms come and go, much to their powerless dismay. When Mitchell Gold's brother told him about a facility that was operating at half-capacity, he inquired. Within a few years, Mitchell Gold took over the whole factory, adding other plants as the firm grew. Since its earliest days, management had a dual mission, to understand both "consumer behavior and employee behavior." Mitchell Gold knew what needed to change in both realms.[924]

First came the need to understand the buying public. Noticing that people were "cocooning," meaning staying home more, the market seemed to cry out for a fresh approach to interior furnishings, so Mitchell Gold and Bob Williams designed for the trend. "As Bob and I have traveled the world, we would see things and think, 'how do people want to live in the near future?' Not how people lived in the past 20 or 30 years." Their initial breakthrough was a dining room chair. Mitchell noticed "a lot of people, when they sit in a dining chair, they like to rock on it a little bit and the joints can break. So we came up with the dining chair that really didn't have joints on it." So sure were they of its durability, the manufacturers included a 25-year warranty, which was unheard of in the industry.[925]

Building a chair with a long-term warranty required expert design and construction. Developing lines to accommodate what they imagined to be the future of furniture use required a workforce that could be relied upon to give their best effort, building pieces that withstood sometimes punishing usage. To get the job done, Mitchell Gold sought to implement the second part of his strategy: to consider the needs of his workforce. Referring to a large manufacturer for whom he had once worked, Mitchell was candid. "They just didn't treat their employees very well." This inspired Gold to do the opposite. He took a sharp interest in the working conditions under which the men and women who built his product toiled. During the first summer of operation, he noticed how unbearably hot the temperature was inside the factory. The owner went to his plant manager, asking for the air-conditioning to be turned on. "He looked at me like I was crazy," said Gold, remembering the moment. The manager replied, "there's no air-conditioning in a furniture factory." The exchange was a quick education in how little traditional management had regarded working conditions. They vowed the MG+BW factory would be different.[926]

The installation of air-conditioning for the next summer was just the first innovation. They followed with good coffee that cost employees a nickel, the price to provide it, not a rate to make a profit. Lighting was improved. Soon, the word got out that Mitchell Gold was a really good place to work. Turnover practically ceased. When workers needed to miss time over daycare concerns, a center was built at the factory. It didn't take long for Mitchell Gold + Bob Williams to become the largest (and according to some, the most beloved) employer in Alexander County.[927]

The industry also noticed. Soon, other companies came calling.

Rowe Furniture, from Virginia eventually went so far as to buy the company. The infusion of capital allowed further enhancements, but the relationship between the two was not what Mitchell Gold hoped it would be. "We thought they were going to take our business and really build it to a new, bigger place," believed Gold. Ultimately, the former owners determined that they could better chart a forward path and bought back the operation with a group of more like-minded investors. The move returned control to a management team that had a deep interest in the product, as well as the working conditions of those who crafted the goods.[928]

The company gained attention in unprecedented ways. Mitchell Gold + Bob Williams' furniture showed up on numerous television shows and films. *Ally McBeal*, *Friends*, *The Good Wife*, *Sex and the City* all sported pieces made in and around Taylorsville. Much thought put into advertising with some print ads featuring Mitchell Gold's dog Lulu modeling chairs and sofas. Others ads were characterized as "provocative" with models sexier than Lulu showing off the furniture, definitely a nontraditional approach. Jerry Epperson, furniture industry analyst pointed out that Mitchell Gold "decided early on he didn't want to be all things to all people." The company head, very cognizant of making such a choice, was surprised by the response, saying "I actually thought we'd get a lot more complaints."[929]

Mitchell Gold + Bob Williams kept the future firmly in view. For the long term, they ensured the company would continue beyond their tenure with the hiring of an outside person for the job of president and CEO. Allison O'Connor joined the firm in 2019, with an eye toward where the company could go in its next 30 years. When the announcement was made, Gold lauded Allison O'Connor's "proven track record." He and Bob Williams believed her experience with an "Australian homewares brand," equipped her for the challenge of "building an omni-channel business with excellence," keeping the company ahead of the industry in its approach.[930]

Even before the worldwide pandemic of 2020, Mitchell Gold + Bob Williams salespeople adapted technology to better serve customers that fit well into the online environment. They began *FaceTime* and *Zoom* calls to discuss design options with potential buyers in the home. Using swatches, tips, and the conversation that goes with it, virtual business grew (especially once COVID hit) to become an important component of what the company offered, along with their website. More importantly, MG+BW maintained their advantage as industry innovators.[931]

A responsible partner in the community, the firm echoed the days when furniture manufacturers made sure the local culture benefitted from the presence of a factory in their midst. Philanthropy infused the MG+BW ethic. Supporting local efforts like Hickory Community Theater and the ALFA (AIDS Leadership-Foothills Area Alliance) gave Mitchell and Bob the opportunity to give back. "I guess a part of it's in Bob's and my DNA," expressed Mitchell. "We want to help people that are less advantaged, less privileged than we are." The experience, which began with air-conditioning and extended into health screenings for each employee, mushroomed into assistance that benefited the entire region. As Mitchell Gold saw it, "it's not just giving back to the community, it's building the community. It's giving the community a good moral direction."[932]

The moral direction of the community was an interesting consideration for a furniture company. In the history of the western North Carolina industry, manufacturers hadn't looked at the business in quite the same way as Gold did. His background set the stage for the ethic he would one day bring to a career as a furniture maker. Growing up Jewish in New Jersey, Mitchell learned the importance of respect from his father. Emphasizing "that people's differences should be appreciated and that everyone deserves fair treatment," the father, Jack sought to convey his views about racial equality to the son. As he matured, Mitchell applied the lesson more broadly.[933]

Recognizing his authentic identity as a gay man was traumatic for Mitchell Gold. Born in 1951, he said "I first realized I was gay as a teen. It was a horrible time. I thought God didn't love me." He vowed suicide if he did not change by the time he turned 21. Fortunately, his father noticed a change in his son and cared enough to get him the help Mitchell needed to process the situation. What he got from his therapy was a fuller understanding of his sexuality and an emerging realization that he needed to help others cope as he did. "Once I got comfortable with who I was, my life changed. My grades got better. I felt born again."[934]

The experience influenced everything he would later achieve. Coming to New York City in 1974, "young, fresh out of college, and closeted," he got a job selling pillows for Bloomingdale's when a faculty advisor at Long Island University talked him out of going to law school. As he began to establish his name in business he also realized that the principle of inclusion taught by his father, included himself. The issue might not have been as controversial but for his eventual creation of a furniture company in Taylorsville. There, conservative religious elements resisted support for gay rights.[935]

Mitchell Gold accepted the challenge. The position in which he and his partner Bob Williams found themselves when they came to Alexander County required a more charitable outlook than what they received. As described in a book on his company entitled *Mitchell Gold + Bob Williams: Who We Are*, "being two gay men, and in Mitchell's case, Jewish, believe us when we say: 'We've met our fair share of bullies. And if those bullies taught us one thing, it's that we'd rather be nice guys'." Ignoring the judgement they felt by the community, the factory namesakes decided to act differently. The ethic carried over to the way Mitchell and Bob treated everyone: their community (though some were adversaries), their customers (who loved their furniture), but perhaps more pivotally, their employees.[936]

The success of Mitchell Gold + Bob Williams was an immediate part of the firm's history from the very start. Before full production began, Mitchell Gold had an order "to make 800 tables and 5000 dining chairs." From there the company never looked back. The positive result of their work afforded MG+BW the opportunity to give back to the community with no malice toward those that opposed their stance on civil rights. In fact, the new scoreboard at Alexander Central High School was underwritten by the furniture maker. It has the firm's logo at the bottom and before each game "the announcer thanks Mitchell Gold and Bob Williams for their support." The school's principal conceded that a few have grimaced to him about it but his response took on a 'put up or shut up' vibe. He told them, "we need a new baseball scoreboard. If your company wants to buy it, come on."[937]

Applying the idea of "comfort" to everything associated with the MG+BW brand, Mitchell Gold wanted his workforce to be as comfortable as his furniture. Beyond the day care center, the "cafe with a full-time chef" and nurse practitioner on staff, Gold and Williams aided employees on an individual basis while challenging community views on the LGBTQ issue. For example, Taylorsville resident and employee Ellen Smith told a reporter from the *Washington Post* about how Mitchell Gold gave care and expressed concern after her son was killed in an auto accident. He provided "anything I

Mitchell Gold is seated (dark shirt, center front row) with scholarship winners during an awards ceremony in the early days of the company. Assisting workers has been a hallmark of the company since it first began in Alexander County in 1989. (Courtesy Mitchell Gold + Bob Williams)

needed," she said. When her daughter was hospitalized, her boss offered "her family a place to stay so they could be closer to the hospital." Characterizing the relationship as a bond, Ellen Smith remarked, "they have been so understanding and so kind, there's no room for any different feelings. No room." As time passed, MG+BW's reputation as an excellent place to work continued to grow.[938]

A benefactor to the community, Mitchell Gold nevertheless stood up for what he believed in. He clearly and persistently stated his views that intolerance was harmful to people who were made to feel inferior, as he had when he was a young man. He edited the book, *Youth in Crisis: What Everyone Should Know About Growing Up Gay* and helped found Faith in America, "a national non-profit organization dedicated to addressing religious-based bigotry," which later merged with the Tyler Clementi Foundation. He also edited *Crisis: 40 Stories Revealing the Personal, Social and Religious Pain and Trauma of Growing Up Gay in America.*[939]

His stance put him in opposition with some in and around Taylorsville, an area described as "dotted with nearly 100 churches, more than half of them Baptist." As an example, the two sides clashed on the establishment of a straight-gay alliance club at the county's high school. The proposal brought a war of words with it in the fall of 2015, especially in the "Letters to the Editor" pages of the *Taylorsville Times*. Condemnation by a few outspoken citizens brought replies from Mitchell, revealing his personal trials. The responses explained why he was committed to helping students avoid the same kind of shame and hurt that he endured. As he answered his critics he reminded them that as "it was wrong to use religious teachings to justify slavery and deny equal rights to women. It is wrong now to promote teachings that cause so much harm."[940]

The situation alarmed the community for reasons other than those verbalized in fundamentalist churches. At about the same time of the debate, the company bought a warehouse in neighboring Iredell County. Locals worried that MG+BW might move production in retaliation. The gossip caused such a stir that Mitchell Gold felt compelled to address the Alexander County Commission in person, assuring citizens that "we are not leaving Alexander County." Breathing a sigh of relief, the commission chairman thanked his county's largest employer for putting "those rumors to rest."[941]

Despite the rancor, the longevity of the company and its economic stature in the area provided Mitchell Gold the ability to affect change. In 2022, when he attended a P.R.I.D.E. (People Respecting Individuality, Diversity and Equality) Club meeting at Alexander Central High School, the room was packed. Afterward, Gold met the newest principal at the school and told him, "it just really astounds me that these kids feel so protected by you." Mitchell had previously asked the students if such was the case and they answered, "yes." As he summed up, Gold told the principle, "that hasn't always been that way." Confiding in one of Mitchell Gold's many letters to the editor, "I see signs of healthy change. I have hope for the future."[942]

Another factory owner might have sought to underplay personal views to minimize risk to the business, but not Mitchell Gold. In an interview with *BusinessNC*, he acknowledged that "we've had a couple of people leave us and say it was because of my activism. We probably have had people not come to work for us. We probably have had customers that haven't bought from us." He accepts the loss, seeing the quandary differently. "Despite common wisdom," he asserted, "doing good does not necessarily conflict with a company's success. We know, because it's our secret to it."[943]

Sales success has certainly aided the community. In 2008, the head of Alexander County's Chamber of Commerce stressed how "community-minded" MG+BW were as she commented, "they're good employers to work for." Others agreed. Once, when Mitchell Gold went to Washington, DC to meet with the area's representative, Cass Ballenger, he expected a "horrible meeting" given their opposing political viewpoints. Gold introduced himself to the congressman, expecting that the 10th Congressional District politician would not know who he was. Instead Representative Ballenger said, "I know exactly who you are." Then, Ballenger commented that "all the furniture manufacturers are complaining about you because you're raising their costs. You're doing benefits that none of them have ever thought about. You're raising the standard of living," asserted the congressman, "and I think it's great."[944]

Accolades came both locally and nationally. Once during a ceremony where MG+BW was receiving an award in California, the former Secretary of Labor during the Clinton Administration, Robert Reich, "was giving a speech about how bad businesses are," citing the way management treated their employees. As Gold remembered the moment he recalled, "he looked over at me and he said, 'well, all except Mitchell Gold's business'." Back in Taylorsville, after the word got out about the fringe benefits offered at the company, folks in the personnel department who knew the local crop of talent began to notice that some of the top craftsmen of the area were applying for jobs. Whether it was affirmation by the federal government or a talented upholsterer, Gold was amazed by the fact that, as he put it, "we really had an awesome responsibility and an opportunity."[945]

Mitchell Gold + Bob Williams established a new trend in furniture making, an ethic that emphasized social responsibility as the ultimate bottom line. From their Taylorsville address of 135 One Comfortable Place, they sought a more responsible way to make furniture. The strategy paid off. Celebrities like award-winning actress Judith Light counted themselves as "furniture groupies," fans of the comfort afforded by the output of the Taylorsville factory, as well as the principled stance taken.[946]

Since 1989, the leadership of MG+BW embraced their emphasis of comfort and stuck to their principles in the most turbulent era the foothills furniture industry had ever seen. They did not follow an established paradigm,

Mitchell Gold and Bob Williams at work. The image is from their book, *Mitchell Gold + Bob Williams: Who We Are* that details the company's philosophy and its history as a unique and consequential manufacturer in the western North Carolina furniture business. (Courtesy of Mitchell Gold + Bob Williams)

far from it. Rather, they chose to commit to following their own individually charted path. If a lesson emerged from the performance of the enterprise, it was that a company could stand for something beyond profit. They successfully bucked industry trends. In a comprehensive history of Alexander County, one historian referenced the accomplishment of Mitchell Gold + Bob Williams by writing, "even though furniture manufacturing has suffered in more recent times, one local company has weathered the storm better than most."[947]

A few other companies would employ less political variations but much of the idea of valuing employees would be the same. Promoting the wellbeing of the community, particularly workers, made good business sense. The collective experience of the furniture tradition could still make a superior product, if those that made it were treated with respect and appreciation.

The face of the 21st century workforce in the western North Carolina furniture industry. These employees are also partial owners of the McCreary Modern, a tangible acknowledgment to their value in the manufacturing process. (Courtesy of McCreary Modern)

Chapter 33
The Son of a Sander

Back when furniture making was still in its glory, a husband and wife team started a new furniture making company. Bill and Dottie Coley took a 7,500 square-foot space in Newton with ten employees and "began crafting wood-framed upholstery pieces" back in 1969, calling the new enterprise Lee Industries. "The furniture industry is not especially hard to get into," recalled Bill Coley about the decision. Dottie agreed, adding "upholstery is fairly easy." Along the way, both acknowledged they learned a lot, as they characterized it, "the hard way."[948]

From the beginning, Lee Industries took a different approach. In an era where traditional styling guaranteed sales, the Coleys banked on the appeal of a contemporary look. Bill brought an architect's eye to designs. Dottie carefully chose fabrics to enhance the appeal. With the arrival of Chic Robinson as executive VP to handle finance, production, and administration, the husband and wife team concentrated on the pieces themselves. One description recognized the distinctiveness of Lee's line, writing that their furniture "doesn't look quite the same as other contemporary chairs. They go off at different angles and have surprising soft curves."[949]

The company toiled to stay ahead of the times. After first showing at the Hickory Home Furnishings Mart, Lee Industries built a showroom at their own factory, then abandoned the western market for High Point, well before everyone else left Hickory. They were well received, gaining a four fold increase in buyer traffic, which resulted in double-digit sales increases at every market. Lee was largely characterized as a "mom and pop" operation, but they were expanding, adding a third factory to their complex by 1980. Even though furniture giant LADD bought the company, the Coleys continued to chart the direction of the firm. Bill and Dottie had crafted "a unique styling statement," with "a look like no one else." Soon, Lee Industries designs were getting knocked off (copied) by a raft of competitors.[950]

Along the way, the lines expanded, allowing Lee to assert several important guiding principles. In addition to expanded fabric offerings, designer collections and outdoor furniture, the company embraced concepts that further set them apart. They championed "environmentally sound manufacturing practices and sustainable initiatives." Taking the attitude of being sustainable into all phases of the company, including "its products, its manufacturing processes and its people," Lee Industries carved out for itself an admirable personality. Products included the development of "soy-based cushions, which replaces part of the petroleum in the cushions with renewable soybean oil." Much of their effort was showcased with the *naturalLEE* line.[951]

To bolster the effort, the Coleys made sure everything associated with *naturalLEE* pieces was subjected to the closest scrutiny. Bill and Dottie insisted that lumber was "certified from renewable resources in managed forests." Lee Industries went so far as to make sure company operations conserved energy, water, and recycled where it could to follow an eco-friendly mission. Lee seriously considered every aspect of furniture making in a world that would eventually warm to the idea of being a good steward of the earth. Company "green teams" were formed to educate, not only the "associates that work" at Lee, but also their suppliers in the ways of being "responsible" for what the furniture company made. The approach was radically different from the principles of anyone else in the region.[952]

Lee Industries remained nimble when it came to promoting its brand. The Coley's son, Norman, at the time operations manager for the company (he would go on to become president), read an interview with Norm Abrams, the host of the PBS series, *The New Yankee Workshop*. In the *USA Today* piece, the local (southern) Norm discovered that the northern Norm had never "upholstered a chair on his show, and he'd like to." Norman Coley emailed the show's producer who called back the same day. As it turned out, the producer knew the work of Lee Industries, having used their furniture for one of his other shows, *This Old House*. Conversations brought Norm Abrams down to Newton where an episode of the show was shot. *The New Yankee Workshop* host was quoted as saying, "the best way to learn is from the masters. That's why we're here." The effort to produce the episode in the heart of the once proud furniture making industry stood out as a real compliment to the expertise that remained, even after the glory days had passed. All Bill Coley could add was, "we were ecstatic."[953]

The other thrust of the company was to embrace their local roots. Engaged in a campaign entitled, "Lee Loves Local," the manufacturer supported a wide range of charitable activities including scholarship programs, service organizations, and educational initiatives. Company reports cited average employee tenure at 15 years. Moving its corporate headquarters to Conover, the company adapted the old Conover Chair facility in 2013, with the help of grants from local and state government. The arrival was well-timed for the Catawba County town. In the seven years prior, Conover had seen its industrial tax base drop by one third as other furniture companies folded. Lee's furniture, crafted in Catawba County, found fans nationwide with over 400 appearances in magazines like *Better Homes & Gardens*, *House Beautiful*, *Southern Living* and *HGTV Magazine*.[954]

Circumstances were not always kind to the path taken by the Coleys. In 2008, Dottie Coley passed away, followed six years later by Norman B. Coley, the son who had taken over as president of the company. In 2016, the company was sold to American Leather Holdings of Texas for an undisclosed amount.[955]

Despite the sale of Lee Industries to outside interests, the effort to remain local remained strong with Bill Coley. Two years after the purchase, the founder retired, but he was not ready to quit. Luckily, he found a new partner in Brian Newton, whose credentials included 15 years with Ethan Allen and a 2020 upholstery startup, the Hickory Oak. An introduction provided Bill with a reason to get back into the furniture business. Originally, Brian Newton wanted to meet Bill Coley because, as Brian put it, Bill was "a legend in the furniture industry." "I met Brian and was very impressed with him," was Bill's first take. Together, they partnered, renaming the business Newton Coley, LLC to reflect the union. The new enterprise followed in some of the same footsteps as Lee Industries, building upholstery for an upscale market.[956]

For Bill Coley, the new furniture venture echoed the old. Starting out in a 8,000 square-foot building with 14 employees felt like 1969 all over again. Fortunately, circumstances allowed for expansion much faster than Lee Industries achieved fifty years earlier. Bill Coley and Brian Newton recognized that the workforce was different. They established flexible work hours and employee lunches with family members invited as a way to create a cohesive environment. Besides, Bill Coley admitted that he hated retirement. Declaring that he "just got bored," Bill relished a return, saying "I just love the furniture business." Bill's wife Laura was amazed by all the tasks she saw her husband tackling at Newton Coley as he led by example. "Every time I walk out into the factory, he's doing another job," she said, which has included cutting fabric, making patterns, sewing, upholstering, loading trucks, even paying bills. She

Refurbishing an old factory, Lee Industries located its headquarters in downtown Conover. Created in 1969, Lee aspired to a different calling than any other furniture maker in the region, to be as environmentally-friendly as possible. In a diminishing industry, Lee has prospered. (Author's collection)

called the effort "amazing."[957]

In the wake of corporate buyouts, much of the furniture industry's energy had withered away. Workers faithful to their jobs were caught in the middle of a squeeze for profits. They had no agency and no one seemed to care for their welfare, or value their ability to still make a product that consumers would buy. To many, the trend of manufacturing was leaving with no way to reclaim it. Case goods production had gone to other shores, with upholstery also in danger if the technique could be mastered elsewhere. A smarter approach, based upon a different model, would have to be found to reestablish furniture in a way that would be profitably sustaining. Some had a desire, a few found an answer.

Bob McCreary grew up in the Caldwell County community of Hudson during the glory days of furniture production in the area. He excelled at football which earned him a scholarship to Wake Forest University, where injuries taught him perseverance. After a medial collateral tear (MCL), the freshman tackle found returning to form much more difficult than he expected.

He almost decided to give up the game that was paving the way for him to be the first in his family to earn a college degree. Then athletic trainer Doc Martin leveled with him. "If you quit now, you'll quit again," he told Bob. Taking the advice, McCreary got back on the field, playing so well that soon the National Football League called. His career started with the Dallas Cowboys, then a season in the Canadian Football League until a concussion landed him in the hospital for two days and ultimately ended his days in the profession.[958]

Weighing his options, Bob returned home to Caldwell County and followed his father's footsteps into the furniture industry. While the elder McCreary had been a sander with Bernhardt, Bob took a job that offered greater possibilities of advancement. He developed his sales ability under Wes Collins, the brains behind Bernhardt's growth. "I thought if I could be like him," Bob McCreary recalled about Wes' tutelage, "I would have arrived. I had much respect for him; he inspired me. I wanted to mold my professional career after him."[959]

Michele Acosta took a different path to furniture. She grew up across the country from Bob McCreary, in California where her grandfather "owned a produce box manufacturing company in the San Joaquin Valley, which he and my father ran," she remembered. While in high school and during her summers away from college, she worked in the family business, putting labels on box ends. "I was paid by the bundle," she recalled, "essentially piece work, making $500+ a week, which was a fortune for a 13-19 year old and would pay for college." She studied interior design in Fresno, then San Francisco, where she also "worked in a furniture store." For a while after graduation, she even managed a small shop.[960]

An interest in furniture was drawing Michele in. "Looking for more experience," she went to work as an assistant buyer for W&J Sloane, a high end furniture seller. She was accustomed to the activity of furniture markets like those in San Francisco, but when she came south, it was a different story.

Her take on the region was much the same as Helen Kelly's, a generation earlier. "I thought I'd stepped back in time," she recalled, recalling her first North Carolina market as "pretty shocking." It must have been surreal for the native Californian, working for a New York based luxury furniture company, finding herself in a world of "strange speaking old white men, terrible accommodations and food, brown bag liquor and so much ugly furniture," by her estimation. Selecting home furnishings that would please her clientele was "truly looking for a needle in a haystack," as she perused the output of southern manufacturers. However, Michele Acosta was persistent. At the Hickory market she discovered an oasis, Sherrill Upholstery, which she saw as becoming "big resource for us." That's where Michele met Bob.[961]

The idea of building something new took Bob McCreary away from Bernhardt. He went to work for Sherrill, hired to help them start up a new, more contemporary division, called Precedent. Two years after he and Michele they met, the two married. Bob drafted Michele into his dream of starting his own company. As she moved from her 79th Street apartment in New York City to Newton, she expected she would become "a southern housewife, get out of retail and do the garden club thing." Instead, together they started McCreary Modern just four months after the wedding.[962]

The McCrearys had long conversations about "how the industry could do better." Together, they visualized what it would look like if they did it "the right way." Those discussions led to them to take out a mortgage on their house to buy "an old two-flood fiber mill" in Newton. Bob quit his "stable, good-paying job" with Precedent at the end of 1985 and on January 1, 1986 started a new one as co-head of a fledgling company. The odds were not in their favor. And they got worse.[963]

Creating McCreary Modern proved to be a formidable challenge. The mutual dream of having their own shop where they could put into action long held beliefs of valuing employees while creating an impressive product was intriguing. Using the lessons Bob had learned at Bernhardt and Precedent and Michele's experience in the design, marketing and retailing of furniture stood on the positive side of the ledger. However, a number of obstacles threatened their success. As Bob's oldest son Robert, an investment analyst, characterized chances for success, the move was "precarious." The first problem involved the building. It "wasn't well-suited to furniture manufacturing," as Robert saw it.[964]

Warped, uneven floors and a dangerous set of stairs were just the beginning of their problems. Within a few months, Bob McCreary was so sick that he was bedridden. It was a moment when he questioned the decision to start the new business. It also gave him time to think. Remembering the good advice he received as a football player sidelined with injury, he and Michele decided to forge ahead.[965]

"I was told by more than one person, do you really know what you are doing?" Bob McCreary recalled about the endeavor. He and Michele knew the undertaking was fraught with danger, but looked at the opportunity analytically. Bob reasoned, "I've always taken a calculated risk, I think, but it's very calculated." Affirming their vision, along with the experience each brought from their knowledge of the industry, the couple continued to move forward as best they could. Bob reached out to his many contacts, saying "I felt confident with the people I knew, the relationships I had put together. I felt confident in my ability to put product together and take it to the customer." Michele agreed with Bob that with payroll to meet, bills coming in for materials and no income, the best path for the company was straight ahead. They must not quit.[966]

Despite the setbacks, the product being made in Newton came along at the right time and in the right way to facilitate an emerging trend in the industry. Instead of trying to brand the factory's output with the McCreary name, Michele and Bob sold to companies who wanted their own name on the furniture. For retailers, having a private label offered distinctive branding advantages. It took about a year and a half with the McCreary Modern team working tirelessly to attract those retailers, but ultimately they turned a corner. "After that, quite honestly, it really became word of mouth and they started coming to us," said Bob looking back on the point when it all came together. Emerging retailers throughout the United States had found a willing partner to supply them with the very products they needed to become household names. In turn, Mr. and Mrs. McCreary found vindication in doing it "the right way," not to mention a promising outlet for the furniture they were producing in their Newton factory.[967]

The intention of the McCreary's when starting the company was to be deliberately thoughtful about how it progressed. For them, controlled growth offered the ability to maintain quality, deepen relationships (especially with their employees) and not let the lure of importing take over just to improve the bottom line. That's not to say they didn't want the company to be profitable. They did, just on their own terms, which meant keeping alive a family atmosphere and assuring both workers and customers that the product would be "made domestically." Over thirty-five years after shipping out the first piece, the company boasted a rate of 98% crafted in McCreary factories.[968]

Though they envisioned a direction of the company, the McCrearys fully acknowledged the value of the people they have worked with as a key to their success. One important find was Rick Coffey who like Bob, got valuable training in the western North Carolina world of furniture before joining the team. As a boy, Coffey remembered, " I used to go to the shop with my dad on Saturday mornings, because my mother got her hair done on Saturday." Because "my dad just cut us loose," Rick roamed the factory floor. That's how he began a career in furniture.[969]

Similar to countless others in the industry, Rick Coffey declared, "it becomes part of you. You love it. You love the people. They were just wonderful, down home folks." Almost by instinct, he could tell when it was genuine and when it was not, although years of experience taught him too. After working for American Drew during summers when he was in college, Rick found himself a plant manager at age 24 for Stanley Furniture in Virginia. Then Broyhill made him an offer that brought the North Carolinian offering great learning opportunities where he "could be running a case goods plant here, in a month from now I might be running an upholstery plant. Paul would just mix them up," a reference to the indomitable Paul Broyhill. In addition, Rick's resume also included a period as vice-president with Thomasville and Drexel Heritage.

In those jobs, Rick Coffey saw the other side of the coin. "I had about all I could stand in corporate America," he admitted. "They were just destroying the companies. The decision making was horrendous." He hated the use of phrases like, "its just business. It's not personal." To someone steeped in the furniture business like he was, the indignity was intolerable. Rick's father was one of the original owners of American/Drew and and at one time company president. Rick Coffey felt that every decision affecting someone's job was personal. His conscience told him, "you're dealing with people's lives and they (outside management) don't understand that. They think they can brush that stuff off. I just can't."

The quandary of remaining in a business that he loved, even though it was changing for the worse, eventually drove Rick Coffey to the same conclusions it had taken Bob and Michele McCreary. Rick went out on his own, restarting an old factory as his new company. He planned to also "produce private label products." Fortunately, one of the visitors to his High Point showroom was Bob McCreary. What Bob noticed was a product Michele had recommended as a fresh direction for McCreary Modern, exposed wood framed upholstery. She believed that "exposed wood chairs, tables and occasional items are the jewelry that makes the outfit." In the summer of 2000, the McCrearys made an offer that Rick said, "I could not refuse, to purchase Morganton Chair, retain all of my staff and make me president and COO (Chief Operating Officer) of McCreary Modern." The union was a match "made in heaven," as Rick described it. His entire career had been in the production end, while Bob and Michele's expertise was sales, design and marketing. Their synergy resulted in a company three times the size of when they first connected.[970]

The atmosphere drew others to it as well, including Bob's son Robert. Like Rick Coffey, he grew up with a dad in the furniture business. In high school and college, Robert worked summers in the factories with which his father was associated, including McCreary Modern. As he described the experience, "I would load trucks. I did a little bit of (upholstery) spring-up, but I did get to meet the people, and I learned the family type culture that was around there." However, Robert McCreary needed time to explore all his options before considering a return to the family business. After college he worked at Morgan Stanley, a New York based investment bank and financial services firm. Then after earning an advanced degree in business school he started his own company. All the while, his father was asking a simple question, "are you ready to come back?" Each had a different view of when the right time would be.[971]

In his years away, Robert McCreary saw some of the same examples of corporate insensitivity as Rick Coffey had observed. Contrasting what he saw and felt at McCreary Modern with his own experiences in the financial world brought him to an epiphany, saying, "I can clearly understand why corporate America has trouble incorporating family values," a reflection on the mismatch. He also saw what Rick, Michele and Bob were doing to combat the trend. He joined the company in 2012.

Robert McCreary returned to a different McCreary Modern, but only in size, not in sensibility. Abandoned factories found new life as the company revitalized the plants and with it furniture manufacturing in the western end. In 1990, McCreary Frame opened in a 76,000 square foot factory in Maiden, just a short drive down the road from Newton. In 2000, they bought Rick Coffey's Morganton Chair, which despite the name, was located in Lenoir. Then they purchased "the old Regency Home Fashions plant in Conover," followed by an old Kincaid factory in the Lenoir suburb of Gamewell, and built newer, more suitable facilities in Newton, which remained their home base. Each plant offered expanded capabilities in design and variety.[972]

The return of the next generation of McCreary settled some important questions for the company. Beyond Bob's query to Robert about coming back home, without a corporate structure to dictate what lay ahead for the company, customers had began to ask about the future direction of the business. As the years passed without clear succession, who would operate McCreary Modern in the coming decades remained an open question. Soon after he joined the enterprise, Robert was named "CEO in waiting," which settled the issue. The designation gave Robert the room necessary to develop his own perspective on the company, its strengths, challenges, and ultimate direction. Early on as a means to train his son, Bob involved Robert in "some pretty important decisions," as Robert recalled, with the elder McCreary saying, "I want your opinion on this." "I'd give him my opinion, 'well it's interesting, but we're not going to do that'" was Robert's recollection of the exchange with his father. Initially, Robert replied, "well, why am I here then?" only to realize, "low and behold, I would find out later that his approach was much more long term." The time together gave father and son the ability to learn from each other and as a result, create a more seamless philosophy to guide the company going forward.[973]

The ongoing success of McCreary Modern has been substantial. In addition to the expansion of facilities, Bob and Michele have taken the company motto seriously, "Employee and family owned. Community focused." In December of 2008, the couple brought all the employees together for an announcement. Bob gave no indication of the meeting's purpose as he stepped up to speak. During his time at Wake Forest he had enjoyed taking theatre classes and demonstrated some acting talent. With his wife beside him, some had the impression that he was going to announce the sale of the company. Michele noted, "people's eyes got bigger and bigger. I could hear their hearts banging in their chests." During Bob's coy meanderings, she stood it as long as she could before she blurted out, "Stop it! Tell them right now." That's when Bob McCreary revealed their unexpected intention to split ownership of McCreary Modern with employees.[974]

Respecting and rewarding the workers who built furniture had become important, perhaps more so than at any time in the history of the western NC furniture industry. The recognition of the employer/employee partnership with its stock option plan committed 30% of the company to employees and reinforced a belief in the shared destiny of everyone who went to work at McCreary Modern each day. To say everyone was invested in the company would be a bad pun, but a good business practice as many have more in their McCreary stock account than they did in their 401k assets.[975]

Just north of the McCreary Modern headquarters stands a billboard recruiting workers for the company. The sign documents the benefits of working with the "employee-owned family" imploring drivers to "turn around and apply." Inset is President and COO, Rick Coffey (Author's collection/McCreary Modern)

Bob and Michele also personally embraced the effort to be "community focused." Their sponsorship included a myriad of grants to local organizations. Hickory's Lenoir-Rhyne University, Newton's Green Room Community Theatre, Bob's hometown of Hudson, and his alma mater, Wake Forest University all had significant needs met by the McCrearys. "We enjoy taking care of the community and our people and their families," is how Michele has described their efforts. "We are very fortunate to be able to give back to our community and make it a better place. Besides, it's fun!"[976]

Sustainability for many of the furniture companies that prospered in the 21st century came from several important factors. First and foremost, these companies took a different look at the furniture business and adapted both their product and their approach. Partnering with lifestyle brands afforded McCreary Modern the unique luxury of letting retailers handle advertising, the paying of commissions and all the other challenges of getting furniture into the houses of consumers. Valuing the contribution of workers by shielding them from offshore replacement created a trust that helped both management and labor live a more assured existence. This ethical stance harkened back to an earlier era in the industry.[977]

These men extend the legacy of a proud furniture tradition. All work at McCreary Modern, where they have the opportunity to share in the success of the company with stock option plan, in addition to other benefits. (Courtesy of McCreary Modern)

Chapter 34
The Work Goes On

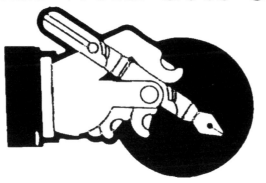

During the early years of the 21st century, only a very few companies had the right formula for success. Operations like Design Foundry, Lee Industries, McCreary Modern, Mitchell Gold + Bob Williams, Sutter Street, even Craftmaster and Southern represented sunny spots in the western region's dimly lit furniture legacy. Most others, especially those corporately controlled, had conceded leadership, thankful they still existed. A few legacy firms retained their ownership much to their credit. Firms like Bernhardt and Century continued what they had done since the last century, operate as a family owned enterprise.

Everyone conceded that the furniture manufacturing landscape had changed. No one operated the way they did a decade or two prior. Reevaluation even applied to Catawba Valley Community College, once tightly tied to training for the industry. The institution questioned the need for furniture education, believing its time had come and gone. When Dr. Garrett D. Hinshaw arrived as the third president of the college in 2006, he surveyed a program that looked like it had reached obsolescence. Commenting on the earlier courses, he said, "the original Furniture Technology program at Catawba Valley Community College served this region for over 40 years and met the needs of a growing industrial sector throughout the United States. The individuals that taught and worked in this program were amazing innovators." Despite the impact of the college, the industry as a whole was in a massive decline when he took over. The school's program took its cue from the manufacturers, which had yet to catch up to the new realities of the economy. As Hinshaw saw it, at the very least, a pause was in order. If the college could not assure graduates of a job, perhaps the program should be abandoned.[978]

The role of the the furniture program had once been a highlight of the school's offerings and firms depended upon it. One of the stalwart instructors of CVCC's furniture technology program since 1994 was D.L. Turbyfill. His career served as a textbook example of learning within the furniture industry. Born and raised in western North Carolina, the Turbyfill name had been prominent in furniture manufacturing for generations. An uncle, "was executive vice president at Vaughn Manufacturing in Galax, Virginia." Clifton Turbyfill, D.L.'s great-uncle spent 45 years rising through the ranks at Hickory Manufacturing on his way to becoming vice-president of manufacturing. After retiring, Clifton moved over to Hickory Chair as a consultant. Clifton's son Basil went through the furniture program at NC State and when D.L. chose a career, he followed suit and also enrolled in Raleigh in the fall of 1977.[979]

During his college years, D.L. took classes from a number of renowned instructors including the esteemed Dr. Anco Prak, who was an "imposing" instructor as D.L. remembered him. In fact, during a random conversation while traveling on a train in Brussels, Belgium some years later, Dr. Prak got into a conversation with a man from North Carolina. After Dr. Prak revealed that he "was a professor at NC State in the furniture program," the man asked if he knew Basil Turbyfill, D.L.'s cousin. From there, Prak lit up, saying that he not only remembered Basil, but also two other Turbyfills from the program, one of which was D.L.[980]

After graduating from N.C. State, D.L. Turbyfill got a job working for his cousin Basil, who was president of Athens Furniture in Tennessee.

That's where he met and married his wife before returning to western North Carolina. He went to work for Cochrane Furniture in Lincolnton, first in engineering, setting up a cost accounting system and then found himself "in the machine room as a supervisor at the age of 23." From there he widened his experience with positions at Clayton Marcus and Craftmaster before coming to CVCC.[981]

"I worked for good companies. All of them were fine," commented Turbyfill on his years in the industry, but it was stressful. "If you're in management, you're going to work 60 hours a week," D.L. said, adding, "that's just the way it is." Instead, he decided, "I wanted to see my son grow up." His varied knowledge with several companies and his education at NC State suited him well for a teaching position. "This program (CVCC) was started because of that program (NC State)." It was a natural fit.[982]

The program he oversaw was a strong asset to the furniture industry in the 1990s. "We had agreements with Kendall College of Art and Design in Grand Rapids, Michigan, which is the premier furniture design school in the US and the world." Down in Catawba County, CVCC's program welcomed students from Ireland, South Africa, the Philippines, and Taiwan, making western North Carolina furniture technology efforts truly international. Turbyfill traveled to Chile and Ireland to teach the same skills he taught on the Hickory campus every semester. Estimates place the number of students who either graduated or gained certificated through CVCC's program at over 2,000 during its run from 1960 to 2006. [983]

Training offshore turned out to be the very thing that eventually spelled doom for CVCC's furniture education efforts. "The industry started moving away" was how D.L. described the events of the early 2000s. He could see where it was going. "Manufacturing has always chased cheap labor," observed D.L., a student of the industry's history. Dejectedly, he commented, "it was devastating, but there was nothing I could do about it." Rather than jump back into an uncertain industry, D.L. Turbyfill "re-upped his skills" and remained an instructor in another area while he watched much of what he had built whither.[984]

A quiet debate took place at CVCC over the future of furniture technology on campus. Relevancy, as with any program the community college offered, was a consideration. Dr. Hinshaw finally called the "time-out," to assess if furniture instruction had become an anachronism. Given some sign of life by companies still producing in the area, there might be a path forward, but the business itself would have to decide. In a last ditch effort, Hinshaw pulled together industry professionals and asked what they needed. They replied that furniture was still viable and needed the school to prepare its future employees, but the program required a fresh approach. The team then went to work, envisioning what a curriculum would look like to accommodate "the future employment preparation for those interested in going into this field."[985]

Intrigued, the furniture community supported the idea with expertise

Governor Pat McCrory at Catawba Valley Community College, touring the Furniture Academy, a reboot of furniture education after a period of decline. The program, also extended to Alexander County, can vitually guarantee graduates with a job in the industry. (Courtesy of Catawba Valley Community College)

and investment. As Hinshaw recalled, "we were able to re-launch a viable program that directly met the current and future needs of the furniture industry." Rebranded, the new effort was dubbed "The Catawba Valley Furniture Academy (CVFA)." The academy model allowed for terms shorter than a two year program, less bound by requirements to teach all aspects of the industry and more concentrated in skills needed for particular jobs. The move paid off quickly. Starting small, graduating classes grew each year. Soon, the program expanded to Alexander County, a service area of CVCC. With space for training, the Alexander Furniture Academy built upon the success of its Catawba County predecessor, to fill a "demand for skilled labor in the region," hardly an expected need in the dark days of furniture's decline, but another sign of life.[986]

The meeting that relaunched furniture education was a strained one, at first. Company presidents sat in a room with their rivals. Each was wary. The president of CVCC remembered the tension. "They wouldn't talk to each other because they were so competitive with each other and had been stealing each other's employees for a long time." He left the mechanics of the new furniture academy to them, since it had to fit their needs. As Hinshaw recalled, "I had to spend a lot of time personally getting them to understand that they all had one problem, a future workforce. We could help them with that if they would allow us to."[987]

One of the individuals at the table that first day was the plant manager of C.R. Laine, Cindy Fulbright. She held the distinction of being the only woman representing a company at the gathering. She also felt the apprehension. "There was a lot of that in that room because we're sitting beside of our competitors who we know have trade secrets that they don't want us to know." Calling the ultimate agreement "one of the most amazing things you've ever seen happen," she agreed that the benefit was worth the effort. The creation of the Furniture Academy required a leader to run the operation, someone who understood the needs of manufacturing. It came a shock to no one, except maybe Fulbright herself that she was asked to become director. As Dr. Hinshaw recognized, "in order to deliver it, I had to have somebody that they trusted in charge of it, and that's why I went and hired Cindy Fulbright." She looked at the move enthusiastically. "What a way to end my career," Fulbright said, "to be able to help other people."[988]

A pioneer in the industry, Cindy Fulbright was one of the first women to manage an entire plant. The climb was not easy. In her twenties, she went to work for Hickory Tavern Furniture, a business owned by the Jones family. When John Jones, Sr. retired, John Jones, Jr. started a new company, J. Royale Furniture. Cindy followed him to the new firm because she felt comfortable in the atmosphere of a family owned concern. While there, a supervisory "lead" job came up.[989]

Over the years, Fulbright had developed her skills in furniture making. Occasionally, her supervisor asked her to fix other people's mistakes. "I would get angry about that to begin with," she recalled, but then started to take a different view. If she corrected the problem, it allowed her to increase her skill set. "I was learning more and more all the time." So when the lead job became available, she felt prepared to handle it. Someone from outside was hired for the position. When she was not selected, she consulted several people whom she regarded as mentors, asking why she was not considered. One told her that she should talk to Mr. Jones.[990]

"Why did you not give me an opportunity to be able to have that job? Why did you have to hire without? Why could you not have promoted from within?" she asked. Standing up for herself and her abilities, she made a good case. Impressed, John Jones, Jr. tried to correct the mistake. "From that conversation, they decided to give me the opportunity to be a lead person," she remembered. From there, she eventually earned the job of plant manager at J. Royale.[991]

As with almost any furniture employee, Cindy Fulbright also faced unemployment when J. Royale later closed. Still a leader, she helped her employees qualify for health insurance since she was able to prove that the North American Free Trade Agreement (NAFTA) served as an integral reason for the shutdown. For a while she attended CVCC as a student, before landing a job with Lexington Home Brands. There she started as a cutting supervisor before ascending to the position of plant superintendent. By then, she held a reputation in the Catawba Valley furniture trade as an experienced manager.[992]

Cindy Fulbright made the most of opportunities when they came. After a year and a half at Lexington, C.R. Laine called, offering a better job. Sonny Roseman impressed her as a "progressive thinker," much the same as she characterized John Jones, Jr. back at J. Royale. At C.R. Laine she said, "We excelled, we did real well while I was there."[993]

Women on the shop floor were not unusual by the time Fulbright entered the business. Chances to advance however, still were. Her work ethic prepared her for all aspects of manufacturing, including the position of plant manager, when Sonny Roseman offered it to her at C.R. Laine. She acknowledged, "I have a different viewpoint than a male does." Analyzing her perspective, she added, "a female has a very good ability to multitask, and can multitask probably better than most men. I think that's the God-given trait that we were given as mothers, that we would have to manage the children and manage the house, and then maybe we had to go to work to help our husbands or whatever." Fulbright put those skills to work on a daily basis.[994]

Over the years, Fulbright's experiences equipped her to analyze the business in ways different from many of her counterparts. Her understanding served her well in her role as head of the Furniture Academy, including its steps to remain relevant in an industry challenged by change. For her, it started with the language used. She believed words that served the furniture making business for a long time came to represent something outmoded. For example, she argued that "one thing we have to do is to change what our perception is of a furniture manufacturing facility." For her, the term 'factory' had connoted to mean "an old, dirty rundown place." For the students she recruited to the Furniture Academy, the emphasis should be changed to reflect a "very clean, facility that has a lot of technology in it." Her approach worked. The Catawba Valley Furniture Academy gained popularity with employers and employees, alike. Importantly, every single student received a job offer the moment they graduated from the program, some even before.[995]

The success of several medium-sized companies and CVCC helped rewrite the narrative of furniture production as the 21st century moved into its second and third decades. Offshoring dealt a massive blow to manufacturers in the area. It took time for them to make a comeback. As with the retooling of furniture training at CVCC, firms looked for a niche in which they could supply a need within the industry. One place Americans had proven superior skills within furniture manufacturing was upholstery. Accepting the loss of producing most case goods, the efficiency and quality of domestic upholstering remained unmatched, which allowed those companies already specializing in upscale upholstery to find their place in a new furniture landscape. Efforts to embody what "reinvention" looked like began to pay off.

The legacy of furniture making in western North Carolina could not be denied. The region that became famous for its output of home furnishings had endured and began to grow again. Even if the glory days had faded, the industry still employed many. In an interesting twist on its past, Hickory's minor league baseball team, the Crawdads, sought to reach out the growing Latinx community in the area by taking on an alternate team mascot. Periodically throughout the season, the Hickory Llamas took the field. The ball club used the alter ego "to embrace the culture and values that resonate local U.S. Hispanic/Latino communities." As part of the design, inside the

Llama's mouth was a chair leg, a nod to "Hickory's furniture-producing industry." Many members of the community found employment in furniture making, further tying the work with the people who make it happen.[996]

As the 21st century emerged, so did the Latinx portion of the population. Data from the Western Piedmont Council of Governments (covering Hickory, Morganton and Lenoir) showed the percentage of the region's population had grown from approximately 5.6% in 2010 to 7.1% in 2020. Statewide, representation is slightly higher at near ten percent. Just under that number (9.4%) were reported employed by Lee Industries in Newton, as an example of the unfolding furniture workforce. Over its 150 year history, industry jobs had been predominately in the hands of white employees but a changing landscape in furniture production widened thought to include diversity as an important goal for the factory floor. Companies like Hickory's Design Foundry created programs to recruit workers from the Hispanic community to "fill hiring gaps." The effort included a program "to bring people from Puerto Rico to Hickory" that not only supplied jobs, but also relocation help with "housing and other resources" to encourage assimilation into the community.[997]

The mindset to create a more inclusive workforce has evolved over time. Catawba County Chamber of Commerce president and CEO Lindsay Keisler cited data arguing, "the more diverse your workplace is, it yields the best talent." Many companies no longer concerned themselves with creating a brand identity for consumers, especially since they made furniture for private labels. Instead, they worked to craft an attractive image for the workers they hoped to employ. In the community where they operated, they sought to build a brand "where people want go to work at a company because of how they treat their people, their benefits, wages, and if they treat people like family," offered Keisler. Catawba County Economic Development Corporation President Scott Millar added that these employers wanted to "attract younger people and people who might not have considered working the sector before" including overlooked populations like "veterans or recovered addicts," not a focus of the industry of old.[998]

Out of necessity, outdated practices in the industry gave way to broader thought. Just as Cindy Fulbright cited a need to revise the language of the factory to reorient perceptions, the new era of furniture production had required recalibration. "I think we are starting to rebound - bottomed out, if you will," was the way Andy Counts, head of "the American Furniture Alliance, a trade organization based in Hickory," saw it. Pronouncing the industry "alive and well." Counts conceded the loss of case goods, along with the some 60,000 jobs that made it, but found hope in the focus on upholstery. He offered the view that "upholstery never really went away." Counts pointed out that American factories "shipped nearly $8.1 billion of upholstered furniture (in 2013), up 3.8 percent from the previous year."[999]

If anything exemplified a new spirit in the industry, it was a third generation pair steeped in furniture making. Since birth, Dee Fry and his sister Cathy found the furniture business to have been a formative part of their lives. As Dee put it, "it was in my blood." Both grew up within the Hickory-Fry Furniture family. The company was started by their grandfather and ultimately taken over by their father and uncles. The 1980s witnessed the family selling out and expecting to walk away, but in 2000, H.D. Fry III (Dee) decided to get back in, building and selling furniture his own way, marketing it on the internet. He started Carolina Chair, an upholstery company that, through its website, gave customers an online option for where they got their sofas and chairs. "Consumers weren't getting anything new, different or better from retail sites than they were from traditional furniture stores," said Dee Fry, about a year after creating his dot-com business. He believed in the direct approach, adding "with us, you're actually going in the factory and buying it." His strategy was fresh in the emerging, but largely unexplored world of furniture e-commerce in the new millennium.[1000]

In a small six-employee factory, Carolina Chair got to work. They touted their "no middle man" advantage, focusing on their output, "instead of spending a lot of money on marketing and fluff," as the company's marketing manager described the emphasis of other firms compared to their own. Dee Fry admitted that his model might be considered an odd way to buy furniture, one where the customer doesn't get to see a chair before buying. He called the sterile encounter "our biggest challenge." A company with only a virtual showroom was new for the furniture buying public, but really not all that different from the way Ed Broyhill III wanted to show his offerings from a catalog in the 1980s. Fry's plan included enticing the uncertain with "free shipping and a 30-day money-back guarantee."[1001]

Carolina Chair had it doubters. One even called up Dee Fry on a Sunday night to tell him that they "couldn't sell top-quality furniture for the prices (Carolina Chair) advertise(d) on the Net." Tactfully, the third-generation manufacturer informed his critic that indeed they could, if the naysayer would "just think about it." Harnessing the new technology of the age was key to delivering an old product in an improved way. Continuing to execute his business plan, Dee and Cathy Fry kept the momentum going, despite objections. In 2017, *Our State* magazine tagged Carolina Chair as one of "four family furniture businesses built to last." The others were Bernhardt, Hickory Furniture Mart, and Century Furniture.[1002]

The Fry siblings were in esteemed company. Smaller by far than the others, Carolina Chair added only three more workers after almost 20 years to continue making their upholstery the old-fashioned way. "A worker builds the frame for a sofa or chair," chronicled one report, while "another cuts the fabric and sends it over to a seamstress, who puts it on the cushions. Someone else assembles the upholstery to the furniture's frame." The process allowed the Frys to customize their output and give their online audience something unique, even if they could not touch it before they bought.

Buyers appreciated the effort. While some Carolina Chair furniture ended up on *The Price is Right*, reminiscent of Broyhill marketing in the 1970s, most of the buzz about the product circulated around the medium where it was offered, online. Cathy Fry called her customers "savvy," saying, "they know how to look on the Internet." With customers from New York to Florida to California, the cyber-word got around.[1003]

Communities across the region began to see their fortunes change, an indication that what seemed like a goodbye to furniture might actually be revived in some form. Communities like Lenoir pondered the future of old furniture buildings, daring to hope that life still existed in them. Not all could be reborn for the industry, but could be repurposed for other use. Along Highway 321 near Lenoir, an elaborately-built showroom, no longer needed with the move of the trade show to High Point was an early relic of the declining industry. With help from a bond referendum and the Broyhill

This building was once a furniture showroom, that in the 1980s was no longer needed for that purpose. Funded by the Broyhill Family Foundation and a county bond referendum, an auditorium was constructed as part of the complex to offer entertainment and meeting space. (Author's collection)

Family Foundation, a concert hall, seating up to 1,000, was added at a cost of $5.1 million, and suddenly, the town had the "best auditorium in the Unifour," according to its first director. The facility was given to Caldwell Community College and Technical Institute for its use and promotion. Broyhill Civic Center began bringing a wide range of culture to Caldwell County, including nationally known acts when it opened its doors to the public in 1993.[1004]

Other Broyhill landmarks morphed into alternative uses as well. In Conover, a "27-acre tract," that once included a factory complex underwent adaptive reuse as the city turned the space into a new facility, known as Conover Station. The former factory and its surroundings became became a "mixed use" campus, sporting a library, an advertising agency and block of offices suitable for rental. The facility also housed Catawba Valley Community College's Manufacturing Solutions Center (MSC). Since the railroad ran by the Broyhill plant in its productive days, a portion of the facility became a train station, anticipating the proposed arrival of high-speed passenger rail service. The grounds around the structure allowed for the creation of a park that featured a walking track and space for concerts and gatherings. A bandshell was erected in 2019 to honor Norman B. Coley, Lee Industries president and son of the founders, who had unexpectedly died five years earlier. The city of Conover "secured $6.5 million in state and federal grants to renovate the property and an abandoned manufacturing building (the Broyhill plant) on it." Once again, the old building served the community anew in a variety of ways that included the MSC. The complex also became a social hub for the city.[1005]

The advent of Conover Station was possible because of tradition set by the earlier Broyhill factory. City manager Donald Duncan believed the success of the property to propel itself forward came from the "population of folks that are predisposed to manufacturing," a reference to the decades of productivity that kept bedroom suites pouring out of the plant. In addition to converting the old factory, CVCC's MSC stood out as a natural fit for the site. Duncan asserted that the faculty could "affect the economy of the entire region and state, as well as Conover." The building that once drove business activity in its day as a furniture producer was expected to do so again, in a much different world and with much different products.[1006]

The impact of the Broyhill plant had come and gone in Conover, but the brand had become indelible. The name drew instant recognition but since its corporate acquisition back in 1980, the identification had lost luster. After declaring bankruptcy, Heritage Home Group sold the brand to Authentic Brands Group (ABG) and SB360 Capital Partners LLC. With the $38.5 million deal also came all the names once owned by Thomasville, including Drexel and Henredon. After outbidding runner-up Big Lots for the Broyhill nameplate, ABG made a deal to spin off the brand.[1007]

The sale revealed the persistence of western North Carolina's furniture legacy. Over the years, the Broyhill name bounced around, "licensed out to others in the marketplace for certain products." With the purchase, Big Lots planned the full return of Broyhill furniture as, quite literally, a centerpiece of the stores. With a variety of accent products ornamenting displays, Big Lots placed its new line in the middle of each location, which improved sight lines and promoted the revitalized furniture line to customers.[1008]

Broyhill's return also upped the game for Big Lots, offering "an excellent brand name" to a new segment of the buying market, according to Jerry Epperson, industry analyst. With an eye toward the long and sometimes torturous journey of the Broyhill brand, he half-jokingly said, "goodness knows several management teams have tried to kill it, but they haven't done it yet." The deal helped Broyhill take on new life in its new home. Retrieved from the bench, the once Lenoir-based family moniker returned from oblivion, lending whatever cachet it had left to a company seeking to use Broyhill for prestige, a novel but encouraging turn of events. Management at Big Lots held high hopes for the move, predicting that the brand would soon become a "billion-dollar brand," bringing in those who fondly remembered the company and its stature.[1009]

The second decade of the 21st century proved to be better for the furniture industry than the first one had been. No longer did massive layoffs spell doom for manufacturing. Granted, as jobs crept back, they were in smaller increments than the previous losses, but still, many analysts would never have believed any would return at all, when the industry started to bleed. Then, another unfortunate curveball hit factories.

The industry had dealt with bad economies, offshoring, and various other obstacles, but nothing could have foreseen what it and the nation faced, when the coronavirus pandemic hit in March of 2020. Immediately, factories shut down as fears of widespread infection became a very real possibility. Employment went down by an average of 30% in a reporting period that started six months prior to the pandemic and extended six months after. The Hickory-Lenoir-Morganton area was second only to Asheville in North Carolina for the most job losses during the crisis. As the summer of 2020 brought no solution to stay-at-home orders, some companies tried to get back in production, a difficult task considering the uncertainty that came with the pandemic. Most employers took a wait-and-see attitude which kept workers sidelined.[1010]

The outbreak caused major disruption the world over, but furniture was among the hardest hit in North Carolina. For many firms, China, a nation that had become a partner/competitor in furniture production felt the effects of the virus first. That caused grave worry on the part of American companies. "All of the supply chain is disrupted," said Alex Shuford III, CEO of Century Furniture. Even before the shutdown of factories, manufacturers like Century felt "ripple effects." Ironically, "most of Century's business is exports rather than imports," as Shuford pointed out, giving Century the opposite problem of most. A significant portion of Century's market were "Chinese customers."

Most companies worried about getting furniture out of China. Century had trouble getting furniture in. COVID-19 hit furniture makers coming and going.[1011]

Newspapers reported local infection and death tolls throughout the crisis, but also kept tabs on how the furniture industry, still the region's largest sector coped with the shutdowns. Like every other business worldwide, Craftmaster closed its factories and sent its employees home. As Roy Calcagne remembered those unprecedented days, the first concern was the workers. He "wanted to make sure they were safe." The company paid everyone for two full weeks even though no one was working to buy time so a plan could emerge. The move cost Craftmaster $1 million but helped keep families whole in a time of crisis. Slowly, Calcagne and his staff started to bring some workers back by June using every precaution against the virus. A few cases, between 15 and 20, erupted requiring even stronger measures to be taken to eradicate the coronavirus from the plant.[1012]

During that period, a curious thing happened; orders continued to roll in. Reports revealed that "backlogs double(d) and triple(d) what they were before the pandemic." The problem proved especially acute for management with more demand for their product during a time when they could not run their factory at anywhere near full capacity. Workers faced added stress too, weighing consequential choices. Some opted to stay home and take care of loved ones while others sought a return to work so they could get a regular paycheck again. Meanwhile, homebound Americans sat on their old sofas as they purchased new ones online. Even with limited productivity, supply worked hard to meet demand but wait times for furniture, not just at Craftmaster but industry-wide, skyrocketed. As work resumed in an unsettled world made so by a disease, delays slowly eased. Each company improvised plans to catch up.[1013]

The business of furniture manufacturing weathered almost every conceivable obstacle in its trek to become a major force in the world economy and a dominant employer in western North Carolina. Each time a difficult situation arose, some portion of the industry survived, figuring out a way to prosper as the times and the economy dictated. Just as with the crafting of a piece of furniture, challenges required reconsideration to overcome the latest obstacle. With ingenuity, manufacturers prevailed, knowing that they were fighting for their economic lives. The successful were unwilling to surrender, refusing to allow the tradition of furniture manufacturing to become a thing of the past. They had done it before; they would do it again.

Throughout its history, the furniture manufacturing business has proven to be as resilient as it needed to be. Winners and losers were never predictable. Even access to adequate capital could not guarantee success. Corporations with deep pockets went bankrupt, causing some of the long-standing names to fall silent. Even as layoffs in the 21st century prophesied doom, the craft of furniture making held on, maybe not to the degree that it once enjoyed, but much more robust than anyone expected in the dark days of 2008, when the region took the double blows of a recession and the loss of its industry. Players new and old created game plans to fit the evolving times. In many ways they were no different from western North Carolina's

This claim could have been made in almost any year. Furniture makers continually asserted optimism even in the most dire of economic times as a way to assure workers that all is well. This ad came from the Broyhill Outlook, a magazine for employees from 1973. (Courtesy of the Caldwell Heritage Museum)

first manufacturers. A successful formula was 'try it. If it works, stick with it. If it doesn't, change it'. They believed that with grit and ingenuity, they, like previous generations of furniture professionals, could meet the trials at their door and devise solutions.

⸻❦⸻

Like many towns that used to rely on the railroad line to bring in wood and take out finished furniture, the railroad is no longer used. In Lenoir, along lower Harper Avenue (a main thoroughfare) the path is paved over, though warning lights to stop traffic are still in place. (Author's Collection)

Chapter 35

A New Deal

"I think there are some fantastic things and some work life balance benefits to an environment like this, to an industry like this. And so you've got to celebrate that."

- Marshall Deal, Wesley Hall Furniture.

The long path of the furniture industry had gone through, saw a variety of twists and turns, just like a piece of wood might as it was molded into use in any given factory, on any given day. Some of those factories endured over time, though their longevity has been anything but assured. However, the human spirit inside those buildings persevered, demonstrating a remarkable resilience.

It may be no surprise that whole families shared in the bounty of furniture making, from working parent to child, along the way leaving practical instruction and a lengthening legacy. Many not only sustained themselves, they prospered. Among those families was one who adapted over five generations, through more than a century and found themselves uniquely placed for the future. Despite repositioning themselves in the business from its hallmark days, the Deal family projected an energy and optimism for whatever laid ahead in an unpredictable industry.

The latest round of furniture heirs has been embodied in a youthful brother and sister duo, Marshall and Emily Deal. They sought to absorb everything they could about how the business had worked in the past as they charted a course ahead, taking the proud craft of building home furnishings forward. Both professionally engaged in the work of the family company, Wesley Hall Furniture.

Just like the family members that preceded them, Marshall and Emily

559

grew up with the business all around. For Marshall, his memories began with trips to showrooms during the furniture market when the Wesley Hall's creative director, Liz Evans fashioned outlandish props to accent new lines. "There would always be a theme," he recalled. "One year there was all kinds of paper mache stuff," he said, vividly remembering the props as his "crazy, over the top" introduction to the world of furniture marketing.[1014]

The family line in furniture stretched all the way back to Edward Marshall (E.M.) Suggs. Born in 1892, E.M. went to work "for many years at Hickory Chair Company," where he did what many other employees did; learned the business of furniture. After the extensive experience he gained at Hickory Chair, E.M. partnered with A.J. Hardin to found an upholstery firm just before World War II. It wasn't until after the war that they officially incorporated as Suggs and Hardin Upholstery Company. The authorization allowed them to raise up to $10,000 for the new works. At the time of the charter, the furniture entrepreneurs only reported $40 in assets. That same year of 1946, E.M. Suggs took part in the purchase of Hickory Fabrics, Inc., a cloth weaving mill where he served as vice-president. Outside his business

This image reveals trends in furniture in the fall 2022 market. Imaginative, eclectic, expansive & varied, these are what buyers saw as they made choices for their retail outlets, the same as they have done for 101 years. The legacy of creative director Liz Evans is still evident. (Courtesy of Wesley Hall Furniture)

interests, E.M. demonstrated his civic-mindedness with successive elections to Hickory's Board of Aldermen, beginning in 1931.[1015]

Just a year after the advent of Suggs and Hardin, E.M.'s son in-law Harold Deal opened Deal Furniture in Hickory with his brother James. In 1959, E.M. Suggs, Harold Deal and James Deal united to begin manufacturing under the name of Highland House Furniture. The family continued its multi-generational legacy when Harold's son Ron started with the company in 1965, a year after the passing of E.M. Suggs.[1016]

Highland House remained very much a family enterprise until sale of the company to Interco in 1986. With the purchase, the St. Louis based conglomerate claimed its position as "the largest furniture manufacturer in the United States," as Broyhill, Ethan Allen and the Lane Co. were also part of Interco's acquisitions. Under different leadership, Highland House chose to indulge in the industry trend of offshoring. The sale marked a temporary end to the Deal's multi-generational run in furniture. It didn't take long however, for a member of the family to feel the sawdust in his veins.[1017]

Harold Deal was out of the furniture business, but his son Ron decided to jump in. A few short years after letting go of Highland House, Ron Deal created another company, using many of the lessons he learned at his father's side. In much the same way that father Harold and grandfather E.M. thought of manufacturing as a family concern, Ron welcomed his own children into the workings of Wesley Hall Furniture. Daughter Anne Deal Bradshaw joined the company in 1999 as Director of Marketing and "equity partner." Once son Eddie Deal finished college at Wake Forest in 1988, he had "a very brief stint working for a large bank and knew that wasn't for me," he recalled. Then, "my father, also a Wake Forest graduate, presented me with the opportunity to be involved in the startup of our upholstery company, Wesley Hall." There, Eddie Deal excelled, taking on various roles that led to the presidency, a position he held until his father's retirement as CEO, when the younger Deal moved into that seat in 2013.[1018]

Wesley Hall Furniture enjoyed the continuity and stable leadership that came from members of the Deal family directing its course, but the company also benefitted from the talents of a number of other key professionals. When Eddie Deal became CEO, Zack Taylor came aboard as president. More recently, "industry veteran Bill McKinney has joined Wesley Hall as vice-president of operations, a new position reflecting the luxury upholstery manufacturers's production and business growth in the past year (2021)."[1019]

One leader who was with the company since its inception handled several jobs. William Whitener's title noted him as Director of Manufacturing, but he also mentored a new breed as they developed. Coming into a business with such a long generational birthright, Marshall Deal highly respected the wisdom William brought to the firm.

> "I think you could count on, certainly no more than two hands, but maybe one hand, people on the face of this planet that have his breadth and depth of knowledge related to this subject matter being how to engineer and build a piece of upholstered furniture and also how to lay out and get it through a plant, a fit with something resembling efficiency."[1020]

The wealth of influences afforded the younger Deals an education well beyond what they received in college. Marshall pointed to a number of people who brought their experiences and knowledge into Wesley Hall, not unlike other furniture operations throughout the region. He cited Zack Taylor for brining "great energy and vision" into the company, as well as CFO Angie Houston, who "grew up in a furniture family herself." Additionally, folks like creative director Darrell Fulbright, a 25 year veteran at Wesley Hall, had plenty to teach Marshall and Emily. They were eager to learn.[1021]

Within the family, it was never assumed that furniture making would become a career for the fifth generation. Marshall revealed, "I felt neither

From a 1999 publication, the Deal furniture family. Father Eddie Deal (COO) is standing (second from the left), while grandfather Ron (Chairman, CEO) is seated with Emily and Marshall Deal, both listed as apprentices. Ginger Miller (center, standing) would go on to work with Em & Marshall as adults. (Courtesy of Wesley Hall Furniture)

forced into it or pushed out of it." The choice of following in the footsteps of his family remained his own. However, there was one incident that might have influenced his decision. As a young man, "I got in trouble for something in school in the sixth or seventh grade," was how Marshall described his first job at Wesley Hall. As punishment, his parents decided that he would spend the summer sweeping floors, cleaning up and bagging scrap cotton, emptying trash, just whatever was needed on the factory floor. The experience gave him his first "appreciation for the people and the work it takes" to keep a furniture operation going.[1022]

For his younger sister Emily (who Marshall calls "Em"), her debut involved an enticement instead of a penalty. Invited to help with a special project, she recalled, "I dabbled a little bit the summer between my junior and senior year of college scanning 20 years worth of spec sheets into the computer." The job promised to aid efficiency at Wesley Hall, as Em described her first experience, "so customer service can pull up specs (specifications) of furniture without having to dig through the filing cabinet." Characterizing herself as a "math person" she demonstrated an aptitude for confronting challenges while enjoying the experience. After that, her grandfather said, "I want to show you how to order fabric," which came in 2019. She jumped at the opportunity, but timing soon made her training more arduous.[1023]

"I was finally starting to get comfortable and not second-guessing myself," Em recalled about the effort just as the COVID pandemic hit. "And so then trying to navigate how to manage our fabric inventory with us having to close down, mills having to shut down, the freight surcharges, the crazy lead times" severely complicated the process for her. She reflected on her initiation into the family business as a time that was "interesting to navigate."[1024]

Unlike Em, Marshall followed a course more like his father. After college, he worked in the corporate environment of Under Armor in Baltimore, Maryland. In that pursuit, he felt fully supported by the family. "Do your thing," was the message he got. However, a change really began after his marriage to another Catawba County native. That's when he reconsidered a life in furniture closer to his roots. Both his father and grandfather were happy to discuss what his role might be. "They spent a lot of time and thought," remembered Marshall about the move, considering the best way to fit him in.[1025]

Both Em and Marshall appreciated the tradition into which they had stepped. Both sought out senior members of the Wesley Hall team to help them understand unexplored aspects of the business. The tutorials ran the gamut from the strategic to the practical, with guides like "Ginger Miller in cutting, Jerry Russell in frame, Rob Setzer in upholstery, and Joel Sigmon in inspection." Each took time to share their expertise. The younger Deals understood the responsibility they assumed regarding the future of the business and the industry. "There's so many people here who still know more than we do, who are out in the factory or in the office," said Marshall about the many tutors he and his sister work with every day. Both have enjoyed the team aspect to their work, relying on the talents of a wide array of professionals, all working toward the same goal of crafting a quality product. As Em put it, "we wouldn't be here without the before."[1026]

While their father may not have expected that at least two of his three children would follow him into the furniture business (a third is just out of school), Eddie Deal taught them something much more important than how to run a factory. "One of my father's least favorite phrases is 'that's not my job'," remarked Em about a long-held family belief that if "something needs to get done, you just step up and do it." The lesson was evident, her brother observed, about his sister's growth within the company. "We needed her to step up and do a lot of stuff." In reply, Em said, "it seemed a bit overwhelming at first, but I know I had tons of people here who would help get me through." She added, "and it's been fun getting to work with my grandfather."[1027]

The mutually supportive world created for the fifth generation of Deals in the furniture industry is one that Em and Marshall have carried forward. The two have developed a keen eye in business, thanks at least in part to the experience they have drawn upon whenever they need. Plus, they enjoyed the process. Marshall confided "it's just fun to be in the room," referring to the inner workings of Wesley Hall. Within those interactions came exciting possibilities which both brother and sister valued. Putting it all together, Marshall said, "it's taking I think, some of the foundational things about what's great about our industry and what's great about what we love about what we do here and just gently massaging those along as we go."[1028]

Like a piece of furniture that came off the line decades ago, maybe even a century past that looks worn and weathered, regained life in the eyes of a rising generation. Instead of antiquated, the beauty and utility of furniture-making is new again. All the industry has ever needed to burn ever brighter was the kind of energized determination that new blood like Marshall and

Em Deal offered. They have committed themselves to the business with enthusiasm, respect, and hard work and vowed to make their product ethically and efficiently. The pitfalls of the industry in earlier eras only informed their path going forward. Taking up the banner of furniture manufacturing in western North Carolina, this new breed has propelled the proud tradition forward with confidence.[1029]

As a side note, one interesting, if coincidental irony of the family is found in their names. The long shadow cast by E.M. Suggs can be found in his great-great grandchildren. E. Deal and M. Deal reflect the initials used by their pioneering ancestor in the furniture industry, a tradition they intend to carry on. They realize that they have benefitted from the cover that shadow has provided, down through son Harold, to their grandfather Ron and father Eddie. The next chapter of furniture history will be written about their time, as they, and their counterparts, step out from under the family shadow and create their own legacy.

Experience equips the next generation. Cutting supervisor Ginger Miller, right, instructs Marshall and Em Deal in the finer aspects of fabrics and patterns. Ginger has been a long-time member of the Deal furniture family (seen in earlier photo) when Em & Marshall were children. (Author's collection)

Epilogue
The Hands

Wood. Oak, maple, cherry, pine, poplar, gum, magnolia. It's all in the western woods of North Carolina. As plentiful as the soil, it grew. For cover, for shelter, for use in a myriad of human needs, wood has always been a resource people could depend upon. So it is no surprise that wood factored strongly into what became the identity of those settling on the eastern slopes of the Appalachian Mountains. Wood, and the taming of it, gave life meaning long before the industrial age came to this mountainous portion of America.

East of the Great Plains, everyone had wood at their disposal. Burn it, build with it, or clear it for crops, pioneers considered the value of the renewable raw material in their lives. Without wood, they would not have survived. The majority of implements in their tool boxes were dedicated to the augmentation of trees to make their existence more livable. And yet, somewhere along the way, an individual here or a group there saw much more potential. As tie passed, no longer was the task of crafting an individual piece for their own family's use a sole consideration. If board feet of lumber could be fashioned into usefulness on a grander scale, money was to be made, employment was to be offered, and the region could find its purpose in the growing and specializing national economy. A perfect plan.

More than a happy accident but less than a grand scheme, furniture-making came along much like any great idea, fortuitously ill-conceived. One step followed another along the path of industrial self-reliance to the point that the foothills of North Carolina sprouted a business model that paid dividends in the products it offered. Fame spread and the work not only provided to the descendants of those who settled in the shadow of North Carolina's mountains, it gave them something to value. Several of the early entrepreneurs had their "big bang" moment when they saw the full potential of devoting all the resources of their region to the work of making furniture. Slowly, the development of an industry in the wood grew only by fits and starts, with times of doubt and failure, followed by renewed hope that citizens could pull together under one banner and have a real impact.

It's staggering to think that even during its height, no furniture company in the United States could claim more than three percent of the market. With numerous "furniture capitals" before them, North Carolina crafters never saw complete dominance in the marketplace the way Ford and Chevy did, or the three television network era of the '60s and '70s, but that meant there was a nation to conquer and plenty of rooms to fill with their factory output.

Furniture making served a vital purpose to the region. It gave western North Carolina an identity. No longer were they looking for a contribution to make in American society. The manufacture of furniture provided them a collective status. Workers put their trust, and their backs, into making well crafted, if sometimes cheap, pieces for use in houses far from their own. They gave it all they had, accepting modest wages and trusted their superiors to grow the industry into something of which they could be proud.

Even if their hands never felt sawdust or their noses never whiffed varnish, the region hung on the idea of furniture making for a central livelihood. In the world of commerce, furniture made every other business possible, from the barbers and beauticians who styled the hair of the labor

Kincaid Furniture, like many area manufacturers, maintained its own fleet of trucks to haul its furniture. Ultimately, the cost of maintenance, along with the drivers was too much. In 1979, Kincaid sold off its fleet, an indicator that the industry had seen its high-water-mark. (Courtesy of the Caldwell Heritage Museum)

force, to the automobile dealers who sold them a new car. If you lived in the area, there was always some connection.

Growing up in western North Carolina, most never realized how firm that connection was. We knew that after 4:30pm each workday, the roads got crowded as the shops "let out." Furnishing our family homes often involved picking up boxed pieces from a warehouse dock where some family member could get furniture at wholesale, thanks to their employment. Most paid little attention to the paternalism of the industrialists, where parks and community venues were named for them, as a present to the towns where they made their money.

In my previous historical inquiries and research, I never flew on a Piedmont Airlines plane, never had polio, and never saw the Ridgeview High Untouchables team play football, but I have worked in a furniture factory. It was my first job. My father drove a truck that carried furniture west, my mother prepared breakfast and lunch as part of a food service company that catered to the first shift at a local factory. My maternal grandparents both worked in furniture, as did many of my aunts and uncles. So it was not a surprise that as soon as I got my driver's license, I would too. Call it tradition.

As a high school junior, I went to class each morning, then in the afternoon, punched in at Kincaid Furniture where I swept, built pallets, and loaded trucks. I made $3.25 per hour for 19 hours of work each week, excluding occasional Saturday hours. While some friends bagged groceries or clerked at retail establishments, I preferred the lack of public contact. What I got instead was a valuable, if sometimes uncomfortable, education in the lives of industrial workers.

A culture was plainly evident in each department within the factory. I was a shipping department person, distinct from the finishing room that I walked through daily from the punch clock to the docks. In my area, the lift drivers ruled. Other than management, these men (and they were all white men) held the preeminent positions. They hunted down items on the manifest in the warehouse, manipulated their squeeze lifts to carry the furniture to the back of the trailer, shoved it in and went for more. Meanwhile, a gang of 2-4 others "grabbed it and grunted," finding the most compact place in the 48-foot trailer for placement. Practical jokes, put downs, and even occasional violence competed with the smell of propane that powered the lift trucks, as stickers affixed to each cardboard box told us where the furniture was heading.

Some couldn't hack it. They quickly moved on to other jobs, occasionally after only a few hours. Others were fixtures. They had been there long before I got there and would be around long after I left. But in the two years I spent observing and participating in the antics that went along with the monotony of loading trucks and taking inventory, I got to know some indelible characters that I'm sure were replicated in every furniture shipping department in every factory in the region and began to unconsciously catalog my experiences.

For many, furniture was a way of life. Their parents had been there before them, and though they hoped better for their children, it was likely those kids would follow them into whatever job the industry offered. Over their careers, they might switch companies for a nickel or dime more per hour as industrial jobs were plentiful in those days and welcoming new blood every day. These were members of a loose brotherhood of workers, most dropping out of high school at 16 to draw a regular paycheck that could buy them a fast car and later raise a family. Often, they wanted more but didn't feel that 'book learning' was their thing. Instead, they gave their labor to the company and took pride, where they could, in their contribution to the larger whole.

The factory culture could be rough at times. Never let anyone know your birthday unless you wanted the legs of your pants forcibly cut from you. A co-worker's weakness was to be exploited as the newcomers got "ragged" for

This snapshot captures workers relaxing from their labor at Hibriten Furniture could have been seen at any factory, at any time. The nature of the job called for employees to find a respite wherever they could. Taking a break without being caught, was a time-honored tradition. (Courtesy of the Caldwell Heritage Museum)

any perceived inadequacy. If coworkers suspected they got under your skin, they piled on the insults, seeing if they could break you. It was a *Lord of the Flies* kind of existence where factions developed, mini-controversies brewed, all while furniture was pumped out of the factory in tractor-trailers and rail cars, along with the occasional pickup truck for employee purchases.

Until you had been there a while, you were targeted constantly. Workers of long standing wanted assurance you could take it; otherwise they would never let you in the 'club.' The jokes were obscene, vulgar, sexist, and sometimes racist. Each person had to figure out how to deal with the situation in order to fit in. Some tried to stay above the fray, while others wallowed in it. Life in the factory got to be so familiar that all one had to do was recite the punch line to get a laugh. "Would I?" was a popular one, whose setup can no longer be quoted.

Up on the rough end where the furniture-making process started, things were scarcely different. A high school friend of mine worked there, and we regularly traded stories about the shenanigans and intrigue that went with groups of people working in a factory setting, their hands but not always their minds devoted to the building of case goods. Kincaid had warehouses from Lenoir to Hudson that stored chairs and we eagerly volunteered for the assignment, with some of us considering ourselves lucky to retrieve that inventory. Being dispatched to bring some back to the main dock was always a task that interrupted the mundane chore of trying to pack furniture faster than the lift driver could deliver it. Everyone, even the lift drivers found little respites that allowed them some time away from the grind. Theirs usually involved filling up the truck's propane tank, which allowed them to take a smoke break, a potentially lethal combination.

The world of a furniture worker was unique. I became a full-time employee one summer, punching in at 7:00am, working until the 9:40 break, when we got ten minutes. Then we put in another effort until the noon whistle blew, signaling the start of a half hour for lunch. At 12:30 we were back at it, our eyes on our watches, anticipating the afternoon break at 2:40 and then the mad scurry that always marked the end of the work day at 4:30, 3:30 on Friday. In between were periods of sometimes great productivity, but often a slog from one task to another as we waited for the whistle, kind of like Pavlov's dog.

If you look at the region, the factory mentality was everywhere. From the school system forward, the idea of compulsory attendance to show management you were committed to the task pervaded just about every aspect of life in the company towns of the foothills. They couldn't help but follow the model created, the one that had run efficiently for decades.

As an adult in 2004, I taught a class on Southern Culture where I pointed out that agrarian life followed a cyclical trajectory, with one season melting into another. Down on the farm, you knew what time of year it was by the work you were doing. Every year followed the pattern of the previous one. In a factory it was quite different. The work was linear and while each day seemed the same, you punched in, you worked, you went home, the itinerary called for progress and a paycheck that helped the leadership reach sales goals, the milestones of which the hands never saw. What we employees got for that was funds for those things we needed and wanted. Loading more cartons of furniture into more trailers for transport across the country was the way to get there, based on a ticking clock. It must have been a stark adjustment for those first farmers to come inside a factory and ignore the warm weather of summer, previously a day made for fishing while the crops grew, what they used to call "laying by time." Now every day had an unending task. Produce more. It's no wonder that the mundanity of whatever job in the shop you were assigned required acting up on occasion to relieve the boredom.

The antics that went on in every department helped to alleviate the sameness and keep workers engaged. The level of mayhem depended on the discipline instilled by the foreman, which varied. We had an ex-Marine who barked and grumbled about the state of things, but generally looked the other way as the hijinks followed their course, all in an attempt to keep the work going. The assistant foreman was older, one of those men who had spent his life with the company and enjoyed telling of the changes he had seen. Much more reflective (and a good cop to the foreman's bad cop), the assistant foreman wore the years of the industry on his face, wearied but thankful that the factory system had allowed him to provide for his children, as they grew up to choose whether to follow in their father's footsteps or find another way.

There was always a pride in closing the door on a well-loaded truck. We then took 15 minutes or so (as much as we could get) to re-energize ourselves for the next one. Those conversations revealed the most about who co-workers were, what they thought about their jobs, and how they saw the world. Often they sized each other up in those rest periods. A few real moments of friendship peaked through amid the verbal jabs of one macho man trying to get the better of the other.

During my time drawing a Kincaid check, I learned much about how the world worked. For one thing, they toughened up a kid who needed to develop his verbal repartee, giving back as good as he got. It also taught me the value of hard, physical work and forced me to make decisions about where I intended to go in life. I gained some understanding of money and what to do with the $40 I took home each week, while the experience gave me insightful tips about how to handle myself in a group setting. Perhaps the most enduring lesson it provided was an appreciation for the working person, whose job was oftentimes one they could perform in their sleep, but they persisted, finding accommodation and pride in their efforts as they showed up day after day. After two years, I decided it was time to move on, so I left the factory, only to be drawn back decades later as a student in search of a local story for my graduate thesis.

As a historian, I already had one memorable occasion to look in on the life and death of a furniture company. I produced and directed a documentary series for the cable television system in Catawba County. The name of the show was *Back Then...* and I took on any subject that presented itself as an interesting story. In one of the 17 episodes (1994-2002) I went to the campus of Catawba Valley Community College at the invitation of Fred Cochran, a deacon from my church. He had spent much of his life in the business of furniture, ultimately becoming a plant manager. His invitation was to attend a reunion of employees from Southern Desk, the institutional furniture maker started by George Ivey, a company that Drexel eventually owned. I brought along my camera. Fred found a number of people, all glad to talk about their time at Southern Desk.

The interviews I conducted were eye-opening. Every single person I talked to told a story of camaraderie and joy as they looked back on their time as a part of the workforce. They cherished the friendships, but just as importantly, the products they made. People told of making sure to be at work every day, even in sickness, to be part of what was happening. Many talked about the pride they felt in seeing their handiwork end up in churches, schools, and municipal buildings throughout the region. They could name them all. I had never talked to individuals so fully committed to their jobs. It rang in contrast to my days loading trucks.

When I later interviewed former employees of Piedmont Airlines for a book and documentary, well after the demise of the Winston-Salem company, I found the same thing. I witnessed lightning striking twice. Both groups loved their work in a way that you just did not typically see in the American workforce. When writing about Piedmont in 2008, I remembered that I had seen it before, at Southern Desk. These were folks who did not buy into the idea of "quitting in place."

At the time, the old Southern Desk factory still stood in Longview. It has since been demolished, just like Drexel's plants in Morganton and in the town of the company's birthplace. For both Piedmont and Southern Desk, these former employees knew the time had passed on the great adventure of their work lives, but were glad to share and celebrate what they had witnessed. The 1999 interviews reflected a world at Southern Desk produced by the World War II generation glad to have a job to sink their teeth into, that gave pride, not just to them but also the community, a pursuit of excellence that other furniture company leadership would kill to claim.

On the other side of the ledger came an experience in 2002. I had only been a community college instructor for a few years. During the same Southern Culture class I was teaching, I got into a conversation with a student who was older than me. He revealed that he was a displaced furniture worker, who had received grants to go back to school. With some dismay, he talked about his years in the shop and how he was now expected to go back and retrain. I remember him saying that the school had put him into a computer technology program. He just shrugged his shoulders, saying he had no real interest in computers. As a trained factory worker, he was expected to be there, so there he was, taking a course that had little to do with what a future job might require. I tried to explain my class in a way that would make it more relevant and he made a strong effort to appreciate the value, but it was evident that he was too steeped in the career in which he had worked all his life to change course and tackle something new at his age, somewhere in his early to mid-50s. He seemed a bit lost. I felt bad, not only for him, but all those others who were enduring the same disruption of their work lives.

This former furniture worker was one of an uncounted thousands of people who made the furniture industry the mighty force it was throughout the 20th century. Encountering them as I did throughout the stages of my life, makes the pursuit of documenting the history of furniture a personal one. They are the people who are the reason living room, dining room, and bedroom suites grace the homes of Americans all across the country. Though they might have seen themselves in a futile job with no real opportunity for advancement, they were actually integral, even indispensable to the process. They were the reason business and economies in western North Carolina flourished. They never got their names on the furniture they made and transported, were never quoted in industry magazines, and never compensated adequately for their toil, but their sweat and ingenuity was in every piece. When they retired or passed away with someone taking their place, they established a legacy that lives on.

This book, the history it includes and the memories it invokes, is for them, "the hands."

It took a cast of thousands to build the furniture industry. This worker from Kent-Coffey epitomizes the character of those who spent their entire lives on the job. He also sports a mischievous look in his eye, suggesting some prank that needs a monkey wrench. (Courtesy of the Caldwell Heritage Museum)

Saws like these were very important to the rise of the furniture industry. Taking raw wood from surrounding forests and adding value brought identity and prosperity to towns like Lenoir, Morganton, Hickory, Statesville and Marion. (Author's Collection)

Acknowledgements

Without the help of so many people this book would never have been possible.

First and foremost is my wife Claudia Ward-Eller. She supported this effort with her kindness, her encouragement but most importantly with her tremendous editing skills. As I got down to what I thought was the final draft, she read it from the perspective of one who knew little about the industry but with her background as a communication instructor, she pointed out places where my words needed clarification. Chapter by chapter she combed through the work (even on our 2022 vacation) to make the pages more understandable. She has my undying gratitude for the effort she put into this, her husband's latest history project.

Also many thanks go to Leroy Lail for his support of this manuscript. He has long been an advocate of the history of furniture in this region and has tirelessly promoted the telling of these stories, some of which he participated in, directly. The industry drew many intelligent people to its ranks, building a foundational presence in the region. Leroy's efforts are a major reason Hickory has remained synonymous with furniture. In terms of innovators, he tops the list, while offering regular encouragement to produce this manuscript.

I would like to thank each of the interviewees who took time from their schedules to offer insight on the business from their perspective. They were there, making a product each day that they and the entire area was proud to say came from western NC. Their expertise made this book more authentic. They include Mitchell Gold, Michele McCreary, Bob McCreary, Robert McCreary, Rick Wilson, Glenn Jarrett, D.L. Turbyfill, Bruce Nelson, Tim Stump, Glenn Hunsucker, Cindy Fulbright, Ed Broyhill, Bill Karslake, Ruth Church, Romey Church, Steve Lackey, Lois Daniel, Ed Harmon, Tony Williams, Margaret Allen, Dr. Garrett D. Hinshaw, Phillip Mosteller, Sonny Roseman, Marshall Deal, Emily Deal, and Ray Keever.

To the many research assistants who have dug out photographs, documents and many other treasures that preserve the memory of the furniture industry, I am most grateful. Thanks to Patrick Daly and Leslie Keller at the

Hickory Landmarks Society, the Historical Association of Catawba County, Cindy Day at the Caldwell Heritage Museum, as well as Steve Hill with the Statesville Historical Collection, the Burke Historical Museum, the Burke County Library, the Catawba County Library System, Patrick Beaver Memorial Library and Patti Holda at the McDowell County Library Archives. Each of these organizations keep something very important to our region and to us. They keep images and information of our past on behalf of all of us. We owe them a great debt. As they might tell you themselves, it's ready and waiting for us to delve into it.

Singular to the research phase and writing of the project was Patrick Beaver Memorial Library and especially Beth Bradshaw. Her offer to host a series on the information I was finding out as I was wrote the book gave me an opportunity to workshop the narrative story line. It took seven sessions over the winter and spring 2022 to tell one version of these events but the series gave me a forum to discuss aspects of production and companies with attendees. The interaction also gave me some important leads. I would never have found Ed Harmon, for example. One attendee said that he knew someone who knew everything about the furniture business in western North Carolina. He was right, as I found out when I met Ed Harmon. For the chain of events that led to meet folks like Ed Harmon, I am most grateful.

To David Moore, who gave me an actual tour of the building that used to house North Hickory Furniture, I appreciate the chance to walk those floors.

I received important background information from a number of individuals who were on the front lines of the industry. Kevin Tolbert provided critical insight and connections on not one but two companies within the manuscript. John Bray has supported the effort throughout and gave great advice on aspects of the story. Plus, he allowed me the honor of seeing his research on furniture history. Alice Lail made an important suggestion about a key portion of the book. Thank you all very much for guiding me through the sometimes tricky ways of furniture company organization.

I owe great thanks to my associates at Redhawk Publications. Editor-in-Chief Robert Canipe and Acquisitions Editor Patty Thompson are the world's best team to work with. Both have supported this project in substantial ways. It is a joy to work with you most every day. Thank you also to Tim Peeler and Aurora King who served as editors.

Great thanks to Dr. Garrett Hinshaw for his support of historical inquiry through the *HandsOnHistory* initiative. His efforts to create the CVCC Furniture Academy are part of furniture industry history as well as the preservation of history through the history section of Redhawk Publications.

A number of students lent their research skills to the project, digging out interesting details on selected furniture companies. Those include Jackson Ammons, Joshlyn Brown, Chloe Bryant, Eli Chellman, Cole Clark, Maverick Davis, Lucas Dunlap, Kylie Ewaka, Shaylee Falder, Katie Foster, Kamonie Frayer, Connor Gordon, Drew Hamby, Emma Huffman, Evan Huynh, Johnathan Jaramillo-Martinez, Brandon Johnson, Megan Lail, Imani Martinez, Keyla Martinez-Garcia, Manny Martinez, Jackson Mullins, Gracin Roseman, Alanna Sigmon, Kaili Sigmon, Kylee Spizzo, and Jaelyn Swagger.

To Melanie Zimmermann, the artist who designed the look of this manuscript, thank you. Your work made a great story even more appealing because of its look. It is great work.

There are several persons who read the manuscript in its earlier stages and offered support and pointers. Primarily, two who were retired from the industry were instrumental. Thank you Earl Wilcox and Keith Orrell. To Jeff and Suzanne Mayo, who took on the entire manuscript and made it all make sense. Their meticulous scrutiny elevated the book tremendously as they caught mistakes I never saw.

As far as any mistakes, either factual or interpretational, those are mine mine and unintentional.

To conclude, I should point out that this book does not reference every furniture company in western North Carolina. To do so would likely swell this volume well beyond its current size. I have sought to find those that throughout the 150+ year history chronicled here, have epitomized the development of furniture making as an industry. There are some that have been left out. If you know of one of these and good history is part of it, hit me up. We can get it into the next edition. The research never ends!

Coming to work in the furniture industry offered an education all its own. During the "golden era" of western North Carolina manufacturing employers like Broyhill offered detailed instruction, especially in its management ranks, about their culture and way of doing business. (Image courtesy of the Caldwell Heritage Museum)

Endnotes

Chapter 1 : The Unexpected Turn

1   Interview with Tony Williams, December 1, 2021, Hickory NC.

2   Tony Williams Interview, 2021

3   Tony Williams Interview, 2021

4   Tony Williams Interview, 2021

5   Tony Williams Interview, 2021; kimballinternational.com/our-history

6   Steve Libby, "Chair Legs Specialty of Williams Wood Carving." National Hardwood
Magazine, February 1998, p.34.

7   Tony Williams Interview, 2021.

8   Tony Williams Interview, 2021.

9   Tony Williams Interview, 2021.

10   Libby, "Chair Legs Specialty of Williams Wood Carving." National Hardwood Magazine,
February 1998, p.34.

11   Libby, "Chair Legs Specialty of Williams Wood Carving." National Hardwood Magazine,
February 1998, p.34.

12   Tony Williams Interview, 2021.

13   nber.org/system/files/working_papers/w21906/w21906.pdf

14   Tony Williams Interview, 2021.

15   Tony Williams Interview, 2021.

16   Tony Williams Interview, 2021.

---◈---

Chapter 2 : Workmanship of Wood, Chisel, and Awl

17   Settlers arriving with family in wagons brought saller items, like chests that stored their
necessities, but larger pieces for storage, like sideboards, cupboards and bedsteads, were not considered
essential since many of those articles could be crafted upon arrival and wagon space was tight.

18   Maude Minish Sutton, "Piedmont N.C. Furniture Industry 150 Years Old, Charlotte Observer,
September 24, 1933, p. 29; Charles J. Preslar, Jr. ed., A History of Catawba County, 1954, p. 17-18.

19   Preslar. ed., A History of Catawba County, p. 55, 57.

20   Edward William Phifer, Jr., Burke: The History of a North Carolina County, 1777-1920,
privately published, p. 240.

21   Nancy Alexander, "Caldwell County's Furniture Industry", Lenoir News-Topic, November 13,
1954, p. 1.

22   The Catawbans, Vol. 1, Gary R. Freeze, p. 7-9; "North Carolina Furniture: 1700-1900", The
North Carolina Museum of History, Division of Archives and History, Department of Cultural
Resources, Robert Winters, ed., 1977, p. 2, 47-48.

23   Lenoir Topic, November 14, 1894, p. 1.

24   Maude Minish Sutton, "Piedmont N.C. Furniture Industry 150 Years Old", Charlotte Observer,

September 24, 1933, p. 29.

25   Sutton, "Piedmont", *Charlotte Observer, September 24, 1933, p. 29.*

26   Sutton, "Piedmont," *CO, September 24, 1933, p. 29; "Furniture-Making is Old Art in State",
Charlotte News, May 19, 1935, p. 58.*

27   Maude Minish Sutton, "Piedmont N.C. Furniture Industry 150 Years Old, *Charlotte Observer,
September 24, 1933, p. 29; https://files.nc.gov/ncdcr/nr/CW0057.pdf, section 8, p. 19. The
National Register of Historic Places application for The Fountain contains a more precise account of
the boundary document.*

28   "Furniture-Making is Old Art in State", *Charlotte News, May 19, 1935, p. 58.*

29   Nancy Alexander, "Caldwell County's Furniture Industry", *Lenoir News-Topic, November 13,
1954, p. 1.*

30   *https://swvatoday.com/smyth_county/news/article_eb3e0bd2-cee1-11e6-9d90-43cf5524aa8f.
html*

31   William Stevens, *Anvil of Adversity, 1968, p. 39-40.*

32   Edward William Phifer, Jr., *Burke: The History of a North Carolina County, 1777-1920,
privately published, p. 241. The southern Catawba plantation belonged to Henry Connor, see https://
files.nc.gov/ncdcr/nr/CT0378.pdf*

33   *https://americanart.si.edu/exhibitions/day*

34   *https://americanart.si.edu/exhibitions/day; https://www.smithsonianmag.com/smithsonian-
institution/the-incredible-true-story-of-master-craftsman-freedman-thomas-day-22569830/; https://
www.npr.org/templates/story/story.php?storyId=128849634; https://www.smithsonianmag.
com/smithsonian-institution/the-incredible-true-story-of-master-craftsman-freedman-thomas-
day-22569830/*

35   *https://ncarchitects.lib.ncsu.edu/people/P000622; https://ncarchitects.lib.ncsu.edu/buildings/
B003507; "Harbison, 101, Oldest Man in Morganton, Dies", Asheville Citizen-Times, August 3,
1957, p. 11.*

36   *Morganton Star, February 22, 1889, p. 3.*

37   Renee Cagle, "Furniture: Burke's Leading Industry", *Morganton News Herald, April 12, 1998,
Section C, p. 1.*

38   L.B. Ivey, "My Memoirs", *Papamoa Press, originalprinting941, digitally reproduced 2018,
books.google.com/books?id=LAOwDwAAQBAJ&pg=PT117&lpg=PT117&dq=
%22azor+shell%22+cabinet&source=bl&ots=tfQhN8jM8z&sig=ACfU3U2
tcCMsCNfhGQ25eFZNSpNIPRCS8g&hl=en&sa=X&ved=2ahUKEwid4-
bkytjtAhWHjFkKHVaYBg0Q6AEwAHoECAEQAg#v=onepage&q=%22azor%20shell%22%20
cabinet&f=false; Maude Minish Sutton, "Piedmont N.C. Furniture Industry 150 Years Old,
Charlotte Observer, September 24, 1933, p. 29; According to one account, Shell also employed as
many as 14 slaves in his operation, Lenoir News-Topic, October 16, 1933, p. 4.*

39   Smith, *The Role of Lenoir, 1968, quoted from excerpt at the Caldwell Heritage Museum.*

40   Nancy Suzanne Smith, *The Role of Lenoir, North Carolina in the Southern Furniture Industry,
Graduate Thesis, Florida State University, 1968, quoted from except at the Caldwell Heritage
Museum, Lenoir, NC.*

41   Maude Minish Sutton, "Piedmont N.C. Furniture Industry 150 Years Old, Charlotte Observer, September 24, 1933, p. 29

42   Michelle Kilbourne-Minor, The Catawba Valley Furniture Industry: The Origins, Composition, and Conditions of Labor, 1879-1939, Graduate Thesis, Appalachian State University,1991, p. 15.

43   L.B. Ivey, "My Memoirs", Papamoa Press, original printing 1941, digitally reproduced 2018, https://books.google.com/s?id=LAOwDwAAQBAJ&pg=PT117&l pg=PT117&dq=%22azor+shell%22+cabinet&source=bl&ots=tfQhN8jM8z&sig=A CfU3U2tcCMsCNfhGQ25eFZNSpNIPRCS8g&hl=en&sa=X&ved=2ahUKEwid4-bkytjtAhWHjFkKHVaYBg0Q6AEwAHoECAEQAg#v=onepage&q=%22azor%20shell%22%20 cabinet&f=false;   Maude Minish Sutton, "Piedmont N.C. Furniture Industry 150 Years Old, Charlotte Observer, September 24, 1933, p. 29; According to one account, Shell also employed as many as 14 slaves in his operation, Lenoir News-Topic, October 16, 1933, p. 4.

44   History of North Carolina: North Carolina Biography, by special staff of writers, 1919, the Lewis Publishing Company, Chicago and New York, p. 103.

⸺⟨⟩⸺

Chapter 3 : The Pivot

45   Stoneman's Last Raid, Ina Woestemeyer Van Noppen, 1961. Various accounts of Stoneman's 1865 raid have been published and are available. The latest in 2010 by Chris J. Hartley.

46   Eric Foner, Reconstruction: America's Unfinished Revolution (1863-1877), This examination provides a comprehensive look during the period when southerners were forced to yield to the nothern pace of business.

47   See Hickory:Now&Then, The Complete History, Redhawk Publications, 2020 by the author for a recap of the town's rise in the region.

48   For an overview of the development of Catawba County towns, see The Catawbans, Vol. 1 by Gary R. Freeze, A History of Catawba County, edited by Charles J. Preslar, Jr.; Richard Eller, Hickory: Then & Now, A Complete History; Richard Eller, Newton: Then & Now, Redhawk Publications, 2002; Valdese, a competitive town to the east of Morganton only came into being after a religious sect, The Waldensians, settled there in 1893.

49   https://www.carolina.com/NC?Towns?Statesville_NC.html; Dwight B. Billings, JR., Planters and the Making of a "New South': Class, Politics, and Development in North Carolina, 1865-1900, University of North Carolina Press, 1979, 9. 48.

50   http://historymatters.gmu.edu/d/5745/. This website includes Grady's funeral story about northern dominance in southern life, epitomizing hsi appeal to create a New South, based on sel-reliance for his region. For a biography of Grady and his message, see "Henry Grady's New South: Atlanta, a Braver and Beautiful City" by Harold E. Davis.

51   The Blue Ridge Blade(Morganton), July 10, 1880, p. 3.

52   Carolina Mountaineer (Morganton), March 31, 1883, p. 1.

53   Carolina Mountaineer, March 31, 1883, p. 1.

54   Blue Ridge Blade (Morganton), October 23, 1880. p. 3.

55   Nancy Alexander, Here Will I Dwell, 1956, p. 192-203.

56   Michelle Kilbourne-Minor, *The Catawba Valley Furniture Industry: The Origins, Composition, and Conditions of Labor, 1879-1939*, Graduate Thesis, Appalachian State University, 1991, p. 16.

57   Kilbourne-Minor, *The Catawba Valley Furniture Industry*, p. 17-18.

58   William Stevens, *Anvil of Adversity*, p. 11; *Morganton Star*, September 25, 1885, p. 1.

59   *Morganton Herald*, February 27, 1890, p. 5.

60   *Morganton Herald*, May 21, 1896, p. 3; *Morgnaton Herald*, April 9, 1896, p. 2.

61   Kilbourne-Minor, *The Catawba Valley Furniture Industry*, p. 28.

62   Dwight B. Billings, Jr., *Planters and the Making of a 'New South': Class, Politics, and Development in North Carolina, 1865-1900*, University of North Carolina Press, 1979, p. 51.

---❧---

Chapter 4 : Stepping Out In Faith

63   *Charlotte Observer (C))*, February 2, 1875, p. 1; *Wilmington Morning Star*, December 11, 1875, p. 2; *Wilmington Morning Star*, September 10, 1882, p. 1; *Wilmington Morning Star*, February20, 1883, p. 1.

64   *Morganton Star*, February 26, 1886, p. 2.

65   *News & Observer (Raleigh)*, February 6, 1878, p. 2; *Laws and Resolutions of the State of North Carolina, Passed by the General Assembly at its Session of 1879*, p. 773.

66   *Lenoir Topic*, June 1, 1878, p. 4.

67   *Lenoir Topic*, June 1, 1878, p. 4; *Asheville Weekly Citizen*, October 17, 1878, p. 4.

68   *Asheville Weekly Citizen*, October 17, 1878, p. 4.

69   *CO*, June 8, 1881, p. 3; *Greensboro Patriot*, February 3, 1885, p. 2.

70   *Alamance Gleaner (Graham)*, November 16, 1882, p. 2.

71   *Observer (Raleigh)*, February 24, 1880, p. 2; *Charlotte Democrat*, May 21, 1880, p. 2; *Morgnaton News-Herald*, September 21, 1905, p. 3 *established relationship between J.W. Wilson and Alex Wilson*; https://www.ncpedia.org/biography/wilson-james-william; *Daily Commercial News (New Bern)*, December 16, 1881, p. 1; *Carolina Mountaineer (Morganton)*, February 20, 1884, p. 3 (*Davidson College attendance*). *Carolina Mountaineer*, April 16, 1884, p. 3; *Carolina Mountaineer*, August 20, 1884 (*graduation*).

72   *Carolina Mountaineer*, August 20, 1884 (*graduation*).

73   *Morganton Star*, March 19, 1886, p. 3.

74   *Weekly Raleigh Register*, April 15, 1885, p. 2.

75   *Weekly Raleigh Register*, April 15, 1885, p. 2; *CO*, February 3, 1885, p. 1; *Daily Journal (New Bern)*, December 14, 1882, p. 2; *Statesville Record & Landmark*, December 15, 1882, p. 1.

76   *Alamance Gleaner (Graham)*, April 2, 1885, p. 3; *By the end of the yewar there is no mention of H.R. Hicks, the enterprise becoming a Wilson and Reid company. W.W. Avery was noted as part of the organization but he was in and out of the ownership structure and an article* (*Carolina Watchman, December 3, 1885*), *refers to him as a "former partner" who was looking to build his own factory in Asheville*; *Daily Review (Wilmington, NC)*, September 7, 1885, p. 4, (*from the Asheville Citizen*).

77   *Morganton Star*, April 3, 1865, p. 3; *Carolina Watchman (Salisbury)*, December 3, 1885, p. 2.

78   *Lenoir Topic*, March 18, 1885, p. 3; *Morganton Star*, May 8, 1885, p. 3; *Morganton Star*, November 13, 1885, p. 1.

79   *Morganton Star, April 2, 1886, p. 3; Morganton Star, March 19, 1886, p. 3.; Morganton Star,* *June 25, 1886, p. 3.*

80   *Morganton Star, February 26, 1886, p. 3; Morganton Star, February 26, 1886, p. 2.*

81   *Morganton Star, March 5, 1886, p. 4.*

82   *Morganton Star, February 26, 1886, p. 3; Morganton Star, February 26, 1886, p. 2.*

83   *Morganton Star, January 21, 1887, p. 3.*

84   *Lenoir Topic, January 26, 1887, p. 2; CO, January 19, 1887, p. 4. Asheville Citizens-Times,* *January 20, 1887, p. 1; Morganton Star, January 21, 1887, p. 3; Asheville citizen-Times. March 30,* *1887, p. 4.*

85   *Morganton Star, March 25, 1887, p. 3; Morganton Herald, November 14, 1889, p. 3;* *Morganton Star, February 26, 1886, p. 3; December 22, 1892, p. 3; Morganton Star, October 24,* *1889, p. 3 (Cumberland Gap Railroad accident). Morganton Herald, March 26, 1891, p. 3 (grip).* *Morganton Herald, April 30, 1896, p. 3 (canal construction); Staunton Spectator, March 11, 1884,* *p. 3; Morganton Herald, March 19, 1891, p. 3; News-Herald (Morganton), December 25, 1902, p. 3* *(railway survey); Morganton Star, January 25, 1889, p. 5 (surveyor).*

86   *The Farmer's Friend (Morganton), November 10, 1898, p. 4; Morganton Herald, January 16,* *1890, p. 3; Morganton Herald, January 16, 1890, p. 3.*

87   *Morganton Star, May 16, 1889, p. 2; Morganton Star, May 23, 1889, p. 4.*

88   *Morganton Herald, April 24, 1890, p. 4; News & Observer, July 5, 1892. p. 2; Marion Record,* *February 7, 1895, p. 4.*

89   *Morganton Herald, December 9, 1897, p. 5; The Farmer's Friend, November 10, 1898, p. 4.*

90   *Morganton Star, May 2, 1889, p. 3.*

91   *The Inter Ocean (Chicago), November 25, 1900, p. 26.*

92   *Morganton Star, February 8, 1889, p. 3; Asheville Citizens-Times, November 22, 1885, p. 1;* *Morganton Herald, May 28, 1891, p. 3.*

93   *Morganton Herald, August 21, 1890, p. 1; Morganton Star, May 23, 1889, p. 2.*

⸺⸙⸺

Chapter 5 : Talk Factory

94   *Lenoir Topic (LT), March 17, 1886. p. 1.*

95   *Lenoir Topic (LT), March 17, 1886, p. 1; LT, April 13, 1887, p. 3. Baldwin's profession named.*

96   *LT, March 3, 1886, p. 2; LT, March 10, 1886, p. 2; LT, January 26, 1887, p. 3.*

97   *LT, May 12, 1886, p. 3; LT, October 27, 1886, p. 2; LT, January 12, 1887, p. 3; LT, February* *29, 1888, p. 3; LT, April 11, 1888, p. 3.*

98   *Robert D. Walker, Jr., "Can't and Never Will: Remembering the Carolina and Northwestern",* *from A History of Railroading in North Carolina by Cary Franklin Poole, Overmountain Press, 1995,* *p. 58-63.*

99   *LT, December 12, 1888, p. 3.*

100   *LT, February 6, 1889, p. 3; LT, January 23, 1889, p. 3.*

101   *LT, March 6, 1889, p. 3.*

102   *LT, March 6, 1889, p. 2.*

103   *LT, March 20, 1889, p. 3; LT, April 3, 1889, p. 3; LT, March 20, 1889, p. 3.*

104   *LT, March 27, 1889, p. 3.*

105   *LT, April 3, 1889, p. 2.*

106   *LT, April 10, 1889, p. 4; For a full background on Tompkins, see George T. Winston's Daniel Augustus Tompkins, A Builder of the New South, 1920.*

107   *https://www.ncpedia.org/biography/harper-george-washington*

108   *Caldwell Messenger, October 2, 1875, p. 3; LT, May 10, 1877, p. 3; LT, October 13, 1877, p. 3.*

109   *LT, January 6, 1881, p. 3.*

110   *LT, October 13, 1881, p. 3; LT, March 15, 1882, p. 3; LT, January 3, 1883, p. 3; www.hpo. ncdcr.gov/nr/CW0423.pdf, p. 8, section 8, application for historic preservation of Bernhardt Planing Mill and Box Factory includes biographical information on J.M. Bernhardt derived from Bernhardt and Harper alumni files at Davidson College, Davidson, NC; LT, January 8, 1884, p. 2; LT (advert), April 7, 1877, p. 3; LT, November 27, 1887, p. 3; LT, December 7, 1887, p. 3.*

111   *LT, March 31, 1881, p. 3; LT, August 11, 1881, p. 3; LT, July 26, 1882, p. 3. Hickory Press, April 5, 1894. p. 5; LT, April 4, 1894. p. 3.*

112   *Lenoir Topic (LT), April 10, 1889, p. 3; LT, May 1, 1889, p. 3; LT, May 22, 1889, p. 3; LT, May 8, 1889, p. 3; LT, May 15, 1889, p. 3.*

---❧---

Chapter 6: Sweet Music

113   *LT, April 24, 1889, p. 3.*

114   *LT, April 24, 1889, p. 3.*

115   *LT, April 24, 1889, p. 3.*

116   *New Era (Shelby), April 19, 1889, p. 3; Alamance Gleaner, May 2, 1889, p. 2.*

117   *LT, May 8, 1889, p. 2; LT, May 8, 1889, p. 3; LT, July 24, 1889, p. 3.*

118   *LT, May 8, 1889, p. 3.*

119   *LT, May 29, 1889, p. 3; Wilmington Morning Star, May 29, 1889, p. 3; LT, June 5, 1889, p. 3; LT, July 24, 1889, p. 3; LT, October 23, 1889, p. 3; Nancy Alexander (column), "Employe of the First Factory", Lenoir News-Topic, June 15, 1964, p. 6.*

120   *The Falcon (Elizabeth City), May 17, 1889, p. 1.; Morganton Star, May 23, 1889, p. 2.*

121   *LT, October 30, 1889, p. 3*

122   *LT, January 8, 1890, p. 3.*

123   *LT, March, 12, 1890, p. 3.*

124   *Asheville Citizen-Times, February 20, 1890, p. 4.*

125   *Asheville Citizen-Times, February 1, 1890, p. 2.*

126   *LT, May 7, 1890, p. 3; LT, May 14, 1890, p. 3.*

127   *LT, May 7, 1890, p. 3.*

128   *LT, March 26, 1890, p. 3; Alamance Gleaner, April 17, 1890, p. 2; LT, June 11, 1890, p.3; LT, June 18, 1890, p. 3.*

129   *LT, July 2, 1890, p. 3; LT, June 11, 1890, p. 3; LT, August 27, 1890, p. 3; LT, July 2, 1890, p. 3; LT, September 10, 1890, p. 3; LT, September 17, 1890, p. 3 4; LT, September 26, 1890, p. 4.*

130   *Statesville Record and Landmark, March 13, 1890, p. 2; Wilmington Morning Star, March 14, 1890, p. 3; Charlotte News, March 15, 1890, p. 5; Asheville Citizen-Times, March 18, 1890, p.1;*

Morganton Herald, August 21, 1890, p. 1.

⸺⬥⬥⬥⸺

Chapter 7: Score One More for Lenoir

131   *Lenoir Topic (LT), November 19, 1890, p. 3.*

132   *LT, October 1, 1890, p. 3; LT, November 19, 1890, p. 3.*

133   *LT, September 11, 1889, p. 3.*

134   *LT, July 2, 1890, p. 3.*

135   *LT, January 7, 1891, p. 3; LT, May 31, 1891, p. 3.*

136   *LT, October 1, 1890, p. 3.*

137   *LT, July 29, 1891, p. 3; LT, May 27, 1880, p. 3; LT, March 14, 1888, p. 2; LT, April 22, 1885, p. 2; LT, February 29, 1888, p. 3; LT, May 6, 1891, p. 3; Hickory Press, June 8, 1992, p. 1; LT, December 13, 1893, p. 2.*

138   *LT, November 26, 1890, p. 3.*

139   *LT, December 10, 1890, p. 3; LT, December 17 & 24, 1890, p. 3.*

140   *LT, December 17 & 24, 1890, p. 3.*

141   *Nancy Alexander, "Employe of the First Factory, Lenoir News-Topic, June 15, 1964, p. 6; LT, February 4, 1891, p. 3.*

142   *LT, April 28, 1891, p. 3; LT, April 29, 1891, p. 3; LT, July 8, 1891, p. 3. LT, October 14, 1891, p. 3; LT, August 5, 1891, p. 3.*

143   *LT, October 14, 1891, p. 2. LT, May 9, 1883, p. 3; LT, October 31, 1883, p. 3. LT, August 12, 1885, p. 3; LT, August 19, 1885, p. 2; LT, January 27, 1886, p. 3; July 29, 1878, p. 4; LT, November 21, 1888, p. 4.*

144   *LT, September 9, 1891, p. 3.*

145   *LT, January 6, 1892, p. 3; LT, January 13, 1892, p. 3.*

146   *LT, August 24, 1892, p. 3; LT, June 8, 1892, p. 3; Weekly Charlotte Observer, March 24, 1892, p. 3; LT, January 11, 1893, p. 3.*

147   *LT, July 27, 1892, p. 3; LT, May 17, 1893, p. 3.*

148   *LT, October 12, 1892, p. 3; Asheville Citizen-Times, October 13, 1892, p. 2; Daily Concord Standard, October 2, 1892, p. 1.*

149   *Asheville Citizen-Times, October 13, 1892, p. 2.*

150   *LT, April 26, 1893, p. 3.*

151   *LT, May 31, 1893, p. 3; http://www.tarheelpress.com/CNW5.html. For a more in-depth understanding of railroading in northwestern North Carolina, see the works of Matt Bumgarner and his series of books on the Carolina and Northwestern Railroad, through Tarheel Press.*

152   *Western Sentinel (Winston), October 26, 1893, p. 1; Western Sentinel, November 30, 1893, p. 4.*

153   *Western Sentinel, October 26, 1893, p. 1; Western Sentinel, November 30, 1893, p. 4.*

154   *Charlotte Observer, April 28, 1894, p. 4; LT, July 4, 1894, p. 3 (a dam broke); Morganton Herald, September 13, 1894, p. 1 (wreck); LT, January 8, 1896, p. 1.*

155   *LT, May 24, 1893, p. 3.*

156   *LT, May 31, 1893, p. 3; LT, September 20, 1893, p. 1; LT, October 10, 1894, p. 1.*

157 LT, October 4, 1893, p. 2

158 LT, October 4, 1893, p. 2.

159 LT, May 30, 1894, p. 3; LT, August 22, 1894, p. 3; LT, October 17, 1894, p. 3; LT, October 24, 1894, p. 3; For background on the Renn Brothers, https://www.ncpedia.org/furniture/industrial-age; LT, October 31, 1894, p. 3.

160 Hickory Press, March 5, 1896, p. 4; Charlotte Democrat, February 28, 1896, p. 3.

161 LT, May 13, 1896.

162 Morganton Herald, October 15, 1896, p. 1.

163 LT, February 16, 1897, p. 3; LT, June 22, 1897, p. 3.

164 LT, March 16, 1898, p. 3; Burke County News, February 23, 1900, p. 2; Burke County News, March 2, 1900, p. 2.

165 Burke County News, March 2, 1900, p. 2.

―❦―

Chapter 8: New Players

166 News and Observer (Raleigh), July 27, 1907, p. 2

167 https://www.ncpedia.org/piedmont-wagon-company

168 Newton Enterprise, January 18, 1901, p. 3; Hickory Press, July 13, 1893, p. 11.

169 https://www.ancestry.com/family-tree/person/tree/57562912/person/382039235195/facts; Jerome Dowd, Sketches of Prominent Living North Carolinians, Edwards & Broughton, 1888, p. 262-4. Karen L. Clinard, Richard Russell, My Dear Father and Mother: The Personal Letters of Livingston N. Clinard, Reminiscing Books, 2007, p. 122, 128; By all indications George W. Hall was the nephew of J.G. Hall, who became president of Piedmont Wagon prior to G.W. Hall's creation of Hickory Furniture.; Charles Preslar, A History of Catawba County, Catawba County Historical Association, p. 486.

170 Charlotte Observer (CO), July 16, 1901, p. 6; Preslar, A History of Catawba County, CCHA, p. 487; CO, November 3, 1901, p. 12.

171 Piedmont Press, October 2, 1875, p. 3; Blue Ridge Blade (Morganton), August 2, 1879, p. 3; CO, December 18, 1886, p. 1.

172 Wilmington Morning Star, August 29, 1883, p. 1; Morganton Star, March 27, 1885, p. 2; Wilmington Morning Star, May 30, 1886, p. 3; Alamance Gleaner (Graham), May 22, 1890, p. 2; Hickory Press, July 4, 1895, p. 8; Newton Enterprise, April 24, 1896, p. 8; Hickory Press, December 10, 1896, p. 5.

173 Weekly Raleigh Register, April 15, 1885, p. 2., The Daily Journal (New Bern), April 15, 1885

174 CO, July 20, 1901, p. 8; Asheville Citizen-Times, July 23, 1901, p. 3. Announcement of the charter also included notification that the capitalization was $100,000, twice what was previously announced; CO, August 4, 1901, p. 2.

175 CO, November 3, 1901, p. 12; Charlotte News, February 6, 1902, p. 2.

176 Charlotte News, February 6, 1902, p. 2; CO, July 26, 1901, p. 2; Hickory Press, January 8, 1890, p. 7; CO, November 3, 1901, p. 12; Some reporting of the era listed W.B. Menzies, brother of K.C. as president of Hickory Furniture, which may have seemed accurate as K.C. remained president of the First National Bank of Hickory during the same time. However, an account of the bank from

1909 clearly states K.C. served as president, see Hickory Democrat, August 26, 1909, p. 4; Raleigh Morning Post, February 18, 1902, p. 6.

177   The Intelligencer (Anderson, SC), August 23, 1893, p. 3; Intelligencer, March 3, 1897, p. 2; Greenville News, December 25, 1901, p. 5; Daily Concord Standard, November 14, 1899, p. 4. Thomas J. Martin was originally from Pelzer, SC but moved to Chester sometime before 1899 where he became a merchant in the commodity of cotton oil. Charlotte Observer, November 3, 1901, p. 12.

178   CO, August 22, 1901, p. 3; CO, July 20, 1901, p. 8

179   CO, July 30, 1901, p. 4; CO, August 21, 1901, p. 2.

180   CO, August 21, 1901, p. 2; Times-Mercury (Hickory), December 18, 1901, p. 5.

181   Michelle Kilbourne-Minor, The Catawba Valley Furniture Industry: The Origins, Composition, and Conditions of Labor, 1879-1939, Graduate Thesis, Appalachian State University,1991, p. 32.

182   Charlotte News, November 20, 1901, p. 1; CO, November 20, 1901, p. 1; Charlotte News, November 20, 1901, p. 1; CO, November 21, 1901, p. 6.

183   The Morning Post (Raleigh), December 19, 1900, p. 3; CO, November 20, 1901, p. 5.

184   Statesville Record and Landmark, February 2, 1883, p. 3; The Farmer and Mechanic (Raleigh), March 26, 1884, p. 4; CO, February 27, 1884, p. 3; CO, June 19, 1886, p. 1; Greensboro North State, July 22, 1886, p. 4; Smithfield Herald, February 19, 1887, p. 3; Concord Times, November 22, 1889, p. 2; Statesville Record & Landmark, January 22, 1891, p. 7; Statesville Record & Landmark, January 28, 1892, p. 4; Ralph Sloan, "Key Tobacco Company Operations, Among Firms Leading to Industrial Growth", Statesville Record & Landmark, July 1, 1975, p. 4; https://www.statesville.com/news/out-of-our-past-nov/article_d8a2226a-66c4-11e4-ac34-001a4bcf6878.html; https://www.ancestry.com/family-tree/person/tree/9286697/person/24438815478/facts. Philip Barton Key was cousin also to another Philip Barton Key, who was the victim of murder at the hands of Congressman Daniel Edgar Sickles. Sensationalized as the "crime of the century" Sickles found out his wife and Key were engaged in an affair. After forcing his wife to confess, the congressman, later Civil War general, spotted Key signaling for another assignation in front of his rented home across from the White House in Washington, D.C. Later claiming temporary insanity, Sickles shot Key then turned himself in. At the time Philip Barton Key was District Attorney of Washington, D.C. The trial turned on Sickles right to protect the marriage bed and his plea of temporary insanity became the first in national jurisprudence to be successful.

185   Statesville Record and Landmark, December 28, 1900, p. 3; Carolina Mascot (Statesville), January 31, 1901, p. 3; Statesville Record and Landmark, November 22, 1901, p. 3.

186   Statesville Record and Landmark, January 2, 1903, p. 3; News and Observer (Raleigh), January 7, 1903, p. 4; Statesville Record and Landmark, January 9, 1903, p. 2.

187   The Weekly High Point Enterprise, January 9, 1903, p. 3.

188   https://www.livingplaces.com/NC/Iredell_County/Statesville_City/East_Broad_Street-Davie_Avenue_Historic_District.html; CO, September 22, 1912, p. 21.

189   Carolina Watchman (Salisbury), April 4, 1906, p. 1; Evening Mascot (Statesville), December 23, 1908, p. 1; Evening Mascot (Statesville), January 1, 1909, p. 1; Statesville Sentinel, August 17, 1911, p. 3; Statesville Sentinel, August 21, 1911, p. 3; Charlotte News, December 6, 1919, p. 10; Greensboro Daily News, December 6, 1919, p. 8.

190   *Statesville Record and Landmark, April 22, 1904, p. 3; Statesville Daily Record, June 22, 1934, p. 1.*

191   *Statesville Record and Landmark, January 29, 1904, p. 3.*

192   "Products of Factories Run Into Million", *CO, April 22, 1923, p. 38; "Statesville Goods Shown", CO, January 24, 1924, p. 32.*

193   https://www.lincolntimesnews.com/news/cochrane-furniture-to-close/article_4db8f675-cd35-56c4-8b8a-af2200c06921.html ; https://www.woodworkingnetwork.com/magazine/fdmc-magazine/new-furniture-manufacturer-brings-it-back-home;

194   *CO, October 28, 1904, p. 3; Hickory Democrat, August 26, 1909, p. 4.*

~~⚜~~

Chapter 9: A Mighty Behemonth

195   *News and Observer, November 12, 1903, p. 2; News-Herald, (NH), (Morganton), November 19, 1903, p. 3.*

196   *Reflections: 1903-1963, p. 10, 21, 74.*

197   *Reflections: 1903-1963, p. 20.*

198   *Morning Post (Raleigh), July 21, 1904, p. 6; Charlotte Observer (CO), August 19, 1904, p. 3; NH, July 27 1905, p. 3.*

199   *NH, September 7, 1905, p. 3.*

200   "Two Ways" Letter to the Editor, *NH, September 21, 1905, p. 2.*

201   *NH, March 22, 1906, p. 1.*

202   *NH, December 13m 1906, p. 5; NH, December 20, 1906, p. 7.*

203   *NH, January 31, 1907, p. 3.*

204   *Reflections: 1903-1963, p. 75.*

205   *Raleigh Times, November 6, 1905, p. 2; Charlotte Observer, November 7, 1905, p. 1; NH, November 9, 1905, p. 3; Semi-Weekly Messenger (Wilmington), November 10, 1905, p. 6; Asheville Times, November 14, 1905, p. 4; Edward William Phifer, Jr., Burke: The History of a North Carolina County, 1777-1920, privately published, p. 241-244.*

206   *NH, June 27, 1907, p. 3; Charlotte News, February 8, 1908, p. 4.*

207   *NH, July 18, 1907, p. 2; NH, July 18, 1907, p. 3; NH, April 1913, p. 2.*

208   *NH, December 10, 1910, p. 3.*

209   *NH, June 10, 1915, p. 5; NH, January 20, 1916.*

210   https://drive.google.com/file/d/1How6JlO8l-MFqX18MGcnvIH-6ZTZi70s/view

211   *Evening Chronicle (Charlotte), October 10, 1913, p. 4; Wilmington Morning Star, October 12, 1913, p. 13.*

212   *NH, October, 27, 1910, p. 4; Greensboro Patriot, November 3, 1910, p. 4; Marion Progress, November 3, 1910, p. 1; Newton Enterprise, November 3, 1910, p. 3.*

213

214   *Edward William Phifer, Jr., Burke: The History of a North Carolina County, 1777-1920, privately published, p. 244.*

215   *Reflections: 1903-1963, p. 22-23.*

216   *Reflections: 1903-1963, p. 23-24.*

217 *http://law2.umkc.edu/faculty/projects/ftrials/conlaw/drexel.html; http://sites.gsu.edu/us-constipedia/bailey-v-drexel-furniture-co-1922/; https://www.ncpedia.org/anchor/child-labor-laws-north.*

218 *Reflections: 1903-1963, p. 23-24.*

219 *https://www.ncpedia.org/biography/huffman-robert-obediah; Reflections: 1903-1963, company publication, p. 27.*

220 *Reflections: 1903-1963, p. 28-29.*

221 *Reflections: 1903-1963, p. 30.*

⸺⧼⧽⸺

Chapter 10: A Buxon Mountain Queen

222 *Charlotte News, April 24, 1905, p. 1; Morning Post (Raleigh), April 25, 1905, p. 8; Wilmington Morning Star, April 26, 1905, p. 3; Weekly News (Lenoir), April 28, 1905, p. 3; Weekly News (Lenoir), October 20, 1905, p. 3; Weekly News, December 14, 1905, p. 3; Weekly News, January 12, 1906, p. 3 Morganton News Herald, March 1, 1906, p. 1.*

223 *Weekly News, March 23, 1906, p. 3; Weekly News, April 13, 1906, p. 3.*

224 *Morganton News-Herald, April 27, 1905, p. 1.*

225 *Statesville Record and Landmark, July 24, 1906, p. 3; Weekly News, April 27, 1906, p. 5.*

226 *"Lenoir Is To Have Another Factory", Raleigh Times, May 24, 1907, p. 6.*

227 *Michelle Kilbourne-Minor, The Catawba Valley Furniture Industry: The Origins, Composition, and Conditions of Labor, 1879-1939, Graduate Thesis, Appalachian State University, 1991, p. 33, 44-5.*

228 *Lenoir Topic, June 21, 1907, p. 3. Charlotte News, April 26, 1905, p. 1; Morning Post, June 3, 1905, p. 8; Weekly News, January 19, 1906, p. 3; Newton Enterprise, May 16, 1907, p. 4.*

229 *History of North Carolina: North Carolina Biography, by special staff of writers, Lewis Publishing Company, Chicago and New York, 1919, p. 103-4.*

230 *Gastonia Gazette, October 24, 1905, p. 2; Charlotte Observer, January 4, 1906, p. 3; Raleigh Times, January 11, 1906, p. 6. Weekly News, May 18, 1906, p. 5; Charlotte Observer, August 1906, p. 6.*

231 *Lenoir News, August 7, 1906, p. 1; "Boy Hurled to Instant Death", Raleigh Times, August 30, 1906, p. 3.*

232 *Lenoir Topic (LT), January 21, 1908, p. 3; LT, July 7, 1908, p. 3; Wilmington Morning Star, November 22, 1908, p. 8; LT, May 18, 1909, p. 3.*

233 *Concord Daily Tribune, January 14, 1909, p. 3; Charlotte Observer, January 16, 1909, p. 9; Raleigh Times, March 30, 1909, p. 8; Evening Chronicle (Charlotte), March 31, 1909, p. 1; News-Herald (Morganton), April 15, 1909, p. 1; LT, May 18, 1909, p. 3; LT, July 9, 1909, p. 3; https://arts.ncsu.edu/wp-content/uploads/2019/01/ANCS_Spring19_final_web.pdf*

234 *The Dispatch (Lexington), February 21, 1900, p. 3; John Hawkins, "The Rest of the Story of T.J. Stone" LNT, Caldwell Heritage Museum Collection; http://www.waitsel.com/art_and_style/T_J_Stone_Furniture.html; https://arts.ncsu.edu/wp-content/uploads/2019/01/ANCS_Spring19_final_web.pdf. In Spring 2019, an exhibition of his work was presented for the first time in North Carolina at the Gregg Museum of Art and Design at North Carolina State University, Raleigh,*

NC, March 21-September 8, 2019.

235 http://www.waitsel.com/art_and_style/T_J_Stone_Furniture.html

236 https://patents.google.com/patent/US2983931

237 https://www.findagrave.com/memorial/191201206/tilden-j-stone

238 http://www.waitsel.com/art_and_style/T_J_Stone_Furniture.html

239 LT, September 28, 1909, p. 3; Charlotte News, September 30, 1909, p. 3.

240 Charlotte Observer, May 19, 1910, p. 16.

241 "Chair Factory Burned", Raleigh Times, November 21, 1910, p. 5; "Plant of Lenoir Chair Co. Is Destroyed by Flames", Charlotte Observer, November 21, 1910, p. 1.

242 Evening Chronicle (Charlotte), December 10, 1910, p. 4.

243 "Two Years For Burning A Factory", Evening Chronicle (Charlotte), March 4, 1911, p. 4.

244 Raleigh Times, December 27, 1910, p. 8; "Stone-Kerley at Lenoir", Charlotte Observer, December 31, 1910, p. 8.

245 Weekly News, November 3, 1905, p. 2; https://en.wikipedia.org/wiki/Lenoir,_North_Carolina

246 News & Observer (Raleigh), March 16, 1906, p. 4; Lenoir News, August 7, 1906, p. 1.

247 "Guarantee Fund Lands Chair Co.", Hickory Democrat, October 11, 1911, p. 1.

248 Guarantee Fund Lands Chair Co.", Hickory Democrat, October 11, 1911, p. 1.

249 Guarantee Fund Lands Chair Co.", Hickory Democrat, October 11, 1911, p. 1; "State News", The Caucasian (Clinton, NC), October 19, 1911, p. 6; "New Enterprises", Raleigh Times, November 2, 1911, p. 2; "Oak Lumber Wanted" (advert), Hickory Democrat, July 11, 1912, p. 4.

250 Dr. R. Wood Brown, "Hickory's Enterprises: Brief Sketches of the Manufacturing Plants of This City", Times-Mercury, June 19, 1912, p. 1. Dr. Brown gives a numerous examples of the working going on at Martin including glue usage (1200 lbs. per month), intricacy of drawer construction (ten pieces of wood are part of each front), number of employees working on an individual piece (ten on a bureau), and production output ("80 different kinds of dressers, side boards, washstands, chiffoineers, chifforobes, beds and princess dressers").

251 Dr. R. Wood Brown, "Hickory's Enterprises", Times-Mercury, June 19, 1912, p. 1.

252 Dr. R. Wood Brown, "Hickory's Enterprises", Times-Mercury, June 19, 1912, p. 1.

--~⧉~--

Chapter 11: Heirs to the Major

253 LT, March 29, 1899, p. 3; Weekly News, August 14, 1903, p. 3; Charlotte Observer, April 21, 1907, p. 13; News and Observer, April 21, 1907, p. 13; North Wilkesboro Hustler, June 21, 1907, p. 5; News and Observer, July 7, 1908, p. 5.

254 News and Observer, January 28, 1903, p. 1; Weekly News, February 27, 1903, p. 3; "The Appalachian Training School" (editorial), Weekly News, October 9, 1903, p. 2; Charlotte Observer, February 13, 1907, p. 6. LT, August 13, 1907, p. 3; "Hard Up For Thunder", News and Observer, October 21, 1906, p. 1. Bernhardt, a Democrat is being defended by a number of papers statewide from Republican allegations that wants to be a commissioner of public roads to benefit his business interests. The papers do not deny that Bernhardt is indeed attempting to do so. They argue that given he amount of business he has created Bernhardt has every right to pursue his interests; LT, September 28, 1909, p. 3.

255 *Lincoln County News*, January 4, 1907, p. 1.

256 "Moore Furniture Factory Sold", *Watauga Democrat*, January 5, 1911, p. 4.

257 LT, December 16, 1913, p. 1. *Charlotte News*, February 14, 1914, p. 8; *Charlotte Observer*, November 30, 1914, p. 8.

258 *Morganton News-Herald*, May 12, 1912, p. 1; *Greensboro Daily News*, December 13, 1912, p. 10; William Stevens, *Anvil of Adversity:Biography of a Furniture Pioneer*, Popular Library, New York, 1968, p. 70-71.

259 Stevens, *Anvil of Adversity*, p. 65, 70-72. William Stevens, the son-in-law of Ed Broyhill provides an insider look at the Broyhill Furniture dynasty. Though intended to spotlight his father-in-law, the book also chronicles T.H. (Tom) Broyhill who is the family pioneer into the world of furniture production. When Ed, 15 years younger than Tom began in the furniture business he did so in the Lenoir Furniture Corporation.

260 "Incorporations", *News and Observer*, July 28, 1905, p. 5.

261 John Hawkins, "The History of Lenoir Veneer Company", *Lenoir News-Topic*, January 15, 2005, Collection of Caldwell Heritage Museum, Lenoir, NC.

262 *Weekly News*, October 27, 1905, p. 3; *Weekly High Point Enterprise*, September 12, 1906, p. 4; "$20,000 Fire at Lenoir", *Concord Daily Tribune*, September 6, 1906, p. 2; *News and Observer*, April 28, 1906, p. 8; *Charlotte Observer*, October 18, 1906, p. 1.

263 *Weekly News*, June 8, 1906, p. 5; *Charlotte Observer*, October 18, 1906, p. 1.

264 https://chiles-house.com/home/james-madison-chiles/; "State Grants Charter", *Charlotte Observer*, December 29, 1906, p. 1.

265 *Charlotte Observer*, September 6, 1907, p. 11.

266 Robert C. Strong (Court Reporter), *North Carolina Reports*, Vol. 167, Cases Argued and Determined in the Supreme Court of North Carolina, Fall Term, 1914, Raleigh, NC, E.M. Uzell and Co., State Printers and Binders, p. 574-5.

267 *Evening Chronicle* (Charlotte), January, 22, 1909, p. 4.

268 *Charlotte Observer*, July 31, 1915, p. 2; "New Factory Will Locate Here", *Weekly News*, September 16, 1916; p. 1; "Lenoir Furniture Men Attending Big Furniture Shows", *Lenoir News*, January 7, 1916, p. 1; "Lenoir Concern Makes Additions to Plant" *Charlotte News*, October 16, 1916, p. 6.

269 "Watch Lenoir Grow", LT, August 27, 1907, p. 3; Kathy Barlow and Sonny Carter, "Lenoir: The Furniture Center of the South", *Tuckers Barn*, Spring/Summer 1982, Compiled by the O&W Comm. Class at West Caldwell High School, p. 10-11; "Washboards and Excelsior", *Evening Chronicle* (Charlotte), May 17, 1911, p. 4; LT, October 22, 1912, p. 3.

270 Jule Hubbard, "Flume Helped Bring About Its Own Demise", June 6, 2016, updated February 8, 2020, *Wilkes Patriot-Journal*, https://www.journalpatriot.com/news/flume-helped-bring-about-its-own-demise/article_1a17985a-2c13-11e6-bc97-5b2d8f29536b.html?fbclid=IwAR376JH2Op8mCqJ-pjEJ-WXH6ZQh1X8h-yoGYxLox3fsHxBK-knPrHwNV9I

271 https://digitalheritage.org/2010/08/floods-of-1916-and-1940/

272 https://www.ncdcr.gov/blog/2014/07/14/the-flood-of-1916-and-unprecedented-destruction-in-western-north-carolina; "Great Damage By Floods at Elkin", *The Western Sentinel*, July 18, 1916, p.

1; Jule Hubbard, "Flume Helped Bring About Its Own Demise", June 6, 2016, updated February 8, 2020, Wilkes Patriot-Journal, https://www.journalpatriot.com/news/flume-helped-bring-about-its-own-demise/article_1a17985a-2c13-11e6-bc97-5b2d8f29536b.html?fbclid=IwAR376JH2Op8mCqJ-pjEJ-WXH6ZQh1X8h-yoGYxLox3fsHxBK-knPrHwNV9I

273 "Catawba County Devastated By A Tremendous Flood", Newton Enterprise, July 18, 1916, p. 1; "The Flood at Glen Alpine", Morganton News-Herald, July 21, 1916, p. 6; "Lenoir Suffers Little Damage", CO, July 24, 1916, p. 12: "Lenoir Isolated From Outer World", Lenoir News, July 18, 1916, p. 1; "8 things to know about North Carolina's Great Flood of 1916, CO, July 17, 2016, p. 16A.

274 https://www.fs.usda.gov/recarea/nfsnc/recarea/?recid=48114

275 "Determined to Nip Labor Union in Bud", LT, March 16, 1917, p. 1.

276 Michelle Kilbourne-Minor, The Catawba Valley Furniture Industry: The Origins, Composition, and Conditions of Labor, 1879-1939, Graduate Thesis, Appalachian State University,1991, p. 52.

277 Lenoir News-Topic, July 28, 1921, p. 1; Lenoir News-Topic, September, 1, 1921, p. 1; "Coffey Bids in the Ethel Chair Company", Lenoir News-Topic, July 7, 1921, p. 5; "New Chair Plant Is to Start Up Soon", Lenoir News-Topic, September 1, 1921, p. 1; "Chair Company Chartered", Lenoir News-Topic, July 28, 1921, p. 1; "Mrs. Mary Harper Beall", Lenoir News, June 30, 1916, p.1.

278 "The Last of the Founders", Lenoir News-Topic, March 31, 1921, p. 3; "Sounds Good", Charlotte Observer, March 31, 1915, p. 4.

--⟨≋⟩--

Chapter 12: A Hustling Business

279 Morganton News-Herald, January 20, 1916, p. 7.

280 Newton Enterprise, August 20, 1914, p. 3; Lenoir Topic, June 17, 1913, p. 3.

281 "South America Will Be Invaded", Statesville Sentinel, August 20, 1914, p. 8.

282 Lincoln County News, October 2, 1916, p. 3.

283 "Lincoln Furniture Manufacturing Co.", Lincoln County News, January 20, 1916, p. 3. Lenoir News, February 6, 1914, p. 1; "Lincoln Furniture Manufacturing Co.", Lincoln County News, January 20, 1916, p. 3; Lincoln County News, June 12, 1914, p. 3; Lenoir News, February 6, 1914, p. 1; Charlotte Observer, December 4, 1914, p. 1; Lincoln County News, March 20, 1916, p. 2, p. 3; "Mr. Rhyne Buys Lincoln Furniture Mfg. Co.", Lincoln County News, July 24, 1916, p. 3; "Gastonian Named Sec.-Treas.", Gastonia Gazette, September 15, 1916, p. 6; "Local Furniture Men Buy Lincolnton Factory", Lenoir News-Topic, September 12, 1919, p. 1.

284 "Rates Reduced", Statesville Sentinel, June 19, 1913, p. 3; Greensboro Daily News, October 24, 1912, p. 6.

285 "Mr. Ivey Makes Additions to Plants", Hickory Daily Record, November 23, 1916, p. 1. Picker sticks were devices used in the textile industry necessary to facilitate the action of a loom.

286 "Statesville Furniture Co.", Statesville Sentinel, January 27, 1916, p. 5; Lenoir News, March 7, 1916, p. 3; Hickory Daily Record, June 1, 1916, p. 3; Lenoir News, August 1, 1916, p.3. Mebane's White Furniture is generally credited as the oldest, continually operating furniture company in North Carolina (1881). It ceased operations in 1985 and was bought and relocated to Hickory.

287 "Struck By Flying Timber", Charlotte Observer, February 16, 1916, p. 8; Lincoln County News, January 27, 1916, p. 3; Charlotte Observer, October 1, 1901, p. 3.

288 *"Labor Dispute at Hickory Chair Co."*, Hickory Daily Record, March 22, 1918, p. 1.

289 *Hickory Daily Record, September 10, 1918, p. 4; Michelle Kilbourne-Minor, The Catawba Valley Furniture Industry: The Origins, Composition, and Conditions of Labor, 1879-1939, Graduate Thesis, Appalachian State University,1991, p. 91, 94.*

290 *John Bray, "An Abbreviated History of Furniture in North Carolina", unpublished script from presentation.*

291 *"Industrial Leadership", Hickory Daily Record, August 15, 1916, p. 3.*

292 *Marion Progress, August 3, 1911, p. 5.*

293 *Greensboro Daily News, August 24, 1906, p. 7, (advert).*

294 *"Marion in Ashes", Marion Record, November 29, 1894, p. 1.*

295 *The Messenger (Marion), April 16, 1897, p. 3; Morganton News-Herald, March 13, 1902, p. 1.*

296 *Morganton Herald, May 14, 1896, p. 1; https://www.findagrave.com/memorial/71902243/ william-avery-conley; Burke County News, July 6, 1900, p. 3. The Messenger (Marion), March 21, 1897, p. 3; The Messenger, July 2, 1897, p. 3; Statesville Record & Landmark, November 19, 1901, p. 3.*

297 *The Messenger (Marion), May 21, 1897, p. 3; https://www.ncpedia.org/biography/wrenn-thomas-f; Morganton Herald, June 3, 1897, p. 1; "Points From High Point", Greensboro Telegram, October 10, 1897, p. 1; The Messenger (Marion), January 21, 1898, p. 3; "Clippings and Cullings", Morning Post (Raleigh), March 15, 1898, p. 2; The Messenger, September 24, 1897, p. 3; The Messenger, April 15, 1898, p. 3; Asheville Citizen-Times, September 2, 1898, p. 3.*

298 *News & Observer (Raleigh), October 10, 1900, p. 8; Raleigh Times, October 11, 1900, p. 3. Each account spells the name of investors differently; Marion Progress (obit), January 22, 1915, p. 1; Marion Progress, September 28, 1916, p. 7.*

299 *"New Furniture Company", News & Observer (Raleigh), March 6, 1902, p. 8; https://www. findagrave.com/memorial/20598870/john-quince-gilkey; Marion Progress, October 26, 1916, p. 5.*

300 *Raleigh Times, January 22, 1909, p. 6; News & Observer, January 23, 1909, p. 8.*

301 *The Sun (Rutherfordton), September 3, 1903, p. 7.*

302 *Greensboro Daily News, February 23, 1906, p. 6.*

303 *Morganton News-Herald, March 6, 1902, p. 1; Gastonia Gazette, January 12, 1904, p. 3; Greensboro Patriot, June 28, 1905, p. 6.*

304 *Lenoir Topic, August 21, 1895, p. 3; The Messenger, May 7, 1897, p. 3; Morganton Herald, June 3, 1897, p. 1; The Messenger, August 6, 1897, p. 3; The Messenger, October 22, 1897, p. 3 (classified); The Messenger, November 12, 1897, p. 3; High Point Weekly Enterprise, January 2, 1907, p. 4 (advertisement); High Point Weekly Enterprise, February 18, 1915, p. 2 (advertisement).*

305 *Asheville Citizen-Times, November 30, 1921, p. 28; "Fire At Marion Takes Property Toll of $35,000", Asheville Citizen-Times, August 20, 1924, p. 3.*

⸺⊗⸺

Chapter 13: A Buxon Mountain Queen

306 *Dan Mabry Lacy, The Beginning of Industrialism in North Carolina, 1865-1900, M.A. Thesis University of North Carolina at Chapel Hill, 1935, p. 125.*

307 *"Hickory Is To Have A Toy Factory Soon", Greensboro Daily News, February 2, 1922, p. 12:*

"George F. Ivey Dies In Hickory", *Charlotte News*, October 1, 1952, p. 1.

308 "Popular Merry Go Round Toy Made by Sou. Toy Co.", CO, July 2, 1922, p. D2.

309 "West Hickory Plants Have Rushing Business", HDR, October 31, 1922, p. 1; https:// californiahistoricalradio.com/wp-content/uploads/2020/11/Radios-become-Furniture-%E2%80%93-Advertising-at-Work.pdf; https://worldradiohistory.com/hd2/IDX-Site-Early-Radio/Archive-Popular-Radio-IDX/IDX/26/Popular-Radio-1926-11-OCR-Page-0064.pdf

310 https://www.ncpedia.org/biography/harper-james

311 *Concord Daily Tribune*, February 1, 1923, p. 1. *Lenoir News-Topic*, February 23, 1923, p. 4.

312 *Lenoir News-Topic*, December 24, 1924, p. 1.

313 *Asheville Citizen-Times*, July 14, 1925, p. 1; *Asheville Citizen-Times*, July 31, 1925, p. 13.

314 https://www.findagrave.com/memorial/136489815/a-g-jonas; *Asheville Citizen-Times*, January 8, 1928, p. 18.

315 "Stockholders' Annual Meet", *The Dispatch* (Lexington), January 12, 1910, p. 1; https://www.caldwellglass.net/history

316 "Corporations Assessed $100 or As Income Taxes", *News & Observer*, September 2, 1925, p. 15.

317 "Furniture Plant is Purchased by Hibriten Firm", *Asheville Citizen-Times*, May 5, 1943, p. 7; Stanley S. Jennings Dies in Lenoir", *Asheville Citizen-Times*, November 30, 1948, p. 3. *Weekly News* (Lenoir), March 21, 1902, p. 3; *Gastonia Gazette*, October 12, 1906, p. 1; *Lenoir Topic*, March 29, 1907, p. 3; *Lenoir Topic*, November 1, 1907, p. 3; "New Enterprise", *Lenoir Topic*, October 27, 1908, p. 3; *Lenoir Topic*, February 19, 1909, p. 3; *Lenoir Topic*, May 6, 1907, p. 3; "Announcements", *Lenoir Topic*, August 2, 1910, p. 4; *Raleigh Times*, December 27, 1910, p. 8. *Weekly News*, July 22, 1915, p. 1; "C.E. Rabb Elected Head of Stubbs Veneer Firm", *Asheville Citizen-Times*, February 11, 1928, p. 5.

318 "New State Charters", *Charlotte Observer*, September 9, 1925, p. 22; "Furniture Plant at Morganton Purchased", *Charlotte Observer*, October 3, 1925, p. 6; "Contract Let for New Factory Building", *News & Observer*, October 17, 1925, p. 3; "Beauty Marks Plant Output", *Charlotte Observer*, November 22, 1930, p. 138; "Firm Nears Agreement on Sale of Plant", *Asheville Citizen-Times*, December 27, 1950, p. 11.

319 Michelle Kilbourne-Minor, *The Catawba Valley Furniture Industry: The Origins, Composition, and Conditions of Labor, 1879-1939*, Graduate Thesis, Appalachian State University, 1991, p. 87.

320 Michelle Kilbourne-Minor, *The Catawba Valley Furniture Industry*, p. 87.

321 Michelle Kilbourne-Minor, *The Catawba Valley Furniture Industry*, p. 106.

322 Michelle Kilbourne-Minor, *The Catawba Valley Furniture Industry*, p. 98-99, 110.

323 Michelle Kilbourne-Minor, *The Catawba Valley Furniture Industry*, p. 111.

324 Michelle Kilbourne-Minor, *The Catawba Valley Furniture Industry*, p. 98.

325 Michelle Kilbourne-Minor, *The Catawba Valley Furniture Industry*, p. 133.

326 Michelle Kilbourne-Minor, *The Catawba Valley Furniture Industry*, p. 109.

327 Sidney Clapp, unpublished manuscript.

328 "Aged Man Injured On Railroad at Lenoir", *Charlotte Observer*, February 26, 1926, p. 2; Sidney Clapp, unpublished manuscript.

◦⟨≈⟩◦

Chapter 14: Family Ties

329 https://files.nc.gov/ncdcr/historic-preservation-office/survey-and-national-register/surveyreports/Lenoir_Architectural_Survey_Final_Report.pdf

330 "Gabriel's Horn", Lenoir Topic (LT), April 26, 1899, p. 3.

331 "Broyhill Buys the Bernhardt Box Factory" (LT), February 2, 1917, p. 1; "Who Will Get the Ring" LT, April 24, 1917, p. 2.

332 "Broyhill Buys the Bernhardt Box Factory" LT, February 2, 1917, p. 1; "Another Big Cotton Mill Now a Certainty", LT, May 17, 1918, p. 1. Broyhill did turn the facility into a cotton mill with a planned opening by October of 1917; "Railroad Clerks Out On A Strike", Durham Morning Herald, September 5, 1917, p. 5; "Many Charters Issued", Greensboro Daily News, September 5, 1917, p. 4; "New Charters Issued by Secretary of State", Twin-City (Winston-Salem) Sentinel, September 7, 1917, p. 7. Durham listed capital at $5,000 while the Greensboro paper reported $25,000. The Winston-Salem newspaper was highest at $45,000.

333 "Pioneer Furniture Manufacturer Dies," Charlotte Observer (CO), January 6, 1935, p. 7.

334 Fred H. May, "Size of Chair Factory is Increased", CO, July 4, 1926, p. 39.

335 Fred H. May, "Size of Chair Factory is Increased", CO, July 4, 1926, p. 39.

336 "Six Hurt, One Missing, after $300,000 Fire", CO, December 1, 1926, p. 1; "Body Found in Lenoir Ruins" CO, December 2, 1926, p. 13.

337 An Oral History with John Christian Bernhardt, Dr. Phillip L Cantelon, interviewer, July 15, 1992 and September 3, 1993, American Furniture Hall of Fame Publication, 2010, p. 5.

338 "Rebuild Lenoir Furniture Plant", Charlotte News, August 9, 1927, p. 13; "Pioneer Furniture Manufacturer Dies", CO, January 6, 1935, p. 7.

339 LNT, November 25, 1920, p. 11.

340 LNT, November 25, 1920, p. 12, 14-16, 20, 22, 24

341 LNT, November 25, 1920, p. 12, 14-16, 20, 22, 24

342 LNT, November 25, 1920, p. 12, 14-16, 20, 22, 24

343 "Furniture Men Are Trying A New Line", LNT, June 16, 1921, p. 1; Greensboro Daily News, December 19, 1915, p. 23 (Margaret Harper relationship); LNT, August 21, 1921, p. 5; William Stevens, Anvil of Adversity: Biography of a Furniture Pioneer, Popular Library, 1968, p. 83. The story of the Broyhill brothers and their rise in the furniture industry is closely chronicled by Ed Broyhill's son-in-law William Stevens. The book is one of the few volumes on western North Carolina furniture pioneers and is accompanied by a film entitled, Bring Me Men to Match My Mountains, https://www.youtube.com/watch?v=dTZ0qLQGbhY

344 Anvil of Adversity, p. 73; Telephone interview with Ed Broyhill II, April 19, 2022.

345 Telephone interview with Ed Broyhill II, April 19, 2022.

346 Anvil of Adversity, p. 73; Telephone interview with Ed Broyhill II, April 19, 2022.

347 Anvil of Adversity, p. 30.

348 "Mr. Grandin's Town", Back Then…, Episode 1, "Mr. Grandin's Town, 1994, Charter Communications, Documentary, produced and directed by Richard Eller.

349 Back Then…, Episode 1, "Mr. Grandin's Town, 1994, Charter Communications; Matthew Bumgarner & Doug Walker, Watauga and Yadkin River Railroad, Tarheel Press, 2002.

350 *Anvil of Adversity, p. 32-3.*

351 *Telephone Interview with Ed Broyhill, April 19, 2022.*

352 *Anvil of Adversity, p. 83-87; Telephone Interview with Ed Broyhill, April 19, 2022.*

353 *Anvil of Adversity, p. 83-87; "New Furniture Plant is Started in Lenoir", Charlotte Observer, December 24, 1926, p. 15.*

354 *Telephone Interview with Ed Broyhill, April 19, 2002; Anvil of Adversity, p. 83.*

355 *"Lenoir Gets Factory as Christmas Present", News & Observer, December 25, 1926, p. 25; Stevens, Anvil of Adversity, p. 87, 89.*

356 *"Lenoir Chair Company Building Addition Two Stories High", Asheville Citizen-Times, March 3, 1928, p. 5; Telephone Interview with Ed Broyhill, April 19, 2022.*

357 *Stevens, Anvil of Adversity, p. 89-90.*

358 *Telephone Interview with Ed Broyhill, April 19, 2022.*

359 *Telephone Interview with Ed Broyhill, April 19, 2022; "Broyhill Furniture Industries a Leader in County and Nation", LNT, June 29, 1996 (Furniture Industry Section), p. 11-12.*

360 *Stevens, Anvil of Adversity, p. 95.*

361 *Stevens, Anvil of Adversity, p. 96-97.*

362 *"Furniture Firm Changes Hands", Charlotte News, December 6, 1929, p. 20; "Harper Furniture is Formed", Asheville Citizen-Times, January 8, 1930, p. 12. The new organization of Harper Furniture featured Tom Broyhill as president, James Marshall as secretary-treasurer and Ed Broyhill as sales manager.*

363 *Anvil of Adversity, p. 66.*

364 *"Broyhill Has Many Employes" CO, November 22, 1930, p. 56.*

Chapter 15: The Western North Carolina Furniture Club

365 *"Hold Furniture Exposition, High Point in June", Lenoir News-Topic (LNT), February 24, 1921, p. 8.*

366 *"Drexel Furniture Co. Is Biggest Plant of Its Kind in the Carolinas" Charlotte Observer, January 23, 1923, p. 25; "High Point's Big Furniture Exposition Greatest Yet Held" Charlotte Observer, January 23, 1923, p. 25-26.*

367 *J.L. Oliver, The Development and Structure of the Furniture Industry, Pergamon Press, p. 113.*

368 *National Register of Historic Places Application for the Bolick Historic District, Catawba County, North Carolina, Section 8, page 1; https://www.southernfurniture.net/about/*

369 *"Southern Furniture: Homegrown, family-owned…" Hickory News, October 12, 1995, p. 5A; "Their first business was buggies", Hickory News (Catawba Report), (Furniture Industry and Trade file, Rhodes Research Room, Catawba County Library, Newton, NC) "Their first business was buggies", Hickory News (Catawba Report), (Furniture Industry and Trade file, Rhodes Research Room, Catawba County Library, Newton, NC); Mabry, Seth, "Southern Style", ONE (Outlook Edition), December 12, 2016, p. 8.*

370 *"New Drexel Plant Ready", Charlotte Observer, August 19, 1923, p. 49.*

371 *"New Furniture Factory for Newton, Catawba News-Enterprise, December 18, 1925, (Furniture Industry and Trade file, Rhodes Research Room, Catawba County Library, Newton, NC)*

372 *"New Table Factory Planned for Hickory"*, Charlotte Observer, January 5, 1923, p. 9; *"New Table Factory"*, News & Observer, January 4, 1923, p. 5; *"Yeager Manufacturing Company"* (advert), Charlotte Observer, January 17, 1923, p. 26. *"Hickory Business Shows Improvement During Year"*, Charlotte Observer, January 4, 1923, p. 7; *"Yeager Company Begins Making Furniture Today"* Charlotte Observer, April 9, 1923, p. 4; *"Fourth Exposition Declared Leader of All"*, Charlotte Observer, October 6, 1924, p. 37. *"Hickory To Get $250,000 Hotel"*, Charlotte Observer, January 1, 1924, p. 9; *"Yeager Company Grows Rapidly in Five Years"*, Charlotte Observer, February 5, 1928, p. 47.

373 *"Chair Factory Partly Destroyed by Fire"*, Charlotte Observer, June 27, 1923, p. 9; *"Fire Takes Heavy Toll at Plant of Hickory Chair Co."*, Asheville Citizen-Times, June 27, 1923, p. 2.

374 *"Hickory Chair Factory is Again in Operation"*, Charlotte Observer, August 28, 1923, p. 13.

375 *"Fire Loss at Hickory Estimated at $150,000"* Charlotte Observer, December 29, 1925, p. 2; *"Resumes Operation"*, Charlotte Observer, March 8, 1926, p. 2.

376 *"Maiden's Fastest Growing Industry"*, Charlotte Observer, July 26, 1925, p. 36; *"Maiden Chair Company Employe(e)s Entertained"*, Charlotte Observer, December 31, 1925, p. 2;

377 *"Receiver's Auction Sale of Manufacturing Property"*, Charlotte Observer, December 1, 1929, p. 45;

378 *"Chair Factory At Maiden Is Burned"*, Statesville Record and Landmark, July 8, 1932, p. 8.

379 *"Chair Company is Facing Suit"*, Charlotte News, March 7, 1937, p. 7.

380 *"Furniture Meet Well Attended"*, March 28, 1929, Caldwell Heritage Museum Collection.

381 *"Manufacturers of Furniture Will Save Huge Sum"*, October 6, 1927, Caldwell Heritage Museum Collection.

382 *"Furniture Men Endorse Proposal"*, December 21, 1922, Caldwell Heritage Museum Collection.

383 *"Furniture Men On Trial in Big Suit"*, March 24, 1927, Caldwell Heritage Museum Collection. *"Declares Mistrial in Furniture Case"* News & Observer, March 22, 1927. Ten jurors voted for conviction but failed to come to unanimous consensus. The trial represented the largest number of defendants ever in a single action up to that time.

384 *"May Establish A Furniture School"*, November 6, 1922.

385 John Hawkins, *"Coffey Furniture"*, an undated draft of a column for the Lenoir News Topic, Caldwell Heritage Museum Collection.

386 *"Brains in Business"*, News & Observer, November 24, 1929, p. 34. Quoted from earlier Lenoir News-Topic story.

——◈◈◈——

Chapter 16: Borax and Depression

387 *"Trade Publication Praises Drexel Enterprises Head"*, Hickory Daily Record reprint from Home Furnishing Daily, November 22, 1963, (Drexel Heritage file, Carolina Room, Patrick Beaver Library, Hickory, NC). John Bray, unpublished presentation on furniture history.

388 *"Trade Publication Praises Drexel Enterprises Head"*, Hickory Daily Record reprint from Home Furnishing Daily, November 22, 1963, (Drexel Heritage file, Carolina Room, Patrick Beaver Library,

Hickory, NC).

389 John Bray, "An Abbreviated History of Furniture in North Carolina", script from presentation, p. 16.

390 http://mid2mod.blogspot.com/2013/05/pssstits-called-borax.html; "Article No. 6" Courier-Journal (Louisville, KY), July 2, 1930, p. 14.

391 http://mid2mod.blogspot.com/2013/05/pssstits-called-borax.html; "Article No. 6" Courier-Journal (Louisville, KY), July 2, 1930, p. 14.

392 Splinters: An Oral History of the Furniture Industry in the Catawba County Area, Lenoir-Rhyne College History Class, 1979-80, edited by Dr. Carolyn Huff, Lenoir-Rhyne College History Department and the Broyhill Institute for Business Leadership, p. 8; Nesbit, William F., "History of Furniture Industry Club Topic", Hickory Daily Record (HDR), February 1, 1972, (Furniture Industry and Trade file, Rhodes Research Room, Catawba County Library, Newton, NC)

393 Southern Furniture Journal, no. 15, January 1909, p. 35; Michelle Kilbourne-Minor, The Catawba Valley Furniture Industry, p. 46.

394 "Furniture Makers Get Rate Reduction", New & Observer, July 3, 1932, p. 6; Michelle Kilbourne-Minor, The Catawba Valley Furniture Industry, p. 46

395 Michelle Kilbourne-Minor, The Catawba Valley Furniture Industry, p. 48.

396 "Weathers Furniture Company" (advert), News & Observer, November 27, 1925, p. 6;

397 "Trade Publication Praises Drexel Enterprises Head", HDR reprint from Home Furnishing Daily, November 22, 1963, (Drexel Heritage file, Carolina Room, Patrick Beaver Library, Hickory, NC). "H.C. Prange Co." (advert), Green Bay Press-Gazette, December 2, 1940, p. 5.

398 "New Organization Takes Over Royal", Lenoir News-Topic (LNT), February 1, 1923, p. 1; "New State Charters", Charlotte Observer (CO), November 24, 1925, p. 16; "Robbins Buy Local Lenoir Chair Plant", LNT, December 11, 1924, p. 1; "Big Furniture Company Sold", CO, May 5, 1943, p. 9.

399 "Women Dental Student First", Baltimore Sun, May 11, 1909, p. 14; "Chair Firm President Dies at 84", CO, November 19, 1960, p. 5; "C.L. Robbins, Prominent N.C. Furnitureman", CO, April 28, 1967, p. 19.

400 "Factories at Lenoir Support Recovery", News & Observer, July 30th, 1933, p. 12.

401 "$1,000,000 Furniture Company is Formed", CO, March 15, 1931, p. 9; "Chair Firm Formed in Elkin", HDR, (Hickory Chair Manufacturing Co. file) Beaver Library, Hickory, NC; Nesbit, William F., "History of Furniture Industry Club Topic", HDR, February 1, 1972, (Furniture Industry and Trade file, Rhodes Research Room, Catawba County Library, Newton, NC); "Hickory Furniture Plant Reopened, Charlotte News, May 18, 1932, p. 1.

402 John Bray, "Hickory's Three Major Furniture Factories Grow and Grow Together", Chapter 2 of unpublished history of furniture in Hickory, p. 29.

403 Sarah Nagem, "Furniture Makers Now Follow Niches", News & Observer, July 22, 2013, p. A1; https://www.carolinachair.com/about.html; "Hickory-Fry Co., Has Diversified Upholstered Line", Hickory Daily Record: 50th Anniversary Edition, September 1965, p. 65.

404 "Number at Work Shows Increase" Statesville Daily Record, October 1, 1931, p. 1; "Veneer Plant Soon to Be In Operation", Statesville Record and Landmark, February 17, 1930. p. 7; "Trustees' Sale

of Real Estate", *Statesville Daily Record*, December 12, 1940, p. 6.

405 "Efird's Made-In-Carolina Sales Exposition Tomorrow", "Display of Furniture Manufactured at Home", CO, February 19, 1930, p. 21.

406 "Newton Furniture Co. Erects New Buildings", CO, February 14, 1926, p. 13; "Special Notices", CO, May 11, 1930, p. 45; "Fire Causes $20,000 Loss at Newton During Heavy Storm", CO, August 2, 1930, p. 4.

407 Stevens, *Anvil of Adversity*, p. 98. Stevens confuses the name of the Newton operation that previously stood but the basic facts of Ed taking over Newton Furniture Company, not to be confused with a retail store of the same name is correct.

408 Stevens, *Anvil of Adversity*, p. 80.

409 Stevens, *Anvil of Adversity*, p. 79.

410 Stevens, *Anvil of Adversity*, p. 107.

411 Telephone Interview with Ed Broyhill, April 19, 2022.

412 "Mr. Broyhill Buys Power Plant", LNT, May 30, 1919, p. 5; "Buffalo Road Will Soon Be Completed", LNT, July 28, 1921, p. 1; Telephone Interview with Ed Broyhill, April 19, 2022.

413 Stevens, *Anvil of Adversity*, p. 107.

414 "Jonas Furniture Firm Bought by Lenoir People", *Asheville Citizen-Times*, February 22, 1936, p. 6; Stevens, *Anvil of Adversity*, p. 101.

415 Benjie Watts, "Early Furniture Days Recalled Fondly", *Lenoir News-Topic*, Caldwell Heritage Museum Collection.

416 Watts, "Early Furniture Days", *Lenoir News-Topic*, Caldwell Heritage Museum Collection.

417 Watts, "Early Furniture Days", *Lenoir News-Topic*, Caldwell Heritage Museum Collection.

418 "Strikes Closes Lenoir Plant; 300 Walk Out", *Charlotte News*, August 20, 1937, p. 4; "Workers Picket Furniture Plant", *Statesville Daily Record*, August 20, 1947, p. 1; "Lenoir Strike Settled 'Very Satisfactorily'", CO, September 4, 1937, p. 16.

419 Michelle Kilbourne-Minor, *The Catawba Valley Furniture Industry*, p. 229, 231, 243.

420 Michelle Kilbourne-Minor, *The Catawba Valley Furniture Industry*, p. 253.

421 "A Colored Wedding", *Hickory Daily Record*, October 18, 1915, p. 1; Michelle Kilbourne-Minor, *The Catawba Valley Furniture Industry*, p. 216.

422 Michelle Kilbourne-Minor, *The Catawba Valley Furniture Industry*, p. 132.

423 "Lenoir Furniture Plant Closes to Avert Strike; State Patrolmen Called", *Hickory Daily Record*, March 25, 1933, p. 1; "Half of Workers Back at Jobs As Lenoir Furniture Plant Re-Opens", *Hickory Daily Record*, March 27, 1933, p. 1. Michelle Kilbourne-Minor, *The Catawba Valley Furniture Industry*, p. 182.

424 "Furniture Men Fight Control", *Hickory Daily Record*, December 10, 1937, p. 4; "Lenoir, Marion Firms Lose War on Security Act", *Hickory Daily Record*, February 8, 1937, p. 2.

425 "Conover Plant Having Trouble", *Hickory Daily Record*, May 31, 1933, p. 1.

426 Jim Church, "Old-fashioned sandwich stand had great food, atmosphere", CO, October 3, 1992, p. 101.

427 Jim Church, "Old-fashioned sandwich stand had great food, atmosphere", CO, October 3, 1992, p. 101.

Chapter 17: War Relieves Depression

428 Kathleen Purvis, "South's Thirst Grew in Fields and Factories", CO, July 26, 2000, p. 3E;
https://www.historysouth.org/the-souths-love-affair-with-soft-drinks/

429 Kathleen Purvis, "South's Thirst Grew in Fields and Factories", CO, July 26, 2000, p. 3E.

430 "Workers To Celebrate Jap New Year's Day By Aiding Red Cross", Asheville Citizen-Times,
January 10, 1942, p. 6.

431 "Industrial Safety Factors Discussed As Meeting Opens", CO, May 21, 1943, p. 17.

432 "Marion Plants are Operating Close to Full Capacity", Asheville Citizen-Times, February 5,
1942, p. 9.

433 "2 Railroads and Seven Manufacturing Plants Face Federal Charges", Asheville Citizen-Times,
February 12, 1942, p. 6; "2 Railroads, 7 Firms Fined $56,000 In Federal Court, Rocky Mount
Telegram, February 25, 1942, p. 1.

434 "Hickory Firm Will Appeal Labor Case", CO, March 18, 1942, p. 9; "Hickory Case Won
by Union", CO, May 30, 1942, p. 14; "Hickory Firm Ordered to Reinstate Workers", High Point
Enterprise, June 25, 1942, p. 11.

435 "Hickory Firm to Hold Special Bond Program", News & Observer, September 25, 1942, p. 6;
"Treasury Raises Flag Over Plant at Hickory" Charlotte News, September 25, 1942, p. 24.

436 "Chair Factory Sold", Charlotte News, February 14, 1944, p. 8; "Sale of Plant Approved", News
& Observer, February 19, 1944, p. 10; "Plant is Purchased", News & Observer, April 11, 1944, p. 2.
The original purchasing company was Harris, Karp, Goldsmith and Company of Cincinnati.

437 "Hickory Manufacturing Company", letter from Joe Moretz to John Bray, date unknown, John
Bray Collection, p. 28.

438 "Treasury Raises Flag Over Plant at Hickory" Charlotte News, September 25, 1942, p. 24.

439 Gary Freeze, The Catawbans: Boomers & Bypasses, Volume 3, Catawba County, 2016, p. 30.

440 "Hickory Manufacturing Company", letter from Joe Moretz to John Bray, date unknown, John
Bray Collection, p. 28.

441 "Hickory Manufacturing Company", letter from Joe Moretz to John Bray, date unknown, John
Bray Collection, p. 27; "Chair Firm Buys Plant Facilities", Charlotte Observer, June 2, 1961, p. 3.f

442 Stevens, "Anvil of Adversity", p. 110.

443 Stevens, "Anvil", p. 80, 107, 195.

444 https://www.madebyhickorychair.com/hickory-chair-a-100-year-story.html

445 Interview with Ruth Church & Romey Church, Hickory, NC, February 15, 2022.

446 https://www.evansfuneralservice.com/obituaries/Mary-Bruce-21131/#!/Obituary; https://
www.ncpedia.org/davenport-college; "Charmed Circle" CO, June 27, 1937, p. 50; "1951 Poetry Day
Winners Announced", Asheville Citizen-Times, October 16, 1951, p. 11.

447 "Bride-Elect Complimented" Charlotte News, July 2, 1933, p. 17; https://www.
evansfuneralservice.com/obituaries/Mary-Bruce-21131/#!/Obituary

448 https://www.hammary.com/about-hammary.php

449 "Comedy Presented by Lenoir Guild", January 27, 1934, p. 5; https://www.ancestry.com/

mediaui-viewer/tree/64455443/person/36384579574/media/91a2feb4-a0df-4d66-aa3b-0aa0fc778e7b?_phsrc=eRy1&_phstart=successSource; https://www.ancestry.com/genealogy/records/hamilton-louden-bruce-24-v2zxjq; "Miss Mary Buys Wedded In Lenoir To Hamilton Bruce", CO, August 22, 1942, p. 8.

450 *https://www.hammary.com/about-hammary.php; Hammary Furniture Company: A Commitment to Excellence Since 1943, Company publication sent to the author, November 1, 1998, p. 1; https://www.evansfuneralservice.com/obituaries/Mary-Bruce-21131/#!/Obituary*

451 "3 W.N.C. Firms Get Incorporation Papers", *Asheville Citizen-Times*, October 26, 1945, p. 14; *Hammary Furniture Company: A Commitment*, p. 1.

452 *Hammary Furniture Company: A Commitment*, p. 1; *https://www.hammary.com/about-hammary.php.*

─◦≪◦─

Chapter 18: Bright Spots and Bitter Battles

453 Stevens, *Anvil of Adversity*, p. 151

454 Stevens, *Anvil of Adversity*, p. 139.

455 Stevens, *Anvil of Adversity*, p. 146.

456 "We the People of North Carolina", Volume XL, Number 11, November 1982, p. 9-12. This magazine listed itself as "the Official Publication of North Carolina Citizens for Business and Industry" and as "the Voice of Business." Its Executive Committee included Broyhill in-law, William E. Stevens, who wrote *Anvil of Adversity*; Carol D. Leonnig, "Broyhill Ends Long Career; Friends Ready Salute", *Charlotte Observer* (CO), June 19, 1991, p. 2B.

457 "We the People", p. 9-12.

458 "New Furniture Firm Started", *Charlotte Observer*, September 30, 1945, p. 6; "Contract Is Granted For Morganton Plant", *News & Observer*, October 1, 1945, p. 10; "New Corporations", *News & Observer*, October 4, 1945, p. 13; Jason Vaughan, "The History of Henredon Furntiure" at the website *https://homesteady.com/facts-5817614-history-henredon-furniture.html*, according the the previous website, "The name Henredon was created from a combination of Henry, Edwards and Donnell."

459 "Burton's Furniture" (advert), *Asheville Citizen-Times*, July 1, 1947, p. 6; "Henry Long Will Succeed Talley", *Statesville Record and Landmark*, July 28, 1947, p. 7.

460 *https://www.stenellaantiques.com/brand-new-furniture/henredon.php;* "Furniture Firm Appoints Merchandise Co-Ordinator" *Charlotte Observer* (CO), January 3, 1949, p. 20.

461 "Furniture Firm Appoints Merchandise Co-Ordinator" CO, January 3, 1949, p. 20.

462 Helen Kelly, "The Old South Merges Into the New", advert for Mecklenburg Furniture, *Charlotte News*, September 12, 1949, p. 17.

463 Helen Kelly, "The Old South Merges Into the New", advert for Mecklenburg Furniture, *Charlotte News*, September 12, 1949, p. 17.

464 Helen Kelly, "The Old South Merges Into the New", advert for Mecklenburg Furniture, *Charlotte News*, September 12, 1949, p. 17; Leroy Lail and Richard Eller, *Hickory Furniture Mart: A Landmark History*, 2020, Redhawk Publications.

465 "Furniture Expert is Visitor Here", *Charlotte News*, May 17, 1949, p. 15; "Heritage-Henredon

Fine Furniture" (advert), Times Dispatch (Richmond, Va), September 22, 1949, p. 32. When a new line of furniture "Circa '60" debuted in 1952, promotion of the line was handled by Don Van Noppen and Henry Wilson, Charlotte News, October 1, 1952, p. 14; CO, September 15, 1953, p. 28.

466 *Frances De Wolf, "Helen Kelly Vacations at Maine Chance", Arizona Republic (Phoenix), February 20, 1949, p. 32.*

467 *Frances De Wolf, "Helen Kelly Vacations at Maine Chance", Arizona Republic (Phoenix), February 20, 1949, p. 32.*

468 *Frances De Wolf, "Helen Kelly Vacations at Maine Chance", Arizona Republic (Phoenix), February 20, 1949, p. 32.*

469 *Frances De Wolf, "Helen Kelly Vacations at Maine Chance", Arizona Republic (Phoenix), February 20, 1949, p. 32.*

470 *Frances De Wolf, "Helen Kelly Vacations at Maine Chance", Arizona Republic (Phoenix), February 20, 1949, p. 32.*

471 *"An Oral History with J. Wade Kincaid" (1988 Interview), American Furniture Hall of Fame Foundation, 2011, p. 1-14.*

472 *https://www.kincaidfurniture.com/history.php*

473 *An Oral History with J. Wade Kincaid, (1988 Interview), American Furniture Hall of Fame Foundation, 2011, p. 18-20.*

474 *An Oral History with J. Wade Kincaid, (1988 Interview), American Furniture Hall of Fame Foundation, 2011, p. 18-20.*

475 *An Oral History with J. Wade Kincaid, (1988 Interview), American Furniture Hall of Fame Foundation, 2011, p. 32.*

476 *An Oral History with J. Wade Kincaid, (1988 Interview), American Furniture Hall of Fame Foundation, 2011, p. 30-1; https://xfer.services.ncdot.gov/gisdot/DOTHD/bios/ACT_Resolution_Jake_Parris_Jr.pdf.*

477 *An Oral History with John Christian Bernhardt, (1993/3 Interview), American Furniture Hall of Fame Foundation, 2010, p. 69; "Charters Given W.N.C. Firms", Asheville Citizen-Times, March 29, 1946, p. 10; '2 Furniture Firms Added by Magnavox", High Point Enterprise, January 6, 1966, p. 11.*

478 *"Captain Nathan McElwee Arrives in States", Statesville Record and Landmark, November 26, 1945, p. 4; "Major A. Long Recounts Some of War Experiences", Statesville Record and Landmark, December 17, 1945; "Group of Local Men Organize Furniture Firm", Statesville Daily Record, January 7, 1946, p. 9; "Dr. McElwee Succumbs at His Home Here", Statesville Record and Landmark, September 9, 1948, p. 7.*

479 *An Oral History with Harley Shuford, Jr., (2008/9 Interview), American Furniture Hall of Fame Foundation, 2011, p. 2.*

480 *An Oral History with Harley Shuford, Jr., (2008/9 Interview), American Furniture Hall of Fame Foundation, 2011, p. 8-13; "Furniture Co. Expands Work", CO, December 10, 1947, p. 12.*

481 *"Two Firms Integrate Programs", Asheville Citizen-Times, May 21, 1948, p. 26; "2 North Carolina Furniture Firms Get US Contracts", Charlotte News, May 14, 1949, p. 16; Asheville Citizen-Times, July 7, 1948, p. 5. Owner David B. Morgan had the distinction of being the father*

of Major (at the time) Robert K. Morgan, pilot of the Memphis Belle (B-17), flying 25 successful missions in the European Theatre of War, then flying another 26 missions in a B-29 in the Pacific Theatre.

482 *"Tarheel Learns About Renegotiation"* (editorial), CO, February 26, 1952, p. 18; *"Government Charges Firm Violated Contract"*, Statesville Record and Landmark, March 28, 1955, p. 10.

483 *"Tarheel Learns About Renegotiation"* (editorial), CO, February 26, 1952, p. 18.

484 *"Tarheel Learns About Renegotiation"* (editorial), CO, February 26, 1952, p. 18.

485 *"Bill Would Relieve Firm of Liability"*, News & Observer, June 22, 1952, p. 13.

486 *"Spainhour Must Pay $119.407.39 to Government"*, Statesville Record and Landmark, March 29, 1955, p. 1.

487 *"2 North Carolina Furniture Firms Gets US Contracts"*, Charlotte News, May 14, 1949, p. 16.

488 *"Unions Charge Unfair Action"*, CO, August 18, 1949, p. 3.

489 *"Drexel Co. Charged"*, Charlotte News, July 27, 1949, p. 15; NLRB Hearing Conducted for Marion Plant", Asheville Citizen-Times, July 29, 1949, p. 37; "AF of L Union Gets Agency", Asheville Citizen-Times, February 1, 1950, p. 11; "Conciliator Fails to Arrive for Morgan Plant Conference", Asheville Citizen-Times, April 2, 1950, p. 33; "Morgan Plant Resumes Work", Asheville Citizen-Times, April 14, 1950, p. 13.

490 *"Elections Won by CIO Unions"*, CO, November 27, 1950, p. 19; *"CIO Loses Vote At Lenoir"*, CO, June 4, 1950, p. 27.

491 *"Union Seeks Votes in Hickory, Statesville"*, High Point Enterprise, November 8, 1950, p. 9; *"Furniture Plant Violence Flares"*, News & Observer, November 30, 1950, p. 10. "Arrest Two as Hickory Strike Trouble Continues", CO, December 1, 1950, p. 12; "More Warrants Served on Hickory Employe(e)s", News & Observer, December 3, 1950, p. 24.

492 *"CIO Union Pushing Furniture Elections"*, CO, November 21, 1950, p. 12.

493 *"NLRB Rules at Hickory"*, News & Observer, September 14, 1951, p. 29; *"CIO Organizer Speaks to Furniture Workers"*, CO, October 14, 1950, p. 3; *"Lenoir Area Furniture Workers Underpaid, Charges CIO"*, CO, March 6, 1951, p. 11.

494 *"Union Loses Election At Plant in Hickory"* CO, January 16, 1951, p. 7; *"Employes Vote Against CIO Union"*, Gaston Gazette, April 26, 1951, p. 5; *"CIO Union Rejected in Furniture Plant"*, News & Observer, May 3, 1951, p. 26; *"Workers of Hibriten Vote Against Union"*, Asheville Citizen-Times, February 19, 1952, p. 9.

495 *"New Corporations"*, New & Observer, April 19, 1950, p. 45; *"Union Seeks NLRB Okay for Election"*, Charlotte News, July 7, 1966, p. 7.

---◁≫◃---

Chapter 19: Upholsters and Upstarts

496 Mamie Zillman, *"Jones Vacation in Color"*, CO, October 20, 1968, p. 69; *"Equitable Leasing Has Loss; Land Net Drops"*, CO, February 24, 1970, p. 19.

497 *"New Corporations"*, News & Observer, September 5, 1945, p. 12; *"Resigns"*, News & Observer, February 5, 1957, p. 17; *"New Corporations"*, News & Observer, June 14, 1947, p. 8.

498 *"Fish Tale"*, News & Observer, July 4, 1955, p. 3; https://files.nc.gov/ncdcr/nr/CT0271.pdf, p. 19; *"New Corporations"*, News & Observer, June 4, 1947, p. 14; Gary Freeze, The Catawbans:

Boomers and Bypasses, Volume 3, Catawba County North Carolina, 2016, p. 30.

499   "Family Tree", Hickory Furniture Mart; *https://www.legacy.com/us/obituaries/hickoryrecord/ name/margaret-shumate-obituary?id=31619805*

500   Telephone interview with C.E. (Sonny) Roseman, Jr., February 3, 2021; "Laine Changes Name", CO, September 30, 1990, Catawba Valley Neighbors Section, p. 26.

501   Telephone interview with C.E. (Sonny) Roseman, Jr., February 3, 2021; "Laine Changes Name", CO, September 30, 1990, Catawba Valley Neighbors Section, p. 26.

502   Telephone interview with C.E. (Sonny) Roseman, Jr., February 3, 2021; "Laine Changes Name", CO, September 30, 1990, Catawba Valley Neighbors Section, p. 26.

503   "New Corporations", News & Observer, June 14, 1947, p. 8; "August Furniture Sale" (advert), News & Observer, August 11, 1961, p. 11; *https://businessnc.com/at-92-buddy-sherrill-still-runs-his-furniture-company/*

504   Harry Snook, "Big Seat", CO, April 28, 1963, p. 21; "Champion Y Opens Road Trip Today", Asheville Citizen-Times, May 24, 1963, p. 24; "Valdese Furniture Company is Fined", CO, April 2, 1969, p. 7.

505   *http://www.kewaunee.com/AboutUs/*

506   "New Industry is Described", Statesville Daily Record, December 1, 1954, p. 6; "Name Change Made by Furniture Firm", Statesville Record and Landmark, July 30, 1959, p. 1.

507   "New Industry is Described", Statesville Daily Record, December 1, 1954, p. 6; "Name Change Made by Furniture Firm", Statesville Record and Landmark, July 30, 1959, p. 1; "New $100,000 Project Slated at Warehouse", Statesville Record and Landmark, October 8, 1959, p. 1.

508   "Architects Show West View and Anthony School Plans" Star Press (Muncie, Indiana), March 29, 1957, p. 10; "North Carolina Firm May Win State Contract", Ironwood Daily Globe (Ironwood, Michigan), March 25, 1961, p. 7; "Southern Firm May Win WMU Bid, Cost State Jobs", Battle Creek Enquirer, March 26, 1961, p. 5.

509   "WMU Order May Go to N.C. Firm", Lansing State Journal, March 25, 1961, p. 12; *https:// projects.kora.matrix.msu.edu/files/157-544-874/OCTOBER201966.pdf*

510   Phone Interview with Bruce Nelson, June 20, 2022.

511   Back Then…, "Behind the Southern Desk", 1999, Charter Communications.

512   Back Then…, "Behind the Southern Desk", 1999, Charter Communications.

513   Back Then…, "Behind the Southern Desk", 1999, Charter Communications.

514   Nashua Telegraph, October 11, 1956, p. 24; Back Then…, "Behind the Southern Desk", 1999, Charter Communications.

515   Interview with Glenn Jarrett, Hickory, NC, September 6, 2022.

516   Interview with Glenn Jarrett, Hickory, NC, September 6, 2022.

517   Interview with Glenn Jarrett, Hickory, NC, September 6, 2022.

518   "Racing Becoming 'Family Affair'", Kingsport Times-News, April 4, 1975, p. 48; Interview with Glenn Jarrett, Hickory, NC, September 6, 2022; Dennis Benfield, "Glenn Jarrett's driven by desire to race full time", CO, October 6, 1993, p. 6V.

519   Interview with Glenn Jarrett, Hickory, NC, September 6, 2022.

520   Interview with Glenn Jarrett, Hickory, NC, September 6, 2022.

521   Interview with Glenn Jarrett, Hickory, NC, September 6, 2022.

522   Interview with Glenn Jarrett, Hickory, NC, September 6, 2022.

523   Interview with Glenn Jarrett, Hickory, NC, September 6, 2022.

524   Interview with Glenn Jarrett, Hickory, NC, September 6, 2022.

525   Interview with Glenn Jarrett, Hickory, NC, September 6, 2022. in that same confrontation with his father, Ned was kicked out of the family home for disobeying his father. However, H.K. Jarrett came to appreciate his son's driving talent as Ned moved up the ranks in NASCAR.

526   Telephone interview with Hank Rullman, January 5, 2021.

527   Telephone interview with Hank Rullman, January 5, 2021.

528   Telephone interview with Hank Rullman, January 5, 2021

529   G. Leroy Lail, Richard Eller, The Bost-Burrus House: A Family Saga, 2021, Redhawk Publications, p. 40; Telephone interview with Hank Rullman, January 5, 2021

530   Telephone interview with Hank Rullman, January 5, 2021

531   "High School Principal Quits for Business Life" CO, May 10, 1946, p. 16; Telephone interview with Hank Rullman, January 5, 2021; "Truck Is Lost In Second Fire", Statesville Daily Record, May 5, 1950, p. 1, a reference to Scales Furniture.

532   Telephone interview with Hank Rullman, January 5, 2021; "Hickory Man to Receive Lutheran Award", CO, March 29, 1984, p. 75.

533   https://www.fandango.com/people/cameron-hawley-278861/biography

⸺⸳⸻

Chapter 20: Upholsters and Upstarts

534   J.L. Oliver, "The Development and Structure of the Furniture Industry", Pergamon Press, p. 117.

535   "Serenity, Classic Design and Functional Elegance", Tampa Bay Magazine, Sept.-Oct. 1988, p. 86. Scott Summers, "Furniture Designer Explains Why 'Traditional' is Popular", Asheville Citizen-Times, May 14, 1961, p. 19.

536   Elizabeth Hillyer, "Versatile New Headboard" St. Louis Post-Dispatch, August 6, 1952, p. 34; Erma Bombeck, "New Furniture Combines Style and Comfort", Journal Herald (Dayton, Ohio), June 14, 1952, p. 19; "Burgdorf's February Bargain Bee" (advert), Courier-Journal (Louisville, KY), February 20, 1953, p. 23.

537   Anne Douglas, "Home Furnishing Tastes in U.S. Rising", Chicago Tribune, June 23, 1957, p. 11; "Alpert furniture for living" (advert), Boston Globe, April 2, 1957, p. 46; Edelen Furniture (advert), Knoxville News-Sentinel, August 5, 1956, p. 10; "Bullock's Pasadena", Los Angeles Times, March 24, 1957, p. 209.

538   An Oral History with Harley Shuford, Jr., (1999), American Furniture Hall of Fame Foundation, 2011, p. 21.

539   "Burgdorf's Budget Shop" (advert), Courier-Journal, April 17, 1955, p. 72; "Miller and Paine" (advert), Lincoln Journal Star, May 15, 1955, p. 29; "Bradford's" (advert), The Tennessean (Nashville), March 16, 1955, p. 17.

540   "Furniture Designer Explains Why 'Traditional' is Popular", Asheville Citizen-Times, May 14, 1961, p. 19.

541 *"Furniture Designer Explains Why 'Traditional' is Popular"*, Asheville Citizen-Times, May 14, 1961, p. 19; *"An Oral History with Harley Shuford, Jr."* (1999), American Furniture Hall of Fame Foundation, 2011, p. 21.

542 *"Furniture Designer Explains Why 'Traditional' is Popular"*, Asheville Citizen-Times, May 14, 1961, p. 19.

543 *"Furniture Mart Sets Open House Today in Hickory"*, Charlotte Observer (CO), November 4, 1951, p. 11; *"Hickory Market Business Spurts"*, *"Buyers Tax Lenoir Accommodations"*, CO, October 28, 1953, p. 7; Paul H. Broyhill, *This is Broyhill*, 2010, Keller Publishing, p. 84.

544 *Telephone interview with Hank Rullman, January 5, 2021.*

545 *"New Furniture Shown"*, News & Observer, October 31, 1951, p. 19; *"Furniture Show Success"*, News & Observer, April 22, 1955, p. 26; *"Waitress Honored"*, CO, May 25, 1988, CVN, p. 6; Beverly Brown, *"Service With A Smile"*, CO, June 1, 1988, CVN, p. 8.

546 *"New Furniture Shown"*, News & Observer, October 31, 1951, p. 19; *"Furniture Show Success"*, News & Observer, April 22, 1955, p. 26; *"Waitress Honored"*, CO, May 25, 1988, CVN, p. 6; Beverly Brown, *"Service With A Smile"*, CO, June 1, 1988, CVN, p. 8.

547 *"Hickory Mart Construction to Begin Soon"*, News & Observer, October 11, 1962, p. 33; *"Six Associates of Asheville"*, Asheville Citizen-Times, October 14, 1962, p. 38; Harry Snook, *"Hickory Home Furnishings Mart Prepares for Opening"*, CO, September 8, 1963, p. 63; Robert Marks, *"For Furniture Marketing, New Air of Cooperation,"* High Point Enterprise, April 22, 1966, p. 18.

548 *"Hickory Mart Construction to Begin Soon"*, News & Observer, October 11, 1962, p. 33; *"Six Associates of Asheville"*, Asheville Citizen-Times, October 14, 1962, p. 38; Harry Snook, *"Hickory Home Furnishings Mart Prepares for Opening"*, CO, September 8, 1963, p. 63; Robert Marks, *"For Furniture Marketing, New Air of Cooperation,"* High Point Enterprise, April 22, 1966, p. 18.

549 *"Hickory Expects 4,000 Furniture Men Today"*, CO, October 20, 1967, p. 3; For an account of Leroy Lail's participation in the furniture sales, see *Win-Win, a memoir and history* of his varied business activities. Also, *Hickory Furniture Mart: A Landmark History*, Leroy Lail & Richard Eller, Redhawk Publications, 2020,

550 Stevens, *Anvil of Adversity*, p. 55-56 with illustration.

551 Carolyn Knuemann, *"Another Tarheel First, You Name it We Make It"*, News and Observer, January 18, 1959, p. 27.

552 *"Hickory To Get New Furniture Plant Soon"*, Charlotte News, November 16, 1932, p. 11; *"Factories at Hickory Work at Top Speed"*, Asheville Citizen-Times, December 18, 1935, p. 21; *"Cox Company in Hickory is Purchased"*, CO, June 20, 1952, p. 6; Carolyn Knuemann, *"Another Tarheel First, You Name it We Make It"*, News and Observer, January 18, 1959, p. 27.

553 Carolyn Knuemann, *"Another Tarheel First, You Name it We Make It"*, News and Observer, January 18, 1959, p. 27; Richard Eller, *"Nelle Burns: She was a furniture pioneer"*, Hickory Daily Record, March 10, 2020, p. 1.

554 Karen Barber, *"Expansion Readies Clayton Marcus for Growth"*, CO, August 15, 1985, p. 83-84.

555 Ashton Chapman, *"Piano Industry Likes N.C."* News & Observer, November 24, 1968, p. 70.

556 http://caldwelljournal.com/kohler-campbell-piano-history/

557   https://www.bluebookofpianos.com/namebrand/agesk.htm; http://caldwelljournal.com/kohler-campbell-piano-history/

558   "Tarheel Dies In Plunge From Hotel In Chicago" Durham Herald-Sun, September 25, 1957, p. 17; https://www.bluebookofpianos.com/namebrand/agesk.htm; "After 58 Years in New York, Kohler & Campbell, Inc. Moves to New One Story Factory in Granite Falls, N.C." Music Trade Review, November 1954, p. 6.

559   Liz Chandler, "Displaced Workers Need Jobs" CO, CVN, p. 10; Rob Urban, "Foul Well May Foul Building Sell", CO, October 16, 1988, CVN, P. 22.

560   https://www.ncpedia.org/pianos; Ashton Chapman, "Piano Industry Likes N.C." News & Observer, November 24, 1968, p. 70; "Marion Piano Factory Burns" Asheville Citizen, April 14, 1970, p. 9; "Kaman Branches Out From Helicopters", Hartford Courant, May 6, 1973, p. 16G; Patti Holda from the McDowell County Historical Society has found documents citing the existence of Westbrook Piano prior to 1994. NCPedia lists 1957 as the year of Westbrooks creation.

561   "Innovations by Currier Piano Brought Firm Special Award", Asheville Citizen-Times, January 26, 1975, p. F13.

562   "New Plant Doubles Currier Plant Production", Asheville Citizen-Times, p. F4; "Innovations by Currier Piano Brought Firm Special Award", Asheville Citizen-Times, January 26, 1975, p. F13.

563   Bob Dennis, "Pac-Man Partly Blamed For Piano Firm Closing", CO, September 25, 1982, p. 7; http://www.ovationfanclub.com/megabbs/forums/thread-view.asp?tid=34014&start=1. A fan site for Ovation guitars included the statement "Marion facility closed in 1985."

564   Conrad Paysour, "'We Didn't Know We Could Build One'", CO, January 12, 1964, p. E6; https://www.evansfuneralservice.com/obituaries/Joseph-Kincaid-2/#!/Obituary

565   Bruce Henderson, "Player Piano, Updated", CO, May 1, 1982, p. C1.

566   https://casetext.com/case/marantz-piano-co-v-kincaid

---∞---

Chapter 21: Buyers Guide

567   "Drexel Tells Plan for Reorganization", High Point Enterprise, October 10, 1960, p. 13.

568   "Drexel Tells Plan for Reorganization", High Point Enterprise, October 10, 1960, p. 13.

569   "Drexel Reports Increased Sales", Asheville Citizen-Times, January 16, 1961, p. 9; "Stockholders To Consider Merger Plan", High Point Enterprise, April 12, 1961, p. 41; Harry Snook, "Drexel Directors Recommend 100 Per Cent Stock Dividend", CO, October 11, 1962, p. 33; "Drexel Furniture Plans Expanded Woodfin Plant", Asheville Citizen-Times, February 14, 1965, p. 3; Dwayne Walls, "Too Much Factory, Too Little Money", CO, March 13, 1966, p. 13.

570   Wake Bridges, "Drexel Industries Head Started Working At 12", High Point Enterprise, July 25, 1963, p. 6; Dick Pierce, "Drexel - A Furniture Complex", CO, April 19, 1964, p. 17; "Now on the New York Stock Exchange" (advert), News & Observer, June 19, 1964, p. 39.

571   "Advertising Put Drexel Out Front", CO, April 19, 1965, p. 17.

572   "Firms Hand out Bonuses", CO, December 19, 1965, p. 57; "In Furniture Manufacturing Country", Charlotte News, April 29, 1966, p. 17; "Drexel Increases Dividend", CO, January 27, 1966, p. 22; Holt McPherson, High Point Enterprise, September 9, 1967, p. 4; "Furniture Merger Called Off", Asheville Citizen-Times, September 22, 1967, p. 23.

573   *"Teens Need Their Own Furnishings"*, CO, October 30, 1967, p. 25.

574   Joann Coker Harris, *"Furry Furniture's Fit for a Cave"*, CO, April 29, 1966, p. 39; Betsy Marsh, *"Furniture Lines Right for the Non-Conformist"*, News & Observer, May 1, 1966, p. 70.

575   *"Drexel Ownership Changes"*, Asheville Citizen-Times, July 10, 1968, p. 22; Guy Munger, *"In Diversity Is Strength"*, News & Observer, July 10, 1968, p. 25.

576   *"Hill Named Drexel Enterprises President"*, High Point Enterprise, November 30, 1965, p. 7; *"Drexel Workers Reject Union"*, Daily Times-News (Burlington), January 16, 1970, p. 20.

577   *"Joint Venture"*, News & Observer, December 8, 1965, p. 23.

578   *"Bassett Buys Prestige Firm"*, Statesville Record & Landmark, October 31, 1963, p. 1.

579   *"Gracious Ladies of Society Learning Bandage Rolling"*, News & Observer, October 8, 1939, p. 20; Sylvia Kidd Ray, Newton:Then&Now, p. 80; *"Firm To Build New Plant Near Newton"*, CO, July 8, 1955, p. 6; *"Yule Party Held By Newton Plant"*, CO, December 25, 1954, p. 5; Robert H. Spillman Interview, American Furniture Hall of Fame, April 4 & 7, 2005, Bassett Virginia, E.L. Briggs, Interviewer; *"Bassett Buys Prestige Firm"*, Statesville Record & Landmark, October 31, 1963, p. 1; *"Bassett Names New Officers, High Point Enterprise, December 31, 1963, p. 2;

580   *Telephone Interview with Glenn Hunsucker, May 10, 2011.*

581   *Telephone Interview with Glenn Hunsucker, May 10, 2011.*

582   *Telephone Interview with Glenn Hunsucker, May 10, 2011.*

583   *Telephone Interview with Glenn Hunsucker, May 10, 2011.*

584   *"Bassett Plans Addition"*, Statesville Record and Landmark, November 5, 1969, p. 9; *Telephone Interview with Glenn Hunsucker, May 10, 2022;* https://greensboro.com/bassett-ceo-to-retire-dean-to-replace-him/article_d1d21664-b593-5b31-9cb6-b5337a5dd9cf.html; https://www.prweb.com/releases/2005/07/prweb264852.htm

585   *Interview with Ed Harmon, Hickory, NC, November 2, 2021.*

586   *Interview with Ed Harmon, Hickory, NC, November 2, 2021.*

587   https://www.lanefurniture.com/page/our-company-history; *"New Corporations"*, News & Observer, April 3, 1946, p. 12.

588   Karen Barber, *"Furniture In Motion"*, CO, August 2, 1984, p. 76.

589   *"Furniture Family Tree"*, Hickory Furniture Mart.

590   *An Oral History with John Bray, American Home Furnishings Hall of Fame, 2017, 2019,* p. 12, 20-21.

591   *An Oral History with John Bray, American Home Furnishings Hall of Fame, 2017, 2019,* p. 20-21.

592   *An Oral History with John Bray, American Home Furnishings Hall of Fame, 2017, 2019,* p. 23.

593   Joann Coker Harris, *"Batman Dons Cape For Furniture Blast"*, CO, April 30, 1966, p. 6.

594   *"Factories Enlarging Showrooms, High Point Enterprise, October 20, 1967, p. 14.

595   https://www.zippia.com/thomasvillefurniture-careers-1147842/history/

596   Mamie Zillman, *"Furniture Designs Run the Gamut"*, CO, April 29, 1968, p. 23.

597   *"1966 Furniture Buyers Guide, First Edition"*, https://archive.org/stream/1966furniturebuy1966smit/1966furniturebuy1966smit_djvu.txt

Chapter 22: Flights of Fortune

598 Nancy Alexander, "Furniture Execs Go Down to the Market in Planes", Charlotte Observer (CO), February 3, 1966, p. 9; "Bernhardt Acquires Orbit Industries", Statesville Record and Landmark, January 1, 1970, p. 6; "New Bernhard Plant is Under Construction", CO, October 7, 1963, p. 1; "Bernhardt Buys Into Hibriten", CO, November 24, 1964, p. 8.

599 Nancy Alexander, "Furniture Execs Go Down to the Market in Planes", CO, February 3, 1966, p. 9.

600 Kay Reimler, "Industry's Centered In Western N.C. Hills", Charlotte News, April 29, 1966, p. 17.

601 Allen Sloan, "Furniture Men Hear Tread of Giants", CO, March 23, 1970, p. 8.

602 Thomas O'Hanlon, "5,350 Companies = A Mixed-Up Furniture Industry", Fortune, Volume LXXV, No. 2, February 1967, p. 145.

603 O'Hanlon, "5,350 Companies", Fortune, February 1967, p. 146-7.

604 O'Hanlon, "5,350 Companies", Fortune, February 1967, p. 145. A "Rube Goldberg" type operation meant that no one craftsman built any piece of furniture. Pieces were moved along on a production line with a given component being added by individuals. Rube Goldberg was a cartoonist that showed a wacky chain-reaction of events leading to the accomplishment of one task, in the case of furniture, a single piece.

605 O'Hanlon, "5,350 Companies", Fortune, February 1967, p. 148.

606 Paul H. Broyhill, This Is Broyhill, 2010, p. 109.

607 Paul H. Broyhill, This Is Broyhill, 2010, p. 110.

608 Paul H. Broyhill, This Is Broyhill, 2010, p. 107.

609 O'Hanlon, "5,350 Companies", Fortune, February 1967, p. 149.

610 O'Hanlon, "5,350 Companies", Fortune, February 1967, p. 180.

611 O'Hanlon, "5,350 Companies", Fortune, February 1967, p. 147.

612 Allen Sloan, "Furniture Men Hear Tread of Giants", CO, March 23, 1970, p. 8.

613 Allen Sloan, "Furniture Men Hear Tread of Giants", CO, March 23, 1970, p. 8.

614 "New Diningroom Furniture Plant for Statesville", CO, September 9, 1923, p. 41; "Sherrill Plant Acquired", Statesville Record and Landmark, April 8, 1974, p. 11L. "New Concept Used by Bernhardt", Statesville Record and Landmark, April 8, 1974, p. 11L.

615 "Phenix Chair Purchased by Thomasville", High Point Enterprise, May 2, 1964, p. 12; "Furniture Firm Acquisition", CO, December 2, 1966, p. 13C; Guy Munger, "Thomasville May Expand", News & Observer, February 7, 1968, p. 23.

616 Guy Munger, "In Diversity is Strength", News & Observer, July 10, 1968, p. 25; Thomasville Furniture Industries: News (Company publication), Vol. 8, No. 6, 1979, p. 3,4,30,39,40.

617 Guy Munger, "In Diversity is Strength", News & Observer, July 10, 1968, p. 25.

618 "Chair Firm's Assets Sold", Statesville Record and Landmark (SRL), October 4, 1967, p. 13; "Route 2 News", SRL, September 22, 1927, p. 6; "Small Roof Fire Monday Afternoon" SRL, December 12, 1933, p. 1; "George Sullivan Loses Right Arm", SRL, February 27, 1939, p. 1; "Way Is Cleared for Road Work", SRL, October 22, 1960, p. 1; "1966 Furniture Buyers Guide"

619   Letter from Mildred Church to her daughter, September 17, 1968; https://www.dol.gov/ agencies/whd/state/minimum-wage/history

620   Interview with Ruth Church & Romey Church, Hickory, NC, February 15, 2022.

621   Interview with Ruth Church & Romey Church, Hickory, NC, February 15, 2022.

622   Interview with Steve Lackey, Hickory, NC, February 17, 2022.

623   Paul Fogleman, "Booming Furniture Industry Closely Ties In With N.C. Four-County Area", Rocky Mount Telegram, April 4, 1970, p. 4; Wilson Daily Times, April 2, 1970, p. 4.

624   Fogleman, "Booming Furniture", Rocky Mount Telegram, April 4, 1970, p. 4; Wilson Daily Times, April 2, 1970, p. 4.

625   Fogleman, "Booming Furniture", Rocky Mount Telegram, April 4, 1970, p. 4; Wilson Daily Times, April 2, 1970, p. 4.

626   "Name of Furniture Firm Here Is Changed", Statesville Daily Record, June 30, 1952, p. 1.

627   Fogleman, "Booming Furniture", Rocky Mount Telegram, April 4, 1970, p. 4; Wilson Daily Times, April 2, 1970, p. 4.

628   Fogleman, "Booming Furniture", Rocky Mount Telegram, April 4, 1970, p. 4; Wilson Daily Times, April 2, 1970, p. 4.

629   "Booming Furniture Furniture Industry Key To Future For Unifour", Charlotte News, April 2, 1970, p. 2.

630   Robert Marks, "Market Outlook Seen as Better", High Point Enterprise, April 22, 1971, p. 27; Robert Marks, "'Cooperative Efforts' Make Market Possible: Gruenbuerg", High Point Enterprise, December 15, 1972, p. 32; Jimmy Dumbell, "Mountain Highway Landslide Creates Major Problems", CO, March 20, 1973, p. 8.

631   Robert Marks, "Gas and Buses Flow At Market", High Point Enterprise, April 19, 1974, p. 5.

632   "Market to Be Open To the Public", Charlotte News, April 19, 1974, p. 16.

633   "Market to Be Open To the Public", Charlotte News, April 19, 1974, p. 16; Ellen Scarborough, "Quiet Mountain Woman Finds Niche in the Furniture World, CO, April 19, 1974, p. 63.

634   Robert Marks, "Debut '72 Sparking Activity at Market", High Point Enterprise, April 23, 1971, p. 5; "House Planned as Grand Prize for Debut '73", Fort Lauderdale News, August 19, 1972, p. 93.

635   Edith Low, "Modern Furniture - Traditional Twist", Charlotte News, July 23, 1971, p. 7.

636   Edith McLean Low, "Quality Furniture Bought Today Could Be Tomorrow's Heirlooms", Charlotte News, April 2, 1970, p. 18.

637   Michelle Kilbourne-Minor, The Catawba Valley Furniture Industry: The Origins, Composition, and Conditions of Labor, 1879-1939, Graduate Thesis, Appalachian State University,1991, p. 62.

638   Edith McLean Low, "Quality Furniture Bought Today Could Be Tomorrow's Heirlooms", Charlotte News, April 2, 1970, p. 18.

639   Telephone Interview with Hank Rullman, January 5, 2021.

640   Allen Sloan, "17-Year-Old Furniture School Quietly Turns Out Experts", CO, March 15, 1970, p. 35.

641   "Catawba Valley Technical Institute Offers Courses in Crafts, Industries", Statesville Record and Landmark, March 20, 1965, p. 2. What began as the Catawba County Industrial Education Center

was then renamed as Catawba Valley Technical Institute, then Catawba Valley Technical College before becoming Catawba Valley Community College in 1979.

642   "Catawba Valley Trains Furniture Specialist in All Fields", CO, January 25, 1970, p. 117.

643   Lloyd H. Hyder, "Will Higher Education Place A Burden On Industry", HMC News Round Up, August 19, 1969, p. 1.

644   Lloyd H. Hyder, "Will Higher Education Place A Burden On Industry", HMC News Round Up, August 19, 1969, p. 1.

645   "New Corporations", News & Observer, August 17, 1928, p. 16; "Business World", CO, January 22, 1970, p. 35; "Open House Set at Warrenton Plant", News & Observer, October 18, 1970, p. 71.

⸺⟨≫⟩⸺

Chapter 24: Plastic Soul

646   "Furniture Industry Turns to Synthetics", CO, January 2, 1970, p. 53.

647   "Furniture Industry Turns to Synthetics", CO, January 2, 1970, p. 53.

648   Allen Sloan, "New Era in Furniture Replacing Days of Sawdust and Sweat", Charlotte Observer (CO), March 22, 1970, p. 12D.

649   Allen Sloan, "Burris Makes His Point: It's Not A Dull Business", CO, March 22, 1970, p. 12D.

650   "New Corporations", News & Observer, September 7, 1946, p. 8; "Colonial Home Near Lincolnton Will Be Scene of Showing in Furniture Styles", CO, June 17, 1951, p. 9D; "Ivey's of Charlotte" (advert), CO, September 9, 1965, p. 4A; Vanessa Gallman, "Furniture Manufacturer Burris, 'A Man's Man,' Dies of Cancer", CO, June 3, 1977, p. 16.

651   Allen Sloan, "Burris Makes His Point: It's Not A Dull Business", CO, March 22, 1970, p. 12D.

652   Allen Sloan, "Burris Makes His Point: It's Not A Dull Business", CO, March 22, 1970, p. 12D.

653   Allen Sloan, "Burris Makes His Point: It's Not A Dull Business", CO, March 22, 1970, p. 12D.

654   Dave Baity, "Lincoln Firm to Build Plastic Homes", CO, February 26, 1970, p. 1B, 8B.

655   Allen Sloan, "Burris Makes His Point: It's Not A Dull Business", CO, March 22, 1970, p. 12D; Allen Sloan, "Maker of Plastic Furniture Enjoying Booming Business", CO, March 24, 1970, p. 20; Allen Sloan, "3M Wood is Better Than Nature's" CO, March 24, 1970, p. 4B.

656   Edith Low, "Squashy Look in Chairs Invites You to Unwind", Charlotte News, June 24, 1971, p. 24.

657   Pat Holecek, "Danish Talent Glows at High Point", Dayton (Ohio) Daily News, October 25, 1971, p. 31.

658   Pat Borden, "'I Can Tell You What Women Will Want'", CO, February 22, 1976, p. 70.

659   Pat Borden, "'I Can Tell You What Women Will Want'", CO, February 22, 1976, p. 70.

660   Pat Borden, "'I Can Tell You What Women Will Want'", CO, February 22, 1976, p. 70.

661   Elizabeth Hillyer, "Plastic Furnishings Win Top Award", Chicago Tribune, January 22, 1972, p. 54.

662   Steve Raymond, "Youth Dollars Pressure Furniture Makers", Tampa Tribune, "April 29, 1973, p. 5H; Allen Sloan, "New Era in Furniture Replacing Days of Sawdust and Sweat", CO, March 22, 1970, p. 12D.

663   The Furniture Industry: Bernhardt Industries, Bernhardt Furniture Industries publication, p.

144-145.

664   Ray Hubbard, "Business Notes", *High Point Enterprise*, January 30, 1966, p. 6; *The Furniture Industry: Bernhardt Industries*, Bernhardt Furniture Industries publication, p. 144-145.

665   Interview with Ed Harmon, Hickory, NC, November 2 & 9, 2021.

666   Interview with Ed Harmon, Hickory, NC, November 2 & 9, 2021.

667   Interview with Ed Harmon, Hickory, NC, November 2 & 9, 2021.

668   Interview with Ed Harmon, Hickory, NC, November 2 & 9, 2021.

669   Interview with Ed Harmon, Hickory, NC, November 2 & 9, 2021.

670   Telephone Interview with Glenn Hunsucker, May 10, 2011.

671   Barbara Ingold, "Designer Sees Plastics as Material of the Future", CO, November 1, 1970, p. 131.

672   Paul H. Broyhill, *This Is Broyhill*, 2010, p. 117, 120-125.

673   Paul H. Broyhill, *This Is Broyhill*, 2010, p. 123-4.

674   Paul H. Broyhill, *This Is Broyhill*, 2010, p. 123-4.

~~~&~~~

Chapter 25: History, Old and New

675   Allen Sloan, "New Era in Furniture Replacing Days of Sawdust and Sweat", CO, March 22, 1970, p. 12D.

676   Allen Sloan, "New Era in Furniture Replacing Days of Sawdust and Sweat", CO, March 22, 1970, p. 12D.

677   Ronald Stockton, "New Furniture Company Shows Line at Drexel", *Asheville-Citizen Times*, April 12, 1970, p. 10C.

678   Ronald Stockton, "New Furniture Company Shows Line at Drexel", *Asheville-Citizen Times*, April 12, 1970, p. 10C.

679   Ronald Stockton, "New Furniture Company Shows Line at Drexel", *Asheville-Citizen Times*, April 12, 1970, p. 10C.

680   Ronald Stockton, "New Furniture Company Shows Line at Drexel", *Asheville-Citizen Times*, April 12, 1970, p. 10C.

681   Barbara Ingold, "Shopping Takes Him Around the World", CO, December 13, 1970, p. 2F.

682   Barbara Ingold, "Shopping Takes Him Around the World", CO, December 13, 1970, p. 2F.

683   Jim Whitfield, "Industrial Wages Rise 8 Per Cent", *News & Observer*, December 30, 1970, p. 15; Tom Wells, "75,000 Tar Heels Unemployed" *Asheville Citizen-Times*, December 13, 1970, p. 31.

684   Mary Yionoulis, "Many NCSU Alumni Successful In Growing Furniture Industry, *Rocky Mount Telegram*, March 29, 1970, p. 4; "Booming Furniture Industry Key To Future of Unifour", *Charlotte News*, April 2, 1970, p. 2; Paul Fogleman, "Booming Furniture Industry Closely Ties In With N.C. Four-County Area", *Rocky Mount Telegram*, April 4, 1970, p. 4; *Wilson Daily Times*, April 2, 1970, p. 4.

685   Bernie Ghilelin, "Wicker Wonder", CO, August 12, 1979, p. 7B; "Venture Has Started Major New Plant, CO, August 12, 1979, p. 7B.

686   Bernie Ghilelin, "Wicker Wonder", CO, August 12, 1979, p. 7B; "Venture Has Started Major New Plant, CO, August 12, 1979, p. 7B.

687 https://www.youtube.com/watch?v=I6ayLfs656o

688 Interview with William Karslake, Hickory, NC, March 1,2022.

689 Interview with William Karslake, Hickory, NC, March 1,2022.

690 Interview with William Karslake, Hickory, NC, March 1,2022.

691 Advert, Charlotte Observer, October 13, 1990, p. 9A; Interview with William Karslake, Hickory, NC, March 1,2022.

692 https://www.wpc.ncep.noaa.gov/tropical/rain/camille1969.html; https://coast.noaa.gov/data/hes/docs/postStorm/H_CAMILLE.pdf; https://www.wwltv.com/article/news/hurricane-camille-50-years-ago-it-was-like-world-war-3/289-299317d2-eb44-4909-9d62-fa85f5b4b0f2; "Flood Victims Get Furniture", High Point Enterprise, September 26, 1969, p. 21.

⸺⧉⸺

Chapter 26: Ingrown Ideas

693 Allen Sloan, "Furniture Tradition to Tumble", Charlotte Observer (CO), April 21, 1971, p. 48.

694 Allen Sloan, "Furniture Tradition to Tumble", CO, April 21, 1971, p. 48.

695 Allen Sloan, "Furniture Tradition to Tumble", CO, April 21, 1971, p. 48; "Furniture President Named", CO, February 1, 1970, p. 33; "Furniture Companies Combine", CO, April 24, 1967, p. 24.

696 Allen Sloan, "Furniture Tradition to Tumble", CO, April 21, 1971, p. 48; "New Manager", High Point Enterprise, September 8, 1974, p. 6.

697 "Darden Assumes Position with Furniture Group", Asheville-Citizen Times, April 9, 1968, p. 24; Bryan Haislip, "He Left Executive Suit for Law School", Charlotte News, November 9, 1970, p. 1.

698 "Firms Combining Management", CO, August 25, 1967, p. 18; "Singer Acquisition" News & Observer, March 20, 1973, p. 19;

699 Interview with Phillip Mosteller, July 6, 2021, Hickory, NC

700 Interview with Phillip Mosteller, July 6, 2021, Hickory, NC

701 Interview with Phillip Mosteller, July 6, 2021, Hickory, NC

702 B.J. Welborn, "Uncertainty Fills Furniture Workers' Lives", CO, November 29, 1976, p. 1-2B.

703 B.J. Welborn, "Uncertainty Fills Furniture Workers' Lives", CO, November 29, 1976, p. 1-2B.

704 B.J. Welborn, "Uncertainty Fills Furniture Workers' Lives", CO, November 29, 1976, p. 1-2B.

705 B.J. Welborn, "Uncertainty Fills Furniture Workers' Lives", CO, November 29, 1976, p. 2B.

706 Lee Weisbecker, "7 Plants Targeted By Union", CO, February 10, 1978, p. 7; Lee Weisbecker, "Company, Carpenters Wait'N'See", CO, February 26, 1978, p. 9.

707 Lee Weisbecker, "Votes are Vital to Labor, Management", CO, February 26, 1978, p. 31-32.

708 Lee Weisbecker, "Union Vote at Broyhill Postponed", CO, March 2, 1978, p. 9; "Union Delays Effort", CO, February 19, 1978, p. 9.

709 "Broyhill Plant Rejects Union By 247-99 Vote", CO, May 11, 1978, p. 47.

710 https://files.nc.gov/ncdcr/historic-preservation-office/survey-and-national-register/surveyreports/AH0716.pdf; "Phenix Chair Purchased by Thomasville", High Point Enterprise, May 2, 1964, p. 12.

711 Lee Weisbecker, "Furniture Plant OK's Union", CO, June 24, 1978, p. 1.

712 "Furniture Workers Get Increases Amid Dispute", News & Observer, December 19, 1978, p. 26; Ken Allen, "Union Rejects Raise, But Firm Grant's It Anyway", CO, December 19, 1978, p. 18;

"Pay Raise Exempts Pro-Union Employees", Rocky Mount Telegram, July 30, 1978, p. 31.

713   "Furniture Union Pact", CO, October 22, 1979, p. 20; William K. Stevens, "Inflation Opens Door For Union Growth in Sunbelt", CO, May 25, 1980. p. 1B-4B; "Recession Halted Trade-Union Momentum", CO, January 2, 1983, p. 53; "Today's Quote", CO, November 22, 1982, p. 2.

714   Jeff Johnson, "Consumers Are Leaning to Wood Furniture", Rocky Mount Telegram, January 6, 1980, p. 17.

715   Jeff Johnson, "Consumers Are Leaning to Wood Furniture", Rocky Mount Telegram, January 6, 1980, p. 17.

716   Jeff Johnson, "Consumers Are Leaning to Wood Furniture", Rocky Mount Telegram, January 6, 1980, p. 17.

717   Jeff Johnson, "Consumers Are Leaning to Wood Furniture", Rocky Mount Telegram, January 6, 1980, p. 17.

718   Jeff Johnson, "Consumers Are Leaning to Wood Furniture", Rocky Mount Telegram, January 6, 1980, p. 17.

719   Monte Plott, "Do-It-Yourself Trend Moves Into Furniture", The Robesonian (Lumberton), November 28, 1977, p. 9, 10.

720   Monte Plott, "Do-It-Yourself Trend Moves Into Furniture", The Robesonian (Lumberton), November 28, 1977, p. 9, 10.

721   Bradley Wyatt, "Tight Credit Boon To Furniture Rental", Charlotte News, March 19, 1980, p. 6.

722   "Broyhill Furniture's President Resigns", CO, September 6, 1979, p. 33; Don Bedwell, "Interco Buying Out Broyhill Furniture", CO, August 12, 1980, p. 19; https://www.smliv.com/stories/king-for-a-century/

723   Rodney Brooks, "Interco Agrees To Buy Broyhill", Asheville Citizen-Times, August 14, 1980. p. 13; "Broyhill Gest OK for Sale", News & Observer, November 27, 1980, p. 50.

724   Don Bedwell, "Furniture Industry Attracts New Suitors", CO, November 2, 1980, p. 38.

725   Don Bedwell, "Telco Acquiring Hickory Furniture", CO, December 2, 1980, p. 29.

726   Don Bedwell, "Furniture: After Rough '80, Industry Braces for '81", CO, January 11, 1981, p. 16H.

727   Interview with Ed Harmon, Hickory, NC, November 2 & 9, 2021.

—◦◦◦—

Chapter 27: The Exodus

728   Karen Barber, "A Search for Quality", Charlotte Observer (CO), April 17, 1983, p. 155; Jane Jeffries, "Salesmen Polish Pitches for Retailers' Onslaught", CO, April 17, 1983, p. 154.

729   Karen Barber, "A Search for Quality", CO, April 17, 1983, p. 155; Jane Jeffries, "Salesmen Polish Pitches for Retailers' Onslaught", CO, April 17, 1983, p. 154.

730   Peter Barnes, "Exhibitors Promote Western Furniture Market", CO, April 17, 1983, p. CVN 14-15.

731   William Mills, "Retail Power Concentrated at Furniture Market", CO, April 19, 1984, p. CVN 2.

732   Karen Barber, "The Little Guy", CO, April 19, 1984, p. CVN 4.

733   William Mills, "Retail Power Concentrated at Furniture Market", CO, April 19, 1984, p. CVN 2; Karen Barber, "The Little Guy", CO, April 19, 1984, p. CVN 4.

734   Karen Barber, "The Little Guy", CO, April 19, 1984, p. CVN 4.

735   Peter W. Barnes, "Western Piedmont Furniture Maker to Move Showroom to High Point", CO, May 3, 1982, p. 43; Karen Barber, "West End of Market Developing Identity of Own, Officials Say", CO, April 19, 1984, p. CVN 1.

736   Diane St. John, "Lure of the East", CO, April 19, 1984, p. CVN 3.

737   Karen Barber, "Home Resource Center Diversifies", CO, April 19, 1984, p. CVN 5.

738   Karen Barber, "Campaign Touts Hickory as Upholstery Market', CO, April 19, 1984, p. CVN 8.

739   Karen Barber, "West End of Market Developing Identity of Own, Officials Say", CO, April 19, 1984, p. CVN 8; Diane St. John, "Lure of the East", CO, April 19, 1984, p. CVN 3.

740   Karen Barber, "Campaign Touts Hickory as Upholstery Market', CO, April 19, 1984, p. CVN 8; "Furniture Experts Debate Permanency of Higher-Priced Trend", News & Observer, February 20, 1984, p. 34.

741   Diane St. John, "Lure of the East", CO, April 19, 1984, p. CVN 3.

742   Tammy Joyner, "Hickory Furniture Mart Reduces Schedule", CO, October 8, 1985, p. 14A.

743   Karen Barber, "Furniture Industry Exposition Starts Friday", CO, February 6, 1986, p. CVN 9.

744   Norman Gomlak, "Bernhardt Realigns, Matching Sales Paths", CO, August 31, 1996, p. 1D; David Olmos & Tammy Joyner, "It's Mostly White, Male at the Top", CO, March 1, 1987, Carolinas Edition, p. 1, 9A.

745   David Olmos & Tammy Joyner, "It's Mostly White, Male at the Top", CO, March 1, 1987, Carolinas Edition, p. 1, 9A.

746   "Workers Aided by Doctrine of Self-Reliance", CO, July 13, 1930, p. 23. A survey of race in furniture factories by the University of Virginia reported some areas where African-American participation in furniture jobs was "numerous" while some found "no negro labor was found." The report was not specific to western North Carolina.

747   David Olmos & Tammy Joyner, "It's Mostly White, Male at the Top", CO, March 1, 1987, Carolinas Edition, p. 1, 9A.

748   Diane St. John, "Banker Brings Dollars and Change to Furniture Industry", CO, October 22, 1984, p. 6C; "DeVille Sold", CO, April 29, 1984, p. 184.

749   Interview with Phillip Mosteller, July 6, 2021, Hickory, NC

750   Diane St. John, "Banker Brings Dollars and Change to Furniture Industry", CO, October 22, 1984, p. 6C.

751   Diane St. John, "Banker Brings Dollars and Change to Furniture Industry", CO, October 22, 1984, p. 6C.

752   Diane St. John, "Banker Brings Dollars and Change to Furniture Industry", CO, October 22, 1984, p. 6C.

753   Tammy Joyner, "Turner Furniture Plans to Buy Dunmore Furniture in Hickory", CO, June 26, 1985, p. 5C; Diane St. John, "Banker Brings Dollars and Change to Furniture Industry", CO, October

22, 1984, p. 6C.

754   Tammy Joyner, "Management Buying 3 Turner Upholstery Units", CO, May 6, 1986, p. 9B.

755   Karen Barber, "New Furniture Maker Fins Home in Old Factory", CO, September 4, 1983, p. CVN 8.

756   Karen Barber, "New Furniture Maker Fins Home in Old Factory", CO, September 4, 1983, p. CVN 8.

757   Rob Urban, "Success Lands Companies in Top 100", CO, June 12, 1987, p.

758   Betty Stone, "Man has job stability", CO, August 8, 2010, p. L6; "Firm Sold, Gets New Name", CO, November 30, 1986, p. 214; John Cleghorn, "Hickory Furniture Company Acquires Herman Chair Inc." CO, March 4, 1987, p. 7B.

759   Interview with Phillip Mosteller, July 6, 2021, Hickory, NC.

760   Interview with Phillip Mosteller, July 6, 2021, Hickory, NC; "Bassett Plans to Buy Impact Furniture Inc.", Charlotte Observer, August 25, 1984, p. 13A; "Bassett Furniture closing divisions, factories", News & Observer, May 23, 1997, p. C10.

Chapter 28: A Short Respite

761   "Furniture Shuttle", Charlotte Observer (CO), March 22, 1984, p. CVN 10; Liz Chandler, "Despite Attendance Declines, Market's Opening Welcome", CO, April 19, 1984, p. CVN10.

762   Diane St. John, "Benchcraft Moving Showroom to High Point", CO, June 12, 1984, p. 14; "Southern Furniture Market Gears Up for October Shows", New & Observer, July 1, 1984, p. 8D; Diane St. John, "Attendance Meager at Furniture Market", CO, October 18, 1984, p. 15.

763   Interview with Leroy Lail, Conover, NC, February 23, 2021.

764   Diane St. John, "Some Hickory Furniture Exhibitors To Remain Open", CO, October 29, 1984, p. 6C.

765   Karen Barber, "Market Weeks Play Smaller Role for Hickory Mart", CO, October 17, 1985, p. CVN 14; For a fuller understanding of the role of Hickory Furniture Mart during the transition from furniture market to consumer mart, see Richard Eller, G. Leroy Lail, Hickory Furniture Mart: A Landmark History, Redhawk Publications, 2020.

766   Karen Barber, "Market Weeks Play Smaller Role for Hickory Mart", CO, October 17, 1985, p. CVN 14.

767   "Workers Pursue Diplomas Without Leaving Plant", CO, December 27, 1984, CVN, p. 7.

768   "Workers Pursue Diplomas Without Leaving Plant", CO, December 27, 1984, CVN, p. 7; Sonja Pashcal Linsley and Scottie Klein Baker, "CCC&TI Program Allows Adults To Receive Diploma" CO, August 12, 1987, p. CVN, p. 3,6.

769   Beverly Brown, "Reading, Writing and Furniture Making?" CO, July 12, 1987, p. CVN 1,7.

770   Rob Urban, "Broyhill Opens Training Center for Retailers, CO, November 19, 1987, p. 2C.

771   "Plant Explosion in Lenoir Kills One Person, Injures 5", Asheville Citizen-Times, November 21, 1994, p. 1; "Fire Officials Say Wood Dust Blasts a Constant Hazard", News & Observer, December 12, 1994, p. 3.

772   "Plant Explosion in Lenoir Kills One Person, Injures 5", Asheville Citizen-Times, November 21, 1994, p. 1; "Fire Officials Say Wood Dust Blasts a Constant Hazard", News & Observer,

December 12, 1994, p. 3.

773 "Machinery Manufacturer Opens Office", CO, November 20, 1987, p. CVN 7.

774 Rob Urban, "Furniture Industry Suppliers Getting Down to Brass Tacks", CO, February 5, 1988, p. CVN 1.

775 https://www.hsmsolutions.com/about/history; Interview with Don Coleman, August 19, 2021, Hickory, NC.

776 "Hickory Springs Change of Guard", CO, November 24, 1996, p. 8V; Phone interview with Don Coleman, August 19, 2021, Hickory , NC; "New Newsletter for Furniture Industry", CO, March 30, 2003, p. 7V.

777 Bill Chapman, "Jobless Figures Show Economy's Growth", CO, December 16, 1987, p. CVN 12.

778 Rob Urban, "Broyhill Plans Drug Tests When Hiring", CO, November 12, 1989, p. 1B.

779 Neil Mara, "College Official Has Hands-On Approach to Hobby", CO, September 23, 1988, p. 81; Laura Zelenko, "History of Furniture Industry Locally to Unfold in New Book", CO, September 18, 1988, p. CVN 18.

780 Shirley Hunter Moore, "Tough Times For Furniture Workers", CO, November 23, 1990, p. 7B.

781 Shirley Hunter Moore, "Broyhill Chief: Workers Shouldn't Worry", CO, January 30, 1991, p. 8C.

782 Shirley Hunter Moore, "Worker's Hands Are Reattached", CO, March 15, 1991, p. 1B.

783 "CVCC Hosts Event To Show Off Furniture Division Building", CO, May 12, 1991, p. CVN 32.

784 Louise Barrett, "College Notes", CO, September 4, 1991, p. CVN 12.

785 Carol D. Leonnig, "Florida Company Takes Over DeVille in Buyout", CO, October 19, 1991, p. CVN 8.

786 Karen Barber, "La-Z-Boy To Buy Kincaid", CO, December 15, 1987, p. 6C.

787 Karen Barber, "Sawdust Settles in Kincaid Battle", CO, December 21, 1987, p. 1, 14C.

788 Karen Barber, "La-Z-Boy To Buy Kincaid", CO, December 15, 1987, p. 5-6C; Karen Barber, "Sawdust Settles in Kincaid Battle", CO, December 21, 1987, p. 1, 14C.

789 "North Carolina Deaths", CO, January 14, 1994, Gaston Observer, p. 6.

790 Tammy Joyner & John Cleghorn, "Lane Stalls Buyout Bid By Interco", CO, November 19, 1986, p. 8B; John Cleghorn, "Interco Makes Bid for Lane", CO, November 25, 1986, p. 13A.

791 John Cleghorn, "Lane Co. Rejects 2 Offers From St. Louis Company", CO, December 9, 1986, p. 14A.

792 "Business Briefly", CO, September 24, 1988, p. 10B; Karen Barber, "Furniture Manufacturer To Build Veneer Factory in Spruce Pine", CO, February 17, 1988, p. 9E; https://en.wikipedia.org/wiki/Ethan_Allen_(company); Karen Barber, "Managers Want to Buy Ethan Allen, CO, October 6, 1988, p. 4C.

793 "Rales Brothers Drop $2.7 Billion Effort to Acquire Interco, Inc.", CO, November 18, 1988, p. 29A; "Business Briefly", CO, May 23, 1989, p. 6D.

794 Suzanne S. Brown, "Blessed are the peacemakers", News & Observer, April 30, 1987, p. 28A.

795 John Cleghorn, "Interco Succeeds in Attempt To Acquire Lane Furniture", CO, December 19, 1986, p. 24A.; "Business Briefly", CO, April 15, 1987, p. 6E; Karen Barber, "Furniture Manufacturer

To Build Veneer Factory in Spruce Pine", CO, February 17, 1988, p. 9E.

--≪≫--

Chapter 29: A Numbers Game

796 *"Furniture Industry Consolidating"*, News & Observer, October, 16, 1988, p. 6I.

797 *"Furniture Industry Consolidating"*, News & Observer, October, 16, 1988, p. 6I.

798 *"Broyhill Scion Shakes Up Furniture Industry"*, News & Observer, April 19, 1987, p. 2I.

799 *"Broyhill Scion Shakes Up Furniture Industry"*, News & Observer, April 19, 1987, p. 2I.

800 *"Broyhill Scion Shakes Up Furniture Industry"*, News & Observer, April 19, 1987, p. 2I.

801 *"Broyhill Scion Shakes Up Furniture Industry"*, News & Observer, April 19, 1987, p. 2I.

802 *"Edgar Broyhill Vows to Keep Toll-Free Phone Lines At Store"*, Asheville Citizen-Times, November 23, 1989, p. 56A.

803 Jim Barnett, *"Furniture Discounters Rethinking Support of Bill to Restrict Makers"*, News & Observer, December 5, 1989, p. 27, 29.

804 C.E. Yandle, *"Tar Heel Recession Looms"*, News & Observer, September 19, 1990, p. 1, 7.

805 James Greiff, *"Clint Eastwood: Cowboy Decorator"*, CO, December 8, 1992, p. D1-2; https://www.youtube.com/watch?v=dAG8MKfgeyo;

806 https://www.youtube.com/watch?v=dAG8MKfgeyo

807 https://www.youtube.com/watch?v=dAG8MKfgeyo

808 https://www.youtube.com/watch?v=dAG8MKfgeyo; Telephone Interview with Ed Broyhill, April 19, 2022.

809 Telephone Interview with Ed Broyhill, April 19, 2022.

810 *"Bankrupt Furniture Firm Offers Settlement"*, News & Observer, February 16, 1996, p. 37; Telephone Interview with Ed Broyhill, April 19, 2022.

811 https://www.furnituretoday.com/business-news/broyhill-enters-race-for-congress-in-nc/; Pamela Sherrod, *"Discount Furniture Catalog Company Files For Bankruptcy"*, Chicago Tribune, November 12, 1995, Section 15, p. 10.

812 Tammy Joyner, *"Michigan-Based Firm Will Acquire Drexel Heritage Furniture in Burke"*, CO, September 23, 1986, p. 13A; Taylor Batten, *"Sale of High Point-Based Furniture Companies Cancelled"*, CO, January 6, 1996, p. 3D; *"Broyhill Scion Shakes Up Furniture Industry"*, News & Observer, April 19, 1987, p. 2I.

813 Norman Gomlak & Shirley Hunter Moore, *"700 Told They'll Lose Jobs"*, Charlotte Observer (CO), December 19, 1996, p. 1.

814 Gomlak & Hunter Moore, *"700 Told They'll Lose Jobs"*, CO, December 19, 1996, p. 1.

815 Gomlak & Hunter Moore, *"700 Told They'll Lose Jobs"*, CO, December 19, 1996, p. 1, 17.

816 Gomlak & Hunter Moore, *"700 Told They'll Lose Jobs"*, CO, December 19, 1996, p. 1, 17.

817 Andrew Shain, *"400-Job Impact Furniture Plant in Hildebran Closing*, CO, May 23, 1997, p. D1-2.

818 *"225 Furniture Layoffs in Spruce Pine"*, CO, July 19, 1997, p. D1; *"Lexington Furniture Announces Layoff"*, News & Observer, July 19, 1997, p. 6D.

819 Chip Wilson, *"Cochrane Shutting Down Newton Plant"*, CO, July 17, 1997, p. L1; Phillip Fiorni, *"Furniture Company Adds 3 New Lines"*, Journal and Courier (Lafayette, Indiana), October

14, 1996, p. 9.

820   Stella M. Hopkins, "Furniture Makers Ponder Puzzling Slump", CO, August 17, 1997, p. D1,6.

821   "Philippines or U.S.A.?" CO, March 12, 1996, p. 5A; "Manufacturers Pass Off Foreign Goods as Made in the USA", Asheville Citizen-Times, March 17, 1996, p. 22.

822   "Manufacturers Pass Off Foreign Goods as Made in the USA", Asheville Citizen-Times, March 17, 1996, p. 22.

823   Powell Nowell, "Furniture Industry Following Computer Trends with SOHO Trend", Rocky Mount Telegram, June 13, 1996, p. 9.

824   Powell Nowell, "Furniture Industry Following Computer Trends with SOHO Trend", Rocky Mount Telegram, June 13, 1996, p. 9.

825   "Tenth Annual Furniture Festival" (advert), CO, July 14, 1996, p. 15V.

826   G. Leroy Lail & Richard Eller, Hickory Furniture Mart: A Landmark History, Redhawk Publications, p. 109-115.

827   "LifeStyle Furnishings Divesting Three Brands, News & Observer, December 7, 2001, p. 16C; John Rega, "Furniture Maker's IPO Could Top $460 Million", CO, July 9, 1998, p. 10D.

828   Stella M. Hopkins, "Furniture Makers Ponder Puzzling Slump", CO, August 17, 1997, p. D1,6.

829   Stella M. Hopkins, "Furniture Makers Ponder Puzzling Slump", CO, August 17, 1997, p. D1,6.

830   Stella M. Hopkins, "Furniture Makers Ponder Puzzling Slump", CO, August 17, 1997, p. D1,6.

831   Stella M. Hopkins, "Furniture Makers Ponder Puzzling Slump", CO, August 17, 1997, p. D1,6.

832   Allen Norwood, "Designer Furniture", CO, October 25, 1997, p. 1E, 10E.

833   "A Brand By Any Other Name Sell Just As Much Furniture", Rocky Mount Telegram, November 2, 1997, p. 8D.

⸻∞⸻

Chapter 30: Slowly Killing the City

834   Heather Howard, Greg Lacour, "1,200 Furniture Jobs Cut in N.C.", Charlotte Observer (CO), June 8, 2005, p. D1,2.

835   Heather Howard, Greg Lacour, "1,200 Furniture Jobs Cut in N.C.", CO, June 8, 2005, p. D1,2.

836   Steve Cannon, "N.C. Leads Another Category: Manufacturing Jobs Lost", News & Observer, February 8, 2001, p. D1.

837   Beth Macy, Factory Man: How One Furniture Maker Battled Offshoring, Stayed Local - And Helped Save An American Town, 2014, Bay Back Books, Macy's research presents a compelling argument for the complicity of the Chinese government in its effort to undercut the American furniture manufacturing sector.

838   Heather Howard, Greg Lacour, "1,200 Furniture Jobs Cut in N.C.", CO, June 8, 2005, p. D1,2; https://www.furnituretoday.com/business-news/fbi-closing-more-plants/

839   Adam Bell, "Newton To Lose Furniture Plant", CO, March 10, 2001, p. 1-2D.

840 *https://www.furnituretoday.com/business-news/fbi-closing-more-plants/*

841 Kerry Hall, *"Furniture Industry Adapts, Remodels"*, CO, June 9, 2005, p. D1,6.

842 Kerry Hall, *"Furniture Industry Adapts, Remodels"*, CO, June 9, 2005, p. D1,6.

843 Hall, *"Furniture Industry Adapts, Remodels"*, CO, June 9, 2005, p. D1,6.

844 Hall, *"Furniture Industry Adapts, Remodels"*, CO, June 9, 2005, p. D1,6.

845 Hall, *"Furniture Industry Adapts, Remodels"*, CO, June 9, 2005, p. D1,6.

846 Hall, *"Furniture Industry Adapts, Remodels"*, CO, June 9, 2005, p. D1,6.

847 Heather Howard, Greg Lacour, *"1,200 Furniture Jobs Cut in N.C."*, CO, June 8, 2005, p. D1,2.

848 John Bray, *"An Abbreviated History of Furniture in North Carolina"*, script from presentation, p. 44.

849 Paul Nowell, *"Bernhardt Riding High one Stewart Line"*, Lenoir News-Topic (LNT), March 9, 2004, p. 1,3A; Paul Teague, *"Bernhardt Lands Smithsonian License"*, LNT, January 16, 2007, p. 1B; Leigh Dyer, *"Domestic Queen's Line Won't Be All Domestic"*, CO, April 7, 2003, 9D.

850 *"Bernhardt Goes Through Corporate Reorganization"*, LNT, May 26, 2009, Caldwell Historical Museum Collection; Leigh Dyer, *"5 Family-Owned Companies That Beat the Odds"*, CO, October 19, 2003, p. 1,4E.

851 Edward Terry, *"Broyhill CEO Resigns"*, LNT, June 27, 2006, p. 1, 3A.

852 Edward Terry, *"Goal: Double Broyhill's Size"*, LNT, Caldwell Heritage Museum Collection.

853 Edward Terry. *"Broyhill Staying"*, LNT, September 12, 2008, p. 1, 6.

854 Edward Terry. *"Broyhill Staying"*, LNT, September 12, 2008, p. 1, 6; Teresa Shore, *"They Should Have Let Broyhill Go"*, LNT, September 19, 2008, Caldwell Heritage Museum Collection.

855 Paul Teague, *"Payouts Under Scrutiny"*, LNT, March 18, 2009, p. 1; Paul Teague, *"New challenges Ahead for Cook"*, LNT, January 15, 2011, p. 1.

856 *"The Pain of Furniture Brands' Workers"* (Lenoir News-Topic editorial), reprinted in the News & Observer, September 19, 2013, p. A9.

857 Virginia Annable, *"'What A Great Company It was'"*, LNT, October 28, 2018, p. 1, 9A.

858 Virginia Annable, *"'What A Great Company It Was'"*, LNT, October 28, 2018, p. 1, 9A.

859 Paul Teague, *"Kincaid Seeks Incentive"*, LNT, March 24, 2009, p. 1,6; Paul Teague, *"Kincaid Incentive Package Approved"*, LNT, May 7, 2009, p. 1,3A.

860 Paul Teague, *"Kincaid Incentive Package Approved"*, LNT, May 7, 2009, p. 1,3A.

861 *"Kim Gilliland, "Kincaid's Closing Will Ripple Hudson"*, LNT, April 20, 2014, p. 1, 7A.

862 *"Kim Gilliland, "Kincaid's Closing Will Ripple Hudson"*, LNT, April 20, 2014, p. 1, 7A.

863 *"Kim Gilliland, "Kincaid's Closing Will Ripple Hudson"*, LNT, April 20, 2014, p. 1, 7A.

864 Edward Terry, *"New Factory Coming"*, LNT, 2004, Caldwell Heritage Museum collection.

865 *"More Furniture Executives Let Go"*, LNT, November 27, 2013, Caldwell Heritage Museum collection; Virginia Annable, *"Fairfield Chair names Mitchell New President"*, LNT, October 10, 2017, p. 1,5A.

866 Guy Lucas, *"Heritage Home Group's CEO Leaves"*, High Point Enterprise, May 19, 2015, p. A1. HHG was formed out of KPS Capital Partners.

867 Telephone Interview with Bruce Nelson, June 20, 2022.

868 *"Furniture Plant Will Close"*, News & Observer, June 28, 2008, p. 2D; https://morganton.

com/news/drexel-heritage-plant-closing-employees-to-lose-jobs/article_538872c8-eb68-11e3-b3c2-001a4bcf6878.html; "Drexel Plant to Close in Morganton", CO, June 4, 2014, p. A8.

869   Telephone Interview with Bruce Nelson, June 20, 2022.

870   Allison Pennell, "Making A Mark", Hickory Daily Record, August 29, 1999; Back Then…, "Behind the Southern Desk", 1999, Charter Communications.

871   Dianne Straley, "Exela Pharma Buys Broyhill HQ" CO, April 21, 2013, p. L1,5.

872   Paul Teague, "For Sale", LNT, July 27, 2011, p. 1; "Furniture Firm Unveils Showplace", Durham Herald-Sun, October 30, 1966, p. 8D.

873   Michael K. Duggan, The Furniture Wars: How America Lost a Fifty Million Dollar Industry, 2009, privately published.

874   https://casetext.com/case/good-v-broyhill-furniture-inc

875   https://casetext.com/case/good-v-broyhill-furniture-inc

876   https://casetext.com/case/good-v-broyhill-furniture-inc

⸺⚮⸺

Chapter 31: Profit and Loss

877   "Business Briefs", Asheville Citizen-Times, October 22, 1986, p. 36.

878   Al Stamboski, "Furniture maker plans Harrods line for autumn", St. Louis Post-Dispatch, January 18, 2000, p. C8; Margaret Allen, "Highland House Furniture and Harrods", email, August 22, 2022.

879   Margaret Allen, "Highland House Furniture and Harrods", email, August 22, 2022.

880   Margaret Allen, "Highland House Furniture and Harrods", email, August 22, 2022.

881   Megan Sexton, "Stories inspire furniture pieces" The Daily Oklahoman, November 2, 2000, p. 18; https://www.furnituretoday.com/business-news/some-highland-house-items-to-survive/; Margaret Allen, "Highland House Furniture and Harrods", email, August 22, 2022.

882   Hannah Mitchell, Jonathan B. Cox, "Is It Worth the Price?", Charlotte Observer (CO), January 19, 2007, p. 1-6A.

883   Scott Mooneyham, "New Robber Barons Running Loose in N.C.", Asheville Citizen-Times, January 21, 2007, p. 11; Hannah Mitchell, Jonathan B. Cox, "Is It Worth the Price?", CO, January 19, 2007, p. 1-6A.

884   Hannah Mitchell, "Furniture Industry Faces Its Future", CO, February 21, 2007, p. D3.

885   "Insider", CO, June 9, 2003, p. 2D.

886   "Asian Firms Rent N.C. Space", News & Observer, March 31, 2007, p. B6.

887   Joe McDonald, "Rising Wages Suggest Change Coming to China", News & Observer, June 9, 2010, p. 14.

888   https://www.forbes.com/sites/pamdanziger/2019/12/03/ethan-allen-turns-the-tables-and-goes-back-to-what-made-it-great/?sh=ca9b78b46545

889   https://www.architecturaldigest.com/story/heritage-home-group-files-for-bankruptcy

890   Jen Aronoff, "Furniture maker celebrates 25 years", CO, March 12, 2006, p. 1V, 14V; https://www.stirdenver.com/partners/hbf/; "60 to be laid off in Hickory", CO, January 25, 2012, p. B2; "Hickory furniture maker outfits Panthers", CO, December 19, 1995, p. D1; https://www.globenewswire.com/news-release/2008/03/31/375525/7151/en/Furniture-Brands-Completes-Sale-

of-HBF-Unit.html

891 Brandy Templeton, "SOLD: Southern Furniture Sold to China", https://www.observernewsonline.com/content/sold%C2%A0-southern-furniture-sold-china

892 Sylvia Ray, "Southern Furniture Acquires Bracewell with Expansion Move", Observer-News-Enterprise (Newton), October 1, 1980, p. 15

893 "Universal Celebrates Anniversary", Hickory Daily Record, October 11, 2020, p. B1, 5.

894 "Universal Celebrates Anniversary", Hickory Daily Record, October 11, 2020, p. B1, 5.

895 Brandy Templeton, "SOLD: Southern Furniture Sold to China", https://www.observernewsonline.com/content/sold%C2%A0-southern-furniture-sold-china

896 Virginia Annable, "Furniture Firm Grows in Conover", Hickory Daily Record, May 7, 2021, p. 1,3; "Universal Celebrates Anniversary", Hickory Daily Record, October 11, 2020, B1.

897 Virginia Annable, "Furniture Firm Grows", Hickory Daily Record, May 7, 2021, p. 1,3.

898 Virginia Annable, "Furniture Firm Grows", Hickory Daily Record, May 7, 2021, p. 1,3.

899 https://www.wfmynews2.com/article/news/local/craftmaster-furniture-sold-to-chinese-company/83-403327371

900 Interview with Steve Lackey, Hickory, NC, January 4, 2022.

901 Interview with Steve Lackey, Hickory, NC, January 4, 2022.

902 Interview with Steve Lackey, Hickory, NC, January 4, 2022.

903 Interview with Steve Lackey, Hickory, NC, January 4, 2022.

904 Interview with Steve Lackey, Hickory, NC, January 4, 2022.

905 Interview with Steve Lackey, Hickory, NC, January 4, 2022.

906 Interview with Steve Lackey, Hickory, NC, January 4, 2022.

907 Telephone interview with Tim Stump, May 16, 2022.

908 https://www.stumpandcompany.com/history/; Telephone interview with Tim Stump, May 16, 2022; Interview with Steve Lackey, Hickory, NC, January 4, 2022.

909 Telephone interview with Tim Stump, May 16, 2022; Interview with Roy Calcagne, Hiddenite, NC, December 6, 2021.

910 https://www.stumpandcompany.com/history/; Telephone interview with Tim Stump, May 16, 2022; Timothy Aeppel, "Transport costs shift factory work to U.S." CO, June 14, 2008, p. 4D.

911 Kerry Hall, "A Bright Spot", CO, June 20, 2006, p. D1,2.

912 Interview with Roy Calcagne, Hiddenite, NC, December 6, 2021.

913 Interview with Roy Calcagne, Hiddenite, NC, December 6, 2021.

914 Interview with Roy Calcagne, Hiddenite, NC, December 6, 2021

915 Interview with Roy Calcagne, Hiddenite, NC, December 6, 2021.

916 https://fortune.com/2020/09/13/milton-friedman-anniversary-business-purpose/

⸺❧⸺

Chapter 32: One Comfortable Place

917 Hannah Mitchell, "Hickory Attracts 820-Job Factory", CO, April 14, 2008, p. 1D.

918 "Claremont's Sutter Street Manufacturing to Expand, Add 72 Jobs" Hickory Daily Record, July 6, 2017 https://hickoryrecord.com/news/claremonts-sutter-street-manufacturing-to-expand-add-72-jobs/article_df1578b2-b68a-57a2-b74a-96471fe6704a.html

919   Deon Roberts, "Furniture-Maker Will Create 200 Jobs in NC With New Plant", Rock Hill Herald (SC), January 13, 2019, p. A11.

920   Deon Roberts, "Furniture-Maker Will Create 200 Jobs in NC With New Plant", Rock Hill Herald (SC), January 13, 2019, p. A11.

921   Jen Pilla Taylor, "Equal Billing for Bob", Charlotte Observer, January 28, 2006, p. I1,4.

922   Telephone interview with Mitchell Gold, July 29, 2021.

923   Elaine Markoutsas, "Good As Gold: Design Mavericks keep it comfortable", Chapel Hill News, October 29, 2006, p. D7.

924   Telephone interview with Mitchell Gold, July 29, 2021.

925   Telephone interview with Mitchell Gold, July 29, 2021.

926   Telephone interview with Mitchell Gold, July 29, 2021.

927   Telephone interview with Mitchell Gold, July 29, 2021.

928   Telephone interview with Mitchell Gold, July 29, 2021.

929   Jen Pilla Taylor, "Equal Billing for Bob", Charlotte Observer, January 28, 2006, p. I4; "Insider", Charlotte Observer, February 23, 1998, p. 2D; Telephone interview with Mitchell Gold, July 29, 2021; Danny C. Flanders, "Pair's casual furniture sits well with boomers", New & Observer, April 29, 200, p. 5E.

930   https://businessofhome.com/articles/mitchell-gold-bob-williams-taps-omnichannel-exec-allison-o-connor-as-new-ceo.

931   Telephone interview with Mitchell Gold, July 29, 2021.

932   Telephone interview with Mitchell Gold, July 29, 2021.

933   Mitchell Gold, Mitchell Gold + Bob Williams: Who We Are, Assouline Publishing, NY, 2014, p. 149.

934   "Letters to the Editor", Taylorsville Times, January 27, 2016, p. 10.

935   Lois Smith Brady, "Mitchell Gold and Tim Scofield", New York Times, https://www.nytimes.com/2010/07/04/fashion/weddings/04VOWS.html; Vanessa Infanzon, "Pillars of North Carolina: Mitchell Gold makes a mark in furniture, civil rights" Business NC, November 1, 2019, https://businessnc.com/pillars-of-north-carolina-mitchell-gold-makes-a-mark-in-furniture-civil-rights/

936   Mitchell Gold, Mitchell Gold + Bob Williams: Who We Are, Assouline Publishing, NY, 2014, p. 87.

937   Guy Raf, How I Built This (podcast transcript), https://steno.ai/how-i-built-this-with-guy/mitchell-gold-bob-williams-home-furnishings-mitchell-gold-and; Tiffany Stanley, "The Last Frontier for Gay Rights", Washington Post, April 2, 2018, https://www.washingtonpost.com/news/style/wp/2018/04/02/feature/the-last-frontier-for-gay-rights/

938   Tiffany Stanley, "The Last Frontier for Gay Rights", Washington Post, April 2, 2018, https://www.washingtonpost.com/news/style/wp/2018/04/02/feature/the-last-frontier-for-gay-rights/

939   http://outrightyouthcv.com/; Mitchell Gold, Mitchell Gold + Bob Williams: Who We Are, Assouline Publishing, NY, 2014, p. 111; Tiffany Stanley, "The Last Frontier for Gay Rights", Washington Post, April 2, 2018, https://www.washingtonpost.com/news/style/wp/2018/04/02/feature/the-last-frontier-for-gay-rights/; Yonat Shimron, "Passion for Justice", News & Observer, November 20, 2008, p. 1D,4D.

940   "Letters to the Editor", *Taylorsville Times*, January 27, 2016, p. 10.

941   Micah Henry, "Engineering planning begins for Shurtape Sewer Project", *Taylorsville Times*, January 20, 2016, p. 1-2.

942   Tiffany Stanley, "The Last Frontier for Gay Rights", *Washington Post*, April 2, 2018, https://www.washingtonpost.com/news/style/wp/2018/04/02/feature/the-last-frontier-for-gay-rights/; Mitchell Gold, phone interview, November 3, 2022; "Letters to the Editor", *Taylorsville Times*, January 27, 2016, p. 10.

943   Mitchell Gold, *Mitchell Gold + Bob Williams: Who We Are*, Assouline Publishing, NY, 2014, p. 85; Vanessa Infanzon, "Pillars of North Carolina: Mitchell Gold makes a mark in furniture, civil rights" *Business NC*, November 1, 2019, https://businessnc.com/pillars-of-north-carolina-mitchell-gold-makes-a-mark-in-furniture-civil-rights/

944   Yonat Shimron, "Passion for Justice", *News & Observer*, November 20, 2008, p. 4D; Mitchell Gold, phone interview, November 3, 2022.

945   Mitchell Gold, phone interview, November 3, 2022.

946   Mitchell Gold, *Mitchell Gold + Bob Williams: Who We Are*, Assouline Publishing, NY, 2014, p. 9.

947   Alexander History Group, LLC, *Alexander County Treasures: A History of Remarkable People and Precious Gems*, Donning Company, 2012, p. 318.

---∞---

Chapter 33: The Son of a Sander

948   "'Mom and pop' make styling statement", *News & Observer*, November 9, 1980, Design for Living Section, p. 2; http://www.leeindustries.com/about/lee/id/3/pid/21/Our%20History

949   "'Mom and pop' make styling statement", *News & Observer*, November 9, 1980, Design for Living Section, p. 2.

950   "'Mom and pop' make styling statement", *News & Observer*, November 9, 1980, Design for Living Section, p. 2; http://www.leeindustries.com/about/lee/id/3/pid/21/Our%20History; Diane St. John, "Furniture Market Sales May Mean More Jobs", CO, May 5, 1984, p. 12A.

951   Heather Howard, "Good, Bad News For Furniture", CO, June 12, 2005, p. V1; Charlene H. Carpenter, "Lee Industries to Renovate Old Factory", CO, June 24, 2012, p. V2; http://www.leeindustries.com/about/lee/id/3/pid/21/Our%20History

952   Heather Howard, "Good, Bad News For Furniture", CO, June 12, 2005, p. V1; Charlene H. Carpenter, "Lee Industries to Renovate Old Factory", CO, June 24, 2012, p. V2.

953   Greg Lacour, "Norm's shop visits Newton", CO, May 3, 2002, CVN, p. 1-2.

954   Beverly Brown, "Firm's Furniture Ends Up in Magazines, Market", CO, March 17, 1987, CVN, p. 9; http://www.leeindustries.com/spotlight; https://hickoryrecord.com/news/furniture-maker-expands-moves-corporate-office-to-conover/article_bec2fd96-249a-11e3-9ff1-001a4bcf6878.html

955   https://www.legacy.com/us/obituaries/hickoryrecord/name/dorcas-coley-obituary?id=27166903; https://www.legacy.com/us/obituaries/limaohio/name/norman-coley-obituary?pid=172248488n=norman-coley&pid=172248488&referrer=0&; https://www.bizjournals.com/charlotte/news/2016/10/13/catawba-county-s-lee-industries-sold-to-texas.html

956 https://www.legacy.com/us/obituaries/hickoryrecord/name/dorcas-coley-obituary?id=27166903; https://www.legacy.com/us/obituaries/limaohio/name/norman-coley-obituary?pid=172248488n=norman-coley&pid=172248488&referrer=0&; https://www.bizjournals.com/charlotte/news/2016/10/13/catawba-county-s-lee-industries-sold-to-texas.html

957 https://homenewsnow.com/blog/2021/12/21/newton-coley-brings-two-industry-veterans-together-at-luxury-upholstery-startup/

958 Elaine Tooley, "The Man Behind the Name", Wake Forest University publication, available at https://www.wfu.edu/stories/2017/man-behind-name/

959 Elaine Tooley, "The Man Behind the Name", Wake Forest University publication, available at https://www.wfu.edu/stories/2017/man-behind-name/

960 Email from Michele McCreary, November 11, 2021.

961 Email from Michele McCreary, November 11, 2021; Elaine Tooley, "The Man Behind the Name", Wake Forest University publication, available at https://www.wfu.edu/stories/2017/man-behind-name/

962 Interview with Bob McCreary, Rick Coffey, Robert McCreary, Newton, NC, February 1, 2022; Email from Michele McCreary, November 11, 2021; Elaine Tooley, "The Man Behind the Name", Wake Forest University publication, available at https://www.wfu.edu/stories/2017/man-behind-name/

963 Email from Michele McCreary, November 11, 2021; Elaine Tooley, "The Man Behind the Name", Wake Forest University publication, available at https://www.wfu.edu/stories/2017/man-behind-name/.

964 Email from Michele McCreary, November 11, 2021; Elaine Tooley, "The Man Behind the Name", Wake Forest University publication, available at https://www.wfu.edu/stories/2017/man-behind-name/; Interview with Bob McCreary, Rick Coffey, Robert McCreary, Newton, NC, February 1, 2022.

965 Interview with Bob McCreary, Rick Coffey, Robert McCreary, Newton, NC, February 1, 2022.

966 Interview with Bob McCreary, Rick Coffey, Robert McCreary, Newton, NC, February 1, 2022.

967 Interview with Bob McCreary, Rick Coffey, Robert McCreary, Newton, NC, February 1, 2022.

968 Interview with Bob McCreary, Rick Coffey, Robert McCreary, Newton, NC, February 1, 2022. "McCreary Buys Chair Company", CO, August 20, 2000, p. V23; Jen Aronoff, "Reopening Planned For Furniture Plant", CO, October 28, 2006, p. 2D.

969 Interview with Bob McCreary, Rick Coffey, Robert McCreary, Newton, NC, February 1, 2022.

970 Email from Rick Coffey to author, April 18, 2022.

971 Interview with Bob McCreary, Rick Coffey, Robert McCreary, Newton, NC, February 1, 2022.

972 "McCreary Buys Chair Company", CO, August 20, 2000, p. V23; Jen Aronoff, "Reopening Planned For Furniture Plant", CO, October 28, 2006, p. 2D; http://mccrearymodern.com

973 Interview with Bob McCreary, Rick Coffey, Robert McCreary, Newton, NC, February 1, 2022.

974 https://www.wfu.edu/stories/2017/man-behind-name/

975 Interview with Bob McCreary, Rick Coffey, Robert McCreary, Newton, NC, February 1, 2022.

976 https://www.wfu.edu/stories/2017/man-behind-name/; https://godeacs.com/news/2014/7/1/Wake_Forest_To_Break_Ground_On_McCreary_Indoor_Center.aspx; https://

godeacs.com/news/2008/9/27/Bob_McCreary_Receives_Gene_Hooks_Achievement_Award.aspx "McCreary Donates $50,000 for 2 Halls", CO, February 18, 2004, p. V2. Bob McCreary has made many other contributions to the community beyond those listed, including substantial endowments to hospitals in both Catawba and Caldwell Counties.

977 Interview with Bob McCreary, Rick Coffey, Robert McCreary, Newton, NC, February 1, 2022.

⸺⸙⸺

Chapter 34: The Work Goes On

978 Interview with Dr. Garrett D. Hinshaw, May 3, 2021.

979 https://hickoryrecord.com/news/mans-two-careers-built-on-furniture/article_ef6e2655-4b3d-562e-9f8e-b923e665bc8e.html; Interview with D.L. Turbyfill, Hickory, NC, August 24, 2022.

980 Interview with D.L. Turbyfill, Hickory, NC, August 24, 2022.

981 Interview with D.L. Turbyfill, Hickory, NC, August 24, 2022.

982 Interview with D.L. Turbyfill, Hickory, NC, August 24, 2022.

983 Leigh Pressley, "College Notes", Charlotte Observer, October 26, 2004, p. V2; Interview with D.L. Turbyfill, Hickory, NC, August 24, 2022; https://www.furnituretoday.com/business-news/catawba-valley-proud-of-comprehensive-furniture-programs/

984 Interview with D.L. Turbyfill, Hickory, NC, August 24, 2022.

985 Interview with Dr. Garrett D. Hinshaw, May 3, 2021.

986 Interview with Dr. Garrett D. Hinshaw, May 3, 2021.

987 Interview with Dr. Garrett D. Hinshaw, May 3, 2021.

988 Interview with Cindy Fulbright, Newton, NC, April 26, 2022; https://www.visithickorymetro.com/articles/post/hickory-the-furniture-capital-of-the-world/; https://www.npr.org/2016/09/01/492203137/demand-for-upholsters-is-great-they-can-sew-up-a-job-in-no-time

989 Interview with Cindy Fulbright, Newton, NC, April 26, 2022

990 Interview with Cindy Fulbright, Newton, NC, April 26, 2022

991 Interview with Cindy Fulbright, Newton, NC, April 26, 2022

992 Interview with Cindy Fulbright, Newton, NC, April 26, 2022

993 Interview with Cindy Fulbright, Newton, NC, April 26, 2022

994 Interview with Cindy Fulbright, Newton, NC, April 26, 2022

995 https://www.npr.org/2016/09/01/492203137/demand-for-upholsters-is-great-they-can-sew-up-a-job-in-no-time; Interview with Cindy Fulbright, Newton, NC, April 26, 2022

996 https://crawdads.milbstore.com/collections/llamas-de-hickory

997 https://businessnc.com/soaring-latino-population-fortifies-north-carolinas-growth-prospects/; https://www.zippia.com/lee-industries-careers-29332/; Virginia Annable, "Employers more flexible to attract needed workers", Hickory Daily Record, May 15, 2022, p. A1,8; Data from Western Piedmont Council of Governments, provided by Taylor Dellinger via email, September 14, 2022.

998 Virginia Annable, "Employers more flexible to attract needed workers", Hickory Daily Record, May 15, 2022, p. A1,8.

999 Sarah Nagem, "Furniture Makers Streamline Process to Fill Niche Markets", CO, July 22, 2013, B1,2B.

1000 Sarah Nagem, "Furniture Makers", CO, July 22, 2013, B1; Paul Howell, "N.C. Furniture

Maker Believes His Dot-Com Company is Different", *Asheville Citizen-Times*, February 25, 2001, p. 17.

1001 Howell, "N.C. Furniture Maker", *Asheville Citizen-Times*, February 25, 2001, p. 17.

1002 Courtney Campbell, "4 Family Furniture Businesses Built to Last", *https://www.ourstate.com/family-furniture-businesses-built-to-last/*

1003 Sarah Nagem, "Furniture Makers Streamline Process to Fill Niche Markets", *CO*, July 22, 2013, B1.

1004 Lisa Pollak, "Civic Center Takes a Bow", *CO*, October 29, 1993, p. V1.

1005 Charlene Carpenter, "Big Plans for Ex-Factory Site", *CO*, May 1, 2011, p. V1; *https://hickoryrecord.com/townnews/building_industry/amphitheater-represents-mans-love-of-conover-music/article_e1c5f3e0-7424-11e9-a434-cb6b099554a2.html*

1006 Charlene Carpenter, "Big Plans for Ex-Factory Site", *CO*, May 1, 2011, p. V4.

1007 Thomas Russell, "Heritage Home Group Identifies $22 Million Bid for Broyhill, Thomasville, Drexel and Henredon", *Furniture Today*, August 31, 2018, *https://www.furnituretoday.com/business-news/heritage-home-group-identifies-22m-bid-broyhill-thomasville-drexel-and-henredon/*; Clint Engel, "The Broyhill Move: Big Lots acquires rights to names, trademarks", *Furniture Today*, February 25, 2019, *https://www.furnituretoday.com/business-news/broyhill-move-big-lots-acquires-rights-name-trademarks/*

1008 Clint Engel, "The Broyhill Move: Big Lots acquires rights to names, trademarks", *Furniture Today*, February 25, 2019, *https://www.furnituretoday.com/business-news/broyhill-move-big-lots-acquires-rights-name-trademarks/*

1009 Clint Engel, "The Broyhill Move: Big Lots acquires rights to names, trademarks", *Furniture Today*, February 25, 2019, *https://www.furnituretoday.com/business-news/broyhill-move-big-lots-acquires-rights-name-trademarks/*; *https://www.courier-tribune.com/story/news/local/2019/02/19/big-lots-buys-broyhill-brand/5920815007/*, the story originally came from Virginia Annable through the Lenoir News Topic, February 2019; Tom Lester, "Big Lots' billion-dollar Broyhill play", *Furniture Today*, October 11, 2012, *https://www.furnituretoday.com/brands-amp-marketing/big-lots-billion-dollar-broyhill-play/*

1010 Kevin Griffin, "Furniture, Textiles Down", December 5, 2020, *Hickory Daily Record*, p. 1, 7, *https://www.newspapers.com/image/697646761/?terms=%22craftmaster%20furniture%22%20taylorsville&match=1*

1011 *https://hickoryrecord.com/hdr/virus-disrupts-supply-chain-hickory-furniture-firms-concerned-about-impact-of-outbreak-in-china/article_115a9f15-9ec4-5126-97d5-487bd5c8b2e0.html*

1012 Virginia Annable, "Change the Message", *Hickory Daily Record*, December 29, 2020, p. 1A, 8A; Interview with Roy Calcagne, Hiddenite, NC, December 6, 2021.

1013 Kevin Griffin, "Furniture, Textiles Down", December 5, 2020, *Hickory Daily Record*, p. 1A, 7A.

⸺⊰≫⊱⸺

Chapter 35: A New Deal

1014 Interview with Marshall and Em Deal, Conover, NC, October 4, 2022.

1015 "E.M. Suggs' Funeral Held", *Statesville Record and Landmark*, September 3, 1964, p. 8; "New

Corporations", *News & Observer*, March 30, 1946, p. 3; "*C.E. Hefner Elected Mayor of Highland*", *News & Observer*, May 3, 1931, p. 14; "*Hickory Election*", CO, June 5, 1946, p. 3; *Obituary for Margaret Suggs Deal, Charlotte Observer*, December 26, 2003, p. 10V; "*New Group Assumes Operation of Mill*", *News & Observer*, January 14, 1946, p. 3; *Obituary for Harold Deal, Charlotte Observer*, April 27, 1997, p. 24.

1016 *Obituary for Harold Deal, Charlotte Observer*, April 27, 1997, p. 24; *Catawba Furniture Mall (advert), Charlotte Observer*, August 11, 2006, p. 10V.

1017 Virginia Hick, "*Lane Accepts Interco's $509 Million Offer, St. Louis Post-Dispatch*, December 19, 1986, p. 10D.

1018 *https://myemail.constantcontact.com/News-from-Wesley-Hall. html?soid=1103432343452&aid=teCMBCB9gdE; https://growjo.com/company/Wesley_Hall; https://www.furnituretoday.com/business-news/high-end-custom-upholstery-specialty-wesley-hall/; https://magazine.wfu.edu/2014/09/22/leaders-by-design/*

1019 *https://www.furnituretoday.com/furniture-people/mckinney-joins-wesley-hall-as-operations-vp/*

1020 *Interview with Marshall and Em Deal, Conover, NC, October 4, 2022.*

1021 *Email from Marshall Deal to author, November 8, 2022.*

1022 *Interview with Marshall and Em Deal, Conover, NC, October 4, 2022.*

1023 *Interview with Marshall and Em Deal, Conover, NC, October 4, 2022.*

1024 *Interview with Marshall and Em Deal, Conover, NC, October 4, 2022.*

1025 *Interview with Marshall and Em Deal, Conover, NC, October 4, 2022.*

1026 *Interview with Marshall and Em Deal, Conover, NC, October 4, 2022.*

1027 *Interview with Marshall and Em Deal, Conover, NC, October 4, 2022.*

1028 *Interview with Marshall and Em Deal, Conover, NC, October 4, 2022.*

1029 *Interview with Marshall and Em Deal, Conover, NC, October 4, 2022.*

Index

I

Icard, NC 42, 43
IKEA 412
Ikerd, W. Steve 433
Williams Wood Carving 12-18, 583
Impact Collection 371
Impact Furniture 336, 371, 404, 430, 433-434, 464, 465, 620, 622
Imperial Furniture Company 123-125, 127, 147, 228
Industrial Education Center 374-375, 614
Ingold, Barbara 395, 616
Interco 413-415, 446-447, 451-453, 462, 470, 495, 561, 618, 621, 632
International Musical Instruments 323
Interstate Commerce Commission 182, 241
Iredell County 36, 39, 121, 161, 591
Ivey, George F. 34, 182, 196, 231, 575, 598
Ivey's Department Store 381
Ivey-Taylor's 297

J

James River Collection 266-267
Jamestown Exposition 111
Janus Collection 312
Jarrett, Dale 301, 304, 306, 502-503
Jarrett, E.T. 135
Jarrett, Glenn 302-305, 579, 608-609
Jarrett, Homer Keith 302
Jarrett Lumber Company 301
Jarrett Lumber Sales 303-304
Jarrett, Ned 301-302, 305
J.E. Broyhill Civic Center 553
Jenkins, Vance 184
Jennings, S.S. 156, 201, 219
Johnson City, TN 106, 188, 284
Johnson, Phil 324
Johnson, P.J. 76
Johnson, W.S. 135
John's River 31, 45
Johnston, Vance 487
Jonas, A.G. 198, 200
Jonas Furniture 199, 252, 603
Jonas Manufacturing 200
Jones, Billy 447
Jones Chairs 319
Jones, Jim 255
Jones, Jr., John 546-547
Jones, Jr., J.R. 293
Jones, Rome 334-338, 389

Made in the USA
Monee, IL
27 March 2023

30293992R00388